INDUSTRIAL RESEARCH DEPARTMENT
WHARTON SCHOOL OF FINANCE AND COMMERCE
UNIVERSITY OF PENNSYLVANIA

RESEARCH STUDIES
XXIX

WHOLESALE PRICES IN PHILADELPHIA
1784-1861

INDUSTRIAL RESEARCH STUDIES

I. Earnings and Working Opportunity in the Upholstery Weavers' Trade in 25 Plants in Philadelphia, by Anne Bezanson. $2.50.

II. Collective Bargaining Among Photo-Engravers in Philadelphia, by Charles Leese. $2.50.

III. Trends in Foundry Production in the Philadelphia Area, by Anne Bezanson and Robert D. Gray. $1.50.

IV. Significant Post-War Changes in the Full-Fashioned Hosiery Industry, by George W. Taylor. $2.00.

V. Earnings in Certain Standard Machine-Tool Occupations in Philadelphia, by H. L. Frain. $1.50.

VI. Help-Wanted Advertising as an Indicator of the Demand for Labor, by Anne Bezanson. $2.00.

VII. An Analysis of Production of Worsted Sales Yarn, by Alfred H. Williams, Martin A. Brumbaugh, and Hiram S. Davis. $2.50.

VIII. The Future Movement of Iron Ore and Coal in Relation to the St. Lawrence Waterway, by Fayette S. Warner. $3.00.

IX. Group Incentives—Some Variations in the Use of Group Bonus and Gang Piece Work, by C. Canby Balderston. $2.50.

X. Wage Methods and Selling Costs, by Anne Bezanson and Miriam Hussey. $4.50.

XI. Wages—A Means of Testing Their Adequacy, by Morris E. Leeds and C. Canby Balderston. $1.50.

XII. Case Studies of Unemployment—Compiled by the Unemployment Committee of the National Federation of Settlements, edited by Marion Elderton. $3.00.

XIII. The Full-Fashioned Hosiery Worker—His Changing Economic Status, by George W. Taylor. $3.00.

XIV. Seasonal Variations in Employment in Manufacturing Industries, by J. Parker Bursk. $2.50.

XV. The Stabilization of Employment in Philadelphia Through the Long-Range Planning of Municipal Improvement Projects, by William N. Loucks. $3.50.

XVI. How Workers Find Jobs—A Study of Four Thousand Hosiery Workers, by Dorothea de Schweinitz. $2.50.

XVII. Savings and Employee Savings Plans, by William J. Carson. $1.50.

XVIII. Workers' Emotions in Shop and Home, by Rexford B. Hersey. $3.00.

XIX. Union Tactics and Economic Change—A Case Study of Three Philadelphia Textile Unions, by Gladys L. Palmer. $2.00.

XX. The Philadelphia Upholstery Weaving Industry, by C. Canby Balderston, Robert P. Brecht, Miriam Hussey, Gladys L. Palmer, and Edward N. Wright. $2.50.

XXI. Wage Rates and Working Time in the Bituminous Coal Industry, 1912-1922, by Waldo E. Fisher and Anne Bezanson. $3.50.

XXII. Ten Thousand Out of Work, by Ewan Clague and Webster Powell. $2.00.

XXIII. A Statistical Study of Profits, by Raymond T. Bowman. $3.00.

XXIV. The Dollar, the Franc, and Inflation, by Eleanor Lansing Dulles. $1.25. (The Macmillan Company.)

XXV. Executive Guidance of Industrial Relations, by C. Canby Balderston. $3.75.

XXVI. Prices in Colonial Pennsylvania, by Anne Bezanson, Robert D. Gray, and Miriam Hussey. $4.00.

XXVII. Earnings of Skilled Workers in a Manufacturing Enterprise, 1878-1930, by Evan Benner Alderfer. $1.50.

XXVIII. Depression and Reconstruction, by Eleanor Lansing Dulles. $3.00.

WHOLESALE PRICES IN PHILADELPHIA 1784-1861

BY

ANNE BEZANSON
ROBERT D. GRAY
MIRIAM HUSSEY
Industrial Research Department
Wharton School of Finance and Commerce
University of Pennsylvania

PHILADELPHIA
UNIVERSITY OF PENNSYLVANIA PRESS
1936

Manufactured in the
UNITED STATES OF AMERICA

In Appreciation

OF HIS EFFORTS

TO STIMULATE COOPERATIVE RESEARCH IN ECONOMICS

THIS VOLUME IS GRATEFULLY DEDICATED

to

DEAN JOSEPH H. WILLITS

PREFACE

Wholesale Prices in Philadelphia from 1784 to 1861 is the second in a series of detailed studies of the history of prices in the Philadelphia area. The data for these 78 years between the close of the Revolutionary War and the beginning of the Civil War differ in many respects from those already presented for the years from 1720 to 1775 in *Prices in Colonial Pennsylvania.* In the Colonial period we were able to include scattered prices of some products and continuous prices of 29 series, which were reduced to 20 by the combination of grades of the same commodity. In the period covered by this volume we are able to include 205 price series from 1818 to 1861, of which 186 are available from 1784 to 1861. Fortunately, nearly all of the commodities quoted regularly in Colonial years persisted in the later period, furnishing an identical group to link the price behavior of the two eras. The contrast between records of wholesale prices before and after the Revolutionary War appears not only in the increase in the number of commodities but also in the introduction of extensive grading, the inclusion of a large list of industrial products, both raw and finished, and in the evolution of specialized market reporting.

Many well-known, and many now almost forgotten, events acted upon prices in the years from 1784 to 1861. Particularly in the first decades of our period, a succession of events, both external and internal, operated to alter rapidly now one part of the economic structure and now another. In the post-Revolutionary-War years the carrying trade, upon which many Philadelphians had long depended, revived slowly, for the most part after 1793, when wars in Europe and insurrections in the Sugar Islands made exporting and shipping especially hazardous. During the same time the European demand for American foodstuffs and West India products, coupled with the local need for certain raw materials and manufactured articles, induced many merchants to assume the risks and to share in the unusual profits of international shipping. As in other war periods, business dealings became highly speculative, and, as prices mounted, the attention of many Philadelphia business men turned to local means of supplying themselves with raw materials and manufactured products.

Probably the effect upon prices of the extension of manufacturing both before and after the Embargo and Non-Intercourse Acts of 1807 and 1809 can never be isolated from the other powerful influences which dominated price behavior during the continental and Napoleonic wars. Domestic industry, encouraged by interferences with the foreign trade of the United States, grew rapidly in importance. With subsequent improvements in techniques the finished products sold at lower and lower prices as the years passed, while the demand for an increasing amount of raw materials tended to sustain their prices better. The opening of the seas to commerce and improved means of transportation contributed largely to an almost steady decline in the prices of many articles, such as spices and Oriental products generally, which were regarded as luxuries even after the Revolution, but were so cheap before the outbreak of the Civil War that they were regarded practically as necessities. Through the development of production at home and abroad, refined sugar was sufficiently reduced in price before the close of our period to enter into ordinary consumption. So, too, improved processes of cultivating and ginning cotton resulted in a downward trend of prices while other agricultural products, notably wheat and corn, maintained a more constant level. The prices of such commodities were sustained by bounties offered by European countries during the early part of the period, by the great demand from a devastated Europe after the close of the Napoleonic wars, by the failures of crops abroad, especially in the forties, by the Mexican War, and by the Crimean War, which shut off Russian supplies of grain.

To relate fully the historical events which brought about these changes in prices is a task beyond the compass of this study. This entails future work by many students equipped with various kinds of information in addition to prices for this area and for other regions. We make no claim to have utilized all of the wealth of historical comment already available for the period. It was not our task to contrast prices in Philadelphia with those in other parts of the United States or in other countries. Though prices in Philadelphia did not fail to be influenced by conditions in the important markets of the world, though much light would be thrown upon factors affecting our own area by a comparison of price movements elsewhere, our primary task, in coöperation with the International Scientific Committee on Price History, was to provide some of the basic data for an inter-regional comparison, which Professor Arthur H. Cole of Harvard University has undertaken in a summary volume on price movements in various parts of the United States.

We were able to undertake two types of interpretation of price movements. As in the Colonial period the comments of merchants offered explanations of many of the short-time factors influencing prices, so in the national period the letters of contemporaries and comments in current market reports suggested many reasons for certain changes in prices. In addition, the diversity of the continuous monthly and annual price series found for the 78 years of this study made possible various statistical analyses. Finally, the variety of the commodities enabled three classifications to be made, each of which isolated diverse movements typical of various parts of the economy. It is these relationships which are emphasized in our discussion.

For students of the economic history of Philadelphia and of Pennsylvania this study of prices from 1720 to 1861 and especially from 1784 to 1861 provides a yardstick by which can be assessed with some accuracy the effect of various changes in the political as well as the economic sphere. With these prices may be compared data of trade, of wages, of land prices, of many other aspects of the economic life of those times.

To students primarily interested in other areas, it furnishes part of the data needed for regional comparisons. To students of the history of economic thought it serves to recreate in part the character of the times in which certain economic theories were generated.

To students of economics in general it supplies part of the background needed in approaching current problems—a realization of previous difficulties and of the gradual method by which the present economic price system developed. Many characteristics of prices may be admitted to differ from those of the present without impairing the comparison of prices after the War of 1812 with those of the recent post-war period. Admitting all the differences between past and present practices in credit and banking and in industrial organization which can be pointed out, it still remains true that the functions performed today had in one way or another to be carried on earlier, and a knowledge of the changes which occurred while the present forms were being evolved will always be necessary for an understanding of the present.

The early stages of this study were carried on at the same time that the first volume was being completed. Together they represent the united efforts of many persons over a considerable number of years. While assuming the responsibility for the interpretation of the data, we gratefully acknowledge the generous coöperation of all those who have made this study possible.

It is to Professor Edwin F. Gay of Harvard University, whose long interest in prices resulted in the formation of the International Scientific Committee on Price History, that we are indebted for the invitation to participate in the group of studies being started in the United States and Europe. Throughout the course of the investigation we have benefited from his rich experience and his helpful suggestions.

Professor Arthur H. Cole of Harvard University, as Financial Representative of the Economic Foundation and as a friend, generously consulted with and advised us in all stages of the work.

Without the interest and faith of Dean Joseph H. Willits of the Wharton School of Finance and Commerce it would not have been possible to complete the studies in their present form. His appreciation and criticism aided us materially. To him we are indebted for a supplement to the funds from the Price Committee which enabled us to expand the work both intensively and extensively.

Fundamentally, it is the individuals and institutions which have carefully preserved the newspapers of the past and the records of merchants which have made our study possible. Many libraries in Philadelphia and elsewhere generously granted us the use of their collections: the Historical Society of Pennsylvania, the Ridgway Branch of the Library Company of Philadelphia, the American Philosophical Society, the Athenaeum of Philadelphia, the Mercantile Library, the Library of Girard College, the libraries of the University of Pennsylvania, the John Carter Brown Library in Providence, the Baker Library of Harvard University, the New York Public

Library, the New York Historical Society, the Massachusetts Historical Society, the Maryland Historical Society, the Historical Society of Delaware, and the Library of Congress. The staffs of all of these libraries assisted in the finding of various sources of prices and comments. Special acknowledgment must be made to the attentions of Miss Mary M. Townsend, Miss Catherine H. Miller, and Mr. George Fairchild of the Historical Society of Pennsylvania and of Mr. Barney Chesnick of the Ridgway Branch of the Library Company of Philadelphia.

Of the collections of historical records outside of libraries, special mention is made of the Wetherill Papers, a complete account of a business which for five generations was in the Wetherill family. Mr. A. P. Wetherill, who has preserved these documents, facilitated our work by permitting us to use many of them at our convenience.

To the price study section of the Industrial Research Department fell the task of collecting the prices and making the computations essential for interpretation. Helen L. Klopfer supervised the first collection of the original data from the newspapers. Gertrude Bancroft assisted in the location of cyclical turning points and undertook a comparison of the depressions of 1837 and 1857 on the basis of individual commodities, which will be made available later. Many other persons assisted at various times in the work, but the greatest credit is due to those who aided at all stages of the study. Blanch Daley and Lillian Davis Shill supplemented many of the newspaper prices and copied a large part of the merchants' records. Both shared in the computation of indices and other statistical summaries. Marjorie C. Denison was invaluable in assisting in coupling material from various sources, in supervising the calculations, in pointing out inconsistencies in the data, in planning charts, and in verifying statements in the manuscript. As in the final stages of other studies we turned to Harold W. Denison for the drafting of charts.

The manuscript was submitted for final criticisms to Professor Edwin F. Gay and Dean Joseph H. Willits. We are indebted throughout the study to the suggestions of our colleagues in the Industrial Research Department, and especially to Professors C. Canby Balderston and Waldo E. Fisher for their reading of the manuscript. We hope that we have taken full advantage of their helpful suggestions.

CONTENTS

CHAPTER PAGE

PREFACE ... vii

I THE GENERAL INDICES OF PRICES ... 1
General Index of Prices ... 2
Classification of Commodities ... 11
Prices of Imported and Domestic Commodities ... 17
Prices of Agricultural and Industrial Commodities ... 21
Outline of Following Chapters ... 25

II DISTRIBUTION OF 140 COMMODITIES AROUND THE GENERAL AVERAGE ... 27
Skewness of the Distribution ... 28

III CHANGES IN PRICE STABILITY ... 34

IV YEAR-TO-YEAR VARIABILITY ... 45
Variability in Different Periods ... 45
Variability of Individual Commodities ... 46
Variability of Major Groups ... 50
Summary ... 52

V FREQUENCY OF MONTHLY PRICE CHANGES ... 53
Major Groups ... 58
Factors Affecting Sensitivity ... 64

VI CHANGES IN SEASONALITY OF SELECTED COMMODITIES ... 66
Effect of the Seasonal Pattern on Frequency of Monthly Price Changes ... 67
Farm Crops ... 74
Corn ... 74
Wheat ... 75
Rice ... 75
James River Tobacco ... 77
Georgia Cotton ... 78
Summary of Farm Crops ... 79
Farm Derivatives ... 79
Flour ... 79
Corn Meal ... 80
Pork ... 81
Dairy Products ... 82

CHAPTER PAGE

Fish 82
Mackerel #1 82
Imported Foods 83
St. Domingo Coffee 84
Hyson Skin Tea 84
Pepper 84
West India Molasses 85
Havana Brown Sugar 85
Summary of Imported Foods 86
Industrial Commodities Ready for Consumption 86
New England Rum 86
Naval Stores 86
Tar 87
Industrial Raw and Semi-Finished Materials 87
Linseed Oil 87
Whale Oil 88
Pig Lead 88
Summary of Industrial Raw and Semi-Finished Materials 89
Indices of Similarity 89
Amplitude of Seasonal Variations 90

VII PRICE MOVEMENTS FROM 1784 TO 1808 94
Monthly Price Movements 95
The Decline to 1789 97
The Rise to 1797 105
The Decline to 1798 114
The Rise to 1801 118
The Decline to 1803 119
The Rise to 1805 121
The Decline to 1808 124
Summary 126
Annual Price Movements 128
Major Groups 128
Sub-Groups 131
Proportion of Commodities Influencing Price Movements 132
Deviation of Annual Group Indices from the General Average 139

VIII PRICE MOVEMENTS FROM 1808 TO 1821 142
Monthly Fluctuations from 1808 to 1811 142

CHAPTER PAGE

Imported and Domestic Commodities 142
Major Groups 148
Sub-Groups 149
Monthly Fluctuations from 1811 to 1821 151
Imported and Domestic Commodities 152
Major Groups 156
Sub-Groups 178
Summary 180
Annual Price Movements 181
Major Groups 181
Sub-Groups 183
Proportion of Commodities Influencing Price Movements 184
Deviations of Annual Group Indices from General Average 188

IX PRICE MOVEMENTS FROM 1821 TO 1843 190
Monthly Price Movements 190
Imported and Domestic Commodities, 1821-1830 190
Major Groups, 1821-1830 193
Sub-Groups, 1821-1830 198
Imported and Domestic Commodities, 1830-1843 201
Major Groups, 1830-1843 211
Sub-Groups, 1830-1843 214
Summary 218
Annual Price Movements 219
Major Groups 219
Sub-Groups 221
Proportion of Commodities Influencing Price Movements 223
Deviations of Annual Group Indices from General Average 228

X PRICE MOVEMENTS FROM 1843 TO 1861 230
Monthly Price Movements 230
Imported and Domestic Commodities, 1843-1849 230
Major Groups, 1843-1849 234
Sub-Groups, 1843-1849 236
Imported and Domestic Commodities, 1849-1861 237
Major Groups, 1849-1861 242
Sub-Groups, 1849-1861 247
Summary 248
Annual Price Movements 249

CHAPTER PAGE

Major Groups 249
Sub-Groups 252
Proportion of Commodities Influencing Price Movements 256
Deviations of Annual Group Indices from General Avage 259

XI Comparison of the Seventeen Cycles 261
The General Index 261
Indices of Sub-Groups 263
Indices of Major Groups 268
Process of Decline 277
Process of Recovery 284
Summary 290

XII Movement of Prices of Identical Commodities, 1720-1861 292
Trends in Commodity Prices 292
Cycles in 20-Commodity and General Indices 297

XIII General Tendencies in Wholesale Price Movements 305

Appendix 329
Method 331
Collection of Data 331
Construction of Index Numbers 336
Cyclical Analysis 340
Analysis of Distribution of Annual Relatives 342
Year-to-Year Variability 343
Seasonality 343
Tables 347

Bibliography 427

Index 433

TABLES

TABLE		PAGE
1	Timing of Cycles in Geometric Index of 140 Commodities, 1784-1861	4
2	Classification of Commodities Included in Study of Prices in Philadelphia, 1784-1861	13-16
3	Relative Semi-Interdecile and Semi-Interquartile Ranges of Annual Distributions of Relatives of 140 Commodities, 1784-1861	29
4	Coëfficient of Skewness of Quartiles of Annual Distributions of Relatives of 140 Commodities, 1784-1861	31
5	Frequency of Years by Percentage of Commodities with No Change in Price from Previous Year, by Periods, 1785-1861	35
6	Frequency of Years by Percentage of Commodities with Price Changes from Previous Year of Less than 2.5 Per Cent, by Periods, 1785-1861	37
7	Classification of Commodities by Major Groups	38
8	Frequency of Years by Percentage of Commodities with Price Changes from Previous Year of Less than 2.5 Per Cent, by Six Largest Major Groups by Periods, 1785-1861	40
9	Relative Year-to-Year Variability of 140 Commodities Classified by Nine Major Groups, by Periods, 1785-1860	48-49
10	Year-to-Year Variability of Nine Major Groups, by Periods, 1785-1860	50
11	Frequency of Price Changes of Selected Commodities by Decades, 1784-1860	67
12	Indices of Similarity of Seasonal Patterns of Selected Commodities for Successive Decades, 1785-1859	90
13	Average Deviation of Seasonal Patterns of Selected Commodities in Each Decade, 1785-1859	91
14	Range of Deviation of Seasonal Patterns of Selected Commodities by Decades, 1785-1859	92
15	Annual Percentage of Change in the Indices of the Major Groups, 1785-1808	129
16	Annual Percentage of Change in the Indices of the Major Groups, 1809-1821	182
17	Process of Expansion of Sub-Groups to the Peak of 1836-1837	215

TABLE		PAGE
18	Annual Percentage of Change in the Indices of the Major Groups, 1822-1843	220
19	Annual Percentage of Change in the Indices of the Major Groups, 1844-1861	249
20	Percentages of Rise of 24 Sub-Groups in 17 Cycles	264-265
21	Percentages of Decline of 24 Sub-Groups in 17 Cycles	266-267
22	Percentages of Rise of Nine Major Groups in 17 Cycles	269
23	Percentages of Decline of Nine Major Groups in 17 Cycles	271
24	Summary of Cyclical Movements of Nine Major Groups	273-275
25	Relation of Initiation of Decline in Major Groups to that in the General Index	278
26	Summary of Order in which Nine Major Groups Contributed to the Initiation of Decline	279
27	Summary of Timing of Initiation of Decline in Nine Major Groups in Relation to that in the General Index	281
28	Relation of Initiation of Recovery in Major Groups to that in the General Index	284
29	Summary of Order in which Nine Major Groups Contributed to the Initiation of Recovery	285
30	Summary of Timing of Initiation of Recovery in Nine Major Groups in Relation to that in the General Index	287
31	Summary of Cyclical Movements of General Index and 20-Commodity Index, 1789-1861	299
32	Summary of Cyclical Movements of 20-Commodity Index, 1732-1775	303

CHARTS

CHART		PAGE
I	Geometric Index of Average Annual Wholesale Prices in Philadelphia, 1784-1861	3
II	Geometric Indices of Average Monthly Wholesale Prices in Philadelphia, 1784-1861 . . . facing	4
III	Median, Quartiles, and Geometric Index of Average Annual Wholesale Prices of 140 Commodities in Philadelphia, 1784-1861	28
IV	Percentage of Commodities with Least Average Changes in Annual Prices, 1785-1861	36
V	Annual Frequency of Monthly Price Changes of 135 Commodities, 1791-1860	54
VI	Distribution of Frequency of Monthly Price Changes by 20-Year Periods	55
VII	Frequency of Monthly Price Changes of 135 Commodities by 20-Year Periods	56-57
VIII	Seasonal Patterns of Selected Commodities by Decades, 1785-1859	70-73
IX	Geometric Indices of Average Monthly Wholesale Prices in Philadelphia by Major Groups, 1784-1809	98-101
X	Geometric Indices of Average Monthly Wholesale Prices in Philadelphia by Major Groups, 1806-1831	158-161
XI	Geometric Indices of Average Monthly Wholesale Prices in Philadelphia by Major Groups, 1820-1845	194-197
XII	Geometric Indices of Average Monthly Wholesale Prices in Philadelphia by Major Groups, 1836-1861	232-235
XIII	Indices of Average Monthly Wholesale Prices in Philadelphia, 1720-1861 . . . facing	300
XIV	Comparison of Average Monthly Wholesale Prices from Merchants' Accounts and from Prices Current	334-335

APPENDIX TABLES

TABLE		PAGE
	Geometric Indices of Average Monthly Wholesale Prices in Philadelphia	
1	140 Commodities, 1784-1861	350
2	157 Commodities, 1818-1861	351
3	69 Domestic Commodities, 1784-1861	352
4	59 Imported Commodities, 1784-1861	353
5	26 Agricultural Commodities, 1784-1861	354
6	67 Industrial Commodities, 1784-1861	355
7	Farm Crops, 1784-1861	356
8	Farm Derivatives, 1784-1861	357
9	Imported Foods, 1784-1861	358
10	Lumber Products and Naval Stores, 1784-1861	359
11	Industrial Raw and Semi-Finished Commodities, 1784-1861	360
12	Industrial Commodities Ready for Consumption, 1784-1861	361
13	Fish, 1784-1861	362
14	Furs, 1784-1861	363
15	Wines, 1784-1861	364
16	Grains, 1784-1861	365
17	Leaf Tobacco, 1784-1861	366
18	Minor Farm Products, 1784-1861	367
19	Grain Products, 1784-1861	368
20	Meats and Meat Products, 1784-1861	369
21	Dairy Products, 1784-1861	370
22	Fruit, 1784-1861	371
23	Beverages, 1784-1861	372
24	Condiments, 1784-1861	373
25	Sugar and Molasses, 1784-1861	374
26	Foods, 1784-1861	375
27	Chemicals, 1784-1861	376
28	Dyes, 1784-1861	377
29	Fuel and Lighting Materials, 1784-1861	378
30	Ferrous Metals and Metal Products, 1784-1861	379
31	Non-Ferrous Metals and Metal Products, 1784-1861	380
32	Wood, 1784-1861	381

TABLE		PAGE
33	Building Materials other than Wood, 1784-1861	382
34	Textile Fibers, 1784-1861	383
35	Textile Fabrics, 1784-1861	384
36	Hides and Leather, 1784-1861	385
37	Spirits, 1784-1861	386
38	Miscellaneous Commodities, 1784-1861	387
39	20 Commodities, 1731-1861	388-389
40	Arithmetic Index of Average Monthly Wholesale Prices of 12 Commodities in Philadelphia, 1720-1861	390-391
	Geometric Indices of Average Annual Wholesale Prices in Philadelphia	
41	Summaries, 1784-1861	392
42	Nine Major Groups, 1784-1861	393
43	Sub-Groups, 1784-1861	394-395
44	20 Commodities, 1731-1861	396
45	Arithmetic Index of Average Annual Wholesale Prices of 12 Commodities in Philadelphia, 1720-1861	396
46	Minima, Maxima, Deciles, Quartiles, and Medians of Relatives of Average Annual Wholesale Prices of 140 Commodities, 1784-1861	397
47	Skewness of Distributions of Relatives of Average Annual Wholesale Prices of 140 Commodities, 1784-1861	398
48	Percentage of Commodities which Increased in Price over the Previous Year—Total and Six Largest Major Groups, 1785-1861	399
49	Percentage of Commodities which Held Same Price as in the Previous Year—Total and Six Largest Major Groups, 1785-1861	400
50	Percentage of Commodities which Decreased in Price from the Previous Year—Total and Six Largest Major Groups, 1785-1861	401
51	Percentage of Commodities which Increased in Price 2.5 Per Cent or More over the Previous Year—Total and Six Largest Major Groups, 1785-1861	402
52	Percentage of Commodities which Changed in Price less than 2.5 Per Cent over the Previous Year—Total and Six Largest Major Groups, 1785-1861	403
53	Percentage of Commodities which Decreased in Price 2.5 Per Cent or More from the Previous Year—Total and Six Largest Major Groups, 1785-1861	404

TABLE PAGE

54 Percentage of Years in which Price of Each Commodity Changed less than 2.5 Per Cent from Previous Year, by Periods, 1785-1861 405-406
55 Percentage of Average Annual Frequency of Monthly Price Changes of 135 Commodities, 1791-1860 407
56 Percentage of Frequency of Monthly Price Changes of 135 Commodities by 20-Year Periods, 1791-1860 408-410
57 Seasonal Patterns of Selected Commodities by Decades, 1785-1859 411-414
58 Summary of Cyclical Movements of 24 Sub-Groups, 1789-1861 . 415-423
59 Annual Percentage of Change in the Indices of the 25 Sub-Groups, 1785-1861 424-425
60 Percentage of Commodities in Six Largest Major Groups which Declined before or with the General Index 426
61 Percentage of Commodities in Six Largest Major Groups which Rose before or with the General Index 426

CHAPTER I

THE GENERAL INDICES OF PRICES

The primary purpose of this study has been to ascertain the wholesale prices in Philadelphia between the Revolution and the Civil War. The chief source of information has been the prices current published in various local newspapers. In addition it has been necessary to supplement these data by the use of prices from merchants' accounts and even, for particular periods and certain commodities, by records of other areas.[1] The method followed in the collection of these data is described in the Appendix, pp. 331-336. The basic material, expressed as relative prices to correct the variations in the monetary and physical units in which prices were quoted, will be published in a subsequent volume.

It is to the analysis and interpretation of these prices that this volume is addressed. In the same sources from which the basic data were derived were found some contemporary explanations as to why particular prices increased or decreased. Before relating the well-known historical events and other factors emphasized by contemporaries to fluctuations in the prices of specific commodities and of groups of commodities, some background of the underlying changes in price behavior is needed. By an analysis of the individual series and of various combinations of them, it is possible to distil from the data some basic conclusions as to the process by which price behavior was modified during the growth of Philadelphia in the first part of the national period.

No adjustments have been made for any changes in the value of gold and silver. The weight and fineness of the Spanish milled dollar, the standard of comparison in the Colonial period, was reduced from time to time. The most significant changes occurred in 1728, when its fineness was lowered from .930 to .916 and its weight by one-half of one per cent, and in 1772, when its fineness was reduced to

[1] A detailed list of the sources used is given in the Bibliography, pp. 427-430.

.902 without a change in weight.[2] Attempts were made to establish a uniform currency under the Articles of Confederation. It was not until 1792, however, that Congress, acting on Hamilton's report of the previous year, established a bimetallic standard based on 24.75 grains of fine gold or 371.25 grains of fine silver, a ratio of 15 : 1. The maintenance of this ratio undervalued gold. By 1795 the market value of silver had declined to 15½ : 1. With the disappearance of gold from circulation, the United States was practically on a silver standard until the Coinage Act of 1834 established a ratio of 16 : 1 by debasing the gold coins 6.26 per cent while the silver dollar remained the same. Since this ratio was higher than the current market ratio, the overvaluation of gold in effect established a gold standard. The final change in the coinage was made by the Act of 1837 which changed the fineness from one-twelfth to one-tenth and increased by .02 grains the amount of gold in the dollar. With the gold dollar containing 23.22 grains of pure gold or 25.8 grains nine-tenths fine and the silver dollar remaining at 371.25, the ratio of gold to silver was 15.98 : 1. It was not until 1853 that the United States formally adopted a gold standard, although it had been in effect since 1834.[3]

Throughout the study, prices were kept in the prevailing currency of the time. As late as 1795 the *Philadelphia Gazette and Universal Daily Advertiser* quoted its prices current in pounds, shillings, and pence. Samuel Wetherill, a prominent Philadelphia merchant, kept his accounts in pounds, shillings, and pence, as late as 1806. Seven shillings 6 pence of Pennsylvania currency equaled the Spanish milled as well as the American dollar, which exchanged at the same time for 4 shillings 6 pence sterling.

General Index of Prices

Out of the changing number of commodities which were sold at wholesale in Philadelphia, continuous price records were secured for 205 series, 186 of which could be used for the period 1784 to 1861. By combining various grades of a commodity, the 186 were consolidated to 140 commodities and commodity-groups and the 205 to 157.

[2] Laughlin, J. Laurence, *Money, Credit, and Prices*, Vol. I, p. 205.
[3] Laughlin, *op. cit.*, pp. 229-240.

A standard was needed as a basis for judging the various price movements of specific articles. For this reason an unweighted geometric average of the relatives and indices of the 140 commodities and commodity-groups was constructed for the entire period. A supplementary index, computed from the 157 commodities and commodity-groups in the original 205 series, covers the period December 1818 to December 1861. This increase of more than 12 per cent in our sample of prices changed but slightly the fluctuations found in the original index. For this reason we have used the index

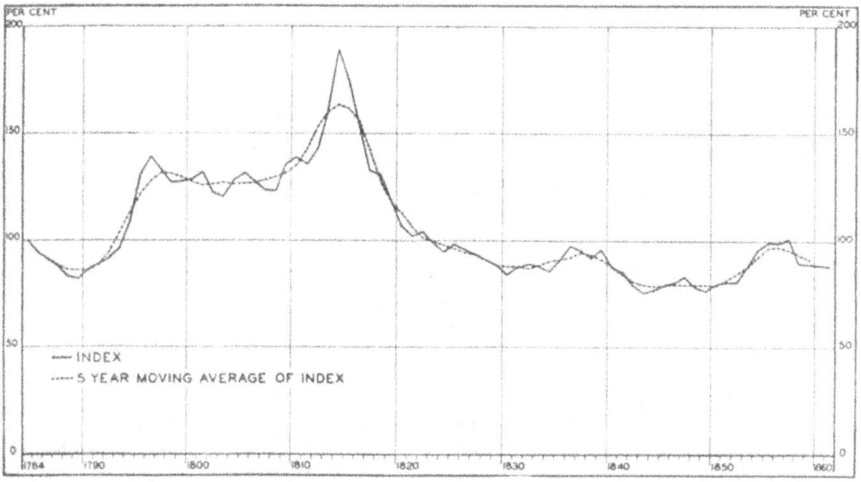

CHART I—GEOMETRIC INDEX OF AVERAGE ANNUAL WHOLESALE PRICES IN PHILADELPHIA, 1784-1861

of the smaller group of commodities available for the whole period (base 1821-1825) as the standard throughout the entire 78 years.

A five-year moving average of the total index on an annual basis shows that the movements of prices may be divided into four distinct periods of moderate length, 1789 to 1803, 1803 to 1830, 1830 to 1843, and 1843 to 1861. In order to separate more clearly the influence on prices of the War of 1812 and the immediate post-war readjustment, the period from 1808 to 1821 has been isolated. For our purposes, therefore, the first period extends from 1784 to 1808, the second from 1808 to 1821, the third from 1821 to 1843, and the final one from 1843 to 1861.

The chart of the monthly indices of average wholesale prices in Philadelphia gives a more exact timing of the end of each period. In addition, it permits the definite location of cycles or swings in prices within each period. The timing of these cycles is indicated in

TABLE I
TIMING OF CYCLES IN GEOMETRIC INDEX OF 140 COMMODITIES
1784–1861
(Base—Monthly Average, 1821–1825)

Beginning of Rise		Peak		End of Recession	
Date	Index	Date	Index	Date	Index
		First Period			
				Apr. 1789	80.2
May 1789	82.0	Jan.–Feb. 1797	140.7	Apr. 1798	124.8
May 1798	125.4	Nov. 1801	133.6	Mar. 1803	118.3
Apr. 1803	118.6	Feb. 1805	133.5	June–July 1808	120.6
		Second Period			
Aug. 1808	120.8	Apr. 1809	140.6	Nov. 1811	130.6
		Oct. 1810	140.4		
		Jan. 1814	197.8		
Dec. 1811	131.2	Nov. 1814	198.8	Apr. 1821	99.5
		Third Period			
May 1821	100.4	Mar. 1822	105.8	Sept. 1824	93.0
Oct. 1824	93.2	May 1825	100.9	June 1828	89.1
July 1828	89.3	Nov. 1828	93.4	July 1830	81.9
Aug. 1830	83.3	Jan. 1832	90.5	June, Sept. 1834	84.6
Oct. 1834	84.8	Feb. 1837	101.3	July 1838	88.8
Aug. 1838	91.3	Apr.–May 1839	97.8	Mar. 1843	74.1
		Fourth Period			
Apr. 1843	74.3	Dec. 1845	83.0	Aug. 1846	77.2
Sept. 1846	77.3	June 1847	85.6	May 1849	74.5
June 1849	74.7	Jan. 1851	81.9	Dec. 1851–Jan. 1852	77.9
Feb. 1852	78.4	Dec. 1855	101.3	June 1856	96.5
July 1856	97.4	June 1857	104.7	Feb. 1858	87.4
Mar. 1858	88.8	May 1859	91.3	July 1861	83.0

Table I, which gives the month when recovery started, the date of the peak, the date of the low, and the position of the general index at each of these significant turning points.

The general index on Chart II traces roughly the significant fluctuations in prices from the close of the Revolution to the outbreak of

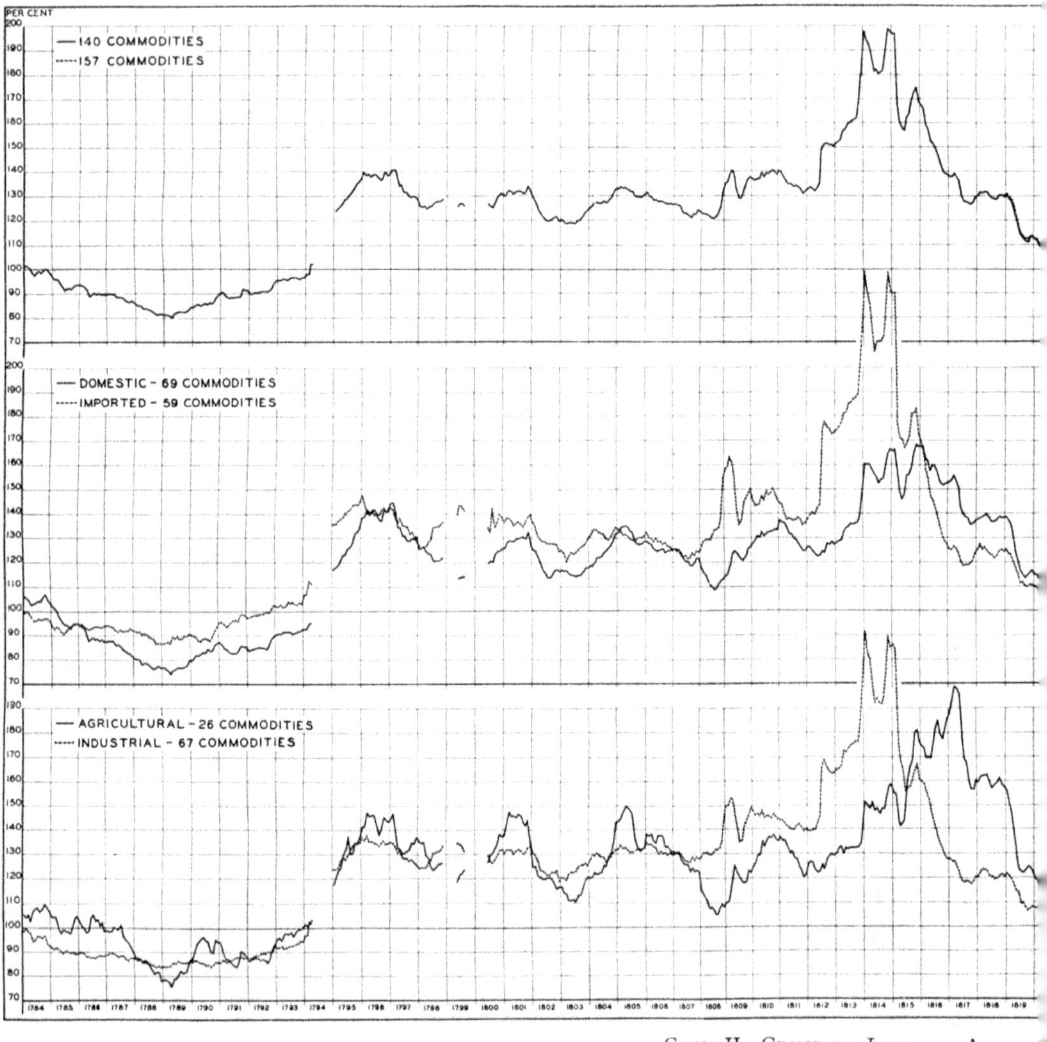

CHART II—GEOMETRIC INDICES OF AVERAG
(Base—M

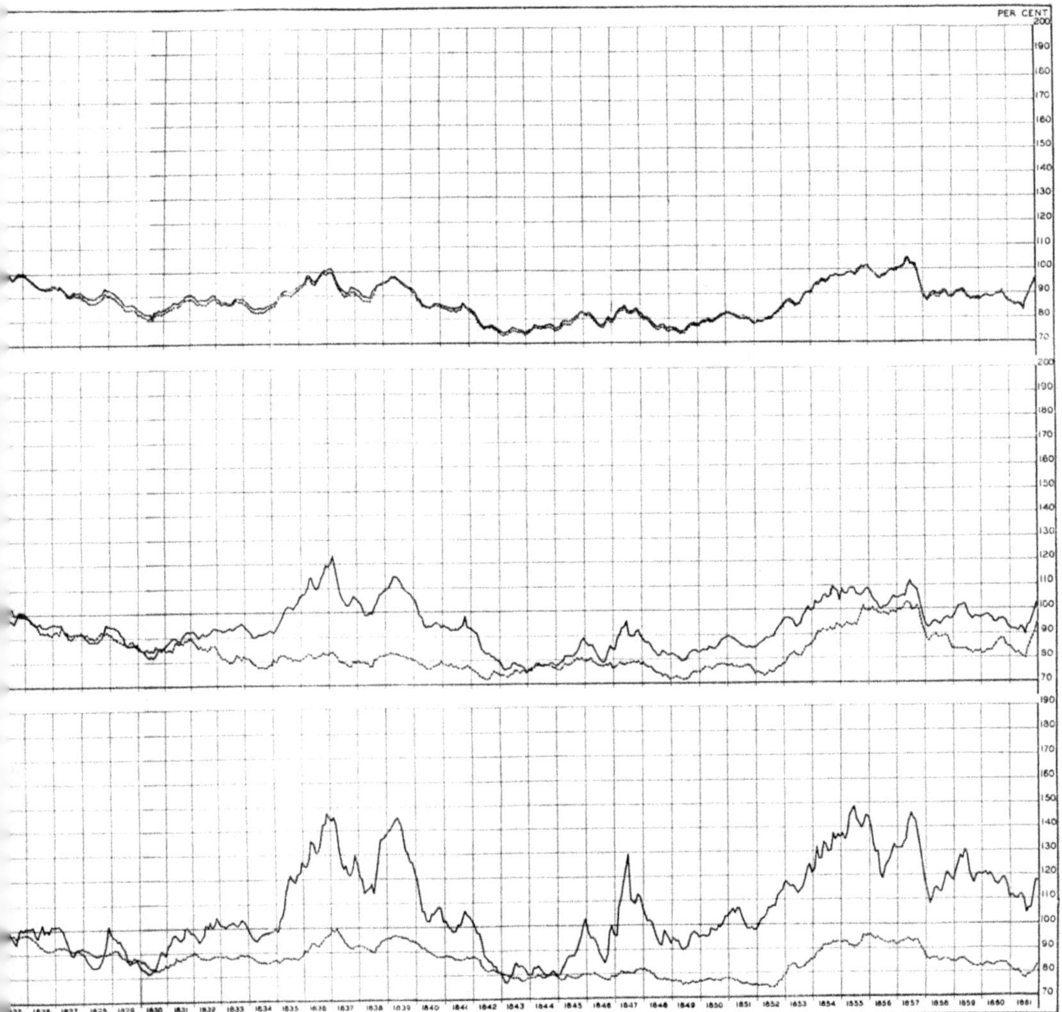

Industrial Research Department, University of Pennsylvania

OLESALE PRICES IN PHILADELPHIA, 1784-1861

(821-1825)

the Civil War. From 1784 to April 1789 prices were contracting from the high level reached during the Revolutionary War. The recession did not proceed at a uniform rate, however. Both in 1784 and 1785, prices advanced slightly for a few months. During part of 1786 and 1787 the decline was practically checked. By the middle of 1787 prices were again slipping downward and continued to recede until about the time of the organization of the federal government.

The next eight years witnessed the most continuous advance in prices of any part of the entire 78 years. The bulk of the rise, which culminated in February 1797, occurred between 1793 and 1796, the early years of the French revolutionary wars. By the beginning of 1795, prices had reached a high level which prevailed for slightly more than two decades. At the peak of February 1797 prices were higher than at any other time in the first major period, 1784 to 1808.

The recession from this peak was abrupt. By April 1798 prices had fallen on the average 11.3 per cent, but were still slightly above the lowest month of 1795. For more than two years, when trade in Philadelphia was hampered by recurrences of epidemics of yellow fever, prices fluctuated around a comparatively low level.

The movements of prices of the next few years reflect to an increasing extent the disturbances arising out of the Napoleonic wars. Changing restrictions on trade imposed by France on the one hand and the Allies on the other, as well as the efforts of the federal government to keep out of the conflict, caused frequent and abrupt changes in prices.

The chief part of the rise from 1798 occurred in the latter part of 1800, but prices continued to rise until November 1801. The certainty of peace had lowered prices sharply by the summer of 1802, but the recession was not definitely checked until after March 1803.

Prices held at a level below that of 1798 to 1800 until the middle of 1803, when they again started to advance rapidly. By February 1805 they had advanced to approximately the level of the peak in 1801. During the following recession, which was longer and more gradual than the advance, prices did not dip as low as they had been in 1803. Nearly all of the contraction occurred between February 1805 and August 1807. In the closing months of that year there was a short-lived, though substantial, recovery; but, with the laying of the embargo, the average of prices again receded, dipping in June and July 1808 slightly below the minimum of 1807.

Thus the first major period includes part of the readjustment following the Revolutionary War and three clearly defined cyclical movements around a high level established on the rise between 1789 and 1797.

The period from 1808 to 1821 was dominated so greatly by the War of 1812 that no cycles can be noted except perhaps one from 1808 to 1811. During 1808 and 1809 prices varied widely, largely because of changes in the commercial policy of the United States. Between July 1808 and April 1809, prices rose on the average 16.6 per cent and in the three months from April to July 1809 lost more than half of the rise. By the close of the year they had recovered to within 2.3 per cent of the peak of April. During most of 1810, prices continued to rise slightly but never reached as high a point as in the previous year. After October 1810 the curve of prices again moved downward, but even by November 1811 they had not dropped as low as in the break of 1809.

As war with Great Britain approached, prices recovered somewhat. The unusually sharp rise between June and July 1812 does not mark the unexpectedness of the outbreak of war as much as it does the effect of the sharp increase in duties imposed to raise revenue to finance the war.

The movements of prices throughout the war period are especially characterized by abrupt changes. Between July 1812 and October 1813 average prices did not advance as much as in the one month from June to July 1812, but between October 1813 and January 1814 they advanced more than they had during the rest of the war years.

In contrast to the generally upward movements of prices in 1812 and 1813 stand the abrupt declines and rises of 1814 and 1815. By July 1814 the total index had fallen 8.9 per cent from the height of January, but by November it had risen slightly above the peak of January. This rise followed the burning of the Capitol at Washington and the suspension of specie payments by the banks. High prices were maintained for four months, but with the news that the treaty of peace had been signed between the United States and Great Britain, prices collapsed and the market in Philadelphia was demoralized.

Between February and March 1815 the total index dropped 14.8 per cent. By June it was 21.2 per cent below the peak of the previous November. That the immediate effect of peace had been overdiscounted explains part of the recovery in the latter part of 1815, but a more positive factor contributing to the rise of 11.4 per cent between June and November 1815 was the demand for American foodstuffs abroad when the European markets were again opened.

The major part of the deflation from the War of 1812 was effected between November 1815 and October 1817. Although by that time the index had dropped lower than in the recession of 1811, it was still slightly above the lowest points of 1798, 1803, and 1808. Prices stiffened and even rose slightly during 1818. Not until after March 1819 did prices drop lower than they had been in 1817. The sharp recession during 1819 of 14.3 per cent between January and September reflects the movement in prices occasioned by the panic of that year. With but slight interruptions the decline continued at a more gradual pace until April 1821, when the recession was checked at the lowest point experienced since the spring of 1794.

The period from 1808 to 1821, therefore, represents, from some points of view, part of a long swing in prices. The rise to a peak in November 1814 was markedly interrupted in 1809, 1811, and 1814, while the decline from November 1814 to April 1821 was broken in 1815 and 1817. In this contraction from the extreme peak of the war years, when the total index was higher than at any other time during the 78 years, prices receded not only to the level prevailing before the outbreak of the war, but even nearly to that prevailing before the beginning of the Napoleonic period.

Part of the third major period, 1821-1843, was influenced by a continuation of the decline from the war peak. The three cycles from 1821 to 1824, 1824 to 1828, and 1828 to 1830 had comparatively short periods of rising prices in which the general index did not reach as high a point as at the crest of each preceding cycle. The recessions were considerably longer than the periods of rise, and at the end of each recession prices were lower than at the end of the previous cycle. The tendency of prices to contract in these years is illustrated by the fact that the peak in 1828 approximated the low of 1824. In July 1830 the general index was 17.7 per cent lower than at the beginning of the period in April 1821.

The movements in prices from 1830 to 1843 are chiefly significant in their tracing of the manner in which prices moved upward until the crisis of 1837 and the unsuccessful attempts at recovery during the next six years. The evidence that part of the rise of prices to 1837 was started in the early thirties rests on the fact that, though the general index receded after a peak in January 1832, it did not drop at any time in 1834 as low as it had been in the summer of 1830. But whenever it was that the factors began to operate, their major influence on prices was felt in the rise from September 1834 to February 1837. In approximately two and a half years prices rose 19.7 per cent with but slight interruptions.

The impact of the crisis in 1837 lowered the index approximately 10 per cent between February and September. Readjustments were slow to be effected and the tendency for expansion persistently appeared. There was a slight recovery before the end of 1837, but prices slid again in 1838. During the latter part of that year and the early months of 1839 they rose materially. In April and May of 1839 the index was within 3.5 per cent of the peak of 1837. Largely because of the failure to clear up the banking difficulties, a widespread recession affected all types of business activity. Prices soon fell lower than at any time in the contraction from 1837 to 1838. Although the recession was somewhat checked during 1840 and 1841, a downward movement persisted until the nadir of March 1843, when the index was not only 24.2 per cent below the peak of 1839 and 26.9 per cent below the peak of 1837 but at the minimum point of the 78 years.

Thus the third major period included more than nine years during which prices continued to recede from the war peak in 1814, as well as the years of expansion from 1830 to 1837 and the contraction which followed.

The final period, from 1843 to 1861, likewise had two rather distinct parts. From 1843 to 1849 prices fluctuated around a low level. The tendencies toward revival which had made some headway by the close of 1845 were largely offset by the discouragement to business resulting from the dispute with Great Britain over the Oregon boundary and the adoption of what appeared to be ill-advised legislation such as the sub-treasury bill and a revision in the tariff.

The causes of the rapid recovery from August 1846 to June 1847 can be traced to the favorable settlement of the Oregon dispute, which helped to restore confidence in the business community, the outbreak of the war with Mexico, which gave rise to a demand for certain war materials and cut off the supply of a few products, and the failure of crops in Europe, climaxed by the Irish famine, which increased the demand for American foodstuffs. With the termination of this unusual demand by the prospects of good crops abroad in 1847 and with the certainty that the war with Mexico would be favorably ended within a short period, prices again turned downward after June 1847. By May 1849 they had fallen nearly as low as they had been in March 1843.

Just as the beginning of the rise to 1837 started in 1830, so the rise to the peak of 1857 started after May 1849. One of the early stimuli to recovery in 1849 was a discounting of the effect of the discovery of gold in California. Before any of the new gold was actually received, contemporaries pointed out that a rise in prices would result.[4] By January 1851 the index had advanced 9.9 per cent. During the rest of the year prices slipped back somewhat.

The major part of the rise to 1857 occurred in the expansion between January 1852 and December 1855. During these three years the general index rose 30.0 per cent with scarcely an interruption. The long period of rise and the height attained by the index may be largely attributed to the effect of the Crimean War, which created a strong demand for American products and cut off an important competitive agricultural area. It was during these years, when grains especially were high, that a concentrated westward expansion developed and a pronounced boom in railroad construction affected prices of building materials and metals.

There was a slight recession in the first half of 1856 in which the index dipped 4.7 per cent. After June, however, the factors of expansion again became dominant. For a year prices rose steadily to a peak in June 1857, the highest point reached by the general index since the early 1820's. As late as September 1857 the index held above the highest prices of 1855. The drastic reaction and panic in the latter part of 1857 is reflected in the collapse of prices between September 1857 and February 1858. In five months the index fell 14.6 per cent.

From February 1858 to November 1860 the general index tended

[4] See Chapter X, p. 238.

to hold, with a few periods of advance. Between February 1858 and May 1859 a slight upward movement raised the index 4.5 per cent. A mild recovery also occurred in 1860. Between October 1860 and July 1861 the general index receded markedly. At the end of this decline prices were 9.1 per cent below the highest point of 1859 and 20.7 per cent below the peak of 1857.

The beginning of the Civil War did not raise prices. As a result of the preparations for secession among the southern states, attempts were made to withdraw balances from the north and to conserve specie. The Richmond and Petersburg banks suspended payment as early as November 21, 1860, and even the Baltimore and Philadelphia banks on the following day. "The Philadelphia money market became very stringent, commercial paper was almost unsalable, rates were quoted at 2½ to 3 per cent per month and public distrust spread rapidly. On November 22 a run started on the banks in Philadelphia and after a hurried meeting of the presidents the suspension of specie payments was ordered once more to take effect at noon."[5] With this financial disturbance, prices receded. Not until after the Battle of Bull Run did they start to advance. By the end of 1861 the general index had soared 15.3 per cent in five months to the highest level reached in four years.

The period 1843-1861 terminates the 78 years of price movements in Philadelphia included in this study. The upward surge of prices which characterized the major part of the period was especially marked between 1852 and 1855. During the closing period improved means of transportation and communication opened up new markets and new sources of commodities. Dealings with other countries were directly affected by disputes between the United States and Great Britain and by the Mexican War and indirectly by the Crimean War and the expedition of England and France against China. The period closed shortly after the outbreak of the Civil War.

During at least part of each of the four periods, prices in Philadelphia were either directly affected by wars at home or abroad or were readjusting themselves after a war to peace-time conditions. Each of the last three periods also included an outstanding crisis and a

[5] Holdsworth, J. T., *Financing an Empire—History of Banking in Pennsylvania*, Vol. I, p. 189.

protracted depression. These and other events will be examined in greater detail and their effect upon various groups of commodities will be given in Chapters VII-X.

Classification of Commodities

The extent to which any composite index oversimplifies the problems confronting contemporary business men by concealing a great diversity of movement of prices is emphasized in the analysis in Chapters II-V. In these chapters the distribution of the 140 commodities and commodity-groups around the average and the changes in prices of specific commodities from year to year will be examined. This discussion will show that commodities differ widely in their scatter around any measure of central tendency. In addition, they differ significantly in the amount by which they tend to change from year to year and in their average variability during each of the four major periods. From the monthly prices, commodities can be further characterized as to the frequency with which changes occurred. Even in the turbulent war years, prices of many articles changed infrequently.

All of these changes in prices, whether considered from the point of view of general behavior throughout the 78 years and in any of the major periods or in the detailed discussion of the fluctuations period by period, would appear chaotic. For practical purposes it is necessary to divide the commodities into groups, homogeneous from some point of view. Three methods of classification are used in examining the relationships of the movements in prices in various parts of the economy.

For one classification, the commodities have been divided into those produced within the United States and those which were imported from foreign countries. Some commodities which were imported during part of the period and produced domestically for the remaining years were omitted from this classification.

A second grouping of the commodities has been made chiefly on the basis of the area of the economy in which they are produced. Domestic agriculture is represented by two groups: *farm crops*, composed of field products; and *farm derivatives*, composed of products of what would now be the milling, baking, meat packing, and dairy industries. For indications of the prices of foreign agricultural commodities in the Philadelphia market we have *imported foods*, consisting chiefly of fruits, beverages, spices, and raw sugar and molasses. In addition, *wines* represent a specialized part of processed foreign agricultural products. Industry is likewise characterized by two groups: *industrial raw and semi-finished commodities* such as dyes, chemicals, ferrous and non-ferrous metals, and materials for paints; and *industrial commodities ready for consumption*, which include a diversified list of manufactured articles such as textile fabrics, refined sugar, soap, glass, and spirits. To typify conditions in the lumber and forest industry we have grouped pine boards, cedar shingles, and oak staves with the naval stores under the heading *lumber products and naval stores*. Two other important sectors, fishing and trapping, are designated by the groups of *fish* and *furs*. This grouping reduces all commodities included in the general index to nine classes which are referred to throughout the text as major groups. The commodities in each group are listed in Table 7, p. 38.

In an attempt to isolate more clearly the commodities contributing to specific fluctuations in prices from 1784 to 1861, a third classification, more detailed than that of the nine major groups, has been used as a supplement. For this purpose we adopted the grouping suggested by the International Scientific Committee on Price History which roughly parallels that used by the United States Bureau of Labor Statistics in its studies of wholesale prices. As we have used it without a house furnishings group but with one of the spirits and wines, it consists of eleven main groups, some of which are subdivided, making a total of twenty-five groups and sub-groups. Fish, furs, and wines remain the same as in the previous classification. Some of the subgroups, such as grains or beverages, represent portions of one of the major groups, while others, such as condiments, pull together commodities from two or more of the major groups.

In order to indicate how the 205 series are combined into 157, how the 186 are consolidated to 140, and how they are classified under each of the three methods, Table 2 has been prepared. The year in which the nineteen series added in the latter part of the period start is given in the last column. None of these were classified as to domestic or foreign origin or by the nine major groups since the

TABLE 2
CLASSIFICATION OF COMMODITIES INCLUDED IN STUDY OF PRICES IN PHILADELPHIA 1784–1861

Commodity	Grade	Detailed Classification: Group	Detailed Classification: Sub-Group	Major Group	Domestic or Imported	Year*
Almonds		Foods	Fruit	Imported Foods	Imported	
Alum		Chemicals and Dyes	Chemicals	Industrial Raw	—	
Ashes	pot	Chemicals and Dyes	Chemicals	Industrial Raw	Domestic	
	pearl	Chemicals and Dyes	Chemicals	Industrial Raw	Domestic	
Bark	Quercitron	Chemicals and Dyes	Dyes	—	—	1803
Beans		Farm Products	Minor	—	—	1815
Beaver		Furs	Furs	Furs	Domestic	
Beef	mess prime	Foods	Meats	Farm Derivatives	Domestic	
Beeswax	white	Miscellaneous	Miscellaneous	Industrial Raw	Domestic	
	yellow	Miscellaneous	Miscellaneous	Industrial Raw	Domestic	
Brandy	French	Spirits and Wines	Spirits	Industrial for Consumption	Imported	
Bread	middling and navy pilot ship smallwater	Foods	Grain Products	Farm Derivatives	Domestic	
Brimstone	crude	Chemicals and Dyes	Chemicals	Industrial Raw	Imported	
	rolls	Chemicals and Dyes	Chemicals	Industrial Raw	Imported	
Bristles		Miscellaneous	Miscellaneous	—	—	1804
Butter		Foods	Dairy Products	Farm Derivatives	Domestic	
Candles	sperm	Fuel and Lighting	Fuel and Lighting	Industrial for Consumption	Domestic	
	tallow dipped tallow mold	Fuel and Lighting	Fuel and Lighting	Industrial for Consumption	Domestic	
Checks	3–4	Textiles	Fabrics	—	—	1818
Cheese		Foods	Dairy Products	Farm Derivatives	Domestic	
Chocolate	Boston Philadelphia	Foods	Condiments	Imported Foods	—	
Cloverseed		Farm Products	Minor	—	—	1795
Cloves		Foods	Condiments	Imported Foods	Imported	
Coal	Virginia (bituminous)	Fuel and Lighting	Fuel and Lighting	Industrial for Consumption	Domestic	
	Lehigh Schuylkill (anthracite)	Fuel and Lighting	Fuel and Lighting	Industrial for Consumption	Domestic	
Cocoa	Island Carracas	Foods	Beverages	Imported Foods	Imported	
Codfish	dried	Foods	Fish	Fish	Domestic	
Coffee	St. Domingo Cuba West India Brazil Java	Foods	Beverages	Imported Foods	Imported	
Copper	old	Metals and Metal Products	Non-Ferrous	Industrial Raw	Imported	
	sheathing	Metals and Metal Products	Non-Ferrous	Industrial Raw	Imported	
Copperas		Chemicals and Dyes	Chemicals	Industrial Raw	—	
Cordage	American	Textiles	Fabrics	Industrial for Consumption	Domestic	
	foreign	Textiles	Fabrics	Industrial for Consumption	Imported	
Cork	velvet bottle	Miscellaneous	Miscellaneous	—	—	1810
Corn	Indian Upper Co. white	Farm Products	Grains	Farm Crops	Domestic	
Corn Meal		Foods	Grain Products	Farm Derivatives	Domestic	
Cotton	Georgia Tennessee La. & Miss.	Textiles	Fibers	Farm Crops	Domestic	

* Year started unless 1784.

TABLE 2 (*Continued*)

Commodity	Grade	Detailed Classification		Major Group	Domestic or Imported	Year*
		Group	Sub-Group			
Currants		Foods	Fruit	Imported Foods	Imported	
Deer Skins	summer and fall	Furs	Furs	Furs	Domestic	
Diaper (linen)	Russian	Textiles	Fabrics	—	—	1808
Duck	ravens	Textiles	Fabrics	Industrial for Consumption	Imported	
	bear ravens	Textiles	Fabrics	Industrial for Consumption	Imported	
Feathers		Miscellaneous	Miscellaneous	Farm Derivatives	Domestic	
Flax		Textiles	Fibers	Farm Crops	Domestic	
Flaxseed		Farm Products	Minor	Farm Crops	Domestic	
Flour	superfine	Foods	Grain Products	Farm Derivatives	Domestic	
Fustic		Chemicals and Dyes	Dyes	Industrial Raw	Imported	
Gin	Holland	Spirits and Wines	Spirits	Industrial for Consumption	Imported	
Ginger	ground	Foods	Condiments	Imported Foods	Imported	
	race	Foods	Condiments	Imported Foods	Imported	
Ginseng		Miscellaneous	Miscellaneous	Farm Derivatives	Domestic	
Glass	8×10	Building Materials	Other than Wood	Industrial for Consumption	Domestic	
Gunpowder		Chemicals and Dyes	Chemicals	Industrial for Consumption	Domestic	
Hams	Jersey and others	Foods	Meats	Farm Derivatives	Domestic	
Hemp	Russian	Textiles	Fibers	Farm Crops	Imported	
Herring		Foods	Fish	Fish	Domestic	
Hides	ox, Buenos Aires raw	Hides and Leathers	Hides and Leather	Farm Derivatives	Imported	
Honey		Foods	Condiments	Imported Foods	Imported	
Hops		Farm Products	Minor	—	—	1790
Indigo	Bengal French	Chemicals and Dyes	Dyes	Industrial Raw	Imported	
Iron	bar, domestic	Metals and Metal Products	Ferrous	Industrial Raw	Domestic	
	bar, foreign English Russian Swedish	Metals and Metal Products	Ferrous	Industrial Raw	Imported	
	hoop	Metals and Metal Products	Ferrous	Industrial Raw	Domestic	
	nail rod	Metals and Metal Products	Ferrous	Industrial Raw	Domestic	
	pig	Metals and Metal Products	Ferrous	Industrial Raw	Domestic	
	sheet	Metals and Metal Products	Ferrous	Industrial Raw	Domestic	
Lard	hogs Jersey	Foods	Meats	Farm Derivatives	Domestic	
Lead	bar pig sheet	Metals and Metal Products	Non-Ferrous	Industrial Raw		
Lead	red dry domestic red dry imported	Building Materials	Other than Wood	Industrial Raw	—	
	white dry domestic white dry imported	Building Materials	Other than Wood	Industrial Raw	—	
	white ground in oil	Building Materials	Other than Wood	Industrial Raw	—	
Leather	slaughter sole	Hides and Leather	Hides and Leather	Industrial Raw	Domestic	
Lemons		Foods	Fruit	Imported Foods	Imported	
Logwood	Campeachy chipt	Chemicals and Dyes	Dyes	Industrial Raw	Imported	
Mace		Foods	Condiments	Imported Foods	Imported	

* Year started unless 1784.

TABLE 2 (*Continued*)

Commodity	Grade	Detailed Classification: Group	Detailed Classification: Sub-Group	Major Group	Domestic or Imported	Year*
Mackerel	#1 #2 #3	Foods	Fish	Fish	Domestic	
Mahogany	Bay St. Domingo	Building Materials	Wood	Industrial Raw	Imported	
Molasses[a]	West India	Foods	Sugar and Molasses	Imported Foods	Imported	
	New Orleans	Foods	Sugar and Molasses	Imported Foods	—	
	Sugar House	Foods	Sugar and Molasses	Imported Foods	—	
Muskrat		Furs	Furs	Furs	Domestic	
Nails		Metals and Metal Products	Ferrous	Industrial for Consumption	Domestic	
Nutmegs		Foods	Condiments	Imported Foods	Imported	
Oats		Farm Products	Grains	Farm Crops	Domestic	
Oil	linseed	Building Materials	Other than Wood	Industrial Raw	Domestic	
	sweet	Foods	Condiments	Imported Foods	Imported	
	sperm	Fuel and Lighting	Fuel and Lighting	Industrial Raw	Domestic	
	whale	Fuel and Lighting	Fuel and Lighting	Industrial Raw	Domestic	
Peas		Farm Products	Minor	Farm Crops	Domestic	
Pepper		Foods	Condiments	Imported Foods	Imported	
Pimento		Foods	Condiments	Imported Foods	Imported	
Pine	heart and plank white panel	Building Materials	Wood	Lumber Products and Naval Stores	Domestic	
	sap	Building Materials	Wood	Lumber Products and Naval Stores	Domestic	
	white	Building Materials	Wood	Lumber Products and Naval Stores	Domestic	
Pitch		Building Materials	Other than Wood	Lumber Products and Naval Stores	Domestic	
Plaster of Paris		Building Materials	Other than Wood	Industrial Raw	Imported	
Pork	Burlington prime	Foods	Meats	Farm Derivatives	Domestic	
Raisins	bloom Malaga Muscatel	Foods	Fruit	Imported Foods	Imported	
Rice		Farm Products	Grains	Farm Crops	Domestic	
Rosin		Building Materials	Other than Wood	Lumber Products and Naval Stores	Domestic	
Rum	Jamaica	Spirits and Wines	Spirits	Industrial for Consumption	Imported	
	New England	Spirits and Wines	Spirits	Industrial for Consumption	Domestic	
	West India	Spirits and Wines	Spirits	Industrial for Consumption	Imported	
Rye		Farm Products	Grains	Farm Crops	Domestic	
Rye Meal		Foods	Grain Products	Farm Derivatives	Domestic	
Salt	fine	Foods	Condiments	Industrial for Consumption	Imported	
	coarse Cadiz Lisbon St. Ubes Turks Isl.	Foods	Condiments	Industrial for Consumption	Imported	
Saltpeter	refined	Chemicals and Dyes	Chemicals	Industrial Raw	Imported	
	rough	Chemicals and Dyes	Chemicals	Industrial Raw	Imported	
Sheeting	Russian brown	Textiles	Fabrics	Industrial for Consumption	Imported	
	Russian white	Textiles	Fabrics	Industrial for Consumption	Imported	
Shingles	long short	Building Materials	Wood	Lumber Products and Naval Stores	Domestic	
Shot		Metals and Metal Products	Non-Ferrous	Industrial for Consumption	—	
Soap	Castile	Miscellaneous	Miscellaneous	Industrial for Consumption	Imported	
	yellow	Miscellaneous	Miscellaneous	Industrial for Consumption	Domestic	

* Year started unless 1784.

[a] The combined molasses index was used three times in combinations except in domestic-imported classifications where only West India was used and the other two series omitted.

TABLE 2 (*Concluded*)

Commodity	Grade	Detailed Classification		Major Group	Domestic or Imported	Year*
		Group	Sub-Group			
soap	white	Miscellaneous	Miscellaneous	Industrial for Consumption	Domestic	
Spanish Brown	dry	Building Materials	Other than Wood	Industrial Raw	—	
	ground in oil	Building Materials	Other than Wood	Industrial Raw	—	
Spelter		Metals and Metal Products	Non-Ferrous	—	—	1810
Spirits of Turpentine		Building Materials	Other than Wood	Lumber Products and Naval Stores	Domestic	
Starch		Miscellaneous	Miscellaneous	Industrial for Consumption	Domestic	
Staves	R O hhd. / W O hhd.	Building Materials	Wood	Lumber Products and Naval Stores	Domestic	
	bbl.	Building Materials	Wood	Lumber Products and Naval Stores	Domestic	
	pipe	Building Materials	Wood	Lumber Products and Naval Stores	Domestic	
Steel	country	Metals and Metal Products	Ferrous	Industrial Raw	Domestic	
	English blistered	Metals and Metal Products	Ferrous	Industrial Raw	Imported	
	German	Metals and Metal Products	Ferrous	Industrial Raw	Imported	
	T. Crowley / Trieste	Metals and Metal Products	Ferrous	Industrial Raw	Imported	
Sugar	Havana white	Foods	Sugar and Molasses	Industrial for Consumption	Imported	
	loaf / lump	Foods	Sugar and Molasses	Industrial for Consumption	Domestic	
	Havana brown / muscovado / muscovado 2 and 3	Foods	Sugar and Molasses	Imported Foods	Imported	
Tallow		Fuel and Lighting	Fuel and Lighting	Farm Derivatives	Domestic	
Tar		Building Materials	Other than Wood	Lumber Products and Naval Stores	Domestic	
Tea	Bohea / Hyson / Hyson skin / Souchong	Foods	Beverages	Imported Foods	Imported	
Timothy Seed		Farm Products	Minor	—	—	1818
Tin	block	Metals and Metal Products	Non-Ferrous	Industrial Raw	Imported	
	plate	Metals and Metal Products	Non-Ferrous	Industrial Raw	Imported	
Tobacco	James River	Farm Products	Tobacco	Farm Crops	Domestic	
	Kentucky	Farm Products	Tobacco	Farm Crops	Domestic	
	St. Domingo	Farm Products	Tobacco	—	—	1815
	Ladies Twist	Farm Products	Tobacco	—	—	1815
Turpentine		Building Materials	Other than Wood	Lumber Products and Naval Stores	Domestic	
Verdigris		Building Materials	Other than Wood	Industrial Raw	Imported	
Wheat		Farm Products	Grains	Farm Crops	Domestic	
Whiskey	apple	Spirits and Wines	Spirits	—	—	1796
	rye	Spirits and Wines	Spirits	—	—	1797
Wine	claret	Spirits and Wines	Wines	Wines	Imported	
	Lisbon	Spirits and Wines	Wines	Wines	Imported	
	Madeira	Spirits and Wines	Wines	Wines	Imported	
	Malaga	Spirits and Wines	Wines	Wines	Imported	
	port	Spirits and Wines	Wines	Wines	Imported	
	sherry	Spirits and Wines	Wines	Wines	Imported	
	Teneriffe cargo	Spirits and Wines	Wines	Wines	Imported	
	Teneriffe particular	Spirits and Wines	Wines	Wines	Imported	
	Sicily Madeira	Spirits and Wines	Wines	—	—	1813
	Marseilles Madeira	Spirits and Wines	Wines	—	—	1813
Wool	¾ clean / ½ clean / Merino clean	Textiles	Fibers	—	—	1813

* Year started unless 1784.

discussion of these classifications will be confined to the series which can be contrasted throughout the entire period.

Prices of Imported and Domestic Commodities

The geometric indices of the average wholesale prices of 69 domestic and 59 foreign commodities for the period 1784 to 1861 are shown on the middle section of Chart II. The movements of these two indices will be analyzed in further detail in Chapters VII-X. Significant differences in level and timing of movements are apparent. At the beginning of the period prices of domestic articles were relatively higher than those of imported commodities. From 1786 to 1815, however, the domestic products usually kept below the imported goods, which were the first to reach the peaks around 1797, 1801, 1805, and 1809.

The most divergent movements of the two indices occurred around 1799 and 1808 when imported goods rose and domestic articles fell in price. This behavior is typical during an embargo period. In 1799 there was a virtual embargo in the port of Philadelphia because of yellow fever. In 1808 the Embargo Acts were in operation.

During the War of 1812 both indices rose, but the index of prices of imported articles rose more rapidly than that of domestic goods. The increase in the distance between the two curves was caused largely by the jump of 20.9 per cent in the prices of foreign commodities between June and July 1812 when the higher duties went into effect. The most significant difference in the movement of these two indices lies in the dating of the time at which the highest point of the 78 years was reached. In January 1814 imported articles were, by a slight margin, at their maximum price. In November of the same year they were almost as high after having fallen substantially in the spring and early summer. Domestic articles, in contrast, after also receding in 1814, were substantially higher in price at the close of the year than they had been at the beginning. Their peak of the war period occurred in February 1815, just before the news of peace arrived, but their maximum of the 78 years was in November 1815.

Both indices fell as soon as it was definitely known that the war had ended. The decline in imported articles apparently overdiscounted the immediate effect of the availability of new supplies. Between June and November 1815 they rose 9.9 per cent, but they were still 23.3 per cent below their war peak. By March 1816 they had receded below the minimum point of the previous year. For domestic articles, in contrast, the opening of European markets created a great demand. Between May and November 1815 their prices rose more than they had declined in the break in the first part of the year. Not until after May 1817 did domestic goods sell for as little as they had in May 1815. Thus imported goods were at their highest point between the Revolution and the Civil War during the War of 1812, but domestic prices in general were at their maximum after the close of the war.

During 1816 the relative position of the two curves changed, the prices of domestic articles being continuously higher than those of imported goods from 1816 to 1820. These five years are to this extent in great contrast to the three previous decades.

From 1821 to 1830 the two curves fluctuated around a similar declining tendency. As in the previous cycles, the prices of foreign commodities were the first to turn down from the peaks of 1822 and 1825. The swing in prices from 1828 to 1830 was largely confined to domestic products.

From 1830 to 1843 the two curves again diverged. The prices of imported goods continued an undulating decline until in 1842 they were 14.7 per cent lower than in 1830. Each of the successive highs in 1831, 1837, and 1839 was lower than the preceding one. In each period of recession prices tended to drop lower than in the previous decline. The exception was the short dip of 1838 when the lowest prices approximated those of 1834. In contrast, the prices of domestic goods completed between 1830 and 1843 three cycles superimposed on a long swing with a peak in 1837.

That the underlying factors which contributed to the crash of prices in 1837 developed during the years after 1830 is indicated by the fact that after the index of domestic prices rose 16.4 per cent between July 1830 and November 1833 it slipped back only 5.6 per cent between November 1833 and May 1834. At this point domestic products were still 9.9 per cent higher in price than in 1830.

The steepest part of the advance to the peak early in 1837 occurred after January 1835. At the peak, the index of domestic articles was approximately 40 points higher than the index of imported goods. Stated differently, the prices of domestic articles were 50.4 per cent higher in 1837 than in 1830 while imported articles were slightly cheaper at the crest in 1837 than they had been at the low of seven years earlier.

Just as the long rise in prices of domestic articles had been broken in 1834, so the decline from 1837 to 1843 was interrupted by a substantial rise from 1838 to 1839 and partially checked during 1840 and 1841. By the close of 1843 the prices of domestic goods had declined to approximately the level of imported articles. At that time both groups were lower than they had been in 1830.

Within a year, however, prices of domestic products were again pulling away from those of foreign goods. From October 1844 to the end of the period the domestic group was always higher than the foreign. The successive swings in prices from 1843 to 1857 tended continuously to raise the level of prices of domestic goods. In each of the recessions in 1846, 1849, 1851, and 1856 domestic products held above the corresponding point in the previous cycle. Only in the rise engendered at the beginning of 1851 did their prices fail to exceed the preceding peak.

Foreign commodities, in contrast, did not begin their rise to 1857 until after June 1849. In the two cycles between 1843 and 1849 the peak of the first exceeded that of the second. In the recession from 1847 to 1849 imported articles dropped below their minimum of 1842.

Both groups had a mild swing between 1849 and 1852, but at no time after the peak of January 1851 did the domestic commodities show an advance from 1849 of less than 7.0 per cent while the foreign commodities fell within 1.8 per cent of the lowest prices at the close of the forties.

The major advance to the peak of 1857 occurred between 1852 and 1855. During these years the domestic commodities led the imported. As early as October 1851 the domestic group resumed its advance, while the foreign continued to decline until the following

April. The next peak of prices of domestic articles occurred in September 1854, although they fluctuated around a high level throughout 1855. Foreign commodities, on the other hand, continued to advance until October 1855 and had an especially sharp rise after July of that year.

The recession in 1856 which preceded the final spurt of prices to a peak in 1857 lowered the domestic index 8.8 per cent below its peak of 1854 while the foreign index dipped only 3.6 per cent below its height in 1855. Before the middle of 1857 both groups had advanced to their maximum prices for the decade.

The movements in prices during the fifties differed from those of the thirties in that both groups shared appreciably in the rise. In 1857 both indices were at least 41 per cent higher than in 1849. The major part of the crash in prices in both groups occurred between September 1857 and February 1858. From the low point of that month imported goods recovered slightly, but before the close of the year the downward movement reasserted itself. By January 1860 their index was 6.2 per cent lower than in February 1858. Between January and September 1860 foreign goods advanced 8.0 per cent, but they dropped again in the latter part of the year and the first part of 1861. By July they were slightly lower than at the beginning of the previous year.

The movements in the prices of domestic articles during the closing years of the period again differed sharply from those of foreign commodities. From the low of February 1858 the domestic products rose until by May 1859 they were 10.7 per cent higher than after the first drop from the peak of 1857. Though domestic articles fell after May 1859, it was not until the beginning of 1861 that their index was lower than it had been in February 1858. The recession continued even after the beginning of the Civil War until in July 1861 the index stood 12.5 per cent below the peak of 1859 and 20.1 per cent below the peak of 1857.

This brief examination of the relation of the movements of the prices of commodities of foreign and domestic origin has given an indication of the diversity of price movements underlying the composite index.

Prices of Agricultural and Industrial Commodities

The second classification of commodities into nine major groups reveals other changes in the relationship of prices representative of such areas of the economy as farming, manufacturing, and lumbering. The detailed discussion of these groups is deferred to Chapters VII-XI, but in order to see the general differences between the two most important sections of the economy, agriculture and industry, we have shown on the lowest section of Chart II a combination of 26 farm crops and farm derivatives as representative of domestic agriculture and a composite of the 67 commodities in the two industrial groups in order to typify the movements of prices representative of manufacturing.

In general, the agricultural index showed wider fluctuations than the industrial. This behaviour was especially marked from 1784 to 1808 and from 1821 to 1830 when the two indices fluctuated around each other, the agricultural index rising above the industrial at every peak and dropping below it in every recession.

The decline from 1784 to 1789 not only started at a lower level in the industrial than in the agricultural group but also proceeded at a more uniform rate. Agricultural prices even increased from January to October 1784 and held at a fairly high level until after July 1787. The bulk of the decline in the agricultural index between 1784 and 1789 was effected between July 1787 and April 1789.

In both groups the long rise in the early nineties culminated in March 1796, nearly a year before the peak in the general index. The greatest difference in the process by which the agricultural and industrial commodities advanced was the pronounced swing in the agricultural index between 1789 and 1791, which contrasts with the more continuous rise in the prices of industrial commodities.

The most divergent movements in the two indices occurred between 1798 and 1800 when the industrial group appeared to complete a minor swing with an intervening peak in 1799 between the highs of 1796 and 1801. Agricultural prices, however, continued during 1798 and 1799 their decline from the peak of 1796 and rose during part of 1799 and throughout 1800 to a peak in 1801.

During the closing years of the first major period, not only was the agricultural index higher at peaks and lower at the end of recessions than the industrial index, but its periods of expansion ended sooner and its recessions lasted longer.

From 1808 to 1821 the two curves showed significant differences. The embargo placed at the close of 1807 checked the decline in the prices of industrial commodities so that they did not fall as low as they had been in 1798 and 1802. The rise which followed, as the effects of the embargo became more pronounced, raised the industrial index before the close of 1808 to a point higher than had been reached even in 1796. The peak of prices of industrial commodities before the War of 1812 was in March and April 1809. At the same time the embargo lowered still further the prices of agricultural commodities, which had been declining from a peak in December 1805. By September 1808 agricultural prices had fallen to the lowest point reached between 1795 and 1820. Between September 1808 and November 1811 agricultural prices completed a well-defined cycle with a peak in October 1810. The industrial commodities, however, did not drop as low in 1811 as they had in the break in 1809.

During the War of 1812 industrial commodities rose to a peak in January 1814. Nearly all of this rise took place from April to August 1812 and from October 1813 to January 1814. After the break in prices from January to August 1814 the industrial index never rose to as high a point as in the beginning of the year. Prices of agricultural commodities rose less extensively during the war than those of industrial products. The break in 1814 was comparatively mild in the agricultural index and in December it stood 4.7 per cent higher than in January.

When it was certain that the war had ended, prices of industrial commodities crashed. Only a slight recovery was effected in the latter part of 1815. On the other hand, agricultural prices receded sharply, but rose between April and July 1815 to a point higher than any reached during the war. Before the close of the year they were 14.2 per cent higher than at the close of 1814. During 1816 and the early part of 1817 the expansion in the prices of agricultural commodities continued in waves which pushed prices progressively higher than at the previous crest and checked their recessions at successively higher levels. By March 1817 the agricultural index was 25.1 per cent higher than in December 1814. During the same time industrial commodities had been steadily falling. In the month when agricultural prices were at their maximum between the Revolution and the Civil War, industrial commodities sold on the average for 42.7 per cent less than at their war peak. Although agricultural prices slumped severely during 1817, their index remained well above the industrial index until 1820.

With the reappearance of cyclical movements in the twenties, the two indices again fluctuated around each other for a decade. At each peak, agricultural prices were relatively higher than those of industrial commodities and at the end of each contraction relatively lower.

During the years after 1830 the agricultural index was continuously above the industrial index except for a few months in 1843 and 1844. The maximum spread between the indices occurred in the late thirties and middle fifties.

In both indices the rise to 1837 started in 1830 inasmuch as neither had a corrective movement in 1834 which brought prices back to the low of 1830. The indices clearly reveal that the rise from 1830 to 1837 affected agriculture more favorably than it did industry. First, the period of rise in the agricultural index exceeded that of the industrial, which had been slower to respond in 1830 and which had tended to sag from the beginning of 1832 to the middle of 1834. Secondly, whether measured from the lows of 1830 or 1834 or from the intervening peak, the rise to November 1836 in the agricultural index surpassed that which terminated in the industrial index in March 1837. Both indices fell during 1837 and part of 1838. In the recovery from 1838 to 1839 the industrial index was, at the peak, 2.5 per cent lower than it had been in 1837, while agricultural prices were within 1.2 per cent of their peak in 1836.

For both of these groups the low of 1843 was not as significant as the corresponding low in the general index or in the indices of imported and domestic commodities. The agricultural index had been slightly lower in 1789 than it was in 1843, while the industrial index was almost continuously lower from 1849 to 1852 than in 1843. Nevertheless, throughout 1843 and 1844 the agricultural index was substantially lower than it had been for more than a decade and the industrial index lower than at any earlier time.

During the rest of the forties the industrial index had but minor fluctuations and after January 1848 tended to recede until the summer of 1852. The agricultural index, in contrast, had wide fluctuations superimposed on a strong rising trend which culminated in the middle fifties. In each succeeding decline agricultural prices held well above the corresponding point of the previous cycle. The demand from Europe for American foodstuffs is especially reflected in the extreme peak of June 1847.

The movements of prices during the fifties as represented by these two indices are chiefly significant in that they minimize the height of prices in 1857. After June 1855 agricultural prices never rose as high as they had been in that month. The peak of industrial prices came in December 1855 and January 1856. Agricultural prices, especially, dropped in 1856. By June they had fallen 20.0 per cent from the peak of the previous year. Most of this loss was regained within the next twelve months. The industrial index sagged mildly throughout 1856 and recovered slightly in the first part of 1857.

The major impact of the crash of 1857 on prices of agricultural commodities was felt between August 1857 and February 1858 and on industrial commodities between September 1857 and February 1858. A generally downward movement characterized the industrial index from February 1858 to July 1861. By that time the prices of industrial commodities were 18.9 per cent lower than at the beginning of 1856. The agricultural index, in contrast, had a clearly defined swing at the close of the 78-year period. From February 1858 to May 1859 it rose 20.4 per cent with only minor interruptions, but in the decline which followed it fell below the minimum of 1858. In July 1861 the agricultural index was 29.8 per cent lower than at the peak of 1855.

A comparison of the five major indices reveals many price movements at certain times which appear to be confined to a portion of the economy. Probably the greatest difference between the curves lies in the length of the downward movement which dominated the fluctuations in prices for many years after the Napoleonic wars or the immediate post-war period. All indices were lower around 1843 than they had been in 1830, but in the total index and in the indices of domestic and agricultural commodities the period of expansion during the thirties was so great that the declining trend may be said to end in 1830. On the other hand, for imported commodities the underlying downward trend persisted clearly until 1842, when the direction changed to practically a horizontal movement. For industrial commodities, however, the downward trend lasted until 1852. The persistence of this declining trend in the prices of industrial commodities, after other important areas of the economy had shifted to a horizontal or even a rising price level, must be indicative of technical improvements in manufacturing processes resulting in lowered costs of production.

Outline of Following Chapters

The remainder of this study is devoted to an intensive analysis of the prices in Philadelphia from 1784 to 1861. In Chapters II-IV the annual averages are used in order to eliminate seasonal changes in price. In these chapters are considered both the manner in which the yearly relatives of the series are scattered around the average and the amount of change from year to year which characterizes the various commodities in each of the four major periods. In Chapter V the emphasis is placed entirely on monthly changes of prices. In this connection the frequency with which quotations changed is examined. It is especially important to ascertain the extent to which the frequency of change was modified as the United States became more developed industrially. Closely related to the number of times that a price changed each year is the seasonality in the prices of particular commodities. For this detailed analysis in Chapter VI a small group of commodities has been selected.

With this background, which gives significant changes in the behavior of prices during the first part of the national period, the four major periods, 1784-1808, 1808-1821, 1821-1843, and 1843-1861, are examined in detail in Chapters VII-X. In these historical chapters the major analysis rests on the interrelation of the movements in the general index, the indices of domestic and imported articles, and the indices of the nine major groups. In addition the fluctuations in the twenty-five sub-groups indicate in greater detail the commodities chiefly contributing to and affected by the successive cycles.

After the historical analysis, the seventeen cycles, defined according to the turning points in the general average, are measured both as to the extent of rise and fall and as to the differences in the time at which the various indices, and even specific commodities, reached their salient turning points. This analysis reveals part of the process by which advances and declines in the general index are effected.

In order to knit together this study of prices in Philadelphia and its predecessor,[6] monthly indices of the prices of 12 and 20 commodities which are available from 1720 and 1731 to 1861 have been constructed. These indices especially stress the differences and similarities in price movements in Philadelphia before and after the Revolution.

In the final chapter are summarized the general tendencies in wholesale price movements noted from 1720 to 1861 and from 1784 to 1861 especially. The changes in prices and the behavior of prices of the various commodities and of groups of them, representative of diverse producing areas of the economy, reveal the progressive modification of the price structure during the economic development preceding the Civil War.

No attempt has been made in this study to separate the statistical and historical analyses. Nevertheless, the discussion does fall into three parts, Chapters II-VI being primarily statistical, Chapters VII-X historical, and Chapters XI-XIII comparative and summary.

[6] Bezanson, Anne, Gray, Robert D., and Hussey, Miriam, *Prices in Colonial Pennsylvania*.

CHAPTER II

DISTRIBUTION OF 140 COMMODITIES AROUND THE GENERAL AVERAGE

That the unweighted index of wholesale prices in Philadelphia from 1784 to 1861 is of greatest use as a standard against which to judge the fluctuations of specific commodities has been partially indicated by the comparison of the movements in the domestic and imported and in the agricultural and industrial groups discussed in the previous chapter. Those analyses dealt with only part of the entire group of commodities. In order to give further indications of the necessity for combining the prices of the various series into an average and at the same time to measure the deviations of the individual series away from the general average, we stress in this chapter the spread between the measures of central tendency and the annual averages of the 140 commodities.

Throughout this discussion it is expedient to substitute the median for the geometric average of relatives. There is in general but little difference between these two measures of central tendency, which are graphically compared on Chart III. In only fourteen years was the median four per cent or more away from the geometric average. The periods of greatest difference were from 1809 to 1817 and from 1856 to 1860. Before 1818 the median fell below the geometric average in all but five years. From 1818 to 1861 the median exceeded the geometric average in a large majority of the years. From 1833 to 1843 and from 1854 to 1861 it was continuously above the geometric average.

The scatter of the individual series around the median is indicated somewhat by the two quartiles drawn on Chart III. Half of the commodities fall in the area between these two curves.

In measuring the distribution of the annual relatives around the median we have selected points which divide the commodities into groups each containing ten per cent. These nine deciles, the quartiles, and the minimum and maximum for each year are given in the Appendix, Table 46. For summary figures we have computed relative semi-interdecile and semi-interquartile ranges, which show the average distance from the median of 20, 40, 50, and 60 per cent of the series. (Table 3)

A majority of the differences between the median and its closest deciles are from five to nine per cent. To include the central two-fifths of the commodities the area must usually be increased to be-

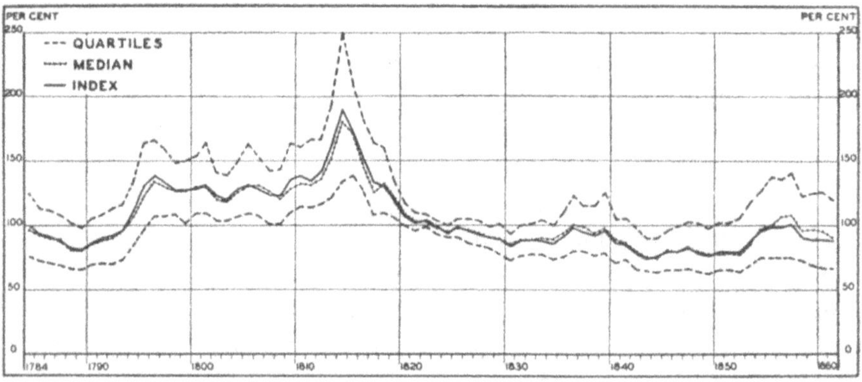

CHART III—MEDIAN, QUARTILES, AND GEOMETRIC INDEX OF AVERAGE ANNUAL WHOLESALE PRICES OF 140 COMMODITIES IN PHILADELPHIA, 1784-1861

tween 13 and 19 per cent of the median, for the middle half of the commodities to between 17 and 24 per cent of the median, and for four-fifths of the series to between 21 and 30 per cent. Thus in order to add more groups of commodities it is necessary to go increasingly further away from the median. In addition, there is less uniformity in the spread away from the median as the proportion of commodities is increased.

SKEWNESS OF THE DISTRIBUTION

These semi-interquartile and semi-interdecile ranges have concealed the tendency for a concentration of commodities sometimes below the median and at other times above. For this reason these measures of dispersion must be supplemented with measures of the skewness of the distribution.

In determining the skewness of the frequency distribution of annual relatives of prices, a geometric measure is more satisfactory than an arithmetic measure since the lower range of the frequency distribution is definitely limited while the upper range is unlimited. Actual charting of the frequencies, using a natural scale for the num-

TABLE 3
RELATIVE SEMI-INTERDECILE AND SEMI-INTERQUARTILE RANGES OF ANNUAL DISTRIBUTIONS OF RELATIVES OF 140 COMMODITIES
1784–1861

Year	D_6-D_4	D_7-D_3	Q_3-Q_1	D_9-D_1	Year	D_6-D_4	D_7-D_3	Q_3-Q_1	D_9-D_1
1784	6.2	18.1	25.6	32.5	1823	2.0	3.8	5.2	6.4
1785	6.5	18.7	22.6	29.2	1824	1.9	3.8	5.0	5.9
1786	8.1	18.0	22.9	31.2	1825	2.4	5.9	7.5	9.3
1787	6.1	18.2	22.1	28.8	1826	4.2	8.0	10.0	12.5
1788	6.6	15.0	21.4	27.8	1827	3.9	6.9	10.4	12.9
1789	9.2	14.0	19.5	26.9	1828	3.8	7.6	9.5	12.1
1790	8.8	16.8	20.7	26.8	1829	3.9	9.9	13.0	16.4
1791	8.1	17.5	20.8	27.3	1830	4.9	10.4	12.4	15.9
1792	8.0	19.2	24.3	28.9	1831	4.0	9.8	13.1	16.6
1793	7.1	17.1	21.9	27.5	1832	5.1	10.6	13.3	15.6
1794	9.9	20.0	23.6	27.5	1833	6.2	10.5	14.7	18.6
1795	6.7	19.5	27.6	33.3	1834	3.7	10.8	14.7	21.4
1796	6.6	15.7	22.1	28.8	1835	8.1	13.9	18.2	24.2
1797	6.2	13.8	20.0	24.1	1836	5.4	14.9	21.6	26.4
1798	7.0	11.7	15.9	22.6	1837	9.2	13.8	17.8	23.1
1799	7.1	13.9	19.3	24.0	1838	7.9	17.1	20.5	26.0
1800	7.7	14.1	17.0	23.4	1839	8.3	16.0	23.9	29.5
1801	8.4	17.5	21.5	25.7	1840	5.9	11.1	18.9	23.8
1802	5.5	13.1	16.1	19.3	1841	7.2	13.2	18.3	23.1
1803	4.7	11.7	15.1	18.3	1842	6.5	16.4	19.5	25.0
1804	8.2	13.6	16.8	20.8	1843	5.6	12.0	16.5	23.5
1805	8.3	15.6	20.9	24.4	1844	7.0	13.9	17.2	23.7
1806	7.2	14.3	17.6	21.0	1845	7.2	13.5	18.5	24.2
1807	4.9	10.8	16.3	20.2	1846	6.6	13.5	20.7	27.0
1808	5.8	14.3	17.9	21.9	1847	10.6	18.4	21.9	29.6
1809	6.6	15.3	20.8	24.5	1848	10.0	19.4	23.8	30.6
1810	6.7	13.1	17.8	24.1	1849	8.3	18.1	22.3	26.1
1811	5.2	12.8	20.9	25.7	1850	7.7	18.2	23.0	29.8
1812	5.7	15.1	19.0	25.9	1851	8.8	19.3	23.0	29.2
1813	9.1	18.7	23.4	32.9	1852	12.0	22.5	27.3	36.5
1814	9.6	24.9	32.1	38.8	1853	11.1	20.7	28.7	34.8
1815	7.1	15.9	19.8	22.4	1854	11.5	21.3	27.4	33.3
1816	6.7	14.1	18.9	24.0	1855	11.2	23.3	31.5	38.7
1817	6.4	16.9	22.3	27.8	1856	13.2	24.6	28.7	34.1
1818	8.0	14.2	19.4	21.6	1857	14.5	24.7	31.0	35.5
1819	3.9	8.5	11.6	13.5	1858	11.7	22.1	26.2	33.2
1820	4.1	6.3	7.6	9.7	1859	11.0	24.2	29.2	34.0
1821	2.4	4.9	6.9	9.5	1860	11.6	23.6	30.7	35.8
1822	1.7	3.2	4.8	5.4	1861	8.4	21.9	29.4	36.3

ber of frequencies and a logarithmic scale for the class intervals, showed that there was some approach to normality in the distribution of the annual figures. This further justifies the use of a geometric measure.

Three indications of skewness were used: first, one measuring the middle of 40 per cent of the distribution. This was accomplished by the formula $(d_7 - d_3) \div (d_7 + d_3)$ in which d_7 is the difference between the logarithm of the seventh decile and the logarithm of the median and d_3 is the difference between the logarithm of the median and the logarithm of the third decile. The second measure of skewness was based on the middle 50 per cent and was computed by the formula $(q_3 - q_1) \div (q_3 + q_1)$. The final measure of skewness covered the middle 60 per cent of the distribution. The formula used was $(d_8 - d_2) \div (d_8 + d_2)$

A comparison of the results of the skewness computed by these three methods gives a rough description of the extent and direction in which the frequency distributions differ from a normal geometric distribution. Changes in skewness in any particular year as represented by the different measures show the influence of including additional sections of the distribution in that year. With the first method, only 20 per cent of the cases on each side of the median are considered. In the successive measurements, additional frequencies are included, enlarging the group from 40 to 50 and then to 60 per cent of the entire distribution.[1]

The skewness for each year derived by these three measures is given in Table 47 in the Appendix. Attention will be centered in our analysis upon the skewness of the quartiles since in only four years did it fail to agree in direction with one or both of the measures of skewness in the deciles. In two-thirds of the years all three agree in direction. There is more variation in the extent of skewness as indicated by the different measures, but in most years there is reasonable conformity.

Following the suggestion of Professor Bowley that skewness of .08 or less in price data is reasonable conformity to a normal distribution, we have selected as distinctly asymmetrical years those with a coëfficient of more than .08.

The annual distributions in the first part of the period from 1784 to 1808 usually approached a moderate symmetry. Only in 1787 and 1793 were the distributions between —.1 and —.2 and in 1788 slightly more than +.1, marking these years as having especially irregular distribution. Between 1801 and 1807, in contrast, every year except 1804 was definitely asymmetrical. A large positive skew-

[1] Any description of frequency distributions by the use of these measures of skewness is incomplete to the extent that no allowance is made for the degree of concentration. For this aspect a measure of kurtosis must be used.

ness characterized the distribution of annual relatives in 1801, 1802, 1803, and 1805, while those in 1806 and 1807 were as definitely negative in skewness.

TABLE 4

COËFFICIENT OF SKEWNESS OF QUARTILES OF ANNUAL DISTRIBUTIONS OF RELATIVES OF 140 COMMODITIES

1784–1861

Year	Extremely Negative	Practically Symmetrical		Extremely Positive	Year	Extremely Negative	Practically Symmetrical		Extremely Positive
		Negative	Positive				Negative	Positive	
1784			.068		1823			.024	
1785		.055			1824			.016	
1786		.036			1825	.105			
1787	.103				1826		.071		
1788				.117	1827	.083			
1789			.032		1828			.041	
1790		.008			1829		.008		
1791			.002		1830	.268			
1792		.038			1831			.001	
1793	.184				1832		.007		
1794		.043			1833			.015	
1795			.075		1834	.192			
1796		.022			1835	.097			
1797			.020		1836		.074		
1798			.035		1837	.194			
1799		.078			1838		.005		
1800		.012			1839			.069	
1801				.176	1840	.154			
1802				.083	1841			.071	
1803				.136	1842		.018		
1804			.061		1843			.047	
1805				.097	1844		.012		
1806	.106				1845		.066		
1807	.289				1846			.072	
1808			.051		1847			.031	
1809				.222	1848			.058	
1810				.118	1849			.020	
1811				.262	1850				.201
1812				.138	1851				.174
1813			.039		1852				.213
1814			.062		1853				.189
1815		.051			1854			.037	
1816				.296	1855			.067	
1817				.310	1856	.187			
1818		.003			1857	.148			
1819	.119				1858		.069		
1820			.048		1859	.150			
1821		.006			1860	.129			
1822				.132	1861		.054		

The high proportions of skewness in these years indicate the existence of a diversity of price movements either contrary in direction or at different rates. Similar diversity is suggested by the frequency of high coëfficients of skewness in the period from 1809 to 1821. The four years from 1809 to 1812 inclusive as well as 1816 and 1817 show a high positive skewness ranging from +.1 in 1810 to more than +.3 in 1817. This was the maximum asymmetry in any of the 78 years.

The positive skewness in most of the years from 1801 to 1812, when average prices were generally moving upward, indicates that a few commodities were rising materially while the bulk of the others lagged behind. The same skewness in 1816 and 1817, however, when prices were contracting, shows that a few fell appreciably less than the average or actually rose when the majority of commodities dropped.

The negative skewness of slightly more than .1 in 1819 suggests that in that year only a few commodities fell markedly and that most commodities fell slightly or even rose somewhat.

The minor peak of 1822 resulted in a positive skewness of .132. Not until 1850 did prices again show a skewness of as much as +.08. Most of the years between 1825 and 1840 had at least a slight tendency to negative asymmetry, and in seven of the years the coëfficient fell between —.08 and —.27. Despite the similarity in distribution, the years 1830 and 1837 especially show a different type of change from the previous year. In 1830 when prices were generally low, and for many commodities still falling, the negative skewness of .27 shows that extensive declines were restricted to a few commodities, while the skewness of —.19 in the crash of 1837 suggests that only a few commodities dropped appreciably that year while the remaining series either fell or continued to advance slightly.

The nine years of generally low prices from 1841 to 1849 had the most normal distributions of any period of similar length between the Revolution and the Civil War. The skewness for nearly a decade did not exceed ±.07. This approximation to a normal distribution is in contrast not only to the preceding years but to the fifties and early sixties.

That the advance of the early fifties was confined to a few commodities with a marked increase in contrast to the more typical mild rise in most commodities is indicated by the positive unbalance of .17 to .21 in each of the years from 1850 to 1853 inclusive. The latter part of the fifties had nearly as extreme asymmetry in the opposite direction, indicating, especially at the peak of 1857, that a small group of commodities had started to fall ahead of the general index. In 1856, 1857, 1859, and 1860 the coëfficient of skewness was between —.13 and —.19.

The degree of unbalance in the distribution of the relative of prices around an average is indicated by the size of the coëfficient of skewness. In years characterized by a high positive or negative asymmetry the composite index is least representative. It is in these years that it is especially necessary to analyze the various classifications of commodities in order to isolate those which contributed to the unbalance by moving less rapidly than others or even moving in an opposite direction.

CHAPTER III

CHANGES IN PRICE STABILITY

The causes of changes in prices have usually been classified as accidental, seasonal, cyclical, and secular. All of these factors exerted a combined influence on the monthly quotations from 1784 to 1861. For purposes of analysis, therefore, it is essential that some factors be removed in order to see the effects of the others more clearly. It is also desirable to have the longer-time changes in mind before attempting the more minute analysis of the monthly prices. For this reason attention must first be given to changes in the annual prices. This procedure eliminates seasonal factors and minimizes the effect of accidental ones.

In order to aid in the appraisal of conditions in each period, the annual prices have been converted into percentages of change from the previous year. This procedure realistically measures the extent of price changes to which business men had to adjust. The manner in which they can adjust to meet these changes has a widespread influence upon the success of individual businesses and consequently upon prosperity or depression.

The first use that can be made of the percentage of change in the annual prices of specific commodities from year to year is the measurement of certain inherent stabilities in these prices. The most stable group consists of those commodities which sold at the same average price for two years either because monthly prices were unchanged or because changes in the monthly prices balanced each other. The number of such series varied considerably from year to year.

In general it can be pointed out that in the period from 1785 to 1808 the percentage of the commodities which did not change from the previous year ranged from 0.0 to 13.6 per cent. In nine of the twenty-four years less than 3 per cent of the commodities did not change in price from the previous year, but in an equal number of years more than 7 per cent maintained the price of the previous year.

Fewer commodities were unchanging in the years from 1809 to 1821. Despite the fact that in one year the prices of 16.4 per cent of the commodities were the same as in the previous year, there were only three other years in which more than 3 per cent of the series showed no change.

The remaining two periods were, in contrast, characterized by an increasing number of commodities which held the same average price for two years or more. In approximately two-thirds of the years from

TABLE 5
FREQUENCY OF YEARS BY PERCENTAGE OF COMMODITIES WITH NO CHANGE IN PRICE FROM PREVIOUS YEAR

Percentage of Commodities	Number of Years in Period			
	1785–1808	1809–1821	1822–1843	1844–1861
Under 1.0	4	2	1	
1.0 and under 2.0	1	3	3	
2.0 " " 3.0	4	4	1	
3.0 " " 4.0	3		2	
4.0 " " 5.0	2			1
5.0 " " 6.0	1	2		4
6.0 " " 7.0				
7.0 " " 8.0	1		8	3
8.0 " " 9.0	2		2	3
9.0 " " 10.0			2	
10.0 " " 11.0	3		2	2
11.0 " " 12.0				
12.0 " " 13.0	2	1	1	4
13.0 " " 14.0	1			1
14.0 " " 15.0				
15.0 " " 16.0				
16.0 " " 17.0		1		
Total	24	13	22	18

1822 to 1843 more than 7 per cent of the commodities were unchanged from one year to the following, while from 1844 to 1861 at least 4 per cent in each year were at the same price as in the previous year and in seven of the 18 years at least 10 per cent of the series did not change.

Most of these instances of great stability were concentrated in four sectors—1787, 1789, 1790, 1793; 1804 and 1805; 1821 to 1824 inclusive; and 1848 to 1852 inclusive. In addition to these fifteen years, 10 per cent or more of the commodities were unchanged in 1813, 1856, and 1860.

There is more inherent stability in the movements of prices than can be indicated by merely the percentage of commodities which sold at the same average price for two consecutive years. For practical purposes, minor changes in the prices of individual commodities can be disregarded. Any decision as to what constitutes a minor change, however, must be purely arbitrary in character. Doubtless, the relative importance of any change in price differs according to the commodity and even from time to time for the same commodity. In order to simplify the problem of measuring the importance of these minor changes, we have adopted the arbitrary procedure of classifying with the commodities which had no change in price those which increased or decreased less than 2.5 per cent from one year to the next.

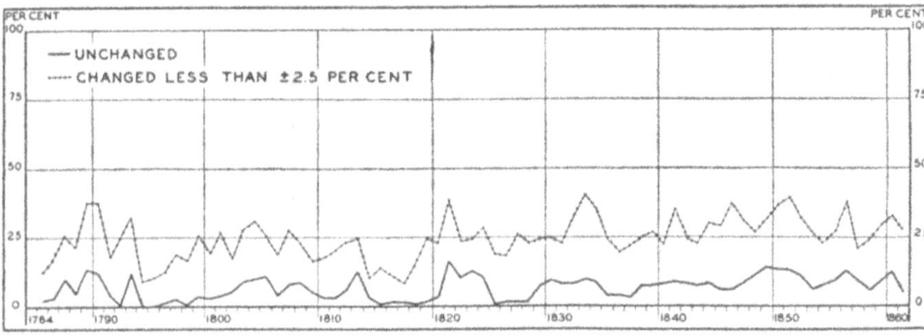

CHART IV—PERCENTAGE OF COMMODITIES WITH LEAST AVERAGE CHANGES IN ANNUAL PRICES, 1785-1861

The summary of the number of years in each period in which various proportions of the commodities were relatively stable brings out clearly the decided tendency for stability in the price system. In the first period the years differed widely with respect to the percentage of commodities which changed less than 2.5 per cent. In most of the years between 15 and 20 or between 25 and 30 per cent of the commodities varied little if at all. During the next period there was a decrease in stability, the bulk of the years having some stability in the prices of 10 to 25 per cent of the commodities. Both of the other periods were characterized by a progressive increase in the number of commodities with little variation. In the typical year between 1822 and 1843 from 20 to 25 per cent of the commodities underwent only minor changes, and there was a tendency for an even larger percentage to be comparatively stable. In no year was there less than 17.5 per cent of the commodities in this class. In each year of the final period, 1844-1861, at least 20 per cent of the commodities had only negligible changes. In half of the years 30 per cent or more of the commodities were in this category.

Since it is clear that there was a tendency for many commodities to increase in the stability of their prices from year to year, it is essential that a further analysis be made with a view to isolating the areas of the economy which contributed most to this development.

TABLE 6

FREQUENCY OF YEARS BY PERCENTAGE OF COMMODITIES WITH PRICE CHANGES FROM PREVIOUS YEAR OF LESS THAN 2.5 PER CENT

Percentage of Commodities	Number of Years in Period			
	1785–1808	1809–1821	1822–1843	1844–1861
Under 5.0				
5.0 and under 10.0	1	1		
10.0 " " 15.0	3	3		
15.0 " " 20.0	7	3	3	
20.0 " " 25.0	2	4	10	3
25.0 " " 30.0	7	1	5	6
30.0 " " 35.0	2		2	5
35.0 " " 40.0	2	1	1	4
40.0 " " 45.0			1	
Total	24	13	22	18

The classification of the 140 series into nine major groups is especially adapted to this purpose. Fish, furs, and wines may be disregarded in this discussion because the number of commodities included in each of these classes is small. The other six groups each include from 12 to 40 series.

The farm crops or agricultural raw products are primarily field crops, much affected by weather and climatic conditions.

The second group of commodities, also originating on farms, represent products of the milling, baking, packing, and dairy industries.

The imported foods, heavily weighted with spices, also include molasses and unrefined sugar.

Table 7
Classification of Commodities by Major Groups

Farm Crops 12

- Corn
- Cotton
- Flax
- Flaxseed
- Hemp
- Oats
- Peas
- Rice
- Rye
- Tobacco
  - James River
  - Kentucky
- Wheat

Imported Foods 21

- Almonds
- Chocolate
- Cloves
- Cocoa
- Coffee
- Currants
- Ginger
  - ground
  - race
- Honey
- Lemons
- Mace
- Molasses
  - New Orleans
  - Sugar House
  - West India
- Nutmegs
- Oil, sweet
- Pepper
- Pimento
- Raisins
- Sugar
  - Havana brown
- Tea

Lumber Products and Naval Stores 12

- Pine boards
  - heart
  - sap
  - white
- Pitch
- Rosin
- Shingles
- Spirits of turpentine
- Staves
  - barrel
  - hogshead
  - pipe
- Tar
- Turpentine

Industrial Ready for Consumption 27

- Brandy, French
- Candles
  - sperm
  - tallow
- Coal
  - anthracite
  - bituminous
- Cordage
  - American
  - foreign
- Duck
  - bear ravens
  - ravens
- Gin, Holland
- Glass
- Gunpowder
- Nails
- Rum
  - Jamaica
  - New England
  - West India
- Salt
  - coarse
  - fine
- Soap
  - castile
  - white
  - yellow or common
- Sheeting
  - Russian brown
  - Russian white
- Shot
- Starch
- Sugar
  - loaf and lump
  - white

Farm Derivatives 14

- Beef
- Bread
- Butter
- Cheese
- Corn meal
- Feathers
- Flour
- Ginseng
- Hams
- Hides
- Lard
- Pork
- Rye meal
- Tallow

Industrial Raw and Semi-Finished 40

- Alum
- Ashes
  - pearl
  - pot
- Beeswax
  - white
  - yellow
- Brimstone
  - crude
  - rolls
- Copper
  - old
  - sheathing
- Copperas
- Fustic
- Indigo
- Iron
  - bar, domestic
  - bar, foreign
  - hoop
  - nail rod
  - pig
  - sheet
- Lead
- Lead
  - red
  - white dry
  - white ground in oil
- Leather
- Logwood
- Mahogany
- Oil
  - linseed
  - sperm
  - whale
- Plaster of Paris
- Saltpeter
  - refined
  - rough
- Spanish brown
  - dry
  - ground in oil
- Steel
  - country
  - English blistered
  - German
  - Crowley-Trieste
- Tin
  - block
  - plate
- Verdigris

Fish 3

- Cod
- Herring
- Mackerel

Furs 3

- Beaver
- Deer
- Muskrat

Wines 8

- Claret
- Lisbon
- Madeira
- Malaga
- Port
- Sherry
- Teneriffe
  - cargo
  - London particular

The lumber products and naval stores include pine boards, cedar shingles, oak staves, and tar and turpentine and their products.

The industrial raw and semi-finished materials consist chiefly of all the dyes and most of the chemicals and drugs, ferrous and non-ferrous metals, and raw materials used in paints.

Among the industrial commodities ready for consumption are classified textile fabrics, spirits, refined sugar, salt, soap, and other processed commodities.

An analysis of the relative stability of each of the six major groups indicates differences in the character of price changes among the groups and from period to period within the groups. The industrial commodities ready for consumption never in any period, and the raw and semi-finished commodities and the imported foods only once, had a year in which none of their commodities varied less than 2.5 per cent. At the other extreme, farm crops had from three to five years and farm derivatives from one to three years in each period when none of their constituent series varied less than 2.5 per cent. The group of lumber products and naval stores was somewhat comparable to farm crops in the first period but was more like the other groups after 1808.

During the four periods considered as a whole, the industrial raw and semi-finished group was the most stable. In a majority of the years 30 per cent or more of its commodities varied less than 2.5 per cent from the price of the previous year. Many of the industrial commodities ready for consumption were nearly as stable. At the other extreme, less than 20 per cent of the farm crops, farm derivatives, and imported foods—the groups with least stability—had only mild changes in prices in a large majority of the years. The lumber products and naval stores were slightly more stable.

Somewhat the same proportion of farm crops and farm derivatives showed little change in all periods. All of the other groups tended to be least stable between 1809 and 1821 but showed usually a progressive increase in stability during the last two periods. The lumber products and naval stores showed in both of the first two periods a majority of years in which less than 17 per cent of their constituents changed mildly, if at all, from one year to another, while in a majority of the years in the last two periods 25 per cent or more of their commodities were stable. Similarly, in imported foods, in more than half of the years from 1785 to 1821 less than

TABLE 8

FREQUENCY OF YEARS BY PERCENTAGE OF COMMODITIES WITH PRICE CHANGES FROM PREVIOUS YEAR OF LESS THAN 2.5 PER CENT BY SIX LARGEST MAJOR GROUPS

Percentage of Commodities	Farm		Imported Foods	Lumber Products & Naval Stores	Industrial	
	Crops	Derivatives			Raw	Consumption
1785–1808						
0.0	5	1		5		
0.1 and under 10.0	5	4	13	4	1	3
10.0 " " 20.0	5	9	5	6	5	5
20.0 " " 30.0	7	9	4	5	6	6
30.0 " " 40.0	1		2		7	6
40.0 " " 50.0	1	1		3	3	4
50.0 " " 60.0				1	2	
Total	24	24	24	24	24	24
1809–1821						
0.0	3	2		1	1	
0.1 and under 10.0	6	4	7	3	1	1
10.0 " " 20.0	2	2	3	3	5	6
20.0 " " 30.0	2	2	3	4	3	5
30.0 " " 40.0		2			2	
40.0 " " 50.0						
50.0 " " 60.0				2	1	1
60.0 " " 70.0		1				
Total	13	13	13	13	13	13
1822–1843						
0.0	4	3	1			
0.1 and under 10.0	7	5	3	2		
10.0 " " 20.0	8	6	11	7		3
20.0 " " 30.0	1	6	6	4	6	11
30.0 " " 40.0	2	2	1	4	12	4
40.0 " " 50.0				5	3	3
50.0 " " 60.0					1	1
Total	22	22	22	22	22	22
1844–1861						
0.0	4	1		1		
0.1 and under 10.0	3	5	1	3		1
10.0 " " 20.0	2	6	3	3	1	
20.0 " " 30.0	5	5	8	4	5	3
30.0 " " 40.0	4	1	4	4	8	6
40.0 " " 50.0			2	1	4	6
50.0 " " 60.0				2		2
Total	18	18	18	18	18	18
1785–1861						
0.0	16	7	1	7	1	
0.1 and under 10.0	21	18	24	12	2	5
10.0 " " 20.0	17	23	22	19	11	14
20.0 " " 30.0	15	22	21	17	20	25
30.0 " " 40.0	7	5	7	8	29	16
40.0 " " 50.0	1	1	2	9	10	13
50.0 " " 60.0				5	4	4
60.0 " " 70.0		1				
Total	77	77	77	77	77	77

10 per cent of the commodities were relatively stable. In the next period more than 10 per cent were usually in this class and after 1844 usually at least 20 per cent.

The industrial groups showed the most striking increase in stability from period to period. In 13 years before 1822 less than 20 per cent of the industrial raw and semi-finished products varied within 2.5 per cent, but after 1822 there was only one year in which as few as 20 per cent varied so slightly. Usually 30 per cent or more had mild variations. Of the industrial commodities ready for consumption, less than 20 per cent were stable in fifteen years of the first two periods and in only four years of the last two periods. From 1822 to 1843 it was an exceptional year when less than 20 per cent of these series were in the stable group and after 1844 it was rare for less than 30 per cent to be in this category.

It is evident that both industrial groups contributed heavily throughout all periods to the number of commodities which changed slightly from year to year. The progressive tendency toward increased stability of prices, however, came not only from these two groups, but also from the lumber products and naval stores and imported foods.

The percentage of the years in each period in which each commodity changed less than 2.5 per cent from the average of the previous year isolates the commodities which contributed to this increased stability. A wide range was covered by the series in each major group, but in some the range was much wider than in others.

That none of the farm crops contributed appreciably to the relatively inert category of commodities is evidenced by the fact that in none of these series were there changes of less than 2.5 per cent in as many as 40 per cent of the years in any period. Only hemp and James River tobacco had as many as 15 per cent of the years in each period when their prices changed less than 2.5 per cent, while Kentucky tobacco had this amount of stability in three periods and flax, flaxseed, oats, and rice in two periods. In contrast, wheat and rye in every year of two periods varied at least 2.5 per cent from the prices of the previous year. The annual prices of corn, cotton, flaxseed, and oats also varied this much in one period.

The farm derivatives had approximately as little stability as the farm crops. In each of the four periods, feathers changed less than 2.5 per cent in 40 per cent of the years. No other commodity had minor changes in even 15 per cent of all the periods, although beef, cheese, ginseng, and hides had at least this amount of stability in three periods and bread, butter, ham, pork, and tallow in two periods. Rye meal, however, was the only commodity which did not have at least one year with a minor change in each of the four periods. In every year from 1822 to 1843 the prices of rye meal differed at least 4.8 per cent from the average of the previous one.

The various imported foods had a greater range in the number of minor changes in prices than the domestic agricultural products. Among the most fluctuating commodities seven in some one of the four periods had no changes in price from one year to another of less than 2.5 per cent: race ginger, lemons, and tea from 1809 to 1821, pimento and raisins from 1822 to 1843, and almonds and currants from 1844 to 1861. The most stable commodities were chocolate, cocoa, and ground ginger, which in more than 55 per cent of the years in at least one period varied less than 2.5 per cent. In another period ground ginger had only minor changes in more than 35 per cent of the years. This much stability appeared also in mace and pepper during one period and in sweet oil during two. That all of these cases of noticeable stability except one in chocolate occurred in the last two periods explains the increase in the number of small changes noted in this group after 1821.

Lumber products and naval stores also differed widely in the amount of price stability characteristic of the constituent series. All of the lumber products except white pine boards had only minor changes in more than 35 per cent of the years in at least one period. The naval stores were more variable. From 1809 to 1821 tar and turpentine changed more than 2.5 per cent every year.

A few of the industrial raw and semi-finished materials tended to undergo large changes from year to year. Thus in the first period whale oil changed at least 3 per cent a year, from 1809 to 1821 copperas, linseed oil, sperm oil, and plaster of Paris varied at least 2.5 per cent from one year to another, and from 1822 to 1843 lead moved 3.5 per cent or more each year. No commodity was as consistently variable after 1843.

Many of the industrial raw and semi-finished materials characteristically had a substantial amount of stability in their annual prices. Except for the period from 1809 to 1821, when because of the influence of the war most prices changed substantially, from 14 to 16 series varied less than 2.5 per cent in 35 per cent of the years. The increased stability after 1821 did not noticeably affect the number of commodities with minor changes in more than 35 per cent of the years in any period, but it is apparent in those in which prices in 50 per cent or more of the years differed less than 2.5 per cent from the previous year. Only one or two series were this stable before 1822, but six fell in this category in each of the last two periods. In general it was the ferrous and non-ferrous metals which had minor price changes in half or more of the years of the last two periods.

The industrial commodities ready for consumption were more uniform in the amount of their stability than the industrial raw and semi-finished materials. All of the highly processed group held at least once in each period within 2.5 per cent of the average price of the previous year except brandy and Jamaica rum from 1809 to 1821. As evidence of the progressive increase in stability of the group as a whole only 8 and 6 series had minor price changes in 35 per cent of the years in the first two periods compared with 10 and 13 in the last two. The number of commodities which in half or more of the years in any period had prices but mildly changed from those of the previous year increased especially after 1843. While only one or two series had been this stable in the first three periods, 10 commodities were in this class from 1844 to 1861. These consisted of all the textile fabrics, gin, glass, gunpowder, and yellow soap.

The three small groups of fish, furs, and wines differed in their amount of stability. Fish usually changed substantially in price from year to year. The greatest range in behavior was from 1809 to 1821 when mackerel always varied at least 3.9 per cent from one year to another, while in four years, or approximately 31 per cent of the period, the prices of herring varied less than 2.5 per cent. Furs were generally more stable than fish and tended somewhat to increase in stability. Between 1844 and 1861 the price of deer skins changed less than 2.5 per cent in nearly 40 per cent of the years and those of beaver and muskrat in slightly more than 55 per cent of the period.

The prices of wines were even more stable, usually varying less than 2.5 per cent in at least a quarter of the years. During at least one period every series except claret changed mildly if at all in more than 35 per cent of the years. From 1844 to 1861 alone all except claret and Teneriffe cargo were comparatively stable in at least seven years or more than 35 per cent of the period and Lisbon, Madeira, Malaga, and port changed less than 2.5 per cent in at least half of those years.

A few series progressively increased in stability from one period to another. Coffee and pepper from the imported foods, country steel from the industrial raw and semi-finished commodities, Castile and yellow soap from the industrial commodities ready for consumption, and sherry wine had in each successive period relatively more years with changes of less than 2.5 per cent than in the previous one. A correspondingly progressive decline occurred in prices of pork from the farm derivatives, almonds from imported foods, and nails from the industrial commodities ready for consumption.

The annual price movements of specific commodities in each period indicate that it was the ferrous and non-ferrous metals and textile fabrics which contributed most to the increased stability of the industrial group. Lumber products, wines, and a few commodities especially in both industrial groups and imported foods also contributed heavily to the increase in stability found in the total group of commodities.

The analysis of the development of increasing stability conceals the fluctuations around the trend within each period. It is important to know the relation of changes in the percentages of commodities with minor variations to the price behavior of particular years. This will be pointed out in Chapters VII-X in which the monthly fluctuations are traced. In those chapters, too, the changes in the percentage of commodities with material increases or decreases will be used to indicate the extent to which various cycles had a widespread or restricted influence on the economy. Fluctuations in prices, which will unavoidably be emphasized, must be considered against these evidences of inherent stability. It is essential to keep in mind the progressive modification in the type of price behavior arising out of the character of the commodity, its changing importance, and its trend in price.

CHAPTER IV

YEAR-TO-YEAR VARIABILITY

A small but increasing proportion of the commodities tended to change in price but little, if at all, from year to year. This conclusion is clear from the analysis in Chapter III. There still remains the question as to what tendencies developed in the variability of specific commodities. In order to find the answer it is necessary to reëxamine and summarize the percentages of change in the annual prices from year to year. For this purpose an index of year-to-year variability has been computed for each commodity in each of the four periods.[1]

This measure was constructed by taking the mean deviation from the mean of the link relatives of the average annual prices of each commodity during the successive periods. In order to make the measurement of the various series comparable, the mean deviation was divided by the mean from which it was computed. This measure is influenced by cyclical swings, to some extent by accidental causes, especially those which affected crops, and to a minor extent by trend. The measure enables one to see the similarities and differences among the various commodities in the same period as well as changes in the variability of the same commodity in different periods.

Variability in Different Periods

Before examining the relative variability of specific commodities, the distribution of the entire group in each period is considered in order to indicate the underlying change from one period to another. From 1809 to 1821 the commodities were more scattered around a higher average than in any other period. The greatest concentration was 41 commodities with a variability of between 12 and 16 per cent. Slightly more than half of the other commodities had an average

[1] To avoid any overlapping, the periods used in this computation were defined as from 1785 to 1808, from 1809 to 1821, from 1822 to 1843, and from 1844 to 1860. Data for 1861 were not available when the indices of variability were computed, but their inclusion would make only slight changes in the indices for the fourth period.

relative variability of less than 12 per cent. The series changing 16 per cent or more were widely distributed. Stated differently, 35 commodities had, from 1809 to 1821, a relative variability of less than 9.65 and an equal number more than 18.1. The median was 13.2. In all of the other periods, the distributions centered around a lower level. The variability from 1785 to 1808 tended to be less than in the war period. The years from 1844 to 1860 were still less variable, while the least relative year-to-year variation occurred from 1822 to 1843.

One method of comparing the distributions in these four periods is the location of the quartiles and median in each.

MEASURES OF RELATIVE YEAR-TO-YEAR VARIABILITY

	1785–1808	1809–1821	1822–1843	1844–1860
Lower Quartile	7.05	9.65	6.00	6.75
Median	10.95	13.20	8.30	9.25
Upper Quartile	14.65	18.10	11.10	11.80

Another way of showing the differences between the distributions in the various periods is to determine the number of commodities in each which would be included within the significant measures of 1809-1821. Instead of 35 commodities having a relative average variability of less than 9.65, as from 1809 to 1821, 52 series for the period 1785-1808, 78 for 1844-1860, and 93 for 1822-1843 had less than 9.65 per cent of changeability. The comparison of the median and upper quartile of the war period with the distribution of the commodities in the other periods shows a somewhat corresponding decline in the number of series with high variability.

NUMBER OF COMMODITIES WITH RELATIVE YEAR-TO-YEAR VARIABILITY

	1785–1808	1809–1821	1822–1843	1844–1860
Less than 9.65	52	35	93	78
More than 13.20	42	70	20	20
More than 18.10	16	35	8	4

VARIABILITY OF INDIVIDUAL COMMODITIES

Among the commodities there were some consistently high or low in their amount of change from year to year, as well as some which fell at one extreme in one period and at the other extreme in others. Six commodities were among the highest 25 per cent of all items in each of the periods. These were corn and rye from the farm crops; currants, lemons, and race ginger from the imported foods; and spirits of turpentine from lumber products and naval stores. In addition, 16 commodities fell in the highest group in three of the four periods. Wheat, Kentucky tobacco, and cotton can be added to the representatives from farm products, raisins to the imported foods group, and turpentine to the lumber products and naval stores group. Some series of the farm derivatives and industrial products ranked among the most variable commodities in three periods. Specifically, these include flour, rye meal, butter, and pork from the farm derivatives; fustic, plaster of Paris, whale oil, and crude brimstone from the industrial raw materials; and coarse salt and brandy from the industrial products ready for consumption. The only other series having as large year-to-year variability as these was muskrat in the furs. None of the fish or wines were represented in the group with consistently high variability.

At the other extreme were the commodities which in all periods fell in the lowest quarter for variability. Three industrial raw materials—nail rod iron, country steel, Spanish brown ground in oil—, three industrial commodities ready for consumption—glass and both grades of Russian sheeting—, and Madeira wine were in each period among the least variable. A large number of items were in the lowest classification in three of the four periods. These were concentrated especially in the two groups of industrial materials. In addition to the three industrial raw materials low in every period, 13 more were among the lowest in three of the periods. Among the industrial products ready for consumption there were two which in three periods had little variability besides the three which were similarly invariable in all of the periods. Only one of the lumber products can be classed among the least variable. It is such series that contributed largely to the stability noted in Chapter III. None of the farm crops, farm derivatives, imported foods, fish, or furs had consistently low variability.

Because of the tendency noted in the general distribution for a marked increase in variability between 1785-1808 and 1809-1821,

TABLE 9

RELATIVE YEAR-TO-YEAR VARIABILITY OF 140 COMMODITIES CLASSIFIED BY NINE MAJOR GROUPS BY PERIODS

Group and Commodity	1785–1808	1809–1821	1822–1843	1844–1860
FARM CROPS				
Hemp	10.8	13.0	7.5	8.1
Peas	11.1	16.0	24.9	14.6
Flax	11.5	11.2	11.0	6.7
Cotton	11.9	22.7	17.6	17.2
Oats	12.2	14.0	20.6	12.4
Tobacco				
James River	12.4	20.6	16.3	11.4
Kentucky	12.6	21.7	16.8	12.3
Flaxseed	15.5	16.2	9.8	7.7
Rye	16.0	19.2	19.5	12.1
Wheat	18.0	17.7	15.2	15.8
Corn	19.7	18.3	19.1	13.2
Rice	20.1	17.7	9.2	12.5
FARM DERIVATIVES				
Feathers	4.9	6.3	8.4	9.1
Hides	8.7	14.2	5.6	10.5
Cheese	11.5	9.9	12.9	9.1
Pork	12.1	18.8	12.4	17.0
Beef	12.1	8.5	7.6	13.1
Ginseng	12.7	14.2	15.5	9.4
Hams	13.6	12.0	8.7	11.4
Bread	13.8	11.8	9.4	10.7
Tallow	14.3	5.6	11.0	7.4
Lard	15.5	13.0	11.6	11.4
Flour	16.7	15.8	14.1	15.9
Corn meal	17.0	17.0	15.5	10.9
Butter	18.1	13.0	16.8	12.2
Rye meal	19.2	15.5	19.2	13.8
IMPORTED FOODS				
Pepper	8.3	13.0	9.8	10.2
Cloves	8.5	12.6	12.2	7.9
Chocolate	9.1	3.5	6.6	5.1
Tea	9.2	19.9	11.3	7.8
Sugar				
Havana brown	9.9	12.2	7.1	11.1
Molasses	10.2	19.3	8.5	13.4
Oil, sweet	10.6	10.6	8.3	7.7
Honey	10.6	20.0	11.3	9.3
Coffee	11.3	12.3	5.2	6.8
Almonds	12.9	10.5	12.5	19.7
Pimento	13.1	14.6	11.9	12.1
Cocoa	14.7	15.2	8.3	5.1
Mace	14.8	8.6	6.5	11.2
Lemons	15.1	22.9	20.5	20.2
Raisins	17.5	14.1	20.3	18.0
Ginger				
race	19.3	24.1	14.8	12.6
ground	22.3	25.2	7.8	10.6
Nutmegs	26.8	16.0	8.0	11.9
Currants	31.4	26.8	17.0	25.5
LUMBER PRODUCTS AND NAVAL STORES				
Staves				
hogshead	8.8	6.8	5.8	10.7
pipe	9.1	5.6	8.3	8.7
Shingles	9.3	6.7	4.8	11.5
Pine Boards				
heart	9.7	7.0	6.4	9.8
Staves				
barre!	11.1	7.8	7.3	9.8
Pine Boards				
sap	11.8	6.3	5.3	4.9
white	13.6	9.2	7.9	5.0
Tar	14.3	22.6	7.4	12.7
Pitch	14.9	18.6	5.1	9.4
Turpentine	15.1	26.9	9.3	13.7
Rosin	18.3	16.7	7.1	10.0
Spirits of Turpentine	20.7	36.3	12.8	12.0

Group and Commodity	1785–1808	1809–1821	1822–1843	1844–1860
INDUSTRIAL RAW AND SEMI-FINISHED				
Tin Plates	3.2	20.9	5.6	2.8
Lead				
white ground in oil	3.8	12.8	5.7	3.8
Steel				
Crowley and Trieste	4.4	9.8	2.4	5.3
country	4.6	4.8	3.1	0.9
Spanish brown				
ground in oil	5.0	4.0	4.8	3.1
Leather	5.1	6.6	4.4	8.3
Tin Blocks	5.4	14.4	7.3	9.5
Spanish Brown				
dry	5.4	14.5	5.5	4.9
Iron				
sheet	5.4	5.4	6.5	5.3
bar, foreign	5.4	9.8	5.2	7.2
Copper				
sheathing	5.6	12.7	5.0	5.1
old	5.6	14.0	8.3	8.1
Iron				
pig	5.7	6.2	8.8	9.7
nail rod	5.7	4.6	4.9	6.6
Lead				
white dry	6.0	12.7	5.7	5.9
Steel				
Eng. blistered	6.3	12.9	1.4	1.3
Beeswax				
white	6.4	9.6	8.8	5.1
yellow	6.4	9.8	5.6	5.9
Steel				
German	6.5	17.0	2.0	4.1
Iron				
hoop	6.6	5.5	3.9	9.1
bar, domestic	6.7	5.3	6.2	8.4
Lead				
red	7.1	14.6	7.3	5.5
Lead	7.2	13.9	9.0	6.4
Indigo	8.2	10.7	10.7	7.4
Ashes				
pearl	8.7	14.5	8.8	10.6
Alum	9.5	13.8	7.3	8.0
Copperas	10.3	28.5	8.0	8.1
Oil				
sperm	11.4	15.7	9.6	9.3
Verdigris	11.8	26.5	8.3	12.3
Mahogany	12.2	25.6	7.9	7.3
Brimstone				
crude	12.2	23.9	18.9	12.9
rolls	12.2	22.0	13.6	9.5
Ashes				
pot	12.5	13.4	11.2	10.5
Logwood	14.6	13.1	8.5	8.5
Oil				
whale	14.8	19.3	9.7	12.2
linseed	15.8	13.1	10.8	10.1
Plaster of Paris	20.0	33.0	13.1	8.5
Fustic	30.5	22.0	10.0	14.7
Saltpeter				
rough	30.7	17.5	6.2	9.2
refined	31.7	14.1	6.4	8.8
INDUSTRIAL READY FOR CONSUMPTION				
Nails	3.3	6.7	7.6	10.2
Sheeting				
Russian white	5.2	6.7	5.5	0.8
Glass	5.2	5.8	4.8	2.8
Sheeting				
Russian brown	5.9	6.5	5.3	1.7
Duck				
bear ravens	6.5	14.6	6.7	1.9
Candles				
sperm	6.6	5.9	10.6	9.0

TABLE 9 (*Concluded*)

Group and Commodity	1785–1808	1809–1821	1822–1843	1844–1860
INDUSTRIAL READY FOR CONSUMPTION (*Continued*)				
Duck				
ravens	7.0	15.4	8.0	1.8
Sugar				
loaf & lump	7.0	11.4	5.1	8.6
Havana white	9.0	11.3	7.6	8.9
Soap				
white	9.3	3.7	8.7	5.7
Coal				
anthracite	9.7	21.9	12.3	8.2
bituminous	9.7	21.6	7.2	9.1
Cordage				
American	10.1	10.0	5.7	5.5
Soap				
yellow	10.4	5.7	3.9	3.4
Cordage				
foreign	10.6	9.8	6.4	9.5
Shot	10.8	12.3	8.1	5.0
Rum				
Jamaica	10.9	13.3	5.6	8.0
West India	11.0	15.8	4.3	8.0
New England	11.9	18.7	7.6	9.9
Candles				
tallow	12.5	7.5	8.9	7.1
Starch	12.6	8.9	7.9	7.3
Gin	15.0	12.0	6.2	4.7
Brandy	15.6	18.3	9.0	18.7
Salt				
coarse	18.1	27.1	8.3	17.6
Soap				
Castile	19.3	8.4	4.9	5.5
Salt				
fine	21.3	27.3	7.6	11.7
Gunpowder	22.5	14.2	1.6	6.6
FISH				
Mackerel	11.9	14.6	10.1	10.7
Cod	12.7	15.8	12.5	9.1
Herring	14.4	9.6	14.0	10.3
FURS				
Deer	9.9	17.9	13.2	11.4
Beaver	11.7	9.7	9.8	6.5
Muskrat	15.7	9.6	12.8	15.3
WINES				
Sherry	5.1	10.9	10.3	7.0
Madeira	5.2	5.0	4.2	5.4
Lisbon	5.6	11.5	5.4	8.2
Teneriffe				
particular	6.3	10.8	4.2	9.9
cargo	6.8	9.5	6.4	13.7
Malaga	8.4	10.5	9.4	9.8
Port	8.6	10.3	6.9	9.3
Claret	10.8	21.3	4.0	14.2

an even more pronounced decrease from 1809-1821 to 1822-1843, followed by a slight increase in the last period, it is not to be expected that many commodities would show a progressive change in their relative variability. Nevertheless, 12 series distributed among the six largest of the major groups had either the same or less variability in each successive period: flax, corn meal, lard, sweet oil, white and sap pine boards, logwood, linseed oil, American cordage, yellow soap, starch, and Holland gin. Even more unusual was the progressive increase in relative year-to-year variability in feathers, pig iron, and nails.

In Table 9 the relative year-to-year variability in each period of the 140 series is presented. The series have been classified according to the nine major groups in order of changeability from 1785 to 1808.

This analysis of the specific commodities within the groups shows that the farm crops, farm derivatives, imported foods, and furs tended to have wide, and the wines more moderate, fluctuations in prices from year to year. Among the lumber products and naval stores and the two industrial groups there was much greater diversity: some commodities were among the most variable while others had relatively minor fluctuations. Especially in the industrial raw and semi-finished commodities was there a proponderance of series which in at least three periods could be classed with the least variable of the 140 series. The fish group did not contain any series which in three or more periods was among the greatest or least fluctuating.

TABLE 10
YEAR-TO-YEAR VARIABILITY OF NINE MAJOR GROUPS BY PERIODS

Group	Average Variability				Relative Deviation from Average Variability			
	1785–1808	1809–1821	1822–1843	1844–1860	1785–1808	1809–1821	1822–1843	1844–1860
Farm								
Crops	14.3	17.4	15.6	12.0	21.0	15.5	26.9	20.0
Derivatives	13.6	12.5	12.1	11.6	20.6	24.0	26.4	17.2
Imported Foods	14.1	16.2	10.7	12.0	33.3	30.2	31.8	31.7
Lumber Products and Naval Stores	13.1	14.2	7.3	9.9	23.7	58.5	20.5	19.2
Industrial								
Raw and Semi-Finished	9.9	14.2	7.4	7.5	51.5	35.9	33.8	32.0
Ready for Consumption	11.0	12.6	6.9	7.3	33.6	40.5	24.6	42.5
Fish	13.0	13.3	12.2	10.0				
Furs	12.4	12.4	11.9	11.1				
Wines	7.1	11.2	6.4	9.7	22.5	23.2	29.7	22.7

VARIABILITY OF MAJOR GROUPS

In order to summarize the variability of the commodities given by groups in Table 9, the average variability of the series included in each group has been computed and is shown in the first part of Table 10. In general these averages reveal from one period to another the same tendencies noted already in the general distribution. The years from 1809 to 1821 were usually the most variable. In no group did the constituent series persistently become more changeable. Farm derivatives had less variability in each successive period, and furs declined in the amount of change from year to year after maintaining the same rate from 1785 to 1821.

Within each period the distribution of the average indices of year-to-year variability differed more among the groups than the total distribution differed from period to period. In the period from 1785 to 1808 farm derivatives, farm crops, and imported foods had a higher average variability than any other groups. The commodities classified as lumber products and naval stores, fish, and furs were but slightly less variable. The two groups of industrial commodities and the wines showed the least amount of changeability from year to year.

In the subsequent periods the various groups tended to conform to this distribution. In the period from 1809 to 1821 all groups except farm derivatives and furs had a higher average variability than in the preceding period. The average for the raw industrial commodities increased so markedly that they ranked among the most variable groups. In the last two periods, 1822-1843 and 1844-1860, all groups had an average variability lower than in either of the first two periods except farm crops from 1822 to 1843 and wines from 1844 to 1860.

Even a glance at Table 9 will show that the specific commodities within each group differed from the average of the group in the amount of year-to-year variability. As a summary figure the relative average deviation of the constituent series from the average variability is given in the second part of Table 10. Since fish and furs each include only three series, this measure for these groups is omitted.

The greatest dissimilarity in any group in any period was in lumber products and naval stores from 1809 to 1821. All of the lumber products had an average year-to-year variability between 5.6 and 9.2, all of the naval stores between 16.7 and 36.3. As a result, the average relative deviation was 58.5 per cent.

Throughout the period as a whole the group with the greatest diversity in the variability of its series was that of industrial raw and semi-finished products. The industrial commodities ready for consumption and imported foods were but slightly more concentrated. The high amount of deviation in these groups would be expected from the fact that although many series in the two industrial groups were as variable as some in the other groups, a substantial number of them were less variable than any in the other classifications. At the other extreme were a few commodities with a high variability from year to year among the imported foods and the industrial raw materials.

The groups with the least deviation from their average variability were the farm crops and farm derivatives. The wines were slightly less uniform in the amount of their variability. Lumber products and naval stores provided the most extreme contrast between periods. From 1809 to 1821 we have seen that they had a greater deviation than any other group, the naval stores being distinctly more variable than the lumber products. From 1822 to 1843, however, when the variability of these series ranged from 4.8 to 12.8, the group had less deviation from its average than any other. Three of the five naval stores varied less from year to year than two of the lumber products.

Summary

The significance of the measure of year-to-year variability rests on its characterization of the relative change from year to year of specific commodities. The period from 1809 to 1821, influenced as it was by the War of 1812 and the world-wide readjustment following the close of the Napoleonic wars, was the severest test of the ability of business men to adapt their dealings to extreme changes in prices. The period from 1785 to 1808, which included the confusion following the Revolutionary War and the added disturbances arising out of the French Revolution, presented nearly as serious problems. Despite the changes in variability from period to period, many commodities were always subject to large fluctuations in their annual prices. This was especially true of farm crops, farm derivatives, and imported foods. Other series, especially some of the industrial materials and wines, underwent only mild changes. Such a generalization conceals the fact that the industrial groups especially included a few extremely variable series. The tendency for certain commodities to change their characteristic variability from year to year indicates the presence of special factors influencing parts of the economy. Such factors as these will be stressed in Chapters VII-X.

CHAPTER V

FREQUENCY OF MONTHLY PRICE CHANGES

By the use of annual averages the four periods have been contrasted in respect to price stability and year-to-year variations. Other changes in the behavior of prices affected the monthly data which form the basis in this chapter for the detailed analysis of the frequency of change and in the following chapter for the study of seasonality in selected commodities. By frequency of change is meant the percentage of the months in each year when the price of a commodity differed from that of the preceding month. This measure of the sensitivity of prices has been applied, in this study, only to the specific grades of commodities which were quoted continuously from 1791 to 1860. Only 135 of the total of 205 commodities were continuous enough or free enough from prices derived from merchants' accounts to be used in a study of monthly changes. The commodities included in this study had a varying number of changes and over a period of time the same commodity was subject to a process of alteration in the frequency of its changes in price. The total effect can be measured by the average number of changes each year.

On Chart V it can be seen that from 1791 to 1834 the percentage of change fluctuated widely from year to year. Often the large percentage of frequency of change occurred in times of high or rising prices. The peak of frequency for these years was in 1815 when prices fluctuated considerably and were especially unsettled by the suddenness of the news of peace, which was accompanied by a drastic dip, followed by a rapid rebound of prices.

The years after 1834 contrast sharply with the earlier years in that there was less variation in the frequency of change from year to year and all of the years had a percentage which would have been regarded as high before 1835.

The shift in the sensitivity of prices is only one factor to be considered in appraising the reasons for the varying frequency of change in the monthly quotations. At any given time there was a greater dispersion in the characteristic frequency of change for different commodities than in the annual averages for the entire period from 1791 to 1860. It is only from a comparison of the typical sensitivity of each commodity and the changes in this sensitivity from time to time that the many divergent factors affecting particular series can be appraised. In all commodities there were some periods when changes in price from one month to the next occurred less frequently than in

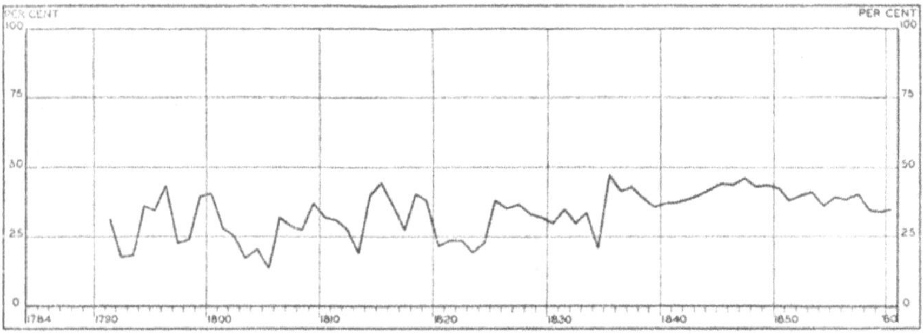

CHART V—ANNUAL FREQUENCY OF MONTHLY PRICE CHANGES OF 135 COMMODITIES, 1791-1860

others. In all periods some types of commodities were subject to frequent changes while other types changed less often.

Basing an assumption solely on the effect of speed of transportation and circulation of news, one would expect two tendencies to be found in any historical survey of prices. In early years when market information passed slowly, the same price would be likely to persist until news of a change in outside trade was received, making a drastic readjustment of price necessary. This influence would lead one to expect less frequent and more abrupt changes as the study of prices is pushed back to early decades. Differently stated, if sensitivity of prices were traceable solely to speed in dissemination of news, changes should become more frequent and more gradual as better means of transportation and communication developed during the century. That this is an oversimplified statement of the factors which enter into frequency of price changes will be clear from the detailed study, which shows that some commodities tended to increase in number of changes, some to decrease, and still others to maintain no definite pattern.

The persistent character of the changes in fluctuations is revealed when the averages of 20-year periods are considered. For this analysis

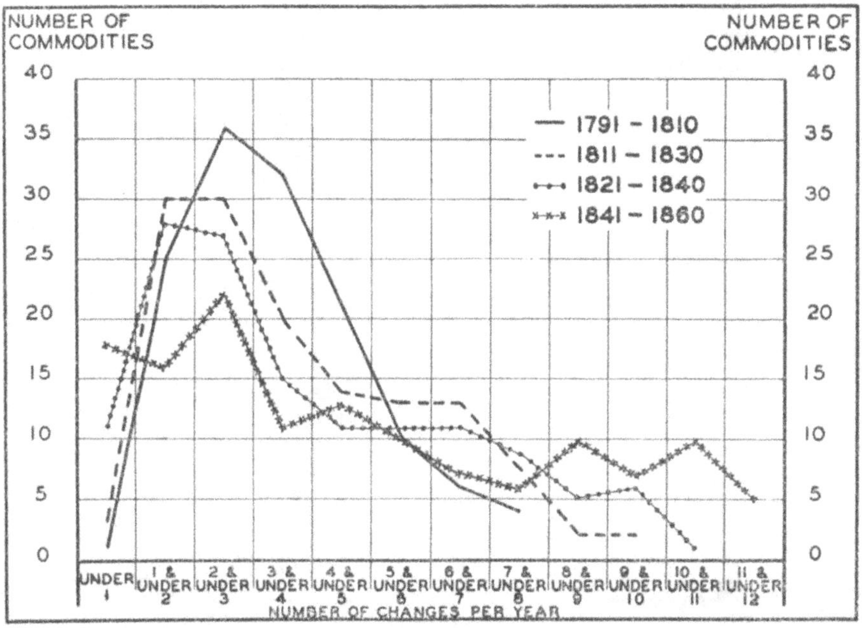

CHART VI—DISTRIBUTION OF FREQUENCY OF MONTHLY PRICE CHANGES BY 20-YEAR PERIODS

the averages of four such periods were computed—1791-1810, 1811-1830, 1821-1840, 1841-1860. This division provided an overlap of 10 years in the two middle periods.

The average number of changes per year in the later periods shows the process by which the commodities diverged from the frequency which characterized the decades from 1791 to 1810. The series which averaged less than one change per year increased from one in the 20-year period from 1791 to 1810, to three in the years from 1811 to 1830, to 11 from 1821 to 1840, and to 18 from 1841 to 1860. An even more marked increase from period to period occurred in the number of commodities which had eight changes or more per year.

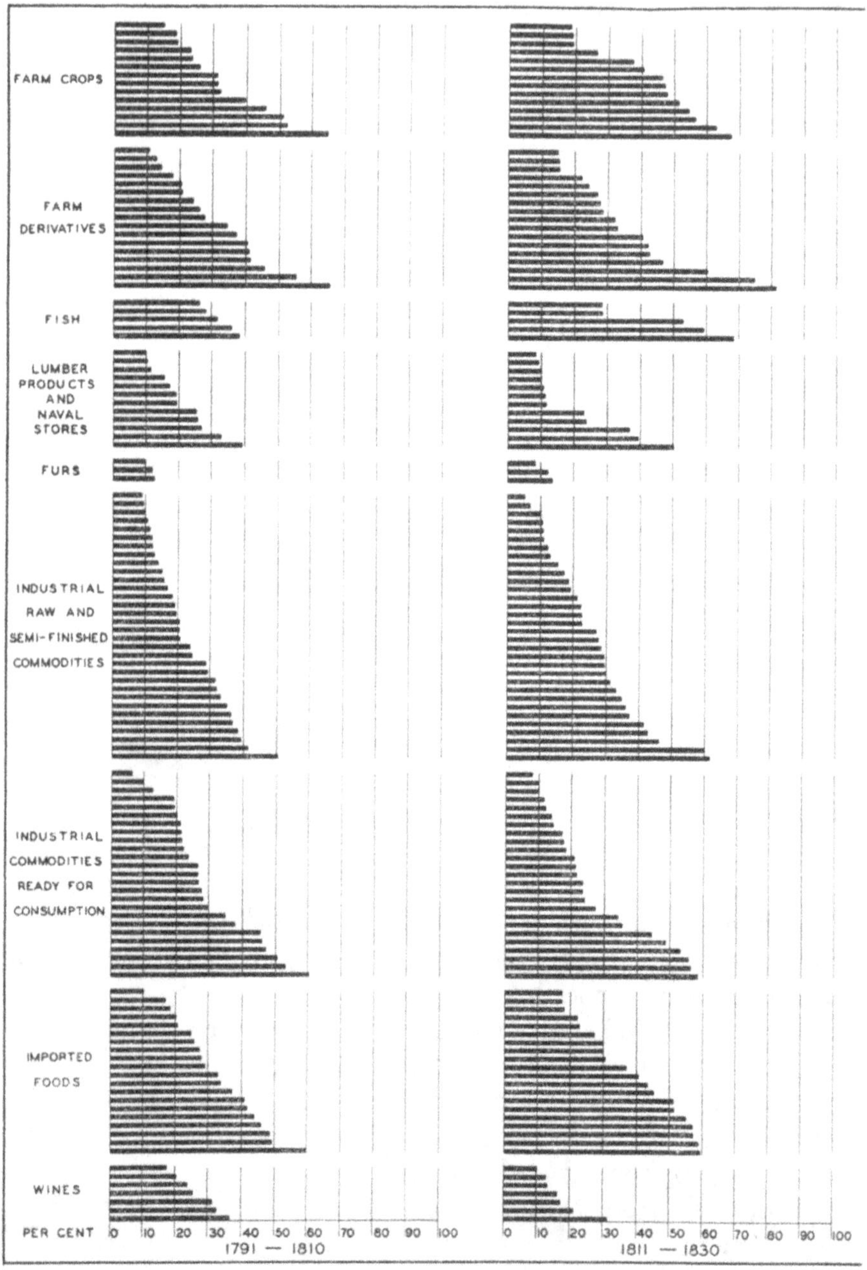

CHART VII—FREQUENCY OF MONTHLY PRICE

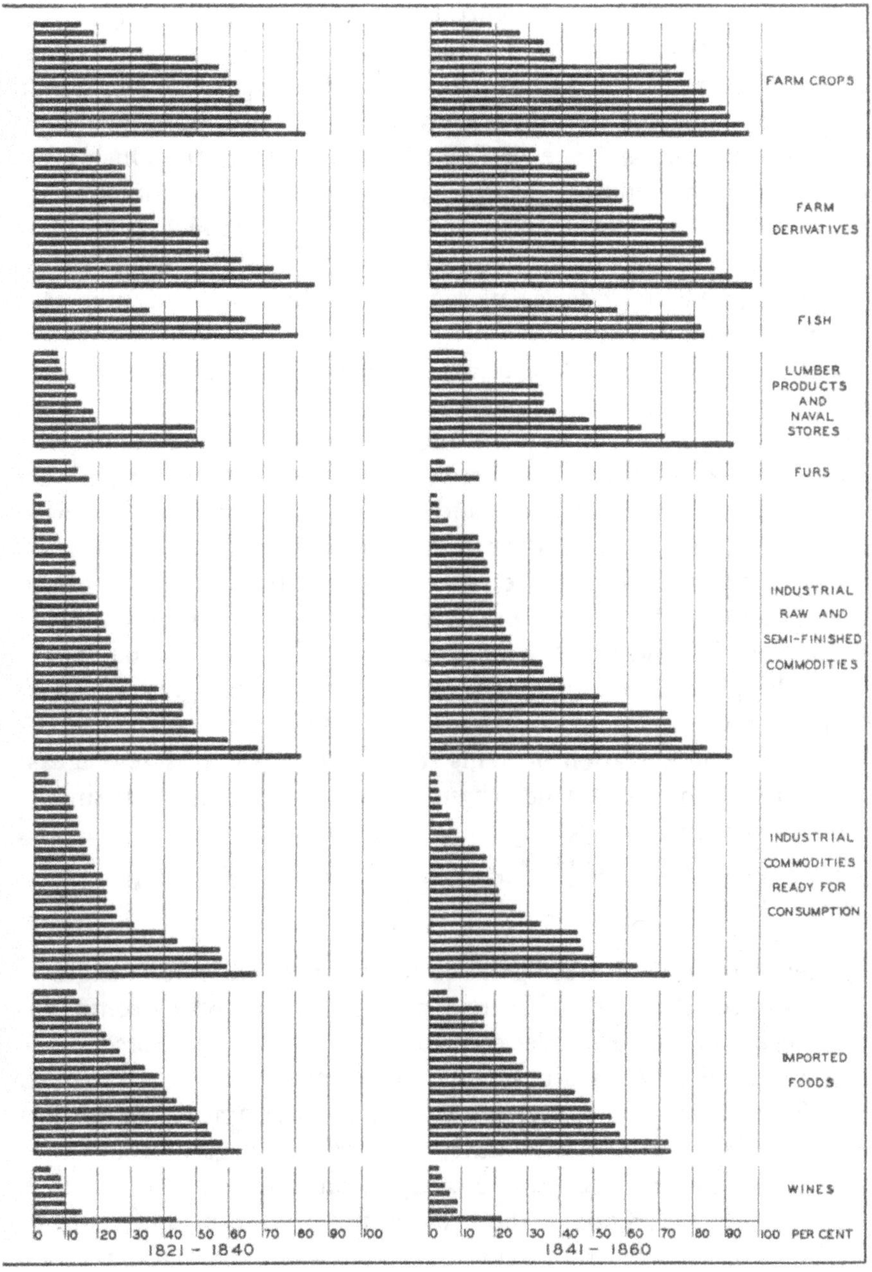

CHANGES OF 135 COMMODITIES BY 20-YEAR PERIODS

In the first period no commodity had as many as eight changes per year. In the next period four commodities not only had as many as eight, but two of these had as many as nine changes. During the 20 years from 1821 to 1840 there were 12 series with more than eight changes per year, and one of them had more than 10. During the final period the number of frequently-changing commodities increased to 32 which were distributed in such a manner as to place more in each of the upper frequencies than appeared in any of the previous periods. Five series averaged more than 11 changes in each year from 1841 to 1860.

The increasing number of commodities with low and high monthly changes in price was accompanied by a progressive decline in the concentration of items in any one interval. In the first period 36 series changed their monthly prices between two and three times per year and 32 changed between three and four times a year. In the period 1811-1830 the maximum of 30 items was concentrated in the interval of one to two and two to three changes per year. During the period 1821-1840 the two highest points were in these same intervals, but the number had declined to 28 and 27. In the final period, 1841-1860, the greatest number of series in any interval was 22 which changed on the average between two and three times a year. The decline in the concentration of items resulted in a progressive decrease of the number of series which changed between two and four times a year. In the intervals between one and two and between four and eight no consistent shift from period to period developed.

Major Groups

After determining these general characteristics of the changes in the sensitivity of prices, it is pertinent to determine which commodities or groups of commodities contributed to the changes noted in the total distribution. Accordingly, the 135 commodities were classified into the nine major groups. No system of classification except one based on the frequency of monthly changes would give groups with all sensitive commodities in one category and all insensitive ones in another. The difference in the relative importance of various commodities and grades would in itself lead one to expect that any group would show diversity in the number of changes in prices.

The appraisal of differences in frequency of change among the groups as well as within them is facilitated by Chart VII. The bars represent individual series within each group and have been arranged in order of frequency of changes in each period. This arrangement does not permit one to follow the same commodity from period to period, but it does reveal the differences in the distribution of each group and the net changes within the group from one period to another.

Farm crops had a marked tendency to increase in number of monthly changes in prices, nine of the series having a greater sensitivity from 1841 to 1860 than the maximum from 1791 to 1810: hops, rice, flaxseed, rye, Georgia cotton, cloverseed, oats, corn, and wheat. In all of these except rice and flaxseed the average number of changes increased progressively from one period to another. Kentucky tobacco also gained continuously in sensitivity. Only one series, James River tobacco, was more insensitive in the last than in the first period. This modification occurred gradually but continuously. Because of this mutation in the prices of James River tobacco, no commodity was consistently the least variable in the farm crops group, but wheat and corn always had the greatest number of monthly changes and oats ranked third from 1811 to 1860.

The farm derivatives tended even more persistently to increase in that the lowest as well as the highest frequencies of change in each period exceeded those of the previous period. All of the commodities in the group changed more frequently between 1841 and 1860 than between 1791 and 1810. Eleven of the 17 series studied in this group progressively intensified their changes in each successive period: hides, small water bread, tallow, butter, Burlington and prime pork, feathers, ginseng, corn meal, rye meal, and flour. No commodity was consistently the least variable of the farm derivatives, but flour and rye meal were the most sensitive commodities from 1791 to 1840 and were among the three most sensitive from 1841 to 1860.

The fish group, which is more homogeneous than the first two groups discussed, developed the most marked increase in frequency of price changes. Only one series—codfish—failed to show an increased sensitivity in each successive period. By 1841 to 1860 the lowest frequency had risen above the highest in the first period. During the same time, however, the difference between the lowest and highest had widened.

The lumber products and naval stores also showed a tendency to more frequent changes in the higher brackets, although the lowest frequency tended to remain. This resulted from a decrease in the frequency of change in the prices of staves while the naval stores especially and pine lumber to a lesser extent increased. Tar and spirits of turpentine were consistently among the three commodities with the most flexible prices in this group, but only spirits of turpentine became progressively more sensitive.

Although the frequency of price changes for beaver and muskrat furs was less from 1841 to 1860 than in any of the three previous periods, most or all of this modification occurred between the last two periods. On the whole, the series in the group of furs were subject to relatively few price changes. The greatest number in any one period was barely more than two per year for deer skins.

The other three large groups—industrial raw and semi-finished products, industrial commodities ready for consumption, and imported foods—tended to show a large increase in the difference between the lowest and highest items. This was occasioned by a drift in some series in each group to a lower frequency of change than in the preceding period, while others rose above the maximum frequency of 1791 to 1810.

Among the industrial raw and semi-finished products this divergent tendency was especially pronounced in eight series in which the frequency of price changes progressively increased and in five which continuously decreased. In each successive period sheet iron, pig iron, Swedish bar iron, pig lead, pearl ashes, copper sheathing, linseed oil, and plaster of Paris became more sensitive. Linseed oil and plaster of Paris always had a greater number of price changes than any of the other industrial raw materials. During the same periods the prices of St. Domingo mahogany, American steel, rolled brimstone, Campeachy logwood, and refined saltpeter were becoming more inert.

The industrial commodities ready for consumption, which likewise tended to diverge, include more series with a decreasing than an increasing frequency of change in their monthly prices. Even New England rum, the only commodity always among the three most variable, did not progressively increase in sensitivity. Only sperm candles and starch had more frequent changes in each successive period than in the previous one. In contrast, the number of changes in the monthly prices of eight of the 25 industrial commodities ready for consumption included in this analysis progressively decreased: American cordage, ravens duck, bear ravens duck, glass, shot, gunpowder, Holland gin, and Jamaica rum.

Imported foods, like the industrial commodities ready for consumption, had more series with a decreasing than an increasing sensitivity. Although St. Domingo coffee consistently ranked among the three most variable of the imported foods, only honey and lemons continuously intensified their sensitivity. Island cocoa, almonds, ground ginger, and Souchong and Hyson skin tea were subject to a continuous decline in the frequency of change.

Wines, like the other homogeneous groups of fish and furs, were more consistent in their behavior than the diversified groups. Prices of all the wines were more insensitive in the last than in the first period. Except for sherry, which had the same frequency of change in the last two periods, and Malaga, which had its greatest sensitivity from 1821 to 1840, the decline in the frequency of change was continuous. Madeira wine was always the least variable and Malaga was consistently among the two with the most frequent number of changes.

The increase in the number of commodities which changed in price less than once a year was caused largely by the decreasing sensitivity in certain series which has already been noted. Many of the commodities, however, which were characterized by a progressive shrinkage in their rate of alteration always averaged more than one change a year. On the other hand, some which had no persistent mutation in frequency of monthly variability had, in at least one period, less than one change a year.

Certain industrial commodities ready for consumption accounted for a large part of the increase in the number of very insensitive commodities which changed in price less than once a year. To this category the industrial commodities ready for consumption contributed nails from 1791 to 1810, white soap from 1811 to 1830, gunpowder and glass from 1821 to 1840, and ravens duck, bear ravens duck, glass, gunpowder, Russian brown sheeting, white soap, and American cordage from 1841 to 1860. All of these series except nails, Russian brown sheeting, and white soap showed a progressive decline in the number of monthly changes in price.

No series in any other group had such a low frequency in the first 20 years, but two of the industrial raw materials—Crowley and American steel—changed in price less than once a year between 1811 and 1830. This number increased to six from 1821 to 1840 when German and English blistered steel, hoop iron, and St. Domingo mahogany in addition to American and Crowley steel were in this class. Four of these—English blistered, German, and American steel, and St. Domingo mahogany—continued to have less than one change per year from 1841 to 1860. Only American steel and St. Domingo mahogany declined continuously from one period to another in their frequency of change.

It was not until the period from 1821 to 1840 that the prices of even Madeira wine, the least sensitive of its group, changed less than once a year. In the closing period, claret, Lisbon, and Teneriffe cargo wines also changed as infrequently. All four of these wines were among those with a persisting modification in the frequency of price change.

The imported foods had started with such a comparatively high frequency for the lowest item, which even increased during the years 1811 to 1830, that it was not until the last period that any of this group changed in price less than once a year. As a result of the decreasing sensitivity in its prices, Island cocoa dropped into this inert class from 1841 to 1860.

Two other groups, lumber products and naval stores and furs, which did not include any series with a continuous decrease in monthly changeability, also contributed to the commodities with less than one change a year. During the period from 1821 to 1840 two of the lumber products—long shingles and sap pine boards—dropped into this inert class, but none of them was so insensitive in any other period. In the last period, beaver and muskrat from the group of furs also fell into this category. None of the farm crops, farm derivatives, or fish was ever this insensitive to change.

Since nearly all of the groups either tended to have an increasing number of price changes per year or tended to diverge, with some series in each group having increased frequency of change, all of the groups except furs and wines had at least one series which changed eight or more times a year by the last period. No other class of frequency of change increased as much during the period of the study as the high-frequency group. Between 1791 and 1810 no commodity averaged as many as eight changes a year. Even in the following 20 years only four series of the farm crops, farm derivatives, and fish had as many as eight changes per year: corn, rye meal, flour, and mackerel #2, all of which increased progressively in sensitivity. In the periods from 1821 to 1840 and 1841 to 1860 the total number of series with frequent changes increased to 12 and then to 32. Not only did certain commodities in the three groups which first had such frequent changes increase in sensitivity, but also some series in four other groups became equally responsive. Thus from 1821 to 1840 the extremely responsive commodities in the group of farm crops included rye, oats, and wheat in addition to corn. In the final period not only did these four commodities continue to be among the most sensitive, but they were joined by hops, rice, flaxseed, cotton, and cloverseed. It is these nine commodities which stand out in the section of farm crops on Chart VII since they exceed the maximum sensitivity of any commodity in this group from 1791 to 1810. Only rice and flaxseed failed to become progressively more sensitive. The representation of farm derivatives in the commodities with eight or more changes a year was increased by the addition of corn meal from 1821 to 1840 and hams, butter, feathers, prime and Burlington pork, and lard from 1841 to 1860. Except for hams and lard the nine farm derivatives, including corn meal, rye meal, and flour, advanced progressively to this extremely changeable category. In a similar way, mackerel #2, which averaged more than eight changes a year from 1811 to 1830, was joined by mackerel #1 from 1821 to 1840 and both by mackerel #3 from 1841 to 1860. All three grades of mackerel were characterized by increasing sensitivity. Two of the industrial raw materials, plaster of Paris and linseed oil, had eight or more changes per year from 1821 to 1840. These two commodities, always the most variable of this group, were joined by yellow beeswax, pearl ashes, whale oil, and pig lead, which also had more than eight changes each year from 1841 to 1860. Only the New England rum of the industrial commodities ready for consumption was in this category either from 1821 to 1840 or from 1841 to 1860. In the last period two of the naval stores, rosin and spirits of turpentine, and two of the imported foods, West India molasses and lemons, also joined the sensitive commodities.

It can be seen that some of the major groups included series from both the sensitive and insensitive classifications. Although none of the imported foods fell at either extreme until the period 1841-1860, when one changed less than once a year and two changed eight or more times, the pull was towards the upper limit, since in three of the four periods at least half the commodities changed four or more times a year. The specific series in the two groups of industrial commodities were widely dispersed. The commodities ready for consumption tended to become, on the whole, less sensitive than in the early period. From 1791 to 1810 only three in this group had fewer than two changes per year. The tendency toward infrequent changes appeared in seven commodities from 1811 to 1830, in nine from 1821 to 1840, and in 10 from 1841 to 1860. At the same time the industrial raw materials tended to gain in frequency of change, increasing from seven commodities with four or more changes per year in 1791-1810, to nine in 1811-1840, and to 12 in 1841-1860. These divergent tendencies in the two groups of industrial commidities have added significance when one realizes that from 1791 to 1810 there were 11 raw materials with less than two changes per year, while eight of those ready for consumption had four or more changes per year. Thus the group which tended to increase in sensitivity of prices was the one which was less sensitive in the early period. As a result, by 1841-1860 their relative position as to sensitivity of price changes had been reversed.

Factors Affecting Sensitivity

That these commodities would differ in the number of times prices changed within a single year is obvious when it is realized that the list of items includes seasonal and non-seasonal commodities, durable and perishable goods, necessities and luxuries, and commodities with an elastic or inelastic demand as well as those priced in large and those in small units. A commodity of one type might tend to hold its price until a change in market conditions forced an abrupt and considerable revision; another might be subject to frequent but minor changes. These various aspects of pricing in a diversified list of commodities account for the range in the frequency of price adjustments in any particular year.

The mutation from 1791 to 1860 in the frequency of change of price quotations for an identical commodity is related in part to the improved means of transportation and communication effected during this period. The frequency of price change of some commodities was influenced by shifts in the usual unit of sale. For example, many articles sold by the hundredweight in the early years were later quoted by the pound. One must also bear in mind the fact that a commodity may have undergone an alteration in its characteristics. This is especially true of those which, in the early years, were regarded as luxuries but had become necessities before 1860. Although no items were added or dropped during the period, the relative importance of the 135 commodities studied was not constant. Commodities which tended to become obsolete were subject to a decline in their frequency of changes in price, while those which increased in demand showed more responsiveness.

CHAPTER VI

CHANGES IN SEASONALITY OF SELECTED COMMODITIES

All types of fluctuations, random, seasonal, and cyclical as well as the long-time trend in prices, contribute to the total of monthly changes. A large part of the fluctuations in any commodity which has a definite seasonal pattern influencing the movement of prices may be traced to the forces underlying its seasonality. It is for this reason that we turn to an examination of the seasonal patterns of 20 series which have been selected for special study. All of the major groups except furs and wines are represented by at least one commodity in this analysis of seasonality. In general, the commodities which were already known to have extremely frequent changes in monthly prices were selected: from the farm crops, corn, wheat, rice, James River tobacco, and Georgia cotton; from farm derivatives, flour, corn meal, pork, and the sub-group of dairy products; from imported foods, St. Domingo coffee, Hyson skin tea, pepper, West India molasses, and Havana brown sugar; from lumber products and naval stores, tar; from industrial raw and semi-finished products, linseed oil, whale oil, and pig lead; from industrial commodities ready for consumption, New England rum; and from fish, mackerel #1.

For each commodity the seasonal patterns for seven periods were constructed. The first period covers the six years from 1785 to 1790, and the remaining periods are successive ten-year intervals. The method used in the construction of each pattern differs but slightly from that developed by Professor Simon Kuznets[1] from the procedure first suggested by Dr. F. R. Macaulay.

[1] Kuznets, Simon, *Seasonal Variations in Industry and Trade*, pp. 27 ff. See *infra*, Appendix, pp. 343 ff., for description of method used in the computation of the seasonal indices.

Effect of the Seasonal Pattern on Frequency of Monthly Price Changes

The most direct method of appraising the effect of seasonality on the frequency of monthly changes in prices is to compare the per-

Table 11

Frequency[a] of Price Changes of Selected Commodities by Decades

Commodity	1784–1790	1791–1800	1801–1810	1811–1820	1821–1830	1831–1840	1841–1850	1851–1860
Changes in Monthly Prices								
Wheat	75.9	66.7	38.3	62.5	63.3	89.2	98.3	94.2
Rice	51.8	55.0	47.5	56.7	46.7	51.7	72.5	80.8
Tobacco, James River	26.5	33.0	14.2	26.7	11.7	25.8	22.5	14.2
Cotton, Georgia	33.7	30.1	61.7	50.0	45.8	79.2	85.0	83.3
Flour	69.9	60.0	71.7	84.2	78.3	92.5	99.2	95.8
Corn meal	72.3	43.3	48.3	53.3	67.5	78.3	85.0	80.8
Mackerel, #1	26.5	26.5	26.7	46.7	72.5	77.5	85.8	80.8
Coffee, St. Domingo	74.7	58.3	61.7	62.5	55.8	58.3	62.5	54.2
Tea, Hyson skin		39.2	58.3	60.0	27.5	20.0	19.2	13.3
Pepper	48.2	42.1	45.0	46.7	55.8	53.3	58.3	40.0
Molasses, West India	65.1	46.7	51.7	65.8	48.3	50.8	75.8	70.0
Sugar, Havana brown	8.4	39.2	44.2	68.3	45.8	61.7	67.5	45.8
Rum, New England	49.4	54.2	66.7	54.2	57.5	78.3	80.8	65.8
Tar	38.6	36.0	42.5	55.8	45.0	53.3	68.3	60.0
Oil								
linseed	61.4	49.2	33.3	48.3	71.7	90.8	96.7	86.7
whale	51.8	37.8	32.5	47.5	45.0	45.8	78.3	70.0
Lead, pig	12.0	10.7	19.2	40.0	45.8	73.3	84.2	68.3
Monthly Changes in Seasonal Pattern								
Corn	100.0	83.3	91.7	83.3	83.3	83.3	91.7	100.0
Wheat	100.0	83.3	75.0	91.7	75.0	91.7	75.0	100.0
Rice	91.7	91.7	91.7	75.0	75.0	91.7	100.0	75.0
Tobacco, James River	58.3	91.7	50.0	91.7	33.3	66.7	83.3	50.0
Cotton, Georgia	66.7	75.0	83.3	75.0	50.0	83.3	75.0	75.0
Flour	75.0	75.0	100.0	100.0	66.7	75.0	83.3	83.3
Corn meal	75.0	75.0	75.0	75.0	83.3	83.3	91.7	91.7
Pork	83.3	66.7	83.3	91.7	66.7	91.7	83.3	75.0
Dairy Products	75.0	91.7	50.0	50.0	58.3	83.3	75.0	75.0
Mackerel, #1	50.0		66.7	75.0	75.0	58.3	91.7	91.7
Coffee, St. Domingo	100.0	91.7	58.3	100.0	75.0	66.7	75.0	58.3
Tea, Hyson skin		58.3	75.0	91.7	58.3	50.0	66.7	50.0
Pepper	91.7	75.0	83.3	91.7	75.0	66.7	66.7	41.7
Molasses, West India	83.3	58.3	100.0	91.7	75.0	91.7	75.0	75.0
Sugar, Havana brown	66.7	83.3	75.0	58.3	58.3	83.3	83.3	66.7
Rum, New England	83.3	66.7	58.3	91.7	58.3	100.0	83.3	83.3
Tar	83.3	91.7	91.7	91.7	91.7	100.0	83.3	91.7
Oil								
linseed	91.7	91.7	91.7	83.3	83.3	75.0	75.0	91.7
whale	75.0		100.0	100.0	75.0	58.3	100.0	75.0
Lead, pig	75.0	41.7	66.7	58.3	50.0	83.3	83.3	75.0

[a] By frequency of change is meant the percentage of the months in each year when the price of a commodity differed from that of the preceding month.

centage of months in the typical seasonal pattern in which there was a change from the preceding month with the percentage of frequency of change in each decade. Although in some cases the frequency in each decade exceeds that of the pattern and in others is approximately the same, it is much more common for the change during the decades to be less than would have been expected from the behavior of the seasonal pattern. If there were no other factors affecting prices, the percentage of change in each decade would exactly tally with the percentage of change in the pattern. The degree to which these two measures fail to conform indicates, therefore, the importance of other factors.

Direct comparisons can justifiably be made for 17 of the series in which the seasonal pattern was computed for the specific grade of commodity used in the measurement of changes in the monthly prices from 1784 to 1860. The items omitted are corn, pork, and dairy products. In none of these 17 commodities did the actual number of changes from 1784 to 1800 even equal the number that might have been expected from seasonal causes alone. In six commodities—tobacco, corn meal, tea, pepper, tar, and whale oil—the frequency of price changes in each decade throughout the entire period fell below the number of changes that could be attributed to purely seasonal factors. Thus, in all of these 17 cases as late as 1800, and in nearly a third of them throughout the entire period, the factors other than seasonality which influenced the "frequency of changes" appear to have diminished rather than to have added to the effects of seasonality. Even of the eleven commodities in which seasonal factors alone could not have produced all of the changes in prices, eight commodities showed the active effect of more than a seasonal factor in only one decade and two in two decades. Flour was the only commodity in which, for the four successive decades from 1821 to 1860, the actual number of changes in its quotations exceeded those of the seasonal pattern. Although at least one commodity showed this relationship in every decade from 1801 to 1860, there were only four in the three decades from 1801 to 1830, while there were three from 1831 to 1840 alone, six from 1841 to 1850, and three from 1851 to 1860. It appears that after 1830, and especially from 1841 to 1850, factors other than seasonality added to the frequency of monthly price changes more than they contributed before 1830. In general, however, throughout the entire period the effects of seasonality on the "frequency of changes" tended to be diminished by other factors. Much of this tendency for the monthly changes in each decade to be less than those expected from seasonality alone can be explained to be on the assumption that the price structure contains inherent inertia.

The method of computing the seasonal patterns followed in this study has been widely tested by others. Nevertheless it is true that in the case of a commodity which had few price changes it would be possible to construct a spurious index of seasonality. It must be remembered, however, that most of the commodities which we have selected for this study of seasonal fluctuations are series which, from their nature, would be expected to have a seasonal pattern and, in addition, most of them were among the most variable of all the commodities. In other words, we have found that even the commodities which changed most frequently from month to month tended to vary less than would be expected from seasonal causes alone.

It is not possible in this study to separate all of these causes which contributed to the disparity between the number of price changes which occurred in each period and the number that might have been expected. There is no doubt, however, that further detailed work on this point will throw much light upon many pricing problems.

Up to this point we have merely considered the commodities in general without examining their individual patterns, nor have we examined changes in the pattern or in the amplitude of fluctuation. All of these problems may seem unrelated to the general problem of pricing. Such a view, however, assumes that prices are only a result of various factors in supply and demand; but when one deals with prices over a long period, account must be taken of the fact that prices may also have acted on and modified many of the forces of supply and demand. It is not possible to distinguish in price data alone effects such as these from the changes both in supply and in demand which originated in new discoveries, in technical improvements, and in changes in the standards of living of individuals.

It is pertinent to this inquiry concerning prices that some attention be given to variations in pattern and in amplitude characteristic of specific commodities. The extent to which neither have changed during the eight periods from 1785 to 1859 creates a strong presumption in favor of the explanation that such seasonality is caused by factors outside the control of the economic system, such as crop years, or that the economic advantages of the seasonal variations in price either to the buyers or sellers of the commodity were not great enough to warrant smoothing or changing the structure of demand and supply.

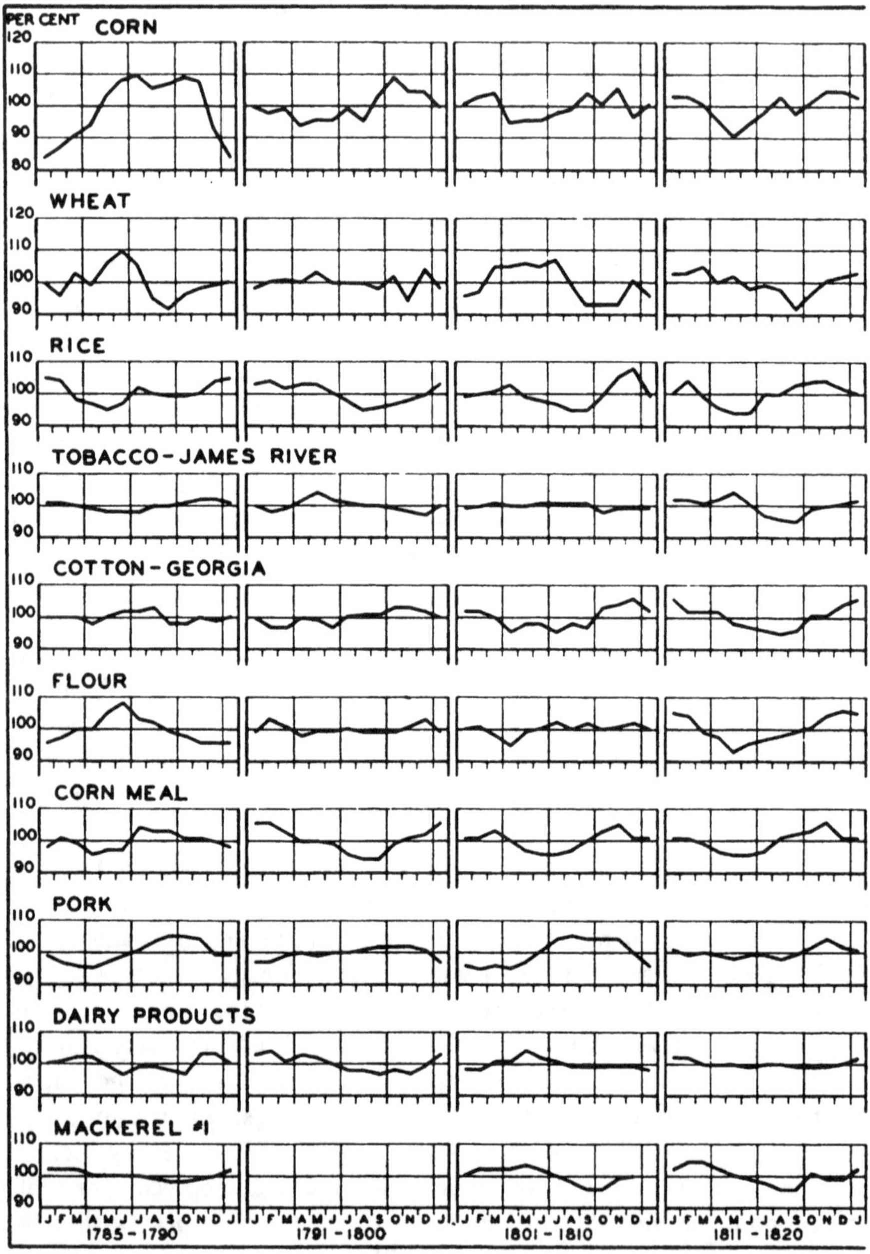

CHART VIII—SEASONAL PATTERNS OF SELECTED

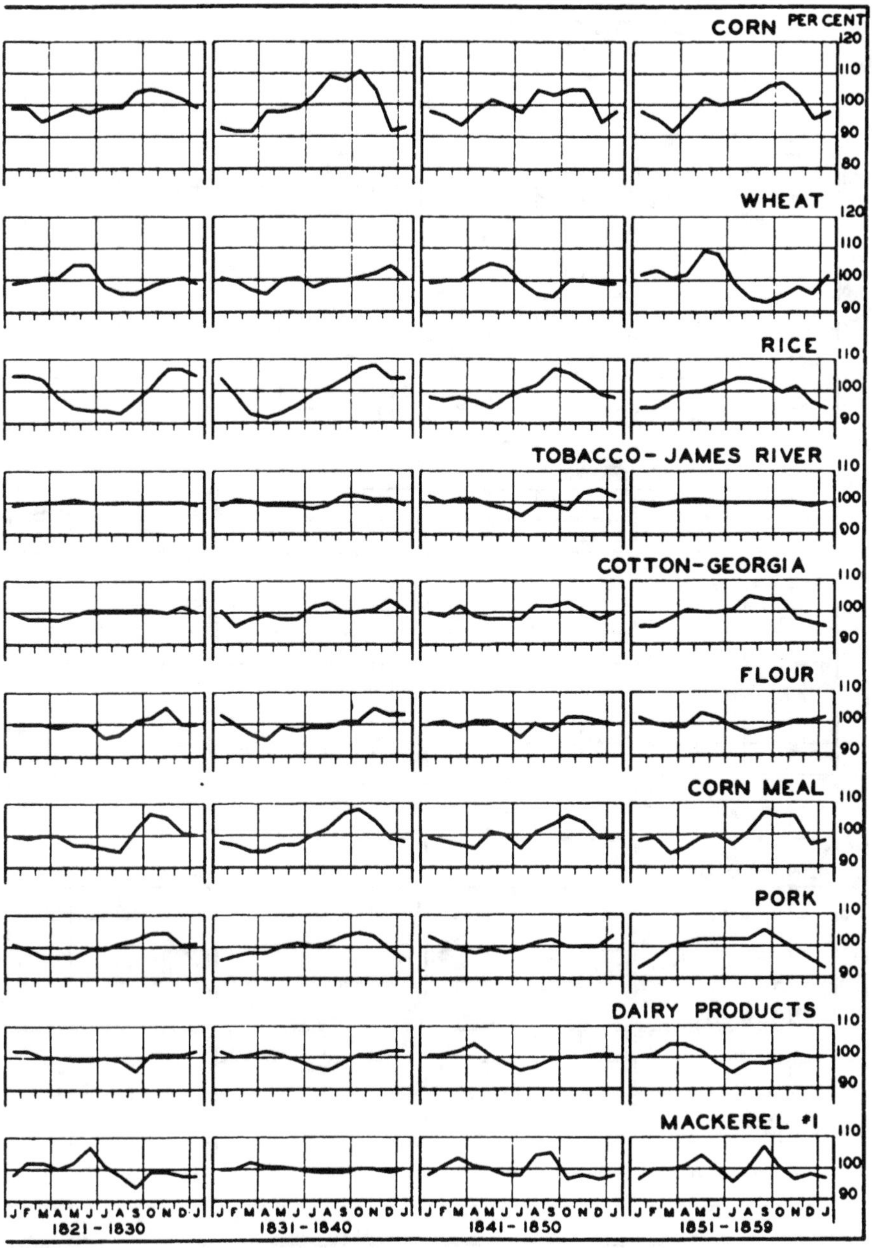

COMMODITIES BY DECADES, 1785-1859

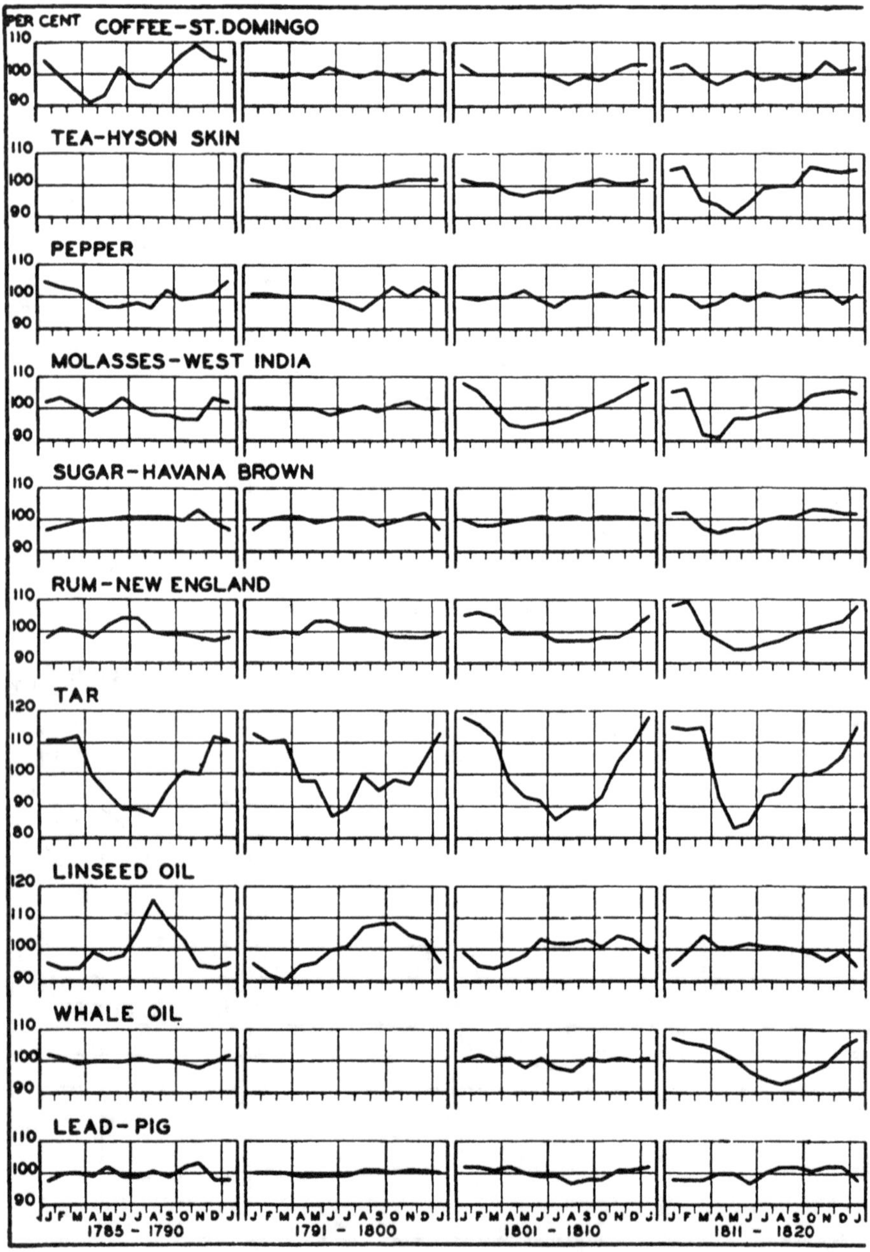

CHART VIII—SEASONAL PATTERNS OF SELECTED

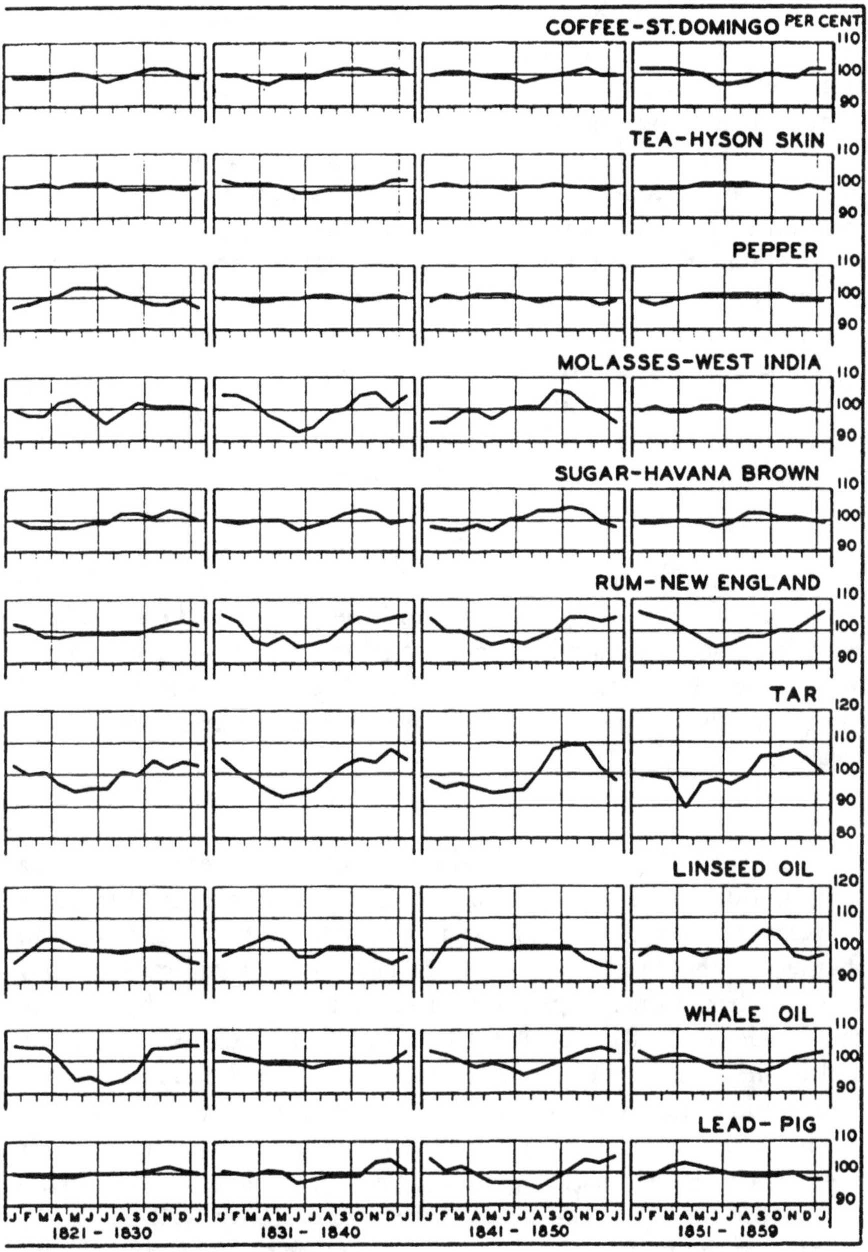

COMMODITIES BY DECADES, 1785-1859, *Concluded*

On the other hand, the extent to which the seasonality in prices appears to have been modified during the period gives some indication of the effectiveness of changes in prices as an incentive for a rearrangement of buying and selling habits.

It must be recognized in advance, however, that any conclusions can only be tentative since there are other factors which might have contributed to a different pattern or to a different degree of seasonality. Among the most important of these is the opening of new areas of supply, especially as the western expansion of the United States continued and as other producing areas throughout the world were developed. Changes in the sources of supply for certain commodities would also result in changes in the time at which shipments of such articles reached the Philadelphia market and would be reflected eventually in a somewhat different seasonality in prices.

Farm Crops

Interest in the seasonality of the five commodities selected from the group of farm crops centers around the time of highest and lowest prices and any variations in seasonality from one decade to another which would suggest that changes had occurred in the use of the commodity or in the relative importance of various producing areas.

Corn

The typical pattern of seasonal movements in prices of corn was a long gradual rise from a low in the spring to a peak in October or November. The contraction of prices was relatively shorter and sharper. In the decade from 1831 to 1840 it was completed as early as December, although prices held low until after March, while in the decade from 1811 to 1820 the contraction continued until May, and in the two decades from 1791 to 1810 it had ended by April. As a result, although April was the lowest month in only two decades, it was the only month throughout the whole period when prices were consistently below the average of the year. Since there was less variation in the timing of the peaks, prices were always well above the average of the year in October and November and even in September, except in one decade.

The persistence in the timing of high and low prices of corn indicates that the greatest demand usually came with or shortly after the harvest season. Although the supplies of corn must usually have been low in the spring, the demand was evidently light, most buyers preferring to wait for the new corn rather than purchase the carried-over crop. The use of corn for fattening livestock would account for a firm fall price.

Wheat

The seasonal pattern underlying the fluctuations in the prices of wheat was not consistent from one decade to another, nor did it show a change throughout the period. This seeming paradox developed because what may be regarded as the typical seasonal pattern reappeared, although several times the movements in the intervening decade differed substantially. The month of highest prices varied more than the lowest month. A relatively long and gradual rise to a peak in May, fairly sustained prices in June, an abrupt drop in July and August, and a further slight drop in September before commencing the rise to a peak late in the following spring is the best generalized description of the seasonal movements. In all decades except 1791-1800 and 1831-1840 the peaks occurred between March and July, while September was as low as or lower than any other month.

Neither wheat nor corn showed a permanent change in the timing of their seasonal fluctuations. An inverse relationship of high and low prices for wheat and corn tended to prevail: corn was low in the spring shortly before wheat was at its peak, while wheat was low in the fall a month before the peak in corn. Thus both tended to have a relatively long seasonal expansion in prices.

Rice

Rice had no consistent seasonal pattern. Unlike the other grains it showed in certain decades two swings in prices each year instead of one. Between 1785 and 1790 it had its major peak in January, five per cent above the average of the year, and a low in May, an equal distance below the average. In the latter part of the year there was usually a more moderate swing that in the first part, with a minor peak in July, followed by a slight recession culminating in September and October. In the two decades from 1801 to 1820, two swings in the seasonal pattern also appeared. Between 1801 and 1810 the pattern showed its greater swing in the latter part of the year. The lowest prices were generally in August and September and the major seasonal peak in December. A short break in January dropped prices to a minor low slightly under the average of the year. Between January and April prices usually rose slightly before starting a gradual but protracted decline to August and September. In the decade from 1811 to 1820 the seasonal pattern was somewhat the same as in the previous decade except that the turning points were reached from one to three months earlier. The two seasonal peaks were equally high. What had been a minor peak in April from 1801 to 1810 appeared as one of the major peaks in February from 1811 to 1820. The major low of August and September in the first decade shifted to May and June in the next, while the major peak of December moved to October and November. Only the minor low of January appeared in the same month of both decades.

Between 1785 and 1820 the seasonal pattern of the series of rice tended to accentuate the two swings in each year. The four decades from 1821 to 1859 have, in contrast, only one swing. The timing of these swings varied in each decade. Between 1821 and 1830, the seasonal peak occurred in November and December. Prices tended to remain well above the average of the year as late as March. Between March and May prices usually dropped and continued to slip until August, when they were at the lowest point of the year. In the next decade the seasonal peak was confined to the month of November, and the recession was more abrupt than in the patterns from 1821 to 1830. From April, when the seasonal index was at its low, to November, an unusually steady and continuous increase characterized the seasonal movements in prices. During the years from 1841 to 1850 the seasonal peak of prices appeared two months earlier and the seasonal low one month later than in the previous decade. This shift lengthened the period of recession and shortened the period of expansion each year. The seasonal rise occurred between May and September while a gradual decline took place between September and May.

A further shift in the seasonal pattern developed in the final decade, the peak continuing to emerge earlier. Between 1851 and 1859 it usually occurred in July and August. The seasonal low, also, appeared earlier than in the previous decade, moving to January and February. This dating corresponds with what had been a minor low in the two decades from 1801 to 1820. From April to November prices tended to hold at or above the average of the year. Although prices of rice did not drop below the yearly average in October, a slight rise in November indicates a tendency to revert to two swings in prices a year which had been generally characteristic before 1821.

The progressive shift in the seasonal pattern of the prices of rice, in contrast to the stability found in wheat and corn, suggests a relationship to the shift in the sources of supply to tidewater areas, to Georgia and Louisiana, and later to the Orient.

James River Tobacco

The most significant seasonality in James River tobacco occurred in the decades from 1791 to 1800, from 1811 to 1820, and from 1841 to 1850. In the other decades, the range from the highest to the lowest seasonal prices was four points or less. Between the three decades with appreciable seasonality there was a change in timing and a shift from two to one swing each year. From 1791 to 1800 the major peak tended to occur in May, after which prices dropped gradually to the major low of December. A second and short fluctuation raised prices in January and dropped them in February before the short rise to the major peak occurred. By 1811-1820 the period of contraction from a major high which still appeared in May had been shortened, the major low coming in September. The secondary swing had practically disappeared and the seasonal index dipped only a point from February to March before advancing to the peak of May. A further shift in the seasonal pattern had occurred by the decade from 1841 to 1850. For that period the index showed a continuation of the tendency for the seasonal low to appear earlier. Usually in that decade the lowest prices were in July instead of in September as from 1811 to 1820 or in December as from 1791 to 1800. The greatest change from 1811-1820 to 1841-1850 was the moving of the highest prices for each year from May to December. This change in the seasonal peak had been indicated between 1831 and 1840 when prices in September and October of each year were higher than those of other months.

The changes in the seasonality of James River tobacco are probably related to the growing importance of tobacco from other regions. As early as 1791, Kentucky tobacco was received in Philadelphia by way of New Orleans.[2] The somewhat different times at which tobacco from areas other than Virginia came to market unquestionably influenced the behavior of prices of James River tobacco. Changes in routes of trade would also result in a different timing of the demand for tobacco for the export trade. Finally the rapid development of the American tobacco industry would result in a new, and perhaps differently timed, demand from that characteristic of the period when England was practically the only market.

Georgia Cotton

The range in the seasonal indices of the prices of Georgia cotton in four periods was six points or less. Frequently more than one swing in prices occurred within the year. Usually the peak in prices appeared between October and December; only between 1785 and 1790 and between 1851 and 1859 did the peak come as early as August and only from 1811 to 1820 was it delayed until January. The lowest prices were usually not as far below the average of the year as the peak was above, and in most of the decades the seasonal lows appeared in three or more months at practically any time of the year except November and December.

Prices of cotton in Philadelphia were largely determined by those prevailing in the Liverpool market, which registered "the fluctuations in world-wide supply and demand."[3] It is significant that the greatest seasonal variations in the price of cotton occurred in the two decades from 1801 to 1820 when trading with Great Britain was often interrupted. Despite the increasing importance of domestic consump-

[2] May 21, 1791, Robert Henderson to William Galt and Company, Richmond.

[3] Gray, Lewis C., *History of Agriculture in the Southern United States to 1860*, Vol. II, p. 694.

tion of cotton, prices in Liverpool maintained their dominant influence throughout the period.

Summary of Farm Crops

Although the timing of the seasonal swings in corn and wheat was somewhat reversed, their patterns persisted throughout the period, showing one swing in prices each year. Rice differed from the other grains in revealing a definite shift in the timing of seasonally high and low prices and, in addition, showed in some decades more than one swing in price in its pattern. Tobacco, in the decades when its seasonality was noticeable, had only one price swing, but shifted the dating of its peaks and lows. Cotton, in contrast, tended to maintain the dating especially of its peaks, but often had more than one swing in its seasonal index.

Farm Derivatives

The commodities which have been selected from the farm derivatives for analysis of seasonality include two processed from the grains, flour and corn meal, in addition to pork and dairy products.

Flour

The successive indices of seasonality in the prices of flour show little similarity. In the four periods when the range in the pattern was nine points or more, there was one well-defined swing each year. In the other four decades, when the range was seven points or less, prices had two well-marked swings or several minor fluctuations. Between the period from 1785 to 1790 and the one from 1811 to 1820 the timing of the seasonal swings was practically reversed. In the earlier period the peak was in June; in the later period the low was in May. In the earlier period the low was from November to January; in the later period the peak was in December.

If the period from 1785 to 1790 be disregarded, some consistency can be found in the dating of the months of highest prices, although there was a progressive tendency for these peaks to occur earlier in successive decades. From 1791 to 1800 the peaks were in December and February; from 1801 to 1810 the peak in December was not far above the average of the year and was equaled by prices in July and

September; from 1811 to 1820 the highest prices were clearly in December; from 1821 to 1840 in November; and from 1841 to 1850 in October and November. Although from 1851 to 1859 the highest prices were in May, the secondary swing gave more than average prices from November to January.

More shifts occurred in the dating of lows than of highs. From 1791 to 1810 the lowest seasonal prices appeared in April; from 1811 to 1820 in May; and from 1821 to 1830 in July. This progressive delay in the reaching of low prices, which shortened the period of rise to the progressively earlier peaks, did not continue. Instead, from 1831 to 1840 the seasonal low reverted to April, from 1841 to 1850 it again appeared in July, and from 1851 to 1859, when the highest peak shifted from the late fall or early winter to a late spring, the lowest prices came in August.

For the major part of the period from 1785 to 1859 flour was at its highest from October to December and at its lowest in April and May or July and August. The seasonality in the prices of flour was thus somewhat the reverse of, and less consistent in timing than, that of wheat.

Corn Meal

The amount of seasonality in the prices of corn meal was comparatively uniform throughout the entire period, but the pattern changed gradually. The most persistent change was in the dating of the peak. From 1785 to 1790 the highest prices usually came in July, from 1791 to 1800 in January and February, from 1801 to 1820 in November, from 1821 to 1850 in October, and from 1851 to 1859 in September. Thus at the beginning of the period the seasonal peak appeared in the summer; in the next 10 years the highest prices were in the late winter. During the following decades this peak tended to come progressively earlier until just before the Civil War the highest prices were usually in the early fall.

Changes also occurred in the date of the low, but the shift was not progressive. From 1785 to 1790, from 1831 to 1840, and from 1851 to 1859 the lowest prices were as early as March or April, while between 1791 and 1800 and between 1821 and 1830 they were as late as August and September. In the other decades the low point fell between these extremes, such as in June and July between 1801 and 1810 and in May and June in 1811-1820, or even tended to fall at both extremes, as when between 1841 and 1850 equally low prices prevailed in April and July.

In addition to these major peaks and troughs in the seasonal pattern, several periods, especially 1785-1790, 1801-1810, and 1841-1850, also had a minor swing. In the two early periods a minor low in December or January was followed by a minor peak in February or March, while in the later period a minor peak in May separated the equally low months of April and July. In the period from 1851 to 1859 the pattern, in contrast to that of any other decade, showed a minor recession in July which interrupted the otherwise continuous increase from the major low in March to the major peak in September. The seasonal contraction in prices during the fall and winter was likewise interrupted by a minor rise in January and February.

The seasonal pattern of the prices of corn meal was more consistent than that of flour. Nevertheless, throughout the period as a whole, both showed somewhat the same datings of highs and lows with the peak of corn meal tending to emerge about a month in advance of that of flour. Unlike the prices of flour, which tended to move inversely to those of its raw material, the prices of corn meal, although less consistent in timing than those of its raw material, had somewhat comparable peaks and troughs in its seasonal index. The closer relationship in the seasonal movements of corn and corn meal than in those of wheat and flour may be regarded as somewhat accidental. Since both corn meal and flour had similar progressive changes in timing, it may be inferred that the seasonal movements in the prices of flour rather than in corn had a dominant influence on the fluctuations of the prices of corn meal.

Pork

The seasonal index in the prices of pork usually rose from a low between January and April to a high between September and November. This pattern persisted throughout except for the decade from 1841 to 1850.

The seasonality in the decade from 1801 to 1810 was unusual in that prices were almost equally low in each month from January to

April and almost equally high in each month from July to November. In the other periods there was a more gradual rise from low to high. In general the contraction of prices each year was effected in a shorter period than the expansion. The timing of the annual peak in prices of pork in practically every decade of the entire period corresponds with the seasonal fluctuations noted by the merchants in the Colonial period. Even before 1775 prices of pork were highest "during the summer and early fall and the merchants counted on the fact that it would drop in price toward the close of the year when new supplies came to market."[4]

Dairy Products

The related products of butter and cheese have been combined in order to give an indication of the seasonality in the prices of dairy products. The most consistent seasonality was that which became especially pronounced in the three decades from 1831 to 1859. During these years the tendency for a peak to occur in March and April followed by a rapid drop to July became increasingly apparent.

The range in the seasonal pattern was extremely uniform except from 1811 to 1820, when it was as small as three points, and in the two decades from 1841 to 1859 when it was larger than in any other period. The average variation in the seasonal index tended to decrease until 1811-1820. In the remaining decades the variation increased.

Fish

Mackerel #1

Fish, in some of its price behavior, resembles farm derivatives, especially meats. For this reason the seasonal indices of mackerel are shown on the first two pages of Chart VIII along with the farm crops and farm derivatives.

The seasonal patterns which describe the yearly movements in the prices of mackerel had in the decades before 1820 one swing with high prices usually prevailing from January to May and low prices from August to October. In contrast, the decade 1821-1830 and the

[4] Bezanson, Anne, Gray, Robert D., and Hussey, Miriam, *Prices in Colonial Pennsylvania*, p. 339.

two decades from 1841 to 1859 had two swings. From 1821 to 1830 the major peak in June was followed by a sharp recession to the major low of September. The general expansion from September to the following June was characterized by a plateau from October to January before the minor peak of February and March. Prices usually slipped back in April before starting a rapid rise to the major peak of June. Probably as a result of the pronounced change from a peak in the first part of the year, which characterized the decades before 1830, to a major peak in the latter half of the year, which was typical of the two decades after 1840, the pattern for the period 1831-1840 reveals practically no seasonality, having a total range of but three points.

The prices of mackerel in the two decades between 1841 and 1859 had two well-defined swings in their seasonal patterns. In both cases the major peak emerged in September. A minor peak in the spring usually occurred in March during the forties and in May during the fifties. June and July were equally low in the first of these two decades, but in both months prices were slightly higher than in October and December, which may be regarded as the major lows from 1841 to 1850. In the following decade, however, July was unquestionably the lowest month, falling under the levels of November and January.

The decades from 1821 to 1830 and from 1851 to 1859 had the greatest range in the seasonal pattern, but the period from 1841 to 1850 had the same average variation as the one from 1821 to 1830, and even the years from 1811 to 1820 had more average variation than those from 1851 to 1859.

The two significant shifts in the seasonal pattern of the prices of mackerel are first, the development of two swings after 1820, and, second, the change from a spring to a fall peak after 1840. The extent of this latter transposition resulted in a tendency for the highest instead of the lowest prices of the year to come in September.

Imported Foods

As a contrast to the domestic agricultural commodities, five imported foods have been selected for analysis of seasonality: St. Domingo coffee, Hyson skin tea, pepper, West India molasses, and Havana brown sugar.

St. Domingo Coffee

Except for the period from 1785 to 1790 the seasonal fluctuations in the prices of St. Domingo coffee were uniformly mild. The most persistent seasonal peak was in November, although between 1831 and 1840 it was reached as early as September and from 1851 to 1859 tended to persist until March. The lowest prices for coffee were usually distributed over several months during the spring and early summer when supplies were abundant and demand somewhat lessened.

Hyson Skin Tea

The only period with an extreme seasonal swing in the prices of Hyson skin tea was from 1811 to 1820. The two earlier periods which were also influenced by the continental and Napoleonic wars had slightly wider seasonal variations than any of the last four decades. The exaggerated pattern of 1811-1820 emphasizes the usual behavior in the prices of tea, especially from 1791 to 1820 and from 1831 to 1840. During these years tea was high in price from October to February and low in May. Usually, prices were but slightly higher in June and even in July.

The fact that from 1821 to 1830 and from 1841 to 1859 the range of the seasonal pattern was restricted to one point above and below the average of the year indicates the increasing rapidity with which supplies of tea could be obtained from other areas. The demand also probably became more uniform. Undoubtedly, merchants could easily hold tea in stock rather than dispose of it at a low price, as they would have to do with a more perishable commodity. The smaller amount of seasonality in tea than in coffee in the later period also reflects the relative decline in the use of tea.

Pepper

The seasonal swings in the prices of pepper were never extreme in any part of the period from 1785 to 1859 and even tended to decrease in amplitude as the period progressed. The maximum range in the pattern for the decades from 1831 to 1859 was only three points.

Throughout the five earliest periods there was no stability in the seasonal patterns. From 1785 to 1790 the peak tended to occur in January and the lowest prices in May, June, and August. By the decade from 1821 to 1830, as a result of continuous changes in the intervening three decades, the pattern was approximately reversed, the peak extending from May to July and the lowest prices occurring in January.

The practical elimination of seasonality in the three decades from 1831 to 1859 indicates a growing diversification in the sources of supply since, with improved transportation and communication, a shortage or a surplus in Philadelphia might be quickly corrected by shipment to or from this area. The elimination of seasonality also suggests that pepper had changed from a luxury with an elastic demand curve to a necessity with a comparatively inelastic demand.

West India Molasses

West India molasses did not have any uniform seasonal pattern. The greatest and also the most uniform seasonality was in the decades 1801-1810 and 1811-1820, when the peaks each year tended to occur between December and February and were followed by an abrupt drop to a low in April or May. The remainder of the year was usually characterized by a gradual and persistent rise.

In contrast to these years of pronounced seasonality were the decades from 1791 to 1800 and from 1851 to 1859 when prices tended to fluctuate mildly around the average of the year. The seasonal patterns for the other decades fell between these extremes, but there was no uniformity among them.

Havana Brown Sugar

The amount of seasonality in the prices of Havana brown sugar differed widely in various decades. Between 1801 and 1810 and between 1851 and 1859 the range of variation as well as the average deviation of the pattern was small. The greatest seasonal fluctuations were in the adjacent decades, 1811-1820 and 1841-1850.

The prices of sugar were always higher in the latter part of the year than in the first part, with the peak usually in October to November. The months of lowest prices were between January and

June; there was a progressive delay in reaching the low in successive decades until 1831-1840.

Summary of Imported Foods

Imported foods, like domestic agricultural products, showed a variety of types of seasonality. Four of the five series studied had only a mild degree of seasonality. The range of variation in West India molasses usually exceeded greatly the fluctuations in the other commodities. The seasonal pattern for coffee and tea tended to persist throughout the entire period. The highest prices for Havana brown sugar usually came at the same time each year, but the lowest prices tended to appear earlier in successive decades. Pepper and West India molasses did not show any consistent timing of seasonally high and low prices. The most striking change occurred in pepper and tea, in which the seasonality practically disappeared well before the close of the period.

Industrial Commodities Ready for Consumption

New England Rum

The seasonal pattern for New England rum showed a progressive shift, especially between 1785 and 1810. Before 1791 the peak tended to occur in June and July and the low in December. Between 1791 and 1800 the seasons advanced, the peaks tending to appear in May and June and the lows from October to December. The greatest advance occurred before 1810. For the decade ending that year the seasonal peak of prices appeared in February and the low from July to September. In the succeeding years there were additional slight advances in the seasonal peak, which commonly occurred in December and January, but the seasonal lows usually came in May and June, although from 1821 to 1830 they were as early as March and April. The tendency to have a peak in the winter followed by a short and abrupt dip in the spring and a persistent upward movement during the remainder of the year is somewhat characteristic of West India molasses from 1801 to 1820.

Naval Stores

All of the naval stores were subject to frequent changes in their monthly quotations and to a high degree of seasonality. Tar was selected as representative of this group since it was the raw material from which pitch was derived and would tend to show more pronounced seasonality than other naval stores.

Tar

The seasonal patterns of the prices of tar displayed wide fluctuations, but those after 1820 were less extreme than those in the earlier part of the period. The four seasonal indices for 1785 to 1820 had a range of 25 to 32 points and an average variation of 6.5 to 10 per cent, while the four patterns for 1821 to 1859 had a range of 10 to 18 points and an average variation of less than 5 per cent. In addition to a change in the amplitude of the seasonal pattern, there was a progressive shift in the timing of seasonal peaks and lows, although just one swing in prices appeared each year. The lowest prices tended to come earlier in each decade: from 1785 to 1790 in August, from 1791 to 1810 in June or July, from 1811 to 1850 in May, and from 1851 to 1859 in April. The highest seasonal prices had a somewhat similar shift; from 1785 to 1820 they were usually between December and March, and from 1821 to 1859 between October and December. That these shifts were exceptionally gradual can be demonstrated by the fact that tar was the only one of the 20 commodities showing a positive index of similarity in each successive decade.[5]

Industrial Raw and Semi-Finished Materials

Such of the industrial raw and semi-finished products as had relatively few changes in their monthly prices were not likely to have much seasonality. From the remaining commodities in this group three articles, representative of three branches of industry, were selected for detailed analysis: linseed oil, whale oil, and pig lead.

Linseed Oil

The seasonal patterns typical of the movements of prices of linseed oil were characterized from 1785 to 1810 by a high but decreasing range and average variation. Low prices always appeared in March, although from 1785 to 1790 they were equally low in December

[5] For the method used in the construction of the index of similarity see Appendix, p. 344. The method followed is that used by Dr. Simon Kuznets, *op. cit.*, pp. 281-282.

and February. The peak of linseed oil prices in these three successive decades tended to appear progressively later: from 1785 to 1790 in August, from 1791 to 1800 in September and October, and from 1801 to 1810 in November.

In the four decades between 1811 and 1850 the seasonal pattern shifted, the low appearing as early as December and January and the peak as early as March and April. In the closing decade, from 1851 to 1859, the seasonal pattern of the prices of linseed oil reverted to a fall peak in September, but the low prices persisted in December.

Throughout the entire period the lowest prices came between December and March, but there was a persistent tendency for the lows to appear earlier in the successive decades. Although February and March, as well as December, were low from 1785 to 1790, after 1810 the low never appeared later than January. The date at which the highest prices appeared shifted more than that of the low. After gradually moving from a peak in August between 1785 and 1790 to a peak in November from 1801 to 1810, it developed a spring peak in March or April between 1811 and 1850, but from 1851 to 1859 a fall peak in September again dominated the seasonal pattern.

Whale Oil

The range in the seasonal pattern of whale oil was moderate in every decade except the two from 1811 to 1830. From 1811 to 1859 the patterns were somewhat similar, showing one swing each year with a low between July and August, although from 1851 to 1859 the seasonal low was delayed until September. The peak was always in December or January except in the irregular pattern which characterized the decade from 1801 to 1810 when the highest prices appeared in February. The persistence of this pattern is further proved by the positive index of similarity in the successive decades from 1811 to 1859.

Pig Lead

The range in the seasonal pattern of pig lead was extremely small from 1791 to 1800 and from 1821 to 1830, never exceeding three points. In four other decades the range was five points. The greatest variation from the month of lowest prices to the month of highest was in the two decades from 1831 to 1850. Despite their smaller range the two periods from 1801 to 1820 had the same average variation as that from 1831 to 1840. There was little consistency in the time at which seasonal highs and lows appeared. Usually the months from June to August were lowest and from November to January highest.

Summary of Industrial Raw and Semi-Finished Materials

The three industrial materials for which seasonal patterns were computed tended to have but one swing in prices each year. Whale oil showed the most persistent timing of seasonal peaks and lows. Linseed oil displayed a gradual shift in the timing of its lowest prices, but the peaks changed abruptly from fall to spring and then reverted to fall. Pig lead, in contrast to both of the other two industrial materials, developed no consistent seasonality or even a progressive change in the timing of its fluctuations within the year.

Indices of Similarity

As a summary and check on the persistence of seasonal patterns, successive indices of similarity have been computed, measuring the likeness between the patterns of adjacent decades.[6] The chief limitation of this procedure is that it does not take account of the reappearance of a similar pattern two or more decades later.

When four of the seven indices for any commodity show a positive resemblance, the seasonality for that commodity must have been somewhat alike throughout most of the period, or at least any change in the time of peaks and lows must have been very gradual. Of the 20 commodities, only tar had a positive similarity throughout the period. Six other commodities displayed a large amount of persistent agreement: New England rum, corn meal, corn, linseed oil, pork, and whale oil. In pork all of the consecutive appearances of a similar pattern were before 1840, in corn meal after 1801, and in whale oil after 1811.

At the other extreme the series of flour and pepper never showed the same pattern in two adjoining decades, while wheat, James River

[6] For the method used in the construction of the index of similarity see Appendix, p. 344. The method followed is that used by Dr. Simon Kuznets, *op. cit.*, pp. 281-282.

tobacco, St. Domingo coffee, and West India molasses were in accord in only one case. That wheat and coffee had any stability in their patterns is due to the fact that similar fluctuations appeared in several decades not adjacent to each other.

Taking the 20 commodities as a whole, there was a tendency for increasing persistence of seasonal patterns as the period advanced. Four series had positive indices of similarity in the two periods from

TABLE 12

INDICES OF SIMILARITY OF SEASONAL PATTERNS OF SELECTED COMMODITIES FOR SUCCESSIVE DECADES

Commodity	1785–1790 / 1791–1800	1791–1800 / 1801–1810	1801–10 / 1811–20	1811–20 / 1821–30	1821–30 / 1831–40	1831–40 / 1841–50	1841–50 / 1851–59
Corn	− .26	+.14	+.22	− .10	+.16	+ .52	+ .58
Wheat	− .38	−.08	−.20	− .08	−.64	− .80	+ .40
Rice	− .42	−.06	−.48	+ .04	0	+ .28	− .10
Tobacco, James River	−1.00	−.16	−.76	− .70	−.86	+ .08	− .90
Cotton, Georgia	− .90	−.16	+.34	− .60	+.28	− .14	− .04
Flour	− .68	−.12	−.24	− .28	−.18	− .22	− .22
Corn meal	− .80	−.08	+.44	+ .32	+.04	+ .50	+ .54
Pork	+ .30	+.36	−.28	+ .20	+.24	− .38	− .60
Dairy Products	− .14	−.10	−.64	− .04	−.02	+ .40	+ .54
Mackerel, #1			+.08	− .12	−.18	− .34	+ .02
Coffee, St. Domingo	− .18	−.60	−.12	− .30	−.16	− .32	+ .14
Tea, Hyson skin		+.44	+.56	−1.00	−.44	− .58	−1.00
Pepper	− .18	−.04	−.56	− .68	−.46	−1.00	− .30
Molasses, West India	− .84	−.42	+.36	− .28	−.28	− .46	− .36
Sugar, Havana brown	− .14	−.52	+.02	+ .36	−.08	− .08	+ .22
Rum, New England	+ .30	−.70	+.28	+ .24	+.52	+ .54	+ .22
Tar	+ .52	+.54	+.48	+ .24	+.62	+ .32	+ .50
Oil							
linseed	+ .22	+.52	−.48	+ .08	+.22	+ .34	− .10
whale			−.02	+ .36	+.26	+ .28	+ .20
Lead, pig	− .28	−.56	−.66	0	−.32	+ .14	− .64

1785 to 1800, five from 1791 to 1810, eight or nine in each 20-year period from 1801 to 1840, and ten from 1831 to 1850, and from 1841 to 1859.

AMPLITUDE OF SEASONAL VARIATIONS

The various commodities displayed considerable diversity in the average deviation in their seasonal patterns throughout the period. Those which, by this measure, had the least amplitude in their seasonal fluctuations were pepper, James River tobacco, Havana brown sugar, pig lead, dairy products, and mackerel #1. In no decade was their average deviation as much as 3 per cent and in five or six of the eight periods, the average variation of pepper, James River tobacco, and Havana brown sugar was less than 1.5 per cent. In addition to these commodities, which were never extremely variable, flour, St. Domingo coffee, and Hyson skin tea had an average deviation of less than 1.5 per cent in four or five decades, and more than 3 per cent in

TABLE 13
AVERAGE DEVIATION OF SEASONAL PATTERNS OF SELECTED COMMODITIES IN EACH DECADE

Commodities	1785-1790	1791-1800	1801-1810	1811-1820	1821-1830	1831-1840	1841-1850	1851-1859
Corn	8.5	3.7	3.2	3.7	2.5	6.0	3.3	3.5
Wheat	4.2	1.7	4.8	2.7	2.2	1.5	2.0	4.2
Rice	2.5	2.7	3.0	2.8	4.8	4.7	3.0	2.5
Tobacco, James River	1.2	1.5	0.8	2.2	0.2	1.2	1.8	0.3
Cotton, Georgia	1.2	1.7	2.8	3.0	1.2	1.8	1.7	2.5
Flour	3.0	1.3	1.3	3.3	1.3	2.2	1.3	1.5
Corn meal	2.2	3.0	2.3	2.5	2.7	3.7	2.5	3.3
Pork	3.0	1.3	3.5	1.5	2.0	2.0	1.2	2.7
Dairy Products	1.8	2.2	1.5	0.7	1.2	1.7	1.7	2.0
Mackerel, #1	1.0		1.8	2.2	2.3	0.7	2.3	2.0
Coffee, St. Domingo	4.7	0.8	1.2	1.8	1.0	1.3	0.8	1.5
Tea, Hyson skin		1.3	1.5	4.3	0.7	1.2	0.3	0.7
Pepper	2.2	1.3	0.8	1.3	1.8	0.5	0.7	1.0
Molasses, West India	2.0	0.7	4.0	4.3	1.7	3.3	2.3	0.8
Sugar, Havana brown	1.2	1.2	0.8	2.3	1.7	1.2	2.3	1.0
Rum, New England	1.8	1.3	2.7	3.8	1.5	3.5	2.5	2.7
Tar	7.8	6.5	10.0	8.7	2.7	4.3	4.8	3.8
Oil								
linseed	5.5	5.2	3.0	1.7	1.3	2.0	2.3	2.0
whale	0.7		1.2	4.3	4.5	1.0	2.2	1.8
Lead, pig	1.3	0.7	1.5	1.5	0.7	1.5	2.7	1.3

at least one decade. Although the deviation in Georgia cotton was only twice less than 1.5 per cent, it was only once as much as 3 per cent.

By the same measure tar and corn stand out as the most variable of all the commodities. Only in one period did either have an average variation of less than 3 per cent while in four decades the average deviation of tar was 6.5 per cent or more and in two that of corn was 6 per cent or more. No other commodity ever had an average annual variation of more than 5.5 per cent. Although tar was always among the three highest in any decade, the extent of its deviations changed abruptly after 1820.

Another measure of the amplitude of the seasonal fluctuations is the range between the months with the highest and lowest prices. The smallest consistent range was in Havana brown sugar in which the greatest difference between the peak and low was seven points. In St. Domingo coffee, Hyson skin tea, pepper, and pig lead the range only once exceeded seven points, while in James River tobacco, Georgia cotton, and dairy products it was never as much as 12 points. Except for flour and mackerel #1, all of the commodities which had

TABLE 14
RANGE OF DEVIATION OF SEASONAL PATTERNS OF SELECTED COMMODITIES BY DECADES

Commodities	1785-1790	1791-1800	1801-1810	1811-1820	1821-1830	1831-1840	1841-1850	1851-1859
Corn	26	15	11	14	10	19	11	15
Wheat	18	10	14	13	9	8	10	16
Rice	10	9	13	10	14	16	12	9
Tobacco, James River	4	7	3	9	2	4	8	2
Cotton, Georgia	5	6	10	11	4	8	5	9
Flour	12	5	7	13	9	10	6	6
Corn meal	8	12	9	10	12	13	10	13
Pork	10	5	10	6	7	8	5	12
Dairy Products	6	7	6	3	6	6	8	9
Mackerel, #1	4		7	8	13	3	8	11
Coffee, St. Domingo	18	4	6	7	4	5	4	5
Tea, Hyson skin		5	5	15	2	4	2	2
Pepper	8	7	5	5	6	2	3	3
Molasses, West India	6	4	14	15	7	12	10	2
Sugar, Havana brown	6	5	3	7	5	6	7	3
Rum, New England	7	5	9	15	5	10	8	11
Tar	25	26	32	30	10	15	15	18
Oil								
linseed	22	18	10	9	7	8	10	9
whale	4		5	14	12	5	8	6
Lead, pig	5	2	5	5	3	7	10	5

the least amplitude by the measure of average deviation were also the commodities with the least range.

Likewise, the extreme amplitude found in the average deviation of corn and tar is corroborated by the range. In no period was it less than 10 points for these two commodities. In addition, the range in wheat, rice, and corn meal was never less than eight points and in linseed oil never less than seven. It is interesting to note that five of the six series with the greatest ranges were grains or products derived from agricultural commodities, while some of the least variable commodities were also farm crops or farm derivatives. The only progressive shift observed in the range of seasonal variation was in pepper and tar, both of which had a decreasing amplitude. This unique tendency was not dependent upon the size of the range since pepper throughout the period had mild while tar had extreme variations.

The detailed seasonal analysis of even 20 selected commodities has shown that in all of these series seasonality alone would account for the frequency of changes in monthly quotations and that in most series studied the frequency of price changes did not equal those of the seasonal pattern. Seasonality, however, would not account for the progressive increase in the frequency of price changes of some commodities. It was observed that very few commodities had the same timing of seasonally high and low prices throughout the period, although more series had a gradual shift in the location of the maximum and minimum prices of each year. The amplitude of the seasonal fluctuations varied substantially from one decade to another, but some commodities could be characterized as usually having a high or a low amount of change within the year.

CHAPTER VII

PRICE MOVEMENTS FROM 1784 TO 1808

Except for the relation in Chapter I of a few outstanding events to the general indices of prices, the discussion of wholesale prices in Philadelphia from 1784 to 1861 has been carried on, up to this point, largely "in a vacuum." Our purpose has been to examine the price data in order to see what fundamental changes occurred in their annual and monthly behavior. In Chapters II-IV the annual averages were studied. Those analyses permitted an examination of the extent and shape of the distribution of the annual averages around their median. It furnished evidence of a small but increasing proportion of commodities with minor, if any, changes in prices from one year to the next. Finally, it provided a mathematical characterization of the various commodities as to the average change from year to year in each of the major periods defined in the first chapter. From the monthly data, the frequency with which changes in prices occurred was studied in Chapters V and VI. In general it was found that commodities differed considerably in their sensitivity even from 1791 to 1810 and that these differences tended to be accentuated in later years. By an intensive analysis of 20 selected series, including many of the most variable, it was possible to appraise the effect of seasonality upon the monthly changes in prices. In addition, this study indicated the extent to which seasonality was modified by shifts in the timing of the yearly recurrence of high and low prices and by increases or decreases in the amplitude of such fluctuations.

With this background, which has revealed significant changes in the behavior of prices from one time to another, the monthly and annual data may be reëxamined in detail. In Chapters VII-X the fluctuations in prices of the 140 commodities classified by each of the three methods described in Chapter I—imported and domestic, nine major groups, and 25 sub-groups—are related to some of the explanations of the factors affecting prices offered by contemporary merchants, by contemporary newspaper and market reports, and by other students of the period between the Revolution and the Civil War. The letters of merchants contributed most in the early years, partly because the collections of letters are more complete than for later years. Besides, as methods of doing business gradually changed, the dealings of the merchants tended to become specialized and reflected less of the general conditions of the market. The concomitant rise of improved market reports provided an invaluable source of general information for the latter part of the period.

The 78 years from 1784 to 1861 were too long and too diversified to be considered as a whole. Accordingly, the chapters from VII-X are organized in terms of the four major periods determined by the price movements of the general index: 1784-1808, 1808-1821, 1821-1843, and 1843-1861.

Monthly Price Movements

In the first six years after our price series start, Pennsylvania, like other areas, was struggling with the preliminary stages of readjustment after the Revolutionary War. Many conditions of trade had changed. Many new charges on the sale of American goods shipped to England made merchants uncertain about what to ship and what weight to give to the prices current upon which they depended for information.[1] In other cases, local supplies were short. Ironmasters, especially, not only felt a lack of workmen which kept stocks of iron scarce, but even were offering passage money to induce iron-workers to immigrate.[2] The West India trade, long a subject of discussion, had been settled by July 1783[3] by the well-known regulations, effective in one form or another for the next ten years, which limited the American trade to the British islands to lumber, flour, bread, grain, vegetables, and live stock and forbade trade in meat, dairy products, and fish. The further restriction to British bottoms hampered Philadelphians more in their carrying trade than in their sale of provisions. In fact, at the close of 1784, the fire at Port au Prince and hurricanes

[1] July 30, 1784, John Clifford to his brother Thomas, Bristol, England.

[2] August 30, 1784, John Clifford to ———.

[3] Channing, Edward, *A History of the United States*, Vol. III, p. 428. Edwards, Bryan, *The History of the British West Indies*, Vol. II, p. 495.

in Jamaica stimulated the demand for lumber to a point at which such cargoes were difficult to obtain.[4]

On the other hand, Europeans, all anxious to start trading with the newly independent states, were at a loss to gauge rightly the demand or the quality of goods to send to the Philadelphia market. Robert Henderson, a Scottish merchant who started in business in Philadelphia after the Revolution, explained in the last quarter of 1784 some of the problems of selecting merchandise. He wrote, "The French undersell us in a great many articles such as laces, silks, gloves, etc.; the Irish undersell us about 10 per cent on linen. Ours is all too high priced. . . . The people want to have good things but they have not the money."[5]

More serious problems, engaging the attention of citizens at this time, had their effect upon prices. The necessity for funding the public securities, or for paying interest on rapidly depreciating certificates, led to the Funding Act of the State of Pennsylvania in 1785.[6] By March 1785, the Assembly, having to deal, as it frequently had in Colonial times, with pressure for the issue of paper money, had passed an act for emitting £150,000 in paper bills which were scarcely issued before they began to depreciate.[7] Regular revenue was sought in this year through the famous Tariff Act of 1785.

Altogether, by May 1785, when the Pennsylvania Assembly hesitated over revoking the charter of the Bank of North America, when sales of goods could only be effected by granting credits of six to nine months, when bankruptcies occurred weekly, Henderson, like others, concluded, "The country will not pay for what is in it for three years to come."[8]

The brighest spot in this year was the maintenance of proportionately high prices for grain. An unusual demand from Spain and Portugal added to the effect of the scant crops of 1785.[9] Not till 1786 was agriculture in Pennsylvania on the way back to what would have been regarded as a normal yield before the American Revolution, and by then all prices were declining drastically.

[4] September 24, 1784, John Clifford to his brother Thomas, Bristol, England.
[5] October 8, 1784, Robert Henderson to ———, Glasgow.
[6] Webster, Pelatiah, *Political Essays*, 1791, pp. 269-305.
[7] Phillips, Henry, Jr., *Historical Sketches of the Paper Currency*, p. 34.
[8] May 3, 1785, Robert Henderson to William Gardiner, Glasgow.
[9] February 27, 1786, John Clifford to Thomas Clifford, Jr., Bristol, England.

It would be easy by attention to the price decline to exaggerate the disorder of the early years of readjustment. Actually the paper currency was not at this time made legal tender.[10] This limitation and the lack of confidence in any issues of paper after the well-remembered experience of the Revolutionary period accelerated the depreciation, which soon reached 30 per cent. Yet it was weak merchants in a position which forced them to push sales who actually were most affected by unstable currency. Those in stronger credit positions delayed sales or resorted to barter.

In general, prices declined from 1784 until the early spring of 1789. Many commodities, however, especially those imported into Pennsylvania, not only dropped less in price than other series but made some recovery in the latter part of 1785 which tended to persist until well into 1787. The index of prices of these imported commodities completed its decline in November 1788, five months before the prices of domestic commodities and the general average reached a corresponding position.

The Decline to 1789

Though the general average of all commodities was, in January 1784, at its maximum of the first six years of our period, two major groups were apparently low in April. One of these, the farm crops, rose to a moderate peak in July 1786 before starting the decline which culminated in April 1789. A return to normal agricultural activity was doubtless aided by this rise in the price of farm crops in 1785 and the first half of 1786. Even in 1787 prices of wheat and flour kept moderately high until the yield from a "generally good"[11] harvest began to come in. That no single factor accounted for the upswing in farm prices is clear from the character of the rise in the constituent farm crop series. Commodities which normally displayed marked unity of behavior were especially far apart in the timing of peaks. Tobacco, rice, corn, and wheat were at their highest prices of the six years in 1784. Four other series—rye, flax, flaxseed, and peas—had peaks in 1785, followed by oats and cotton in 1786 and hemp in 1787. In addition, the tobacco series had a minor peak in 1787.

[10] Webster, Pelatiah, *op. cit.*, p. 270, n. 3.

[11] July 12, 1787, Levi Hollingsworth to Richard Brodhurst, Kingston, Jamaica.

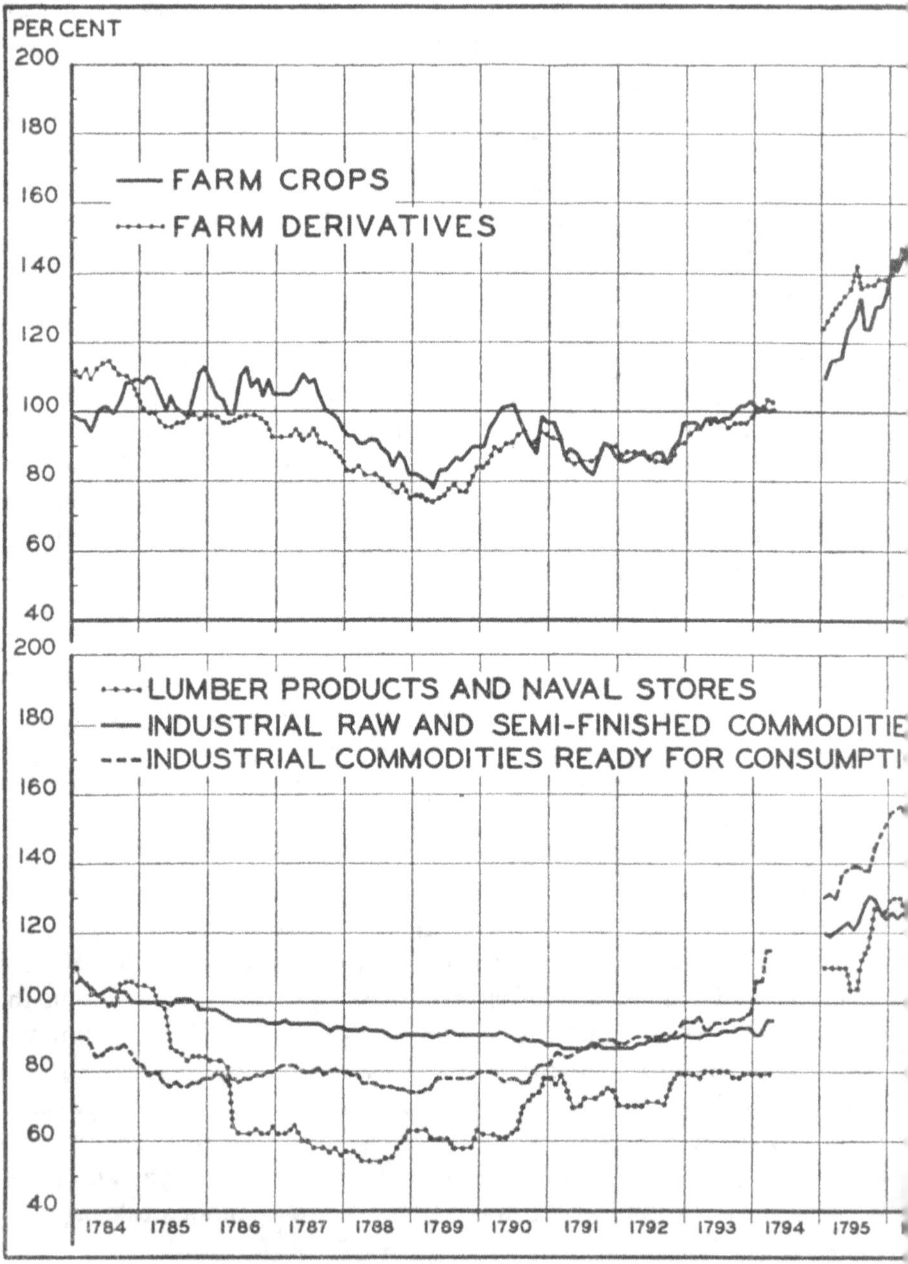

CHART IX—GEOMETRIC INDICES OF AVERAGE MONTHLY WHOLE
(Base—Mo

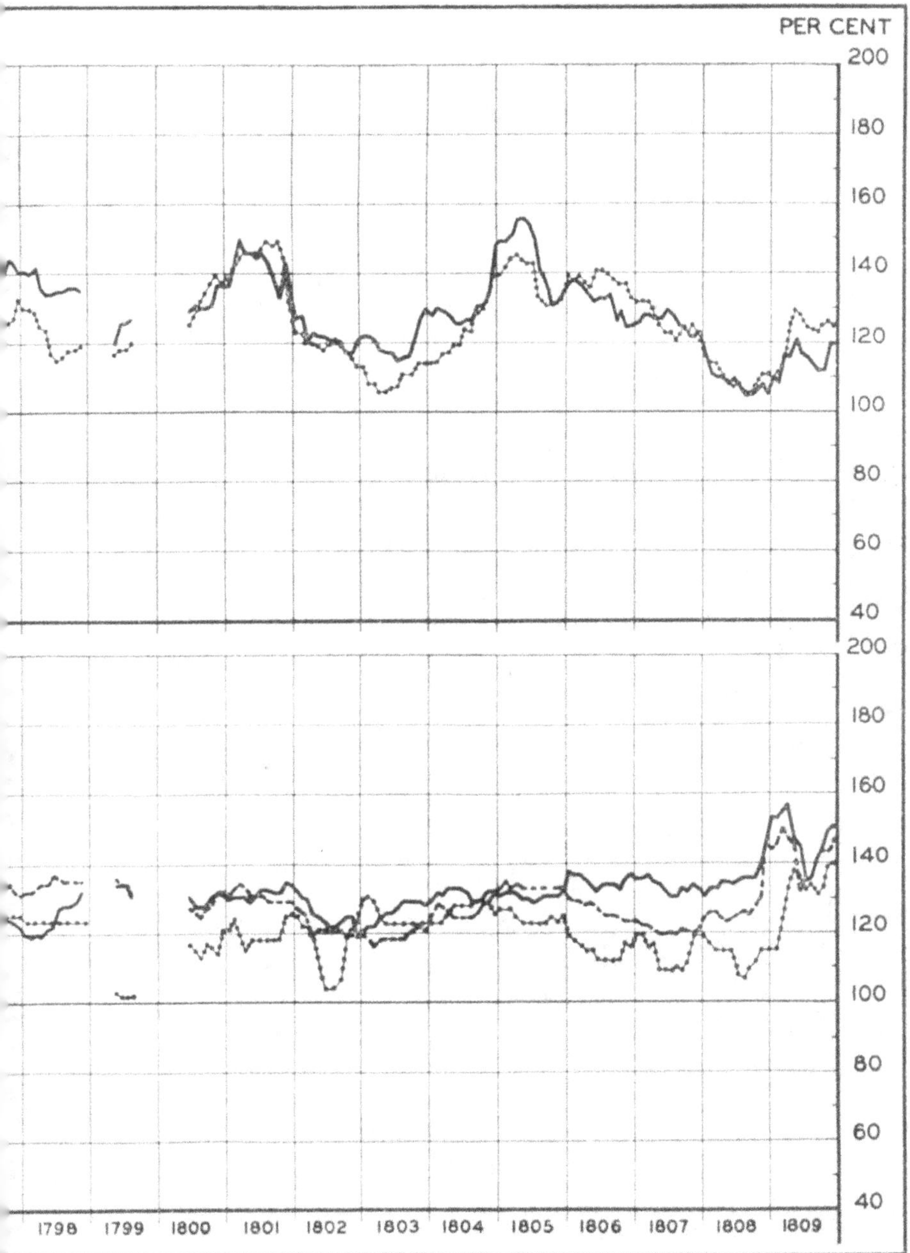

CES IN PHILADELPHIA BY MAJOR GROUPS, 1784-1809
rage, 1821-1825)

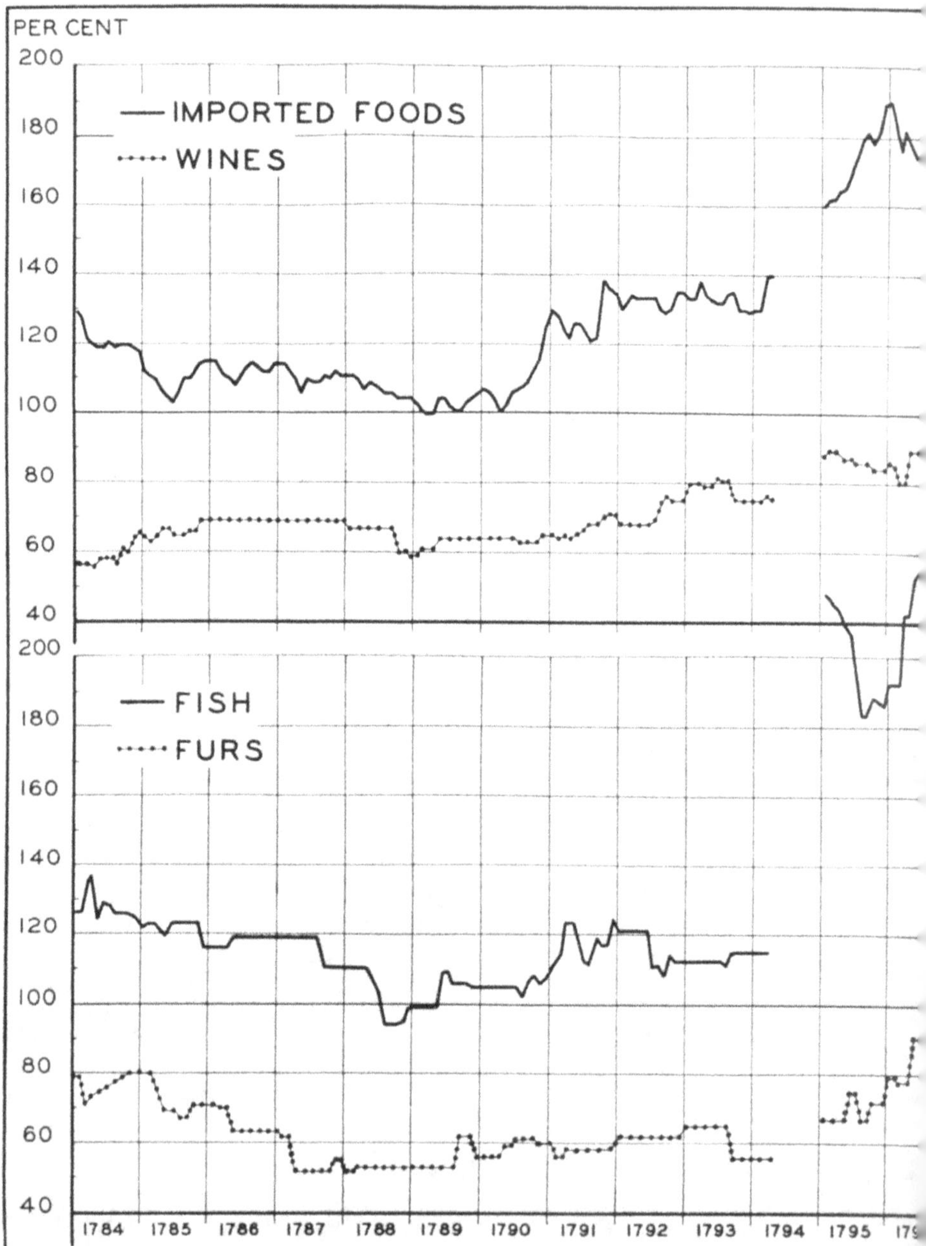

CHART IX—GEOMETRIC INDICES OF AVERAGE MONTHLY WHOLES
(Base—Mon

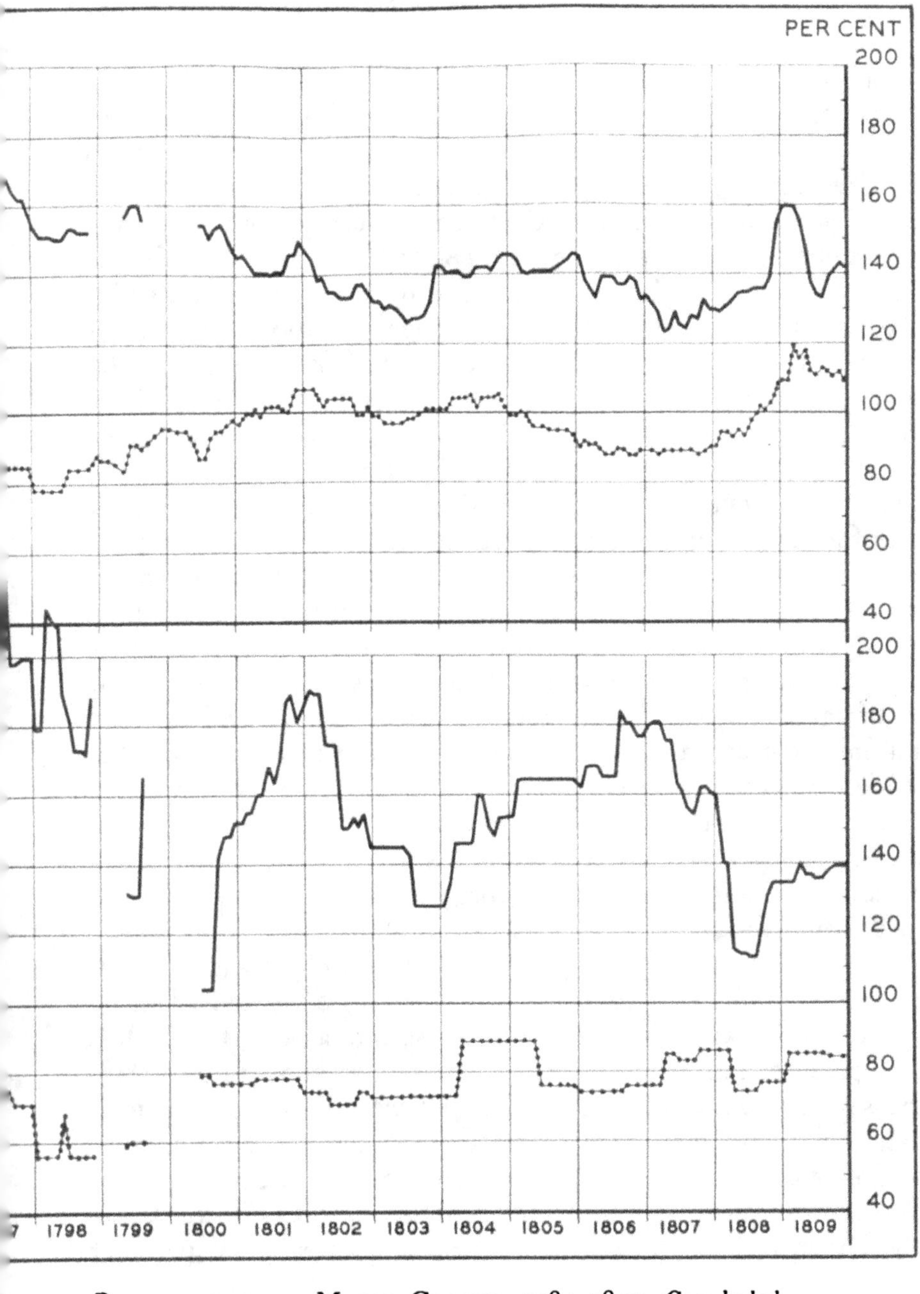

CES IN PHILADELPHIA BY MAJOR GROUPS, 1784-1809, *Concluded*
erage, 1821-1825)

The other major group which was low in April 1784—wines—advanced to a plateau which was maintained from November 1785 to December 1787.

Two other major groups had within the period from 1784 to 1789 a distinct swing in prices which began later than that in farm crops and wines. After June 1785 the imported food group rose 12.5 per cent in eight months. Its subsequent decline during more than three years reduced prices only 2.9 per cent below June 1785. The advance in the prices of industrial commodities ready for consumption which started after September 1785 was of longer duration than that of imported foods, but during the year and a half prices rose only 8.3 per cent. During the next two years the prices of these commodities receded, reaching, in February 1789, a point 10.5 per cent below the peak of 1787 and 18.4 per cent below February 1784.

The other groups fell persistently during the period. The highest prices for lumber products and naval stores during these years occurred in January 1784. The decline of these prices was more abrupt than that of any other group and was completed more quickly than in any other of the six largest groups. In July 1788 the index of prices of lumber products and naval stores was 51.0 per cent below that of January 1784. In contrast, the group of industrial raw and semi-finished materials, which was at its highest in February 1784, had declined only 19.1 per cent by May 1791. No other group had such a protracted decline. In fact many of these groups which were low in 1788 or 1789 had another swing in prices in the early nineties which was well started before the industrial raw materials ended their long decline.

The farm derivatives reached a peak in July 1784. By the following June the index of this group had fallen 17.0 per cent. During 1785 and 1786 when farm crops were rising to a peak, the decline in the prices of farm derivatives was checked. In the middle 1780's increases in prices among the derivatives were confined to animal products and corn meal and the total rise in these was not concentrated enough in time or large enough in amount to cause a rise in the average of the group. The maximum prices in 1786 occurred in July, but in this month, when the farm crops were 20.0 per cent higher than in 1784, the derivatives were 13.7 per cent lower. Both groups completed their decline in April 1789.

The two smaller groups of fish and furs had a comparatively short period of recession. The index of the fish group, which declined from its peak between April 1784 and August 1788, held its low price for three months. The furs, which maintained a comparatively high level from November 1784 to March 1785, ended this recession in February 1788.

Disregarding the swings in price between 1784 and 1789, the downward movement in prices during this period was completed in:

February 1788 in furs
July 1788 in lumber products and naval stores
October 1788 in fish
January 1789 in wines
February 1789 in industrial commodities ready for consumption
April 1789 in imported foods
April 1789 in farm crops
April 1789 in farm derivatives
May 1791 in industrial raw and semi-finished products

The downswing of prices, manifest in the total curve from the beginning of 1784 to April 1789, conceals many contrary short movements in particular sub-groups as well as in the major groups. Some even completed a mild swing in prices in these years. In various months in 1785, chemicals and drugs, beverages, minor farm crops, and wines rose to higher peaks than they averaged in any month in 1784. Grains fluctuated around a high level until the last half of 1786. A much larger number, especially those including West India products, continued to advance or sustained, until 1787, a high level already made. Those with a peak in 1787, which they reached in the order named, were: spirits, sugar and molasses, textile fabrics, tobacco, and wines. Dyes even held the maximum price of these early years through January 1788. The most persistent upward tendency, however, appeared in the non-ferrous metals, which advanced from November 1784 to November 1788.

These contrary movements against the growing momentum of recession account for the diversity of opinion as to when the recovery of this period really started. It has often been dated as early as 1786 and equally often in 1788. The fact is that in each of these years the prices of substantial numbers of commodities rose, especially between the latter half of 1784 and the end of 1787. Yet improvement in these served only to impede rather than to halt the general decline.

Tench Coxe, a contemporary, felt that the conditions of trade were precarious throughout 1786. His comment, written later, was, "Notwithstanding the actual prosperity of the United States at this time, it is a fact, which ought not to be concealed, that their affairs had fallen into a very disagreeable condition in the year 1786."[12] This is amply borne out by the need for convening mercantile citizens in the fall of 1786 at Annapolis and reconvening them in Philadelphia in the spring of 1787.[12] Yet in the last half of 1787, when merchants were seeking new sources for articles which they had been long accustomed to buy in England, and were failing to get easy deliveries, when specie was disappearing and currency was depreciating, Levi Hollingsworth, one of the most prominent merchants of his time, wrote, "We are not in that confusion here that the people of Europe suppose—our laws are well administered in the old counties and some of the new."[13]

Among modern writers, Channing, summarizing various types of evidence, points out that "between 1783 and 1787 the country had passed through a period of economic readjustment." He concludes that, despite the pessimism of contemporaries, the evidence shows that "commercially and industrially the country had regained its prosperity by 1788 and was on the high road to it in 1786."[14] Such a conclusion must rest on other evidence than the movement of prices in Philadelphia. From the prices alone we would have to conclude that the improvement of 1786 affected a limited number of commodities and even in these was not a long sustained advance. Levi Hollingsworth was optimistic about the future by the spring of 1788. "The commerce of this city," he wrote in April, "seems to revive a little this spring. Great quantities of wheat are shipping off for Portugal and flour for Spain and I flatter myself that on the Federal Government taking place a new spring will be given to trade and agri-

[12] Coxe, Tench, *A View of the United States of America*, pp. 3-4.

[13] October 10, 1787, Levi Hollingsworth to Enoch Story, London.

[14] Channing, Edward, *op. cit.*, Vol. III, p. 481.

culture."[15] By the close of 1788 a basis for recovery seems to have been laid and a mild start to higher prices was in progress. Yet before the spring of 1789 no widespread advance sufficient to change the direction of average prices was under way.

The economic conditions toward the close of this long post-war decline and the character of the readjustment which had taken place are well summarized in a letter of Thomas Clifford, Jr., of Bristol, England, to his wife at home. "It appears to me," he wrote from New York, "that this country taking it at large is in a very thriving state, though individuals, the traders of all kinds, are suffering very much. The imports from Great Britain are daily lessening and, I believe, in a few years will be very inconsiderable. The people are raising and manufacturing almost every article that the country wants. It is supposed [that] this state and New Jersey will manufacture this year almost the whole of their linen; the stock of wool is increasing; a variety of articles are made in the iron way; almost the whole of their nails and other heavy articles is daily increasing so that, I believe, it will be only the finer kinds of those goods that will be had from England. Some glass houses are getting to work and will lessen the consumption of Bristol glass much. If I am not mistaken, this country will soon be in a situation to pay all it owes if peace and harmony should prevail among them, but its imports and exports will be inconsiderable to what they have been. . . . You may naturally suppose if this country should be in the flourishing state I expect, that payments would be more regular. This would be the case provided that no more people embarked in the trade than it would support, but there is reason to fear it will always be more or less overstocked with such traders. . . . The exports directly to England from these parts are very inconsiderable in value and if England should put America on the same footing as other countries, it will be much lessened. The duties on lumber and iron paid by other nations would almost entirely destroy this trade."[16]

The Rise to 1797

Our prices justify the feeling that a basis for recovery was being laid, since three of the nine major groups, furs, lumber products and

[15] April 21, 1788, Levi Hollingsworth to Mark Pragers, London.
[16] August 1, 1788, Thomas Clifford, Jr., to his wife in Bristol, England.

naval stores, and fish, started their recovery between February and October 1788 and wines, industrial commodities ready for consumption, imported foods, farm crops, and farm derivatives between February and May 1789. In fact, all groups except industrial raw and semi-finished materials began to rise by May 1789.

It was in this order that commodities started the rise which culminated between the fall of 1795 and the spring of 1797. The eight years following 1789 were generally marked by rising prices which mounted with especial rapidity from 1793 through 1796. It was during these years that while conditions became more settled in Pennsylvania after the adoption of the federal constitution, business abroad was unsettled by the outbreak of the French Revolution which later drew all Europe into the Napoleonic wars.

In the early nineties many commodities of domestic origin had a minor swing in price. The index of the prices of domestic commodities rose 17.6 per cent from April 1789 to January 1791. By August it had declined 5.1 per cent. With some fluctuations it continued below the peak of 1791 until near the close of 1792.

By 1795, nearly all prices had reached a level considerably higher than in any of the eleven preceding years. For more than twenty years thereafter prices tended to fluctuate around this level. In January 1796 the index of the average prices of imported commodities was at the peak of the period from 1784 to 1808. At that time the index was 70.3 per cent above the low of November 1788. The peak of prices of domestic commodities and for the general index was in February 1797, more than a year after the corresponding point in the curve of prices of imported commodities. These peaks were widely separated in time but were relatively near together in amount.

Although the total curve of prices had only minor fluctuations during this period of expansion, all but the two industrial groups had a marked swing in prices in the early nineties. The farm crops and farm derivatives, among the last of the groups to end their recession, were the first to reach a minor peak. In June 1790 the farm crops were 30.8 per cent higher than in the spring of the previous year. The derivatives reached their peak in August 1790. This relation of the derivatives to farm crops was reversed in the following recession, which was completed in May 1791 in the derivatives but not until

August 1791 in the farm crops. The derivatives held near the low level for approximately a year and a half. Lumber products and naval stores did not reach a minor peak until after the derivatives, but both completed their recession at the same time. Prices of fish continued to rise until after the other three groups composed chiefly of domestic articles (farm crops, derivatives, and lumber products and naval stores) had completed their recession. As a result, the decline in the fish index was postponed and confined to the months between December 1791 and September 1792. Imported foods, which started upward in 1789 at the same time as the farm crops and derivatives, reached a peak in October 1791 after both of the other groups had completed their recessions. The minor peaks in the indices of wines and furs were not reached until the summer of 1793 after all of the other groups except imported foods had ended their declines. As a result it was as late as April 1794 that the wines and furs completed theirs. During these years when the other groups were having a distinct swing, the industrial goods ready for consumption were steadily advancing, while the industrial raw materials sagged continuously until May 1791 before starting a gradual rise.

Probably at no other time between 1784 and 1861 did the general curve conceal such diversity of movements among the groups as from 1789 to 1792. Although most of them had a swing in prices within that period, the timing was so diverse that they tended to cancel each other and the general curve shows a relatively unbroken advance. Nevertheless, after 1788 there was an increasing number of commodities rising, but not until 1790 did the annual prices of half of the commodities advance. In 1792 and 1793 about 85 commodities rose. In 1794 and 1795 the pull upward became more pronounced. In the first of these years 114 commodities rose and only 26 declined, and in the next year 118 advanced and 22 declined. Not even during the War of 1812 or in the years preceding 1837 or 1857 did as many commodities rise in a single year as in either 1794 or 1795. By the time the peak in the annual index was reached in 1796, as many as 44 commodities were falling in price. This increase in the number of commodities declining foreshadowed the widespread decline in the next two years.

All major groups reached peaks between the fall of 1795 and the spring of 1797. The industrial raw materials, which had been the last to turn upward after the decline from 1784, attained their peak in September 1795. In spite of the fact that this group did not have a swing in the early nineties, its rise of 52 months was shorter than that of any other group except imported foods, which had been the last of the six major groups to complete its swing after a peak in 1791. By January 1796 the imported foods had risen 47.2 per cent in 25 months, five months less than the rise to the minor peak of 1791.

Two months later the peaks of prices for farm derivatives and for industrial commodities ready for consumption occurred. These four groups which were the first to reach peaks include 102 of the 140 series. In spite of the fact that many of these commodities reached their highest prices in 1796, as many as 36 had a lower average price that year than in 1795. Only eight series among the other groups fell in 1796 and half of these were in the wine group, which had its peak in August 1796. In reaching this peak the wines were midway between both the farm derivatives and industrial products ready for consumption, which had attained peaks in March 1796, and the furs, which did not turn downward until after January 1797. In the first three months of 1797 prices of farm crops, lumber products and naval stores, and fish also were at the crest of this swing.

The rise in prices during the early nineties has special significance because of the fact that during those years some series rose to the highest prices of the period from 1784 to 1861 and most sold at the highest prices between 1784 and 1808. In addition, most of the series did not recede to a level as low as that from 1784 to 1789 until several years after the close of the War of 1812.

There is no doubt about the source of the stimulus to the rise in prices which changed the partial upturn of 1788 into a widespread advance in the next year. The uninterrupted rise from 1789 to 1797 in the general index of prices had been foreshadowed as early as the fall of 1787 in the prices of ferrous metals and building materials other than wood. In the early months of 1788 they were joined by grain products, furs, and wood. It is striking that both groups of building materials were among the first to rise, while the ferrous metals started their upward movement three and one-half years before the non-ferrous metals and the grain products fifteen months ahead of grains. During 1788 two other food groups, beverages and fish, added a rising impetus to that of grain products. Spirits and chemicals and drugs were also moving upward before the close of the year. By that time nine sub-groups were rising.

Within a year not only had the general average "turned the corner" but the number of groups showing an unmistakable rise had doubled. Farm products and foods were the chief contributors to the rise in 1789. Rye meal had been reported as "scarce and not always to be had"[17] early in February 1789, but it was the exportation in the summer and fall, especially of grain and flour, which accounted for the comment that "Philadelphia seems to enjoy a better trade at present than it has done for some time past."[18] In the middle of December Henderson wrote that from the "quantity of flour and wheat that is exported this fall, flour will not be lower till near harvest next." He added, "There never was so much of these articles exported in one year since Pennsylvania has been known."[19]

Increases in the prices of grains and minor farm products, followed by advances in sugar and molasses, fruits, meats and meat products, and dairy products, were supplemented by gains in wines, fuel and lighting, and hides and leather. The general curve rose for two and one-half years before all of the other six groups added their impetus to the rise.

In 1790 the rise in prices gained momentum. Early in January, wheat and flour were reported to be in brisk demand and supplies still being sought. The extent to which farming areas had been combed for grain was explained by John Clifford, in February, when he wrote to his brother, "It is supposed that the western shores of Maryland and Virginia, the Delaware state and the country bordering the navigable rivers have generally sent their wheat to market and that there is but little more than sufficient left for their own use until next harvest. This is a circumstance that has rarely happened heretofore and will doubtless occasion flour to keep up its price. . . . Our dependence now principally rests on the western

[17] February 4, 1789, Levi Hollingsworth to George Walker, New York.

[18] November 5, 1789, John Lewis to James Jones, New Orleans in Reed and Forde Papers.

[19] December 12, 1789, Robert Henderson to David Lamb, Charleston. See also December 29, 1789, John Clifford to Thomas Clifford, Jr., Bristol, England.

country and I do not expect there is any considerable quantity remaining there. It appears to me as if flour will still rise and I think it not improbable but it may get to $8.00 per barrel."[20]

Besides the vigorous demand for grain and foods, the most important factors which can be isolated as contributing to an increase in prices in the early nineties were:

1. shortages of certain raw materials
2. an unusually active period of local building
3. the redemption of certificates which all holders had expected to be useless.

Among the ferrous metals in 1790 both bar and rod iron were scarce and advancing in price. Late in March, Hollingsworth believed that quotations could not fall "unless an importation takes place from Europe as the supply from our iron works is not equal to the demand."[21] Lumber also was scarce. The large number of vessels which had been able to enter the port of Philadelphia throughout the whole mild winter and spring without any interruption by ice had by June 1790 carried away enough lumber in their cargoes to raise prices. The increase in prices of pine boards caused Clifford to write in June, "Lumber of all kinds is high now owing to so many vessels coming for freights. Pine boards such as I formerly paid 60 to 70 shillings are now at 90."[22]

The rise in prices of lumber furnishes evidence also apparent in other materials of a sizable boom in local building which raised the price of glass and the raw materials used in paints. Inquiries were made for white lead ground in oil and Clement Biddle explained, in July, to a correspondent, "Painters oil has risen within three weeks near 18 pence per gallon, and now is very scarce at 4 shillings 6 pence to 5 shillings 9 pence."[23]

The rise of 12.9 per cent in the group index of lumber products and naval stores between July and September 1790 can be explained both by "a scarcity of water at the sawmills and the great demand for boards for the consumption of the place," which, in Clifford's words,

[20] February 1, 1790, John Clifford to Thomas Clifford, Jr., Bristol, England.
[21] March 20, 1790, Levi Hollingsworth to Solomon Townsend, New York.
[22] June 21 (about), 1790, John Clifford to Thomas Clifford, Jr., Bristol.
[23] July 29, 1790, Clement Biddle to Tobias Lear, New York.

"made boards scarce and high."[24] Actually the boom in local building started after the price of lumber had been raised by shipments to other areas. The proportions of the stimulus to construction in 1790 can be illustrated by the fact that "bricks for building" advanced 56 per cent between spring and September.[24] One explanation given for the spurt in local building was that "the Congress having adjourned to meet at this place has occasioned a demand for houses and, of course, an advance in the rent. This has occasioned an advance in the wages of almost all the tradesmen, has set the carpenters at work to building and repairing."[24]

The enhanced price for farm produce and foods and the activity in shipping and building speeded up the circulation of money[25] even before the national Funding Act of August 4, 1790[26] gave some basis for the great rise in public securities which occurred "within these few days"[27] or toward the middle of December.

Despite the vigor of the advance in the early nineties, six groups were slow to participate. Condiments ended their recession only in May 1790. Both textile fibers and textile fabrics followed in October, but the non-ferrous metals did not start to rise until after April 1791 and tobacco and dyes lagged still further behind all the other groups. Not until December 1791 did the most sluggish groups contribute to the upward movement in prices. By that time some of the groups which had provided an initial impetus to the general rise from 1789 had completed a minor recession and were again helping to sustain the total index.

At certain times between 1789 and 1794, 10 of the sub-groups in addition to those that were late in ending the decline displayed a marked tendency to fall in price, despite the general upward movement of the total index. Each of these sub-groups had a well-marked swing in prices with a peak between 1789 and 1793 and a low between 1791 and 1794. Two months after the general curve started to rise in 1789 the beverages, which had turned upward in the middle of the preceding year, attained a minor peak.

The greatest concentration of these relatively minor peaks was in

[24] September 25, 1790, John Clifford to Thomas Clifford, Jr., Bristol.

[25] May 23, 1790, Clement Biddle to Richard Smith, London.

[26] Webster, Peletiah, *op. cit.*, see footnote p. 342, for provisions.

[27] December 22, 1790, Robert Henderson to William Galt and Company, Richmond.

1790. In that year the rise in four groups was not only halted but was followed by a considerable recession which, in grain products, lasted for 16 months, in building materials other than wood for 18 months, in grains for nearly two and a half years, and in chemicals and drugs for nearly four years.

In each of the three years from 1791 to 1793 one or two other groups also started a substantial decline. The recessions in spirits, ferrous metals, furs, and sugar and molasses were completed within a year, but the decline in the fruit group persisted for more than a year and a half. Because of the variation in the time at which these groups again joined the advance it was not until after April 1794 that all were contributing to the rise which culminated in 1797.

The rapidity of the advance in the general index after 1789 is manifested not only by the continuous increases but more especially by the speeding up of the rate of increase in 1793, 1794, and 1795. The average annual index in 1792 was 2 per cent more than in 1791 though many commodities were declining and stocks and rates of exchange falling "owing to the banks stopping discount[ing]."[28] In the following year the rate of increase more than doubled, the annual index of the total curve rising 5.2 per cent. In the first part of this year Philadelphians were concerned over "the many failures in England [which] have affected merchants here."[29] As the year advanced they anticipated that "the war in Europe [would] cause a continued demand for provisions and naval stores."[30] In 1794 the rate of increase again more than doubled, the general curve rising 13.8 per cent that year. Prices continued to advance so rapidly in 1795 that the average was 19.3 per cent above that of the previous year. Even during the War of 1812 prices did not increase so continuously and at such a rapid rate. In 1793, the first of these years of rapidly rising prices, 36 commodities declined, 17 held at the same price as in 1792, and 87—only four more than in the previous year —increased. That the total index rose more than in the previous year is partly explained by the fact that the number of commodities which decreased in price was 20 less than in the previous year, but the more

[28] December 9, 1792, Robert Henderson to William Galt, Richmond.

[29] May 25, 1793, Samuel Wetherill to Brandrams, Templeton and Jacques, London.

[30] June 3, 1793, Reed and Forde to Richard Lemmon.

positive factor which led to the speeding up of the advance was the fact that 72 of the 87 series which rose showed a greater percentage of increase in 1793 than in 1792. The continuation of the marked rise into 1794 can be attributed to a further reduction of 10 in the number of commodities which declined in price. All of the remaining series rose and 87 of these rose at a faster pace than in 1793. Many series, like the general index, advanced at an increased rate in both years. The final spurt in the acceleration of the rate of increase came in 1795 when only 22 commodities sold for less than in the previous year and when 87 of the 118 which rose showed an even greater rise than in 1794.

The continuation of rising tendencies in 1793 and 1794 is striking in view of the succession of epidemics of fever in the city in both years. At its worst stages, houses, stores, and shops were closed and in September 1793 it was stated that "most of the merchants [have] fled to the country and no business [is] doing."[31] The embargo in the spring of 1794 which crippled commerce for nearly three months[32] did not cease until May 25.[33] This and the protest of the western counties against the taxes on distilling, which resulted in an open outbreak between July 15 and August 29, interfered with the sending of supplies to Philadelphia.[34] By fall, flour was scarce; yet prices were considered unduly high. Hollingsworth wrote at this time, "Many of the merchants refuse to load at the prices and we think it probable that the price may recant."[35] How completely mistaken was this judgment is clear from the continued rise in most commodity prices. By December wheat and flour were both scarce, and Girard, who was exporting both, wanted the consul at Bordeaux advised "of the rapid rise of our produce and give him to understand that the price of wheat quoted in the invoice of the ship *Good Friends'* cargo is far below [that] of the present. Flour is here $9.00

[31] September 25, 1793, Levi Hollingsworth and Son to Thomas Contee, Nottingham.

[32] May 16, 1794, Stephen Girard to Gy. Lavaud, Tortuga.

[33] May 27, 1794, James McCurrach and Company to Donaldson and Thomson, London.

[34] October 5, 1794, Reed and Forde to Daniel Clark, Jr., New Orleans. For a description of the Whiskey Rebellion see *The Life of Albert Gallatin* by Henry Adams, pp. 123-144.

[35] October 10, 1794, Levi Hollingsworth and Son to Herman Stump, Hartford.

per barrel and it is a difficult matter to procure that article at that price."[36] Prices increased still further in the following year.

The Decline to 1798

Though the advance of the general index continued until February 1797, the momentum of the rise was slowing down in 1796. The ensuing decline was first completed in the prices of imported commodities. In February 1798 their index was 14.7 per cent less than at the peak. The general index declined for two months after the average of the imported commodities ceased to decline. The prices of domestic commodities, which had reached their peak thirteen months after the peak of imported commodities, did not end their recession until May 1799, fifteen months after the low of the imported commodities. Although the decline in the prices of domestic goods was but slightly longer than that of imported commodities, it was much more severe. In 27 months the prices of domestic commodities fell 21.5 per cent while those of imported articles dropped only 14.7 per cent in 25 months.

In appraising the fluctuations in prices from 1796 to 1808 one must bear in mind that all groups held at a higher level than in the period from 1784 to 1789. Secondly, the swings in prices were, on the whole, shorter than the fall in prices from 1784 to 1789. Most of the swings after 1796 were similar to the minor swing which, in many groups, interrupted the general rise in prices from 1789 to 1796. Regardless of whether the general curve was moving up or down there was always a considerable number of commodities moving in the opposite direction and often a small but important group which held at the same price.

The decline from the peak around 1796 was first checked among the major groups in the industrial commodities ready for consumption. By December 1797, a year and three-quarters after their peak, their average price had dropped 17 per cent. This was not a severe decline compared with that into which many groups fell, but it was the most severe drop in this group between 1784 and 1808 and was completed in the shortest time. Even after this recession, prices were 77.3 per cent above those of 1789. In the 32 months from December

[36] December 8, 1794, Stephen Girard to William Douglas, Petersburg, Virginia.

1797, when the industrial commodities ready for consumption reached a low point, to August 1800, when the last of the major groups halted its decline from the peak in the spring of 1797, the industrial goods ready for consumption completed another minor swing.

Most of the groups ended their decline in 1798. In April of that year the group of raw and semi-finished industrial products ended its contraction. In July the imported foods and wines, in the next month the farm derivatives, and in December the furs started to advance. Two of the major groups continued to decline until 1799, the farm crops reaching their low in May and the lumber products and naval stores in August. It was a year after all other groups had started to rise that the prices of fish ended this decline and that the industrial commodities ready for consumption completed an additional minor swing.

Some indication of the factors initiating the decline from one of the most extreme peaks of the 78 years may be found in the order in which the sub-groups took part in the contraction. Four started to decline in 1795. The first of these, hides and leather, which had been rising for 67 months, began to fall after January. It was six months before any other group joined the hides and leather series in a downward price movement. Before the end of the year, dairy products, dyes, and chemicals and drugs broke away from the upward trend then dominating other groups. During the next year, grains, grain products, and foods of all kinds, both imported and domestic, except sugar and molasses and fish, added ten more groups with declining prices to the four which began to recede in 1795. The change in the general direction of the movement of prices heralded by this concentrated decline of 1796 took place early in 1797.

It is of interest that the recession in food prices, though spread over a year and a half, was so generally felt before the close of 1796. It is significant that so few foods are represented among the commodities which continued to advance until the next year. In 1797, furs, textile fibers, wood, building materials other than wood, sugar and molasses, fish, and textile fabrics started to decline between January and August. Even then the rise in prices of tobacco and ferrous and non-ferrous metals had not been checked. Tobacco continued to rise until 1798, non-ferrous metals until 1799, and ferrous metals until 1801.

From the movement of prices alone it would be hazardous to point to any one factor which initiated the decline. That the forces working toward higher prices must have been particularly strong is evident by the continued rising tendency in ten groups after fourteen had begun to fall.

Before the end of 1796 merchants were cautious both in placing orders and in sending ships to sea. It was in this year that the British "fleet was forced to abandon the Mediterranean"[37] and so, if one follows the reasoning of Captain Mahan, decreased the protection of neutral vessels in the trade to the south of Europe.[38] West India trade was dull enough to elicit the comment: "Our late advices from the West Indies are discouraging to the exportation of flour. The French have taken many of our vessels and say they will condemn all provision vessels bound to British ports. Our merchants decline shipping at this time."[39] Just as there was hesitation about sending out cargoes, so orders were delayed. At the close of 1796, Samuel and Miers Fisher wrote, "At present the prospect of trade does not look favorable on many accounts, so that [we] have not sent forward any orders for next fall and it seems to require further time to deliberate upon."[40] A few days later a similar policy was outlined to their Liverpool correspondent.[41]

In 1797 business was still further slowed down by an epidemic of fever which, though less severe in mortality than the epidemic of 1793, was so dreaded that in the summer "much more than half of the inhabitants were out of the city and business of most kinds at

[37] Mahan, Alfred T., *Sea Power in Its Relations to the War of 1812*, Vol. I, p. 74.

[38] The interest of two Philadelphia merchants in the happenings in the south of Europe appears in a letter of November 1797 inquiring about the effect of the Treaty. "The relative situation of Portugal with England and France, being attended by a late treaty which we have just seen, but have not had time to consider, we should be glad to have your observation thereon for our government in future, and especially how it may affect American vessels bound from hence to ports in Portugal with cargoes truly American or truly Portuguese property." November 16, 1797, Samuel and Miers Fisher to Holford Gonne and Company, Lisbon.

[39] October 18, 1796, Levi Hollingsworth to Libby, Carne and Slade, Alexandria.

[40] December 17, 1796, Samuel and Miers Fisher to Nevins and Gatliffe, Leeds, England.

[41] December 19, 1796, Samuel and Miers Fisher to Rathbone, Benson and Company, Liverpool.

an entire stand, save that some shops and stores continue open."[42]

Yet prices of some articles began to recover while others were declining. As early as 1796 dyes ended their contraction. While they did not contribute much to an advance, they held at an intermediate point until the beginning of 1798, when they began their rapid rise to an extreme peak in 1799. Besides, beverages, dairy products, and hides and leather began another expansion before the close of 1797. Consequently the year 1798 started with seven groups, three of which had not attained their peaks, rising against the downward trend of others. It required only the addition to these of one group, chemicals and drugs, in April 1798 to offset sufficiently the mild decline in others to change the direction of the general average.

The termination of the decline from peaks established in 1795 and the following years was, like the peaks, spread out over various months of three or more years. In contrast to the rise, however, the decline from 1797 was mild in that the fall in prices was arrested without establishing, in any group of commodities, prices as low as in 1789. Only two of the 15 sub-groups which had a mild swing in prices in the early nineties were pulled down in the recession from the peaks of 1795-1797 below the prices of the early part of the decade. Both recessions may be considered as mild, but they differ in character. In the earlier one only 15 groups showed a definite break in their advance; in the recession which culminated on the general curve in April 1798, prices of all groups except ferrous metals fell substantially at one time or another. In the general index the fall was gradual because of the slowness with which the price decline was disseminated and because of the counterbalancing effect of the rise of others.

The extent of the decline in many commodities is indicated by the fact that the averages of six sub-groups dropped between 40 and 68 per cent below the prices held at their maxima. These include chemicals and drugs, grains, grain products, tobacco, fish, and minor farm products. The mildest decline was in beverages, non-ferrous metals, wines, wood, textile fabrics, and textile fibers, all of which dropped at least 10 per cent but none more than 20 per cent.

[42] September 11, 1797, Samuel and Miers Fisher to Joseph Jacob Hollander and Sons, Altona.

The Rise to 1801

Most commodity groups had two more swings in prices before 1808. In general, prices were high in 1801 and 1805 and low in 1803 and 1808.

During the first part of this major period the imported commodities had tended to reach their successive lows and highs progressively earlier than the domestic commodities. Thus, in the low of 1789, the curve of prices of foreign commodities was moving five months ahead of that of the domestic commodities. By the peak of 1797 it was 13 months ahead and by the low of 1798 it was 15 months in advance of the corresponding low in the prices of domestic commodities. This tendency was climaxed at the peak which was reached in November 1801 in the general index and in the domestic index, but which had appeared 29 months earlier in the curve of prices of imported commodities. In fact, the peak of June 1799 in the imported index came just one month after the low in the prices of the domestic series. Imported commodities rose 14.1 per cent in 16 months, and domestic 16.8 per cent in 30 months. The main difference was that the imported index tended to maintain a high level while the domestic commodities were rising to their peak in November 1801.

Though the general index rose for 43 months after April 1798 to November 1801, the rise had none of the momentum of the years from 1793 to 1795 when price increase was piled upon increase. The most marked advance of this short rise occurred in 1799 when prices of 73 commodities advanced and 58 of these at a higher rate of increase than in the previous year.

Among the major groups the peaks in this swing were divergent. The imported foods were highest in July 1799 and the furs a year later. These two groups had risen from their lows in 1798 before the fish had completed its recession from 1797. All of the other groups reached their peaks within a period of 12 months between March 1801 and February 1802. The farm crops and industrial commodities ready for consumption were at their crests in March 1801, five months earlier than the corresponding point in the curve of prices of farm derivatives. The remaining groups—industrial raw materials, lumber products and naval stores, fish, and wines—reached their peaks in successive months from November 1801 to February 1802.

Long before the Peace of Amiens could be foreseen, a slackening of the rate of advance appeared. Though the general average increased until November 1801, only 53 commodities showed a higher percentage of increase in 1800 than in 1799 and by 1801 the number rising faster than they had in the previous year had been reduced to 44 commodities.

More agreement can be found in the timing of the sub-groups at the peak of 1801 than in the peak of 1797. Twelve groups reached their maxima between March and December 1801; seven had begun to contract earlier, leaving only five with an upward tendency at the close of 1801. All of these except sugar and molasses and hides and leather had turned downward by April 1802.

The Decline to 1803

Caution in the conduct of business in Philadelphia seems to have been exercised even before there was a widespread decline in prices. At the close of 1799 Samuel Wetherill, a prominent Philadelphia business man, referring to the failure of the house of Cheap and Loughnan in London, wrote, "We note with concern your observations respecting failures in London and Hamburg and shall be cautious of whom we purchase bills. Our shipping merchants must certainly feel the effects of these failures."[43] Early in the next year the effect of the mercantile depression hampered payment by making the rate of exchange on Hamburg and London too uncertain for Philadelphians to procure bills.[44] That domestic prices did not generally recede until 1801 was attributed to the "immense shipments" to Europe which made flour, beef, and pork "both scarce and high."[45]

To European demand may be attributed the mildness of the

[43] December 26, 1799, Samuel Wetherill to Brandrams, Templeman and Jacques, London.

[44] February 6, 1800, Samuel and Miers Fisher to John Burstall, Jr., Kingston-upon-Hull, England; February 13, 1800, Samuel and Miers Fisher to Joseph Walker, Leeds, England; March 25, 1800, Samuel and Miers Fisher to Thomas Cullen, Oratava in the Teneriffe.

[45] June 5, 1801, Reed and Forde to John O'Bannon, Kentucky.

decline in Philadelphia produce from the peak of 1801. Reversing the order maintained from 1789 to 1801, the index of domestic commodities, after declining 13.9 per cent in nine months, ended its recession in August 1802, seven months ahead of both the general curve and the index of foreign commodities. This is the only critical turning point from 1784 to 1808 in which imported commodities failed to precede domestic articles. The total decline in the index of imported commodities amounted to 16.2 per cent over a period of 45 months, but the bulk of the fall in prices occurred in the last 15 months.

The major groups differed more in the time of reaching the low after these peaks than in recording the high. The furs, which had been the second group to reach the peak, were the second to reach the low, but the imported foods, which had been the first to start downward, were nearly the last to complete the decline. The group of lumber products and naval stores, which had been among the last to attain a peak around 1801, dropped 17.2 per cent in eight months, ending its decline in August 1802. It was, thus, the first group to reach a low. Furs followed in the next month and the industrial raw and semi-finished commodities in December. The decline in all but one of the other groups ended between March and July 1803. Only fish, which had been the next to the last to reach a peak, continued to decline until January 1804.

The recession from November 1801 to March 1803 associated with the lull in hostilities[46] was intensified in Philadelphia by another of the frequent recurrences of yellow fever which caused a "deranged state of business here and [the] flight of the inhabitants,"[47] as well as by the unfavorable markets in Europe. The European factors as summarized by Hollingsworth, were in part the result of the restoration of peace effected by the Peace of Amiens, for which preliminaries were agreed to in London in October 1801, and in part connected with plentiful harvests. "Since the news of peace," he wrote at the beginning of 1802, "our markets have been regularly

[46] Smith, Walter Buckingham and Cole, Arthur Harrison, *Fluctuations in American Business, 1790-1860*, p. 17.

[47] Between August and October 1802, Levi Hollingsworth and Son to Thomas Bodley, Lexington, Kentucky.

declining in price and by no means settled, neither will they for the ensuing summer. Commerce must and will change its direction and new channels will open. The late harvest of grains and all kinds of provisions in England, France, and up the Baltic was very great. They have a considerable surplusage which will in general supply their West India colonies. Spain has already shut her ports of Havana, St. Jago de Cuba against us. Portugal is so glutted with wheat from the Baltic and corn and flour from this country that Mr. Buckly, our consul at Lisbon, writes his father-in-law in this city not to ship to that market, alleging that they have six months' supply there at market and the prices very low. . . . We may conclude that bread provisions will be low in the United States all this season."[48]

The timing of the end of the decline in the sub-groups suggests the effect of the reopening of warfare. Although 11 groups of commodities reached their lowest point before the close of 1802, many of these include imported commodities and raw materials for local consumption. Few of the agricultural staples, except tobacco and cotton, and no groups of domestic foods advanced before April 1803. Between then and September meats and meat products, wines, grain products, condiments, dairy products, fruit, minor farm crops, and grains started a vigorous advance. It is of interest that wines and fruit from the south of Europe and East India spices along with all the important domestic foods rose in 1803.

The Rise to 1805

In the same month in which the general rise started "very unfavorable accounts of the prices of provisions in Europe" reached Philadelphia. "From the advices received," wrote Hollingsworth, "the prices at Lisbon and the ports on the Bay of Biscay had suffered a reduction of 10 to 12 per cent. On the Mediterranean they are yet maintained but it is almost too late to make adventures there as the harvest would be on nearly as soon as the vessel could arrive."[49] The rise in the general curve, however, lasted from April 1803 to February 1805.

[48] January 29, 1802, Levi Hollingsworth to Thomas Bodley, Lexington, Kentucky.
[49] April 6, 1803, Levi Hollingsworth to William Hartshorne, Alexandria.

The final peak of prices in the first major period occurred in December 1804 in foreign commodities and in April 1805 in the domestic series. Here the imported commodities reasserted their tendency to precede the domestic commodities in reaching highs and lows. Both groups attained approximately the same index at their peaks although they were four months apart in timing.

The peak of prices in 1805 was largely confined to five of the nine major groups: industrial commodities ready for consumption, in February; farm derivatives, in April; farm crops and furs, in May; and imported foods, in December. With these groups might also be considered the industrial raw and semi-finished commodities which were moderately high in 1805, but were higher in the following year with a peak in January 1806. The prices of lumber products and naval stores reached their highest point in this swing in February 1803 only six months after their low of 1802. This group maintained a relatively high level until the close of 1805 and was nearly as high in the fall of 1804 as at the peak in the previous year. The wines also reached a peak before 1805; the highest prices were in June 1804. Although a high level was maintained during all of that year there was a pronounced drop in 1805. One other group besides the industrial raw and semi-finished materials, although high in 1805, continued to advance in 1806; the prices of fish did not reach a peak until August of the latter year.

The 41 months of expansion in prices from 1803 to 1805 were a repetition in many respects of the 43 months from 1798 to 1801. The difference is that the forces contributing to the advance outlasted the change in the direction of the general average in more sub-groups in 1803-1805 than in the earlier swing, especially in those of domestic origin. In fact the total curve of all imported commodities began to recede at the close of 1804. Though this change in direction of prices is evident in only six sub-groups composed mainly of imported articles, it applies also to imported commodities included in a number of others. The indices of sugar and molasses, dyes, non-ferrous metals, wines, and beverages all decreased before December 1804. Within a year, minor farm products, both series of building materials, grain products, furs, grains, dairy products, fuel and lighting, and condiments began to contract. In this year no recovery occurred in any of the groups which declined first; consequently the maintenance of an advance in textile fibers, fruit, fish, meats, and chemicals and drugs into 1806, in tobacco until 1807, and in spirits, ferrous metals, and textile fabrics until 1809 shows the unusual strength of the upward movement in these groups.

At the peak of 1805, in contrast to that of 1801, most domestic staples continued to advance until after the direction of the general curve had changed, adding to the evidence from other sources that part of the rise of 1805 was occasioned as much by scanty crops as by the benefits of neutral trade. In the middle of February 1805, a letter sent to Norfolk by Hollingsworth gave the information that "the last advices received from England and Spain gives us a prospect of a British demand for flour and corn and hath advanced the prices here."[50] Later in the same month he believed prices would "keep up till May."[51] It was in March that the tone of the correspondence began to change. Advices had just reached the Philadelphia merchants of an "offer of negotiations for peace on the part of the French Government" which "has very much dampened the spirit of speculation for your market in this city. A few or no new purchases have been made since the information reached us."[52] This merchant refrained from extending his undertakings as he had previously planned, having in mind "the great losses always experienced at the termination of hostilities on speculations made to Europe."[52] At this time he preferred to await the result of negotiations between Great Britain and France. As spring advanced, evidences appeared of less voluntary limitation of activities. On March 20, Hollingsworth's request was, "Advise us that we may make arrangements for getting our funds home, for in the present unsettled state of the West Indies we wish to have as little there as possible."[53] A week later, he was urgent in the request for withdrawing funds, pointing out that "the unsettled state of things in the West Indies from the arrival and success of the French fleet as it renders property precarious there, induces a solicitude on the subject of any funds that may

[50] February 14, 1805, Levi Hollingsworth to John Cowper and Company, Norfolk.

[51] February 20, 1805, Levi Hollingsworth to William Thomas, near Chestertown, Maryland.

[52] March 11, 1805, Levi Hollingsworth to Daniel Crommelin and Sons, Amsterdam.

[53] March 20, 1805, Levi Hollingsworth and Son to Robert Hollingsworth, Guadeloupe.

be in your hands. . . . At the same time we expect that the precariousness of property there and success of the French fleet, should their superiority in those seas continue, will occasion great fluctuations in the prices of the cargoes of their prizes and afford good opportunity for advantageous speculations."[54]

By the fall of 1805 the clearest indication of a contraction in business had emerged in the prevailing liberal terms of credit. It was explained in October, "We are and have been obliged to give 90 and 150 days credit on our sales all the present season and the custom has obtained so currently here that it is only a long season of brisk demand will break it."[55] About this time it was learned that the prices of products, and especially of flour and wheat, had "considerably fallen both in London and at Cadiz."[56]

The Decline to 1808

The decline in the general curve of prices in Philadelphia lasted from February 1805 to July 1808. During this period of general recession, the prices of some of the major groups showed varied movements. Furs completed an extra swing. Their recession from the high plateau of prices which lasted from April 1804 to May 1805 was completed by August 1806. Prices of furs then advanced and by October 1807 were only 3.4 per cent less than in 1804-1805. This high level was held as late as March 1808, after which prices dropped to slightly less than they had been in 1806. No other group had a comparable short swing in prices. The imported foods reached their low in April 1807. Between June and October of that year the decline in three other groups—wines and both classes of industrial commodities—was checked. The contraction in the remaining groups continued until August 1808, when farm crops, lumber products and naval stores, furs, and fish completed their swings. The end of the decline in the prices of farm derivatives occurred in the following month. In seven of the sub-groups the decline from 1805 was arrested between May and October 1807. These were condi-

[54] March 27, 1805, Levi Hollingsworth and Son to Robert Hollingsworth, Guadeloupe. At this time Robert Hollingsworth was intrusted with about $20,000 to invest in goods.

[55] October 16, 1805, Levi Hollingsworth and Son to Levi Hollingsworth, Jr., Baltimore.

[56] October 21, 1805, Levi Hollingsworth and Son to Cooch and Hollingsworth.

ments, fruit, building materials other than wood, chemicals and drugs, spirits, sugar and molasses, and wines.

To some extent the rise in prices of these seven groups of commodities corresponded with the later stages of the restrictions on neutral trade arising from the British Orders in Council and the series of decrees by Napoleon authorizing seizures of neutral vessels which obeyed the mandate to call and pay duty at English ports. It is significant that there is a gap of seven months between the start of a rise in the last of the seven groups and the beginning of recovery in any others and that this first affected dyes and beverages.

After December 1807 shipping from American ports was definitely restricted. As months of the embargo period passed, products of domestic origin dropped still lower. Prices of relatively perishable commodities suffered most from the restrictions. Grains, which in 1806 dropped 20 per cent below their average in 1805, in 1807 slowed down in their pace of decline to 8.7 per cent below the price of the previous year. Yet the decline of 1808, after two years of dwindling quotations, was 24.3, a larger percentage of decrease from one year to the next than occurred in grain prices at any other time in this major period. Grain products, which declined slightly more than grains in 1806, suffered a less severe contraction in 1807 and 1808, though even in this group the average of 1808 was 12.9 per cent below that of the previous year. Meats and meat products with a decrease of 22.6 per cent, fish with 23.6 per cent, and dairy products with 15.5 per cent were the groups in which the price decline from 1807 to 1808 seems to have been intensified.

The recession from 1805 to 1808 brought about lower grain prices than had been known since 1792, lower in fact than occurred again until 1820. Meats and meat products were lower than in any year since 1793, and grain products were only slightly above their average in 1794.

The prices of imported commodities had shown, since 1796, an underlying downward movement which was especially apparent in the fact that the low in 1803 was less than that of 1798 and the peaks of 1796, 1799, and 1804 were progressively lower. This tendency was not so pronounced in the prices of domestic commodities. Although the peaks of 1805 and 1801 were not as high as the maximum of 1797, the peak of 1805 exceeded that of 1801 and the index in 1802 did not fall as low as in 1799.

At the end of the first major period, the prices of imported commodities were moving still further ahead of those of domestic origin than at the preceding peaks. Although the decline had started only four months earlier in the index of imported goods, the recession was completed in July 1807, but the prices of domestic commodities continued to decline for another 13 months. By August 1808 the average prices of these commodities had dropped 19.7 per cent from their peak in 1805 and were lower than in either of the two preceding depressions. The price of imported commodities declined only 9.7 per cent and held above the low of 1803. By August 1808 when the domestic series ended their recession, the prices of imported commodities had risen 9.7 per cent and before the close of that year were higher than at any other time in the 25-year period.

Summary

A contrast between the curve of farm crops and that of raw and semi-finished industrial commodities can be made on the basis of long-time differences in behavior. From 1784 to 1787 the farm crops varied without much change in the general level until a prolonged and almost uninterrupted decline set in which was not ended until the spring of 1789. In this period the industrial commodities continued a gradual decline which lasted until well into 1791. This decline in the raw materials was going on despite a considerable though short advance in the average of farm crops. A more striking contrast between the two may be made in the behavior of the middle 1790's. Both groups were rising together at a somewhat similar pace until the latter part of 1795, when the advance in prices of industrial raw materials slowed down and the farm crops made the steepest part of their rise. As a result, farm crops kept relatively far above the raw materials until 1798. Looked at generally, the farm crops in the rest of the period fluctuated around a higher level established in the rise of 1795. On the other hand, the industrial raw materials, by a mildly rising tendency, often interrupted, worked gradually to still higher prices than they had reached in the rise of the middle 1790's. By the end of the period the industrial raw materials were relatively not only far above the curve of farm products and moving in the opposite direction from it, but diverged more than in any of the other extreme periods in these years.

The contrast between the movements of farm crops and industrial raw and semi-finished commodities has shown their tendency to spread apart in the last decade of this major period though the groups were not relatively far apart in the first decade, despite differences in fluctuations. An opposite tendency appeared in the lumber products and naval stores. The decline in this group of commodities from 1785 to 1788 was severe enough to depress its annual index in 1787 as much as 42.5 per cent below that of farm crops. Despite the fact that lumber products and naval stores began to advance in price nearly a year before farm crops and continued that advance without marked interruption, it was not until 1795 that the series pulled relatively close together, reaching their extreme peaks not only at about the same time, but also at about the same amount. In the rest of the period, despite a considerable difference in timing, the behavior of price movements of lumber products and naval stores was like that found in farm crops and free from a general rising movement which affected industrial raw materials.

No such extreme contrast can be made for farm derivatives and industrial commodities ready for consumption. The two groups were relatively far apart at the beginning of the price decline in 1784. The discrepancy narrowed in the course of the decline to 1789. At times there were short periods both at peaks and lows when the groups were moving in opposite directions, and each group had swings not apparent in the other, but in general the movements of these two groups of consumers' goods were more similar than those of the corresponding groups of raw materials.

Throughout this first major period, manufacturing plants of one type or another were being started which more and more reduced the dependence upon European producers. At the end of the period a Philadelphia merchant interested in the development of manufactures wrote, "The situation of our country as respects England and France is really unpleasant. . . . It appears extraordinary that those nations should not know their interests. Our Government is certainly disposed to be at peace with all the world. We have a constant surplus of produce which those nations and their dependencies are in want of, and we are receiving of them manufactures of various kinds, thus enabling them with greater facility to carry on the war. Your government does not seem to be aware that if the Embargo continues (and it certainly will while their Orders in Council are in force) that the people of the United States must manufacture the greater part of the articles which have heretofore been imported from England. Manufactures of cotton and linen goods are now establishing. Two large buildings are erecting for making shot in this City. A manufactory of red lead is lately established and there is one for white lead in contemplation. If manufactories are once completely established in this country, England in all probability will never regain the loss."[67] Thus, even before the end of the first period covered by our study of prices, a shift in the relative importance of domestic and foreign commodities was being sensed.

Annual Price Movements

The outstanding movements in prices from 1784 to 1808 may be summarized by the use of the annual indices. Such data are especially useful in measuring the amount and direction of change.

Major Groups

From 1784 to 1789 the general index declined continuously, but the greatest declines, of nearly 6 per cent, occurred from 1784 to 1785 and from 1787 to 1788. The final decline in 1789 before the steep and continuous rise of the nineties was barely more than one per cent. The various major groups differed widely from this general behavior. Although the decline from year to year in the index of the industrial raw and semi-finished commodities was usually less than that of the general curve, it lasted two years longer. The group of farm derivatives was the only other one with a continuous decline from 1784 to 1789. Like those of the general curve, its greatest recessions, of 12 per cent or more, were in 1785 and 1788. Fish, which fell from 1784 to 1788, maintained its price of 1788 in 1789, while furs and lumber products and naval stores, which also fell continuously from 1784, advanced in 1789. Imported foods made a

[67] July 8, 1808, Samuel Wetherill to Brandrams, Templeman and Company, London.

slight increase in 1786 which interrupted the recession. In contrast to the other groups, farm crops did not begin to decline until 1787, having risen from 1784 to 1786. The industrial commodities ready for consumption had the fewest years of decline, dropping only in 1785 and 1788.

All groups except industrial raw and semi-finished articles turned upward in 1790. The general index rose continuously from 1789 to 1796. This rise was paralleled by similar increases in imported foods and wines and exceeded in duration by the industrial com-

TABLE 15
ANNUAL PERCENTAGE OF CHANGE IN THE INDICES OF THE MAJOR GROUPS
1785–1808

Year	Farm		Im-ported Foods	Lumber Products and Naval Stores	Industrial		Fish	Furs	Wines	General Index
	Crops	Deriv-atives			Raw	Con-sumption				
1785	+ 4.1	−12.0	− 9.3	−11.4	− 3.2	−10.4	− 4.7	− 5.9	+11.7	− 5.9
1786	+ 0.2	− 0.5	+ 2.1	−24.7	− 4.7	+ 0.5	− 3.4	− 9.7	+ 4.7	− 3.3
1787	− 1.8	− 5.9	− 1.9	−13.9	− 2.3	+ 2.7	− 1.4	−15.4	0.0	− 2.9
1788	−14.3	−12.5	− 3.1	− 5.7	− 2.1	− 5.0	−10.9	− 4.5	− 5.6	− 5.8
1789	− 5.3	− 4.0	− 4.5	+ 7.1	− 0.7	+ 0.4	0.0	+ 5.7	− 3.8	− 1.1
1790	+14.2	+17.3	+ 6.4	+10.7	− 1.3	+ 2.7	+ 1.9	+ 5.6	+ 2.1	+ 5.0
1791	− 8.6	− 2.6	+17.7	+10.7	− 2.9	+ 9.2	+11.0	− 2.0	+ 4.8	+ 3.7
1792	+ 0.1	− 0.8	+ 3.0	− 2.4	+ 1.6	+ 4.7	− 0.5	+ 7.8	+ 6.3	+ 2.0
1793	+11.8	+10.5	+ 0.6	+ 9.3	+ 3.4	+ 4.2	− 2.3	− 0.5	+10.2	+ 5.2
1794	+ 5.9	+15.9	+ 7.8	+ 9.5	+13.6	+28.2	+24.7	− 4.2	+ 6.0	+13.8
1795	+18.6	+19.9	+20.6	+31.9	+19.9	+14.8	+41.2	+18.2	+ 3.8	+19.3
1796	+19.1	+ 5.3	+ 2.9	+14.4	+ 1.0	+ 9.4	+ 5.3	+22.3	+ 0.7	+ 6.4
1797	− 3.4	− 8.2	− 5.0	+ 2.4	− 0.6	− 9.8	+ 7.3	−12.4	− 1.6	− 4.0
1798	− 4.3	− 6.0	−10.0	− 8.4	0.0	− 1.8	−16.3	−22.6	− 4.9	− 4.8
1799	− 6.7	− 2.0	+ 4.2	−14.6	+ 6.0	− 0.3	−22.8	+ 4.1	+10.3	+ 0.2
1800	+ 1.3	+ 8.4	− 2.1	+10.9	− 1.1	− 3.8	−14.8	+23.0	+ 4.4	+ 0.8
1801	+10.6	+11.3	− 7.1	+ 3.7	+ 0.5	+ 1.4	+36.0	+ 4.3	+ 8.3	+ 2.8
1802	−14.7	−17.5	− 4.8	− 4.4	− 4.8	− 7.3	− 1.4	− 6.7	+ 1.9	− 7.1
1803	− 0.9	− 8.0	− 4.7	+ 8.5	+ 0.3	− 2.1	−17.3	+ 0.7	− 4.7	− 1.9
1804	+ 8.5	+12.3	+ 8.7	+ 1.3	+ 4.4	+ 6.4	+ 7.0	+17.0	+ 4.9	+ 6.6
1805	+11 2	+12.6	+ 0.4	− 1.5	− 0.5	+ 5.4	+10.2	− 4.2	− 6.6	+ 2.7
1806	− 9.1	− 0.6	− 3.2	− 7.9	+ 3.4	− 5.2	+ 5.3	− 8.2	− 7.5	− 2.6
1807	− 4.8	− 8.8	− 6.9	− 0.4	− 1.0	− 4.5	− 2.4	+10.3	− 0.3	− 3.4
1808	−13.7	−12.7	+ 5.4	− 0.3	+ 1.8	+ 5.6	−23.6	− 5.1	+ 9.7	− 0.5

modities ready for consumption, which had started an advance a year earlier. The other five groups which recovered in 1789 or 1790 underwent a minor interruption to their expansion of the early nineties. Farm crops receded in 1791, farm derivatives in both 1791 and 1792, lumber products and naval stores in 1792, fish in both 1792 and 1793, and furs in 1791, 1793, and 1794. With the industrial raw materials increasing after 1791, six of the major groups rose in 1792, seven in 1793, eight in 1794, and all in 1795 and 1796.

In contrast to these years of widespread expansion stand the years of equally pervasive decline, 1797 and 1798. Only the lumber products and naval stores continued to rise in 1797 and no group was higher in 1798 than in the previous year, although the industrial raw and semi-finished commodities maintained the same average price.

The recovery from 1798 to 1801 was mild in the general index. The advance in both 1799 and 1800 amounted to less than one per cent and even in 1801 less than three per cent. Only furs and wines rose in all three years. In 1799 these groups were joined by the industrial raw and semi-finished articles and imported foods, and in 1800 by farm crops, farm derivatives, and lumber products and naval stores. Although the rise in 1801 was small in the total and in many of the groups, it affected all except the imported foods.

Most of the decline from 1801 to 1803 occurred in 1802, when only wines continued to advance and when the farm crops and farm derivatives fell approximately 15 to 18 per cent. In spite of the fact that wines dropped in 1803 and fish fell more that year than in the previous year, the total receded less than 2 per cent, because lumber products and naval stores, industrial raw and semi-finished materials, and furs rose. The declines in the remaining groups were less than in 1802.

All major groups again rose in 1804, when the bulk of the advance to the peak of 1805 occurred. Most groups foreshadowed the decline to 1808 either by receding in 1805 or by advancing that year at a slower pace than in the previous one. The most outstanding contributors to the peak of 1805 were the groups of farm crops, farm derivatives, and fish which, with further increases of 10 per cent or more, rose proportionately more in 1805 than in 1804.

During 1806 and 1807 a mild but widespread recession characterized the movements of most groups. Only industrial raw and semi-finished commodities and fish advanced in 1806 and only furs in 1807. In 1808, when the embargo caused divergent movements in the prices of imported and domestic commodities, the total index receded one-half of one per cent. Most of the groups composed chiefly of domestic commodities dropped appreciably, especially farm crops, farm derivatives, and fish, which fell between 12.5 and 24 per cent. Lumber products and naval stores, however, were only 0.3 per cent lower than in the previous year and furs 5.1 per cent lower. The other groups, heavily weighted with imported commodities, advanced.

In spite of the variety of commodities included in the nine major groups, the annual averages from 1784 to 1808 show a surprising amount of conformity in the direction of change from year to year. In four years all groups conformed, in six there was only one exception to the general movement, and in five others only two exceptions. Throughout the period most of the forces affecting prices contributed to expansion. This is evident not only in the rise of the general index, but also in the fact that prices conformed more on the rise than on the decline and that the one or two exceptions to the general movement took more often an upward than a downward direction.

Sub-Groups

The sub-groups show in greater detail than the major groups the movements in the annual averages of prices from 1784 to 1808. At least 14 sub-groups declined in each of the four years, 1785-1788 inclusive. The special severity of the recession in 1785 and 1788 is indicated by the fact that about 20 groups declined in both years. Only three groups paralleled the general curve in showing no recovery until 1790: meats and meat products, dairy products, and fruit. Six other sub-groups ended their recessions in 1788: grains, grain products, fish, wood, building materials other than wood, and furs. Fourteen other groups made at least a minor recovery in 1785, 1786, or 1787, while ferrous metals rose from 1787 to 1792 and non-ferrous from 1784 to 1789.

The upturn in 1790 affected 17 of the sub-groups. Tobacco and textile fabrics maintained, that year, the prices of the previous one; chemicals, dyes, non-ferrous metals, textile fibers, and the miscellaneous group declined less than 7 per cent; only beverages took a severe drop of approximately 14 per cent. During 1791 and 1792 a rising tendency persisted, although at least 11 of the sub-groups declined in each of the two years. The speeding-up of the rate of advance after 1792 is evidenced by the increase in prices in 17 of the 25 groups in 1793, in 24 in 1794, and in all of them in 1795. Even in 1796 the rise continued in all groups except dairy products, condiments, chemicals, dyes, and hides and leather. During the general expansion from 1789 to 1796 most groups were either slow to rise or receded in 1791 or 1792. As a result, meats and meat products and wines were the only sub-groups paralleling the increase in the composite index, and only the wood group, which advanced for nine years from 1788 to 1797, had a longer rise.

The decline to 1798 and the rise to 1801 were much less widespread than the increases from 1792 to 1796. No more than 16 groups moved in the direction of the general curve in any year after the peak of 1796 until the recession in 1802. Only tobacco, ferrous metals, hides and leather, and wines continued to rise that year. The low of 1803 was accompanied by a decline in 15 groups, while 10 rose contrary to the general direction.

Just as in 1802 between the high of 1801 and the low of 1803, so in 1804 between the low of 1803 and the peak of 1805 most groups were moving in the same direction. Only ferrous metals and spirits continued to recede in 1804.

During 1805 and 1806 many groups moved contrary to the general curve. Only 13 were like the average in having a higher index in 1805 than in 1804 and only 15 fell in 1806. The continued recession in 1807 and 1808 affected at least 17 groups. Condiments advanced in both years and textile fabrics continued an uninterrupted rise which had started after 1802. The other increases in 1807 were in tobacco, ferrous metals, wood, and furs, while in 1808, as a result of the embargo, fruit, sugar and molasses, chemicals, building materials other than wood, spirits, and wines rose in addition to condiments and textile fabrics.

Although the 25 sub-groups show more diversity in movements than the nine major groups, the prices of as many as 20 of the sub-groups moved in the same direction in six years.

Proportion of Commodities Influencing Price Movements

In the years from 1784 to 1789 when the total curve was falling, the number of items showing an increase over the previous year varied from 27 to 46 per cent, the smallest number occurring in 1788. At the end of the decline in 1789 only 41.4 per cent of the commodities were at a lower price than in 1788, while 13.6 per cent were unchanged and 45 per cent were rising in advance of the general curve.

In the upswing which reached a peak in 1796, the percentage of commodities advancing from the previous year increased continuously until, in 1795, 84.3 per cent of the commodities were rising and only 15.7 per cent declining while none sold at the same price as in 1794. The continuation to the peak in 1796 was confined to 67.1 per cent of the series. Practically all of the others started to decline after 1795. As a result of this seven-year rise in the general curve the average of 1796 was 68.8 per cent above that of 1789. At this time prices were higher than at any other time from 1784 to 1861, except during and immediately after the war from 1812 to 1814.

During the next two years (1797-1798) the average of prices declined although in both years at least 40 per cent of the commodities increased. In 1798 the general curve was only 8.6 per cent lower than in 1796 and still more than 50 per cent above its low point in 1789.

The cycle from 1798 to 1803 was comparatively mild, especially in its expansion phase from 1798 to 1801. During each of these three years barely 55 per cent of the commodities rose. The decline from the peak in 1801, when prices were still 5.2 per cent below 1796, was more abrupt. In two years prices dropped 8.9 per cent to the lowest point between 1796 and the War of 1812. In 1802 nearly 70 per cent of the commodities dipped, 5 per cent maintaining the level of 1801 and only one-fourth of the commodities moving upwards. Thus the drop was slightly more widespread than that of 1788. In addition, in 1803 a decline in 50 per cent of the commodities more than offset the rise in 41.4 per cent.

The final cycle in prices in the period from 1784 to 1808 was somewhat the reverse of the previous one in that it had two years of expansion from 1803 to 1805, followed by three years of contraction from 1805 to 1808, in which prices did not fall as low as they had been in 1803. The five-year swing from 1798 to 1803 had included three years of expansion followed by two years of contraction in which prices dropped below those of 1798. The peaks of 1801 and 1805 were approximately equal. The rise was more abrupt in 1804 and 1805 than it had been before 1801, although the percentage of commodities rising fell off in 1805 instead of slightly increasing as in 1801. The rise, even in 1804, when 66.4 per cent of the commodities advanced, was far from equaling in pervasiveness that of 1794 to 1796. In 1805 slightly more than 52 per cent of the series increased. In both 1804 and 1805 at least 10 per cent did not change in price from the previous year. As a result less than one-fourth of the commodities declined in 1804 and less than three-eighths in 1805.

The decline from 1805 to 1808 did not affect as large a number of the commodities as had the rise from 1803 to 1805. The number declining was 62.9 per cent in 1807. In 1808, when the recession was checked, 52.1 per cent of the series fell. In each of the last three years approximately 30 to 40 per cent of the commodities made an advance over the previous year.

Thus far in describing the three and a half cycles between 1784 and 1808 it has been indicated that there was usually a substantial number of commodities which, at any one time, moved contrary to the general direction. What these commodities are can be roughly shown by an examination of the percentage of items which increased or decreased in each of the six largest groups.

The unbroken decline from 1784 to 1789 in the general curve was interrupted in some of the groups, especially in imported foods and industrial products ready for consumption. During the first four years of the decline a smaller percentage of the commodities among the imported foods sold at a price below that of the previous year than of the aggregate. This disparity was most marked in 1786 when less than 30 per cent of the imported foods declined in contrast to the more than 50 per cent among all the commodities. The industrial goods ready for consumption did not differ so persistently from the total. In fact, in 1785 and 1788 more than a proportionate share of these commodities declined, but in 1786 and 1787, when half of all the commodities were declining, only a quarter of the series of industrial goods ready for consumption fell in price. In addition to these two groups, other sections of the economy differed from the average, especially in 1789 at the end of the contraction. Prior to that, however, the farm crops in 1785 declined less generally than any of the other six major groups. From 1787 to 1789 the recession was more marked in farm products than in some other sections. Throughout the contraction the proportion of the farm derivatives which declined equaled and usually exceeded that of farm crops as well as of the total. From 1785 to 1788 at least three-fourths of the lumber products and naval stores dropped each year, a higher average of declining items than occurred in any other group. In 1789 barely a quarter of the commodities in this group fell, the lowest percentage of any of the groups. The industrial raw materials showed each year a progressive shrinkage in the percentage of commodities which sold for less than the previous year—in 1785 and 1786 as many as 60 per cent decreased, but in 1789 only 32.5 per cent.

It has already been noted that in 1789 two-thirds of the lumber products had started to rise. Not only did this group start upwards ahead of any of the others, but it also persisted upwards for a longer period. In all the following years until after 1797 at least two-thirds of this group sold above the price of the previous year. The industrial goods ready for consumption, in which at least 50 per cent of the commodities advanced in price every year, did not start upwards until a year after the lumber products and naval stores, and two-thirds of this group declined a year before the lumber products and naval stores. The other four main groups showed a recession in the early 1790's not reflected in the general curve. Barely half of the industrial raw materials made any advance in 1789. In the next two years less than a third of these series rose. It was not until after 1791 that the raw materials started to move up. In each of the next ten years, however, more than half of them increased each year over the previous year. This is one explanation of the mildness of the price recessions in the swings in industrial raw materials during these years.

The rise in farm crops from 1789 to 1796 was more erratic. Although 58.3 per cent of the commodities rose in 1790 from the low of the previous year, only a third advanced in 1791. Though a larger number rose in the following year, the percentage was well below half. In the next four years 83.3 per cent or more of these series advanced except in 1794, when only two-thirds rose. The maximum percentage which increased in any one year was 91.7 in 1796. The unusual character of this advance in farm crops is indicated by the fact that not until 1836 did as many of these commodities rise in any one year.

Of farm derivatives, which appear to be a more homogeneous group than the farm crops, 78.6 per cent increased in 1790. No other group had such a widespread rise that year. The recession in 1791 and 1792 was marked among the farm derivatives; only 42.9 per cent advanced in 1791 and slightly more than a third in 1792. The final four years of expansion culminating in 1796 were slightly more pervasive in this group than in the farm crops. In 1793 an approximately equal percentage of these groups advanced. In the following year, when only two-thirds of the farm crops rose, 92.9 per cent of the derivatives advanced, while in 1795 and 1796, when the number of farm crops which sold for more than in the previous year expanded, the rise in the farm derivatives tapered off.

The decline in 1797 was most severe in the farm derivatives. In this group 78.6 per cent of the series fell while only 53.6 per cent of all commodities receded that year. Barely a third of the lumber products and naval stores and only 40 per cent of the industrial raw materials receded, while between a half and three-fourths of the series in the other groups declined. In 1798 the decline was more widespread in farm crops, imported foods, and lumber products and naval stores than it had been the previous year. In these groups prices of two-thirds or more of the series fell.

In contrast to all of the other groups, the industrial raw and semi-finished commodities had an upward tendency. In fact, in every year from 1792 to 1801 inclusive more than half of these series were higher than in the previous one. Apart from this group, the recovery of 1799 was largely confined to imported foods. More than three-quarters of these series advanced, while only a third or less of the farm crops, industrial commodities ready for consumption, and lumber products and naval stores, and 42.9 per cent of the farm derivatives rose. The failure of the industrial commodities ready for consumption to rise before 1804 is best illustrated by the fact that in no year from 1797 to 1803 inclusive did the prices of as many as 41 per cent of these series advance.

The continuation of the general rise in 1800 and 1801 was more widespread than the start had been in 1799. Farm crops and farm derivatives increased in the number of series rising until in 1801 three-quarters or more of these series were advancing. Increases in imported foods, in contrast, which had provided a large part of the initial impetus, tapered off, less than a quarter of these commodities rising in 1801. The lumber products and naval stores contributed more than any other group in 1800 when three-quarters of the series rose, but only half of them were higher in 1801 than in 1800.

The decline to 1803 was especially pronounced in 1802 when the prices of more than 80 per cent of the imported foods and industrial commodities ready for consumption and more than 70 per cent of the farm derivatives and lumber products and naval stores fell. The group of farm crops was less affected than any other group; less than 60 per cent of its series receded. The slowing down of the decline in 1803, when prices of only half the commodities decreased, is indicated by a shrinkage of the number of series which declined in every group except farm derivatives, which had the same number of of decreases as in 1802.

The rise to 1805 had been foreshadowed as early as 1803 when 55 per cent or more of the lumber products and naval stores and industrial raw and semi-finished commodities rose. In 1804, when nearly two-thirds of all the commodities advanced, 85.7 per cent of the farm derivatives and more than 70 per cent of the imported foods and the industrial commodities ready for consumption moved upwards. Only in the group of lumber products and naval stores did less than half of the commodities increase in price. The peak of 1805 was more related to the farm crops and farm derivatives than to any other groups. Three-quarters or more of all the articles in these classes were higher in 1805 than in 1804. Between 50 and 52 per cent of the lumber products and naval stores and the industrial commodities ready for consumption rose in 1805. Of the imported foods and industrial raw and semi-finished goods 45 per cent or less increased in price that year.

The general decline from 1805 to 1808 was aided by three-fourths or more of the lumber products and naval stores and the industrial commodities ready for consumption in 1806, of the farm derivatives and industrial commodities ready for consumption in 1807, and of farm crops and farm derivatives in 1808. At the other extreme were the industrial raw and semi-finished articles, of which no more than 25 to 45 per cent declined in any of the three years. At least half of the series in all of the other groups fell in 1806 and 1807. In 1808, however, less than half of the imported foods and the industrial commodities ready for consumption receded.

No attention has yet been given to the percentage of commodities which did not change in price from one year to the next. The times at which 10 per cent or more of the commodities in any of the six largest groups maintained the same average price for two years indicate the areas of greatest stability. Since in two-thirds of the years from 1784 to 1808 none of the series in the farm crops were unchanged, the three years 1789, 1790, and 1803 (two of which terminate recessions), in which 16.7 to 25 per cent of these commodities had the same average price as in the previous year, stand out as unusually stable. In only one year, 1787, did more than 10 per cent of the farm derivatives remain unchanged. The imported foods were never even this stable. In the group of lumber products and naval stores in 1790 and again in 1804, years following lows in the general curve, one-sixth of the items remained unchanged. The group with the greatest stability was industrial raw and semi-finished products, which in seven years showed more than 10 per cent of its items unchanged from the previous year. In four years more than 10 per cent of the industrial commodities ready for consumption did not vary in price.

Further tendencies toward stability in the various groups can be indicated by adding the percentage of commodities which varied less than 2.5 per cent to the percentage which did not change from one year to the next. In this large group of comparatively stable items the years when 10 per cent of the commodities changed less than 2.5 per cent, if at all, become so numerous as to lose significance. But when years with minor changes in 25 per cent or more of the series are considered, the nine years with most stability for farm crops would include the closing years of every major recession except 1808. On the other hand, only one major peak, that of 1801, would be included as a year of consequential stability for the farm crops. The farm derivatives evinced more stability for this major period in years between the peaks and lows than at the turning points. In fact, no one of the four years in which as many as 25 per cent of the derivatives changed less than 2.5 per cent in price was a crucial one in the general index. From their ranking in minor changes, imported foods rarely added a high percentage of stability in the period from 1784 to 1808. In three years, 1793, 1799, and 1803, more than 25 per cent of these series changed less than 2.5 per cent. These represent a low, a high, and an intermediate year in the price fluctuations of imported foods. It is difficult to generalize about the stability of prices of lumber products and naval stores since in some years they showed a marked stability and in others extreme instability. Like farm crops, all series of the group of lumber products and naval stores varied more than 2.5 per cent in five years. Like the farm crops again, in nine years 25 per cent or more were affected by minor changes. These years included the turning points in the general curve, except the peak of 1796 and the low of 1803. The highest percentage of items subject to minor changes occurred in the group of industrial raw and semi-finished commodities. Among these, in 15 years 25 per cent or more of the items changed less than 2.5 per cent and in only one year in the entire period less than 10 per cent underwent mild changes. Marked stability typified, also, the annual price relationship of the series of industrial commodities ready for consumption. In 14 of the 24 years, 25 per cent or more of the commodities in this group varied less than 2.5 per cent.

Deviation of Annual Group Indices from the General Average

In the period from 1784 to 1808 the farm derivatives and the industrial raw and semi-finished commodities fluctuated nearer to the general average than any other groups. The farm crops and the industrial commodities ready for consumption were usually not far from the general average, but the farm crops were usually above it and the industrial materials ready for consumption were more often below than above. The remaining five groups differed markedly: the imported foods were always above the general index, and the fish remained above in every year except 1800; the lumber products and naval stores were below the general curve except in three years, and the wines were always at least 15 per cent below the general curve and furs at least 20 per cent.

Not only did the major groups differ in their general relation to the total index but they also differed in their response to cyclical fluctuations. The extent to which the farm derivatives and the farm crops varied from the general curve appears to have been dependent upon the current phase of the successive cycles. The 11 years in which the index of farm derivatives was below the general index are the years in which recessions were terminated and those immediately before and after. At such times the farm crops were also either below the general index or less than 3 per cent above it. Both groups tended to reach their maximum variation from the general curve at the peak of the major as well as minor cycles.

None of the other groups appear to have been influenced appreciably by the cycles in prices. Instead, each shows an individual long-time relationship with the general index. Although the industrial raw and semi-finished commodities were, like the farm derivatives, closely distributed around the general index, they did not fluctuate around it like the derivatives. From 1784 to 1790 the industrial raw and semi-finished commodities were above the general index, from 1791 to 1798 they were below it, and from 1799 to 1808 they were again above the general index except in 1805.

The variations of the industrial commodities ready for consumption from the general index were approximately the reverse of those of the industrial raw and semi-finished. From 1784 to 1793 the industrial commodities ready for consumption held below the general index. From 1794 to 1800 they were above it, but they again held below from 1801 to 1807, except in 1805.

For the imported foods the period from 1784 to 1808 must be divided. Between 1784 and 1800 this group was always at least 17.6 per cent above the general index. The climax came in the five years from 1791 to 1795 when it was continuously more than 30 per cent above the average of all commodities. In contrast, during the eight years from 1801 to 1808 the imported foods were only from 4.1 per cent to 12.1 per cent above the general index.

An inverse movement characterized the variations of the index of lumber and naval stores from the general index. This group held at least 17.3 per cent below the general curve from 1786 to 1794, but in the latter part of this major period it never dropped this low except in 1799.

The general behavior of the three smaller groups has been described above. The fish, which held above the general curve in every year except 1800, attained their greatest disparity between 1795 and 1798 when for four years they were at least 49.1 per cent above the general index. This variation marked the climax of the years from 1784 to 1798 when the fish were always at least 18.2 per cent above the average of all commodities. Wines and furs were further away from the general average than any other groups. During this period the wines were always 15.4 per cent or more below the total index and from 1795 to 1798 they were at least 33.8 per cent below it. The furs, which were still further below the average of all the commodities, always held at least 23.1 per cent below the general curve and from 1787 to 1808 were more than 30 per cent below it.

CHAPTER VIII

PRICE MOVEMENTS FROM 1808 TO 1821

During the years from 1808 to 1821 prices in Philadelphia fluctuated more violently than at any other period between 1784 and 1861. The price movements of these years are not susceptible to cyclical analysis. This period should be considered as one which includes the precipitating influences leading up to the war, the war from 1812 to 1814 with its alternation of successes and reverses, and the long period of readjustment after this and the Napoleonic wars.

Monthly Fluctuations from 1808 to 1811

Between 1808 and 1811 most commodities completed a swing in prices. The total index rose from July 1808 to a peak in April 1809 slightly higher than another peak in October 1810. Its recession from these peaks terminated in November 1811.

Imported and Domestic Commodities

The direction of price movements for each commodity during 1807 and 1808 was largely determined by whether it was exported or imported. The various restrictions on shipping in these years, especially, operated to reduce the supply and raise the prices of foreign goods in Philadelphia. The same factors cut off the foreign demand for domestic commodities entering into exportation and consequently lowered their price.

Throughout this period the prices of imported commodities reached their turning points in advance of the prices of domestic goods. This order at critical turning points had appeared earlier. Imported commodities completed their recession from the peak of 1805 in July 1807, more than a year before the comparable point for the domestic commodities. After July the average prices of imported commodities started to rise while those of domestic commodities continued to decline. The divergent effect on these goods of the embargo placed in December 1807 can best be illustrated by the fact that prices of domestic commodities, which had risen slightly in the latter part of 1807, fell 11.0 per cent from November of that year to August 1808, while in the same nine months the imported series rose 7.0 per cent. This contrary movement clearly separated the curves which in 1807 had been relatively at the same level.

During all the period from 1808 to the close of 1815 the index of imported commodities was continuously and substantially above that of the domestic commodities. When, after August 1808, domestic commodities also started to advance, the rate of increase in the price of foreign commodities accelerated. The peak of prices for imported commodities occurred in March 1809, the month the embargo was repealed. At that time the index for imported commodities was 34.4 per cent above the low of July 1807. Both groups receded sharply for a few months, but during 1810 and 1811 the prices of imported commodities never rose to as high a point as they had reached in the early months of 1809. In contrast, the domestic commodities soon recovered and before the close of 1809 were higher than they had been in May. Their advance continued until in January 1811 they were 10.1 per cent above the minor peak of May 1809 and 26.9 per cent above the low of August 1808. Even this rise over a period of nearly two and a half years did not restore the prices of domestic commodities to a relative parity with those of imported commodities either at their peak or even at their current position, near the end of their recession.

In November 1811 the index of imported commodities ended its decline from the peak of March 1809. During those 32 months the average decline in the prices of these commodities was 17.1 per cent. In spite of this substantial decline the index of imported commodities was approximately as high relatively as the domestic index had been at its peak 10 months earlier. By November, however, the domestic commodities had fallen 9.5 per cent, but their recession was not completed until the following May when their index was 11.1 per cent below the peak.

It would be unwise for a period of sudden shifts in enforcement of trade restrictions to attempt to relate the timing of price changes minutely to historical events. Though the Non-Intercourse Act did not become effective until March 1809, merchants were aware by January that it would "no doubt be carried into effect."[1] Their dealings were influenced by the interpretation they put upon the restrictive decrees of other countries, the character of their own business, the source of their correspondence, and the flexibility with which they could turn from one channel of trade to another. For instance, the response of a specialized firm such as Wetherill's to trade restrictions was to turn to means of insuring supplies of raw materials, especially those needed in the making of paints. Samuel Wetherill began to reduce or delay his orders to foreign merchants because quotations of raw stuffs were rising enough to make unpredictable the price at which an order could be filled.[2] By July 1809 there was even some doubt about the means of making payments which led Wetherill to write, "The times are so precarious we are more cautious than usual of whom we purchase bills."[3] At the beginning of the next year a complete change in the plans of this firm was announced. "We regret," wrote Samuel Wetherill, "that affairs between this country and England is such as to prevent our receiving the usual supply of goods. This circumstance renders it unnecessary to inclose an order at this time."[4] He had long been accustomed to order raw materials for paints from Brandrams, Templeman and Company, London. In his letter at this time he explained both the immediate and permanent factors which led him to change, with full awareness that because of the "advantageous terms on which we have for many years past received red and white lead from you, we have been enabled to vend very great quantities of those articles at a moderate profit, but there has been three manufactories of them established in this city and, though they have not yet made a sufficient quantity to meet the demands, yet as they vend to consumers, it has totally deprived us of any profit on red lead (having sold the last we had of you at upwards of a dollar per hundred loss), and nearly deprived us of profit on the white lead. And as we cannot consent to lose that portion of our

[1] January 3, 1809, Samuel Wetherill to Brandrams, Templeman and Company, London.

[2] June 9, 1809, Samuel Wetherill to Brandrams, Templeman and Company, London.

[3] July 8, 1809, Samuel Wetherill to Brandrams, Templeman and Company, London.

[4] January 10, 1810, Samuel Wetherill to Brandrams, Templeman and Company, London.

business, they being the principal and leading articles in the color line, we have been reduced to the necessity of establishing a manufactory of them which will shortly be in operation on an extensive scale. It is evident from the great quantity of lead in this country and the low price of vinegar[5] that those manufactories must succeed, though we have in some measure been compelled to undertake it in order to retain our business."[4]

The same factors which led a specialized business to integrate caused Stephen Girard to spread out to take advantage of the various shifts in the interpretation of trade regulations. He had reasoned that the American embargo would reduce the prices of native staples and bought heavily of Upland cotton when it was low.[6] He later turned his attention to coffee and sugar. In doing this, often at the risk of having to store the articles, he was reasoning that "the decrees of Berlin, Milan and Rambouillet, and the embargo with its supplementary acts, could not fail to put up the price of these staples in our country, and put down the price in the islands where they were produced."[7] He was influenced in the choice of commodities and in the choice of places to dispatch his vessels by wide acquaintance and contacts in many countries which brought information, often belated, about the conditions of trade. When Baring and Brothers wrote to him in March 1809 their ideas of the effect of the non-intercourse bill, their guess was, "We presume that the produce of your country will find its way here circuitously, probably through Lisbon, Madeira, or some other intermediate place, but it is not possible to calculate with any certainty, and still less to recommend any particular plan of proceeding until we can place more reliance on the course your Government will take."[8] In this is indicated one of the factors that led to roundabout routes of trade and lags in the movement of prices of similar and related products.

The decline in the general price level which occurred from April 1809 to November 1811 was particularly severe in the groups of im-

[4] January 10, 1810, Samuel Wetherill to Brandrams, Templeman and Company, London.

[5] Acetic acid or "vinegar" is used in the manufacture of white lead by the Old Dutch process.

[6] McMaster, John Bach, *The Life and Times of Stephen Girard*, Vol. II, p. 63.

[7] McMaster, John Bach, *op. cit.*, p. 76.

[8] McMaster, John Bach, *op. cit.*, p. 84.

ported commodities. It was dealers in these articles who were cheered by the prospect of "better" prices in the last quarter of 1810. In October a Philadelphia merchant wrote to a New York correspondent: "The news we received from Washington . . . yesterday, which you have before this time, has caused a great sensation with us. The holders of coffee, sugar, and Hyson tea are looking for advance prices. What it may turn out is uncertain."[9] He followed this with a letter to another correspondent explaining that "the news from Washington is the President's proclamation assuring a free intercourse with France, etc., as well [as] admitting her vessels of war to the waters of the United States and a proviso that a non-intercourse shall be renewed against Great Britain in case she shall not have withdrawn her orders in council by the 2nd of February next."[10]

Though it is difficult at this date to see the general reasoning of such comments, it is true that most of the groups which established peaks between May and December 1810 were chiefly composed of commodities of foreign origin.

The same factors upset completely the plans of other shippers. Hollingsworth wrote in November 1810, "The [ship] *Jane* was purchased . . . with the intention of keeping her as a regular trader between Liverpool and this port, but a prospect of the renewal of restrictions of intercourse between England and the United States alarms us. The vague manner in which the instructions of the Secretary of the Treasury to the Collectors of our Ports is worded excites doubts whether vessels leaving England prior to the second of February will not (in case of the non-compliance on the part of the British Government with the wishes of ours by refusing to rescind the orders in Council) be subject to the penalties of the non-intercourse Law. Those that leave England subsequent[ly] will."[11]

Though the immediate effect of the revival of domestic restrictions on trade was not as serious as many feared, a substantial decline in prices traceable to many causes occurred in 1811. It was this year which marked the closing of the First Bank of the United States when Congress failed to renew its charter. According to Dr. J. T.

[9] October 23, 1810, John Hamilton to Keelso and Crump, New York.

[10] November 3, 1810, John Hamilton to I. and C. Van Cleef.

[11] November 21, 1810, Levi Hollingsworth and Son to Hobsons and Bolton, Liverpool.

Holdsworth, "the liquidation of the one bank that over-shadowed all others in resources, in influence, and in service to Government and business, created a very serious monetary and financial situation. Though it did not close its doors until March 3, 1811, it had, in anticipation of unfavorable action by Congress, begun in 1810 to curtail loans and draw in bank balances."[12] This action necessarily drained many other banks of specie, many loans had to be called, and new accommodations were virtually prohibited. These operations were ultimately reflected in a period of contracting prices in which many firms failed.[13] In fact, as many as 52 failures were reported in the summer of 1811,[14] yet some goods were scarce and their prices high. Textile fabrics were limited enough in supply to receive special comment.[15] Girard, in explaining the demand and high prices prevailing for good grades of tea, wrote, "I do not recollect more than three or four ships sailing this season from this port for Canton."[16]

In this period, especially, fluctuations in the prices of particular commodities are of more interest than changes in the total. Often also the rise in price in the country of origin is of more significance than many of the "decrees" in appraising price variations. It is this rise which induced permanent shifts in the importance of many commodities and encouraged attempts to produce the most needed ones. Since many manufacturing ventures arose in this period, it is of interest to recall the result of "the advance of glassware lately taken place on Liverpool" before the War of 1812. "On comparing the present with the former prices," Wetherill wrote, "we find the difference so great that there is no prospect of selling here to any advantage. . . . On calculation we find the advance exceeds 75 per cent. There are two glass manufactories lately established near this city which are now in operation; at one of them they are making vials of different kinds and selling considerably below the prices they will cost to import. The advance on English glass is greatly in favor of those manufacturers. In effect, it amounts [to] a prohibition of the

[12] Holdsworth, J. T., *Financing an Empire—History of Banking in Pennsylvania*, Vol. I, pp. 62-63.

[13] September 16, 1811, James N. Weems to William Harris, Chestertown, Maryland.

[14] September 27, 1811, Edward Hand to Adam Reigart, Jr., Lancaster, Pennsylvania.

[15] September 16, 1811, James N. Weems to William Harris, Chestertown, Maryland.

[16] October 16, 1811, Stephen Girard to William H. Thomas, New York.

articles. Should a singular advance take place in England on red and white lead we shall be highly gratified."[17]

Major Groups

Since, as we have already shown, significant differences developed in the movements of prices of domestic and imported commodities from 1807 to 1811, it is to be expected that the movements in the prices of smaller groups of commodities were largely influenced by the extent to which they are composed of products of domestic or foreign origin.

The only groups continuing advances which started in 1807 were imported foods, industrial raw and semi-finished materials, industrial commodities ready for consumption, and wines. Not only did these groups alone undergo a rise which started between May and November 1807, but they were also the only ones to reach a peak between February and April 1809. Two of these groups—industrial raw and semi-finished materials and industrial commodities ready for consumption—also had minor peaks between December 1809 and May 1810, while the wines reached, in October 1810, a peak well above that of March 1809.

In contrast, the groups composed primarily of domestic commodities—farm crops, farm derivatives, lumber products and naval stores, fish, and furs—did not start to rise until September or October 1808 and did not reach their peaks before August 1810 to June 1811.

The termination of the recession during 1811 or 1812 is not so clearly related to the origin of the commodities. The first two groups which ended their contraction (in February and April 1811) were wines and industrial commodities ready for consumption. Both of these were chiefly imported. Four groups—fish, farm crops, imported foods, and industrial raw and semi-finished products—came to the end of their decline between September 1811 and February 1812. Thus, by the time that all the imported commodities reached their low points, two groups of domestic commodities had also reached theirs. It was not until June and August 1812 that the farm derivatives and lumber products and naval stores ceased to decline, while the remaining group of domestic commodities—furs—continued to recede until January 1814.

[17] March 13, 1812, Samuel Wetherill to Alexander W. Walker, Philadelphia.

Sub-Groups

In following the price changes of this period among the sub-groups, it is of interest that the embargo, which had been in force from December 1807 to March 1809, was mitigated by the provisions of the Non-Intercourse Act between March and June 1809 and that trade to this extent was free from restrictions imposed by the United States from June 1809 to November 1810.

Four sub-groups can be disregarded in the discussion of these years since they did not have turning points between 1807 and 1811. Hides and leather, textile fabrics, and ferrous metals rose during this period from lows in January 1805 or earlier to peaks in 1809 or 1810, while tobacco declined from a peak in 1807 to a low in January 1812.

Seven groups started to rise between June and November 1807. Condiments, fruits, spirits, sugar and molasses, and wines were either entirely composed of, or at least heavily weighted by, imported commodities. Chemicals and building materials other than wood, the other groups to turn up at this time, included a considerable number of domestic as well as foreign commodities. Not until June 1808 did any other group start to rise. At that time beverages and dyes, both of which consisted of imported articles, joined in the upward movement. By that time every group composed of imported commodities had started to rise, except the non-ferrous metals, which did not reach its low until October 1808.

The rise in domestic commodities was especially concentrated between September and November 1808. During those three months the prices of seven groups made up almost entirely of domestic commodities—fish, furs, textile fibers, grain products, meats, wood, and fuel and lighting—began to mount. The other three groups consisting wholly of domestic commodities turned upward later: grains in January 1809, dairy products in April, and minor farm crops in January 1810.

The dates at which the various groups reached peaks can be divided into three periods:

1. January-May 1809
2. May-December 1810
3. April 1811 and after.

Nine sub-groups attained their peaks in the first period. Of these, spirits, condiments, beverages, non-ferrous metals, fruit, and textile fabrics include a large proportion of imported commodities. It should be especially noted that non-ferrous metals, which had been late in ending the recession in 1808, rose quickly and had a peak in conformity with many other imports. There was also three groups weighted with domestic commodities with peaks in this first period: chemicals, ferrous metals, and textile fibers.

In the second period, from May to December 1810, seven sub-groups reached their highs. Of these, building materials other than wood, hides and leather, wines, sugar and molasses, and dyes were largely influenced by prices of imported commodities. Only wood and grain products were primarily of domestic origin.

The remaining sub-groups are all made up entirely of domestic products and all except tobacco, which had been declining gradually during this period, were slow to reach their peaks. In fact, fuel and lighting materials did not recede substantially until after January 1815 and grain prices even tended upward until after May 1817. These were the extreme cases. Meats and meat products and fish rose until April and May 1811, dairy products and furs until September and October 1811, and minor farm products until July 1812.

No such contrary movement developed as a result of the repeal of the Non-Intercourse Act in December 1810 as had resulted from the complete embargo of December 1807. In fact most groups ended their recession in 1811 or 1812. The sub-groups first to complete their contraction were spirits and chemicals in June and July 1809 and fruit in June 1810. During the first four months of 1811, ferrous metals, wines, and sugar and molasses reached their lowest points, while non-ferrous metals, hides and leather, and fish followed in the four months from June to September. The greatest concentration of low points occurred between November 1811 and January 1812. In those three months, textile fibers, beverages, condiments, dyes, and tobacco ended their declines. Most of the remaining groups followed as war with Great Britain became more certain and as hostilities actually commenced. Only three groups persisted in their decline for more than six months after the declaration of war. Wood receded until April 1813, minor farm crops until October, and furs until January 1814.

Monthly Fluctuations from 1811 to 1821

From 1812 to 1815 the prices of nearly all commodities, although generally tending upward, were subject to wide fluctuations associated with various victories and defeats during the war. In the first half of 1812 the average prices were higher than at the close of the previous year, but no substantial change came until between June and July, when the index rose 10.7 per cent. This level was maintained until after March 1813. Between March and November the index rose 10.2 per cent. The greatest rise of the war period occurred between November 1813 and January 1814. In those two months prices soared 17.4 per cent, reaching the highest point since the Revolutionary War. In the next four months they dropped 8.4 per cent and held around this level from May to September. In the late fall prices again advanced and in November, after Washington had been burned and the Philadelphia banks had suspended, the total index was 10.4 per cent higher than in the lowest part of the summer of 1814 and even 0.5 per cent higher than it had been in January 1814. At this peak average prices were higher than at all other times between the Revolutionary War and the Civil War.

Although prices dropped slightly in December 1814, they maintained for three months a level just slightly below the two peaks of January and November. Between February and March 1815 the index dropped 14.8 per cent from the level prevailing just before the news of peace arrived on February 12 and demoralized trading. The recession continued at a slower pace until in June prices were 21.2 per cent lower than at the peak.

Not only was the decline halted at this point, but in the next five months prices rose continuously and regained nearly half of what had been lost in the sharp break. Although in November 1815 the index was 12.3 per cent less than it had been in the previous year, it was 11.4 per cent above its position in June. After this rally the general index dropped for nearly two years with only minor interruptions. By October 1817 it was 36.4 per cent less than at the peak of 1814 and 27.5 per cent less than at the minor peak of 1815.

With prices at their lowest points since the close of 1808, the rise occasioned by the war appears to have been offset. At this level prices stiffened. The general index even showed a slight rise. Not until April 1819, a year and a half later, did prices fall below the average of October 1817. Once prices headed definitely downward, the fall was continuous and rapid; between January and September 1819 the index shrank 14.3 per cent. During the fall and winter of 1819-20 the recession was again checked, but after February 1820 the contraction in prices reasserted itself. A general and gradual decline persisted until in April 1821 the index was lower than it had been at any earlier time after February 1794. The decline in those two years completed the transition from the general high average of prices which had characterized the years between 1794 and 1819.

Imported and Domestic Commodities

It is to be expected that the war would raise the prices of imported commodities relatively higher than those of domestic origin. Early in 1812, even before war was declared, the prices of imported commodities rose. By May they were 5.0 per cent higher than at the low of the previous November. In the same six months, the prices of domestic commodities fell slightly. An abrupt rise occurred during the month following the declaration of war. The index of imported commodities jumped 20.9 per cent between June and July when higher duties were imposed. After August, however, prices sagged slightly.

The stagnation in the prices of certain imported articles in the summer of 1812 was frequently commented upon by contemporaries. It arose from the happenings in the period necessary to relay the news of the declaration of war by the United States and of the repeal of the British Order in Council the day before war was declared. Immediately upon the repeal, ships were loaded and sent to America. All summer the effect of the arrival and the release of these goods was felt. In August, James N. Weems wrote to the agent of a domestic manufacturer of textiles, "From the daily expectation of British goods, sales are almost entirely suspended from want of purchasers though [I] hope in a few weeks trade will again revive. . . . I think domestic goods [textiles] will scarcely bring as good prices as they have done."[18] While many of the vessels intended for New York and Philadelphia were captured,[19] enough textiles were received to lead Weems to write in September, "Since the arrival of British goods there appears almost to be a total stop to the sale of domestic, and some persons are sending them to auction in this place which serve to depress the sales, also."[20] Toward the close of the year Grotjan explained in detail some of the factors influencing prices throughout the summer of 1812.

> . . . A general depression of commerce has manifested itself since the middle of last month, and but very few articles of all those which have come to our knowledge, have sold brisk. Amongst the latter, sugar and molasses have still continued to be in demand, and maintained a steady price. We have observed with satisfaction that, during this period, the market has not been too much pressed by foreign sales, as it is our opinion, that this general depression will be but temporary. No alteration in the political concerns of this country have taken place, which could warrant a different view. Amongst the most prominent causes which have affected the present stagnation in business, we count the approach of winter, and the sudden cessation of those important sales, effected by our merchants during the last two months, for the supply of the western country which, we believe, have this fall exceeded any former sales of the same season. The vast quantity of foreign productions which have arrived in this country during the summer and autumn, would undoubtedly have occasioned a considerable fall in the prices of every prominent article, if the continuation of new supplies could reasonably be expected; but as immense quantities of many articles will be consumed during the winter, there is every reason to expect that prices in general will be higher toward spring. Our own staple articles, however, may not be included in this estimate, unless a more advantageous opening to some part of the continent should present itself by that time. Flour, wheat, rye meal, Indian corn, rice, etc., will probably experience a further depreciation, which the approach of winter alone would be likely to produce, independent of the effect which the prohibition of the licensed trade, would have on these articles.
>
> The sales of the dry goods in general are likely to remain heavy during the winter, unless circumstances should occur which would warrant pur-

[18] August 24, 1812, James N. Weems to Gideon Thornton, agent for the Natick Manufacturing Company, Massachusetts.

[19] September 15, 1812, James N. Weems to James Brown.

[20] September 22, 1812, James N. Weems to Gideon Thornton, agent for the Natick Manufacturing Co., Massachusetts.

chases on speculation, which is not unlikely. At all events, the regular spring trade will no doubt be brisk, and advantageous to holders of dry goods.

The quantity of Russia goods in the market is very considerable, and therefore not likely to experience a great advance for the next six months.[21]

In December the rise in prices of imported articles started again. It continued without interruption and even accelerated its climb after October 1813, with the result that in January 1814 imported commodities were 76.7 per cent higher than in November 1811. This was, by a very slight margin, the peak of prices for imported goods. Within four months prices had receded 13.6 per cent. In spite of this precipitous drop, prices of imported commodities were still higher than they had been in November 1813. During the summer prices rose slightly, but between September and November 1814 they again soared, reaching a peak almost equal to that of the preceding January. Lower, but still extremely high, prices prevailed as late as February 1815.

The movements in the prices of domestic commodities during the war, although more extreme than at any other time between the Revolution and the Civil War, appear dwarfed in comparison with the more violent fluctuations already noted in prices of imported commodities. The average prices of domestic commodities were also sluggish in responding. The largest increase in any one month in 1812 was 2.9 per cent between August and September, which is insignificant compared with the increase in imported commodities between June and July. The rise in prices of domestic commodities was persistent, however, although by November 1813 they were only 13.9 per cent above the low of May 1812. The most salient increase occurred between November 1813 and January 1814 when in two months the index soared 15.3 per cent. This acceleration is comparable to the speeding up of the rate of increase in the prices of imported commodities between October 1813 and January 1814. In the early part of 1814 the prices of domestic commodities sagged, but

[21] December 7, 1812, *Grotjan's Philadelphia Public Sale Report.* This weekly publication included shipping and market comments as well as prices current.

the decline of 5.2 per cent between January and July was less than in the imported commodities and required two months longer for its completion.

The advance in the closing months of 1814 affected the domestic commodities more than the imported in that their prices continued to rise until February 1815 and in the four months after October 1814 were considerably higher than in the peak at the beginning of the year. Just before the news of peace reached Philadelphia, prices of domestic commodities were 9.4 per cent above those prevailing in the previous summer and 3.7 per cent above those of January 1814.

The collapse of prices in the spring of 1815 affected the imported commodities more severely than the domestic. In the single month from February to March the index of imported commodities dropped 22.6 per cent and by the time the recession was checked in June prices were 30.2 per cent below the war peak. The contraction in domestic prices was more gradual and was completed one month earlier. Even these commodities declined 12.6 per cent in the three months from February to May.

In the latter part of the year prices again increased. For the imported commodities this appears as but a mild rally breaking the sharp decline from November 1814 to July 1817. Although their prices had risen 9.9 per cent by November 1815 they were still 23.3 per cent lower than at the war peak. In contrast, the domestic commodities had advanced 15.5 per cent by November 1815, so that their average stood above the war peak; they were at this time at the highest point between the Revolution and the Civil War.

Prices of domestic commodities held near this high level for four months before starting their broken decline. The imported commodities, however, dropped immediately after the peak of November, with scarcely an interruption, until by July 1817 they were 35.3 per cent below the minor peak of November 1815 and 50.4 per cent below the war peak. On this decline the imported commodities not only fell more rapidly than the domestic but dropped relatively below them after February 1816. This marks the end of the period beginning in 1807 during which the imported commodities were relatively above the commodities of domestic origin. The corresponding decline in the prices of domestic commodities was completed in October 1817 when their index was 19.6 per cent below the post-war peak.

For the imported commodities the decline from 1814 to 1817 lowered prices below the level from which they started their rise before the War of 1812, and in fact lower than they had been at any time since 1794. The smaller decline in the domestic commodities prevented such a complete readjustment. Thus, in October 1817 their prices were not only above the low levels of 1808 and the first part of 1812, but were even above the peaks of 1801 and 1805 and but slightly below the one of 1811.

The decline of both the imported and the exported commodities met with a pronounced check in 1817 and 1818. The index of imported commodities even rose 7.2 per cent between September 1817 and February 1818 and held above the lows of July and September 1817 until after April 1819. The domestic commodities rose less than the imported and by March 1819 had again dropped as low as in October 1817.

During the spring and summer of 1819 prices dropped abruptly and by September were 16.1 per cent lower than they had been six months earlier. At the same time the imported commodities dropped 10.3 per cent. For several months the imported commodities declined gradually, but in the early part of 1820 they again dipped sharply. In June and August of that year, when their recession was completed, their index was at the lowest point it had touched since November 1792. The domestic commodities after dropping steadily from December 1819 to April 1821 were lower than they had been since 1794. Because of the upturn in the imported commodities in September 1820, while the domestic commodities continued to fall until the following spring, the index of the domestic commodities again dropped relatively below the foreign index after November 1820.

Major Groups

From the contrast of the fluctuations of prices of foreign and domestic commodities between 1812 and 1821, it is clear that critical turning points in the two sets of data, and often the direction of movements, differed. Between February 1811 and August 1812 all major groups except furs ended declines from the peaks of 1809, 1810, or 1811. Special significance attaches to the timing of this advance because of the ninety-day embargo laid upon shipping April 4, 1812. Actually all major groups except farm derivatives, lumber products and naval stores, and furs were rising before April. Three of the groups by the end of March 1812 had only increased a few points from their lowest month of 1811. The most marked increases before April 1812 had been in wines, which, from a low in February 1811, advanced 12.9 per cent; in fish, which, beginning to rise after September 1811, advanced 13.0 per cent in February and April; and in farm crops, which were 9.8 per cent higher in March 1812 than in November 1811. The prices of wine in April were identical with those of March but dropped a trifle lower in the next two months—mild movements in comparison with the marked rise which took place in July after the declaration of war. Fish held the same price from February to July 1812, except for a slight decline in May. Although prices of farm crops rose from November 1811 to February 1812, they dropped from then until May and, except for a temporary advance in July, showed little response even to the declaration of war until October 1812.

The most that one can say about the effect of the embargo of April 1812 is that it did not depress domestic commodities as much as usually occurred in earlier embargo periods such as 1808, or in Colonial years. Farm derivatives, which had been declining from August 1810, dropped 3.0 per cent between March and April and even a trifle lower in May and June. Lumber products and naval stores went on declining until August 1812.

With the declaration of war in June and the increased duty on imported articles, the indices of the groups heavily weighted with imported commodities rose steeply between June and July. The group of imported foods made the largest gain in that month—nearly 25 per cent. The upward movement continued for two more months, though at a greatly reduced pace. The wines, also composed entirely of imported commodities, rose 14 per cent and failed to rise higher in the next month. The comparatively small increase in this group must be discounted by the fact that it had been at a high level in the early part of 1812. Even the two industrial groups which are some-

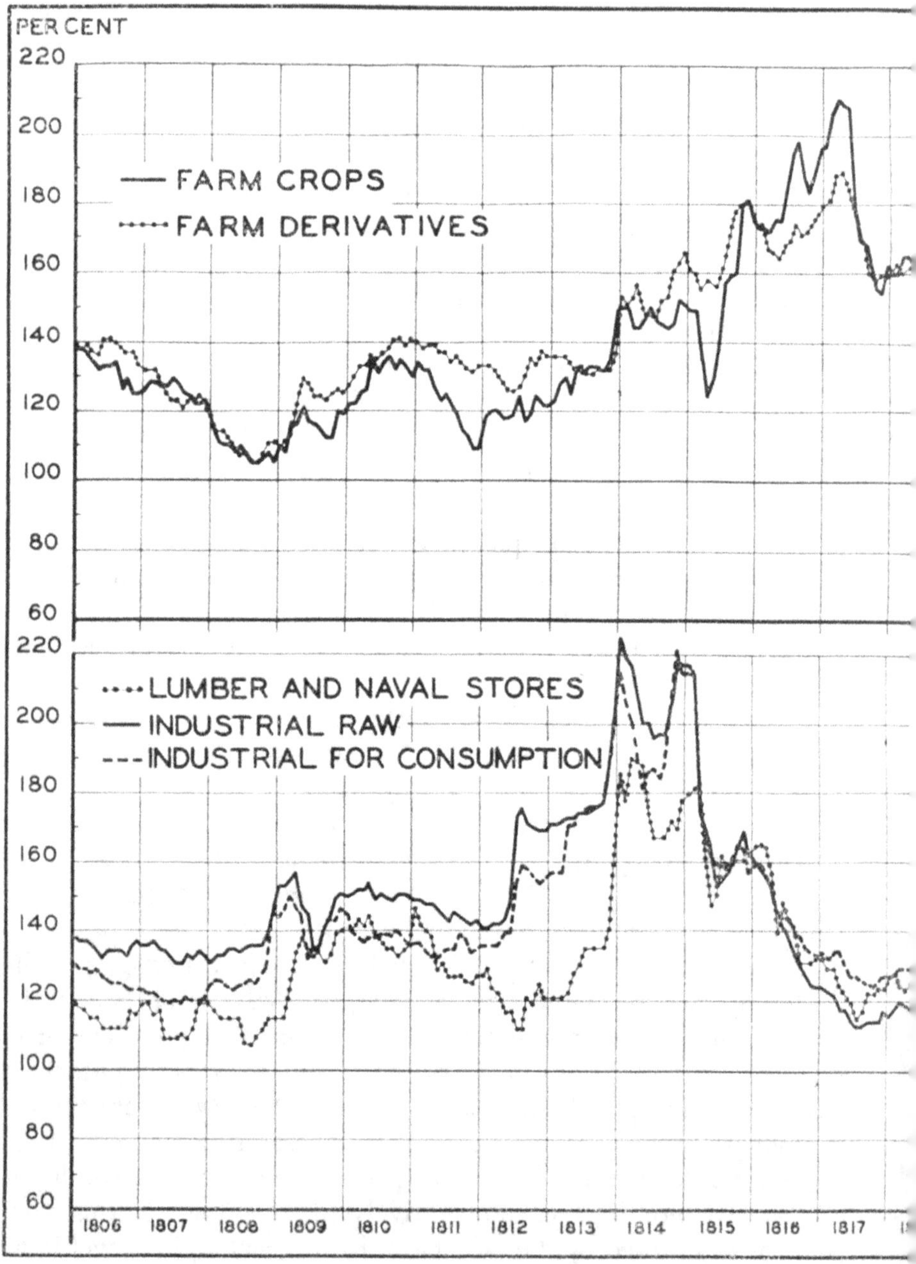

CHART X—GEOMETRIC INDICES OF AVERAGE MONTHLY WHOLE
(Base—Mo

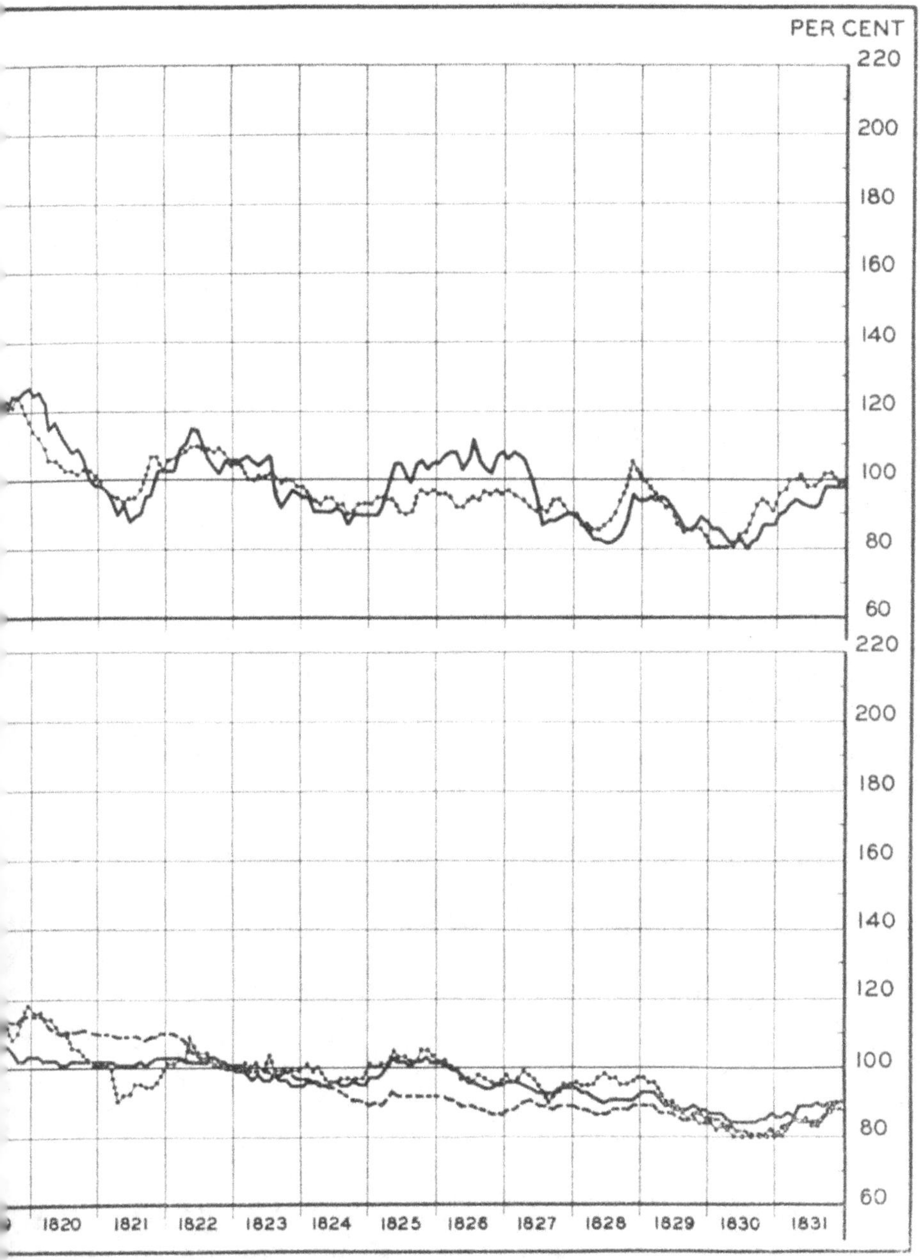

CES IN PHILADELPHIA BY MAJOR GROUPS, 1806-1831
rage, 1821-1825)

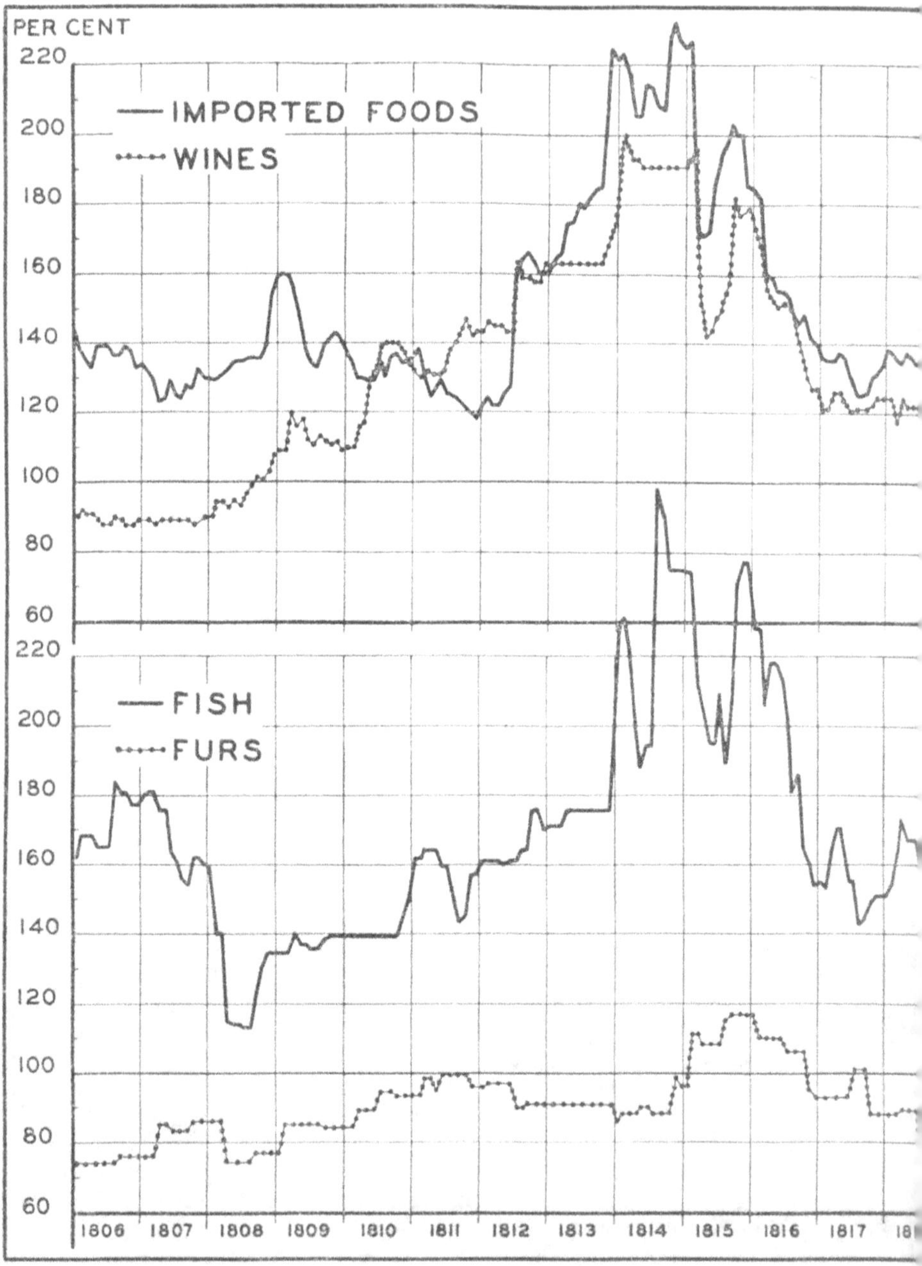

CHART X—GEOMETRIC INDICES OF AVERAGE MONTHLY WHOLES
(Base—Mor

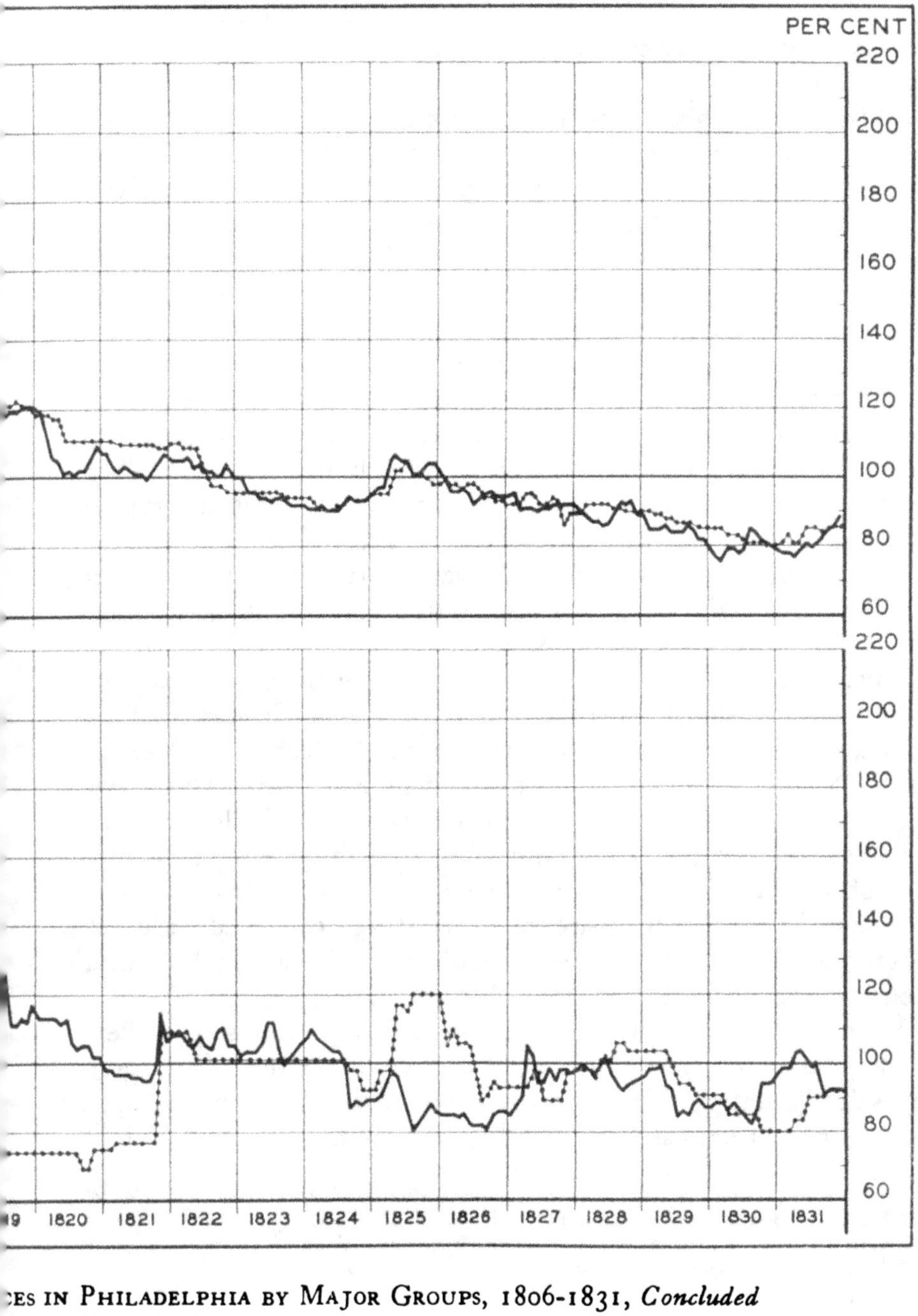

ces in Philadelphia by Major Groups, 1806-1831, *Concluded*
rage, 1821-1825)

what influenced by the inclusion of some domestic commodities rose between 11 and 16 per cent in July and increased further the following month.

In contrast, the groups dominated by domestic commodities failed to share in this abrupt rise. Farm crops rose 4.4 per cent in July, but in August they dropped to a lower price than that of June. Farm derivatives, the only other domestic group to show any increase, was less than one per cent higher in July than in June. Fish did not change in price in July and lumber products and naval stores and furs declined between 3.5 and 7 per cent.

Since neutral vessels were not restricted from entering the port from the outbreak of the war until the spring of 1813, there was not an increasing scarcity of imported goods. As a result their prices sagged somewhat after their initial rise in the summer of 1812. When the usual increase in trade, after the winter dullness, was interrupted with the British blockade, there were substantial advances in the prices of imported commodities in Philadelphia. This rise came after a period when sales of most commodities, except coffee, had been reported to be dull[22] and prices wavering. About the middle of March a Philadelphia merchant writing to New York explained, "From the news of the British being in considerable force in our Bay, speculation has once more got on tiptoe in consequence of which the holders of goods will not sell without at advanced prices."[23] In the next two weeks persistent rumors of an armistice, which would lower prices for those who had been conserving their stock, and news of the capture of Girard's incoming vessel laden with goods from Canton, which would advance the prices of some articles, competed with each other in a market in which goods would not sell "at anything near the prices that had been obtained."[24]

Even on April 12, 1813 Grotjan was still reporting sales as "extremely languid." In casting about for a reason for the lull in prices and sales he stated, "The reported armistice whether founded upon solid ground or not has undoubtedly given the first check."[25] Judged

[22] February 1, 1813, also March 1, 1813, *Grotjan's Philadelphia Public Sale Report.*
[23] March 17, 1813, John Hamilton to David Wylie, New York.
[24] March 31, 1813, John Hamilton to David Wylie, New York.
[25] April 12, 1813, *Grotjan's Philadelphia Public Sale Report.*

from the movement of prices, the remarks in *Grotjan's Philadelphia Public Sale Report* in the middle of May suggest a more adequate reason for the slow advance of prices in the first part of 1813. Up to then, except for a few articles, Philadelphia had been moderately well supplied by her own incoming vessels and by the free entry of neutrals to the port. It was this which led Grotjan to write: "The prices of British dry goods have maintained themselves better than could have been expected, considering the quantities which have been introduced during the last summer and fall. The late sales have, on an average, been certainly lower, and the difference between the prices obtained for many articles in February, March, and April, is very perceptible and varies from 5 to 25 per cent. Woolen goods, in general, have depreciated most."[26]

The movements in prices between the spring and fall of 1813 were chiefly influenced by the restriction of the sea trade of Philadelphia. Imported foods rose 4.6 per cent between March and April 1813 and by October were 11.4 per cent higher than before the blockade. The industrial commodities ready for consumption rose even more abruptly in April. Their index that month was 8.9 per cent higher than in March. Although they continued to increase during the year, they were only 3.4 per cent higher in October than in April. The industrial raw and semi-finished comodities were less affected, being only 2.1 per cent higher in October than in the previous spring and but slightly more than at the peak of the previous year. Wines sold for nearly the same price from December 1812 to October 1813.

Among the domestic commodities, the lumber products and naval stores had the most abrupt rise. As early as July 1813 they were 12.3 per cent above the level of the first three months of that year. This high level was maintained as late as October. Farm crops took a more gradual and persistent rise of 10.1 per cent between January and November. The only other domestic group to show a rise in 1813 was fish, which advanced 2.1 per cent between March and April and held at this level for the rest of the year. Furs did not change in price. The group of farm derivatives was the only one which did not rise during the major part of 1813. As late as November its index was still 2.9 per cent lower than in February.

[26] May 17, 1813, *Grotjan's Philadelphia Public Sale Report.*

The period of inertness, during which the prices of domestic goods were sustained at a very high level or were mildly increasing despite the blockade at the capes of the Delaware, ended in the last quarter of 1813. Farm crops, which advanced 12.4 per cent from October to December, continued a slight increase even in the opening months of the next year. Farm derivatives, which made little advance until December, rose 11.8 per cent between December and January. The index of lumber products and naval stores, after holding at the same level from July to October, mounted in each of the next months, gaining in all 37.4 per cent. In the other two groups of domestic commodities, fish and furs, prices were unchanged during the closing months of 1813. The likeness of the price behavior of the two groups ended in January 1814 when fish advanced 30.1 per cent and furs declined further.

The market observation by Grotjan on the first of November after the unequal advances was: "The state of our commercial affairs and the consequent enhancement in the price of many indispensable articles, or such which have become so through habit, make it daily more difficult to form a correct opinion on their future rise or fall. For some time past judgment has been out of the question, and common prudence has, no doubt, prevented many a merchant from entering as deep into speculations as from the present result might have been done with great success."[27]

The merchants were continually faced with the problem of how to conduct their business in order to guard against the extreme changes in prices which would result from an unexpected end of the war. "It, therefore, seems to become peculiarly necessary," Grotjan wrote, "to discriminate between such articles as are subject to sudden depreciations in price and those which are not."[27] He rated as subject to sudden depreciation goods which "can be obtained in our market within a short period of time, either from foreign places in the neighborhood of the United States or from other states in the union."[27] Grotjan attributed the rise in these prices more to the blockade than to the war in general. Such articles might be subject to substantial fluctuations in prices. Even among these commodities there were two distinct classes, first, those used chiefly for domestic consumption,

[27] November 1, 1813, *Grotjan's Philadelphia Public Sale Report.*

which had already advanced in price more than most and would, therefore, be expected to fall most. The other class of goods which could be quickly obtained, more important as exports or reëxports than for local use, were not expected by Grotjan to be liable to "so great a depreciation in price."[27]

The second large class of goods were those usually imported from Europe. Because stocks of such merchandise were depleted throughout the United States, Grotjan felt their present prices would not materially fall. He erred in thinking that it would take some time after peace was effected to replenish the stocks in the hands of merchants because he failed to take into account the fact that the results of negotations would be known in Europe before the news reached here. New merchandise would be shipped either on consignment by British merchants or to fill orders received indirectly from American traders. Such goods could arrive almost as soon as actual news of peace.

Grotjan called special attention to those goods which had been largely imported from Europe but were by 1813 being supplied by "successful manufactories established here." The scarcity of such foreign articles had raised "the value of our own manufactured goods" and had acted "as a powerful protection to enable the enterprising undertakers to overcome the difficulties and bear the expenses connected with the commencement of such establishments."[27] Grotjan, stressing as he was the immediate effects of a change in war activities, did not visualize then the intense competition which would arise in this class of goods when British firms attempted to regain their dominance in this market. A very specific account of this rivalry is to be found in the correspondence of Wetherill. More widespread effects can be indicated by the pressure for protective tariffs which developed in the immediate post-war years.[28]

The final category of merchandise discussed by Grotjan consisted of "such goods as are imported into this country from India." Compared with other articles he considered these "least liable to a great and sudden depreciation." He added, "Although there is not yet an absolute scarcity of any of these articles, many of which have ad-

[27] November 1, 1813, *Grotjan's Philadelphia Public Sale Report.*

[28] See discussion pp. 176 ff.

vanced to nearly three times their former price, yet it is certain that even in case of immediate peace no new supplies can reach the market in less than fifteen months and it is very likely that none will reach us in less than two years and a half."[27]

The rise in domestic commodities attracted the attention of contemporaries less than that of imported goods. One of the disturbing factors which added to the effectiveness of the blockade in curtailing the interchange of commodities by sea routes was an embargo placed on December 17, 1813. It prohibited any vessel except those of foreign neutrals from leaving an American harbor and even these must clear with such cargo as was already loaded at the time the law went into effect. Doubtless the fear that supplies could not soon be replenished stimulated a rise already in process in goods of foreign origin.

Toward the close of December 1813, Grotjan felt that the activity in the market had "in some measure subsided." He added, "We have found this week as much inclination to sell, as there was manifested to purchase. The market has therefore become rather more regular and, although no great depreciation in the prices of foreign articles can be anticipated, it is presumable that most of them will be gradual and moderate during the winter. These premises are founded upon the supposition that the matter contained in the President's message relative to our foreign affairs, the operation of new and additional duties and taxes, and the last embargo act were necessary to support the continuance of the high prices produced by the sudden and unexampled rise of last week."[28]

Imported foods, which tended slowly upward in each month of 1813, advanced 21.7 per cent between October and December to a peak so extreme that it was only slightly surpassed in the latter months of the war. Prices of wines started their rise more gradually than imported foods, but continued to increase until in February 1814 the index was 22.3 per cent higher than in October, with prices at the maximum for the war years. Prices of industrial raw and semifinished commodities were enhanced 27.6 per cent between October 1813 and January 1814, reaching then their maximum for the war,

[27] November 1, 1813, *Grotjan's Philadelphia Public Sale Report.*

[28] December 27, 1813, *Grotjan's Philadelphia Public Sale Report.*

though industrial commodities ready for consumption made higher peaks later in the war than were attained in their advance of 21.4 per cent between October 1813 and January 1814.

The critical year 1814 opened with farm crops, foods, and foodstuffs, imported and domestic, at the highest prices they had yet reached in the war. Four of the five groups rose a trifle higher in February and then declined in the spring and summer months. The rise in farm derivatives persisted until April.

By the last week in January, Grotjan, who two weeks earlier had been stressing the rising tendencies in prices, reported the market as "very unsettled," a condition which he attributed both to usual seasonal factors and to the embargo.[30] Even at the close of March, Grotjan was able to report optimistically: "The unusual depression which our market has experienced during the last two months begins gradually to wear off as the spring season approaches. The sales of this week have been much more lively and the prices . . . are improving."[31]

The outlook, however, changed rapidly. Early in April a Philadelphia merchant wrote, "Since the President's recommendation to both houses respecting the [lifting of the] embargo, etc., business has experienced some check. The country merchants who were coming in pretty fast seem to suspend their purchases of dry goods and buy very sparingly both of British and domestic."[32] Grotjan also recognized the immediate effect of this new factor on prices. "At the moment when the market prices of the most important articles of trade began to mend we received the President's message recommending the repeal of the embargo and other restrictive commercial measures. The consequences which will result from so great a change in our commercial affairs, however beneficial it may prove to future operations, has apparently checked the spirit for adventure at present and thereby caused an unexpected depression in the market."[33]

Like the prices of foods, those of lumber products and naval stores increased slightly above the high of January, but their decline after March lasted longer than the recession in foodstuffs. The industrial

[30] January 24, 1814, *Grotjan's Philadelphia Public Sale Report.*

[31] March 28, 1814, *Grotjan's Philadelphia Public Sale Report.*

[32] April 14, 1814, James N. Weems to Gideon Thornton, agent for the Natick Manufacturing Company, Massachusetts.

[33] April 11, 1814, *Grotjan's Philadelphia Public Sale Report.*

commodities ready for consumption were higher in January 1814 than they were again until November. The industrial raw materials attained their maximum war peak in January 1814.

The most substantial decline in the spring and summer of 1814 occurred in imported articles. It was the rise in these and more especially in sugar, coffee, tea, and other tropical products which brought consumers' protests at the beginning of 1814;[34] it was the decline in the prices of these in the spring which made the calculations of merchants uncertain.

The recessions in imported foods and fish differed appreciably from those of the other groups. In imported foods the decline from the peak in February lasted only two months and the index began to rise again after April. The movements in the prices of fish differed more in that the three months of decline from February to May were followed by three months of rising prices in which the index climbed far above the earlier peak. Although prices dropped in the closing months of the year, they held above the early peak. The rapid advance of these prices after May and their continuance at a high level may reflect the effectiveness of the British blockade, which was extended to New England during the summer.

The other commodities, both imported and domestic, underwent a somewhat longer recession, terminating between July and September, followed by a rise after the burning of Washington[35] and the suspension of specie payments by the banks to peaks in the closing months of 1814 or the beginning of 1815. Only wines, industrial raw materials, and lumber products and naval stores failed to exceed at that time their peaks in the opening months of 1814.

[34] Scharf, J. Thomas, and Westcott, Thompson, *History of Philadelphia, 1609-1884,* Vol. I, p. 569.

[35] The alarm of Philadelphians caused by the landing of the British and their raids into Maryland is described in McMaster's *Life and Times of Stephen Girard* (Vol. II, p. 276 f.). An interesting sidelight is provided by Grotjan's "Note to Subscribers" in the issue of September 5, 1814. "The threatening posture of our enemy who has landed on our shores and commenced to carry fire and destruction through our beloved country, the danger which approaches our city and our firesides, makes it an indispensable duty for every able citizen to hold himself in readiness promptly to answer to the call of his country. Being fully impressed with this sacred duty, and intending to waive every other consideration this is to notify our subscribers that in case no report should be issued from our office next week that the editor is temporarily prevented from performing his duty to his subscribers by performing a duty due to his country."

The imported foods paralleled the industrial commodities ready for consumption in that both groups in November 1814 were at the maximum of the war period. Farm crops were also at their maximum in November, but the derivatives continued their advance for another month. Wines and lumber products and naval stores were the only groups to advance beyond December. Although wines rose as late as February 1815 and the lumber products and naval stores as late as March, neither group achieved as high a level as in the early part of 1814.

Probably because of the previous disappointments arising out of the long-continued negotiations for peace which were reflected in successive waves of contraction and expansion in trading, the favorable result of the work of the commissioners at Ghent was not anticipated. Two days after the treaty was signed, but more than a month and a half before news of it reached Philadelphia, Grotjan commented, "During the course of the week, prices have rather improved and although commerce remains languishing nothing has occurred to indicate a sudden depreciation."[36]

Over and over during the war, prices had fluctuated as rumors of peace were circulated. The belated news of the actual peace, received in Philadelphia in the middle of February 1815, was followed by a drastic drop in prices. As usual, imported commodities reacted most. None of the imported groups had declined by February 1815 as much as 3 per cent below their peaks near the close of 1814. By March, however, both groups of industrial materials were slightly more than 19 per cent lower than at the peak while wines were 21 per cent and imported foods nearly 26 per cent lower.

Only fish, among the domestic commodities, had a comparable decline. By February 1815 the fish group was 9 per cent lower than at the peak of the previous August, but by March it had dropped approximately 21 per cent below the peak. The farm crops and derivatives showed slight declines. In February both were less than 4 per cent below their war peaks, while in March the derivatives were only 6.3 per cent less than at the peak and the farm crops only 11.7 per cent. Furs did not change in price during February and March, and the lumber products and naval stores even advanced slightly.

[36] December 26, 1814, *Grotjan's Philadelphia Public Sale Report.*

After the severe initial decline in March, most of the groups continued to recede for a few months longer but at a much slower rate. Imported foods and wines were the first foreign commodities to end their decline; both groups turned upward after April when they were slightly more than 26 per cent below the previous peak.

Contemporaries at this time did not fail to give special attention to the likely course of prices of industrial articles. For his analysis Grotjan felt that these should be subdivided according to the country of origin. He gave most attention, however, to British goods. After pointing out that the decline in the price of British goods had been especially great partly at least because of the fact that "large quantities of British manufactured goods remained on hand in this country to be disposed of when the news of peace arrived," he listed the chief ways in which these supplies reached the country:

1. by prizes taken and brought in
2. by Letters of Marque trading to Saint Barts and other places
3. by means of neutral importations from Lake Champlain and St. Andrews since the cessation of the non-intercourse law
4. by means of smuggling.

As a result of these irregular sources of supply there were great disparities in the assortment of goods. Grotjan noted that "larger quantities of some, less of others, and none of many articles otherwise regularly imported"[37] figured in the inventories of the merchants. The indices of the two industrial groups do not reveal any of these diverse price movements.

After having fallen by June 30.3 per cent below their index of November 1814, the industrial raw and semi-finished materials turned upward. Two months more were required for the industrial commodities ready for consumption to end their decline of 28.4 per cent from November 1814 to August 1815.

The fall in prices of imported articles was occasioned not only by the realization of the merchants that their stocks on hand must be liquidated but also by the speedy arrival of new merchandise which had been shipped from abroad before the news of peace reached Philadelphia. Americans, too, were prompt in reopening connections with

[37] March 20, 1815, *Grotjan's Philadelphia Public Sale Report.*

British houses.[38] Grotjan summarized in July the developments in trade during the spring and early summer:

> The revolution in the prices of merchandise of every description has been great since the return of peace, but the equilibrium which a regular and uninterrupted commerce produces is not yet reëstablished. . . . The immense quantity of British goods which have reached this country since that period [spring], have naturally lowered and moderated the prices of articles imported from that country; notwithstanding which the prices which can still be obtained are highly favorable to the importer. The importations from France have not been near adequate to the demands, for which reasons many articles, particularly brandy, sell at a very advanced price. The productions from the Mediterranean are much in the same situation. . . . Drugs remain scarce. . . . Importations from Germany have just commenced to make their appearance. . . . India goods remain high and find a quick sale. . . . Amongst the West India productions the article of coffee has remained most stationary . . . sugar, molasses and salt have fluctuated much and are at present nearly down to such prices as would leave to the importer only a saving profit.[39]

The most drastic declines among the domestic products occurred in fish, which by August was nearly 30 per cent below the war peak, and in lumber products and naval stores, which dropped nearly 20 per cent between March and May 1815. The farm crops had started to decline after November 1814, a month before the derivatives; they continued to decline until April 1815, a month after the farm derivatives turned upward. Their total decline was 18.1 per cent compared with only 6.3 per cent in the farm derivatives. In fact, the demand for foodstuffs for immediate shipment after the news of peace was so great that the prices of farm derivatives were but momentarily depressed. In every month of 1815 after June the prices of derivatives not only were higher than in April but tended to advance more each month and as early as August were higher than at any time during the war. In the rise in the latter part of 1815 two other groups of domestic commodities, farm crops and furs, also reached prices higher than at any time during the war. Although lumber products and naval stores advanced more than 12 per cent between May 1815 and

[38] April 11, 1815, Joseph N. Paul to Cropper Benson and Company, Liverpool, in Robeson and Paul's letter book. See also McMaster, *op. cit.*, Vol. II, Ch. IX.

[39] July 17, 1815, *Grotjan's Philadelphia Public Sale Report.*

January 1816 and fish more than 30 per cent between August and November 1815, neither group reached the level of the war peak. The same is true of the groups of foreign commodities. The steepest rise in these groups came between April and September 1815 when the index of imported foods increased 19.1 per cent and wines 27.7 per cent. The industrial commodities were much less affected. Between June and November the industrial raw and semi-finished products advanced barely more than 10 per cent, while the maximum rise in industrial commodities ready for consumption was less than 5 per cent between August and October.

After January 1816 all groups were definitely receding from their war and post-war peaks, except farm crops and farm derivatives. The general downswing in prices aggravated the previous weakness of the trading part of the community. As early as May, one Philadelphian reported to an English house: "Business generally is very dull in America. Every person that I have seen is complaining and not without a cause. The country is overstocked with goods particularly in the dry goods lines."[40] The only encouragement was the organization of the Second Bank of the United States. According to Hildeburn, "The national Bank which is to be a specie bank commences its operations in July next and is confidently expected will, in the course of two or three years, equalize the exchange between our states which is now a serious evil being from 5 to 15 per cent between one state and another."[40]

The difficulty of trading when the currency issued by every bank was subject to varying rates of discount in different communities handicapped merchants throughout the period from the Revolution to the Civil War. It was especially acute in 1816. One description of the current situation was given in the same letter by Hildeburn. "The bank paper through the whole western country even to within ten miles of our city is at a discount with us of at least 12 per cent and . . . consequently persons residing to the westward of us cannot think of making purchases in our city until compelled which we have depended much on. . . . With the banks not paying specie all confidence is lost among them as they have now no check on each other and will not receive other than city paper."[40] This situation was aptly

[40] May 25, 1816, Samuel Hildeburn to Bradshaw and Ryley, Liverpool.

described by Wetherill's pun, "You will observe by the discount at which paper west of the mountains is passing that it is literally on the wrong side."[41]

In the same year Mathew Carey summarized "the calamitous state of trade and commerce" in a ten-point outline.

> 1. Remittances from the country, on which a great portion of our citizens depend for the discharge of their engagements, fall miserably short of what they had a right to expect.
>
> 2. Western notes, which form a large proportion of the few remittances received, are at a discount of from 6 to 15 per cent.
>
> 3. The regular sales of goods are very slow and dull.
>
> 4. Goods, foreign and domestic, when sold at auction, are sacrificed at a loss of from 20 to 45 per cent.
>
> 5. It is hardly possible to raise money on real estate of any description.
>
> 6. Those who hold bills receivable, intended to meet and discharge their bills payable, are obliged to prolong the period of payment, from the inability of their debtors to pay, and from the danger of forcing those debtors to stop payment altogether.
>
> 7. Thus pent up and shut out from their resources, many of our citizens, besides their bank engagements, owe heavily to the government for duties, and to individuals for goods purchased.
>
> 8. Money cannot be had of the brokers but at the rate of from 18 to 30 per cent per annum.
>
> 9. It is extremely difficult, and hardly possible, to procure new discounts at Bank for any note, how solvent soever the drawer and indorser may be. New accommodation notes are absolutely proscribed.
>
> 10. Various bankruptcies have taken place and many persons are "*tottering to their fall,*" and hanging on the very verge of the precipice of bankruptcy.*
>
> * It is proper to state that this picture applies to towns and cities only. The agricultural part of our citizens are generally in a state of as high prosperity as they ever were before.[42]

One of the most salient factors in 1816 is that which is briefly alluded to in the note at the end of Carey's statement in regard to the favorable situation in agriculture. Although prices of both farm crops and farm derivatives fell in some months, their underlying tendency

[41] October 3, 1816, Samuel Wetherill to George L. Mayer, Baltimore.

[42] September 21, 1816, Carey, Mathew, *Letter II to Bank Directors.*

was unmistakably upward. In March 1817 farm crops were higher in price than at any other time between the Revolution and the Civil War and 93.8 per cent higher than in the closing months of 1811 when the rise started. Farm derivatives reached a comparable point a month later after a rise of 50.2 per cent from the low in the early summer of 1812. The continuation of this extreme rise in the face of generally declining prices reflects the unusual demands from Europe because of shortages of foodstuffs as well as the restricted supplies here after the cold season and poor crops of 1816.

In the fall of that year Grotjan devoted a considerable space to his explanation of the high prices for many domestic foodstuffs and his reasons for expecting even further advances.

> This article [flour], as will be observed by the general prices current, has experienced a great and sudden rise; owing to intelligence received from Europe that the crops of grain have failed in several countries, it is to be expected that large demands will be made on our surplus. As our crops of wheat and rye have been considerable, this surplus might perhaps have been sufficient to answer the expected foreign demand, without unreasonably enhancing the current prices of former weeks, if not a great proportion thereof was necessary to compensate for the lamentable deficiency of the crops of Indian corn which, in consequence of the remarkable cool season experienced during the summer months, have been greatly deficient in the states of New Jersey and Pennsylvania, and perhaps more so in the states of Maryland and Virginia; few farmers having been able to raise sufficient for their own use. The present extraordinary, and we may say, double prices are therefore likely not alone to maintain themselves, but still to experience a further advance.[43]

In addition, Grotjan commented that pork, butter, and tobacco were especially scarce.

After reaching peaks in the early months of 1817 the prices of farm crops and farm derivatives collapsed. Between April and October the index of the derivatives fell 17.0 per cent, while from March to November that of farm crops dropped 27.1 per cent. These sharp recessions were followed by more than a year in which prices held around, or even above, this level. A comparison of these two groups of domestic commodities with the other groups of either

[43] November 18, 1816, *Grotjan's Philadelphia Public Sale Report.*

domestic or foreign origin shows that the farm crops and derivatives belatedly took in a few months of 1817 the decline which the other groups had taken more gradually but more persistently after the end of 1815 or the beginning of 1816. Thus all groups except furs checked their recessions between June and November 1817 and tended, at least, to hold for a year or more. Several groups even showed a substantial rise during 1818. This recovery closely followed the resumption of specie payments at the end of 1818.

The timing of the movements between 1817 and 1819 shows distinct periods of concentration. Most groups reached their lowest prices in 1817 between June and August. Only farm crops, farm derivatives, and the industrial commodities ready for consumption continued to decline as late as October and November. Not only were these groups the last to start their recovery but they were also the first to complete it and made, in general, the smallest gains. Between February and April 1818 they were, at their minor peaks, only from 3 to 7 per cent above their lowest prices in 1817. The industrial raw and semi-finished group also completed its rise in March 1818, showing a net increase of only 6.2 per cent. The other groups of foreign and domestic commodities continued to rise. Wines, the only other group which rose less than 7 per cent, turned downward in December 1818, a month after the imported foods, which had risen 10.6 per cent. Lumber products and naval stores and fish, which had been among the first to rise, increased more and continued their advance longer than the other groups. At their peak in February 1819 lumber products and naval stores were 17.4 per cent and fish 23.5 per cent above their lowest price in 1817. Even the groups which had their peaks early in 1818, except farm derivatives, held above the low of 1817 throughout the year. Although as late as October 1818 this group was above its low of 1817, it had been lower for three months during the preceding summer. All of the other groups, except lumber products and naval stores and wines, had well-sustained prices until between March and May 1819. The most drastic contraction was that of fish which in four months dropped more than it had risen in 18 months; at the other extreme were the lumber products and naval stores, which held above their low of 1817 until after July 1819 and rose above the low again in the closing months of that year and the beginning of 1820. Similarly, wines sustained their prices until after November 1819.

Once prices had dipped below the average of 1818, their recession was sharply accelerated. This contraction in prices marks the effect of the financial disturbances in 1819. As usual, the first evidence of the overextension of trading was in such comments as, "Our market is now stocked with British articles of every description . . . hoping for more prosperous times."[44] By the close of May the situation had become so aggravated that Grotjan felt it necessary to analyze it at length.

> The state of the commerce of the United States, in general, is at this moment placed in such a situation as to make it a matter of the greatest difficulty to predicate on the future. From the present aspect it appears inevitable that the ruin of many families must take place before business settles into an even channel. The causes, of which the united effects are now so severely felt, are various; but we believe the largest head of the hydra to be the enormous system of banking, from which source has proceeded the raising of artificial capital, which has thrown out inducements to speculation beyond prudence, and, therefore, has caused the constant high prices of our staple articles, which to our merchants has proved a loss in foreign markets. Whereas without the pernicious excess of the banking system no speculations except those founded upon solid reasoning could have been made; our own staple articles could have been purchased at such prices as to insure a profit in other countries, and the manufactures of Europe etc. would not have commanded such prices as to induce foreigners and speculators to inundate the country and by that means produce a pernicious balance of trade against us.[45]

Trading in all of the post-war years had been marked by an intense competition between British manufacturers who were attempting to regain their dominance in the American market and the many domestic producers who had been encouraged by the interruptions of trade during the Napoleonic wars, and especially after the Embargo Act and throughout the War of 1812—a situation which had been foreseen by Grotjan as early as March 1815.[46] Pressure was continuously being exerted upon Congress to maintain or raise tariffs

[44] January 27, 1819, Samuel Wetherill to Brandrams, Templeman and Company, London.

[45] May 31, 1819, *Grotjan's Philadelphia Public Sale Report.*

[46] March 20, 1815, *Grotjan's Philadelphia Public Sale Report.*

and even to place an embargo on certain imported articles. The conflicting interests of various manufacturers and the far-reaching effects expected from even a slight change in tariffs can be illustrated by a letter of Wetherill's to Adam Seybert when Congress proposed levying an additional duty on shot. "I observe by the paper of Saturday last, that you reported a Bill proposing an additional duty of one Cent per pound on Shot, which would if carried into effect make the duty on that article the same as it now is on White Lead and Red Lead—Permit me to observe, that the reason which operates to add to the duty on Shot, will in my opinion apply with much greater force to increasing the duty on White and Red Lead: in Manufacturing the latter articles a greater number of persons are employed, a much large[r] Capital necessary in consequence of the very slow process of corrosion, and you are aware, that the expense of Buildings, Steam Engine, Pots, etc., for carrying on a White Lead Manufactory, must far exceed the expense necessary for making Shot. (My Works independent of the Stock of Lead has not cost less than 25,000 Dollars) and when the use to which those articles are applied are taken into consideration, it will appear that White Lead and Red Lead are far more important to the Community.

"The object of this letter is to request that when the Bill may be call[ed] up, you will amend it by including White Lead and Red Lead, fixing an additional duty on those articles of one Cent per pound. If this cannot be effected, it is important to the White Lead Manufacturers that the Duty *should not be increased on Shot;* for if the additional duty on Shot should prevent the importation of that article it would of course increase the demand for Pig Lead (our mines at present not being adequate to the Supply) the White Lead manufacturers would consequently pay higher for the raw material and thereby be placed in a much worse situation than they are at present: there are at this time a great[er] number of White Lead Manufacturers established than is necessary to supply the demand of that article, there consequently will be a competition, and as our Country abounds in Lead it certainly is of importance to the community that the manufacturers of those articles should be protected."[47]

[47] April 18, 1818, Samuel Wetherill to Adam Seybert, Washington.

Although the decline in prices in 1819 tapered off, there were only minor interruptions until most groups reached a low in the spring and summer of 1821. Two groups, furs and industrial raw and semi-finished materials, did complete their decline in 1819 and 1820. At the other extreme were wines, which tended to fall until the second quarter of 1824, and the industrial commodities ready for consumption in which the contraction was so persistent and dominant that no cyclical variations were again apparent until after August 1830. The other major groups ended their recession between April and September 1821.

Sub-Groups

From 1812 to 1821 the sub-groups show a maze of increases and decreases reflecting the succession of events at home and abroad during and after the War of 1812. The variations in these changes in prices are of especial significance to students who attempt to trace the trade of Philadelphia with any particular locality. For general purposes, however, we may attempt to clarify the situation by isolating the periods in which the various groups reached their war or post-war maxima. Not only can the groups be divided on the basis of whether their highest prices were reached during or after the war but also by the part of the war or post-war period in which their most extreme expansion occurred.

Four periods stand out as times at which various groups reached their peaks.

1. December 1813-April 1814
2. October 1814-March 1815
3. September 1815-March 1816
4. March-August 1817

The only exception to this classification is fish. Its peak in August 1814 seems more closely related to the peaks in other commodities between October 1814 and March 1815, than to those in the earlier part of the war.

During the period from December 1813 to April 1814, nine sub-groups reached their highest prices: sugar and molasses, chemicals and drugs, dyes, textile fibers, textile fabrics, wines, building materials other than wood, hides and leather, and fruit. Primarily these consist of imported commodities. The chief exceptions are textile fibers and building materials other than wood. Since the war interfered with trade by sea between Pennsylvania and other states, many domestic commodities had a restricted market.

The next period, from October 1814 to March 1815, in which beverages, spirits, condiments, non-ferrous metals, fuel and lighting, ferrous metals, and wood reached their maxima, marks the final spurt in prices between the time when Washington was burned and the banks suspended specie payment and when news of peace reached Philadelphia. Most of the commodities affected at this time also were of foreign origin, the chief exceptions being fuel and lighting, wood, and some ferrous metals. Meats, furs, and tobacco, all of domestic origin, attained their peaks in the first post-war period from September 1815 to March 1816. The remaining groups—grain products, dairy products, grains, and minor farm crops—rose for at least another year, not reaching their peaks until March-August 1817.

This analysis shows that although some groups of domestic commodities sold at the highest prices in one of the two war periods, no group including even one imported commodity reached a higher price after the war than it had during the war. All of the groups of domestic commodities which had their highest peaks after the war were of agricultural origin except furs.

That the major groups conceal some diverse fluctuations in the underlying sub-groups is especially apparent in the timing of the end of the recession from the war and post-war peaks. First, the major groups conceal the different classes of goods which reached a low in 1819 and 1820. Among the first to reach their lows were beverages, spirits, dairy products, and fruit, in addition to furs, chemicals and drugs, dyes, and hides and leather. The second fact concealed is that although many groups continued to fall after 1821—specifically: meats and meat products, textile fibers, condiments, wines, fuel and lighting, ferrous metals, tobacco, and textile fabrics—the decline in all of them was definitely checked by the end of 1826, although the group of industrial commodities ready for consumption averaged out the turning points in its constituent series and showed a persistent decline until the summer of 1830.

Summary

A summary of the most significant movements in prices during the period from 1808 to 1821 reveals little similarity in the behavior of the various groups. In the recession of prices immediately prior to the outbreak of the War of 1812, farm crops, lumber products and naval stores, and imported foods dropped 20 per cent or more, while none of the other groups declined as much as 15 per cent. It is not possible to say that the decline was greatest in raw materials, for the industrial raw materials declined approximately 10 per cent while the farm crops and lumber and naval stores, which may also be regarded as raw materials, fell between 20 and 24 per cent. Nor was it the domestic agricultural situation which was chiefly affected, for although farm crops fell 20 per cent, farm derivatives receded less than 11 per cent. It cannot be said that imported commodities were chiefly affected, because only the imported foods showed a substantial decline while other groups wholly or largely influenced by imported commodities declined less severely and two groups of domestic commodities, farm crops and lumber and naval stores, fell nearly as much as the imported foods.

Even the length of recession seems to have had little influence on the severity. In ending the decline from the pre-war peak the groups may be classified into four sections. First, the wines and industrial commodities ready for consumption checked their recession between February and April 1811; both of these groups suffered relatively mild declines. The recessions in the second section of the groups including fish, farm crops, imported foods, and industrial raw and semi-finished materials ended between September 1811 and February 1812. Two of these underwent severe declines of 20 per cent or more and the other two 13 per cent or less. The third section consists of farm derivatives and lumber products and naval stores, which declined until the summer of 1812. One of these groups fell approximately 24 per cent and the other 11 per cent. The remaining group, furs, fell less than 15 per cent but did not end its recession until after January 1814.

The greatest difference in the behavior of commodities in this second main period was the dating of their maximum prices. The industrial raw and semi-finished commodities, wines, and lumber products and naval stores were at their highest between January and March 1814, fish in August 1814, and the industrial commodities ready for consumption and imported foods in November 1814. This difference in behavior emphasizes the fact that the War of 1812 did not result in a consistent rise in prices. Of greater significance is the fact that three groups continued to advance after the close of the war and reached their maxima in the immediate post-war years: furs in January 1816 and farm crops and farm derivatives in March and April 1817. Thus it was chiefly domestic agricultural articles which, under the impetus of demands from Europe and a restricted supply at home, were substantially higher in price after the war than at any time during it. Other domestic commodities, especially lumber products and naval stores and fish, and all imported commodities reached higher prices during the war than later.

The effect of the panic of 1819 is largely concealed by the general downward sweep of prices from the war and post-war peaks to 1821 or beyond. It is highly significant, however, that all groups except furs and wines were marked by a sharp recession confined to a few months of 1819.

At the close of the period in 1821 furs had been advancing since March 1819 without making much headway, and industrial raw and semi-finished commodities since June 1820, while wines and industrial commodities ready for consumption continued to recede into the twenties. The other five groups, lumber products and naval stores, farm derivatives, farm crops, fish, and imported foods, showed an upward movement which started between May and October 1821.

Annual Price Movements

Major Groups

The annual averages show the persistent tendencies to rise or fall at various periods by eliminating the seasonal and minimizing the random changes. These figures show that in 1809 all groups rose 6 to 16 per cent above their prices of the previous year. Most groups continued to advance further in 1810, but imported foods and industrial commodities ready for consumption, which had been among the first to advance, declined that year and continued to fall in 1811. During 1811 all groups except fish, furs, and wines declined. Farm derivatives were only one-tenth of one per cent less than in the previous year, while farm crops, which fell more than any other group, were 6.2 per cent less than in 1810.

The fact that most of the domestic commodities advanced but little even in the second half of 1812 explains why four groups, composed chiefly of these commodities, farm crops, farm derivatives, furs, and lumber products and naval stores, were on the average from one to 9 per cent lower in 1812 than in the previous year. The only group of domestic commodities to show a rise that year was fish, which increased less than 5 per cent. The groups heavily weighted with imported commodities advanced from 8 to 13 per cent that year. During

TABLE 16

ANNUAL PERCENTAGE OF CHANGE IN THE INDICES OF THE MAJOR GROUPS 1809–1821

Year	Farm		Imported Foods	Lumber Products and Naval Stores	Industrial		Fish	Furs	Wines	General Index
	Crops	Derivatives			Raw	Consumption				
1809	+ 6.4	+11.4	+ 8.2	+15.3	+ 8.7	+11.9	+ 6.9	+ 6.8	+15.7	+10.2
1810	+12.6	+11.1	− 8.6	+ 5.6	+ 2.2	− 2.6	+ 2.4	+ 8.2	+14.1	+ 2.3
1811	− 6.2	− 0.1	− 5.4	− 4.4	− 3.4	− 2.3	+12.5	+ 7.6	+ 6.3	− 2.5
1812	− 1.4	− 3.2	+13.2	− 8.9	+ 8.4	+ 8.3	+ 4.6	− 4.2	+10.9	+ 5.2
1813	+10.5	+ 1.6	+26.8	+10.1	+11.8	+18.5	+ 5.9	− 3.0	+ 8.3	+13.1
1814	+10.7	+15.9	+19.4	+32.9	+18.4	+14.8	+30.4	− 1.2	+16.7	+17.8
1815	+ 4.5	+ 8.0	−10.5	− 6.1	−16.4	−12.5	− 3.2	+24.4	−13.0	− 8.8
1816	+20.1	+ 2.7	−19.0	−11.8	−19.0	−17.1	−10.7	− 4.0	−11.5	−12.2
1817	− 0.8	+ 1.0	−15.7	−15.7	−17.3	−11.2	−21.2	−12.4	−17.0	−12.7
1818	−11.4	− 8.7	+ 2.7	+ 2.8	+ 0.9	− 1.4	+ 6.0	−14.3	+ 0.2	− 1.5
1819	−15.9	−18.2	− 7.7	− 4.3	− 7.4	− 6.0	−16.1	− 6.6	− 0.2	− 8.6
1820	−17.4	−18.1	−14.6	−10.2	− 7.1	− 6.4	−21.3	− 2.1	− 7.2	−10.7
1821	−15.6	− 6.4	− 3.9	−12.4	0.0	− 2.2	− 8.6	+12.5	− 4.1	− 4.3

1813 and 1814 all groups except furs rose continuously and only imported foods and industrial commodities ready for consumption failed to rise by a larger percentage in 1814 than in the previous year.

The drop apparent in the annual averages of six groups in 1815 followed two years of advancing prices in lumber products and naval stores, three years of expansion in imported foods and both groups of industrial commodities, six years of unbroken advance in fish, and seven years in wines.

Three groups of domestic commodities reached higher points in 1815 than they had attained previously. In furs the rise of 24.4 per cent in 1815 followed three years of gradually declining prices and was followed by five years of contraction. Farm crops and derivatives, the other groups to rise in 1815, had been advancing since 1812 and continued to advance in 1816. Farm derivatives were even 1.0 per cent higher on the average in 1817 than in 1816, while farm crops declined less than 1.0 per cent. All of the other groups declined more than 10 per cent in both 1816 and 1817 except furs, which only dropped 4 per cent in 1816.

The stability after the latter part of 1817 was especially apparent in fish prices, which were 6 per cent higher in 1818 than in the previous year, and to a lesser extent in wines, industrial raw materials, imported foods, and lumber products and naval stores, which increased less than 3 per cent, while the industrial commodities ready for consumption declined only 1.4 per cent. Although the annual averages for 1818 conceal the stability in the prices of farm crops and derivatives, they do show that the declines in that year were less than in the next two. All groups declined during 1819 and 1820, and most of them were still low in 1821. The end of the recession was apparent only in furs, which were 12.5 per cent higher in 1821 than in the previous year, and in the industrial raw and semi-finished commodities, which were at the same price in both years. After 1821, however, all commodities rose except wines, in which the average annual prices continued to fall as late as 1824, and the industrial commodities ready for consumption, in which the decline persisted as late as 1830.

Sub-Groups

The sub-groups show some of the general characteristics found in the major groups, but, as might be expected, they also show some significant deviations from the more typical behavior. Only sugar and molasses and spirits behaved like the wines in rising every year between 1808 and 1814. The only group to rise continuously from 1809 to 1814, like the fish, was another domestic group—grains. The advance in the grains from 1812 to 1814 was distinctly unusual, especially as grain products declined mildly but persistently during the same years. Only two other groups rose uninterruptedly to peaks in 1814: fuel and lighting from 1810 to 1814 and fruit from 1811 to 1814. All other groups experienced some break in their expansion, usually in 1811 or 1812.

The widespread character of the rise in 1813 and 1814 is evidenced by the fact that only four groups failed to advance in 1813, namely, minor farm products, grain products, furs, and miscellaneous articles, and only three in 1814, furs, grain products, and textile fabrics. The decline in none of these in 1814 was as much as 2.5 per cent.

In the face of the general decline after the close of the war, there were several outstanding cases of advances to still higher prices. Beverages rose from 1812 to 1815 and meats and meat products and wood increased continuously from 1813 to 1815. Tobacco and dairy products sold at higher average prices each year from 1813 to 1816, and the miscellaneous group advanced from 1814 to 1816. The only groups to rise as late as 1817 were minor farm products, which had an unbroken rise from 1814, grain products, from 1815, and grains, from 1816.

During the years when these groups composed primarily of domestic agricultural commodities rose, other groups began an unbroken decline. Chemicals fell from 1815 to 1820; sugar and molasses from 1815 to 1821; and condiments, fuel and lighting, and ferrous metals from 1815 to 1824. Somewhat shorter declines dominated the prices of wood which, after a rise from 1813 to 1815, fell from 1816 to 1821; furs dropped from 1816 to 1820, and hides and leather from 1817 to 1820.

The check to the decline in 1818 is indicated by the fact that 11 groups advanced that year, while eight others dropped less than 5.5 per cent.

The final contraction in prices from the war and post-war peaks was accelerated in 1819, when only one group rose, and in 1820, when every group showed at least a slight decline. Eight sub-groups ended their recession that year and showed higher prices in 1821. The fall of nine more sub-groups was checked in 1821, seven of the remaining eight continued to decline until 1823 or 1824, and one persisted in its decline as late as 1826. The annual averages thus bear out what was noted in the monthly figures; although one of the major groups, the industrial commodities ready for consumption, continued to decline until 1830, every sub-group had shown a rise by 1826.

Proportion of Commodities Influencing Price Movements

The greatest stability in prices between 1809 and 1821, as measured by the percentage of commodities which sold at the same average price in two years, occurred from 1812 to 1813 and from 1820 to 1821. As many as 12.1 per cent of the commodities sold at the same average price in 1813 as in 1812 and 16.4 per cent were unchanged from 1820 to 1821. That these years showed unusual stability for this period is evidenced by the fact that in every other year less than 6 per cent of the commodities failed to change in price and in all of the other years, except 1809 and 1812, less than 3 per cent sold at the same price for two years.

If commodities which changed less than 2.5 per cent from the previous year are also regarded as stable and are added to the number which did not change at all, the year 1821 still stands out because of its unusual stability. In that year nearly 40 per cent of the commodities were unchanged in price or varied less than 2.5 per cent. The year 1813 is less marked, for, although 24.3 per cent of the commodities were at least comparatively stable that year, in 1819 a fourth of the commodities, and in 1811, 1812, and 1820 between 20 and 24 per cent of the commodities, changed less than 2.5 per cent if at all.

The least stable years were 1814, 1816, and 1817. At the peak of war prices, 10 per cent of the commodities varied less than 2.5 per cent, while in 1816 less than 11 per cent and in 1817 less than 8 per cent were this stable. In the remaining years, 1809, 1810, 1815, and 1818, approximately 14 to 17 per cent of the commodities were subject to but minor changes.

The distribution of the commodities which rose or declined 2.5 per cent or more reflects primarily the upward or downward movement characteristic of any particular year. In 1809, 1813, and 1814 when prices were generally rising, between 62 and 72 per cent of the commodities advanced at least 2.5 per cent. In 1818, when the decline from the war and post-war peaks was checked in many commodities, 38.6 per cent of them rose 2.5 per cent or more, but 46.4 per cent dropped a corresponding amount. In 1810 slightly more than half the commodities advanced appreciably, but in 1811 and 1812 between a third and a half were similarly raised. On the downswing after the war peak there was no year, except 1818, in which more than 30 per cent of the commodities rose as much as 2.5 per cent. The year with the least evidence of rise was 1820, when only

6.4 per cent of the commodities were appreciably higher than in 1819. The percentage of commodities which declined 2.5 per cent or more in any one year was especially high in 1817 and 1820, when between 70 and 80 per cent of the commodities dropped materially. More than 40 per cent suffered a noticeable decline in 1811 and in all of the post-war years from 1815 to 1821. More than 13 per cent fell this much in every year and even at the peak of 1814 approximately 18 per cent of the commodities were at least 2.5 per cent lower than in 1813.

Even when the three small groups of furs, fish, and wines are omitted, the remaining six major groups showed in the period from 1809 to 1821 marked contrasts between some years of high and others of low instability. Imported foods and industrial commodities ready for consumption were the only groups in which there was always at least one commodity that changed less than 2.5 per cent from one year to the next. All of the farm crops in 1813, 1815, and 1817 changed at least 2.5 per cent. This is also true of farm derivatives in 1816 and 1820, of lumber products and naval stores in 1818, and of industrial raw and semi-finished materials in 1814.

During the same period all groups except farm crops and imported foods had at least one year in which as many as half of the commodities changed less than 2.5 per cent. In 1813 nearly 65 per cent of the farm derivatives were within 2.5 per cent of their prices in the previous year. In 1821 between 52 and 56 per cent of both industrial groups of commodities showed a change of less than 2.5 per cent, and in 1812 and 1813 half of the lumber products and naval stores were comparatively stable, but in no year of this period did more than a fourth of the farm crops and imported foods show as much stability.

The difference in the percentage of commodities in the various groups which increased 2.5 per cent or more in any year emphasizes the difference in timing of their peak of prices. In the three years from 1812 to 1814 between 55 and 86 per cent of the imported foods and both industrial groups showed a noticeable rise, but in the post-war years from 1815 to 1821 never as much as 30 per cent of these groups rose appreciably except in 1818, when between 33.3 and 47.6 per cent rose at least 2.5 per cent. In contrast, between 50 and 75 per cent of the lumber products and naval stores rose appreciably in each of the years from 1813 to 1815, while a similar percentage of the farm crops advanced in each year from 1813 to 1817, and between 50 and 65 per cent of farm derivatives from 1814 to 1817. In the remaining years of this period no more than a quarter of the commodities in these domestic groups rose substantially except in the group of lumber products and naval stores in 1818, when nearly 60 per cent advanced noticeably.

The downward movement in the post-war period is emphasized by the fact that among the three groups influenced largely by imported commodities[48] between 48 and 90 per cent of the commodities declined each year from 1815 to 1820 except in 1818, when between 37 and 43 per cent fell substantially. The most widespread drop in these groups occurred in 1817 when 85 to 90 per cent of the series in each group fell. Not until after 1817 did more than half of the farm crops and farm derivatives decline appreciably, but from 1818 to 1821 between 64 and 100 per cent of the series in these groups declined at least 2.5 per cent.

The lumber products and naval stores were, from 1816 to 1818, more like the imported than the domestic commodities. Between 75 and 92 per cent of the group decreased at least 2.5 per cent in 1816 and 1817, but less than 42 per cent fell that much in 1818. From 1819 to 1821 they declined in somewhat the same proportion as other domestic commodities.

The difference in 1821 between the three groups most affected by imported commodities and the three composed almost entirely of commodities of domestic origin is brought out clearly by the relative proportion of the various groups which declined that year. Only between 20 and 43 per cent of the commodities in the groups dominated by articles of foreign origin declined noticeably while among the domestic groups between 64 and 83 per cent of the commodities were affected.

The groups differed both in the extent of stability and the times at which a substantial portion of the commodities underwent minor, if any, changes. Throughout the period from 1809 to 1821 never as many as 10 per cent of the farm crops and imported foods sold at the

[48] Imported foods, industrial raw and semi-finished products, and industrial commodities ready for consumption.

same price in two consecutive years. This much stability did appear in the other groups at various times: in 1809 in the industrial raw and semi-finished materials, in 1812 in the farm derivatives, in 1813 in the farm derivatives, lumber products, and industrial raw and semi-finished materials, in 1814 in lumber products, and in 1821 in both industrial groups.

When the series which changed less than 2.5 per cent from one year to another are added to those with no change in price, other years also show marked stability. The only case when 10 per cent of the series were unchanged but when less than 25 per cent varied mildly if at all was in the industrial raw and semi-finished articles in 1813. In many cases, however, 25 per cent or more of the series differed in price less than 2.5 per cent from the previous year, although fewer than 10 per cent had been unchanged: farm crops in 1809 and 1812, farm derivatives in 1811 and 1815, lumber products and naval stores in 1810-1812 and 1819, industrial raw and semi-finished materials in 1819 and 1820, and industrial commodities ready for consumption in 1811, 1812, and 1818-1820. Generally speaking, the farm crops were most stable before 1813, lumber products before 1815, farm derivatives before 1816, industrial materials ready for consumption after 1817, and industrial raw and semi-finished materials after 1818. In no year from 1809 to 1821 did as many as 10 per cent of the imported foods remain unchanged from the previous year, nor did 25 per cent ever vary less than 2.5 per cent.

Deviations of Annual Group Indices from General Average

Despite the extreme fluctuations in prices during this period, five groups had only minor variations away from the general average. The industrial commodities ready for consumption were never more than 8.2 per cent above the general average nor more than 4.5 per cent below it, the average deviation being 3.5 per cent. The only years in which the industrial commodities ready for consumption were relatively below the total index were from 1816 to 1818 inclusive. Wines, lumber products and naval stores, imported foods, and industrial raw and semi-finished materials deviated on the average from the total index by 5.5 to 7.7 per cent. Of these, wines fluctuated closest to the general curve, being below it in 1809 and 1810, above it from

1811 to 1814, below it from 1815 to 1818, and above it from 1819 to 1821. Imported foods were always higher than the general average except in 1810 and 1811, and the lumber products and naval stores were always below except in 1819 and 1820, mainly because of the low prices of lumber during most of the period. The group of industrial raw and semi-finished materials exceeded the average from 1809 to 1815, but dropped below from 1816 to 1821. The greatest deviations of the index of these industrial products occurred from 1809 to 1814, when it was always at least 8 per cent above the general average, and from 1817 to 1819, when it was more than 8 per cent below.

The other four groups deviated more widely from the general index. Usually farm derivatives were at least 10 per cent away from the average of all commodities. The index of farm derivatives was lower than the composite index except in 1811 and from 1816 to 1819, the greatest deviations, of more than 13 per cent, being from 1816 to 1818. During 1813 and 1814, when it failed to rise in proportion to most groups, it was 17 per cent or more below the composite index. Farm crops fluctuated from 1809 to 1815 around a lower level than the average and from 1816 to 1820 at a higher one. In 1809 and from 1812 to 1815 farm crops were 11 to 22 per cent cheaper relatively than most commodities, while from 1816 to 1819 they were 14 to 38 per cent dearer. Fish held above the general average except in 1821. The greatest deviations were in 1815, 1816, and 1818 when this group was more than 25 per cent higher than the composite index. In all of the years from 1811 to 1819 inclusive, except 1813, fish exceeded the total by more than 15 per cent. From 1809 to 1821 furs averaged nearly 35 per cent below the general index.

CHAPTER IX

PRICE MOVEMENTS FROM 1821 TO 1843

Monthly Price Movements

The period from 1821 to 1843 differs from the other major periods in that the price movements were relatively free from the direct effect of war. Nevertheless, the period is not one in which a uniform price behavior prevailed. From 1821 to 1830 the general curve of prices showed a persistent underlying decline from the peaks established during and immediately after the War of 1812. Although the movements reverted to their cyclical appearance, the three oscillations between 1821 and 1830 showed relatively short periods of expansion in which prices did not rise as high as at the previous peak, followed by much longer periods of recession in which prices dropped lower than in the previous decline.

From 1830 to 1843, in contrast, prices displayed a long underlying swing which dominated three cycles. Most commodities reached their major peaks in 1836 or the early months of 1837, but others, although relatively high in those years, recovered quickly from the abrupt decline in 1837 and 1838 and reached in 1839 prices higher than those of 1837. The decline after 1839 generally continued with but minor interruptions, especially in 1841, until in 1843 the general index was slightly lower than at any other time in the four periods.

Imported and Domestic Commodities, 1821-1830

These characteristics of the general movements in prices from 1821 to 1843 are emphasized in the index of domestic commodities, while the index of imported commodities differs substantially in several respects.

From 1821 to 1830, when it might be said that prices were still receding from the peaks of the war and post-war period, both the general and domestic indices completed three cycles, but the last one, which had a peak in 1828, did not affect noticeably the index of imported commodities.

In the first cycles of this period the index of imported commodities reached its turning points in advance of that of domestic commodities. The peak in the spring of 1822 in the imported series was just one month ahead of the domestic. The recession in the imported group was completed in May and June 1824 while the domestic index continued to fall until September.

The rise in the next cycle was again short, although substantial. As early as February 1825 Nicholas Biddle, as president of the Second Bank of the United States, was using some of its resources to support the rate of exchange on London. He urged the cashier of the branch office in Savannah to "proceed to purchase largely undoubted bills of exchange on London." Biddle explained in detail the reasons for this move: "The late rise in Europe in the price of the great staple of the South [cotton], together with the amount of exchange which will be furnished by the governments of Mexico and Colombia must contribute to depress exchange below its present rate."[1] The situation to which Biddle referred with respect to cotton was its rapid increase in price in Liverpool after March 1824 and the later speculation in the United States as well as in Great Britain when it was felt "that cotton production had reached its limit while demand was rapidly increasing and European stocks were very low."[2] Another evidence that part of the recession which started in 1825 arose largely from conditions outside the United States is that the peak of prices in the commodities of foreign origin occurred in May 1825, five months earlier than in the domestic group.

Biddle tried to place the bank in a position where it could meet any emergency that might arise. As early as April he outlined his plans in a letter to the Boston branch: "Having parted with much of our own specie for the China trade, we are desirous of concentrating our resources at some point where they may be disposable so as to protect immediately any quarter which may be exposed. We should prefer, therefore, that this special deposit should be at New York

[1] February 8, 1825, Nicholas Biddle to James Hunter, Savannah.

[2] Gray, Lewis C., *History of Agriculture in the Southern United States to 1860*, Vol. II, p. 698.

rather than at Boston. . . . If you and Mr. Frothingham think that, having passed the crisis of the first instant, the money is not necessary for the protection of your office, you will have the goodness to send it to the office at New York."[3]

Throughout the recession Biddle attempted to avoid calling loans unnecessarily. In response to the estimates made by the Boston banks as to their probable demand for specie on October 1, he wrote in August, "Our great object is to pass that period if possible without any diminution of our discounts. . . . We shall exert ourselves to give you such funds as we can spare, but having more than three millions two hundred thousand dollars to pay here we may not be able to remit largely."[4] In dealing with the situation in the fall of 1825 one historian of the Second Bank of the United States comments, "Unfortunately the bank at this moment was compelled to act with extreme circumspection, because it had to expend on the 1st of October, $7,000,000 of the public funds in redemption of the national debt."[5]

As the recession continued, Biddle was forced to warn the Savannah branch against expanding its demands on the other branches: "In the precarious state of private credit at this time, owing to the failures which have already occurred and are still expected, it is not I think desirable for your office to increase the responsibilities of either banks or individuals as would be the case if you checked on the North. In the meantime the Bank and the northern offices are at the present moment making very heavy disbursements on account of the government which calls for all the funds they can command."[6]

Near the close of the year Biddle summarized the factors which had handicapped the bank: "The state of affairs in this quarter has for some time past been extremely critical. In addition to other causes with which you are perfectly acquainted, there has been within the last two or three weeks a heavy demand for specie for Canada and elsewhere, which has produced among the state banks the natural consequences, alarm and curtailment of business. To this succeeded more recently a very considerable call for specie amounting to about

[3] April 11, 1825, Nicholas Biddle to Gardner Greene, Boston.
[4] August 6, 1825, Nicholas Biddle to Samuel Frothingham, Boston.
[5] Catterall, R. C. H., *Second Bank of the United States*, p. 107.
[6] October 7, 1825, Nicholas Biddle to William P. Hunter, Savannah.

$400,000 to pay the instalment of the Louisiana Bank . . . on the 1st of January which threatened seriously to affect the banks of Philadelphia and New York after the late exhausting demand which they have undergone."[7]

The decline in the prices of imported commodities was very rapid until the summer of 1826, when the rate of fall was noticeably lessened. During 1827 and 1828 these prices were relatively firm, but the highest price in 1828 was only 1.0 per cent above the lowest price in 1826. After the opening of 1829 prices of imported goods again declined rapidly until in July 1830 they were 18.3 per cent below the peak of 1825.

It was in this latter part of the twenties that the domestic group took a distinct swing not apparent in the prices of imported commodities. By July 1828 the domestic group was 11.3 per cent lower than at its peak in 1825, a drop which corresponds with the decline of 13.2 per cent in the imported group from its highest price in 1825 to its lowest in 1828. For the domestic group, however, most of this decline had come within two short periods, from January to May 1826 and from April to August 1827. As a result its sharp rally of 8.0 per cent between July and November 1828 did not raise the index much above the lowest point of 1826. In spite of this extra swing, the domestic group first reached its low in May 1830, two months before the imported commodities ended their decline. The domestic group dipped again to this same low level in July 1830.

Major Groups, 1821-1830

The rise which began in the spring and summer of 1821 in most of the nine major groups had got under way in 1819 in furs and in 1820 in the industrial raw and semi-finished products. Lumber products and naval stores, which turned up after April 1821, were followed during the next five months by farm derivatives, farm crops, fish, and imported foods in rapid succession. Only the wines and the industrial commodities ready for consumption failed to show a noticeable rise. The peaks were soon reached in the closing months of 1821 and the first few months of 1822. In November 1821 both fish and furs reached their peaks. The furs held this high level as late as

[7] November 26, 1825, Nicholas Biddle to John A. Fort, New Orleans.

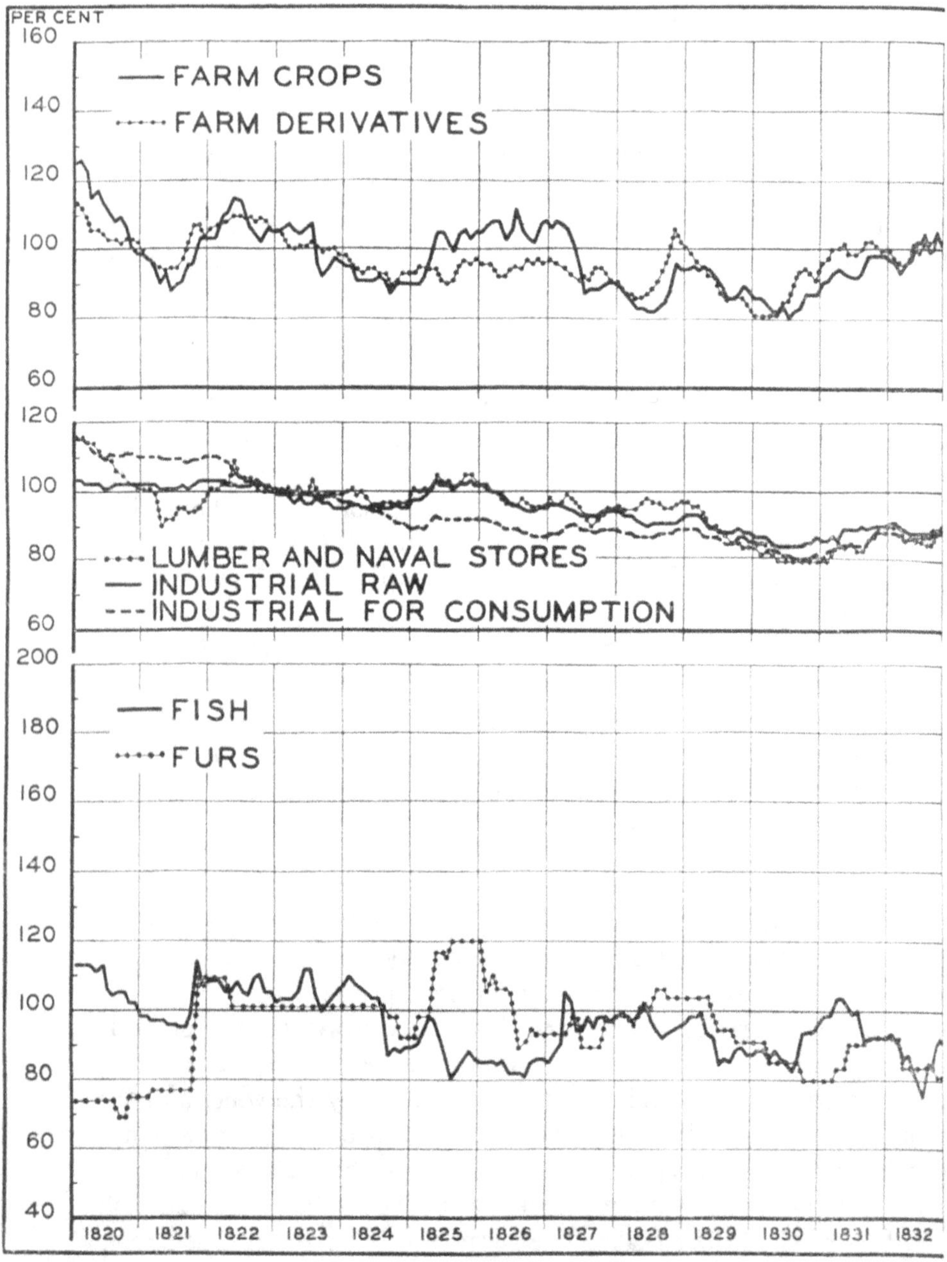

CHART XI—GEOMETRIC INDICES OF AVERAGE MONTHLY WHOLESAL

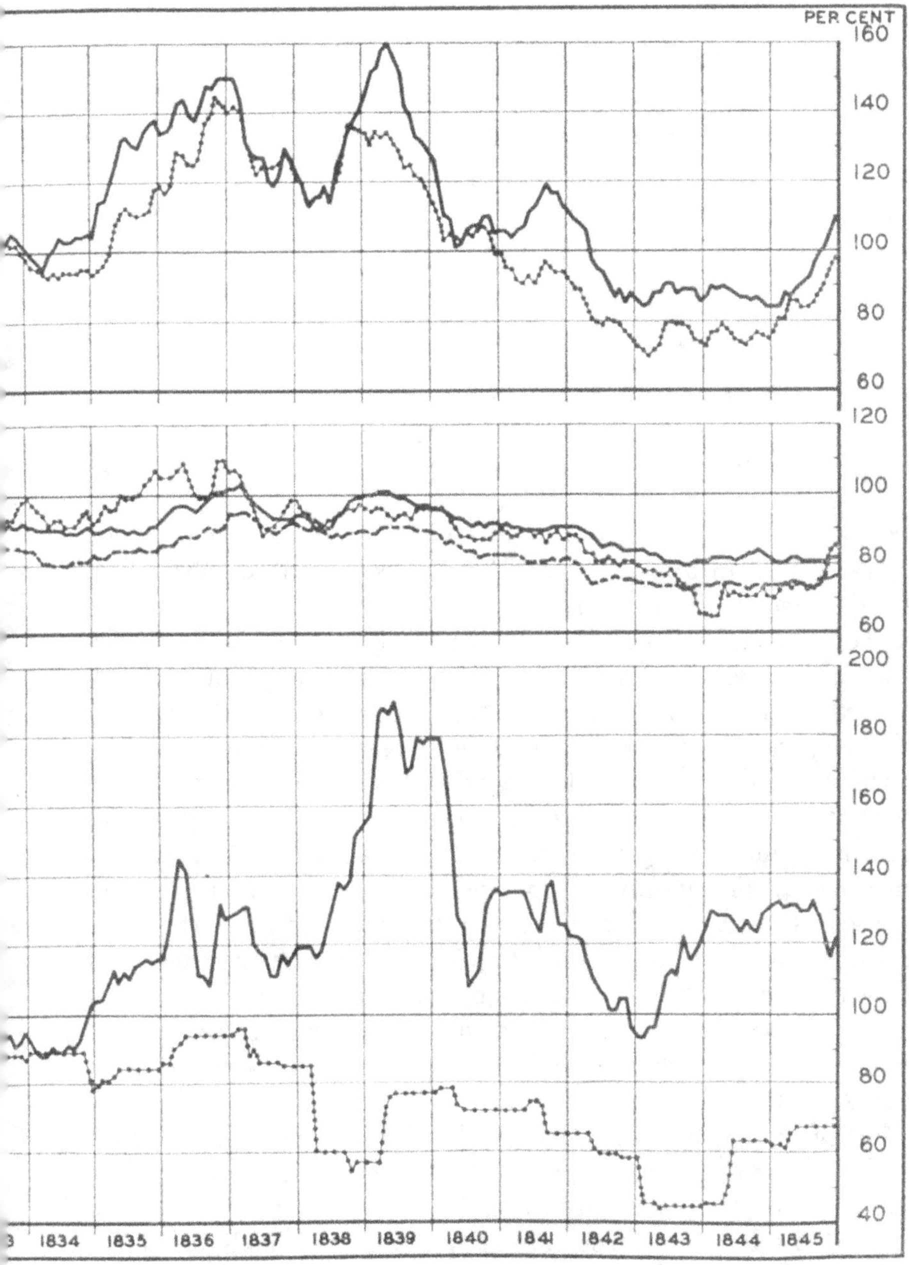

s in Philadelphia by Major Groups, 1820-1845
ge, 1821-1825)

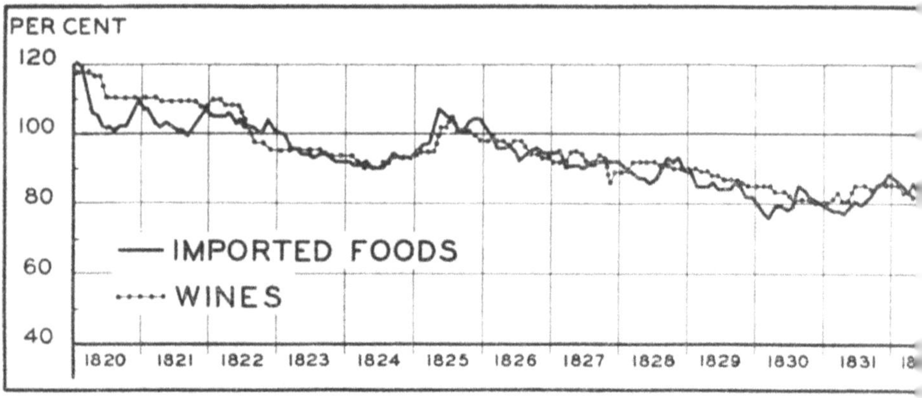

CHART XI—GEOMETRIC INDICES OF AVERAGE MONTHLY WHOLE
(Base—Mo

April 1822 and fish fluctuated slightly below its peak for more than two years. The third group to end its rise was imported foods. The industrial raw and semi-finished products rose only 2.7 per cent over a period of 20 months and turned down after February 1822. Farm crops, farm derivatives, and lumber products and naval stores, which advanced until May or June 1822, were the last to turn down.

The beginning of the rise to a peak in 1825 was concentrated in the summer and fall of 1824. Only the industrial commodities ready for consumption, which declined until 1830, failed to share this rise, which in all the other groups occurred within four months of September 1824. The industrial raw and semi-finished materials, the first group to end its recession, turned upward after May 1824. Its rise was followed within a month by wines and lumber products and naval stores and within two months by imported foods. Farm crops, farm derivatives, and fish turned upward together after September. Furs continued to decline until November and turned upward after January 1825.

Most of the groups were declining by the fall of 1825. The fish, one of the last to begin to rise, had a shorter period of expansion than any other group. It definitely turned down after April 1825. The industrial raw and semi-finished materials, imported foods, and lumber products and naval stores began to recede the following month.

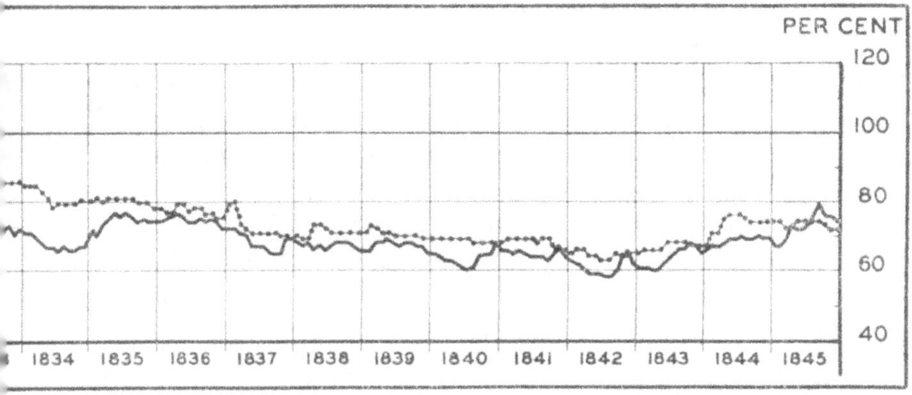

ES IN PHILADELPHIA BY MAJOR GROUPS, 1820-1845, *Concluded*
age, 1821-1825)

Wines started to fall in price after July and furs after September. Farm crops and derivatives were again the last groups to recede. Not until they had risen 28.5 per cent between September 1824 and July 1826 did the farm crops start their recession, which was mild until after the spring of 1827. Farm derivatives, having the longest and one of the mildest increases of this period, did not turn downward until after January 1827.

After their peaks in 1825, imported foods and industrial raw and semi-finished products, like the industrial commodities ready for consumption, continued to fall until 1830. The other groups recovered, rising to peaks generally in the latter part of 1828.

Prices of furs started to rise slightly after August 1826, but made no sustained advance until the closing months of 1827. In contrast, fish, which also turned up in 1826, rose rapidly to a peak in April 1827 and sustained a high level for two years. No other group ended its recession from the high prices in 1825 until lumber products and naval stores began to rise after August 1827 and wines after November. Farm derivatives and farm crops, the last to turn down, did not show any recovery until after April and July 1828.

The final contraction which completed the general decline underlying price movements from 1821 to 1830 started in the wines after March 1828. The imported foods and both industrial groups had been falling while other groups had been rising in 1828 and fish had reached a peak in April 1827, 14 months before the general curve had completed its contraction from the peak of 1825. Lumber products and naval stores started, after June 1828, a mild decline which became more precipitous after the following spring. Furs started their final decline of the twenties after September 1828, while farm crops and farm derivatives started theirs after November 1828.

In the three recessions from peaks in 1822, 1825, and 1828, farm crops and derivatives were the last to turn down. These groups, however, were more prompt in contributing to recovery, especially in 1821 and 1824. Only in the advance of 1828 were they the last groups to start to rise.

Sub-Groups, 1821-1830

The 24 sub-groups, excluding the miscellaneous, show the cycles in prices between 1821 and 1830 in greater detail. The impetus to the recovery in 1821 came in a series of waves. The first appeared in furs after March 1819 and chemicals after December. Between April and August 1820 six other groups started to advance. Among these were many imported commodities—dyes, beverages, hides, and fruit—and also some domestic commodities such as leather and dairy products. In 1821 the increases were concentrated in April and May, when grain products, grains, and wood started up, in August and September, when sugar and molasses and fish started their advance, and in November and December, which marked the beginning of recovery in building materials other than wood, minor farm products, and nonferrous metals. None of the remaining groups showed any response to the swing in prices from 1821 to 1824.

The advances in the 16 groups which were affected by this cycle were generally completed in the closing months of 1821 or in 1822. Only wood, minor farm products, and dyes failed to turn down before the end of 1822.

The declines from these peaks were generally longer than the preceding increases. The chief exceptions were the last five groups to start their recession. Only one group which had a peak before October 1822 declined for a shorter period than it had risen. This exception was furs, which started to rise in the spring of 1819.

The most significant fact about the recession, which generally persisted until the latter part of 1824, is that eight groups did not decline to as low a point in that depression as they had fallen to in the previous one. The groups are grains, minor farm products, grain products, chemicals, dyes, wood, furs, and hides and leather. The decline in the general index, in both imported and exported commodities, and in most of the major groups to a lower level in 1824 than in 1821 was caused by the other 16 sub-groups, which either did not rise in 1821 and 1822 or which dropped lower after their rise than they had been before.

The rise to the second peak of prices between 1821 and 1830 started between April and August 1823 in meats and meat products and textile fibers, which had not been affected by the previous rise, and in chemicals and fruit, which had been among the first to rise in the previous swing. Nearly a year elapsed before any other group began to advance, but after June 1824 several groups started to rise. By April 1825 all of the others had turned upwards except grain products, which delayed until after July 1825, and textile fabrics, in which the rise after November 1826 appears unrelated to this cycle.

The general downward pull in prices is evidenced by the fact that only seven groups climbed relatively higher around 1825 than they had around 1822. Four of these sub-groups, minor farm products, dyes, furs, and hides and leather, had shown a resistance to the declining trend when their recessions in 1824 were checked above the lows of 1821. Fruit, sugar and molasses, and non-ferrous metals, after dropping lower in 1824 than in 1821, exceeded around 1825 the peaks which they had established around 1822.

On the upswing, meats and meat products continued to be among the leaders and after its peak of November 1824 was the first subgroup to turn down. Fourteen other groups started their recessions after rising to peaks between March and October 1825. Hides and leather did not turn down until after January 1826. Many domestic agricultural commodities, especially grains, minor farm crops, grain products, and dairy products, did not begin to recede until, or even after, the latter part of 1826. Three other domestic groups—textile fibers, fuel and lighting, and wood—attained peaks in the early months of 1827 about midway between the peaks of May 1825 and

November 1828 in the general curve. The most unusual movement of prices was that in spirits which, taking its rise belatedly after January 1825, did not recede until after August 1828. Several other groups also showed peaks around April and May 1827 which did not belong clearly to the general peak of either 1825 or 1828. The sub-groups which failed to bring higher prices in 1828 or 1829 than in the spring of 1827 include hides and leather, fish, condiments, and dyes, in addition to the textile fibers, wood, and fuel and lighting previously noted. Wines differed from all other sub-groups in declining after a peak in March 1828, three months before the total curve reached its low.

The peak of November 1828 on the general curve is primarily related to somewhat similar peaks in spirits, meats and meat products, furs, fruit, grains, and grain products, reached between August and November 1828, and to those in chemicals, building materials other than wood, minor farm crops, and dairy products attained between February and April 1829. Tobacco varied considerably from other groups in that its decline from October 1825 to March 1829 was followed by a year in which prices rose rapidly to a peak in March 1830—its closest approach to the 1828 peak in the general curve.

The variations from the general peak of 1828 are not merely in the scattered periods at which the different sub-groups reached peaks at all comparable to the general one, but also in the fact that five important sub-groups failed to respond. After November 1826 textile fabrics tended persistently upward and did not turn definitely downward until after March 1832. In contrast, the decline in beverages, sugar and molasses, ferrous metals, and non-ferrous metals from peaks in July or October 1825 was not checked until the closing months of 1830 or even late in 1831.

The definite character of the low on the general curve in July 1830 is evidenced by the fact that all but two of the groups completed their contractions within 13 months of that date. One of the exceptions, tobacco, continued to decline until February 1832 from its peak in March 1830, while the other exception, textile fabrics, continued its persistent advance.

The extent of the changes in the annual indices of the sub-groups may be used to isolate the commodities which were most extremely influenced in particular years. Grains, grain products, and dairy products rose so steeply from 1821 to 1822 that their annual indices increased from 39 to 45 per cent. At the same time furs rose slightly more than 25 per cent and wood, dyes, and fruit between 10 and 16 per cent.

The advances of 1825 and 1828 differed especially from that of 1822 in that in these later cycles no group rose as much as three important agricultural sub-groups had in 1822. In 1825 textile fibers advanced nearly 20 per cent, non-ferrous metals less than 16 per cent, while condiments, fruit, furs, and sugar and molasses rose between 10 and 14 per cent. The major part of the rise of domestic agricultural produce was delayed until the next year, when grains after advancing slightly in 1825, rose nearly 26 per cent. Dairy products and minor farm crops also made their major advance of from 18 to 21 per cent, and grain products theirs of 12 per cent, in that year. Although the general peak of 1825 failed to attain as substantial increases as that of 1822 and although it was spread over two years among all of the groups, fruit, furs, grains, grain products, and dairy products, which had risen more than any other groups in 1822, were among the 10 with the largest advances in 1825 and 1826.

The peak of 1828, like that of 1825, was not confined to one year. The expansion was in general less extreme than in 1825 and affected fewer sub-groups. The most significant fact is that fruit, which advanced 17 per cent in 1828, and grains and grain products, which increased between 10 and 12 per cent in 1829, had also been both in 1822 and 1825-26 among the groups with the greatest rise.

Imported and Domestic Commodities, 1830-1843

The year 1830 marks the beginning of a distinct change in the trend underlying the movements of prices of domestic commodities. From 1815 to 1830 there was an unmistakable downward trend which affected most of the prices in this group. From 1830 to 1837, however, and in some even until 1839, there was an equally unmistakable upward movement in prices. The imported commodities, in contrast, continued to reflect the persistence of at least a slight downward trend as late as 1842.

The effect of the difference in trend after 1830 is apparent as early as the crest of the cycle from 1830 to 1834. The peak of December 1831 in the prices of imported products was only 5.9 per cent above the low of the previous year. The domestic index, in contrast, continued to advance for nearly two years more and by November 1833 was approximately at the level of its peak in 1828 or 16.4 per cent above its low of 1830. Even after its short contraction from November 1833 to May 1834 it was still 9.9 per cent higher than in July 1830.

The decline in the prices of imported articles long before any recession in the prices of domestic goods, which resulted in the separation of the two indices, had a deleterious effect on Philadelphia merchants. As early as September 1832 one of them reported that there had been "about 70 failures in this city since January."[8] The index of foreign prices not only started its decline earlier than the domestic but continued to recede until September and October 1834, falling 13.5 per cent in nearly three years. At the end of this decline the foreign index was 8.4 per cent less than in July 1830.

The short run-down in the prices of domestic goods between November 1833 and May 1834, and an acceleration in the decline of prices of imported goods about the same time, appear to be related to uncertainty as to the future of the Bank of the United States and to the subsequent removal of the government deposits. In writing to several English houses, Warder commented on the banking policies, especially as they affected Philadelphia, and speculated as to their effect on business. Early in January 1834 he wrote: "For the continuation of the internal improvements 2 or 3 million of dollars will have to be provided next year, and if the money affairs of this country remain as they now are it will be impossible to procure the money at home. We think the Bank of the United States have their affairs in as narrow a compass as is necessary for their safety, and, as soon as Congress determines the courses to be pursued in relation to that Institution, they will extend their business. Of course the state banks will do the same and render money much more abundant. At this time the state banks are generally indebted to the United States Bank

[8] September 13, 1832, Wilson and Potts, Philadelphia, to G. M. Coates, Philadelphia, in Coates Letter Book.

as largely as they consider safe. In this city the aggregate balance is half a million of dollars. The banks thus far have lost very little by failures and the dividends now making are at the usual rates."[9]

From the correspondence of Nicholas Biddle one can see the steps he took when "the present situation of the Bank and the country and the measures of hostility to the institution which are understood to be in contemplation" rendered "it expedient to provide for its entire safety against all contingencies." Accordingly, he started to reduce the discounts of the bank gradually and fix the rates of exchange between New York and the branch offices of Pittsburgh, Lexington, Louisville, Cincinnati, St. Louis, Nashville, and Natchez at 2½ per cent, between New York and Mobile and New Orleans at 2 per cent and between New York and any other branch south of Washington at 1 per cent.[10]

Before the close of the month, Warder reported that the first effects of the removal of the government deposits from the Bank of the United States "caused much embarrassment in the money affairs of this country."[11] Within a few days he wrote in more detail to a firm of London bankers and contrasted the situation in Philadelphia and New York: "The arbitrary removal of the Government deposits from the Bank of the United States has caused a want of confidence and consequent scarcity of money. . . . In this city we have had few failures of persons in good credit. In New York business is carried to a much larger amount and they have had many heavy failures. The exchange [on] London is now lower than for many years owing to the deranged state of money affairs."[12]

The change in status of the Second Bank of the United States from a central to merely a large bank provoked Biddle to summarize its contribution to the country as a whole and to indicate the course which it was prepared to follow in the future. "Up to the 1st of October 1833, the Bank of the United States was directly responsible for the condition of the currency and of all the great interests dependent on

[9] January 7, 1834, Warder and Brothers to Comerford Son and Girdler, London.

[10] January 21, 1834, Nicholas Biddle to Isaac Laurence, Presidents Office, Discount and Deposit, New York.

[11] January 30, 1834, Warder and Brothers to William Eliot, Dorsetshire.

[12] February 4, 1834, Warder and Brothers to Smith, Payne, and Smith, London.

it. After the labor of many years and at great expense, it had succeeded in giving a general uniformity of value to the circulating medium, in reducing to their lowest charge the internal exchanges, in preventing sudden fluctuation in those with foreign nations, and thus securing to the country a currency, uniting in a higher degree than probably existed elsewhere the advantages of safety and flexibility. In the same spirit, whenever any event threatened to disorder that currency, the Bank felt bound to employ all its resources to avert or to mitigate every inconvenience to the community. It was for this that it interposed in the disastrous crisis of 1825—for this that it expanded its business in 1831, until the country could recover from the overexcitements of its excessive importations—for this that in 1832 it defrayed out of its own means the expense of deferring the payment of the public debt, to protect the community from being disturbed by the sudden withdrawal of it from the commercial service—for this that in the same year it again, at its own expense, postponed the claims of foreigners for the public debt, lest their demands might add to the evils of a pestilence which was deranging the business of the country. These were the natural duties of its position.

"That position is now changed. On the 1st of October 1833 all its responsibilities for the currency ceased. The public revenue passed into other hands, and with it departed from the institution all guardianship of the circulating medium and all control over the pecuniary concerns of the country. The Bank of the United States as a component part of the financial system established by Congress, in which the public revenue was to be the support of the public currency, exists no longer. Henceforward the Bank is the property of the stockholders, to be administered for their interest. . . .

"They [the Bank directors] cannot, however, be insensible to the extraordinary position in which the country is placed. . . . What the Bank hopes to do—and will try to do—is this: In the general confusion into which the affairs of the country are hastening, it may be of great importance to have some strong point, by rallying to which the public fortunes can be retrieved. That point may be the Bank of the United States. It is accordingly preparing itself for that crisis. It has now nearly eleven millions of dollars in its vaults. It has sent to Europe for large additional amounts of specie, and it is gradually reducing its loans and its issues so as to place its credit beyond the reach of all contingencies.'"[13]

Before the close of February, Warder saw some signs of recovery. In writing to a New York correspondent, he reported: "Our money market is evidently easier and confidence increased which is probably partly owing to a larger western business having set in than was generally anticipated which brings a large amount of funds to our city. There has been no failure of any consequence for a week, and from the beginning of our difficulties not a single wholesale dry goods house and only two hardware houses have failed that we have heard of."[14] By August 1834 when prices of domestic articles had started upward and the long recession in the prices of imported articles had been practically completed, Warder commented, "Business has improved, but it is not so brisk as it was before the derangement in our currency."[15]

The upward movement in prices of goods produced in the United States continued at an accelerated rate from 1834 to 1837 with but slight interruption. By February 1837 this index, 36.8 per cent higher than in May 1834, was at the highest point reached between 1819 and the Civil War.

The corresponding rise in the prices of imported articles was only 8.3 per cent between October 1834 and February 1837 and the bulk of this increase had occurred by May 1835. The slightness of this rise is indicated by the fact that even at the peak of February 1837 the index of imported commodities was below what it had been in the low of 1830.

During these years of expanding prices the comments of merchants reveal several particular factors which contributed to the rise. During most of 1835 Warder was disturbed by the probability of a war with France.[16] At one time it even appeared that a non-intercourse law or some other form of economic pressure might be adopted by Congress.[17] Not until the special message of the President to Con-

[13] February 22, 1834, Nicholas Biddle to John A. Stevens, Chairman of the Committee of Correspondence of the Union Committee of New York.

[14] February 21, 1834, Warder and Brothers to Masters and Markoe, New York.

[15] August 6, 1834, Warder and Brothers to Nicholas Naftel, Guernsey Island.

[16] February 19, 1835, Warder and Brothers to Comerford Son and Girdler, London.

[17] February 19, 1835, Warder and Brothers to F. B. Swaby, Espytown, Pennsylvania.

gress early in 1836, which was "more specific than was anticipated," was Warder able to say, "There is little danger of war with France."[18]

In addition, the rising prices in 1835 precipitated some labor disturbances. In the summer of that year it was noted, "The general strike for higher wages or compensation extended to the boatmen on the Schuylkill which much impeded the navigation for the first three weeks of last month."[19]

The effects of the Specie Circular were minimized by "the large imports of specie" which made money "rather more abundant," but, nevertheless, Warder expected that "the demands from the West will be very considerable as our government have passed an order to prevent anything but gold and silver being received in payment for lands which will lock up a large amount of the precious metals."[20]

Philadelphians appeared serenely confident that the expansion would continue. Even when it was said in August 1836 that "money remains very scarce and by last accounts from England it was in great demand there," the worst that was expected was that it probably would not become "abundant in this country for some months."[21]

By November the pressure was more apparent. "Money is exceedingly scarce," Warder wrote, "but we have had no failures of any consequence. How long this will be the case should there be no relief it is impossible to foresee."[22]

With the news in March 1837 of several failures at New Orleans[23] prices dropped. Early in May the financial situation was acute. "There appears to be an entire want of confidence in our banks as well as individuals," Warder explained. "They now refuse to receive on deposit checks on other banks in this city . . . which indicates that their silver is very low. As to gold, I believe they have little or none."[24] By the middle of May when the banks suspended specie payments,

[18] January 30, 1836, Warder and Brothers to Comerford Son and Girdler, London.
[19] August 5, 1835, Warder and Brothers to Comerford Son and Girdler, London.
[20] August 6, 1836, Warder and Brothers to Smith, Payne, and Smith, London.
[21] August 29, 1836, Warder and Brothers to Joseph Naftel, Palmyra, New York.
[22] November 14, 1836, Warder and Brothers to Highfield and Birch, Liverpool.
[23] March 17, 1837, *Commercial List and Philadelphia Price Current.*
[24] May 6, 1837, Warder and Brothers to Comerford Son and Girdler, London.

the index of domestic commodities had fallen 11.5 per cent. Prices continued to decline, but at a slower rate, and in August and September 1837 the index of domestic articles was 16.6 per cent below its peak. By this time confidence had been somewhat restored. The *Commercial List* reported, on September 16: "We learn that the general condition of the sixteen banks in this city and the Liberties[25] is sound and favorable compared with their situation on the 11th of May. Their stock of specie has increased, their circulation and the amount of discounts have decreased more than two millions of dollars, while their deposits remain about the same as at that period."[26]

The prices of imported commodities also dropped. In October they were 7.2 per cent lower than in February. This decline, although slight in comparison with the decline in the prices of domestic products, lowered the index of foreign commodities to approximately its depressed levels of 1834, while the domestic commodities in 1837 held approximately 14 per cent above their lowest prices in 1834.

The prices of domestic articles rallied in October and November 1837, resumed their decline in December, and by May 1838 were 19.8 per cent below their peak of the previous year. A similar movement occurred in the prices of imported commodities, which tended to lag a month or two behind those of domestic origin. In June and July 1838 they were a trifle lower than in the previous October.

The upturn in prices of domestic articles after May had been foreshadowed by a comment in the *Commercial List* on April 28, 1838 that "business continues quite active, and confidence, the great mainspring of commercial enterprise, is gradually reviving." The New York banks had resumed specie payment and the editor called upon the Philadelphia banks to "without delay commence paying out specie for all amounts under one dollar." He continued, "This would at once relieve the community from a host of Loan Office tickets, many of them nearly illegible, and would bring into circulation hundreds of thousands of dollars in specie, which had been carefully hoarded up since May last."

The recovery in June was nearly cancelled by a revival of uncer-

[25] Then a separate section, now part of the city proper.

[26] September 16, 1837, *Commercial List and Philadelphia Price Current.*

tainties. "The new Treasury Circular and the apprehension felt by the business community of the passage of the Sub-Treasury Law by Congress, added to the unusually warm weather, have considerably checked and paralyzed business operations. Buyers hold back, waiting for the decision of Congress. Capitalists refuse to lend their money or make investments until the decision of Congress is known as regards the Sub-Treasury bill. The banks have commenced curtailing, and the idea of an immediate resumption of specie payments is scarcely named. In short, all classes of the community here are anxiously looking to Washington to learn the fate of the Sub-Treasury bill."[27] With the defeat of the Sub-Treasury bill and with the expectation that banks in Philadelphia would resume specie payment on the first of August, prices advanced.

Near the middle of August the *Commercial List* reported, "Business is becoming more active and confidence is daily becoming more firmly re-established."[28] Prices of domestic products continued steadily upward until in April and May they were 15.8 per cent above the bottom of the previous year, but still 7.1 per cent below the peak of February 1837.

Prices of foreign goods recovered even more in that, although they had only risen 7.1 per cent, by March 1839 they were within 0.7 per cent of their 1837 peak. At the crest of prices the editor of the *Commercial List* commented, "Money is more abundant, and the general aspect of affairs is bright and cheering."[29]

Instead of advancing further, prices contracted sharply; before the end of the year the index of domestic commodities had fallen 7.4 per cent. Near the close of November it was reported that "most of the dealers and manufacturers decline operating to any extent at present, owing to the embarrassed situation of our monetary affairs. A considerable number of hands have recently been discharged from the various factories in the city and suburbs, and we regret to learn that a further reduction is to take place."[30] Less than a month later Philadelphians were "startled by the announcement" that a bank official

[27] June 16, 1838, *Commercial List and Philadelphia Price Current.*
[28] August 18, 1838, *Commercial List and Philadelphia Price Current.*
[29] May 4, 1839, *Commercial List and Philadelphia Price Current.*
[30] November 22, 1839, *Commercial List and Philadelphia Price Current.*

had so involved the Schuylkill Bank that it was forced to close. Since this was the first failure of a bank in Philadelphia, the confidence of the community was severely shaken.[31]

The rapid decline in prices continued until in June 1840 the index of domestic commodities was 18.0 per cent below the peak of 1839. The index of imported commodities fell 8.2 per cent in the same period. The checking of the decline in the summer of 1840 followed soon after the Legislature of Pennsylvania had set January 15, 1841 as the date when specie payments should be resumed by the banks upon penalty of losing their charters. In the fall of 1840 prices even advanced slightly. Specie payments were resumed in January 1841, but early in February the United States Bank again suspended, followed within 24 hours by the other banks.

The decline in prices in 1841 lowered domestic commodities only slightly under the low of 1840 while imported commodities even held slightly above the bottom of 1840.

Again in the autumn of 1841 prices rose slightly, but after January 1842 declined precipitously. Contemporaries blamed this contraction on the Pennsylvania Legislature. Shortly after the stoppage of the Girard Bank near the close of January[32] resolutions were introduced into the legislature calling for an immediate resumption of specie payments by the banks or the surrender of their charters.[33] By the middle of March it was known that the governor had signed the bill. The editor of the *Commercial List* reported, "This measure, as impolitic as it was wicked under existing circumstances, left the banks no alternative, although it was well known that measures were in progress for a general resumption on or before the first of August next. Each bank was therefore compelled to take care of itself and leave the community and the other banks to shift for themselves."[34] Runs were immediate on most of the banks and many were forced to close. Several business houses also failed.[35]

In the weekly market report published late in June 1842 it was noted, "The resumption circle is gradually extending and, as there

[31] December 20, 1839, *Commercial List and Philadelphia Price Current.*
[32] January 28, 1842, *Commercial List and Philadelphia Price Current.*
[33] February 11, 1842, *Commercial List and Philadelphia Price Current.*
[34] March 18, 1842, *Commercial List and Philadelphia Price Current.*
[35] April 8, 1842, *Commercial List and Philadelphia Price Current.*

will probably be an abundant crop of winter grain, we may reasonably soon look for a better state of affairs than has been experienced during the last six months."[36]

The prices of foreign commodities turned upward after July. This revival, which occurred after the index had dropped 13.4 per cent from the peak of 1839, marks the end of the underlying decline which had dominated the movements of these prices after 1814. Only in the late spring and early summer of 1849 did the index of imported commodities fall below the low of July 1842.

Early in August, Warder felt that, despite the "general suspension of business" which had developed, the financial difficulties were on the verge of mending. He added in greater detail, "Such of the banks of the United States as do not shortly resume will be compelled to close their business, and in a few months we may calculate on a specie currency through the whole union, when it is probable there will be a much better state of things. Manufactured goods as well as the produce of the soil in a general way are very low."[37]

Although domestic commodities continued to fall with but slight interruptions until the spring of 1843, the "mercantile community" reported a "decidedly better feeling" although transactions were not on "an extensive scale."[38] Substantial signs of recovery were apparent by November when the *Commercial List* cited as evidences of revival "a large number of houses which had remained empty for months past have recently been rented, but at low prices. Taken all together there is a better feeling pervading the community, and a number of new firms are springing up in place of those which have become embarrassed and are winding up their business."[39]

During the spring and summer of 1843 prices of domestic articles as well as imported goods advanced. At the end of June the *Commercial List* noted other signs of expansion: "There is an increased desire manifested by capitalists to make permanent investments. Several factories which had been standing idle for one or two years have been put into operation, and the hum of cheerful industry is again

[36] June 24, 1842, *Commercial List and Philadelphia Price Current.*
[37] August 9, 1842, Warder and Brothers to Joseph Naftel, Guernsey Island.
[38] September 9, 1842, *Commercial List and Philadelphia Price Current.*
[39] November 18, 1842, *Commercial List and Philadelphia Price Current.*

beginning to be seen and felt in the suburbs of our city."[40] Although the prices of domestic articles receded from July to December 1843, when they were lower than at any time after 1789, the prices of imported articles were consistently higher in the latter part of 1843 than at the beginning of the year. The prospects for 1844 were "much brighter than those at the close of last year."[41] Specifically, the market reporter pointed out: "The stocks of goods generally on hand on the first instant were less than during any similar period for the last twelve years. There is a good feeling in the market and money continues abundant. As soon as fresh supplies arrive, business will probably open very active."[42]

Major Groups, 1830-1843

The recovery of 1830 appeared almost simultaneously in all groups. Farm derivatives and imported foods turned upward in March and April. These leaders were followed by farm crops, lumber products and naval stores, fish, and both groups of industrial commodities between August and October. Wines advanced after November. Only in furs was the rise delayed until the following spring.

The rise persisted in general, at least until the beginning of 1832. Lumber products and naval stores, however, continued to rise until in January 1834 they were 24.2 per cent above the low of 1830. The expansion in farm crops lasted until October 1833, while farm derivatives, wines, and industrial commodities ready for consumption were at their crest near the close of 1832. Only fish had a brief and sharp advance terminating as early as April 1831.

All groups, except industrial raw and semi-finished products, showed a contraction in prices around 1834. In this group of industrial commodities the rise in the early part of the thirties was gradual and but slightly interrupted.

The recessions after the peaks of 1832 to 1834 were mild in farm crops, farm derivatives, and lumber products and naval stores in comparison to their rise after 1830. In none of these groups did the

[40] June 30, 1843, *Commercial List and Philadelphia Price Current.*
[41] December 29, 1843, *Commercial List and Philadelphia Price Current.*
[42] January 5, 1844, *Commercial List and Philadelphia Price Current.*

indices in 1834 fall as low as in 1830, and in farm crops even what was called a depressed level in 1834 approximated the peak of 1828. Imported foods, industrial commodities ready for consumption, fish, furs, and wines dropped lower after the rise than they had been in 1830. In fish the recession had been completed by August 1832, while, at the other extreme, wines not only were lower in 1834 than they had been in 1830 but continued to decline with only slight interruptions until the summer of 1842.

The divergent behavior of prices in the early thirties requires that the total rise to 1837 be judged from 1830 for farm crops, derivatives, lumber products and naval stores, and industrial raw and semi-finished materials, from 1832 for fish, from 1834 for imported foods, furs, and industrial commodities ready for consumption. If 1834 were used as a basis of comparison for all groups, part of the initial impetus to the extreme peaks of 1837 would be missed.

The rapid increase which occurred between 1834 and 1837 raised most prices to the highest point between the years around the War of 1812 and the late fifties, or even until the Civil War. The first signs that a period of expansion was ended appeared when the prices of fish and imported foods turned downward after April 1836. All other groups expanded further for more than six months. The increase in the prices of farm crops, farm derivatives, and lumber products and naval stores was checked in November and December 1836. The downward turn of furs and both industrial groups after March and April 1837 shows the prompt response of all prices to the shrinkage in business in the early part of 1837. Lumber products and naval stores dropped approximately 20 per cent between December 1836 and July 1837. Nearly half of this drop had been recovered by the beginning of 1838 when a downward movement again set in which continued with many interruptions until the early months of 1844.

Prices of fish, which had been among the first to start a decline, began to recover as early as October 1837. In farm crops the decline was not decisively checked until after March 1838, in farm derivatives and industrial raw and semi-finished products until after July, and in furs until after October. In all of these groups the recovery which started in 1837 and 1838 followed a decline of 20 per cent or more except in the industrial raw and semi-finished products in which the fall amounted to approximately 12 per cent. Imported foods and industrial commodities ready for consumption showed no substantial advance at this time and, like wines, declined until the early forties.

The revival after July 1838 was restricted to farm crops, farm derivatives, industrial raw and semi-finished commodities, fish, and furs. The period of advance was short in farm derivatives, which turned downward after October 1838, and in industrial raw and semi-finished articles, which ended an eight-month rise in March 1839. Furs, the last group to recover in 1838, continued its advance until April 1840. The most striking increase in prices between 1838 and 1839 occurred in farm crops and fish, which at their peaks in May and June 1839 were higher than at their peaks in 1836. The fact that farm crops were 6.2 per cent higher in 1839 than at the preceding peak is distinctly unusual, but even this is dwarfed by the increase in the prices of fish, which were 31.3 per cent higher in 1839 than in 1836.

On the decline after 1839 farm crops and fish continued to move somewhat differently from the other major groups. Between May and July 1840 the declines in both farm crops and fish were checked and were followed by substantial advances culminating in September and October 1841. It was only after the secondary recovery that these groups finally started their recessions, which, like those of other groups, terminated in the early forties. Even here, however, farm crops and fish differed in that they were the only groups which were higher at the close of the recession in the early forties than they had been in 1830.

At the end of the long contraction after the peaks of 1837 and 1839, the prices of most commodities were at their nadir of the entire 78-year period from 1784 to 1861. There was less conformity than in 1830 as to the time at which the recession terminated. Imported foods, which had been declining from early in 1836, and wines, which had been falling from the close of 1832, showed in August and September 1842 the first signs of revival. Not until after the beginning of 1843 did any other group turn upward. Then in rapid succession fish started to rise in March, farm derivatives in April, and furs in June. In the fall of that year both industrial groups rose. The most sluggish groups to respond to the long-expected revival were lumber products and naval stores, which rose abruptly in April 1844, and farm crops which, after making several thwarted attempts at revival during the two-year period of very low prices, finally started upward after January 1845.

Sub-Groups, 1830-1843

The dates of revival around 1830 in the various sub-groups were more diverse than in the main groups. Nevertheless, all sub-groups started to rise within 13 months of August 1830 except the textile fabrics, which had been rising from a low near the end of 1826, and tobacco, which underwent an unusual swing from March 1829 to February 1832, reaching a peak in the latter part of 1829 and the beginning of 1830.

The peaks of the expansion beginning around 1830 were scattered over a period of nearly three and a half years, not counting those of tobacco and non-ferrous metals, which continued to advance to 1836-1837. The first groups to turn down were meats and meat products, fish, and chemicals, which had reached their peaks between October 1830 and May 1831. The most usual recession occurred after peaks between November 1831 and May 1832. During these seven months condiments, beverages, fruit, hides and leather, minor farm crops, furs, wood, textile fabrics, and textile fibers ceased to advance. Another large and important number of sub-groups began to decline between September 1832 and June 1833: grains, grain products, wines, fuel and lighting, spirits, and dairy products. The other groups—sugar and molasses, ferrous metals, building materials other than wood, and dyes—continued to rise until the close of 1833 or the beginning of 1834.

In the recession that generally terminated in 1834 three groups may be overlooked: non-ferrous metals and tobacco, which continued to advance in the face of the widespread decline, and wines, in which the decline after 1832 continued for nearly a decade.

Chemicals and fish, among the first to decline, started to rise again after July and August 1832. All other groups declined for at least a year and a half more, but all the remaining sub-groups except dyes, textile fabrics, and hides and leather completed their recessions between February 1834 and March 1835. Such concentration in the time at which diverse groups started to rise gives a strong presupposition to the influence of a common factor in 1834 which made for recovery. Special factors must have been present, however, to cause dyes and fabrics to continue their declines as late as November 1835 and hides and leather until February 1836.

TABLE 17
PROCESS OF EXPANSION OF SUB-GROUPS TO THE PEAK OF 1836–1837

Sub-Groups	Low		High		Rise	
	Date	Index	Date	Index	Number of Months	Percentage
Minor Farm Products	Sept. 1829	78.0	Apr. 1836	201.9	79	258.8
Meats and Meat Products	Feb. 1830	79.2	Oct. 1836	145.5	80	183.7
Grains	Mar. 1830	82.6	Feb. 1837	185.4	83	224.5
Grain Products	Mar. 1830	85.8	Mar. 1837	195.9	84	228.3
Dairy Products	May 1830	71.8	Nov. 1836	158.0	78	220.1
Chemicals	May 1830	85.8	Jan. 1836	114.8	68	133.8
Building Materials Other Than Wood	May 1830	77.1	Dec. 1836	102.9	79	133.5
Textile Fibers	June 1830	81.1	Aug. 1836	115.2	74	142.0
Fuel and Lighting	July 1830	77.0	Mar. 1837	120.1	80	156.0
Spirits	July 1830	97.3	Mar. 1837	124.3	80	127.7
Non-Ferrous Metals	Nov. 1830	72.7	Apr. 1837	113.2	77	155.7
Wood	Jan. 1831	82.9	July 1836	101.0	66	121.8
Sugar and Molasses	July 1831	80.9	Apr. 1836	121.5	57	150.2
Tobacco	Feb. 1832	61.2	Aug. 1836	139.1	54	227.3
Fish	Aug. 1832	75.3	Apr. 1836	144.8	44	192.3
Fruit	May 1834	48.8	July 1835	79.0	14	161.9
Condiments	Sept. 1834	62.7	Mar. 1836	72.2	18	115.2
Furs	Dec. 1834	78.2	Mar. 1837	96.1	27	122.9
Beverages	Feb. 1835	52.7	Sept. 1835	63.8	7	121.1
Ferrous Metals	Mar. 1835	84.0	Apr. 1837	103.9	25	123.7
Dyes	Nov. 1835	64.4	Feb. 1837	81.5	15	126.6
Textile Fabrics	Nov. 1835	75.1	Jan. 1838	91.8	26	122.2
Hides and Leather	Feb. 1836	75.2	Nov. 1836	88.0	9	117.0

The most fundamental contrast in the behavior of the various groups in this recession centers around the level at which each group checked its decline. As in the case of the major groups, it is essential that a distinction be made between those sub-groups which started their recovery around 1834 at a higher point than in 1830 and those which in the general recession from 1832 to 1834 fell to points lower than in 1830.

The sub-groups which, after their recovery from 1830, did not drop as low as they had been that year include (in addition to the rising groups of tobacco and non-ferrous metals) chemicals, which resumed their advance in 1832, grains, minor farm crops, grain products, meats and meat products, dairy products, sugar and molasses, building materials other than wood, textile fibers, and spirits, which started to rise in 1834, and fuel and lighting and wood, which advanced in the early part of 1835. In these 14 sub-groups the rise to 1837 should be measured from the low of 1830, since part of their behavior in the next years is related to the stimulus of these years. Although the remaining 10 groups include fish, which had ended its recession as early as August 1832, as well as fruits, condiments, and furs, which started to rise in 1834, the chief constituents were five of the six groups last to rise in the middle thirties and the wines, which declined until 1842. In these groups the rise to 1837 should be measured only from their lowest point in the first half of the decade, when their levels fell below the lows of 1830.

The end of the expansion of prices can be seen first in fruit and beverages, which declined after July and September 1835. In the early months of 1836 chemicals, condiments, sugar and molasses, fish, and minor farm crops added their weight to retard the rise. In the summer the upward movement ended in wood, tobacco, and textile fibers. Practically all of the other groups dropped after the closing months of 1836 and the beginning of 1837. Only textile fabrics continued to advance after April 1837. In this group the decline did not set in until after the beginning of 1838.

The most definite brakes to the rapid decline of the movement of prices in 1837 were the increases in chemicals, building materials other than wood, sugar and molasses, fuel and lighting, hides and leather, fish, tobacco, and fruit which began between June and November. Many other groups also showed some recovery in the latter part of the year, but they fell again to still lower levels in 1838.

The exceptions to recovery after the collapse of 1837 occurred in the sub-groups of wood and textile fabrics which, although somewhat high in the late thirties, tended to decline to 1843-1844. In general the rise after the low of 1837-1838 was completed between January and July 1839. The most striking fact about this recovery was that a few groups reached a higher point at this time than they had before the crisis of 1837. It has been noted earlier (page 213) that both fish and farm crops reached their major peak of the thirties at this time. The sub-groups show that it was tobacco and minor farm crops rather than grains or textile fibers which accounted for the magnitude of the rise in farm crops. In addition, dyes were higher at the close of 1838 than they had been in 1837, and hides and leather at their peak of February 1839 exceeded their preceding peak at the end of 1836.

In nearly all groups another rapid decline started between November 1838 and August 1839 which, although often retarded, especially in 1840 and 1841, persisted until the early forties. A few sub-groups met with definite checks in their decline followed by substantial increases. For meats and meat products and fruit this recovery terminated in the last quarter of 1840. The most unusual rise in this period was that of beverages, which, in March 1841, were substantially higher than at their previous crest in 1835. The extent of this rise grew out of the war between Great Britain and China, which greatly raised the price of tea.[43] Several other groups advanced to noticeable peaks in the latter part of 1841: grains, grain products, fish, textile fibers, and hides and leather.

The first group to end its decline at the close of the third major period was spirits in November 1841. Between May and August 1842 condiments, fruit, wines, sugar and molasses, and tobacco completed their contractions. The prices of half of the groups continued to decline until between February and December 1843. Meats and meat products, building materials other than wood, textile fabrics, and minor farm crops did not reach their lowest points until the latter part of 1844. Two groups failed to recover in the early forties; the prices of chemicals continued to sag until September 1846 and those of beverages until February 1849.

That most prices were at their nadir in the early forties is evidenced by the fact that only tobacco, minor farm crops, fish, and spirits were higher than they had been around 1830. Even when allowance is made for the fact that some groups were lower in 1834

[43] The substantial increase in the price of tea began in the previous August when the Philadelphia tea market was "in an excited state." August 29, 1840, *Commercial List and Philadelphia Price Current.*

than in 1830, only beverages, dyes, and textile fabrics can be added to those groups which did not in this period decline lower after the peaks of 1837 and 1839 than they had been before the rise of the middle thirties.

Summary

Since the base period, 1821-1825, used in the computation of the indices, includes the first few years of this major period, the behavior of the group indices in the remainder of the period indicates especially the divergences in trend which developed after 1825. The downward drift in four major groups was so marked that even in 1836 and 1837 their indices did not equal the average of the base period. The industrial commodities ready for consumption after 1823, wines after 1825, imported foods after 1826, and furs after 1829 kept continuously below the average of 1821-1825 throughout the remainder of the period. The groups of industrial raw and semi-finished materials and lumber products and naval stores held at higher levels and at least in 1837 were slightly higher than on the average in the first part of the twenties. It was the two domestic agricultural groups—farm crops and farm derivatives—as well as fish that contributed most to the height of prices in 1837.

The most marked difference in behavior, however, between the indices of fish and farm crops and those of the other groups lay in the extreme height of prices in these two groups in 1839 when their indices even exceeded those of 1836-1837.

Regardless of the height of prices reached in the latter part of the thirties, all groups dropped in the following recession at least slightly below the base average. Lumber products and naval stores after 1837, industrial raw and semi-finished materials after 1839, farm derivatives after 1840, and farm crops after 1842 kept below the average of 1821-1825 for the remainder of the period. Fish prices, however, dipped under the base in only a few months of 1842 and 1843.

At the turning points which mark the end of the third major period, the index of furs was more than 55 per cent below the average used as a base, imported foods more than 40 per cent, wines and lumber products and naval stores approximately 35 per cent, farm derivatives and industrial commodities ready for consumption more than 25 per cent, industrial raw and semi-finished products and farm crops 15 to 20 per cent, and fish less than 7 per cent below the average of 1821-1825.

Annual Price Movements

Major Groups

The amount and direction of change in the various major groups from year to year emphasize the characteristics of price movements between 1822 and 1843. In 1822 all groups rose except wines, which declined to 1824, and industrial commodities ready for consumption, which declined to 1830. Imported foods and industrial raw and semi-finished commodities rose less than half of one per cent from their low in 1821, but the expansion in the other groups ranged from 7 to 26 per cent. During 1823 and 1824 all groups dropped to successively lower levels. For fish this decline persisted through 1826. All other groups, except the industrial ready for consumption, advanced in 1825. In farm derivatives only a slight advance of less than half of one per cent occurred; in lumber products and naval stores, industrial raw and semi-finished articles, and wines there were more substantial advances of 5 to 8 per cent. The largest increases in that year—from 10 to 13 per cent—were found in farm crops, imported foods, and furs. Only the groups dominated by domestic agricultural commodities continued to advance in 1826, but these, like all other groups except fish, fell in 1827. The decline that year was most severe in furs and farm crops, which were 7 to 10 per cent lower than in 1826. No other group declined as much as 5 per cent. The prices of fish even increased more than 13 per cent in 1827 and made a further slight rise the next year. In 1828, lumber products and naval stores also rose slightly, and furs rose nearly 9 per cent. The other groups, except farm crops, which rose 5 per cent in 1829, continued an uninterrupted decline to 1830.

The underlying decline during the twenties is apparent in that in seven years all or most of the groups declined and in only two years did more than three groups increase. The peaks of 1822 and 1825 affected nearly all of the groups, but that of 1828-1829 was confined to farm crops, lumber products and naval stores, fish, and furs.

TABLE 18

ANNUAL PERCENTAGE OF CHANGE IN THE INDICES OF THE MAJOR GROUPS 1822–1843

Year	Farm		Imported Foods	Lumber Products and Naval Stores	Industrial		Fish	Furs	Wines	General Index
	Crops	Derivatives			Raw	Consumption				
1822	+13.0	+ 8.8	+ 0.1	+7.2	+0.4	−4.0	+ 7.7	+25.7	−5.4	+2.2
1823	− 5.5	− 6.3	− 8.0	−2.3	−4.5	−5.5	− 1.7	− 2.7	−7.7	−5.4
1824	−10.2	− 7.5	− 3.1	−2.3	−2.2	−5.2	− 5.3	− 2.0	−3.5	−4.4
1825	+10.0	+ 0.4	+10.9	+5.1	+5.8	−2.7	−10.2	+12.9	+7.6	+4.5
1826	+ 6.0	+ 1.1	− 6.2	−4.7	−3.8	−2.2	− 5.8	− 9.7	−2.7	−2.6
1827	− 9.3	− 1.8	− 4.4	−2.6	−2.9	−0.4	+13.4	− 7.8	−4.4	−3.0
1828	−10.6	− 1.3	− 2.0	+0.7	−2.8	−1.2	+ 1.0	+ 8.9	−1.4	−2.2
1829	+ 5.3	− 1.6	− 5.8	−6.7	−2.1	−1.0	− 5.2	− 3.7	−3.6	−2.4
1830	− 7.5	− 0.9	− 4.9	−9.9	−5.1	−4.9	− 3.7	−12.7	−5.8	−5.4
1831	+11.9	+10.6	+ 0.6	+4.7	+3.9	+2.7	+10.3	+ 1.9	+1.0	+4.4
1832	+ 5.6	+ 0.4	+ 3.9	+3.2	+0.1	+3.1	−11.1	− 2.2	+1.8	+1.8
1833	+ 2.6	+ 1.9	−15.0	+4.8	+1.6	−2.1	+ 7.5	+ 0.6	+1.3	−1.3
1834	− 0.9	− 7.0	− 5.2	+2.7	0.0	−5.1	− 1.1	+ 3.5	−5.0	−2.6
1835	+25.0	+12.6	+10.0	+5.2	−0.2	+2.8	+21.5	− 5.9	−1.7	+5.7
1836	+12.8	+21.9	+ 0.3	+6.3	+8.3	+6.0	+12.0	+10.8	−3.6	+7.6
1837	− 7.6	+ 0.4	− 8.7	−7.2	−0.2	+4.5	− 3.7	− 3.7	−6.3	−2.4
1838	− 6.1	− 5.7	− 1.6	−3.7	−2.6	−3.2	+ 8.6	−25.6	−1.7	−3.6
1839	+18.4	+ 4.6	− 0.3	+1.1	+4.9	+1.0	+35.8	+ 8.9	−0.8	+4.4
1840	−25.4	−17.5	− 5.2	−5.2	−6.2	−5.9	−21.3	+ 3.2	−2.7	−8.9
1841	+ 2.1	−10.8	+ 2.0	−1.7	−2.4	−4.0	− 5.7	− 5.5	−1.0	−2.5
1842	−13.1	−12.7	− 6.5	−6.3	−4.1	−5.3	−17.1	−13.0	−4.9	−7.2
1843	− 9.4	− 8.6	+ 5.8	−8.8	−6.3	−4.1	− 1.5	−25.7	+2.8	−4.7

That 1830 marks a significant turning point is evidenced by the fact that 1831 was the first year after 1809 when all major groups showed at least a slight advance. The rise which started after 1830 persisted until 1836 in lumber products and naval stores. Industrial raw and semi-finished commodities and farm crops also tended to rise from 1830 to 1836; in no year did either decline as much as one per cent. In the remaining years more severe breaks occurred in the rise. Fish and furs declined in 1832; the advances of imported foods and industrial commodities ready for consumption in 1831 and 1832 were followed by declines in 1833 and 1834. Farm derivatives, after rising from 1830 to 1833, dropped 7.0 per cent in 1834, but rose again in each of the next three years, while wines, which had increased slightly from 1830 to 1833, declined continuously until 1842. In each of the years from 1832 to 1835 inclusive the prices of at least two groups receded.

Not until 1836 did all groups except wines show at least a slight increase. In that year imported foods were on the average less than 0.5 per cent above their prices in 1835. The increases in lumber products and naval stores and both industrial groups amounted to 6 to

8 per cent, in furs, fish, and farm crops to 11 to 13 per cent, and in farm derivatives to approximately 22 per cent. In the face of a general decline in 1837 and 1838 farm derivatives increased slightly in 1837, industrial commodities ready for consumption rose nearly 5 per cent the same year, and fish, which had dropped less than 4 per cent in 1837, advanced nearly 9 per cent in 1838. The rapidity of the decline and advance in the monthly prices of 1837 and 1838 minimizes the change in the annual averages. The group of furs, which dropped slightly more than 25 per cent in 1838, was the only one which in either year fell as much as 9 per cent. The rally after the low of 1838 raised at least slightly all groups except imported foods and wines. Prices of lumber products and naval stores and industrial commodities ready for consumption were only about one per cent higher in 1839 than in 1838. Farm derivatives and industrial raw and semi-finished materials advanced nearly 5 per cent and furs about 9 per cent. The outstanding increases in 1839 were those of 18.4 per cent in farm crops and 35.8 per cent in fish. Only furs continued to advance in 1840 when all other groups except wines declined more than 5 per cent.

The slowing up of the rate of decline in the general curve in 1841 was influenced by increases of about 2 per cent in two groups and by the fact that, although all other groups declined, only farm derivatives fell as much as 6 per cent. The decline was greatly accelerated the next year when all groups dropped more than 4 per cent and farm crops, farm derivatives, fish, and furs more than 12 per cent.

The first groups to show, in their annual averages, the end of the recession were wines and imported foods in 1843. Farm derivatives, industrial raw and semi-finished commodities, fish, and furs rose at least slightly in 1844, but farm crops, lumber products and naval stores, and industrial commodities ready for consumption did not show positive signs of recovery until 1845.

Sub-Groups

Although the general average was higher in 1822 than in 1821, as many as 12 sub-groups receded. The decline in the next two years was more widespread. Only tobacco and dyes increased in 1823, and tobacco, meats and meat products, fruit, chemicals, and textile fibers in 1824. The expansion to the peak in 1825 nearly reversed the proportion of groups rising and falling. Except for meats and meat products, fish, beverages, textile fabrics, spirits, and miscellaneous articles, all groups advanced that year. The remainder of the decade was characterized by a widespread decline in most groups. The recovery around 1828 was so restricted in its effect and so distributed among the groups which did rise that from 1826 to 1829 only seven to nine groups advanced in any year. Even fewer groups rose in 1830. Grain products, meats and meat products, textile fabrics, and hides and leather were the only sub-groups that made any headway in 1830 against the downward drift of the others.

In contrast to the decline in the five previous years, a widespread advance characterized those from 1831 to 1836, except 1834, when only tobacco, chemicals, dyes, and furs continued their advances. The interruption to the expansion culminating in 1836 is evidenced not only by the 21 series which fell in 1834 but also by the 10 which fell in both 1833 and 1834. There is little relation between the length of this decline in the annual averages and the relation of monthly prices in 1834 to those in 1830. Although the annual prices of grains, minor farm crops, grain products, and non-ferrous metals dropped in both 1833 and 1834, it has been noted that their monthly prices held above the low of 1830. On the other hand, the monthly prices of fish, ferrous metals, and wines were lower in 1834 than in 1830 although the annual prices did not drop in 1833.

The resumption of the general advance in 1835 and its continuance in 1836 affected every group except wines in one year or the other. In addition to wines, which fell continuously from 1833 to 1842, dyes, ferrous metals, furs, textile fabrics, and hides and leather dropped in 1835 and fruit, beverages, condiments, and chemicals in 1836.

The crash in 1837 and the further recession in 1838 affected 17 groups in each year, 11 of which fell in both years. Eight groups, however, including grains, grain products, dyes, ferrous metals, non-ferrous metals, textile fabrics, spirits, and miscellaneous articles continued to rise in 1837 and tobacco, fish, fruit, sugar and molasses, chemicals, dyes, textile fabrics, and hides and leather made some recovery in 1838. Of these only fruit, sugar and molasses, and textile fabrics failed to advance further in 1839. In addition to the five sub-groups which rose in both 1838 and 1839, the marked recovery of the latter year was aided by 13 other sub-groups.

The closing four years of the third major period were marked by a sweeping decline. Twelve sub-groups dropped continuously in all four years and eight in three of the four years. Only fruit dropped in one and grain products, beverages, condiments, and spirits in two years.

Proportion of Commodities Influencing Price Movements

The period from 1822 to 1843 when compared with the two preceding major periods shows a marked increase in the importance of prices which did not change from year to year or which changed less than 2.5 per cent. Within the period itself certain segments may be sharply distinguished from others by the percentage of commodities which did not change in price from the previous year. Between 1822 and 1824 as many as 10 per cent of the individual series had the same average price for at least two consecutive years, but between 1825 and 1828 the number of commodities unchanged in price from one year to the next was continuously less than 1.5 per cent. Between 1829 and 1834 at least 7 per cent of the commodities held the same average price for two consecutive years. From 1835 to 1837 the number of such series never constituted as much as 4 per cent of the total, but from 1838 to 1843 at least 7 per cent of the commodities were stable.

When the number of commodities increasing or decreasing less than 2.5 per cent in each year is added to those unchanged, the total number of these relatively stable commodities does not show any distinguishing characteristics for consecutive years. Throughout this period at least 18 per cent of the commodities were relatively stable each year. The most marked stability occurred from 1832 to 1834, when between 32 and 40 per cent of the commodities changed less than 2.5 per cent, and in 1841 when 35 per cent showed little, if any, change.

The percentage of commodities undergoing a substantial change may be used to summarize the extent to which various parts of the economy participated in the successive periods of expansion and contraction.

Between 1821 and 1830 three peaks have been noted, namely:

1822, 1825, and 1828-1829. The most widespread rise occurred in 1825, but even in that year scarcely 53 per cent of the commodities rose noticeably higher than they had been in the previous year. Less than 40 per cent rose as much as 2.5 per cent in 1822 and in 1828-1829 only 26 to 28 per cent. In fact, in terms of the number of commodities showing a substantial rise, the years 1828 and 1829 differ little from 1826 and 1827.

The general downward movement of prices during the twenties is evidenced by the fact that, except in 1822 and 1825, more than 49 per cent of the commodities declined noticeably each year. In 1823, 1824, and 1826 the number declining was between 50 and 58 per cent, and in 1830 it was over 60 per cent.

The increases in prices during the thirties, especially in 1831, 1835, and 1836, were distributed among 50 to 60 per cent of the commodities. Even in 1832, when 42.1 per cent of the series rose at least 2.5 per cent, there were more commodities rising than falling substantially. The same situation existed at the peak of 1839.

The decrease after 1830 was not as widespread as that in the first part of this major period. Only in four years in the late thirties and early forties did as many as 49 per cent of the commodities decline materially, yet in eight years the number of commodities with a marked decrease exceeded the number with a corresponding increase: 1833 and 1834, 1837 and 1838, and 1840 to 1843 inclusive.

The tendency for many commodities to decline during the twenties and, after the extreme peaks of 1837 and 1839, to drop to their nadir in the early forties influenced the significant difference between the percentage of commodities which increased in various years and the percentage which decreased. In every year from 1822 to 1843 more than 20 per cent of the commodities showed a significant decrease, but in six years less than 20 per cent showed a corresponding increase. At the other extreme were three years in which 60 per cent or more of the commodities decreased at least 2.5 per cent, while in no year did as many as 60 per cent of the commodities increase that much.

The mildness of the rise in the annual data in 1822 is indicated by the fact that 50 per cent or more of only farm crops, lumber products and naval stores, and farm derivatives increased 2.5 per cent or more that year. The more general decline in 1823 lowered substantially half or more of all the major groups except lumber products and naval stores. Imported foods showed the greatest proportion of declining items, 81 per cent of these commodities falling at least 2.5 per cent. In 1824, however, less than 60 per cent of any of the major groups receded substantially and only in farm crops and imported foods did half of the commodities drop appreciably.

The peak of 1825 was widely distributed: a majority of the series in the major groups, except farm derivatives and industrial commodities ready for consumption, rose materially. Throughout the remainder of the twenties, while the general average was still contracting from the peak reached in the War of 1812, only in farm crops in 1829 did as many as half of its constituents increase as much as 2.5 per cent. This was the only case in the five years from 1826 to 1830 when more commodities advanced noticeably than decreased an equal amount, although in 1827 in farm derivatives, and in 1828 in lumber products and naval stores, as many series rose as fell as much as 2.5 per cent. The most concentrated declines, when two-thirds or more of the series in any group decreased substantially, occurred in imported foods in 1826, in farm crops in 1827 and 1828, in lumber products and naval stores in 1829, and in imported foods and lumber products and naval stores in 1830.

The proportion of commodities rising emphasizes the pervasive character of the expansion during most of the early thirties. In 1831 more commodities in each group advanced at least 2.5 per cent than fell a corresponding amount. Two-thirds of the farm crops and lumber products and naval stores and more than 90 per cent of the farm derivatives advanced noticeably. A slackening of the rise was apparent in 1832, when only imported foods rose more generally than in 1831, while in the farm derivatives there were as many substantial recessions as advances and in the industrial raw and semi-finished materials even more.

In 1833 and 1834 lumber products and naval stores was the only group which advanced and had a larger proportion of constituent series rising appreciably than falling. In addition, the index of industrial raw and semi-finished articles increased slightly in 1833 and held the same average the next year. Yet no more than a quarter of its commodities advanced materially in either year. The other groups receded, especially in 1834, when two-thirds or more of the farm crops and farm derivatives and more than 60 per cent of the imported foods dropped at least as much as 2.5 per cent.

Although the resumption of the rise in 1835 affected all groups except the industrial raw and semi-finished materials to the extent that more series rose noticeably than fell, its greatest impact was on farm crops and farm derivatives, of which more than 80 per cent rose substantially. Even in 1836, when in all groups a larger percentage of series increased as much as 2.5 per cent than decreased and when more than 55 per cent of the series in all groups except imported foods fell in this class, only in farm derivatives did more than 85 per cent and in farm crops as many as 75 per cent advance materially.

The collapse in 1837 was slow in affecting the annual prices of both industrial groups as was evidenced by the fact that more series in these groups rose than fell markedly. Of farm crops and farm derivatives an equal proportion of the series advanced and contracted as much as 2.5 per cent. In 1838, when in all groups more series receded noticeably than rose, two-thirds of the farm crops and half of the lumber products and naval stores and farm derivatives decreased substantially in price.

During the recovery of 1839 the tendency in all groups except imported foods was upward in that more series made a material advance than declined. More than 64 per cent of the farm derivatives and farm crops increased at least 2.5 per cent, but less than 50 per cent of the other groups rose similarly.

The downward drift in prices in the four years after the peak of 1839 was most pronounced in 1840 when 62.5 per cent or more of the series in each of the six largest groups dropped 2.5 per cent or more. Approximately 93 per cent of the farm derivatives and 83 per cent of the farm crops fell that much. The recession was modified in the following year when a smaller percentage of every group receded. Although half or more of the lumber products and naval stores, of the industrial commodities ready for consumption, and of the farm derivatives decreased noticeably in price, a larger proportion of the series of farm crops and imported foods advanced substantially than declined. As many as 50 per cent of the farm crops made considerable headway against the general decline. Renewed deflation characterized price movements in 1842. The number of items in each of the six major groups falling markedly again exceeded those rising. More than 50 per cent of the imported foods, approximately 60 per cent of the industrial commodities ready for consumption, and 75 per cent or more of the farm crops, farm derivatives, and lumber products and naval stores were at least 2.5 per cent lower than in 1841. Only the slightest evidences of recovery appeared in the annual averages of 1843. Although more than 60 per cent of the imported foods increased noticeably, in none of the other groups did as many as 20 per cent of the commodities increase similarly. In fact, more series in the farm crops and both industrial groups took pronounced decreases in 1843 than in 1842. The same proportion of the lumber products and naval stores fell 2.5 per cent or more in both years, while of the farm derivatives, in which the decline in 1843 was less comprehensive than in 1842, more than 70 per cent of the series still decreased appreciably in price.

During the years from 1822 to 1843, farm crops, farm derivatives, and imported foods had relatively little stability by comparison with lumber products and naval stores and both industrial groups. Only in one year did even one series of the farm derivatives maintain the same average price as in the previous year; in all but one year at least one of the industrial raw and semi-finished articles was unchanged in price. Never were as many as 10 per cent of the farm derivatives and imported foods invariable and only in 1830 did the farm crops have this much stability. In contrast, the lumber products and naval stores in three years, the industrial commodities ready for consumption in seven years, and the industrial raw and semi-finished materials in 15 years included 10 per cent or more of such insensitive commodities.

The contrast between farm crops, farm derivatives, and imported foods on the one hand and the lumber products and naval stores and both industrial groups on the other is even more marked when the commodities that varied less than 2.5 per cent are added to those which did not change at all. Twenty-five per cent of the series of farm crops in only three years between 1828 and 1833, of farm derivatives in seven years between 1823 and 1834, and of imported foods in four years somewhat scattered through the period showed only minor price changes. In the other groups, however, for from 13 to 21 years the prices of 25 per cent or more of the constituent series were within 2.5 per cent of those of the previous year. The most extreme stability appeared in the industrial raw and semi-finished group, in which in every year at least 10 per cent of the series were unchanged or 25 per cent changed only mildly. One of the most fundamental differences which distinguishes the period 1821-1843 from the two earlier ones is this marked increase in stability, especially among the industrial commodities. A progressively increasing number of these commodities became subject to only slight changes in prices from year to year.

Deviations of Annual Group Indices from General Average

The movements in prices from 1821 to 1843 may be summarized by comparing the annual indices of each of the nine major groups with the general average. Lumber products and naval stores and both industrial groups were, on the whole, close to the general index, having an average deviation of less than 4 per cent. Farm derivatives, imported foods, furs, and wines underwent more extreme variations, usually differing from the average by 9 to 13 per cent. The most extreme deviations of 18 per cent or more were in farm crops and fish.

Even among the groups which most closely approximated the general average, significant differences can be noted. Lumber products and naval stores were usually above the average, the greatest difference being in 1834 and 1835 when they were more than 9 per cent above. Only in 1822, 1830, 1831, 1832, and 1839 did they fall below the composite index. The industrial raw and semi-finished materials were somewhat similar to the lumber products and naval stores in that their index was above the general average except in 1822, 1823, 1832, 1835, and 1836. It is especially significant that the industrial raw and semi-finished materials were continuously above the average from 1837 to 1843, the greatest variation being slightly more than 10 per cent in 1842. In contrast, the industrial commodities ready for consumption from 1824 to 1843 were always lower than the general index, deviating more than 9 per cent in 1836.

Among the groups with greater but not extreme deviations, only the farm derivatives were usually above the general index. From 1836 to 1839 this group was approximately a third or more higher than the composite index. Imported foods, furs, and wines were usually below the general average. Although the group of furs from 1823 to 1830 and again in 1834 exceeded the average, it had dropped nearly 40 per cent below by 1843. Imported foods and wines, except in 1825 and 1826, were continuously below the average, the spread tending to increase until in 1839 both were more than 25 per cent below the general index.

The extreme deviations in farm crops and fish tended to lift their indices well above the average. Farm crops, except in 1824 and 1828, and fish, except in 1825, 1826, and 1832, were relatively dearer than most commodities. From 1835 to 1841 the index of the farm crops exceeded the average by more than 25 per cent, rising in 1839 as much as 53 per cent above it. The fish group was even higher. Not only was it more than 25 per cent above the average from 1836 to 1843, but in 1839 it was more than 85 per cent and in 1840 and 1841 more than 54 per cent higher than the general curve.

CHAPTER X

PRICE MOVEMENTS FROM 1843 TO 1861

Monthly Price Movements

The period from 1843 to 1861 shows a general upward movement of prices in contrast with the general decline during the previous period. The major part of the rise was concentrated between 1849 and 1857. As is characteristic of periods of rising prices, the length of the advances culminating in peaks in 1845, 1847, 1851, 1855, 1857, and 1859 were usually longer than the periods of recession ending in 1846, 1849, 1852, 1856, 1858, and 1861. Only the declines from 1847 to 1849 and 1859 to 1861 exceeded the length of the preceding expansion. In both of these cycles prices fell lower during the contraction than they had been at the beginning of the previous rise. The only other depressed period in which prices dropped lower at the close of the swing than at the beginning was the brief but severe drop from June 1857 to February 1858 when, in eight months, the general index fell 16.5 per cent.

It appears that the rise in prices in 1861, after the outbreak of the Civil War, terminated what might have been a long period of receding prices. Although in 1861 the general index was still higher than it had been at the low of 1852, a general downward movement is indicated by the progressive dropping of prices in each successive swing lower than they had been in the previous one and by the lengthening of the period of recession in relation to the period of expansion.

Imported and Domestic Commodities, 1843-1849

Only in the rise around 1843 did prices of foreign goods advance before those of domestic, but from the peaks both foreign and domestic commodities shared equally in starting to decline before the other group had completed its expansion.

The recovery of 1843 affected the various commodities slowly. Although the prices of imported goods turned upward after July 1842, it was not until after December 1843 that the domestic series definitely rose. At the end of 1843 when the index of imported goods was only 4.3 per cent higher than at its low nearly a year and a half earlier, both indices were at practically the same point. Even in 1844 the advance was gradual. By the close of 1844 both groups were less than 4 per cent higher than they had been the year before. During 1845 the prices of domestic articles especially soared and in December were 18.6 per cent higher than at their low in 1843. The imported commodities had reached a peak a month earlier, having advanced 11.8 per cent in three and a third years.

In most fluctuations in this period, domestic articles characteristically rose by a larger percentage than the goods of foreign origin. Declines, too, were generally more severe in the index of domestic goods than in that of the foreign. The decline from the peak near the close of 1845 was completed in the prices of domestic commodities as early as August 1846, but the slight recovery in imported articles was offset by a drop in December 1846 and January 1847. In fact this group of commodities showed little advance during any part of the Mexican War. Uncertainty as to what might happen curtailed many business undertakings. Only the commodities generally necessary for war and those usually imported from Mexico brought relatively high prices.[1]

The extreme rise of 21.7 per cent between August 1846 and June 1847 originated in the demand for American foodstuffs to offset the shortages in Europe rather than in the effects of the Mexican War. The famine in Ireland, especially, is of importance in accounting for the sharpness of the rise. In those ten crucial months the indices of grains and grain products more than doubled, of meats and meat products rose nearly as much, and of minor farm crops soared approximately 60 per cent.

Practically two years were required to complete the contraction of prices from a peak reached in but ten months of expansion. With several interruptions the index of domestic commodities slid 17.4 per cent between June 1847 and May 1849. Imported commodities had risen only 3.0 per cent between January and November 1847, but by June 1849 this group was 9.7 per cent lower than at the peak.

[1] May 15, 1846, *Commercial List and Philadelphia Price Current.*

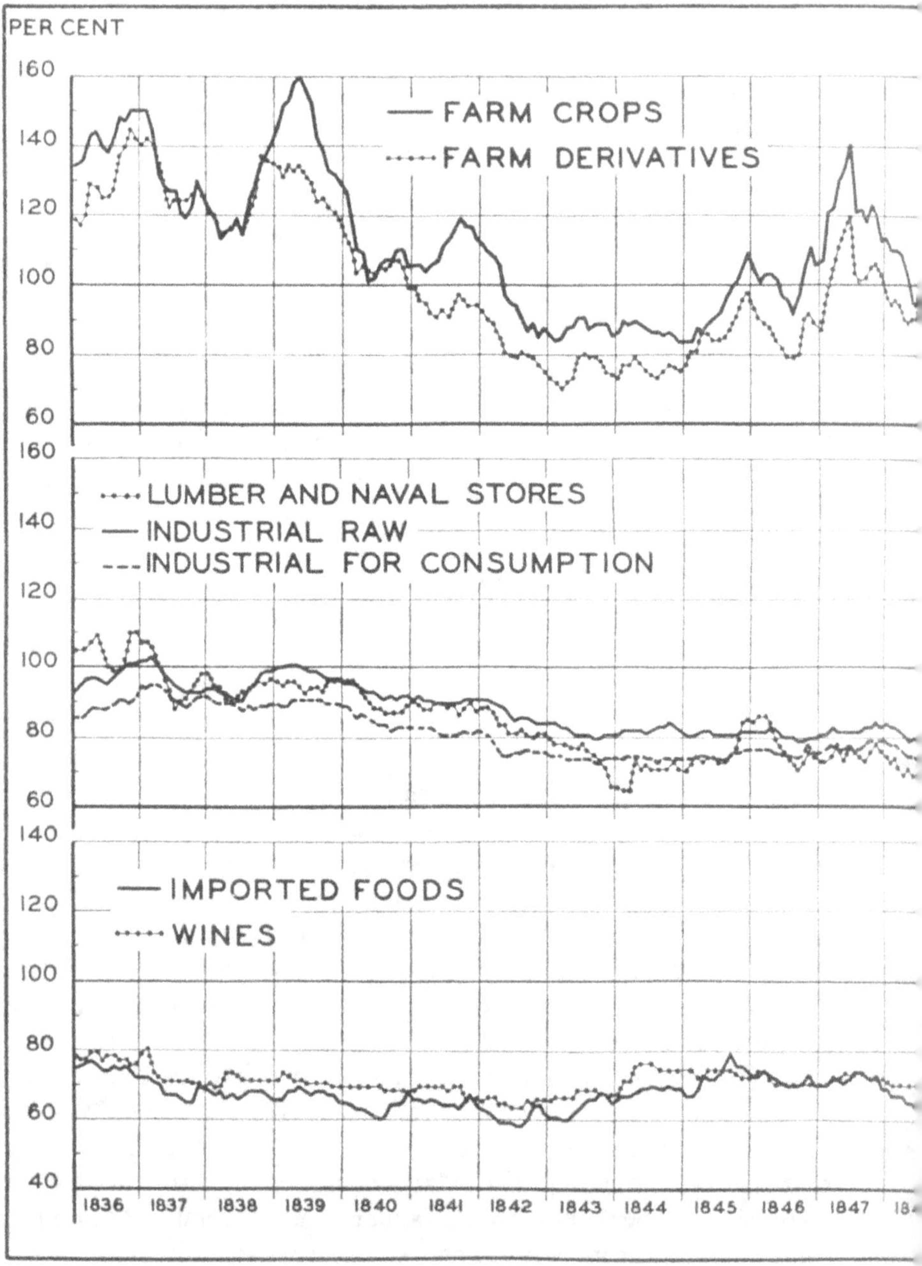

CHART XII—GEOMETRIC INDICES OF AVERAGE MONTHLY WHOLES
(Base—Mon

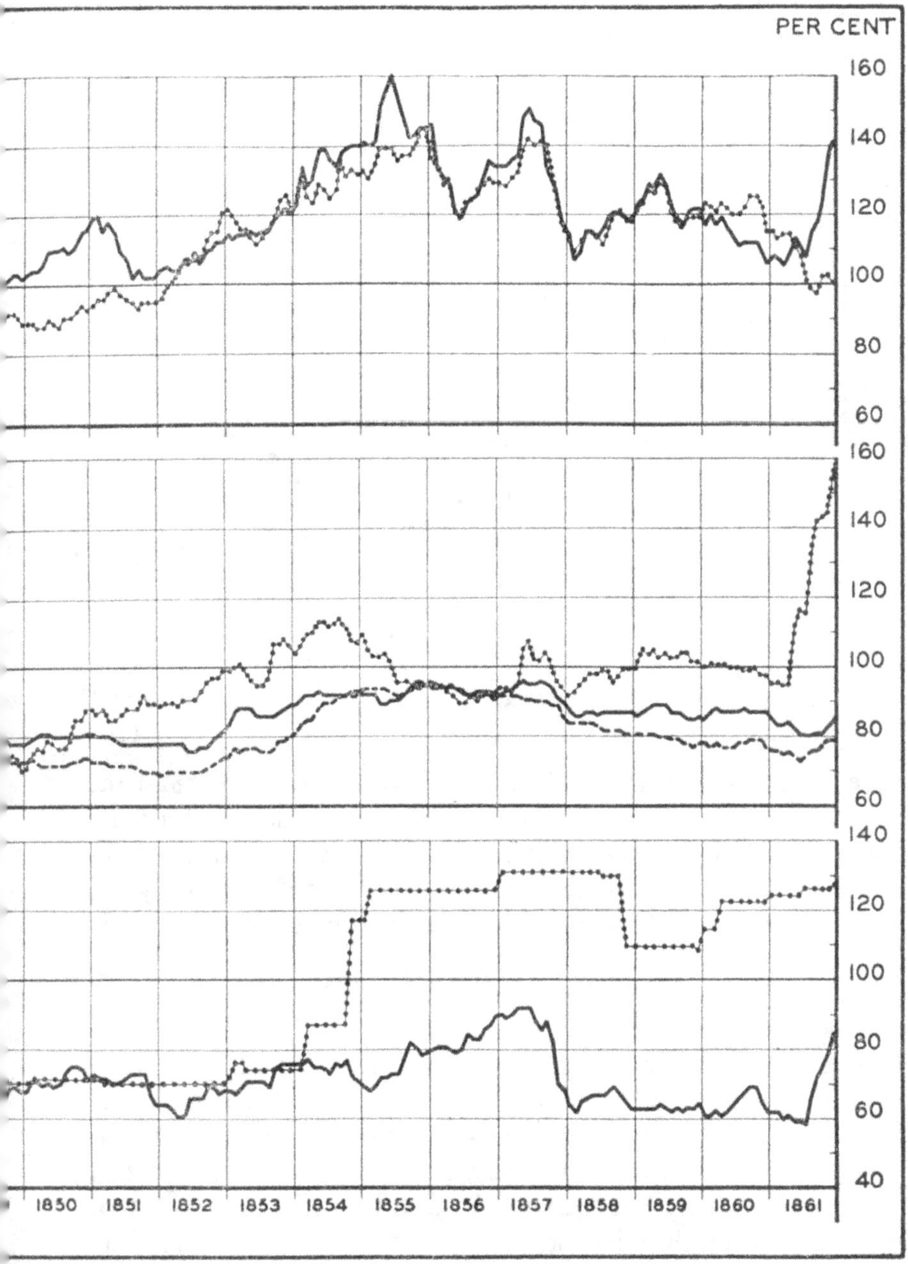

ES IN PHILADELPHIA BY MAJOR GROUPS, 1836-1861
age, 1821-1825)

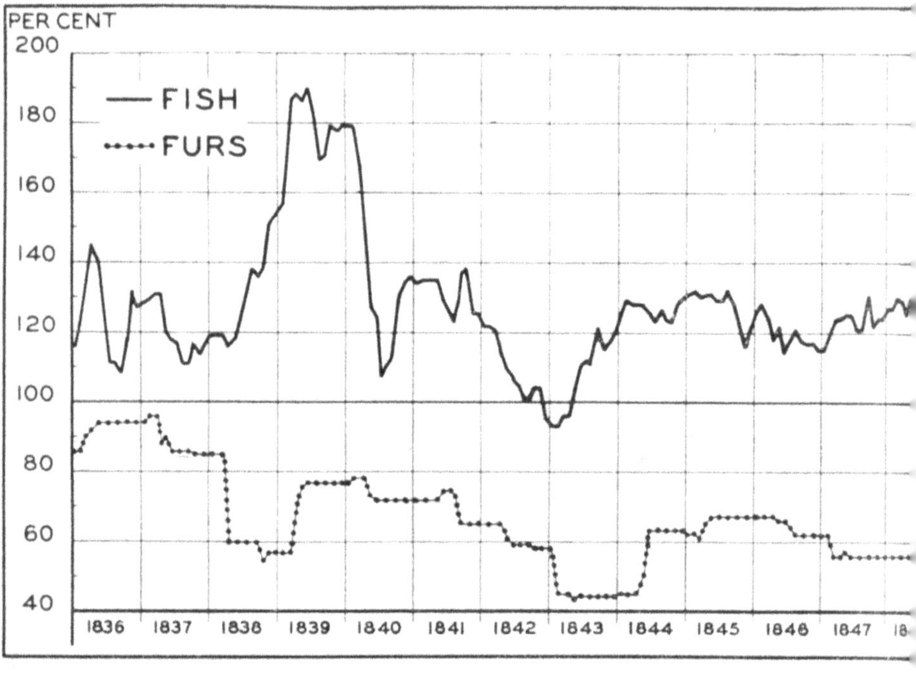

CHART XII—GEOMETRIC INDICES OF AVERAGE MONTHLY WHOLE
(Base—Mo

Since 1844 the two groups had tended to diverge. By 1849 the separation was so pronounced that, while prices of domestic articles that year were slightly higher than at the low of 1846 and 5.5 per cent higher than in 1843, imported commodities were not only 7.0 per cent lower than in 1846 but were even slightly lower than in 1842.

Major Groups, 1843-1849

The recovery around 1843 was slow in affecting all the major groups, little advance being made before 1845. Wines and industrial raw and semi-finished materials showed smaller increases than the other groups and turned downward after June 1844. All the other major groups advanced at least until the following August, but by May 1846 all except the industrial commodities ready for consumption had started to fall. The fact that the prices of six groups broke

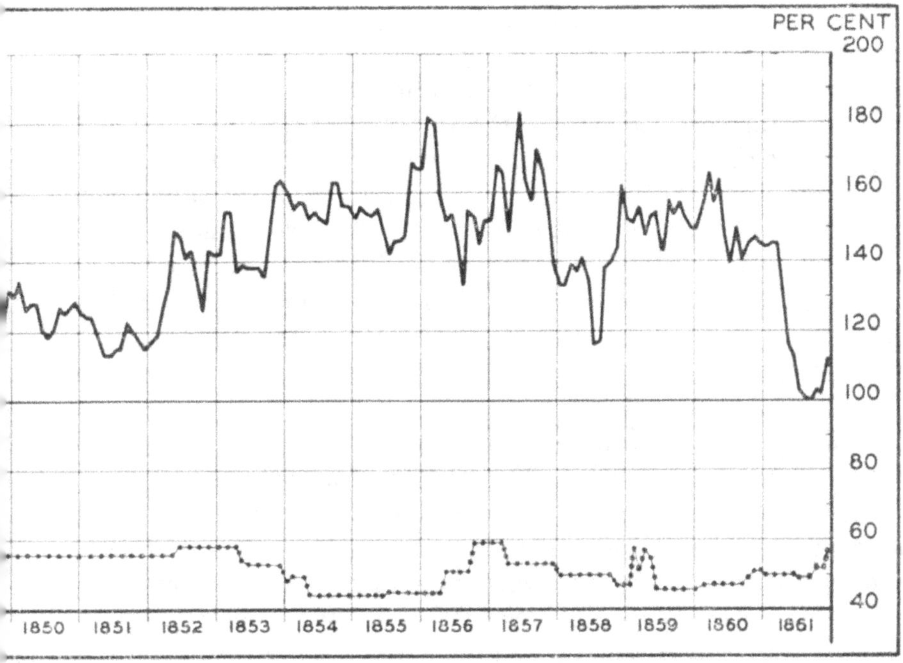

IN PHILADELPHIA BY MAJOR GROUPS, 1836-1861, *Concluded*
ge, 1821-1825)

within four months of December 1845 shows how widespread was the pressure for contraction. Contemporaries related this to the uncertainty of business men over the proposed sub-treasury bill, the agitation for a change in the tariff, and the dispute between the United States and Great Britain over the boundary of Oregon.[2]

After a short decline of eight to ten months, farm crops, farm derivatives, and fish started to rise between July and September 1846. The industrial raw and semi-finished articles recovered in the fall. Wines followed early in 1847. Rising prices among these important groups of commodities resulted from conditions abroad. At home, although there was optimism as a result of the favorable settlement of the Oregon boundary,[3] there was considerable gloom in the business community because of the passage of the new tariff bill, the sub-treas-

[2] April 24, 1846, *Commercial List and Philadelphia Price Current.*
[3] June 19, 1846, *Commercial List and Philadelphia Price Current.*

ury bill, and the warehouse bill. In addition, the federal government was confronted with a deficit. In Philadelphia confidence was especially impaired by the failure of several firms.[4]

The demand for foodstuffs in the fall of 1846 and the spring of 1847 because of the general failure of crops in Europe accounts for the extensive rise in the prices of farm crops and farm derivatives and the smaller, but substantial, rise in fish. While these commodities as well as wines and both industrial groups advanced, imported foods, lumber products and naval stores, and furs continued to decline. The boom of 1847 was short. Abundant harvests abroad lowered the prices of farm crops and derivatives after June, and by February 1848 all groups were falling.

In most groups the duration of the decline exceeded the previous rise. The first indications that the general contraction was nearing its close came when lumber products and naval stores in August 1848 and farm crops in September turned upward. In the first part of 1849 imported foods, fish, farm derivatives, and industrial raw and semi-finished products began to recover. Wines showed no tendency to rise until after August. The only groups which continued to decline in the face of the strong upward movement starting in 1849 were industrial commodities ready for consumption and furs. Not until February 1852 did the group of highly-processed industrial commodities advance, while furs tended downward until the latter part of 1854 and the beginning of 1855.

Sub-Groups, 1843-1849

Except for chemicals, which declined from 1839 to 1846, and beverages, which declined from 1841 to 1849, all sub-groups started to rise between December 1841 and December 1844. As in the case of the major groups, the rise was generally terminated in the latter part of 1845 or the first few months of 1846. Only hides and leather failed to rise after September 1843, and textile fibers, wines, and dyes reached the summit of their expansion between February and August 1844. At the other extreme, fuel and lighting and non-ferrous metals continued to advance until the closing months of 1847 and the beginning of 1848. The prices of textile fabrics varied only slightly

[4] August 14, 1846, *Commercial List and Philadelphia Price Current.*

from 1844 to 1853. The end of the following recession came in nearly all of the groups which suffered decline between June 1846 and February 1847. For six sub-groups the start of recovery was concentrated in the two months of September and October 1846.

The end of the rise was less concentrated, although seven groups, primarily agricultural products—grains, grain products, minor farm crops, meats and meat products, textile fibers, sugar and molasses, and dyes—turned downward between April and July 1847; tobacco had not advanced after May 1846. Several important groups did not begin to recede until the latter part of 1847 and five even delayed until the first part of 1848: chemicals, spirits, non-ferrous metals, hides and leather, and dairy products. The timing of the series indicates how definitely agricultural commodities contributed to the first phase of sharp recession.

Only three groups failed to turn up again in 1848 or 1849: textile fabrics, which varied only slightly during this period; ferrous metals, which declined until the middle of 1852; and furs, which tended to sag until the spring of 1855. The first evidences of recovery were the increases in the prices of eight groups between June and October 1848: sugar and molasses, meats and meat products, building materials other than wood, chemicals and drugs, fuel and lighting, wood, tobacco, and textile fibers. The others followed in rapid succession between February and December 1849.

The nearly simultaneous appearance of this rise in diversified types of commodities gives a strong presumption that a common factor was affecting most prices. The less detailed classification of commodities into nine major groups shows a corresponding concentration: lumber products and naval stores and farm crops led upward in August and September 1848 and the other groups rose by September 1849, except industrial commodities ready for consumption and furs, which were comparatively stable during this period, but tended to decline in the early fifties.

Imported and Domestic Commodities, 1849-1861

The grouping of commodities according to domestic or foreign origin reveals that, on the average, the prices of domestic products rose after May and of foreign after June 1849. The close similarity of these dates adds corroborative evidence of the working of a common factor. It is significant that on June 15, 1849 the market reviewer of the *Commercial List* predicted, "The influx of gold dust from California will soon begin to be felt, and real estate which has been comparatively neglected for several years past will be more sought after for investments, and prices for all desirable properties will advance." Such a comment suggests that the discovery of gold in California had a substantial effect on prices before any addition of the metal was actually made to the currency system. Undoubtedly this discovery aided in the beginning of an underlying upward trend in the prices of imported commodities and in the acceleration of the upward trend in the prices of domestic commodities. In fact, the discovery of gold may have given the appearance of an upward trend to the prices of domestic commodities from 1843 to 1849 by halting the recession which followed 1847 at a higher level than might have been maintained otherwise.[5]

Although both the index of domestic commodities and that of imported commodities rose in the latter part of 1849 and in 1850, the prices of foreign commodities increased for a shorter period and advanced less in amount than those of domestic. The expansion ended as early as October 1850 at a point 9.1 per cent above the low of 1849 in the index of imported goods; that of domestic products advanced for another three months to a point 12.9 per cent above its low of 1849. The ensuing recession had, however, less effect on the domestic goods than on the foreign. In the domestic series the decline was halted in September 1851 at a point 7.0 per cent above the low of 1849. Imported commodities not only started to decline ahead of the other group but continued to fall until April 1852, when they were only 1.8 per cent above the corresponding point in 1849.

In both groups prices rose steeply and with but minor recessions from 1852 to 1854. By September 1854, the domestic index was 38.3 per cent higher than in 1849. During the next year these commodities fluctuated around a slightly lower level, but suffered no appreciable decline until in the first part of 1856, when the index dropped 7.1 per cent between January and June. Imported commodities ad-

[5] Cf. Smith, Walter Buckingham and Cole, Arthur Harrison, *Fluctuations in American Business, 1790-1860*, p. 94.

vanced more slowly between 1852 and 1854. At the time when the domestic index was at its peak, the imported index was also higher than it had been in 1849. Foreign commodities, however, did not turn down after September 1854; instead they continued to advance but at a slow rate until July 1855. Between July and October the average of these commodities increased 8.4 per cent to a point 42.2 per cent higher than in 1849. There was only a slight recession from this peak during 1856, when the index was always within 3.6 per cent of the peak of 1855.

Underneath the fluctuations in prices during 1854 and 1855 and before the ultimate break in 1857, there was an acute stringency in business, especially among the financial houses. Before the close of 1854 Jay Cooke, then associated with the investment firm of E. W. Clark and Company in Philadelphia, was subtly warned by his older brother, "I do hope you will weather the long storm in which every business firm is now contending for existence and that in a few years more you will be able to take things quietly and get out of the vortex."[6] Jay Cooke at least presented a cheerful impression to his family. "I am glad to hear you keep easy in your Philadelphia house," his brother replied early in 1855. "It seems to me I would dissolve connections with so many houses, but you know best. . . . Telegraph says three more banking houses failed in St. Louis yesterday. I hope yours is not one of the number."[7]

Evidently Jay Cooke felt that the developments during 1855 were not unduly serious, for he returned to Sandusky in the autumn to visit his parents. While he was there E. W. Clark wrote, "We are not very busy just now and do not particularly need your services except in the financial line. All moves on smoothly even in that line, barring that everybody we owe anything to seems disposed to make us pay. We have paid some $400,000 within thirty days and are getting tired of the game inasmuch as all our cash is used up and more too. . . . The New York office cannot help us and they say we may consider ourselves well off if we do not have to help them. The bears have been running this matter into the ground and we can hardly have any news from abroad that will not help the money market.

[6] November 21, 1854, Pitt Cooke, Sandusky, Ohio, to Jay Cooke, Philadelphia.

[7] January 18, 1855, Pitt Cooke, Sandusky, Ohio, to Jay Cooke, Philadelphia.

The shipment of specie must be at an end soon—they cannot have gold and food too from us."[8]

After the sharp break in 1856 domestic commodities recovered rapidly. Between June 1856 and June 1857 their index climbed 12.3 per cent to the highest point reached after 1839. Foreign commodities took a shorter and milder rise of 5.3 per cent between September 1856 and May 1857. At that time their prices were higher than at any time since the peak of 1825.

Prices collapsed in the latter part of 1857 and the first months of 1858. By February 1858 domestic commodities had fallen 17.5 per cent and imported commodities 15.8 per cent from their peaks.

The pressure in the money market continued in the first part of 1857. E. W. Clark and Company was informed by Jay Cooke, who was traveling in the Middle West, that the condition of the crops was favorable. Clark commented that business continued "fair" with the firm although there had been a few isolated failures.[9] Even near the close of July the situation did not appear critical. "I have been thinking over the condition of the money market," wrote E. W. Clark, "and am quite confident that before long we shall have higher rates. The current of gold from the West will cease soon and some go in that direction to handle the crops. The steady payment of $200,000 to $500,000 into the sub-treasury daily must after a while have an effect, and the imports are very large indeed, which will soon renew the shipments [of specie] to Europe. Business is once more becoming active and money will be wanted by the merchants. I think there is no cause for alarm."[10]

The financial troubles of the three previous years were climaxed by the disastrous debacle in the autumn of 1857. Several banks in Philadelphia as well as throughout the country failed before the close of August. During the week of September twelfth alone nine Philadelphia banks closed. A general suspension was expected, but the banks continued to redeem their five-dollar notes.[11] Such action looked

[8] October 24, 1855, E. W. Clark, Philadelphia, to Jay Cooke, visiting in Sandusky, Ohio.

[9] June 4, 1857, E. W. Clark, Philadelphia, to Jay Cooke.

[10] July 21, 1857, E. W. Clark vacationing at Long Branch to Jay Cooke, Philadelphia.

[11] McMaster, John Bach, *A History of the People of the United States*, Vol. VIII, pp. 291-293.

to a Baltimore banker "like a determination on the part of the banks to assist the merchants at the risk of having to suspend themselves."[12] These fears were not groundless, for within a few days all banks suspended specie payment in Philadelphia, followed soon by practically all of the banks in other areas. Before the close of September, Clark wrote from New York: "They are having the same sort of fun here as we had in Philadelphia last week. Money is *not tight—it is not to be had at all.* No money, no confidence, and no value to anything. A week more of such times and the banks will fail. Our position is precarious only because the money market is in this state. . . . The fact is people don't much care who fails."[13] Four days later all of the branches of E. W. Clark and Company suspended. Only the Philadelphia house carried on, and it was forced to reorganize.[14] Commenting on the "sad times in Philadelphia," a friend wrote to Cooke, "It must be melancholy to see old establishments that had stood the storm of 1837 totally wrecked in 1857."[15]

After the contraction from 1857 to 1858 the prices of imported and domestic commodities moved in opposite directions. During 1858 the decline in the prices of imported commodities was checked, their index holding as late as October slightly above the low of February. A further sharp recession occurred in the last two months of the year, and a gradual but persistent decline continued throughout 1859 with the result that in January 1860 their index was 6.2 per cent lower than in February 1858 and 21.1 per cent below the peak of 1857. During 1860 prices of imported articles advanced until by September they had more than recovered from the decline between 1858 and 1860. After September, however, they receded rapidly, falling 9.5 per cent by July 1861, when the index was even 2.2 per cent lower than in January 1860. In contrast, prices of domestic articles recovered substantially in 1858 and by May 1859 had climbed 10.7 per cent above the low of the previous year. They slumped sharply after this peak, falling 6.1 per cent in four months. During the closing months of 1859 and the first part of 1860 these prices stiffened, only to slide again in the latter part of that year and the first part of

[12] September 22, 1857, Samuel Harris and Sons, Baltimore to Jay Cooke, Philadelphia.
[13] September 29, 1857, E. W. Clark in New York to Jay Cooke, Philadelphia.
[14] Oberholtzer, Ellis Paxson, *Jay Cooke, Financier of the Civil War*, Vol. I, pp. 88-89.
[15] November 9, 1859, S. Marks, Huron, to Jay Cooke, Philadelphia.

1861. In July 1861 they were 12.5 per cent lower than at the peak of 1859 and even slightly lower than in 1858.

Major Groups, 1849-1861

The general advance from 1849 to 1857 had two important interruptions, first in the early fifties and second in 1856. The most significant declines in the early fifties occurred in the prices of imported foods and the industrial raw and semi-finished commodities, which at their lows of April and June 1852 were slightly lower than before the advance culminating in 1850. The fluctuations from 1849 to 1852 in the group of industrial raw and semi-finished articles were very slight. The only other groups which were lower in the first part of the fifties than in 1849 were the industrial commodities ready for consumption and furs, which had not risen to peaks in 1850 or 1851.

Three other groups had a swing in prices at this time, but in all of these the recessions terminated at points above the lows of 1848 or 1849. In fish this swing was nearly completed before the expansion in the prices of farm crops ended. Between January 1849 and February 1850 the prices of fish increased 48.9 per cent. The sharpest part of this rise came between October and December 1849. For approximately a year fish had sold continuously at prices lower than at any other time after 1843. This drop had occurred as increasing amounts of fish were received in the market and as news reached the city that an unusually large catch had been taken.[16] The rise which restored the prices of fish to approximately the level of 1847 and the early part of 1848 came with the accounts that the catch that year was "decidedly short of an average."[17] The swing in the prices of farm crops reached a crest in February 1851 after a long advance from the summer of 1848. Nearly two-thirds of this gain, however, was lost between February and November 1851. Not until the last quarter of 1853 did farm crops again command as high a price as at the beginning of 1851. Farm derivatives had a milder rise than farm crops from 1849 to 1851 and declined moderately from May to September 1851. Their greatest peak of the early fifties came in January 1853 when the index was 22.2 per cent higher than at any time in

[16] October 14, 1848, *Commercial List and Philadelphia Price Current.*
[17] October 27, 1849, *Commercial List and Trade and Statistical Register.*

1851 and 44.6 per cent above the low of 1849. The sharp drop of 8.9 per cent in the five months from January to June 1853 was followed by an even more rapid advance which by October had more than offset the decline.

Wines and lumber products and naval stores suffered no marked recessions in the early fifties. In wines there was only a mild advance until after the beginning of 1854. Lumber products and naval stores, in contrast to all other groups, showed a strong underlying upward movement around which prices fluctuated slightly from July 1848 to September 1854. During this six-year period these prices nearly doubled. Naval stores rather than lumber products account for the steadiness of this expansion.

Regardless of when the initial impetus to rise appeared, all groups except furs contributed to the mounting level of prices after the first part of 1853. The increasing rate at which prices advanced and the widespread character of the expansion coincided with the beginning of the movement of fleets to the Dardanelles which preceded the Crimean War and antedated, slightly, the actual outbreak of war between Russia and Turkey. With the formal declaration of war by England and France against Russia in the spring of 1854, an added impetus was given. Not only were supplies needed for the war, but, more important to the American farmers, the Crimean War removed Russian wheat from the world markets.

Not until near the close of 1854 did any group start to decline. Lumber products and naval stores and imported foods turned down in October and November. During 1855, as the outcome of the Crimean War become more certain, farm crops started to fall as early as July and farm derivatives in December. Both industrial groups and fish fell in the first three months of 1856. Only furs and wines had failed to decline by this time.

The height of prices in 1855 is often minimized because the general index rose to a higher point in 1857 than in 1855. An examination of the nine major groups shows that farm crops, farm derivatives, lumber products and naval stores, and industrial commodities ready for consumption were higher between 1854 and 1856 than at any other time in the latter part of the fifties. The industrial raw and semi-finished materials at their peak in January 1856 averaged only one-tenth of a point lower than at the later peak of May 1857 and the index of fish in February 1856 was within one-half of one per cent of its peak in the next year. Thus only imported foods, wines, and furs advanced substantially higher in 1857 than two years earlier.

This evidence of widespread high prices in 1855 justifies the complaints of contemporaries, especially since the low prices of much of the forties and the early fifties were still clearly in their minds and formed a basis for comparison. By 1857 the business community must have adapted itself to a high level of prices. These high prices were encouraging to many business men but presented a pressing problem of readjustment to those depending upon wages or fixed income. The incidence of these new conditions on various segments of the population was discussed in the following article on "High Prices" which appeared on May 5, 1855 in the *Commercial List and Philadelphia Price Current.*

> The high rates at which breadstuffs are held is alarming to men of ordinary means, and of a character to drive poor men to desperation. The cost of living in the principal cities seems to have trebled within the recollection of those who are still young in years. The prices of the ordinary articles of food have kept pace with the advance in rents, until to live decently and comfortably and save something for a rainy day has become to many hard working men an obsolete state of existence.—When butter reaches 35 cents per pound, flour $11 per barrel, and potatoes $1.50 to $2 per bushel, the mechanic of family, who is even well paid for his work, must struggle bravely and manage economically to keep his head above water and escape the incubus of debt. Day after day he reads in the market reports "breadstuffs have advanced," and a continual "improvement" in the rates;—and while the merchant and speculator are more than satisfied, as they harvest the fruits of their enterprising operations, the heart of him who sees his daily food rapidly rising beyond his reach sinks into despair.
>
> Yet there is something cheering in the aspect of a thriving trade, and the prospect of its continuance. While the cry of "starvation prices" is raised by the Jeremiahs of society, we behold the various channels of trade filled with the tide of business, and are conscious of a slow but certain improvement in all the branches of industry. If the laboring man must pay more to live comfortably, it is equally apparent to us that it will not be long before he is much better paid than he has ever been. With the revival of business this spring, we have witnessed the relief of the pressure of excessive

competition by the departure of large numbers of working men for the great West which offers so broad a field for energy, shrewdness, and enterprise, and still this emigration continues. Our farmers are making a loud demand for additional help, and numbers of Germans and others who gained a knowledge of farm-work in the old world are leaving the fierce and hot struggle maintained in the various mechanical trades to seek their fortunes in the country.—The result, it is easily seen, will be the solid gain of those who remain among us. With the diminution of laborers, wages must improve, and the cry of "starvation prices" will cease.

Speculation is rife in regard to the probable continuance of the present high rates of provisions. As regards flour, it is the prevailing impression among well-informed business men that with the opening of the lake navigation there will come such an influx from the Northwest as to make a material reduction in rates. But it is argued that while this great arrival may affect the home demand, the events which are now going on in Europe will have a tendency to sustain prices. By the struggle which is now raging in the East, not only a vast number of hands have been withdrawn from the cultivation of the soil, but an extensive wheat region in the vicinity of the Black Sea is given over to desolation by hostile armies. Should the state of things continue, it is argued that the demand for flour abroad will become so great as to keep the article at comparative high rates or take it even beyond them.

In regard to other articles of provisions, the probabilities are in favor of a reduction in prices as the season advances, although, at the first glance—seeing how well rates are maintained, and how certain articles continue steadily to improve—we might draw a different inference. It is apparent that articles which depend entirely upon home consumption must fall as the season pours them into the market and as the varieties of food are increased by the addition of fish, vegetables, etc. Adventitious circumstances may occasionally prevent the operation of this plain law, but in general it holds good. In conclusion, we have only to say that we are exceedingly gratified at the prospect of an active and improving trade, even though "starvation prices" rings in our ears.

The recession in 1856, although less than 5 per cent for the general index, affected many groups seriously. Between June and August 1856 farm crops, farm derivatives, lumber products and naval stores, and fish fell 18 to 27 per cent below their prices at the peaks between 1854 and 1856. In all but lumber products and naval stores these declines had been effected within a year. As usual, the industrial raw and semi-finished products declined less than others, but even this group fell nearly 5 per cent in the seven months from January to August 1856. The industrial commodities ready for consumption declined only slightly during 1856, but, unlike any other group, did not recover in the latter part of that year. Their recession from the peak of December 1855 was not completed until the middle of 1861. That the total index did not drop more than 4.7 per cent in 1856 can be attributed to industrial commodities which had relatively slight declines, to wines and furs whose prices tended to rise, and to imported foods which, despite a drop of 12.2 per cent from October 1854 to February 1855, recovered so rapidly that after July 1855 they were above their index of the corresponding period in the previous year.

Since the industrial commodities ready for consumption did not show a peak in 1857, only eight major groups are considered here. All of these reached peaks between October 1856 and June 1857, imported foods, wines, and furs rising higher than they had been earlier in the decade.

The collapse in 1857 first affected between April and July the prices of all groups except wines, which held their high prices until after June 1858. This recession was generally terminated in January and February 1858. In from seven to nine months the industrial raw and semi-finished materials had dropped 10.8 per cent, lumber products and naval stores 15 per cent, farm derivatives 23.2 per cent, farm crops 28.9 per cent, and imported foods 32.9 per cent. Only fish and furs tended downward for more than a year. Fish ended a 13-month drop of 36.5 per cent in July 1858. Furs, the last group to end its contraction in this decline, was 19.3 per cent lower from November 1858 to January 1859 than it had been at its height in the last quarter of 1856 and the first quarter of 1857.

The final peak of prices before the Civil War occurred, in general, between February and May 1859. Only fish reached a definitely higher point early in 1860 than at any other time after 1858. Imported foods had only minor fluctuations after February 1858 until the sharp rise in the latter part of 1861. After the minor peaks around 1859, the contraction in prices from the extreme peaks of 1855 or 1857 was resumed. Mild evidences of recovery occurred in 1860, but the certainty of the secession of some of the southern states after the election of Lincoln and the suspension of specie payment before the close of November depressed prices further. In general, prices fell until the seriousness of the Civil War was realized when the Union forces were routed at Bull Run. The lowest prices intervening between the peaks in the latter part of the fifties and those resulting from the Civil War appeared first in furs between June 1859 and January 1860 and next in wines in December 1859. All other groups continued to fall until the farm crops turned upward after December 1860. Lumber products and naval stores fell until April 1861. The other five groups completed their contractions between June and September of that year. The most extreme advances in the closing months of 1861 appeared in farm crops, imported foods, and especially in lumber products and naval stores, which after May were increasingly higher than even at the peak of 1854.

Sub-Groups, 1849-1861

The rise in prices which generally started in 1849 and had its greatest effect in the middle and latter part of the fifties affected all of the sub-groups. The greatest significance of this rise was not merely the extent of it, but rather the time at which the expansion was completed. As early as 1853 ferrous and non-ferrous metals had both completed a sharp rise, the peak of which was not exceeded later in the decade. In 1854 condiments and building materials other than wood were at their greatest height. During 1855 five important groups reached heights not exceeded later: grains, grain products, dairy products, chemicals and drugs, and fuel and lighting. The prices of minor farm crops and textile fabrics were at their highest in the early months of 1856.

In contrast to these groups which did not rise after the recession of 1856 to the levels attained earlier stand 13 groups which, between December 1856 and the early part of 1858, exceeded the heights reached in any other part of the decade. These were tobacco, meats and meat products, fish, fruit, beverages, sugar and molasses, dyes, wood, furs, textile fibers, hides and leather, spirits, and wines.

The recovery of 1859 affected 14 groups. The most unusual increase at that time was that in the prices of grain products, which were higher than they had been in 1857 although still well below the extreme peak of 1855. No other group rose enough to offset the collapse in prices in the latter part of 1857.

Regardless of whether the decline started as early as 1853, as in the case of ferrous metals, or as late as August 1860, as in the case of dyes, the end of the decline in most groups was intensely concentrated. More than half of the groups touched their low between July and October 1861. Only the seven which had started to rise by November 1860 were apparently unaffected by the general slump in prices occasioned by the financial difficulties at the close of 1860 and the beginning of 1861.

Summary

When considering the movements in prices from 1843 to 1861 in relation to the average of 1821-1825 it is possible to indicate roughly the different trends of the various major groups. The groups with a somewhat downward movement, at least after the base period, are furs, imported foods, and both groups of industrial materials. The indices for these groups in the last of the four main periods never equaled the average of 1821-1825.

Lumber products and naval stores were comparatively low until the upward movement of the early fifties began. After 1852 the index of this group fluctuated around the average of the first part of the twenties. Wines held low until the increases of 1854 and 1855 raised the level of the curve well above its base.

The three remaining groups—farm crops, farm derivatives, and fish—showed a more persistent upward sweep than the wines and lumber products and naval stores. After 1849 the farm crops and after 1852 the farm derivatives kept continuously above the average of the base period except for a slight dip in farm derivatives in 1861. For fish the upward trend began well before the 1843-1861 period with the result that, except for a few months in 1843, 1848, 1849, and 1861, the index fluctuated substantially above the average of 1821-1825. The spread tended to increase as late as 1857.

Throughout the analysis in this chapter, little attention was paid to this fanning out of the indices of the groups. This tendency is related to long-time changes in demand on one side and techniques of production on the other. These slow but progressive changes in the relative importance of various commodities are inherent in any study of prices over such a long period, especially one which involves a rapid development of manufacturing and transportation facilities.

Annual Price Movements

The percentage of change from year to year in the annual figures emphasizes the longer-time movements which are often obscured by the monthly fluctuations. The timing of recovery and recession is somewhat altered by this form of analysis, however, because of the relative slowness of annual figures to reveal a change in direction.

Table 19
Annual Percentage of Change in the Indices of the Major Groups
1844–1861

Year	Farm		Imported Foods	Lumber Products and Naval Stores	Industrial		Fish	Furs	Wines	General Index
	Crops	Derivatives			Raw	Consumption				
1844	− 0.3	+ 0.5	+ 6.7	− 7.3	+ 0.9	− 0.1	+17.5	+24.7	+10.7	+ 2.0
1845	+ 7.4	+14.1	+ 6.6	+ 7.5	− 1.2	+ 0.7	+ 1.4	+15.7	− 0.3	+ 3.6
1846	+ 8.0	− 0.2	− 1.9	+ 3.8	− 0.6	+ 1.9	− 6.8	− 1.5	− 3.1	+ 0.5
1847	+21.0	+21.1	+ 0.7	− 4.0	+ 2.1	+ 2.1	+ 2.9	−11.2	+ 1.1	+ 4.2
1848	−15.8	−11.7	−10.2	− 3.6	− 2.4	− 2.3	− 3.8	− 2.3	− 2.8	− 6.0
1849	− 3.5	− 3.6	− 0.8	+ 0.8	− 3.1	− 3.7	−12.2	0.0	− 1.7	− 2.5
1850	+ 9.1	+ 1.3	+11.2	+ 8.1	+ 2.6	− 0.4	+21.3	0.0	+ 2.8	+ 4.4
1851	+ 0.7	+ 6.2	− 0.3	+11.1	− 1.5	− 1.6	− 5.9	0.0	− 0.4	+ 0.5
1852	− 2.2	+12.3	− 8.3	+ 5.7	− 0.9	− 1.3	+14.3	+ 2.0	0.0	+ 0.1
1853	+ 8.2	+ 9.8	+ 9.8	+ 8.9	+11.0	+ 9.2	+ 8.0	− 4.6	+ 5.5	+ 9.1
1854	+16.4	+ 8.8	+ 4.6	+ 9.7	+ 6.1	+15.0	+ 7.0	−16.7	+21.8	+ 9.2
1855	+ 9.0	+ 7.4	0.0	− 9.7	+ 0.7	+ 5.4	− 2.1	− 2.2	+38.9	+ 3.7
1856	−12.1	− 7.5	+10.5	− 7.7	+ 1.7	− 0.2	+ 2.2	+15.8	+ 0.6	− 0.2
1857	+ 5.3	+ 4.1	+ 4.2	+ 8.0	− 0.5	− 3.1	+ 3.3	+ 5.6	+ 3.5	+ 1.8
1858	−15.5	−13.4	−23.7	− 2.7	− 7.4	− 8.4	−15.7	− 9.0	− 2.8	−11.1
1859	+ 7.5	+ 6.3	− 4.4	+ 6.3	+ 0.2	− 4.0	+11.6	+ 1.0	−14.7	− 0.3
1860	− 8.4	− 0.6	+ 2.5	− 3.2	− 0.1	− 2.3	− 1.0	− 4.6	+12.6	− 0.7
1861	+ 3.6	−12.6	+ 4.0	+25.0	− 5.2	− 2.1	−21.4	+ 6.3	+ 2.3	− 0.7

Major Groups

These figures for the major groups show that the revival in the first part of the forties started in the imported foods and wines in 1843, followed by the farm derivatives, industrial raw and semi-finished materials, fish, and furs in 1844. The remaining groups, farm crops, industrial products ready for consumption, and lumber products and naval stores, did not definitely rise until 1845.

The abruptness of the contraction and expansion of prices in 1846 accounts for the fact that the annual averages conceal the severity of that recession. The annual index of all commodities shows continuous advances from 1844 to 1847. The recession in 1846 appears merely as the smallest rise in the general index between 1844 and 1847, an increase of 0.5 per cent.

The nine major groups show the effect of recession more clearly. Although six or seven had risen in 1844 or 1845, only three groups showed any average advance in 1846. The most substantial rise in the annual figures in 1846 occurred in farm crops, which were 8 per cent higher than in 1845. Industrial commodities ready for consumption and lumber products and naval stores rose 2 to 4 per cent. The other groups suffered slight declines. Although fish dropped nearly 7 per cent and wines slightly more than 3 per cent, the other four groups averaged within 2 per cent of their prices in 1845.

The general index rose 4.2 per cent in 1847, the largest increase in any year in this decade. Part of this expansion may be attributed to the widespread character of the rise, which affected all groups except lumber products and naval stores and furs. The extent of the enhancement, however, resulted from the increases of 21 per cent in farm crops and farm derivatives; none of the other groups rose as much as 3 per cent.

The recession in 1848 and 1849 affected all groups. Furs, which maintained the same price in 1849 as in 1848, and lumber products and naval stores, which rose less than 1.0 per cent in 1849, were the only groups which failed to decline in both years. The significance of the slight increase in lumber products and naval stores rests chiefly on the fact that it marks the beginning of the expansion which culminated in the general curve in 1857.

From 1850 to 1855 the general index showed at least a slight increase each year. Then, after dipping only two-tenths of one per cent in 1856, it advanced nearly 2 per cent to the peak in 1857. The rise started in 1850 with a slightly larger advance than at any time in the previous decade. All groups participated except furs, which held at the average price of 1848 through 1851, and the industrial commodities ready for consumption, which did not check their fall from the peak in 1847 until after 1852. The most substantial increases among the groups in 1850 were those of 11 per cent in imported foods and 21 per cent in fish. An increase of only 1.3 per cent in farm derivatives, though slight, is especially important since it marked the beginning of a continuous rise to 1855. Thus farm derivatives and lumber products and naval stores were the only groups which in every year of the early fifties contributed to the rise in the general index. In 1851 they were assisted by a gain of less than 1.0 per cent in farm crops and in 1852 by more substantial increases in fish and furs. The general index shows the effect of the widespread, although slight, declines in 1851 and 1852 by rising only one-half of one per cent in 1851 and only one-tenth of one per cent in 1852.

The speeding up of the advance during 1853 and 1854 is reflected in the further increases of 9 per cent each year in the general index. All groups rose in both years except furs, which declined until after 1855. The most salient fact about the advance of 1853 was its uniformity among most of the groups—seven of the eight groups increased between 8 and 11 per cent that year. In 1854, in contrast, three groups rose 15 per cent or more while the other five rose less than 10 per cent. The range in the increases was from 4.6 to 21.8 per cent. The tapering off in the expansion is indicated in the general index by an increase of 3.7 per cent in 1855 compared with more than 9 per cent in the two preceding years. Among the groups only wines continued to advance at a faster pace than in 1854. Imported foods held their average price of the previous year and lumber products and naval stores and fish declined.

Again the annual averages conceal the impact of a recession—in 1856 the general curve slipped only two-tenths of a point from the level of 1855. The most serious recessions in 1856 occurred in farm crops, farm derivatives, and lumber products and naval stores, which were 7.5 to 12.1 per cent lower in 1856 than in 1855. The only other group to show any recession was the industrial commodities ready for consumption, which, after starting to decline in 1856, did not rise again until after 1861. The only substantial increases effected in 1856 were those of 10.5 per cent in imported foods and 15.8 per cent in furs. The other three groups advanced less than 2.5 per cent. Except for the two classes of industrial commodities, all groups recovered in 1857 or continued to advance. In view of the high levels at which most prices kept, even with the decline in 1856, and considering that the collapse of 1857 affected the average of the year, it is not surprising that no group except lumber products and naval stores showed an annual increase of as much as 6 per cent.

The sharp drop of prices in 1857 appears in the annual averages of 1858. All groups declined that year: imported foods 23.7 per cent; fish, farm crops, and farm derivatives 13 to 16 per cent; furs and both industrial groups 7 to 9 per cent; and wines and lumber products and naval stores 2.5 to 3 per cent.

Although the general index showed further slight declines of less than 1.0 per cent in both 1859 and 1860, the behavior of the groups exhibits a marked contrast in the two years. In 1859 the continuation of the recession was confined to imported foods and industrial commodities ready for consumption, which fell between 4 and 4.5 per cent, and wines, which dropped nearly 15 per cent. All other groups increased at least slightly. The industrial raw and semi-finished materials and furs rose 1.0 per cent or less, lumber products and naval stores, farm derivatives, and farm crops 6 to 7.5 per cent, and fish 11.6 per cent. In 1860, however, only two groups advanced—imported foods 2.5 per cent, and wines 12.6 per cent. Farm derivatives, industrial raw and semi-finished articles, and fish dipped 1.0 per cent or less. Industrial commodities ready for consumption, lumber products and naval stores, and furs dropped between 2 and 5 per cent. The most severe contraction was 8.4 per cent in farm crops. In 1861 the rise in imported foods and wines continued and was strengthened by increases in farm crops, lumber products and naval stores, and furs. The advances in the other groups in the latter part of 1861 were not sufficient to raise their annual averages.

Sub-Groups

The analysis of the changes in the annual indices of the 25 subgroups isolates still further the commodities contributing most to the various fluctuations. In each year from 1844 to 1847, although the general index moved upward, a substantial number of groups declined. The only groups which did not rise in at least two of these four years were chemicals and hides and leather, both of which declined from 1844 to 1846, and beverages, which declined in 1844, 1845, and 1847. On the other hand, all groups receded in at least one year except grains and dairy products.

The rise in 1845 was confined to 15 groups, only six of which increased more than 10 per cent. Grains, fruit, and furs advanced between 11 and 16 per cent, dairy products 26 per cent, and tobacco and meats and meat products between 30 and 34 per cent. Of the 10 groups which declined that year only dyes dropped more than 8 per cent.

The recession of 1846 in the monthly indices in the sub-groups is concealed in the annual averages. Fourteen groups even show an average advance that year, although only one rose more than 8.5 per cent. The declines were also limited in extent, only one being as much as 10.3 per cent.

The peak of 1847 was more definite than that of 1845, although as many as eight groups did not rise. The greatest declines were 11.2 per cent in furs and 7.1 per cent in tobacco; the other recessions were less than 3 per cent. The effect of the demand from Europe for foodstuffs is reflected in the rise in dairy products of 10.4 per cent, in grains of 27.9 per cent, in grain products of 28.8 per cent, in minor farm crops of 34.8 per cent, and in meats and meat products of 40.7 per cent. Dyes, fuel and lighting, and textile fibers also showed substantial advances of 10 to 23 per cent. The other nine groups advanced less than 7 per cent.

The contraction of prices during 1848 and 1849 was extremely widespread. Only chemicals failed to decline in either year. Most groups declined in both years. Textile fabrics and miscellaneous articles rose in 1848 against the general trend, while tobacco, meats and meat products, beverages, sugar and molasses, fuel and lighting, building materials other than wood, and textile fibers anticipated the boom of the early fifties by starting upwards in 1849.

The general curve started in 1850 a six-year advance. No group of commodities, however, showed the same sustained rise. One of the nearest approaches is found in building materials other than wood, which, influenced by naval stores, advanced continuously from 1849 to 1854. The most continuous rise appears in hides and leather, which mounted from 1850 to 1857. Although in one year it rose only two-tenths of one per cent, in three years the advance was between 19 and 23 per cent, and in two others nearly 14 per cent. By 1857 the annual average was nearly two and a half times what it had been in 1849. The third group to start an unbroken ascent was non-ferrous metals, which advanced continuously from 1851 to 1854. All other groups, except meats and meat products and furs, declined either in 1851 or 1852. Despite recessions in 1851, six groups started an unbroken advance in 1852: fish and ferrous metals increased from 1852 to 1854 and grains, grain products, dairy products, and spirits from 1852 to 1855.

The rise during 1853 and 1854 was distributed among most of the groups. The only groups which did not mount in both of these years were meats and meat products and furs, which declined in both 1853 and 1854 in the face of the general advance; chemicals, fuel and lighting, and textile fabrics, which fell in 1853; and sugar and molasses, which dipped in 1854. The most outstanding advance which started in 1853 was that in tobacco, which moved steadily upward until 1857. In 1854 chemicals commenced an unbroken rise which also culminated in 1857.

The tapering off in the momentum of the rise is indicated by the fact that in 1855 ten groups which had advanced for two or three years previously turned down. We have already seen that the index of fish was among the first to recede. The sub-groups show that the check at this time in the advance in imported foods was caused chiefly by recessions in fruits and condiments. In addition, dyes, textile fibers, and the miscellaneous group began to contract. The most important declines indicating the end of the expansion period occurred in ferrous and non-ferrous metals, wood, and other building materials. The recessions in these groups reflect, in part, the certainty as to the outcome of the Crimean War, but, more important from the American standpoint, they also indicate the end of a building boom. In two groups the decline in 1855 marks the beginning of a long period of contraction; condiments fell continuously from 1855 to 1859 and building materials other than wood from 1855 to 1860, except for a rise of about 1.0 per cent in 1857.

The recession in 1856 was confined to 12 groups, 10 of which dipped less than 9 per cent. One of these, textile fabrics, began to recede in 1856 as supplies of Russian sailcloth became available, and continued to decline to 1861. The outstanding decreases of nearly 30 per cent in both grains and grain products marked the collapse of these prices after four years of unusual advance and coincided with the end of the shipments stimulated by the Crimean War.

Ten of the groups which rose in 1856 continued to advance in 1857. In addition, eight which had receded the previous year recovered in 1857. Of these groups, the greatest recovery was in beverages. Its rise of approximately 17 per cent was influenced by the French and English expedition against China. Fuel and lighting and ferrous metals did not participate in the recovery of 1857, but joined the groups which had continuous declines to 1860 or 1861.

The revulsion of prices in 1857 is shown in the annual prices of 1858. With the prices of tea increasing during the continuation of the friction in China, beverages rose slightly. All other groups declined. Fruits and sugar and molasses fell between 30 and 38 per cent; tobacco and hides and leather dropped between 20 and 24 per cent. The remaining groups were equally divided, half showing declines of less than 10 per cent and the other half declining between 10 and 19 per cent. In general, the largest declines were those in farm crops and other foodstuffs. Metals, building materials, chemicals, and textile fabrics were the most important groups with relatively small recessions.

As in the case of the major groups, a sharp distinction in the behavior of the sub-groups occurred during 1859 and 1860, although the general curve declined slightly in both years. The individual groups showed a great diversity of movement in these two years. Dairy products, chemicals and drugs, dyes, non-ferrous metals, and miscellaneous articles rose in both years. In addition, nine other groups had a peak in 1859. The rise of 18.2 per cent in grains exceeded all other advances. Fish, grain products, and hides and leather also reached substantial peaks, 11 to 14 per cent above the low of 1858. In 1860 only three groups, fruit, wines, and condiments, rose in addition to the five which increased in both years. All others declined. The most extreme recessions in 1860 were those of 11 and 13 per cent in textile fibers and tobacco. In most of the other groups the contraction was less than 5 per cent.

The increases in the annual averages of 1861 were confined to 11 groups, three of which had started to rise in 1860. The only group of those increasing in both 1859 and 1860 which continued to advance in 1861 was dyes. The other 10 groups with a net gain in 1861 include tobacco and textile fibers, which had had the largest decreases in 1860; imported foods, such as beverages, fruit, and condiments; other imported commodities, specifically textile fabrics, wines, and spirits; building materials other than wood; and furs.

Fourteen groups declined in 1861. In ferrous metals and fuel and lighting this marks the fifth consecutive year of recession and in meats and meat products the fourth.

Proportion of Commodities Influencing Price Movements

The proportion of commodities with only slight changes in prices from year to year was extremely high between 1844 and 1861. Only in years of advance like 1854 and 1857 and in a year of sharp recession like 1858 did less than 25 per cent of the commodities show resistance to extreme price changes. Even in these three years at least 20 per cent of the series varied less than 2.5 per cent from the prices of the previous year. The greatest stability occurred in 1851 and 1856, when nearly 40 per cent of the commodities showed little if any change. In seven other years at least 30 per cent of the commodities were stable.

In the peaks of 1845 and 1847 and the recovery of 1850, 41 to 48 per cent of the series rose 2.5 per cent and more. The most sustained period of advance was that from 1853 to 1855. During the first two of these three years nearly 60 per cent of the commodities rose appreciably, but in 1855 only 44 per cent had a corresponding rise. This shrinkage in the proportion of commodities rising is another indication of the approaching end of the expansion period. The peak of 1857 also was shared by only 44 per cent of the commodities and the recovery in 1859 appeared to an appreciable extent in only about a third of the series.

The recession of 1846 affected by at least 2.5 per cent the annual averages of only 30 per cent of all commodities. Nearly as many fell 2.5 per cent or more in the peak of 1847. The contraction during 1848 and 1849 was more serious. In the first of these years nearly 60 per cent of the series and in the next year 45 per cent fell noticeably.

The general rise in prices during the early fifties was accompanied by a marked reduction in the proportion of commodities declining.

In no year from 1850 to 1854 did as many commodities fall at least 2.5 per cent as rose the same amount. In 1856 the number declining noticeably exceeded the number rising, although the declines were confined to 36 per cent of the series. Nearly as many fell in the peak year of 1857. The decline in the annual averages in 1858 was so widespread that more than two-thirds of the commodities fell 2.5 per cent or more and less than 10 per cent increased that much. From 1859 through 1861 the proportion decreasing continued to exceed the number rising, although only 37 to 46 per cent of the series fell materially.

The period from 1844 to 1861 differs from the three preceding periods in the increased number of commodities which varied less than 2.5 per cent from year to year. The upward movement in prices from 1844 to 1861 contrasts sharply with the persistently sagging tendency prevalent from 1822 to 1843. The pervasiveness of this general expansion is indicated by the fact that only in 1848, 1849, 1856, and 1858-1861 did more commodities recede substantially than advance.

In the peak of 1845 at least 75 per cent of the farm crops and derivatives advanced 2.5 per cent or more and two-thirds of the lumber products and naval stores were similarly affected. Among the imported foods and the two industrial groups, 35 to 43 per cent of the constituent series rose appreciably.

The peak of 1847 was even more predominantly confined to agricultural products. Between 78 and 83 per cent of the derivatives and farm crops advanced materially that year. In none of the other four major groups was more than 43 per cent of the series affected.

The upswing of the early fifties appeared at first predominantly in the lumber products and naval stores and farm crops, in which from two-thirds to three-fourths of the series rose substantially. In the other groups the proportion rising 2.5 per cent or more was approximately between a quarter and a half. The strong advance in lumber products and naval stores was intensified in 1851, when more than nine-tenths of these series increased materially. The group of farm derivatives was the only other one in which as many as half of the constituent series rose noticeably. That the further expansion was extremely widespread is indicated by the fact that more than 55 per cent of the commodities in each of the six major groups except imported foods rose in 1853 and 1854. Even in 1855 more than 55 per cent of farm crops, derivatives, and industrial commodities ready for consumption advanced noticeably. It is very significant that of the lumber products and naval stores, in which half or more of the series had risen every year from 1850 to 1854 inclusive, no series increased as much as 2.5 per cent in 1855.

The advance to the peak of 1857 was, likewise, widespread: more than half of the commodities in the four non-industrial groups rose substantially. Even among the industrial commodities approximately a third showed an upward lift. In contrast, the slight recovery of 1859 affected one-half or more of only lumber products and naval stores, farm crops, and farm derivatives. The least advance that year was the one in industrial commodities ready for consumption, of which 7 per cent of the series rose as much as 2.5 per cent.

During 1860 less than 40 per cent of the commodities in any of the six large major groups increased materially, but in 1861 slightly more than 40 per cent of the lumber products and naval stores and 57 per cent of the imported foods showed an early rise in response to the war. A third of the farm crops and of the industrial commodities ready for consumption, a tenth of the industrial raw and semi-finished articles, and none of the farm derivatives rose as much as 2.5 per cent.

Throughout the period from 1844 to 1861 most of the series which maintained the same price for two consecutive years belonged to the two industrial groups. Never were as many as 10 per cent of the farm crops or farm derivatives this stable, while only in 1855 did the imported foods and in 1854 and 1860 did the lumber products and naval stores contribute 10 per cent or more of their constituent series to this inert class. In contrast, at least 10 per cent of the industrial raw and semi-finished materials showed no variation in price from the previous year in 1844, from 1847 to 1850, and from 1855 to 1857. The greatest stability throughout this major period was that of the industrial commodities ready for consumption, of which not only did 10 per cent or more sell at the same price for two consecutive years except in 1857, 1858, and 1861, but more than 22 per cent were this stable from 1848 to 1852 and in 1859 and 1860.

The inclusion of the series which changed less than 2.5 per cent from one year to another indicates further the inherent stability in the prices of both groups of industrial materials. Only in 1853, 1857, and 1858 did less than 25 per cent of the industrial raw and semi-finished products change but mildly, if at all, and only in 1857 did less than 25 per cent of the industrial commodities ready for consumption show equally marked stability. The addition of the series with less than a 2.5 per cent change in prices from one year to another shows that the farm crops, imported foods, and lumber products and naval stores had more stability than was indicated merely by the number of their constituents which did not change in price for at least two years. Imported foods in eight years, farm crops in nine years, and lumber products and naval stores in 11 years, had 25 per cent or more of their commodities but slightly changed in price. The group of farm derivatives stands out as having the least stability—1844, 1850, and 1853 were the only years when as many as 25 per cent of its series varied little if at all.

Deviations of Annual Group Indices from General Average

The comparison of the annual indices of the nine major groups with the general average indicates the groups which had the greatest deviations from the composite index as well as those which were relatively higher or lower. Fish and farm crops were continuously the highest groups. The index of fish from 1844 to 1861 always held more than 34 per cent above the total curve, and on the average it was 56 per cent higher. Farm crops, usually about 33 per cent above the composite index, was always at least 14 per cent above it. Farm derivatives, too, except in 1844, exceeded the average of all commodities. From 1847 to 1861 it held 13 per cent or more above the general curve. The greatest deviations of these groups occurred in 1852, 1853, and 1859, when fish exceeded the average by 67 per cent or more, in 1847, 1854, and 1855, when farm crops rose more than 41 per cent above it, and in 1855, 1859, and 1860, when farm derivatives varied more than 36 per cent from it.

At the other extreme the industrial commodities ready for consumption, imported foods, and furs were consistently below the general curve, but only furs had an average deviation larger than that of either farm crops or farm derivatives. No group was as far below the average from 1844 to 1861 as fish was above. The industrial commodities ready for consumption, always at least 3.3 per cent below the composite index, were usually about 8 per cent below and even deviated as much as 12 per cent in 1852, 1853, 1860, and 1861. Imported foods were in every year even further below the general curve than were the industrial commodities ready for consumption. Never rising to within 8 per cent of the general index, imported foods tended to fluctuate about 18 per cent below and from 1858 to 1860 were more than 26 per cent under the average. Throughout this final major period furs consistently oscillated below even the imported foods. The annual index of the prices of furs deviated from the general index by approximately 18 to 55 per cent, averaging slightly more than 36 per cent. The maximum differences of more than 46 per cent between the two curves occurred from 1854 to 1857 and in 1860.

The other three major groups fluctuated around the general average, not being consistently above or below it. The industrial raw and semi-finished materials had the smallest deviation, while lumber products and naval stores had a higher average percentage of deviation than the industrial commodities ready for consumption, and wines varied more than even the imported foods. In relation to the composite index, the group of industrial raw and semi-finished materials had a downward trend, falling from 7.2 per cent above the general curve in 1844 to 7.0 per cent below it in 1857. From 1844 to 1850, except in 1847, these industrial products were above the average, but from 1851 to 1861 they were persistently below it. The index of lumber products and naval stores had an inverse movement. It fluctuated below the general average from 1844 to 1850 and above it from 1851 to 1861 except in 1856 and 1857. The greatest deviations were in 1844 and 1847 when lumber products and naval stores were more than 8 per cent below the average, from 1852 to 1854 and in 1859, when they were 15 to 16 per cent above it, and in 1861 when they exceeded the general index by 41.7 per cent. In the prices of wines there was a still more abrupt shift in their relation to the total. From 1844 to 1854 they held approximately 4 to 15 per cent below the general average while from 1855 to 1861 they were more than 21 per cent above it, the greatest deviations of approximately 42 per cent occurring in 1858 and 1861.

CHAPTER XI

COMPARISON OF THE SEVENTEEN CYCLES

The discussion in the four previous chapters has centered around the successive cycles in prices from 1784 to 1861. The chief emphasis has been placed on the comparisons and contrasts of the various groups of commodities in each cycle. In this chapter the historical factors will be largely disregarded and attention focused upon the comparison and contrast of the 17 cycles apparent in the general curve.

For the composite index it is significant to compare the duration of the swings, their relative variability, and the difference in length of the expanding and contracting phases of each. Similar measurements can be made of the corresponding cycles in the nine major groups and 24 of the sub-groups. The order in which the indices of the major groups began to contract or expand shows the steps by which an expansion of prices turned into a recession and by which the following recovery was effected. As a supplement, a study of the times at which the specific commodities began to rise and fall compared with the turning points in the general curve gives the proportion of the series in each group which contributed to the initiation of changes in the direction of the composite index.

The General Index[1]

The 17 cycles from 1789 to 1861 in the general index differ markedly in length. Two of them, the one from 1789 to 1798 and the other from 1811 to 1821, were extraordinarily long, nine years or more in duration, because of the peculiar conditions in those periods. At the other extreme were two short cycles: the one from 1856 to 1858 lasted only 20 months and that from 1828 to 1830 only 25 months. If these extremes be disregarded, the remaining 13 cycles show a definite tendency to last from 40 to 46 months.

[1] The data are presented in Table 24, pp. 273 ff.

Six of the cycles fall within these limits. Of the other seven, two required only 32 or 33 months for completion and the other five between 50 and 64 months.

The four largest increases in the general curve were, in the order of their importance, those from 1789 to 1797, from 1811 to 1814, from 1852 to 1855, and from 1834 to 1837. Even these differed markedly in extent, the peak of 1797 being slightly more than 75 per cent above the bottom of 1789 and the peak of 1837 approximately 20 per cent above the low of 1834. Two peaks, 1828 and 1859, were less than 5 per cent above and five others, 1801, 1822, 1825, 1851, and 1857, less than 10 per cent above the previous low.

The greatest declines were associated with the maximum increases, but did not always follow them immediately. The advances from 1789 to 1797 and from 1811 to 1814 were followed by a drop of nearly 50 per cent from 1814 to 1821. The bulk of the contraction after the rise from 1834 to 1837 came in the drop of nearly 25 per cent from 1839 to 1843. Likewise the outstanding recession associated with the rise from 1852 to 1855 was the slump of 16.5 per cent in eight months from 1857 to 1858. From no other peak did the total index fall more than 13 per cent and the declines from the peaks in 1809, 1832, 1845, 1851, and 1855 were less than 7.5 per cent; neither in the amount of rise nor of fall did any progressive tendency appear to intensify or to moderate them.

Another measurement of the cycles, the "index of cyclical variability," was computed by averaging the percentages of the intervening peak represented by the preceding and succeeding lows.[2] Except for the two unusually long periods, which also had the highest index of cyclical variability, there was no relation between the length of the cycle and its severity as measured by this computation of variability. The cycles varied considerably in their average height, two being as low as 6.5 to 7. The nearest approach to any concentration was the clustering of six cycles between the indices of 8 to 10.

The two mildest swings were those from 1858 to 1861 and from 1849 to 1852, while the most severe, disregarding the two longest, were those from 1834 to 1838 and from 1838 to 1843. These cycles

[2] The method followed is that used by Professor F. C. Mills, *Behavior of Prices*, pp. 84 ff.

reflect the influence of the price changes around 1837. It is significant that the two cycles from 1852 to 1858, which were influenced by conditions around 1857, also had high variability.

The measurements of the cycles in the general index do not reveal any progressive change throughout the period. Although the four longest cycles occurred before 1821, swings of 50 months or more appeared from 1830 to 1834, from 1838 to 1843, and from 1852 to 1856. The most severe cycles were the two long ones which occurred before 1821. The two cycles between 1834 and 1843, the one from 1846 to 1849, and the two from 1852 to 1858, were more severe than any of the three from 1798 to 1811, while those from 1828 to 1830, from 1830 to 1834, from 1843 to 1846, from 1849 to 1852, and from 1858 to 1861 were less severe.

The final factor to be considered in the analysis of the cycles in the general index is the relative duration of the periods of expanding and contracting prices. It is to be expected that, in a period when an upward trend in prices underlies the fluctuations of several successive cycles, most of the swings will characteristically have a longer period of rise than of fall. As corollaries, the cycles on a long downward trend usually have a longer fall than rise, and on a horizontal trend the length of the period of rise and fall might be equal or alternating in successive cycles. In the light of the price movements previously discussed, it is not surprising that in the two cycles from 1789 to 1803 the number of months of rise exceeded the number of months of fall. This relationship was reversed in the seven cycles from 1803 to 1834. The periods of rise and fall alternately exceeded each other in length in the four swings from 1834 to 1849. In the three cycles from 1849 to 1858 the period of rise was again longer than the period of fall while in the closing cycle from 1858 to 1861 the recession became dominant.

Indices of Sub-Groups

The cyclical variations of the indices of all the sub-groups except miscellaneous articles have been considered in Chapters VII-X. As a summary, their significant measures can be compared. When any of the sub-groups failed to reflect a swing apparent in the average, it was necessary to measure as one swing the movements in prices over two or more general cycles.

TABL

PERCENTAGES OF RISE O

Year of Peak	Farm Products			Foods									Ch ic
	Grains	Tobacco	Other	Grain Products	Meats	Dairy Products	Fish	Fruit	Beverages	Condiments	Sugar and Molasses		
1797	191.8	246.0	138.5	210.9	155.3	153.0	168.9	163.4	81.0	113.5	147.6		145
1801	56.9	22.5	79.7	79.7	63.6	33.2	82.4	34.5	28.7	15.7			28
1805	80.4	17.9	20.7	83.5	61.4	95.8	44.1	96.1	32.1	12.6	28.7		19
1809			61.2	70.3	45.7	38.1	45.6	25.6	24.2	41.8	37.7		72
1814	209.0	298.9	102.7	86.3	77.2	69.2	87.5	94.0	197.5	125.9	160.6		131
1822	94.9		47.6	73.2		61.3	19.8	42.9	7.0		11.9		1c
1825	60.1	27.0	84.0	35.3	18.0	51.6	12.6	44.7	7.9	19.8	28.4		6
1828	43.7	27.0	22.4	68.6	22.0	19.3	29.3	64.5		7.7			11
1832	61.5		28.6	43.9	36.2	60.3	25.9	30.5	13.8	17.4	25.2		21
1837	87.7	127.3	143.0	103.6	58.5	70.8	92.3	61.9	21.1	15.2	35.5		30
1839	39.1	143.7	59.6	27.1	39.3	25.9	72.0	43.0	48.0	6.1	15.8		22
1845	72.6	66.6	13.0	53.3	54.6	81.2	41.3	88.2		29.5	41.6		
1847	105.4	21.9	59.8	102.9	76.3	36.4	14.1				10.7		15
1851	24.6	113.1	27.4	13.6	83.5	31.4	48.9	85.9	30.2	15.2	22.8		14
1855	118.8		77.6	119.3	30.2	63.9	61.7	162.6	25.0	30.7			36
1857	53.0	65.0	26.0	31.9	28.9	17.2	37.0	55.9	31.1		123.6		13
1859	52.3		26.4	45.6		23.9	43.0	23.5			29.6		14

The first measure of the cycles, that of their duration, necessarily corresponds roughly to that of the general index, since the cycles have been defined in relation to its turning points. The only exceptions are the cases when a sub-group missed a cycle. Even in such cases, however, there was no progressive tendency for an increase in length. (Appendix Table 58.)

Although the four greatest increases in the general curve were those from 1789 to 1797, from 1811 to 1814, from 1852 to 1855, and from 1834 to 1837, the four maximum advances in each of the sub-groups were more widely distributed. Even so, the pervasiveness of the unusual increases to peaks in 1797 and 1814 is indicated by the fact that every sub-group had one of its four largest increases in at least one of these times and that all but five had in these two advances two of their four largest ones.

The extent of the advance to the peaks in 1855 and 1837 was especially aided by the groups which at that time had one of their most substantial increases. Twelve sub-groups thus contributed materially to the peak of 1855 and eight to the peak of 1837. A listing of these groups brings out the difference in the character of the advance in the two periods. Only three sub-groups noticeably aided both advances: grain products, fuel and lighting materials, and ferrous metals. The importance of agricultural products in stimulating the advance to a peak in 1837 is shown by the fact that tobacco, minor

GRO PS IN 17 CYCLES

Fuel and Lighting	Metals		Building Materials		Furs	Textiles		Hides and Leather	Spirits	Wines	Year of Peak
	Ferrous	Non-Ferrous	Wood	Other		Fibers	Fabrics				
99.6		61.6	152.7	87.1	80.2	82.8	60.7	48.8	252.1	52.2	1797
22.5	60.8	11.1	11.6	21.7	40.1	31.9	24.4		15.3	36.5	1801
34.9		22.5	16.6	15.7	26.2	34.1				8.0	1805
	22.2	15.3	18.4	45.8	35.4	24.6	85.9	52.2	72.0	59.4	1809
125.8	36.0	140.1	33.7	94.4	36.2	102.3	47.0	123.4	161.5	53.9	1814
		3.3	19.9	6.8	52.4			35.7	11.1		1822
16.0	9.4	25.8		7.8	30.7	52.3		9.4		15.2	1825
			9.5	7.2	19.3	25.1		7.5	19.8	7.8	1828
32.3	6.4		19.1	21.8	15.2	17.4	15.5	14.8	16.1	8.9	1832
38.5	23.7	55.7	16.2	22.5	22.9	34.0	22.2	17.0	20.4		1837
20.8	6.0	7.8		14.8	44.5	28.8		19.0	6.3		1839
	16.0		27.7	17.5	54.1	20.4		13.1	34.0	20.2	1845
30.4		25.6	13.6			51.7		18.3	13.8	3.9	1847
21.3		54.6				31.5		32.1	6.7		1851
40.6	31.4	17.4	41.6	47.1		23.7	24.4	59.1	69.9		1855
		13.8	21.7	8.8	34.2	16.5		71.1	14.6		1857
		8.8	10.9	8.5	22.0	5.0		25.0		96.7	1859

farm crops, and dairy products, in addition to the grain products, made at this time one of their outstanding gains. The other groups which also contributed to this peak were fish and non-ferrous metals. In contrast, the peak of 1855 was built up from unusual increases in many different parts of the economy. Domestic agriculture was represented only by grains in addition to grain products; the other contributing groups, besides fuel and lighting materials and ferrous metals, were fruit, condiments, chemicals, wood, building materials other than wood, hides and leather, textile fabrics, and spirits.

To a lesser extent the groups which attained one of their four major advances in other periods of expansion also suggest the different characteristics of the successive waves in the movements of prices from 1784 to 1861. Thus the mildness of the advance stands out in 1822 when only furs increased unusually, and in 1859 when wines, terminating a long advance, showed also one of its largest gains. Even more mild were the peaks of 1828 and 1832, when no group had one of its most sizable increases. Similarly, the importance of cotton in the peak of 1825 is suggested when it is seen that only minor farm crops and textile fibers made unusual gains in that expansion. Again, the effect around 1847 of the shortage of foodstuffs in Europe is emphasized by the material increases of prices of grains, grain products, and meats and meat products. The group of textile fibers was the only other one with a similar behavior in that cycle.

TA

PERCENTAGES OF DECLINE OF

Year of Peak	Farm Products			Foods								
	Grains	Tobacco	Other	Grain Products	Meats	Dairy Products	Fish	Fruit	Beverages	Condiments	Sugar and Molasses
1797	45.0	54.3	49.6	52.9	31.4	33.5	58.8	25.6	11.0	38.9	34.0
1801	34.5	5.1	22.2	41.6	40.2	36.8	32.5	44.1	31.3	17.2	
1805	55.4	36.9	36.2	45.4	42.4	41.1	38.8	38.6	28.1	13.2	33.4
1809			33.9	21.9	13.9	21.4	13.0	29.2	55.5	35.6	10.8
1814	75.2	67.6	62.7	73.5	57.6	57.6	64.6	49.9	42.5	69.0	71.8
1822	39.4		19.2	35.5		49.4	23.4	30.7	17.3		15.1
1825	35.7	41.3	54.8	26.4	21.4	27.1	17.6	44.6	37.8	11.2	31.0
1828	30.6	28.8	13.4	37.8	24.6	22.0	21.7	39.9		21.4	
1832	25.9		17.1	22.1	14.9	19.6	26.9	39.9	22.8	32.5	11.5
1837	48.5	38.5	36.0	37.4	29.3	27.4	23.7	34.9	20.7	14.3	22.8
1839	38.3	68.5	51.1	48.7	59.8	54.6	51.0	35.4	29.2	14.8	40.1
1845	30.2	17.2	12.0	30.4	27.0	27.0	13.1	41.2		21.0	17.6
1847	51.5	38.1	36.0	48.9	35.9	32.4	31.0				25.9
1851	14.8	39.2	12.5	13.2	17.1	11.7	16.0	47.4	32.2	12.3	19.2
1855	48.3		31.1	47.3	16.0	20.0	26.8	35.5	7.7	36.1	
1857	39.0	36.3	27.3	30.0	47.4	27.3	36.5	54.2	16.7		47.5
1859	34.3		26.1	33.0	.	33.0	39.5	33.6			33.4

It is difficult to say whether the cycles of the sub-groups became more or less severe during the period. In dyes and textile fabrics the increases in four of the first five cycles were more than in any later ones, except one of textile fabrics which, covering two cycles, equaled the smallest of the four. In all other groups the four largest increases were distributed before and after the period from 1821 to 1834.

In the outstanding decline of the whole period from the peak of 1814 to the low of 1821 the general average dropped nearly 50 per cent. Since the various sub-groups did not reach their maxima at the same time, the general average minimizes their recessions. All but five of the sub-groups dropped as much or more than the general curve. For 19 groups this recession was the most extreme of any in the entire period and for all it was at least one of the four largest declines. Chemicals, grains, grain products, and sugar and molasses dropped during these years more than 70 per cent. Nine other groups fell more than 60 per cent. All groups except furs and hides and leather receded at least 40 per cent and even these two declined more than 37 per cent.

The other two pronounced declines in the general curve were those from 1839 to 1843 and from 1857 to 1858. Among 12 sub-groups the decline after 1839 was also one of the three most severe. In tobacco, meats and meat products, and furs it was actually the

-GRO PS IN 7 CYCLES

es	Fuel and Lighting	Metals		Building Materials		Furs	Textiles		Hides and Leather	Spirits	Wines	Year of Peak
		Ferrous	Non-Ferrous	Wood	Other		Fibers	Fabrics				
7	26.4		12.3	15.2	30.7	39.3	19.6	15.8	32.2	37.8	13.7	1797
9	14.7	12.9	11.3	14.7	11.6	10.5	33.8	22.9		34.7	8.6	1801
4	27.6		13.0	6.5	13.7	16.8	19.9				16.2	1805
6		9.7	20.3	5.9	22.1	14.7	43.7	43.2	33.8	25.0	7.5	1809
2	67.3	41.1	66.6	47.0	63.9	38.5	55.5	53.8	37.4	68.0	55.0	1814
2			9.2	4.7	14.3	15.7			8.1	22.2		1822
3	20.1	15.9	36.7		16.4	26.5	29.7		16.1		17.5	1825
1				23.0	14.2	24.4	26.3		9.4	7.4	13.7	1828
0	14.9	7.6		12.0	10.5	14.9	9.7	18.3	24.4	8.7	27.0	1832
6	21.4	11.6	24.9	37.4	18.5	43.6	28.0	16.1	14.1	7.7		1837
3	34.6	23.4	24.9		26.0	44.6	36.3		24.8	15.6		1839
3		27.1		12.8	17.1	34.8	19.5		18.0	4.6	8.1	1845
0	14.7		10.5	13.5			23.7		20.9	21.8	8.5	1847
4	12.0		18.0				16.4		7.1	10.6		1851
5	26.8	25.2	12.3	13.4	16.1		9.2	11.2	12.3	8.3		1855
[illegible]			19.6	14.5	8.6	19.3	18.8		33.6	38.4		1857
7			14.1	11.4	11.9	19.6	17.6		24.3		17.1	1859

most extreme decline. The contraction after 1857 does not stand out clearly in most of the sub-groups. Only fruit took its major drop and only meats and meat products, sugar and molasses, hides and leather, and spirits had one of their three major declines at that time. In contrast, the recession of 1797 was more severe in the sub-groups, most of them falling more than they did in 1857. One of three pronounced declines in each group occurred at this time in eight of the sub-groups, but the beginning and end of the decline which in the general curve lasted from 1797 to 1798 were so diversified that much of the fall was concealed in the general average. Even after 1809 as many groups fell off severely as after 1857.

Among the cycles the extreme decreases were more widely distributed than the advances. In every period of contraction at least one group had one of its four chief declines and except for the contraction from 1859 to 1861 at least one group had one of its three largest recessions.

The variability of the sub-groups in each cycle can be indicated by the average percentage that the preceding and following lows were below the intervening peak. On the whole the greatest variability is found in the domestic agricultural groups—grains, grain products, minor farm crops, meats and meat products, and dairy products—as well as fruit and fish. At the other extreme, construction materials —specifically ferrous metals, wood, and other building materials—

and textile fabrics, wines, chemicals, and condiments had the smallest indices of cyclical variability. Among the commodities intermediate in variability, tobacco, beverages, sugar and molasses, dyes, textile fibers, and furs tended to have more pronounced cycles than fuel and lighting materials, non-ferrous metals, hides and leather, and spirits.

Indices of Major Groups

The length of the cycles of the major groups is somewhat determined by the method of relating their turning points to those of the general curve. In the cases in which a group completed more than one swing within a cycle of the general curve, the movements have been consolidated. At other times the swing in the prices of a group might extend over two or more cycles on the general curve. The total measurements for these swings appear in the cycle of the general curve to which its peak corresponds while the other cycles covered by the swing are blank.

Farm crops, farm derivatives, and fish were the only groups with cycles which corresponded to every one in the composite curve. At the other extreme, the industrial commodities ready for consumption tended after 1811 to reflect only the extreme peaks of the general curve. As a result this group reflected only nine of the 17 cycles. Five of its swings lasted 100 months or more. Prices of wines were subject to behavior somewhat similar to that of the industrial commodities ready for consumption. As a result only 11 cycles were completed in the wines, and four lasted 113 months or more. The other groups also failed to reflect some of the cycles in the general curve, completing only 14 or 15 cycles in the entire period. In furs the cycles from 1846 to 1856, in industrial raw and semi-finished commodities those from 1828 to 1834, and in lumber products and naval stores those from 1846 to 1852 are concealed. The cycles missed by the imported foods were somewhat distributed. This group did not respond to the cycles of 1828-1830, of 1838-1843, or of 1846-1849.

Like the movements of the general curve, the amount of rise and fall in the cycles of the nine major groups showed no progressive tendency to increase or decrease during the period as a whole. The relative extent of expansion to the various peaks as noted in the composite index was not uniform among the groups. As in the average, the rise from 1789 to 1797 in fish, furs, industrial commodities ready for consumption, farm crops, farm derivatives, and lumber products and naval stores exceeded any other advance. In imported foods, and industrial raw and semi-finished products, however, the rise from 1811 to 1814 exceeded that of 1789 to 1797. In wines even more extreme advances occurred to peaks in 1859, 1809, and 1814 than in 1797.

TABLE 22

PERCENTAGES OF RISE OF NINE MAJOR GROUPS IN 17 CYCLES

Year of Peak	Farm		Imported Foods	Lumber Products and Naval Stores	Industrial		Fish	Furs	Wines	General Index
	Crops	Derivatives			Raw	Consumption				
1797	98.2	101.4	91.1	184.4	50.8	113.7	168.9	80.2	52.2	75.4
1801	24.6	29.6	6.7	22.8	13.7	2.3	82.4	40.1	36.5	7.1
1805	35.2	37.4	16.1	25.9	15.4	16.2	44.1	26.2	8.0	12.8
1809	29.4	33.8	29.5	36.8	19.8	25.4	45.6	35.4	59.4	16.6
1814	93.8	50.2	95.9	69.0	59.5	66.3	87.5	36.2	53.9	52.2
1822	30.1	16.4	8.7	21.3	2.7		19.8	52.4		6.3
1825	28.5	8.2	18.2	9.8	9.0		12.6	30.7	15.2	8.5
1828	17.2	23.1		9.1			29.3	19.3	7.8	4.8
1832	30.7	28.5	15.1	24.2		9.8	25.9	15.2	8.9	10.5
1837	57.7	55.7	17.6	21.1	22.4	19.0	92.3	22.9		19.7
1839	41.0	19.9		11.2	12.0		72.0	44.5		10.1
1845	29.8	38.8	35.1	31.6	4.8		41.3	54.1	20.2	12.0
1847	53.6	51.6			6.5	8.5	14.1		3.9	10.9
1851	27.7	44.6	24.1		5.1		48.9			9.9
1855	58.3	31.1	28.8	66.3	26.3	37.2	61.7			30.0
1857	26.6	19.9	35.8	20.4	4.8		37.0	34.2		8.5
1859	22.9	18.4	10.7	14.1	4.0		43.0	22.0	96.7	4.5

There was less conformity in the importance of the peak of 1814. Only in farm crops, lumber products and naval stores, and industrial commodities ready for consumption did the expansions which corresponded to that from 1811 to 1814 in the general curve rank as second in amount of rise. That it was so large in the general curve is in part explained by the fact that it was the maximum for the groups of imported foods and industrial raw and semi-finished articles.

The other two unusually extensive increases in the general curve were those from 1834 to 1837 and from 1852 to 1855, the peak of 1855 being further above its previous low than was the peak of 1837. Such a relationship also characterized the corresponding cycles in farm crops, imported foods, lumber products and naval stores, and both industrial groups.

Considering the period as a whole, the major groups differed widely in amount of rise in most cycles. Usually those which contributed least to the rise comprised the two industrial groups, wines, and imported foods. Including the swings in the general curve which were not reflected in their movements, the increases in these groups were less than 20 per cent in 10 to 13 cycles.

The groups with the most substantial advances were farm crops and fish, two of the three which completed every cycle that appeared in the general average. The least increase in farm crops was 17.2 per cent in 1828, the only cycle in which it rose less than 22 per cent. Ten of its advances were roughly between 20 and 40 per cent and four between 40 and 60 per cent. The other two increases, those of 1797 and 1814, were over 90 per cent. The smallest rise in the index of fish prices in any cycle was 12.6 per cent from 1824 to 1825. In two other expansions the increases were also less than 20 per cent. In only three cycles was the rise between 20 and 40 per cent. In 11 cycles the advance exceeded 40 per cent, five being as much as 40 to 60 per cent, two from 60 to 80 per cent, and four over 80 per cent. In farm derivatives, lumber products and naval stores, and furs the increases tended to be more extreme than those in the two industrial groups, imported foods, and wines on the one hand, and less extreme than those in farm crops and fish on the other. Farm derivatives, lumber products and naval stores, and furs rose less than 20 per cent in at least five cycles and less than 40 per cent in at least 12.

The decline from 1814 to 1821, in which prices contracted from the rise between 1789 and 1797 as well as from that between 1811 and 1814, was in all groups except furs like that in the general group in that it was more severe than any other recession. The decline in furs at that time was 38.5 per cent compared with recessions of 50 to 65 per cent in the other major groups.

The next most severe drop in prices in farm crops, farm derivatives, lumber products and naval stores, industrial raw and semi-finished materials, and fish, as well as in the general curve, was that from 1839 to 1843 when prices receded from the rise which had been especially marked between 1834 and 1837. In farm crops, farm derivatives, and fish, the decrease in those years was between 47.5 and 51 per cent; lumber products and naval stores fell nearly 35 per cent, and industrial raw and semi-finished materials more than 20 per cent.

The imported foods and industrial commodities ready for consumption missed this recession because they did not recover in 1839

TABLE 23

PERCENTAGES OF DECLINE OF NINE MAJOR GROUPS IN 17 CYCLES

Year of Peak	Farm		Imported Foods	Lumber Products and Naval Stores	Industrial		Fish	Furs	Wines	General Index
	Crops	Derivatives			Raw	Consumption				
1797	22.4	22.4	21.3	33.0	9.0	17.0	48.8	39.3	13.7	11.3
1801	23.1	29.2	21.1	17.2	11.8	13.1	32.5	10.5	8.6	11.5
1805	32.8	27.3	15.8	18.0	4.7	11.6	38.8	16.8	16.2	9.7
1809	19.6	10.6	25.9	23.6	10.1	11.2	13.0	14.7	7.5	7.1
1814	58.2	50.2	57.4	52.8	55.3	63.5	64.6	38.5	55.0	49.9
1822	23.9	18.4	15.9	12.1	8.3		23.4	15.7		12.1
1825	27.2	11.4	28.7	14.5	18.8		17.6	26.5	17.5	11.7
1828	16.2	23.9		18.8			21.7	24.4	13.7	12.3
1832	9.2	10.4	24.8	8.1		9.7	26.9	14.9	27.0	6.5
1837	24.7	21.0	24.9	19.7	11.9	23.2	23.7	43.6		12.3
1839	47.7	48.6		33.6	21.3		51.0	44.6		24.2
1845	15.3	19.4	22.8	20.1	5.9		13.1	34.8	8.1	7.0
1847	33.5	29.6			8.2	12.4	31.0		8.5	13.0
1851	15.3	8.9	20.2		5.8		16.0			4.9
1855	25.9	18.6	12.2	21.0	4.5	22.9	26.8			4.7
1857	28.9	23.2	32.9	15.0	10.8		36.5	19.3		16.5
1859	19.7	24.4	14.9	9.7	10.4		39.5	19.6	17.1	9.1

but fell from 1837 to 1843. This recession, which amounted to 23 to 25 per cent, is somewhat comparable in effect to that from 1839 to 1843 in most of the other major groups and in the industrial commodities ready for consumption was exceeded only by the fall from 1814 to 1821. In imported foods, however, it was exceeded by the contractions from 1857 to 1858, from 1825 to 1828, and from 1809 to 1811, as well as by that from 1814 to 1821.

In the general curve it has been noted that the recession from 1857 to 1858 ranked third in severity. This, however, was not the case in any of the major groups. Among lumber products and naval stores, fish, and furs, the third most severe decline was that from 1797 to 1798, when their indices dropped between 33 and 50 per cent. The correspondingly severe contraction in imported foods, industrial raw and semi-finished products, and wines was that from the peak of 1825. Wines receded 17.5 per cent between 1825 and 1828 while industrial raw and semi-finished materials and imported foods, which continued to fall until 1830, decreased in all nearly 20 per cent and 30 per cent respectively. For farm crops and farm derivatives, the declines of nearly 30 to 35 per cent between 1847 and 1849 were exceeded only by their recessions from the peaks around 1814 and 1839. Just as the industrial commodities ready for consumption did not recover in 1839 after a decline set in from the peak in 1837, so after the peak of 1855 they failed to recover in either 1857 or 1859, but dropped approximately 23 per cent between 1855 and 1861. In this group only the decreases following the peaks of 1814 and 1837 were more severe.

In the amount by which they usually receded, the major groups do not have the same relative importance as was noted in their typical extent of advance. Both industrial groups and the wines which, counting the cycles they missed, declined less than 10 per cent in at least nine contractions and less than 20 per cent in at least 14, as a rule receded much less than any other group. At the other extreme the group of fish stood out as participating in the most violent decreases. It not only completed every cycle that appeared in the general index, but it never dropped less than 13 per cent. In only four cycles did it fail to contract more than 20 per cent from the preceding peak. The declines of all of the other major groups fall between these extremes. Imported foods, which had been among the groups rising the least, usually fell more than the lumber products and naval stores and furs. These two groups, in at least 10 cycles, declined less than 20 per cent, while the imported foods and both domestic agricultural groups suffered an equal or even larger number of decreases of more than 20 per cent.

As evidence of the minimizing of changes by the total index, the indices of cyclical variability were usually larger for the groups than for the composite. In 12 of the cycles, fish had more extreme movements than any other group. Furs three times, lumber products and

Table 24
Summary of Cyclical Movements of Nine Major Groups

Group	End of Preceding Recession	Peak	End of Succeeding Low	Number of Months			Index of Cyclical Variability
				Rise	Fall	Total Cycle	
General Index	Apr. 1789	Feb. 1797	Apr. 1798	94	14	108	27.1
Farm							
Crops	Apr. 1789	Feb. 1797	May 1799	94	27	121	35.9
Derivatives	Apr. 1789	Mar. 1796	July 1798	83	28	111	36.3
Imported Foods	Apr. 1789	Jan. 1796	June 1798	81	29	110	34.5
Lumber Products and Naval Stores	July 1788	Feb. 1797	Aug. 1799	103	30	133	48.9
Industrial							
Raw and Semi-Finished	May 1791	Sept. 1795	Apr. 1798	52	31	83	21.3
Ready for Consumption	Feb. 1789	Mar. 1796	Dec. 1797	85	21	106	35.1
Fish	Oct. 1788	Mar. 1797	Aug. 1800	101	41	142	60.8
Furs	Feb. 1788	Jan. 1797	Nov. 1798	107	22	129	41.9
Wines	Jan. 1789	Aug. 1796	June 1798	91	22	113	24.0
General Index	Apr. 1798	Nov. 1801	Mar. 1803	43	16	59	9.0
Farm							
Crops	May 1799	Mar. 1801	July 1803	22	28	50	21.4
Derivatives	July 1798	Aug. 1801	Apr. 1803	37	20	57	26.0
Imported Foods	June 1798	July 1799	July 1803	13	48	61	13.7
Lumber Products and Naval Stores	Aug. 1799	Dec. 1801	Aug. 1802	28	8	36	17.9
Industrial							
Raw and Semi-Finished	Apr. 1798	Nov. 1801	Dec. 1802	43	13	56	11.9
Ready for Consumption	Dec. 1797	Mar. 1801	Mar. 1803	39	24	63	7.6
Fish	Aug. 1800	Jan. 1802	Jan. 1804	17	24	41	38.8
Furs	Nov. 1798	July 1800	Sept. 1802	20	26	46	19.5
Wines	June 1798	Feb. 1802	June 1803	44	16	60	17.7
General Index	Mar. 1803	Feb. 1805	July 1808	23	41	64	10.5
Farm							
Crops	July 1803	May 1805	Aug. 1808	22	39	61	29.4
Derivatives	Apr. 1803	Apr. 1805	Sept. 1808	24	41	65	27.2
Imported Foods	July 1803	Dec. 1805	Apr. 1807	29	16	45	14.8
Lumber Products and Naval Stores	Aug. 1802	Feb. 1803	Aug. 1808	6	66	72	19.3
Industrial							
Raw and Semi-Finished	Dec. 1802	Jan. 1806	July 1807	37	18	55	9.0
Ready for Consumption	Mar. 1803	Feb. 1805	Aug. 1807	23	30	53	12.7
Fish	Jan. 1804	Aug. 1806	Aug. 1808	31	24	55	34.7
Furs	Sept. 1802	May 1805	Aug. 1808	32	39	71	18.8
Wines	June 1803	June 1804	Oct. 1807	12	40	52	11.8
General Index	July 1808	Apr. 1809	Nov. 1811	9	31	40	10.6
Farm							
Crops	Aug. 1808	Aug. 1810	Nov. 1811	24	15	39	21.1
Derivatives	Sept. 1808	Oct. 1810	June 1812	25	20	45	17.9
Imported Foods	Apr. 1807	Feb. 1809	Dec. 1811	22	34	56	24.3
Lumber Products and Naval Stores	Aug. 1808	Jan. 1811	Aug. 1812	29	19	48	25.2
Industrial							
Raw and Semi-Finished	July 1807	Apr. 1809	Feb. 1812	21	34	55	13.3
Ready for Consumption	Aug. 1807	Mar. 1809	Apr. 1811	19	25	44	15.7
Fish	Aug. 1808	May 1811	Sept. 1811	33	4	37	22.1
Furs	Aug. 1808	Oct. 1811	Jan. 1814	38	27	65	20.4
Wines	Oct. 1807	Oct. 1810	Feb. 1811	36	4	40	22.4
General Index	Nov. 1811	Nov. 1814	Apr. 1821	36	77	113	42.1
Farm							
Crops	Nov. 1811	Mar. 1817	June 1821	64	51	115	53.3
Derivatives	June 1812	Apr. 1817	May 1821	58	49	107	41.8
Imported Foods	Dec. 1811	Nov. 1814	Sept. 1821	35	82	117	53.1
Lumber Products and Naval Stores	Aug. 1812	Mar. 1814	Apr. 1821	19	85	104	46.8
Industrial							
Raw and Semi-Finished	Feb. 1812	Jan. 1814	June 1820	23	77	100	46.3
Ready for Consumption	Apr. 1811	Nov. 1814	Aug. 1830	43	189	232	51.7
Fish	Sept. 1811	Aug. 1814	Aug. 1821	35	84	119	55.6
Furs	Jan. 1814	Jan. 1816	Mar. 1819	24	38	62	32.5
Wines	Feb. 1811	Feb. 1814	June 1824	36	124	160	45.0
General Index	Apr. 1821	Mar. 1822	Sept. 1824	11	30	41	9.0
Farm							
Crops	June 1821	May 1822	Sept. 1824	11	28	39	23.5
Derivatives	May 1821	June 1822	Sept. 1824	13	27	40	16.2

TABLE 24 (*Continued*)

Group	End of Preceding Recession	Peak	End of Succeeding Low	Number of Months: Rise	Number of Months: Fall	Number of Months: Total Cycle	Index of Cyclical Variability
Imported Foods	Sept. 1821	Dec. 1821	July 1824	3	31	34	11.9
Lumber Products and Naval Stores	Apr. 1821	May 1822	June 1824	13	25	38	14.8
Industrial							
Raw and Semi-Finished	June 1820	Feb. 1822	May 1824	20	27	47	5.4
Ready for Consumption							
Fish	Aug. 1821	Nov. 1821	Sept. 1824	3	34	37	19.9
Furs	Mar. 1819	Apr. 1822	Jan. 1825	37	33	70	25.0
Wines							
General Index	Sept. 1824	May 1825	June 1828	8	37	45	9.7
Farm							
Crops	Sept. 1824	July 1826	July 1828	22	24	46	24.7
Derivatives	Sept. 1824	Jan. 1827	Apr. 1828	28	15	43	9.5
Imported Foods	July 1824	May 1825	Mar. 1830	10	58	68	22.0
Lumber Products and Naval Stores	June 1824	May 1825	Aug. 1827	11	27	38	11.7
Industrial							
Raw and Semi-Finished	May 1824	May 1825	Sept. 1830	12	64	76	13.5
Ready for Consumption							
Fish	Sept. 1824	Apr. 1825	Sept. 1826	7	17	24	14.4
Furs	Jan. 1825	Sept. 1825	Aug. 1826	8	11	19	25.0
Wines	June 1824	July 1825	Nov. 1827	13	28	41	15.3
General Index	June 1828	Nov. 1828	July 1830	5	20	25	8.4
Farm							
Crops	July 1828	Nov. 1828	July 1830	4	20	24	15.4
Derivatives	Apr. 1828	Nov. 1828	Feb. 1830	7	15	22	21.3
Imported Foods							
Lumber Products and Naval Stores	Aug. 1827	June 1828	July 1830	10	25	35	13.6
Industrial							
Raw and Semi-Finished							
Ready for Consumption							
Fish	Sept. 1826	Apr. 1827	Aug. 1830	7	40	47	22.2
Furs	Aug. 1826	Sept. 1828	Mar. 1831	25	30	55	20.3
Wines	Nov. 1827	Mar. 1828	Nov. 1830	4	32	36	10.5
General Index	July 1830	Jan. 1832	Sept. 1834	18	32	50	8.0
Farm							
Crops	July 1830	Oct. 1833	Apr. 1834	39	6	45	16.3
Derivatives	Feb. 1830	Nov. 1832	May 1834	33	18	51	16.3
Imported Foods	Mar. 1830	Dec. 1831	July 1834	21	31	52	18.9
Lumber Products and Naval Stores	July 1830	Jan. 1834	Oct. 1834	42	9	51	13.8
Industrial							
Raw and Semi-Finished							
Ready for Consumption	Aug. 1830	Dec. 1832	June 1834	28	18	46	9.3
Fish	Aug. 1830	Apr. 1831	Aug. 1832	8	16	24	23.7
Furs	Mar. 1831	Mar. 1832	Dec. 1834	12	33	45	14.0
Wines	Nov. 1830	Nov. 1832	Aug. 1842	24	117	141	17.6
General Index	Sept. 1834	Feb. 1837	July 1838	29	17	46	14.4
Farm							
Crops	Apr. 1834	Nov. 1836	Mar. 1838	31	16	47	30.6
Derivatives	May 1834	Nov. 1836	July 1838	30	20	50	28.4
Imported Foods	July 1834	Apr. 1836	July 1842	21	75	96	19.9
Lumber Products and Naval Stores	Oct. 1834	Dec. 1836	July 1837	26	7	33	18.5
Industrial							
Raw and Semi-Finished	Sept. 1830	Mar. 1837	July 1838	78	16	94	15.1
Ready for Consumption	June 1834	Apr. 1837	Sept. 1843	34	77	111	19.6
Fish	Aug. 1832	Apr. 1836	Sept. 1837	44	17	61	35.8
Furs	Dec. 1834	Mar. 1837	Oct. 1838	27	19	46	31.1
Wines							
General Index	July 1838	May 1839	Mar. 1843	10	46	56	16.7
Farm							
Crops	Mar. 1838	May 1839	Jan. 1845	14	68	82	38.4
Derivatives	July 1838	Oct. 1838	Mar. 1843	3	53	56	32.6
Imported Foods							
Lumber Products and Naval Stores	July 1837	Jan. 1838	Mar. 1844	6	74	80	21.8
Industrial							
Raw and Semi-Finished	July 1838	Mar. 1839	Sept. 1843	8	54	62	16.0
Ready for Consumption							
Fish	Sept. 1837	June 1839	Feb. 1843	21	44	65	46.4
Furs	Oct. 1838	Apr. 1840	May 1843	18	37	55	37.7
Wines							

TABLE 24 (*Concluded*)

Group	End of Preceding Recession	Peak	End of Succeeding Low	Number of Months: Rise	Number of Months: Fall	Number of Months: Total Cycle	Index of Cyclical Variability
General Index	Mar. 1843	Dec. 1845	Aug. 1846	33	8	41	8.8
Farm							
Crops	Jan. 1845	Dec. 1845	Aug. 1846	11	8	19	19.1
Derivatives	Mar. 1843	Dec. 1845	Aug. 1846	33	8	41	23.6
Imported Foods	July 1842	Sept. 1845	Dec. 1848	38	39	77	24.4
Lumber Products and Naval Stores	Mar. 1844	Mar. 1846	July 1848	24	28	52	22.0
Industrial							
Raw and Semi-Finished	Sept. 1843	Oct. 1844	Oct. 1846	13	24	37	5.2
Ready for Consumption							
Fish	Feb. 1843	Aug. 1845	June 1846	30	10	40	21.1
Furs	May 1843	Apr. 1846	Apr. 1855	35	108	143	34.9
Wines	Aug. 1842	June 1844	Feb. 1847	22	32	54	12.4
General Index	Aug. 1846	June 1847	May 1849	10	23	33	11.4
Farm							
Crops	Aug. 1846	June 1847	Aug. 1848	10	14	24	34.2
Derivatives	Aug. 1846	June 1847	May 1849	10	23	33	31.8
Imported Foods							
Lumber Products and Naval Stores							
Industrial							
Raw and Semi-Finished	Oct. 1846	Nov. 1847	May 1849	13	18	31	7.1
Ready for Consumption	Sept. 1843	Jan. 1848	Jan. 1852	52	48	100	10.1
Fish	June 1846	Sept. 1847	Jan. 1849	15	16	31	21.6
Furs							
Wines	Feb. 1847	Aug. 1847	Aug. 1849	6	24	30	6.1
General Index	May 1849	Jan. 1851	Jan. 1852	20	12	32	6.9
Farm							
Crops	Aug. 1848	Feb. 1851	Nov. 1851	30	9	39	18.5
Derivatives	May 1849	Jan. 1853	June 1853	44	5	49	19.9
Imported Foods	Dec. 1848	Oct. 1850	Apr. 1852	22	18	40	19.8
Lumber Products and Naval Stores							
Industrial							
Raw and Semi-Finished	May 1849	May 1850	June 1852	12	25	37	5.3
Ready for Consumption							
Fish	Jan. 1849	Feb. 1850	May 1851	13	15	28	24.4
Furs							
Wines							
General Index	Jan. 1852	Dec. 1855	June 1856	47	6	53	13.9
Farm							
Crops	Nov. 1851	June 1855	June 1856	43	12	55	31.3
Derivatives	June 1853	Nov. 1855	June 1856	29	7	36	21.1
Imported Foods	Apr. 1852	Oct. 1854	Feb. 1855	30	4	34	17.3
Lumber Products and Naval Stores	July 1848	Sept. 1854	July 1856	74	22	96	30.4
Industrial							
Raw and Semi-Finished	June 1852	Jan. 1856	Aug. 1856	43	7	50	12.6
Ready for Consumption	Jan. 1852	Dec. 1855	June 1861	47	66	113	25.0
Fish	May 1851	Feb. 1856	Aug. 1856	57	6	63	32.5
Furs							
Wines							
General Index	June 1856	June 1857	Feb. 1858	12	8	20	12.1
Farm							
Crops	June 1856	June 1857	Feb. 1858	12	8	20	24.9
Derivatives	June 1856	June 1857	Feb. 1858	12	8	20	19.9
Imported Foods	Feb. 1855	May 1857	Feb. 1858	27	9	36	29.6
Lumber Products and Naval Stores	July 1856	June 1857	Jan. 1858	11	7	18	16.0
Industrial							
Raw and Semi-Finished	Aug. 1856	May 1857	Feb. 1858	9	9	18	7.7
Ready for Consumption							
Fish	Aug. 1856	June 1857	July 1858	10	13	23	31.7
Furs	Apr. 1855	Mar. 1857	Jan. 1859	23	22	45	22.4
Wines							
General Index	Feb. 1858	May 1859	July 1861	15	26	41	6.7
Farm							
Crops	Feb. 1858	May 1859	Dec. 1860	15	19	34	19.1
Derivatives	Feb. 1858	May 1859	Sept. 1861	15	28	43	19.9
Imported Foods	Feb. 1858	Oct. 1860	July 1861	32	9	41	12.2
Lumber Products and Naval Stores	Jan. 1858	Apr. 1859	Apr. 1861	15	24	39	11.0
Industrial							
Raw and Semi-Finished	Feb. 1858	May 1859	July 1861	15	26	41	7.1
Ready for Consumption							
Fish	July 1858	Mar. 1860	Sept. 1861	20	18	38	34.8
Furs	Jan. 1859	Feb. 1859	Jan. 1860	1	11	12	18.8
Wines	Aug. 1849	June 1858	Dec. 1859	106	18	124	33.1

naval stores once, and farm crops once had the greatest variability. That fish and furs so frequently had the greatest average fluctuation from high to low may be attributed, at least in part, to the small number and great homogeneity of their constituent series. When only the six largest major groups are considered, farm crops stand out as the most variable in eight cycles, farm derivatives in four, imported foods in three, and lumber products and naval stores in two cycles.

The least variable group was predominantly the industrial raw and semi-finished articles. In 11 of the 15 cycles completed in this group, it had the lowest index of variability and in two others the next to the lowest. The group of lumber products and naval stores was never the lowest, but in seven cycles it ranked next to the lowest in variability. All of the other groups except fish and farm crops ranked at least once at or close to the bottom of the list in extent of variability.

It is highly significant that, like the general curve, none of the groups showed any persistent tendency to increase or decrease in variability. This applies not only to those with consistently high variability, such as fish and farm crops, and to those of low variability, such as industrial raw and semi-finished articles, but also to the other groups which were sometimes relatively high and other times relatively low.

Just as the difference between the period of rise and the period of fall in the general index indicated the underlying trend of various periods, so a comparison between the number of months of expansion and contraction in the cycles of the various groups emphasizes their trends. That the farm crops and farm derivatives had at least a slight upward trend throughout much of the 78 years is revealed by the frequency with which the length of the rise exceeded that of the decline. Except in six isolated cycles, the farm derivatives rose for a longer time than they fell after reaching a peak. Farm crops had fewer swings before 1830 in which the rise exceeded the fall than did the farm derivatives, but after 1830 both groups in the same six cycles had longer periods of expansion than of contraction.

The two groups with the most pronounced downward trend, industrial commodities ready for consumption and wines, had only four cycles in which the length of the rise exceeded that of the fall.

In wines only one of these cycles appeared after 1811 and in the consumers' goods only two after 1803.

In the cycles of the industrial raw and semi-finished articles and in furs the period of fall also characteristically exceeded the rise. Only five times did these groups rise for a longer period than they fell and three of these cycles were located in the early part of the period.

Imported foods, lumber products and naval stores, and fish corresponded closely to the general curve in having six or seven cycles with a longer period of rise than of fall. In lumber products and naval stores and fish, however, these cycles were somewhat distributed throughout the period. In imported foods, in contrast, the underlying decline during the major part of the period is indicated by the fact that in no cycle from 1808 to 1849 did these prices rise for as long a period as they fell.

The concentration of the times at which the duration of rise in the various groups exceeded the length of the fall indicates clearly the periods of greatest expansion in prices. All of the groups show this type of price behavior in the cycle from 1789 to 1798. The continuation of the rise at a slower rate is emphasized in the cycles of 1798 to 1803 and 1808 to 1811, when five or six groups had a longer rise than fall. As a result of the unusual rise in the prices of farm crops and farm derivatives after the War of 1812, these two groups were the only ones to rise for more months than they fell in the cycle from 1811 to 1821.

The continuation of the downward sweep of prices from 1821 to 1830 explains the sparcity of groups with a longer period of rise than of fall. The cycles from 1838 to 1852 also show falling prices. In contrast, in the cycles including the peaks of 1837, 1855, and 1857 most groups had a longer rise than fall.

Process of Decline

The 17 cycles have been shown to differ in length and in extent of rise and fall. Some admittedly were minor cycles. To the extent that the less severe cycles were generated from different causes or were mitigated by special happenings, one might expect some divergence in the timing of groups at their peaks. Yet it seems worth while to consider first the 17 cycles without emphasis upon their unlikeness.

One preliminary inquiry concerns the order in which groups of commodities changed their direction from an upward to a downward one. All groups which began to fall before the general average may be said to have been factors in precipitating the decline; those which turned down at the same time as the general average exerted a similar influence. Those which continued to rise after the general index had begun to fall may be regarded as having mitigated at least the

TABLE 25
RELATION OF INITIATION OF DECLINE IN MAJOR GROUPS TO THAT IN THE GENERAL INDEX

Year of Peak	Number of Groups Falling		
	Before	Coincident	After
1797	6	2	1
1801	4	1	4
1805	2	1	6
1809	3	1	5
1814	4	3	2
1822	5	0	4
1825	2	3	4
1828	7	2	0
1832	2	0	7
1837	6	0	3
1839	5	1	3
1845	4	2	3
1847	2	2	5
1851	4	0	5
1855	4	1	4
1857	4	4	1
1859	4	3	2

initial severity of the recession. Part of the character of the decline in different cycles is shown by the time at which the various groups started to fall in relation to the similar turning point in the general average.

From this tabulation it is clear that the declines in 1805, 1809, 1832, 1847, and 1851 were mitigated by the persistence of firm or even rising tendencies in five or more groups after the general average had begun to recede. In contrast, the severe declines from peaks in 1797, 1828, and 1857 were so widespread that not more than one group maintained a rising tendency.

Since the cycles differ in the number of groups contributing to a decline, some interest attaches to a study of those groups which initiated the decline. In this, as in the inquiry above, we are concerned only with the time when the index of each group began to contribute to the decline. That there was some tendency for the same groups to lead in the decline in various cycles is indicated by the fact that imported foods were eight times among the first two groups to decline and 13 times among the first four. The industrial commodities ready for consumption led the decline seven times and was 11 times among

TABLE 26
SUMMARY OF ORDER IN WHICH NINE MAJOR GROUPS CONTRIBUTED TO THE INITIATION OF DECLINE

Group	Order of Decline from High[a]			
	First	Second	Third	Fourth
Farm				
Crops		1	2	1
Derivatives			2	6
Imported Foods	4	4	2	3
Lumber Products and Naval Stores	3		2	1
Industrial				
Raw and Semi-Finished	3	1	3	1
Ready for Consumption	7	2	2	
Fish	1	3	2	2
Furs	1	1	2	
Wines	4	4		1

[a] When two or more groups started to decline in the same month, they are given the same rank.

the first four groups to fall. Farm derivatives never appeared among the first two items leading the decline, though they became important in contributing to the decline after as many as three other groups had started to recede. The group of farm crops was never among the first and only once among the second in the initiation of a recession.

The tabulation of the number of times which each group was among the first four contributing to the contraction emphasizes the preponderance of a few groups in initiating the decline.

The recessions in which the group of imported foods was not among the first four to decline were 1801, 1805, 1814, and 1859. Those in which the industrial commodities ready for consumption did not constitute one of the first four groups to decline were 1814, 1832,

1837, 1845, 1847, and 1855. Thus, only in the decline starting in 1814, which was initiated by industrial raw and semi-finished materials, wines, lumber products and naval stores, and fish in the order named, did neither imported foods nor industrial commodities ready for consumption contribute to the early stages of contraction.

A tabulation of the number of months by which each group preceded or followed the start of a decline in the general curve gives an indication of their sensitivity to price decrease. From this it is clear that farm crops followed more closely than other groups the turning points in the general curve, having in eight of the 17 depressions turned downward in the same month as the average. In the other cycles there was more tendency for farm crops to reach a peak after than before the general curve. Farm derivatives differed from farm crops by more frequently anticipating the decline in the general curve. The derivatives declined in advance of the average of all commodities in five cycles against three for farm crops. Imported foods more conclusively than any other group declined in advance of the general curve, normally having anticipated a decline by one to 14 months. Both lumber products and naval stores and industrial raw and semi-finished articles show a diversity of behavior. In no more than nine recessions did either group turn downward within three months of the start of the decline in the general average, while in the other periods of contraction they began to fall at widely different times. The industrial products ready for consumption normally anticipated the decline in the general average. In seven cases, however, this arose from the failure of the curve of consumption goods to share at all in the peak. The group thus lacked response to the factors causing the preceding rise. Wines, like imported foods, often dropped before the general index. Fish, like farm derivatives, held up in about half the cycles after the general curve had turned down.

Up to this point the contribution of the groups to the initiation of declines has been based upon the turning points in their indices. Since a recession in a group could arise either from a general decrease which affected all or most of the constituent series or from a severe drop in the prices of a few items in the group, it is important to know what percentage of the series in each group contributed to the various declines. Rarely could it happen that all of the commodities in any group would decline at exactly the same time. Yet, if 50 per cent or more of them were declining, only a substantial contrary movement in the others would prevent a decline in the average of the group.

In only six cycles did farm crops fail to contribute to the initial decline. The index of this group as well as less than 50 per cent

TABLE 27

SUMMARY OF TIMING OF INITIATION OF DECLINE IN NINE MAJOR GROUPS IN RELATION TO THAT IN THE GENERAL INDEX

		Farm		Imported Foods	Lumber Products and Naval Stores	Industrial		Fish	Furs	Wines
		Crops	Derivatives			Raw	Consumption			
	Falling			3	1	1	7			3
Number of Months Before	22–24				1					
	19–21							1		
	16–18					1			1	1
	13–15			2	1	1				
	10–12		1	1		1	1	2		1
	7–9	1	1		1	1	1	1		3
	4–6	1			1			2		1
	1–3	1	3	6	2	3	1	2	4	1
	Same	8	5	2	3	4	3	1		
	Holding								2	
Number of Months After	1–3	3	3	1	3	2	1	5	4	3
	4–6					1			2	
	7–9						1			
	10–12		1	1		1	1	1	1	1
	13–15	1							1	
	16–18	1	1	1				1		
	19–21	1	1		2					
	22–24		1		1					
	25–27							1		
	28–30								1	
	Holding High									1
	Rising				1	1	1		1	2

of the constituent series did not recede before or with the general index in the peaks of 1805, 1809, 1822, 1825, 1832, and 1851. Besides, in 1839, when the average of the group dropped with the general curve, only 33 per cent of the commodities participated. The importance of farm crops in declines rests upon the fact that in 10 of the depressions 50 per cent or more of the series dropped in price either before or at the same time as the general curve.

More than 50 per cent of the farm derivatives declined with or in advance of the general curve in 10 of the 17 cycles, though in only eight of these was the movement of the group in accord with that of the majority of the items. In 1805, 1809, 1814, 1822, and 1851 farm derivatives were not a factor in bringing about the initial declines.

Imported foods, either by a decline in the average or by a drop in the price of 50 per cent or more of the items in the group, may be said to have been an important factor in initiating every recession, though in only eight cases was the movement of the group and the percentage of items in accord.

These three groups seem to be more clear in their tendencies than others. For instance, on the basis of the turning points in their average lumber products and naval stores declined before or with the general curve from 10 peaks, yet in only four of these was the proportion of items which declined as much as 50 per cent. The lumber products and naval stores group did not contribute to the declines of 1809, 1822, 1832, 1845, and 1851 and in all of these cases less than a third of the items declined with or before the general index.

The group curve of industrial raw and semi-finished commodities preceded the general average in eight peaks and corresponded with it in four others. In seven of these the recession was widespread enough to affect 50 per cent or more of the items. The group was not a factor in contributing to the declines starting in 1805, in 1832, or in 1847. The diversity of behavior among the series in the industrial raw and semi-finished group is evident from the relatively small percentage of items sharing in the early stages of most declines since from only three peaks—namely, 1845, 1857, and 1859—did more than 55 per cent of the series of the group decline in advance or coincidentally with the general average.

Considered without taking into account the percentage of items affected in the early stages of decline, the group of industrial commodities ready for consumption gives an impression of carrying more weight in recessions than is warranted by a careful analysis of the time of turning points in the series. From the twenties this group was subject to minor movements on a gradually declining trend. The lack of conformity to the general average is indicated by the fact that in seven cycles the group fell throughout the whole period of the rise in most other groups. The industrial commodities ready for consumption contributed significantly in percentage of items involved in 1797, 1801, 1822, 1828, 1839, and 1857. They did not contribute to the declines in 1832, 1837, 1845, or 1847. In the other seven peaks the group average began to decline before the general curve though normally less than 49 per cent of the constituents were affected.

The group of fish, which is made up of a small number of items, is equally divided between cycles in which the decline in the series begins before and after the general curve; in only one cycle did the decline come in the same month in both. In seven peaks the fish group did not contribute to the initial decline, though in all but three it turned down within three months after the direction of the general curve changed.

Furs contributed less often than any other group. In 1797 and again in 1857 the majority of the items as well as the average declined in advance of the general curve. In 1837 the rise in one series offset the decline in two others. On the whole, the fur series may be said to have contributed rarely to the initiation of a decline; in 11 peaks neither a large percentage of the items nor the index of the group contributed to the recession.

The wine group displayed some of the characteristics of the imported foods, though it less frequently anticipated declines and at seven peaks did not contribute to the following recession in the general index.

In summary, if emphasis is given only to the number of times each group anticipated the recession in the general curve by declining in advance of the average, imported foods, industrial commodities ready for consumption, and wines stand out as contributing most frequently in the early stages of the process of decline. The other groups contributed in the following order: industrial raw and semi-finished products, fish, lumber products and naval stores, furs, farm derivatives, and farm crops.

The inclusion of the times at which the indices of the groups declined with the general curve would change the ranking of some of the groups. Imported foods and industrial commodities ready for consumption were the most frequent contributors, and the industrial raw and semi-finished group was a close third. The greatest shift in position was that made by farm crops from last to fourth place.

When another measure of contribution to decline is added—the proportion of the commodities in the group which declined before or coincidentally with the general average—a slight revision in the relative importance of groups in the process of decline must be made. Imported foods and both industrial groups still head the list. The revised order for the other groups is: farm derivatives, lumber products and naval stores, farm crops, fish, wines, and furs. The greatest importance of farm crops and farm derivatives in initiating declines arises from the fact that their turning points tended to coincide with that of the general index; thus they appear to be the determining factor in the actual location of the peak. The last four groups listed tended to lag somewhat behind the other groups and even behind the general curve.

Process of Recovery

A comparison of the dates at which each of the nine major groups ended its decline in any swing with the corresponding date in the general index of prices gives one indication of the sensitivity or slug-

TABLE 28

RELATION OF INITIATION OF RECOVERY IN MAJOR GROUPS TO THAT IN THE GENERAL INDEX

Year of Low	Number of Groups Rising		
	Before	Coincident	After
1789	5	3	1
1798	1	1	7
1803	3	1	5
1808	4	0	5
1811	3	1	5
1821	2	1	6
1824	4	3	2
1828	5	0	4
1830	2	2	5
1834	6	0	3
1838	2	2	5
1843	3	1	5
1846	2	2	5
1849	4	2	3
1852	4	1	4
1856	3	2	4
1858	2	4	3
1861	5	2	2

TABLE 29
SUMMARY OF ORDER IN WHICH NINE MAJOR GROUPS CONTRIBUTED TO THE INITIATION OF RECOVERY

Group	Order of Recovery from Low[a]									
	1st	2nd	3rd	4th	5th	6th	7th	8th	9th	Last
Farm										
Crops		2	5	3	3	2	2		1	1
Derivatives	1		3	4	5	1	1	1	2	3
Imported Foods	3	1	3	1	1	4	5			3
Lumber Products and Naval Stores	3	3	3	1	1	2	2	3		2
Industrial										
Raw and Semi-Finished	2	3	3		2	3	3	1	1	2
Ready for Consumption	2	1	1	1	5	2	1	1	4	7
Fish	1	3	4	1	3	1	2	1	2	3
Furs	4	2			3	2	2	3	2	3
Wines	5	2	1	3		3		3	1	3

[a] When two or more groups started to rise in the same month, they are given the same rank.

gishness of the prices of various groups in responding to changes in other groups. Only in the recoveries of 1789, 1828, 1834, and 1861 did more than half of the groups move upward in advance of the general index. At the other extreme were nine periods of recovery—1798, 1803, 1808, 1811, 1821, 1830, 1838, 1843, and 1846—in which five or more groups did not rise until after the general index had started upwards. The most sluggish recoveries were those in 1798, 1838, 1843, and 1846, when four groups did not advance until six months or more after the general index, and in 1821, when four groups delayed more than three months before starting to advance.

There was little consistency in the order in which the groups rose after every depression. Every group except farm crops was at least once the first to end its decline and all groups were at least once the last to register a recovery. In the 18 recoveries, the group of lumber products and naval stores was nine times among the first three to rise, and the industrial raw and semi-finished commodities and fish and wines were eight times among the three leaders. The farm derivatives tended to maintain a rather central position. In 12 upswings they were among the third to fifth groups to rise. The group of industrial materials ready for consumption appears to have been the most sluggish in that seven times it was the last to rise. But these were cases in which the group, not showing a recovery within the limits of the general curve, was recorded as falling.

Even an examination of the actual number of months between the time when the general index turned upward and the corresponding date in each of the groups does not reveal a persistent tendency for any group to lead in the recovery process. In nine swings the prices of fish started to advance before the general index showed an upward movement. The prices of wine rose ahead of the general index in seven swings and in three others were rising or holding high. At the other extreme were the farm crops and industrial raw and semi-finished commodities, which rose ahead of the general curve in only five swings, and the farm derivatives, which turned upwards in only three swings before the general index.

The farm crops and farm derivatives, however, were the most important groups in determining the location of the start of the upswing in the general curve. In seven swings the date of the end of the recession in the prices of farm crops and in eight swings the corresponding date in the curve of prices of farm derivatives coincided with the end of the recession in the general index.

When it is realized that the upswing in the general curve is aided by those groups which turned upwards at the same time as well as by those which had turned up in advance or which had been rising or holding high, it can be seen that farm crops contributed to the upswing in 12 cycles, farm derivatives in 11, and fish, imported foods, lumber products and naval stores, industrial raw and semi-finished commodities, and wines in 10 cycles.

Just as the general index conceals the differences in the timing of the groups, so does the curve of each group conceal the variations in the timing of the swings in the prices of the commodities within the group. A relatively strong movement in the prices of a small proportion of the commodities can offset a less vigorous movement among the others. In some cases this would mean that the group would show a rise when only a small proportion of the series was involved. At other times, when a large proportion of the commodities had shown a rise before or coincidentally with the upswing in the general index, a relatively strong downward movement in the other prices would delay the end of the recession in the group. This situation is clarified by the computation of the percentage of the commodities which contributed to the rise, including the series which rose in advance of the general curve, those which rose at the same time as the general index, and those which were rising or holding high.

TABLE 30
SUMMARY OF TIMING OF INITIATION OF RECOVERY IN NINE MAJOR GROUPS IN RELATION TO THAT IN THE GENERAL INDEX

		Farm		Imported Foods	Lumber Products and Naval Stores	Industrial		Fish	Furs	Wines
		Crops	Derivatives			Raw	Consumption			
	Rising			1	1	1	1		1	2
	Holding High									1
Number of Months Before	25–27							1	1	
	22–24								1	
	19–21							1		1
	16–18								1	
	13–15			1					1	
	10–12				2	2	1	1		
	7–9	2		1	2		1	1		4
	4–6	2	2	2		1	1	2	1	
	1–3	1	1	2	3	1	3	3		2
	Same	7	8	3	2	5	2	1		
	Holding								2	
Number of Months After	1–3	3	5	3	3	4	1	4	4	3
	4–6	1		2		2	1	2	1	2
	7–9		1		1				2	
	10–12				1			1	1	
	13–15	1								
	16–18		1		1					
	19–21									
	22–24	1								
	25–27					1				
	28–30							1		
	Falling			3	2	1	7		2	3

The use of two measures, the date of the end of the recession and the percentage of the commodities involved, qualifies the conclusions based solely on the comparison of the timing of the movement of the group index in comparison with that of the general curve. In the recovery of 1789 only three of the eight groups which rose before or with the general curve were affected in a majority of their series. The rise that year was, from this point of view, most significant in the imported foods, lumber products and naval stores, and fish. In 1824, when seven major groups rose before or with the general index, in only four—farm crops, farm derivatives, imported foods, and wines—did 50 per cent or more of their series move upward. The rise in 1828 substantially affected all but the industrial groups. Farm derivatives, lumber products and naval stores, fish, and furs turned up before the general curve as the result of a similar movement in more than 50 per cent of the commodities in each group. Wines rose before the general curve although less than half of these series advanced. Farm crops began to rise one month after the general curve although two-thirds of the commodities in the group ended their recessions before or with the general curve. The index of imported foods did not show any marked recovery in 1828 although more than half of its series turned upward with or before the total average.

The recovery in 1834 was also one of the most widespread. Six groups rose before the general curve, but in only two—farm crops and fish—were more than 50 per cent of the series affected. In these two groups the rise was so general that two-thirds or more of their series rose before or with the general index. The lumber products and naval stores were also a factor in the recovery of 1834, since 50 per cent of these commodities had ended their recessions by the time the general curve had reached its corresponding position and the curve for the whole group of lumber products and naval stores reached a similar point just one month later.

The recovery of 1861 appeared in all groups except farm derivatives and fish before or at the same time as it was evinced in the general curve. More than 58 per cent of the constituent series in each of these seven contributory groups participated in this revival except in the industrial raw and semi-finished commodities. Only 30 per cent of this industrial group turned up before or at the same time as the general index. Not only did the farm derivatives and fish delay in showing any recovery, but less than 8 per cent of the commodities in these two groups accompanied or preceded the composite index.

The use of the percentage of commodities within each group rising with or before the general index also modifies the interpretation of those periods of recovery in which more than half of the groups did not start to advance until after an increase had appeared in the general index. In 1821, when only three groups, furs, industrial raw and semi-finished products, and lumber products and naval stores, had ended their recessions by April, three other groups, imported foods, farm crops, and wines, showed that half or more of their commodities had advanced with or before the general curve. Similarly, in 1803 and 1838 when only four groups turned upwards with the general curve, there were two other groups, imported foods and wines, in which a rise in 50 per cent of the commodities accompanied or preceded the beginning of the upswing in the general index.

The recoveries of 1798 and 1846 stand out as being initially the least widespread of any of the 18 similar periods of price expansion from 1789 to 1861. In 1798 only the industrial groups moved up with or in advance of the general index, and in only the raw and semi-finished industrial products were more than half of the series rising. In 1846, when four groups began their expansions before or with the general curve, only two showed increases in more than 50 per cent of their commodities. These are the only two recoveries when less than half of the groups contributed to the general advance by a rise either in their averages or in 50 per cent or more of their commodities before or with the general curve.

Considering the period from 1789 to 1861 as a whole, it appears that 50 per cent or more of the farm crops were rising with or before the general curve in 12 recoveries. Furthermore, these recoveries were the 11 consecutive ones from 1821 to 1856 inclusive and the one in 1861. Half or more of the commodities in the groups of imported foods and wines contributed to the recovery in 10 periods, and in that of fish in nine periods, scattered between 1789 and 1861. At the other extreme are the groups of industrial commodities ready for consumption, furs, and industrial raw and semi-finished products. In only one period of recovery did as many as half of the industrial commodities ready for consumption rise with or before the general index. Only in 1821, 1828, and 1861 did as many as two series in the fur group contribute to the initial recovery. In just four periods, 1798, 1803, 1811, and 1838, were 50 per cent or more of the industrial raw and semi-finished commodities rising with or before the general curve.

A group can be considered to have contributed to a recovery either if a small percentage of its commodities exerts an influence strong enough to raise its curve with or before the general index, or if half or more of its series rise even though their influence may be offset by a smaller group which held or continued to fall. Using this definition of "contribution to recovery," it appears that farm crops was the most recurrent group in facilitating recovery. In 15 of the 18 periods of recovery between 1789 and 1861 inclusive and in all from 1811 to 1861 inclusive the group of farm crops was an important element. The farm derivatives contributed to 12 periods of recovery, 11 of which were in the consecutive cycles from 1824 to 1858 inclusive. The imported foods were a factor in 14 recoveries, the wines in 13, the lumber products and naval stores in 12, and industrial raw and semi-finished commodities and fish in 11. The two groups of industrial products tended to contribute to the recoveries in the first part of the period, but became unimportant factors later. Five of the nine recoveries in which the industrial commodities ready for consumption participated were confined to the consecutive recoveries from 1789 to 1811 inclusive. Similarly, six of the 11 times in which the industrial raw and semi-finished commodities contributed to the advances were the consecutive recoveries from 1798 to 1824 inclusive. The furs were a negligible factor not only because they represented just three series, but also because they contributed to only six recoveries.

Summary

This analysis of the 17 cycles in the general index and their counterparts in the nine major groups has emphasized the unusual length and severity of the two long swings from 1789 to 1798 and from 1811 to 1821. The first of these marked the beginning of the series of events culminating in the Napoleonic wars and the second included the War of 1812 and the readjustment made necessary not only by the end of this war but also by the world-wide readjustments upon the restoration of peace in Europe. The comparison of the different cycles also threw into relief the widespread and extensive fluctuations in prices around 1837 and 1855-1857.

Price movements in Philadelphia from 1784 to 1861 were also subject to an underlying trend which, at times, was upward, at other times downward, and at still other times somewhat horizontal. The difference in the length of the periods of expansion and contraction has helped in isolating the times at which the trend of the general index changed as well as in suggesting the extent to which the trends of the various major groups corresponded to or varied from the general trend.

Of greater significance than the length or extent of the cyclical movements is the relation between the time at which the general index started to fall or rise and the corresponding points in the indices of the major groups. Imported foods and industrial commodities ready for consumption were the most consistent in contributing to the start of recessions. No group was so consistent in contributing to initial recovery. The industrial commodities ready for consumption were especially important until after 1811, and the industrial raw and semi-finished until after 1824. Between 1811 and 1824 there was a shift in the relative importance of industrial and agricultural products. Beginning in 1811 farm crops continuously contributed to recovery, and beginning in 1824 farm derivatives also aided in every revival except that of 1861. The importance of farm crops and derivatives was not in leading the recovery or recession, but in determining the dates at which the general curve not only started to rise but also started to decline.

CHAPTER XII

MOVEMENT OF PRICES OF IDENTICAL COMMODITIES 1720-1861

By the use of the material collected for prices in Philadelphia for the years before the Revolution,[1] it is possible to examine the price movements of some commodities for nearly a century and a half, except for the period of the Revolutionary War, and of even more commodities for over a century and a quarter from 1731 to 1861. The prices of the 20 identical commodities which were used from 1731 to 1775 have been isolated for the period from 1784 to 1861 except for a few grades which disappeared. For example, only two of the four kinds of bread found in the Colonial period were continuously quoted in later years. These data permit the finding of definite answers to such questions as: to what extent did the upward trend in prices found in the Colonial period persist after the Revolution? Did any change occur in the later period in the type of cyclical fluctuations found in these commodities when Pennsylvania was a proprietary colony? How did the fluctuations in the prices of these commodities compare with those of the total group after 1784? In addition, these data show other progressive changes as industry developed and agriculture became relatively less important. These shifts will be stressed in the final chapter.

Trends in Commodity Prices

In dealing with the 20 commodities in the Colonial period it was found that the various grades or specifications of salt, staves, and bread had similar trends. The long-time movement differed, however, in muscovado and loaf sugar and in West India and New England rum. From 1784 to 1861 the trends of the grades of salt, staves, and bread continued to be similar, while those in the grades of sugar

[1] Bezanson, Anne, Gray, Robert D., and Hussey, Miriam, *Prices in Colonial Pennsylvania.*

and rum persistently differed. It is, therefore, necessary to discuss the long-time movements in both periods in 22 series. Specifically the commodities used in the later period are:

beef, prime	pork, Burlington	sugar
bread	rice	Havana brown
ship	rum	(muscovado)
middling	West India	loaf
corn, Indian	New England	tar
cotton, Georgia	salt	tobacco, James River
flour	fine	turpentine
gunpowder	coarse (Lisbon)	wheat
indigo, French	staves, white oak	wine, Madeira
molasses, West India	barrel	
pitch	hogshead	
	pipe	

Before the Revolution only turpentine and loaf sugar showed a downward trend in price in Philadelphia. The fluctuations in pitch, tar, salt, rice, and gunpowder centered around a horizontal trend. All other commodities either showed an upward movement, distributed over the major part of the period from 1720 to 1775, or advanced in a series of steps with relatively short but steep increases followed by a horizontal trend.

The tracing of the long-time movements in these same commodities to 1861 is handicapped by two factors: first, the present lack of data on price movements from 1775 to 1784; and second, the influence of the wars in Europe from 1792 to 1815, climaxed in the United States by the War of 1812, which dominated the movements and levels of prices for at least a quarter of a century. For these reasons the discussion of trends in the later period is divided into an examination of any change in level between the decade before and the one following the Revolution, an analysis of the substantial swings in prices from 1789 to the war or post-war peak, and a determination of the underlying movements from 1821 to 1861. In order to smooth the fluctuations in annual prices a five-year moving average has been used throughout these analyses.

The successive five-year moving averages from 1765 to the Revolution and for the first decade of the later period warrant a classification of the series on the basis of their net change in level between these two periods. The most significant increases evident in the decade following the Revolution are found in those commodities which in every consecutive five-year period between 1784 and 1861 were higher than in any similar period from 1720 to 1775. Such an increase affected the prices of James River tobacco, flour, wheat, rice, staves, and Madeira wine. Five other commodities rose as much or more between the years immediately before and after the Revolution: Havana brown sugar, West India molasses, cotton, West India rum, and New England rum. Although both Havana brown sugar and cotton were consistently higher in the decade after the Revolution than at their previous maxima, molasses and New England rum not only were lower in the first decade of the later period than at the highest point in Colonial years, but also dropped further below later. Of these five series, West India rum approached nearest to the six commodities with the most significant rise, for, although from 1786 to 1789 its five-year moving averages were lower than those of 1759 to 1761, those of all of the remaining periods were well above the Colonial peak. None of the remaining commodities showed such substantial changes except gunpowder, which definitely was lower immediately after the Revolution than before. Loaf sugar, pork, corn, salt, and pitch tended to be slightly higher at the beginning of the later period than at the close of the Colonial period, and bread, turpentine, and tar were slightly lower. Indigo and beef sold at approximately the same levels immediately after the Revolution as they did before.

The general movements in the group of 20 commodities from 1784 to 1821 may be roughly described as a decline from 1784 to 1789, a rise to 1797, a decline from 1797 to 1808, and a rise to 1815 before starting the recession which lasted to 1821 or later.

The first rise after the Revolutionary War is evident in the five-year moving averages of the specific commodities between 1787 and 1794. The three most important products from the West Indies—molasses, Havana brown sugar, and rum—together with the related products—loaf sugar and New England rum—started upward between 1787 and 1788. Important domestic commodities, specifically flour, wheat, and tar, also began a rise at the same time. In each of the next two years three more commodities showed the beginning of a rise: pitch, salt, and turpentine between 1788 and 1789, and staves, corn, and Madeira wine between 1789 and 1790. The remaining commodities turned upward in rapid succession: pork, bread, beef, and indigo between 1790 and 1791, and gunpowder and rice between 1791 and 1792. Only James River tobacco continued to decline until 1793, while cotton had an underlying downward movement until 1810.

The rise which began in all of these commodities except cotton in the latter part of the eighties or early nineties generally persisted until 1797 or even later. Only corn reached its crest as early as 1795 and pork and New England rum in 1796. Seven of the commodities ended their rise in 1797, but molasses and West India rum persisted upward until 1798, tar and loaf sugar until 1799, beef and rice until 1803, and salt until 1806. These 17 commodities suffered severe recessions before the War of 1812 and cotton a long general decline from 1784 to 1810. In contrast pitch, staves, and Madeira wine had an underlying upward movement until the war or immediate post-war years and indigo tended to advance until 1825.

That there was a great diversity in the time at which the rise to the war or post-war peaks started is indicated not only by the fact that some commodities tended to advance continuously from the latter part of the eighties or early nineties but also by the lack of conformity in the time at which the other commodities recovered from their recession in the latter part of the nineties and the early years of the nineteenth century. The most concentrated rise was after 1809 and 1810 when seven commodities ended their decline. The recessions in the other 11 commodities ended between 1800 and 1808.

Compared with this diversification, the end of the rise, although distributed over six years, appears concentrated. Only gunpowder reached its highest five-year average as early as 1812. In each of the next three years, three commodities were at their maxima. Most of the important domestic staples such as cotton, wheat, flour, bread, corn, beef, pork, James River tobacco, staves, and turpentine continued to rise until 1816 or 1817. Madeira wine was the only imported commodity to rise still further after the war. Although the prices of indigo receded somewhat between 1813 and 1819, their underlying movement was upward until 1825. The other commodities declined abruptly from their peaks.

Although the deflation from the Napoleonic war period generally persisted beyond 1821, it is possible to judge the trends and changes in trends of the prices of specific commodities from 1821 to 1861 free from the severe fluctuations noted generally between 1784 and 1821. Only in salt did the downward trend last until the beginning of the Civil War. The five-year moving averages of gunpowder declined until 1851 and those of molasses and both grades of sugar until 1850, but all of these series showed a rising trend in the decade of the fifties. The prices of indigo also had a long decline, for, although they rose until 1825, their decline after 1825 persisted until the end of the period.

Eleven other commodities had a somewhat shorter downward movement. Staves and pitch fell until 1847, cotton until 1844, and New England rum until 1842, but in the closing years they, too, had an upward trend. In no other series did the recession persist after 1833. West India rum tended upward after 1824, corn after 1826, rice after 1828, and tobacco, turpentine, and tar after 1830. The prices of Madeira wine tended to fall until 1833 and fluctuated around a somewhat constant level until 1847 before starting a continuous advance.

The other five commodities exhibited a very different trend. The fluctuations in flour, wheat, bread, and beef centered around a horizontal plane from 1821 to 1861. The trend underlying the movements in the prices of pork was horizontal until 1844, when a definite upward movement asserted itself.

The long-time movements in the prices of these commodities have been most clearly indicated by the foregoing analysis. In a few there was such a definite upward or downward movement that it is possible to give for these a generalized description for all or most of the period. Although cotton, Havana brown sugar, and loaf sugar showed a rising trend near the close of the period, they tended to decline throughout the major part of the 78 years. The most extreme decline was in the prices of cotton, but the decreasing tendency in the prices of loaf sugar has additional significance in that it marks the continuation of a declining trend noted in the Colonial period.

Five other commodities moved upward noticeably from 1784 to 1861: corn, rice, tar, turpentine, and West India rum. In both corn and West India rum the upward movement thus extends throughout most of the period from 1720 to 1861. In the Colonial period the advancing tendencies were more pronounced in corn than in rum, but this relationship was reversed in the period after the Revolution.

Certain commodities also showed a distinct change between the Colonial and later years in the level around which their prices fluctuated. Rice not only tended upward from 1784 to 1861, but its five-year moving average kept continuously higher than in the Colonial period. A similar comparison reveals that wheat, flour, James River tobacco, staves, and Madeira wine maintained, throughout the later period, the advances made earlier and even exceeded the pre-Revolutionary-War peaks. The five-year moving averages for all of these commodities never dropped as low between 1784 and 1861 as the highest average between 1720 and 1775.

Cycles in 20-Commodity and General Indices

Before reviewing the movements of prices in the geometric index of 20 commodities during the Colonial period, it is pertinent to compare this index with that of the total of 140 commodities from 1784 to 1861. The smaller group shows all of the 17 cycles between 1789 and 1861 and in addition a well-marked swing from 1789 to 1791 which was not apparent in the general curve. It is necessary to combine the two swings in the index of 20 commodities from 1789 to 1791 and from 1791 to 1799 in order to have a movement comparable to that of 1789 to 1798 in the composite index. With this reduction to the same number of cycles in both curves, it is possible to compare their critical turning points, their variability in each cycle, and the number of months of rise in relation to the number of months of decline.

Considering the fact that the smaller group of commodities is heavily weighted with farm crops and farm derivatives, which the previous analysis has shown to be important in determining the location of turning points in the general curve, it is not surprising that eight of the 18 lows and eight of the 17 peaks occurred at the same time in both indices. Adding the times when the smaller group turned down in advance of the general curve to those when both turned down together, it can be said that the group of 20 commodities contributed to the initiation of 14 of the 17 recessions. Even of the three apparent exceptions, one may be disregarded because the index of the smaller group did not advance after the general curve turned downward and even started a recession just one month after the decline began in the composite index. In both of the other two cycles, when the group of 20 commodities delayed 22 months before starting its decline, special factors were present which should be noted. The peak of April 1809 in the general index was caused chiefly by the extreme rise of many imported commodities after the passage of the Embargo Act. The concomitant decline in the prices of domestic articles affected the smaller group more than it did the general index. The rise and even the peak in the 20 commodities practically corresponded with those in the index of domestic commodities in the cycle between 1808 and 1812. The other recession which was delayed for 22 months in the 20-commodity index occurred in the early thirties when the peak in the general index was reached in January 1832. In this cycle, also, domestic commodities, especially those of agricultural origin, tended to advance until late in 1833. As a result, the peak of November 1833 in the index of 20 commodities coincided with the index of domestic commodities rather than with the general index.

The group of 20 commodities did not contribute as frequently to recoveries as it did to declines although in five revivals the start of recovery in the smaller group preceded the upturn of the composite curve. In addition to the eight times when both turned together, there were five upswings in which the group of 20 was delayed. Four of these were in recoveries of 1824 and earlier. The fact that this small group of commodities contributed more to the initiation of recoveries after 1824 than it did earlier again corresponds somewhat to the shift already noted in the behavior of farm crops and farm derivatives, which became important in determining the start of revival in the latter part of the period.

The cyclical variability of the index of 20 commodities was always more extreme than that of the general index. As in the case of the general curve and the major groups, the two long swings from 1789 to 1798 and from 1811 to 1821 were far more variable than any of

TABLE 31
SUMMARY OF CYCLICAL MOVEMENTS OF GENERAL INDEX AND 20-COMMODITY INDEX
1789–1861

Indices	End of Preceding Recession	Peak	End of Succeeding Low	Number of Months: Rise	Fall	Total Cycle	Index of Cyclical Variability
General	Apr. 1789	Feb. 1797	Apr. 1798	94	14	108	27.1
20-Commodity	Apr. 1789	Mar. 1796	Aug. 1799	83	41	124	40.3
General	Apr. 1798	Nov. 1801	Mar. 1803	43	16	59	9.0
20-Commodity	Aug. 1799	Feb. 1801	Aug. 1802	18	18	36	17.6
General	Mar. 1803	Feb. 1805	July 1808	23	41	64	10.5
20-Commodity	Aug. 1802	Mar. 1805	Aug. 1808	31	41	72	22.9
General	July 1808	Apr. 1809	Nov. 1811	9	31	40	10.6
20-Commodity	Aug. 1808	Feb. 1811	May 1812	30	15	45	21.2
General	Nov. 1811	Nov. 1814	Apr. 1821	36	77	113	42.1
20-Commodity	May 1812	Oct. 1814	Apr. 1821	29	78	107	48.6
General	Apr. 1821	Mar. 1822	Sept. 1824	11	30	41	9.0
20-Commodity	Apr. 1821	May 1822	Dec. 1824	13	31	44	14.4
General	Sept. 1824	May 1825	June 1828	8	37	45	9.7
20-Commodity	Dec. 1824	May 1825	Apr. 1828	5	35	40	11.7
General	June 1828	Nov. 1828	July 1830	5	20	25	8.4
20-Commodity	Apr. 1828	Nov. 1828	July 1830	7	20	27	15.8
General	July 1830	Jan. 1832	Sept. 1834	18	32	50	8.0
20-Commodity	July 1830	Nov. 1833	May 1834	40	6	46	14.4
General	Sept. 1834	Feb. 1837	July 1838	29	17	46	14.4
20-Commodity	May 1834	Feb. 1837	July 1838	33	17	50	22.1
General	July 1838	May 1839	Mar. 1843	10	46	56	16.7
20-Commodity	July 1838	Oct. 1838	Mar. 1843	3	53	56	25.5
General	Mar. 1843	Dec. 1845	Aug. 1846	33	8	41	8.8
20-Commodity	Mar. 1843	Dec. 1845	Aug. 1846	33	8	41	18.5
General	Aug. 1846	June 1847	May 1849	10	23	33	11.4
20-Commodity	Aug. 1846	June 1847	July 1848	10	13	23	24.5
General	May 1849	Jan. 1851	Jan. 1852	20	12	32	6.9
20-Commodity	July 1848	Oct. 1850	Apr. 1852	27	18	45	11.2
General	Jan. 1852	Dec. 1855	June 1856	47	6	53	13.9
20-Commodity	Apr. 1852	May 1855	June 1856	37	13	50	24.5
General	June 1856	June 1857	Feb. 1858	12	8	20	12.1
20-Commodity	June 1856	June 1857	Feb. 1858	12	8	20	18.8
General	Feb. 1858	May 1859	July 1861	15	26	41	6.7
20-Commodity	Feb. 1858	May 1859	Dec. 1860	15	19	34	11.9

the others. The most important fact, however, is that, as already noted in the general and group indices, no tendency appeared for either an increasing or decreasing cyclical variability from 1789 to 1861.

In general, the small group of 20 commodities had a proportion of rise and fall in the various cycles similar to that in the total. From

1798 to 1803 the expansion in the general curve to a peak in 1801 was longer than its contraction. The smaller group had a reverse relationship largely because it started to rise nearly a year and a half later than the general group and reached its peak nine months earlier. In the swings from 1808 to 1812 and from 1830 to 1834 when, because of special factors, the peaks in the 20-commodity index came 22 months after those in the general curve, the length of rise in the smaller group exceeded the length of the decline. This longer period of rise than of decline is especially significant in the cycle from 1830 to 1834, since it shows the beginning of the long expansion from the low in 1830 to the peak in 1837. Except for these three cycles from 1798 to 1803, from 1808 to 1812, and from 1830 to 1834, both the small group and the total show a similar relationship between the expansion and contraction periods of each cycle.

Three indices of prices in Philadelphia are compared on Chart XIII. The vertical scale is logarithmic in order to aid in judging the severity of the various fluctuations. The top line indicates the composite index of 12 commodities from 1720 to 1861 in relation to their average from 1741 to 1745.[2] The lower solid line traces the movements from 1731 to 1861 in the index of 20 commodities in relation to the average of 1821 to 1825. To facilitate other comparisons the total index from 1784 to 1861, also based on the average of 1821 to 1825, is indicated by the broken line. This is the same index as that shown by the solid line on the top section of Chart II, but it has been plotted in terms of a logarithmic, instead of a natural, vertical scale. The 12-commodity index differs from the other two indices not only in the base period used, but also in that it is an arithmetic instead of a geometric average of the relatives of the constituent commodities.

In our study of the Colonial period, when the arithmetic average of 12 commodities was compared with the arithmetic average of 20, it was found that the smaller group of commodities fluctuated around a lower level than did the larger. A further comparison of the arithmetic and geometric averages of the 20 commodities showed a lower general average for the geometric than for the arithmetic. Since the arithmetic average of 12 commodities based on the average of 1741-

[2] The eight of the 20 commodities not included in this index are: cotton, gunpowder, indigo, rice, staves, James River tobacco, turpentine, and Madeira wine.

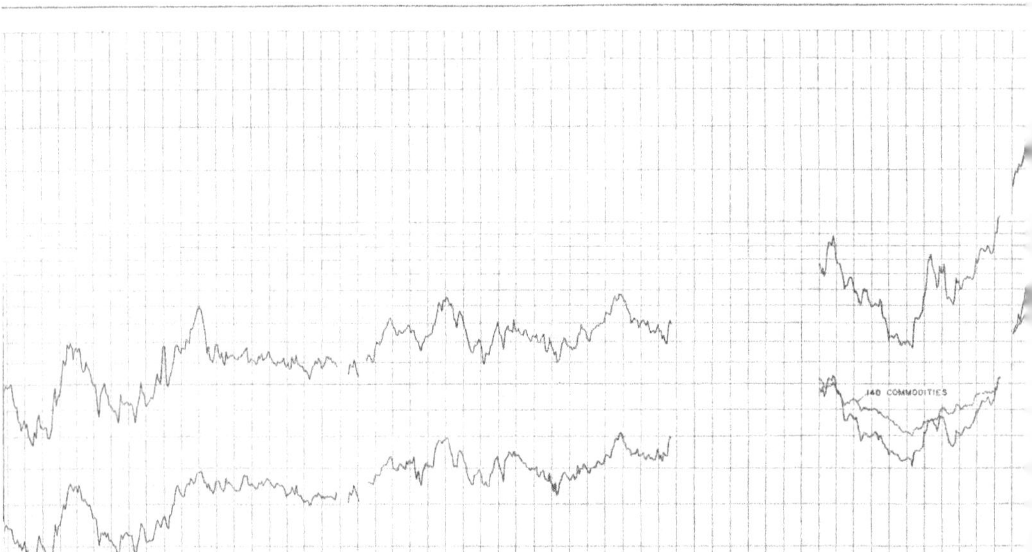

CHART XIII—INDICES OF AVERAGE MONTHLY WHOLESALE PRICES IN PHILADELPHIA, 1720-1861 (arithmetic average of 12 commodities, base—

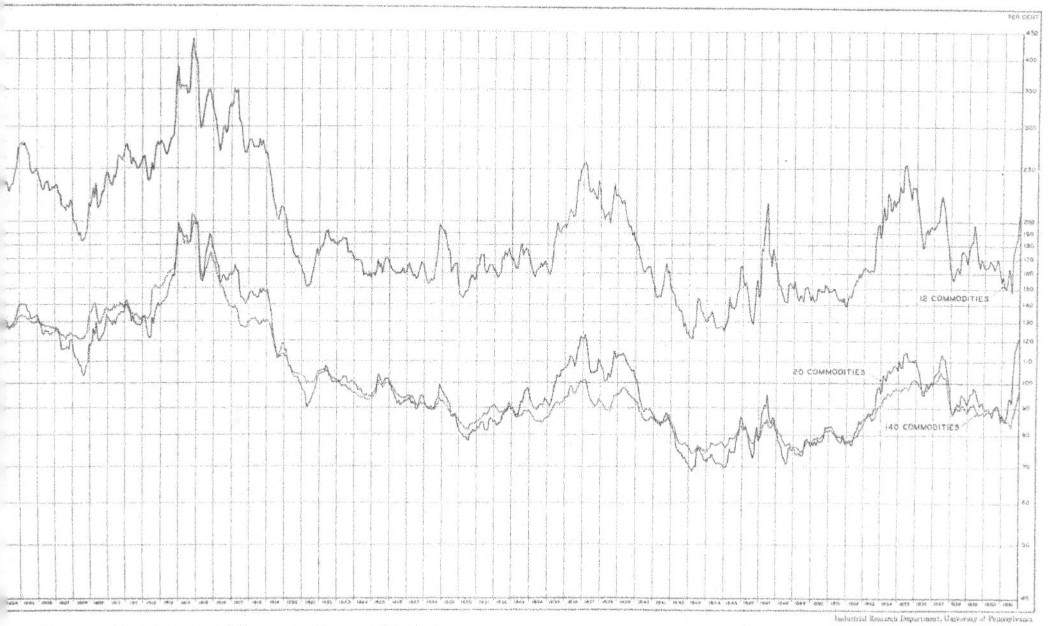

geometric averages of 20 and 140 commodities, base—monthly average, 1821-1825)

1745 agreed closely with the geometric average of 20 commodities on the same base, the difference in level between the arithmetic average of 12 commodities on the early-period base and the geometric average of 20 commodities on an 1821-1825 base reflects chiefly the substantial increase in level of prices between the two base periods.

Another measure of the general increase between 1741-1745 and 1821-1825 can be secured by averaging the index of 20 commodities for both periods. This procedure shows that, in general, prices increased 78 per cent between the two base periods. A large part of this increase occurred in the latter part of the Colonial period, but after the Revolution prices tended to hold still higher; not until the early forties did they drop as low as in 1788 and 1789. At no time did prices fall as low as they had been a few years before the outbreak of the Revolution.

The events associated with the movements of prices of specific commodities as well as with those of the general indices during the Colonial period were discussed in detail in the preceding volume and the events from 1784 to 1861 have been associated with the movements of the composite and group indices in Chapters I and VII-X.

On the ratio chart the monthly index of the 20 commodities and that of the 140 commodities and commodity-groups are graphically compared. As would be expected from the measurements already made of the length and severity of the cycles in the two curves, the indices tend to rise and fall together, the smaller group showing more extreme increases and decreases than the total group. The chart brings out, however, an even more important relationship between the two curves which the cyclical measurements did not even suggest—throughout the entire period from 1784 to 1861 both indices fluctuated about a similar level. As a result of the greater variability of the smaller group its curve usually exceeded that of the total at peaks and fell below it before the end of the recessions.

The most marked differences between the two curves appear from 1784 to 1797, from 1807 to 1813, from 1816 to 1819, from 1833 to 1839, from 1854 to 1857, and in 1861. On the downswing from 1784 to 1789 the index of 20 commodities fell substantially more than the general index. Even on the upswing it tended to fluctuate at a lower level than the general index, although in 1790 and 1791, around the peak of a minor swing which did not show in the general index, the group of 20 commodities rose for a few months to approximately the level of the general curve. At the close of 1793 the smaller group was still relatively below the total. Not only did the smaller group rise from 1789 to 1794 at a faster rate than the total but it also continued to advance at a more rapid rate, reaching a peak early in 1796 nearly a year in advance of the general index. Despite a drop after the peak, the group of 20 commodities brought relatively higher prices as late as 1798 than the 140 commodities.

In addition to being lower than the general index in 1807, the average of the 20 commodities receded still further in 1808 and generally held below the total until near the close of 1813. On the decline from the war peak, in contrast, the smaller group of commodities was relatively higher than the general average, especially from the middle of 1816 to the early months of 1819.

Another period of considerable dissimilarity between the two indices was the years preceding and following the peak of 1837. The rise from 1830 to 1834 was extremely marked in the smaller group of commodities. In spite of the fact that in the early thirties the index of 20 commodities had risen to a greater extent than the general, the smaller group continued to increase at a faster rate. At the peak of 1837 the index of 20 commodities was higher than at any time between the break in 1819 and the increase in prices during the Civil War. The general curve, in contrast, was not as high at its peak in 1837 as in the peaks of 1822, 1855, and 1857 and barely exceeded the height reached in 1825. Throughout 1838 and 1839 the index of 20 commodities continued to fluctuate at a higher level than the general index. Although the distance between the two curves narrowed, especially in 1840, it was not until early in 1841 that the smaller group fell below the average of the total.

The expansion of prices during the fifties was also more rapid in the 20 commodities than in the general average of wholesale prices. The greatest contrast between the two curves in this cycle was that the index of 20 commodities was higher in 1855 than in 1857, when the general curve was at its maximum of the decade. The contraction of prices in 1856 was more severe in the small group of commodities than in the total.

At the close of the 78-year period, the index of 20 commodities was again pulling away from the average of all commodities. It not only started upwards seven months in advance but after September 1861 was higher than at any time after the secondary peak in 1838.

Despite the fact that the group of 20 commodities passed through more extreme cycles than the total index and despite the fact that the two curves often separated, the most striking conclusion based on their behavior during the 78 years is that they did tend to move usually in similar directions around the same level. Stated differently, the disparity between these selected commodities and the total index

TABLE 32
SUMMARY OF CYCLICAL MOVEMENTS OF 20-COMMODITY INDEX
1732–1775

End of Previous Recession	Peak	End of Succeeding Low	Number of Months			Index of Cyclical Variability
			Rise	Fall	Total Cycle	
May 1732	Mar. 1735	Apr. 1737	32	27	59	15.3
Apr. 1737	Nov. 1737	May 1740	7	30	37	15.7
May 1740	Aug. 1741	May 1745	15	45	60	27.6
May 1745	Feb. 1749	Apr. 1755	45	74	119	22.4
Apr. 1755	Nov. 1759	Aug. 1761	55	21	76	15.6
Aug. 1761	Jan. 1763	June 1765	17	29	46	19.0
June 1765	Nov. 1766	Apr. 1769	17	29	46	15.9
Apr. 1769	Nov. 1772	Mar. 1775	43	28	71	17.8

which developed during the expansion of prices was somewhat compensated by a reverse disparity in the contraction of prices.

There still remains a comparison of the variability and length of the cycles for the entire period from 1731 to 1861. We have already seen that the cycles after 1789 in the 20-commodity and composite indices were of similar length and did not tend to change in duration. Furthermore, although the smaller index was more variable than the total, neither tended to change in the extent of their fluctuations. Adding the eight complete cycles from 1732 to 1775 in the index of 20 commodities to the 17 from 1789 to 1860, we can compare the duration and variability of 25 cycles in the average of 20 identical commodities. Over a period of more than a century and a quarter the length and extent of cyclical swings were not progressively altered.

One cycle after 1784 lasted longer than any in the Colonial period and others longer than most of the early cycles. On the other hand, five of the cycles after 1789 were shorter than any preceding one. Two of the later cycles varied considerably more than any in the Colonial period. If the conditions from 1789 to 1799 and from 1812 to 1821 were so unusual that these periods should not be compared with others, the cycle from 1740 to 1745 could also be excluded. Disregarding these three cycles, there still remain four in the later period more variable than any in the Colonial period. On the other hand, five of the cycles after 1789 were less variable than any before 1775. Throughout both periods the longest and most extreme cycles are those associated with wars.

Up to this point certain phases of the behavior of prices from 1784 to 1861 have been analyzed. In addition, the movements of groups of commodities, reflecting varied conditions, have been examined. Finally, by the use of an identical group of commodities, the movements in prices before the Revolution have been compared with those between the Revolution and the Civil War. In certain aspects, progressive changes have been noted; in others, a comparatively uniform behavior has persisted. It is to the summary and interpretation of these changes and stability in the relationships of prices that the final chapter is devoted.

CHAPTER XIII

GENERAL TENDENCIES IN WHOLESALE PRICE MOVEMENTS

It has often been said that the economic system is always in a "new era." To contemporaries, recent developments often appear so new and startling, so different from previous conditions, that a revolution seems to have been accomplished. Too little attention is given to the fact that some of the new developments may have been gradually emerging in previous years and that many of the former characteristics persist in inconspicuous places.

From 1784 to 1861 many changes in Philadelphia and in other parts of the country had repercussions upon the prices in Philadelphia. The manufacturing industries established before the Revolution, notably milling, baking, shipbuilding, distilling, and sugar refining in addition to the fabricating of wood, iron, and coarse textile products, developed further and steadily increased throughout the later years. The need of obtaining a self-sufficient economy colored the discussion of the early years of the national period and grew more intense as commercial reprisals gave place to actual warfare.

Events early in the nineties affected the maritime interests of the inhabitants and the trade of the port of Philadelphia. Too much emphasis cannot be given to the series of epidemics of fever which finally induced some of the merchants to move permanently to other areas and especially to New York. Others who had depended upon foreign sources for their supplies abandoned this trade and concentrated their capital in manufacturing enterprises, leaving a few specialized importers. More and more Philadelphians became primarily interested in the domestic markets which arose out of the internal development of the country. Canals, improved roads, and finally railroads widened the area from which the city drew its supplies and for which it acted as a distributing center. Such forces dominated the later years particularly.

When dealing with prices in Philadelphia from the close of the Revolution to the Civil War, as well as in the half century before, we may be far enough removed from the confused events of those years to appraise the underlying developments and to trace the gradual modification of certain phases of the price structure. In this interpretation of our data presented in the foregoing chapters, we shall examine first the changes apparent in the prices of specific commodities before reviewing the general tendencies in the aggregate of wholesale prices.

It is easy in a study of prices over a stretch of years to concentrate attention on significant changes which occurred from one time to another. The years from 1784 to 1861 alone contain at least three outstanding periods of expansion and contraction frequently referred to in general discussion. Concealed especially by the fluctuations in the general average were the small changes in prices which characterized the variations from year to year in a few commodities.

After 1821 the stability of prices was especially marked, at least 17.5 per cent of the commodities varying less than 2.5 per cent from one year to another. In half of the years after 1843 at least 30 per cent of the commodities fell in this category. This marked tendency towards increasing stability was caused largely by ferrous and non-ferrous metals from the industrial raw and semi-finished products and textile fabrics and a few other series from the class of industrial commodities ready for consumption, in addition to wines as a group, lumber products, and a few of the imported foods. Farm crops, farm derivatives, naval stores, and fish included no series with noticeable or increasing stability.

The tendency towards more mild price changes in the later than in the earlier decades from 1784 to 1861 has also been indicated by the extent of year-to-year variability of individual commodities in each of the four major periods. Although many commodities were consistently among the most or least variable in as many as three of the periods, the general decrease in variability was so substantial that 96 of the 140 series showed a smaller average variation from 1844 to 1860 than from 1785 to 1808. Twelve of these—flax, lard, corn meal, sweet oil, sap and white pine boards, logwood, linseed oil, American cordage, yellow soap, starch, and gin—decreased progressively from period to period in extent of changeability except that the index of year-to-year variability for sweet oil and logwood was the same in two consecutive periods.

The most shifting characteristic of the price behavior of individual commodities was the frequency with which their monthly prices changed. As many as 60 of 135 series or approximately 45 per cent of the entire group showed a progressive alteration in the number of times their prices changed from one month to the next. Most of the series in the farm crops, farm derivatives, and fish groups showed progressively more sensitivity. In fish the frequency of price changes increased so markedly that all of the series were more changeable in monthly prices from 1841 to 1860 than the most variable series from 1791 to 1810. A progressive intensification of changes also characterized honey and lemons in the imported foods, spirits of turpentine in the naval stores, pig iron, sheet iron, Swedish bar iron, pig lead, pearl ashes, copper sheathing, linseed oil, and plaster of Paris in the industrial raw and semi-finished group, and sperm candles and starch in the industrial commodities ready for consumption. These 35 series with progressively increasing sensitivity show in some cases the increasing importance of that commodity or grade of commodity and indicate in others the more continuous supply of and demand for the commodity.

During the same years 25 series maintained an equally progressive decreasing sensitivity. None of the fish, farm derivatives, or lumber products and naval stores, and only James River tobacco of the farm crops manifested such a tendency. In each of the two industrial groups, in imported foods, and in wines, however, from five to eight series showed a decreasing frequency of change in successive periods. Some of these series consist of commodities or grades of commodities which were declining in relative importance, at least in the Philadelphia market, as well as of products for which the demand became relatively inelastic, thus requiring substantial but less frequent alterations in price. In the small group of furs there was no series with a tendency to increase or decrease in sensitivity.

No commodity was consistently among the least variable in its group. On the other hand, wheat, corn, and oats were usually the most variable of all the farm crops, flour and rye meal of the farm derivatives, St. Domingo coffee of the imported foods, tar and spirits of turpentine of the lumber products and naval stores, linseed oil and plaster of Paris of the industrial raw and semi-finished materials, and New England rum of the industrial commodities ready for consumption. All of these except St. Domingo coffee, tar, and New England rum were also among the series which continuously increased in sensitivity.

The detailed analysis of seasonality in 20 selected commodities revealed the fact that even some of those with the most frequent change in monthly prices were not as sensitive as might have been expected from seasonality alone. There was no evidence, however, that increasing seasonality would account for the increasing frequency of change. Nine of the 20 commodities included in this analysis of seasonality were characterized by progressive increases in the frequency of monthly price changes: corn, wheat, Georgia cotton, flour, corn meal, pork, pig lead, linseed oil, and mackerel #1. Only in corn meal and mackerel #1, however, did the frequency of change in the seasonal pattern tend to increase continuously. It appears, therefore, that the enhanced sensitivity of the monthly prices in the latter decades was largely caused by factors other than seasonality. On the other hand, the tendency for some commodities to become inert with respect to monthly changes in prices may be partially attributed to a decrease in seasonality. In James River tobacco and Hyson skin tea a reduction in the number of changes in prices per year was accompanied by a decline in the number of changes in their seasonal patterns, especially between 1811 and 1820, and 1821 and 1830.

The most stable seasonal patterns were those of tar, New England rum, corn meal, corn, linseed oil, pork, and whale oil. Wheat and St. Domingo coffee showed some persistence in the timing of their seasonal highs and lows although not in adjacent decades. On the whole, the seasonal patterns of any commodity were more alike in the later than in the earlier decades. Even with this resemblance, however, many series gradually shifted the timing of the maximum or minimum prices of the year as new sources of supply were opened up or as the buying habits of the community were altered.

In appraising the movements in prices from 1784 to 1861, the 140 commodities and commodity groups were combined into 25 sub-groups, reclassified into nine major groups, and combined into a total. Although each of the 25 sub-groups contains too few series for certain types of analysis, its index does suggest the typical behavior of a small part of the wholesale price structure. To this extent the 24 indices, excluding that of the miscellaneous group, permit a more detailed comparison of price movements than do those of the major groups.

A small number of groups usually showed the most extreme increases in each cycle. These included the domestic agricultural groups of grains, minor farm crops, and the related groups of grain products, meats and meat products, and dairy products, besides fish and fruit. All of these contributed signally to 10 or more of the 17 expansions. Grains and grain products were especially important, being among the groups with the greatest increases in 14 cycles. The dominance of these groups in the rise of the thirties is indicated by the fact that in the expansion from 1830 to 1832 and the following one from 1834 to 1837 all of them were among the third of the groups with the greatest amount of rise. The recurrent character of their impetus in expansions can be illustrated by the cycles in which all but one appeared among the third which advanced most, 1797, 1805, 1828, and 1855, and even to a considerable extent by those of 1801, 1822, 1825, 1845, 1847, and 1859 when all but two sub-groups increased markedly. In other words, it was only in the increases to peaks in 1809, 1814, 1839, 1851, and 1857 that these groups did not dominate the start of expansion.

It is to the remaining groups which in general contributed slightly that one must look for a large part of these advances. Imported commodities were especially affected by the embargo of 1808 and the blockades during the War of 1812; thus chemicals, building materials other than wood, textile fabrics, hides and leather, spirits, and wines were among the third of the groups with the greatest increases in 1809, and beverages, condiments, sugar and molasses, chemicals, non-ferrous metals, and spirits rose similarly from 1811 to 1814. The only corresponding increases in domestic agricultural products occurred in minor farm crops and grain products in the rise to 1809 and in grains and tobacco in the expansion to war or post-war peaks.

The increases to the three peaks of 1839, 1851, and 1857 were more dependent on the seven groups which usually rose most than had been the advances of 1809 and 1814. Fish and fruit contributed noticeably to all three, meats and meat products to two, and the other four to one. These were distributed in such a way that four of the most sensitive groups appeared among the third with the greatest increases in each rise. In all three they were aided by increases in tobacco and, in addition, in the advance to 1839 by beverages, dyes, and furs, in 1851 by non-ferrous metals, textile fibers, and hides and leather, and in 1857 by sugar and molasses, furs, and hides and leather.

Thus a few groups took the outstanding increases in most cycles. Only under the unusual impact of events associated with the Napoleonic wars and the War of 1812 did they fail to account for at least half of the eight groups with the maximum increases in each cycle. Their failure to participate as extensively in 1839, 1851, and 1857 is in part due to the marked severity of the rise in tobacco in those three periods and in hides and leather in each of the four advances after 1849. Of greater importance, however, was the tendency of grains, minor farm crops, grain products, meats and meat products, dairy products, fish, and fruit in a long period of expansion to make their increases early. Thus they made unusual gains in the upswings of 1832 and 1837 but failed to recover relatively as much as others after the crash in the latter year; so too in the expansion of the early fifties these groups made their major advances before 1855 and thus failed to participate vigorously in the final spurt from 1856 to 1857.

The amount of contraction in the various sub-groups from the successive peaks was influenced in a few cases by the pronounced downward trend underlying several consecutive cycles in particular series. As a result, an analysis of the groups composing the third with the greatest decline in each recession differs from the preceding examination of the groups with the maximum increases. Nevertheless, all of the seven groups with the largest increases except dairy products declined very noticeably in at least nine downswings. Specifically, the declines in grains were marked in 14 contractions, grain products in 13, fruit in 12, fish in 10, and minor farm crops and meats and meat products in nine. The group of dairy products, which dropped severely in only seven declines, was replaced in importance by that of tobacco, which fell markedly in 10 recessions.

In no period of decline, however, did all of these seven groups fall enough to be classed in the third with the greatest recessions. Yet, six were in this class after the peaks of 1805, 1837, and 1847, and five after 1797, 1822, 1828, 1839, 1855, 1857, and 1859. Thus, in the declines after 1801, 1809, 1814, 1825, 1832, 1845, and 1851, half or more of the severely falling groups were those which commonly underwent only mild contractions. In five of these periods the seven sensitive groups accounted for half of the extreme declines, being supplemented in 1801 by dairy products, dyes, textile fibers, and spirits, in 1825 by textile fibers, beverages, sugar and molasses, and non-ferrous metals, in 1832 by beverages, condiments, hides and leather, and wines, and in 1845 by dairy products, dyes, ferrous metals, and furs. The roll-down from 1851 had on many groups a similar effect to that from 1825. Among the sensitive groups, fruit and tobacco fell in both recessions, but the greatest similarity was in the groups which usually suffered moderate or slight declines, of which textile fibers, beverages, sugar and molasses, and non-ferrous metals fell so markedly in these contractions that they ranked among the upper third of the sub-groups.

The recessions after 1809 and 1814 were the most affected by the groups commonly insensitive. From the war and post-war peaks very severe declines in grains, tobacco, and grain products were accompanied by corresponding ones in condiments, sugar and molasses, chemicals, fuel and lighting, and spirits. In the decreases from 1809, after the modification of trade restrictions, the greatest contractions were those in minor farm crops, textile fibers, and many groups of imported commodities—beverages, condiments, chemicals, dyes, textile fabrics, and hides and leather.

It appears from this analysis that the momentum toward recession was more widely distributed than that towards revival. This conclusion is further substantiated by an examination of the number of times that sub-groups other than grains, grain products, fruit, tobacco, fish, minor farm crops, and meats and meat products were among the third of the groups with the greatest decreases. Dairy products and sugar and molasses dropped relatively this much seven times; beverages, condiments, dyes, furs, and textile fibers five times; hides and leather and spirits four times; chemicals three times; ferrous metals, non-ferrous metals, and fuel and lighting materials twice; and wood, wines, and textile fabrics once. Building materials other than wood never dropped drastically.

Throughout the 17 cycles practically the same small number of groups of commodities tended toward the most extreme advances and declines. Yet the severe decreases were less concentrated than the increases. That some groups were more important in the amount of momentum which they added to contraction than they did to expansion is due largely to their downward trend for at least a part of the 78-year period. The permanence of the characteristic amount of rise and fall in specific groups is indicated by the failure of any shift to develop in their relative importance.

The index of cyclical variability, which shows the combined effect of rise and fall by expressing both as a percentage of the peak, merely confirms the previous findings. The seven groups with the greatest increases had the most variability and tobacco, which had been one of the groups with most pronounced declines, ranked next. The mildest cycles were, in general, those of textile fabrics, ferrous metals, condiments, chemicals, wood, building materials other than wood, and wines. None of the groups tended to increase or decrease progressively in the extent of their variation in the successive cycles.

The 17 cycles from 1789 to 1861 can also be described by the number and types of groups which initiated the declines and revivals by falling or rising in advance of the general average. Before the composite index reached its peaks of 1797, 1801, 1828, and 1855 as many as 16 sub-groups had started to fall, and in 1837 and 1859 as many as 15. The declines originating in 1814, 1822, 1839, 1845, 1851, and 1857 were preceded by the beginning of contractions in 11 to 13 sub-groups. The other recessions—1805, 1809, 1825, 1832, and 1847—were apparent early in fewer groups, only 10 in 1847 and five in 1809 and 1825 having started to fall before the average.

The contribution of the various groups to the initiation of declines ranged from four times for grains to 12 times for condiments and sugar and molasses and 14 times for beverages. The dominance of these last three groups recalls the fact that imported foods, among the major groups, usually led in declines. For this reason it is pertinent to examine first the four groups composed largely or entirely of imported foods: fruits, beverages, condiments, and sugar and molasses. All of these were among the groups which fell in advance of the general average in the declines of 1828, 1837, 1847, and 1859. Three of them anticipated the recessions from the peaks of 1797, 1801, 1814, 1822, 1845, 1851, and 1855, and two led those from 1805, 1809, 1832, 1839, and 1857. Only in the roll-down from the peak of 1825 did just one of these sub-groups begin its contraction ahead of the average. Thus every shrinkage in the composite index was preceded by a fall in at least one of these four sub-groups.

Eight other groups contributed to more than half of the 17 contractions by starting to decline in advance of the average: meats, dyes, and textile fibers 11 times, spirits 10 times, and minor farm crops, chemicals, hides and leather, and wines nine times. These 12 groups contributed in varying degrees to the successive decreases in the average. Eleven of them anticipated the recessions from 1797, ten from 1828, 1837, and 1845, nine from 1801, 1855, and 1859, eight from 1814, 1822, and 1839, seven from 1847, six from 1805 and 1857, five from 1851, four from 1809 and 1832, and three from 1825. In every recession early declines in these groups were accompanied by similar contractions in other sub-groups, but in 15 cycles these groups accounted for more than half of those which fell before the composite index started to drop. The recessions from the peaks in 1851 and 1857 were unique in that they were more largely initiated than any of the others by groups which did not commonly show the first signs that the expansion period was slowing down. Fuel and lighting materials and ferrous metals made early contributions to the declines from both of these peaks. The prices of fish also began to recede before the general peak of 1851. In the initiation of that roll-down domestic agriculture was unusually dominant, the indices of grains, grain products, and dairy products turning ahead of the composite index. The start of the contraction in 1857 originated in different groups, early declines in tobacco, non-ferrous metals, furs, and textile fabrics adding their weight to similar decreases in fuel and lighting materials, ferrous metals, and six of the groups which usually declined first. It may be inferred that whenever a group led a decline its constituent commodities were among those for which there was relatively the least demand.

Just as the start of recessions had been foreshadowed by early declines in certain groups, so the revivals in the general index were preceded by advances in a varying number of sub-groups. Thirteen or more of the sub-groups started an early recovery from the lows of 1803, 1808, 1828, 1838, and 1849, 10 to 12 from the depressed levels of 1789, 1811, 1824, 1830, 1834, 1843, and 1852, and eight or nine before the general curve turned upward in 1821, 1846, and 1856. Only three groups anticipated the recovery of 1858 and five that of 1798.

All groups at one time or another developed a rising tendency earlier than the composite index, but their contribution was not as concentrated as it was in the start of recession. Only 10 sub-groups began to recover sooner than the average in more than half of the cycles: chemicals 11 times; fruit, textile fibers, hides and leather, and wines 10 times; and fish, sugar and molasses, fuel and lighting, building materials other than wood, and spirits nine times. All of the other groups anticipated the general rise at least four times. Of the groups which most frequently rose in advance of the total all but fish, fuel and lighting, and building materials other than wood had also contributed substantially to the initiation of declines.

Of greatest interest is the shift in the relative importance of various groups in showing the first signs of recovery. The five times when ferrous metals started upward before the composite index were concentrated in the five consecutive revivals from 1789 to 1811 inclusive. In contrast, the seven groups—grains, tobacco, minor farm crops, textile fibers, grain products, meats and meat products, and dairy products—which include practically all of the farm crops and derivatives, showed early revivals in the recoveries from 1828 to 1856 especially. Before 1828 no more than two of these seven groups had risen earlier than the average, but this behavior was evident in six of them in 1830 and 1834, in five in 1838, 1849, and 1852, in four in 1856, and in three in 1828, 1843, and 1846.

This analysis emphasizes the groups which rose or fell in advance of the average in the various cycles. It is such diversity of movements, concealed by the composite index, which makes the general average at some times minimize and at others exaggerate the extent of increases or decreases in prices in certain cycles.

For the main part of our analysis it was expedient to reclassify the commodities into nine major groups, representative of the diverse sections of the economy from which the wholesale prices had been selected. Domestic agriculture is represented by farm crops, and to some extent by farm derivatives, which included the products of what would now be regarded as the meat packing, milling, baking, and dairy industries. Other manufacturing industries are represented by the industrial raw and semi-finished products and industrial commodities ready for consumption. The other major groups likewise represent specific areas of enterprise, imported foods, lumber products and naval stores, fish, furs, and wines. It is from these nine groups, and especially from the six largest ones, which include 126 of the 140 series, that more general conclusions can be drawn than from the individual commodities or the small sub-groups and that more specific findings can be secured than from the aggregate.

At least a small amount of stability characterized all of the six largest major groups. In farm crops and farm derivatives about the same slight proportion of the constituent commodities tended to show little change in price in all periods. The other groups, and especially the two industrial groups, showed a marked increase in stability from one period to another. In many of the years after 1821, at least 30 per cent of the annual prices of the industrial products changed less than 2.5 per cent.

The relative amount of year-to-year variability of the major groups was in inverse order to their stability. Typically, the farm derivatives, farm crops, and imported foods showed the highest average amount of change in their annual indices. The groups of lumber products and naval stores, fish, and furs were but slightly less variable. The least amount of changeability from year to year was in the two industrial groups and in wines. Although the groups tended to keep somewhat in this order, all increased in variability for the period from 1809 to 1821 in comparison with that of 1785 to 1808 except farm derivatives and furs. In the last two periods such a decrease in variability occurred that all groups had a lower average than in either of the first two periods except farm crops from 1822 to 1843 and wines from 1844 to 1860.

In the behavior of their monthly prices the major groups show significant differences as well as progressive changes. In general, farm crops, farm derivatives, and fish always underwent a moderate number of price changes each year and developed a tendency toward even more frequent changes. In farm derivatives, as a result of this progressive increase, all series changed more frequently from 1841 to 1860 than from 1791 to 1810. The constantly increasing sensitivity of the prices of fish was so marked that in the closing period all grades of fish were more changeable than the highest frequency in the group from 1791 to 1810. The development of the tendencies for increasingly frequent changes in price among these important commodities paralleled the internal development of the country and the rapid improvement of facilities for transportation and communication. The net result of these physical changes in conditions affecting trade was a somewhat continuous interchange of products and news in contrast to the intermittent arrival of vessels by way of the Delaware in the earlier period.

At the other extreme stood wines and furs, which never changed frequently in price and which even tended to become more insensitive. This latter development was especially pronounced in wines. This somewhat similar evolution arose from different factors. Although furs and wines might both be regarded as luxury goods which would not be expected to change frequently in price, other conditions related to sensitivity of prices were dissimilar. During the period under consideration Philadelphia declined in importance as a fur market and accordingly local prices of furs were less responsive to slight changes of supply and demand than were prices in active markets. In addition, new supplies of furs were received during a relatively short part of the year when most of the trading was done. At other times prices might be regarded as being almost nominal—the last price paid tending to be quoted for some time. Supplies of wines, in contrast, arrived more and more frequently which assured adequate stocks at practically all times. On the other hand, since wine is nonperishable, it was seldom that merchants were forced to dispose of an over-supply below the usual price. In addition, an increase occurred in the variety of wine offered for sale. This development modified the frequency with which any particular series changed in price.

The other groups—lumber products and naval stores, both classes of industrial products, and imported foods—include series with a diversity of behavior. In all groups some commodities increased in frequency and in all except lumber products and naval stores some declined. Such a development is to be expected in these diversified groups with seasonal and non-seasonal commodities, durable and perishable goods, and necessities and luxuries.

The spreading apart of the series in these groups and the pronounced but opposite developments in farm crops, farm derivatives, and fish on the one hand and furs and wines on the other is reflected in an increasing diversity in the frequency of price change. From 1791 to 1810 only one series, an industrial commodity ready for consumption, changed on the average less than once a year. In the last two periods many commodities, including some from all groups except farm crops, farm derivatives, and fish, were in this inert class. Even more commodities gradually shifted into the high-frequency class. Between 1791 and 1810 no commodity averaged as many as eight changes a year, but after 1841 all groups except furs and wines included at least one series with this average number of price changes.

In summarizing the cyclical movements of the nine major groups, it has been shown that in their influence on the time of the initiation of recovery the two industrial groups were especially important in the early cycles and that the farm crops and farm derivatives were important in the later ones.

The amount of rise in the various periods of expansion is also pertinent in any appraisal of the contribution of groups to recovery. Perhaps of greatest importance are those groups which did not show the general cyclical movement because they continued to rise during the entire swing in the composite index. Such was the case in the industrial raw and semi-finished products at the peak of 1832 when they continued an advance from 1830 to 1837, in the industrial commodities ready for consumption when they continued their advance from 1843 to 1848 through the peak of 1845, in lumber products and naval stores when they continued to rise from 1848 to 1854 through the peak of 1851, in furs when they started to increase in price eight months before the general peak of 1855 and continued upward until 1857, and in wines when, advancing from 1849, they rose through the peaks of 1851 and 1855 and held the peak of 1857 as late as June 1858.

The three groups in each cycle which had the greatest amount of rise from low to peak merit special consideration. Throughout the period as a whole the group of fish was the most dominant among the extremely advancing group. Only in the increases to peaks in 1822 and 1825 did it fail to be among the three rising most. In seven cycles the advance in this group exceeded that in all others, in five it was second, and in three third. Farm crops also contributed substantial increases to most cycles, being first in the peaks of 1832 and 1847, second in four, and third in five advances. Only in the peaks of 1797, 1801, 1809, 1828, 1845, and 1857 did it fail to increase sufficiently to be classed among the three with the most extreme advances. No other group aided substantially more than seven peaks. Furs were first in three, second in two, and third in two; farm derivatives were second in five and third in two. Lumber products and naval stores increased most unusually to peaks in 1797 and 1855, when they rose more than any other group, and in 1809 and 1822, when only two groups showed a greater increase. Imported foods contributed relatively their most to the advances of 1814, 1857, and 1825, and wines in 1809, 1859, and 1801. Only to the peak of 1797 did the industrial commodities ready for consumption rise sufficiently to be among the three with the greatest increases. The group of industrial raw and semi-finished products was never in this class.

The two peaks of 1822 and 1825, to which fish did not contribute extremely, were alike in that furs and farm crops made the two greatest advances in both. These were aided in 1822 by lumber products and naval stores and in 1825 by imported foods. The joint contribution of farm crops, farm derivatives, and fish was most apparent in the peaks of 1805, 1832, 1837, 1847, and 1851 when they rose more extremely than any other groups. In two of these, 1832 and 1847, farm crops and farm derivatives and in two others, 1805 and 1851, in addition to 1828, fish and farm derivatives exceeded all other groups.

The analysis of the groups with the largest increases in each cycle isolates those which characteristically made substantial advances, but it does not show the times at which outstanding increases were made.

For this purpose it is necessary to examine the dates at which each group had its four most extreme expansions. The rise to 1797 stands out in all groups, being the largest in six and the second in imported foods and industrial raw and semi-finished articles and the fourth in wines. The advance to 1814 was nearly as pronounced. Only in furs did it fail to be one of the four main increases.

The expansions to 1837 and 1855 were less widespread. That of 1837 was most pronounced in farm derivatives, fish, farm crops, and the industrial raw and semi-finished products, while that of 1855 was also marked in farm crops and industrial raw and semi-finished materials, in addition to lumber products and naval stores and industrial commodities ready for consumption. Eight other periods of expansion were marked in certain groups: 1801 in fish, 1809 in wines, lumber products and naval stores, and industrial commodities ready for consumption, 1822 and 1839 in furs, 1845 in furs and imported foods, and 1859 in wines, which had advanced from 1849.

In summarizing the process of decline in the major groups it was noted that imported foods and the industrial commodities ready for consumption were most consistent in contributing to the start of recessions by turning in advance of the general curve. Farm crops and farm derivatives were important in determining the date at which the composite index began to recede. The amount of contraction after the peaks in the successive cycles must also be considered in any examination of the effects of the various groups on the decline in the general curve. Of peculiar importance are those groups which, not having shared in the preceding rise, continued to fall for two or more cycles. This behavior affected the prices of imported foods in 1828 when they were declining from 1825 to 1830, in 1839 when they were falling from 1836 to 1842, and in 1847 when they fell from 1845 to 1848. Prices of lumber products and naval stores also missed the peak of 1847 by their downward drift from 1846 to 1848. In the group of industrial raw and semi-finished materials which receded from 1825 to 1830 the peak of 1828 did not appear. Furs failed to reflect the crests of 1847 and of 1851, although the decline from 1846 to 1855 was checked. Wines missed the peak of 1822 because the contraction from 1814 was not halted until 1824. This group also did not develop a peak either in 1837 or 1839 but fell from 1832 to 1842. The most persistingly falling group was that of industrial commodities ready for consumption. From the peak of 1814 it contracted until 1830 without reacting to the intervening peaks of 1822, 1825, or 1828. Similarly, it fell from 1837 to 1843 without showing a peak in 1839, from 1848 to 1852 without attaining a peak in 1851, and from 1855 to 1861 without registering a peak in either 1857 or 1859.

The relative importance of the declines in the major groups compared with their advances is especially modified by the trend underlying several cycles. Groups moving upward would not fall as much as they had advanced, while groups with a downward trend would be subjected to more severe recessions. Nevertheless, fish and farm crops, which made the most extreme advances, also suffered the greatest declines. Fish ranked among the first three groups in extent of recession in every slump except those from the peaks of 1809, 1825, 1837, and 1845 and farm crops were similarly depressed markedly except after 1797, 1828, 1832, and 1845. The declines to which these groups contributed most were 1805, 1822, 1847, and 1855, when they fell more than any others. Farm derivatives and imported foods each in seven different cycles were among the groups with the most appreciable recessions. The farm derivatives contributed largely to the declines from 1801, 1805, 1822, 1828, 1839, 1847, and 1859. In all of these contractions except that from 1828 the other two groups with large decreases were farm crops and fish. Imported foods were an especially important factor in the slumps following peaks in 1809, 1825, 1832, 1837, 1845, 1851, and 1857. Only in the last two did both farm crops and fish also recede markedly. The other groups were dominant in only a small number of contractions: furs in those from 1797, 1825, 1828, 1837, and 1845; lumber products and naval stores in those from 1797, 1809, and 1845; industrial commodities ready for consumption in those from 1814 and 1855; and wines in that from 1832.

Since the groups differed in their characteristic amount of decline, it is expedient to take the four largest recessions in each group in order to see the times at which the various groups underwent the most substantial contractions. The drop in prices after 1814 stands out in all groups. Only in furs, in which three other recessions were more severe, did it fail to be the most drastic. The less severe recession of 1839 was nearly as widespread, affecting to an unusual extent all groups except imported foods, industrial commodities ready for consumption, and wines, all of which failed to reach a peak in 1839. The decline after 1797, although moderate in the general curve, was extreme in lumber products and naval stores, fish, furs, and industrial commodities ready for consumption. No other downswing markedly affected more than three groups, the one after 1825 being relatively most severe in imported foods, industrial raw and semi-finished materials, and wines, and the one after 1837 in both industrial groups and furs. In eight other declines one or two groups were drastically lowered: farm derivatives after 1801, farm crops after 1805, imported foods and lumber products and naval stores after 1809, wines after 1832, farm crops and derivatives after 1847, industrial commodities ready for consumption after 1855, imported foods after 1857, and fish and wines after 1859.

It is significant that the decline in the general index can conceal the severity of the declines in the constituent groups. This is especially clear in the crash of 1857, which in the general index was exceeded only by those of 1814 and 1839. This importance came only as a result of the closeness in timing of the fall in most of the groups. Actually, except in imported foods, for which this break was more severe than any other except that of 1814, the other groups which fell in 1857 passed through from four to 10 contractions more severe than this one.

The combined effect of the rise and fall of prices in each swing has been measured by the index of cyclical variability, the average percentage distance from the high to both the preceding and succeeding lows. Thus the rise is made comparable to the decline. The group of fish stands out as having the most extreme cycles, being the most variable in 12 out of the 17 and third in two others. Only in the cycles from 1808 to 1811, from 1824 to 1828, and from 1843 to 1846 did it fail to be in the three groups with the greatest variability. The cycles in farm crops were but slightly less extreme, this group ranking among the first three in 10 cycles. Farm derivatives, imported foods, and furs had about the same moderate swings in prices, each being in seven cycles among the three most fluctuating groups. Lumber products and naval stores were extremely variable only in 1797, 1809, and 1855 and wines in 1809, 1832, and 1859. Neither of the industrial groups ever had high cyclical variability.

Regardless of the different characteristic amount of fluctuation in the various groups, two of the four most extreme cycles in each were the long swings from 1789 to 1798 and from 1811 to 1821. Another extremely variable cycle was that from 1838 to 1843, which affected several groups especially farm crops, furs, farm derivatives, industrial raw and semi-finished materials, and fish. The other extreme cycles in each group were widely distributed. That from 1798 to 1803 was especially pronounced in fish, the one from 1808 to 1811 in lumber products and naval stores and wines, the one from 1834 to 1838 in both industrial groups, the one from 1843 to 1846 in furs and imported foods, the one from 1846 to 1849 in farm crops and derivatives, the one from 1852 to 1856 in lumber products and naval stores and industrial commodities ready for consumption, the one from 1856 to 1858 in imported foods, and the one from 1858 to 1861 in wines.

The most salient aspect of the fluctuations of the major groups was that no progressive change developed during the entire period in either the length or severity of their cycles.

The movements of the indices of the major groups have been contrasted with those of the composite index by measuring the relative distances each year between the general average and the various groups. Two relationships are important: first, the amount of deviation in any group away from the average; second, the position of a particular group above or below the average.

On the whole, the groups that held closest to the general average were the two industrial ones. Their average deviation from the total curve was approximately 5 per cent. The greatest deviations occurred from 1809 to 1821 in the industrial raw and semi-finished materials when they averaged nearly 8 per cent away from the composite index and from 1844 to 1861 when the industrial commodities ready for consumption tended to be slightly more than 8 per cent below the average.

From 1784 to 1808 the two industrial groups moved inversely to each other in relation to the general curve. From 1808 to 1815 both groups were above the average. During the descent of prices after the war both fell below, the raw materials continuing to be more depressed than the general index as late as 1823 while from 1820 to 1823 the industrial commodities ready for consumption recovered enough to rise above the average. From 1824 to 1861 they were continuously below the general average. The industrial raw and semi-finished materials, in contrast, were better sustained in price, being higher than the average from 1824 to 1831, in 1833 and 1834, from 1837 to 1846, and from 1848 to 1850.

The average prices of lumber products and naval stores deviated slightly more from the average than did those of the industrial groups. For the period as a whole their fluctuations were more than 8 per cent; from 1784 to 1808 and 1844 to 1861 they were usually between 10 and 13 per cent away from the composite index, but in the other two major periods they varied less than 6 per cent. Before 1823 lumber products and naval stores tended to fluctuate below the general average, rising above it only in 1784, 1797, 1803, 1819, and 1820. For the remainder of the period the group held above the composite index except from 1830 to 1832, in 1839, from 1844 to 1850, and in 1856 and 1857.

Farm derivatives, imported foods, wines, and farm crops varied still more widely from the average of the 140 commodities. For the 78 years their average deviations were from 12 to slightly more than 17 per cent. Farm crops and derivatives showed a progressive increase in the extent of their fluctuations away from the general average in each successive major period. Imported foods and wines, in contrast, attained their greatest deviations from 1784 to 1808 and their mildest ones from 1809 to 1821, followed by larger variations in the last two periods. Farm derivatives always deviated less than farm crops. As a result, in practically an equal number of years before 1827 farm derivatives were below and above the total index, while the farm crops were more often above than below. In the later years, however, both groups tended to be well above the general average. From 1827 to 1861 farm derivatives held above the composite curve except in 1844, and the farm crops were continuously above from 1829 to 1861.

The imported foods and wines tended to vary more widely from the average than the farm derivatives but less than the farm crops. As evidence of the downward trend of the movements of imported foods for a substantial part of the entire period, the fluctuations from 1784 to 1821 were above those of the general curve except in 1810 and 1811 and those from 1822 to 1861 were below except in 1825 and 1826. In contrast, the average relative prices of wines from 1784 to 1810 were less than those of the average of the 140 commodities. From 1811 to 1826 the indices of this group and the total were closer together, wines rising above the average for a short stretch and then dropping below again. During this time wines were never continuously above or below the composite index for more than four years. From 1827 to 1854 this group kept below the general index, but the rise in prices, especially in 1854, was so marked that from 1855 to 1861 wines were continuously more than 20 per cent above the average.

The greatest divergences from the general index occurred in fish and furs. On the average they deviated approximately 30 per cent, but their fluctuations tended to balance each other. Throughout the period fish moved well above the average, dropping below it only in five years; furs were below the average except in nine years, eight of which were from 1823 to 1830.

The differences in trends which developed after the post-war readjustment are reflected in the extent to which fish, farm crops, and farm derivatives especially, and lumber products and naval stores in less degree, kept their fluctuations above the general average during the latter part of the period. In contrast, imported foods, industrial commodities ready for consumption, and wines were usually below the composite index. The industrial raw and semi-finished products generally held closely to or slightly above the general index. The chief times when the prices of this group were relatively below the average occurred between 1791 and 1798, between 1816 and 1823, and between 1851 and 1861.

To summarize the diverse changes noted in the individual series and in the various groups and to appraise their net result in the structure of wholesale prices, we turn to the aggregate of the 140 commodities and commodity-groups. Although influenced by the choice of the base period, the changes in the distribution of the annual relatives around the median of each year suggest the type and extent of variation which occurred from one year to another. In the years when the distribution was but mildly skewed either negatively or positively, many of the series changed but slightly, if at all, or else larger changes in some series canceled each other or modified the asymmetry of the previous year. The large positive skewness in the years of advancing prices, as in the early years of the nineteenth century before the War of 1812 or during the expansion of the early fifties, reflects a substantial advance in a few commodities while the majority lagged behind. The negative skewness during the rise to 1837 shows a different type of unbalance—many series advancing and a small number falling or rising slowly.

The most outstanding examples of positive asymmetry when the total index was falling occurred in 1787, 1816, and 1817. It was in these years that while most prices fell a few rose. Likewise, the extreme negative skewness accompanying the crashes of 1837 and 1857 resulted from a severe drop in a relatively small number of commodities and a milder recession, if not even a slight advance, in the others.

Throughout the period it has been explained that some commodities tended to undergo few if any changes in price and others tended towards greater stability in the latter decades than in the early ones. For the aggregate this development resulted in the greatest stability in 1821 when more than 16 per cent of the commodities maintained the same average price as they had in the previous year. The most sustained stability, however, occurred in the 23 years from 1838 to 1860 when at least 5.7 per cent of the series held the same price for two consecutive years. In contrast, 32 of the 53 previous years showed a smaller percentage of invariable prices.

The inclusion of the series which changed less than 2.5 per cent from one year to another increases the stability apparent in every year. In 1833 as many as 40 per cent of the commodities were in this class and in every year after 1836 at least 20 per cent. In fact, after 1818 there were only three years—1825, 1826, and 1836—when less than 20 per cent of the series sustained only minor, if any, changes in price. It is to the other series with more substantial changes in price that we must look for the impetus to successive expansions and contractions which characterized the movements of the total index.

Even the extent of substantial changes was markedly reduced in the two periods after 1821 from what it previously had been. The year-to-year variability in each period for individual commodities showed such a shrinkage that while 16 had varied less than 18.1 per cent on the average from 1785 to 1808 and 35 from 1809 to 1821, only eight were as variable from 1822 to 1843 and four in the closing period.

Other mutations appeared in the frequency with which monthly prices changed. In the aggregate, this percentage fluctuated widely from 1791 to 1834. In 1796, 1800, 1815, and 1818 more than 40 per cent of the monthly prices of 135 commodities available for this analysis changed from one month to the next. At other times prices were much less fluctuating. In 1792, 1793, 1803, 1805, 1813, and 1823 less than 20 per cent of the potential number of changes occurred.

The years after 1834 stand in marked contrast to the previous ones. The wide variation in the number of price changes was modified, but a much higher frequency of change prevailed. From a third to nearly a half of all monthly prices changed in each year. While in an individual commodity such a shift might be largely due to a change in its characteristics, this pronounced shift in the aggregate reflects largely the improvements in transportation and communication which had been effected. As both news and goods began to be received continuously rather than intermittently the market became better organized and prices reacted more frequently than before to changes in outside markets.

The 20 commodities studied for the period 1720 to 1775 can be matched, except for a few specifications, in the years from 1784 to 1861. The same cycles which occurred in the total index appeared also in the average of the small group of commodities. In general, the two indices fluctuated around the same level, but as the cycles in the group of 20 commodities were more extreme than those in the total index, the smaller group rose above the average at peaks and dropped below during the contractions. Only from 1784 to 1797, from 1807 to 1813, from 1816 to 1819, from 1833 to 1839, from

1854 to 1857, and in 1861 were the curves markedly different. The cycles in the index of 20 commodities showed no tendency to increase or decrease in duration or severity from 1784 to 1861 or even from 1731 to 1861.

By the use of the commodities included in the analysis of prices for more than a century and a quarter it is possible to appraise the extent to which prices were higher after the Revolution than before it as well as the diverse trends which developed especially after 1821. Most commodities were at least slightly higher at the beginning of the national period than at the close of the Colonial period. Only gunpowder was definitely lower, although bread, turpentine, and tar were slightly cheaper in some years of the first decade after the Revolution than in the decade preceding it. Loaf sugar, pork, corn, salt, and pitch tended to be slightly higher. Havana brown sugar, West India molasses, Georgia cotton, West India rum, and New England rum had made more pronounced gains in price. The most significant contrasts between prices before and after the Revolution were in James River tobacco, flour, wheat, rice, staves, and Madeira wine which averaged higher in every consecutive five-year period between 1784 and 1861 than in any similar period from 1720 to 1775.

Between the Revolution and the Civil War, no persistent trend affected the underlying movements of these specific commodities, with a few exceptions. Despite a rising trend near the close of the period, cotton, Havana brown sugar, and loaf sugar tended to decline throughout the major part of the 78 years. Of these the downward movement in the prices of loaf sugar was most significant since it marks the continuation of a similar trend noted in the Colonial period. A noticeable upward movement underlay the fluctuations of corn, rice, tar, turpentine, and West India rum from 1784 to 1861. As both corn and West India rum had a similar trend in the early period, most of their variations in price from 1720 to 1861 centered around a steadily increasing plane.

In spite of many divergences, the trends from 1784 to 1861 can best be described by dividing the period into sections. From 1784 to 1821 the general movements in the group of 20 commodities consisted of a decline from 1784 to 1789, a rise from 1789 to 1797, a decline from 1797 to 1808, a rise from 1808 to 1815, and a recession from 1815 to 1821 or later. In salt this declining tendency lasted until the beginning of the Civil War, in gunpowder until 1851, and in molasses and both grades of sugar until 1850. In 11 other commodities the downward movement had a somewhat shorter course. The prices of staves and pitch receded until 1847, cotton until 1844, and New England rum until 1842. No other series had a falling trend from the war and post-war peaks which persisted after 1833. Regardless of whether the underlying contraction continued until the forties or fifties or was checked in 1824 as in West India rum, in 1826 in corn, in 1828 in rice, and in 1830 in tobacco, turpentine, and tar, the prices for the remainder of the period moved around an upward trend. The prices of Madeira wine, however, which tended to fall until 1833, fluctuated around a somewhat constant level before starting a continuous advance after 1847. Although pork had a horizontal trend until 1844, its prices too showed a definite upward movement in the later years. The trend underlying the prices of indigo was unique in that it rose until 1825 with only a slight setback between 1813 and 1819. The decline which set in after 1825 persisted until the end of the period. In contrast to these changes in the direction of trend which appeared at various times between 1824 and 1851 are the constant horizontal planes around which, from 1821 to 1861, fluctuated the prices of flour, wheat, bread, and beef.

This analysis of prices so clearly indicates the dominance of progressive factors which influence their relationships that it may well provide a background against which modern prices should be considered. It is safe to conclude that at any given time the structure of wholesale prices contains a great diversity of price behavior. Each group of related commodities and perhaps each commodity is moving in response to its own seasonal and secular pattern and is influenced by and contributes to the more general cyclical variations to a different extent.

APPENDIX

METHOD

Collection of Data

As a first step in the collection of the original prices the files of old Philadelphia newspapers were examined. Local libraries, especially the Historical Society of Pennsylvania, the Ridgway Branch of the Library Company of Philadelphia, the Athenaeum of Philadelphia, the Mercantile Library, the American Philosophical Society, and the libraries of the University of Pennsylvania, were consulted. The search for papers not in their files was extended to include other depositories, notably the Library of Congress in Washington and the New York Public Library and the New York Historical Society in New York City.

The first Philadelphia newspaper to carry prices after the Revolution was the *Pennsylvania Mercury and Universal Advertiser* of August 20, 1784. The list of the newspaper sources and the years for which they are used is given in the bibliography, pp. 427-429. In the early part of the period, when the lists in each paper were short and did not always appear continuously, it was necessary to use a large number of papers. Early attempts had been made to establish specialized price reporting such as the *Philadelphia Price Current* published by John McPherson, the *Complete Counting House Companion* by Mathew Carey as a supplement to the *Pennsylvania Evening Herald* from 1785 to 1789, and *Finlay's American Naval and Commercial Register* from December 1795 to December 1797. With the starting of *Hope's Philadelphia Price Current* in 1804 a continuous series of specialized commercial newspapers began in Philadelphia. *Grotjan's Philadelphia Public Sale Report*, started in May 1812, was carried on by other editors from 1825 to 1827 and the *Philadelphia Price Current and Commercial List*, beginning in 1827, continued under various names, throughout the period. Even with such sources available, however, it was necessary to consult other Philadelphia newspapers in order to secure continuous records of prices for some commodities. In collecting the prices from the newspapers the quotations published nearest the 15th of each month were used. Whenever a range of prices was given, the low and the high were averaged.

These data, when collected and posted by series, were broken by many gaps, especially in the early years. The next step was to supplement the prices obtained from newspapers with others secured from merchants' letters and account books. The complete list of the sources used is given in the bibliography, pp. 429-430. The Historical Society of Pennsylvania has preserved many fine records of the Biddles, Cliffords, Hollingsworths, and Whartons, of Chaloner and White, Reed and Forde, Warder and Brothers, Lippincott and Company, and many other prominent business firms. The Library of Girard College made many of the records of Stephen Girard available to us. Other account books were found in the possession of individuals, especially the unusually complete records of the firm of Wetherill and Brother starting with the accounts and letters of Samuel Wetherill, which have been carefully preserved by Mr. A. P. Wetherill. The search for Philadelphia material was extended to other areas, the Library of Congress yielding the Stephen Collins papers; the John Carter Brown Library in Providence, letters from Hewes and Anthony of Philadelphia; the Boston Historical Society, the Wetmore papers, which contained many letters from Hewes and Anthony and other Philadelphians; and the Baker Library of Harvard University, the Trotter collection. Whenever possible, more than one but no more than 11 quotations in any month were taken from the merchants' accounts and the range of the high and low prices averaged.

Even with this number of supplementary sources there were certain commodities, especially in the latter part of the period, which were not quoted in the local papers nor dealt in extensively by merchants. In order to preserve the same group of series throughout the 78 years we were finally forced to use a few prices from the Baltimore and New York markets. In all of these cases, however, a test was first made on an overlapping period to determine that the prices of these commodities in either Baltimore or New York had been approximately equal to and moving with the local prices.

Thus starting with the framework of prices from local newspapers, we supplemented these data with prices from other local sources and finally with a limited amount of material from other areas. At every step in the process we carefully scrutinized the prices, checking and verifying them before proceeding further, always keeping in mind that the validity of the final result rested fundamentally upon the accuracy of the basic data. In only a few places was it necessary to estimate prices on the basis of related commodities or to interpolate arbitrarily for a few months.

Even with all of this work it was not possible to fill in completely the months from May to December 1794, from December 1798 to April 1799, and from September 1799 to May 1800. These gaps were caused primarily by the severe epidemics of fever during which trading in Philadelphia came to a standstill. During some of these same months Pennsylvania especially was disturbed by internal friction over the collection of excise taxes, culminating in the Whiskey Rebellion in 1794 and Fries Rebellion in 1799.[1]

As an example of the reliability of the newspaper prices, such data for three commodities, linseed oil, spirits of turpentine, and copper sheathing, are compared on Chart XIV with average monthly prices for the same commodities secured from merchants' records. Those of linseed oil and spirits of turpentine were compiled from the account books of Wetherill and Brother and those of copper sheathing[2] from the records of Nathan Trotter and Company. Certain differences are to be expected. The newspapers usually quoted the high and low prices of the sales of the week, representing slight differences in quality. The account book prices, however, are the average of from one to eleven sales, weighted by the volume of each. This procedure introduces many slight fluctuations in prices because a change could appear merely because of a shift in the relative amount sold at slightly different prices. In addition, since both of these firms specialized in the highest grade of materials, their prices would tend to be slightly above the average of the market as a whole. The same type of comparison can be shown for many other commodities, but this analysis is deferred to a later study, when the records of these companies will

[1] Dunaway, Wayland Fuller, *A History of Pennsylvania*, pp. 411-419.

[2] The similarity of the two lines is the only point emphasized by the chart. It should be noted that the lowest section is not plotted from 0.

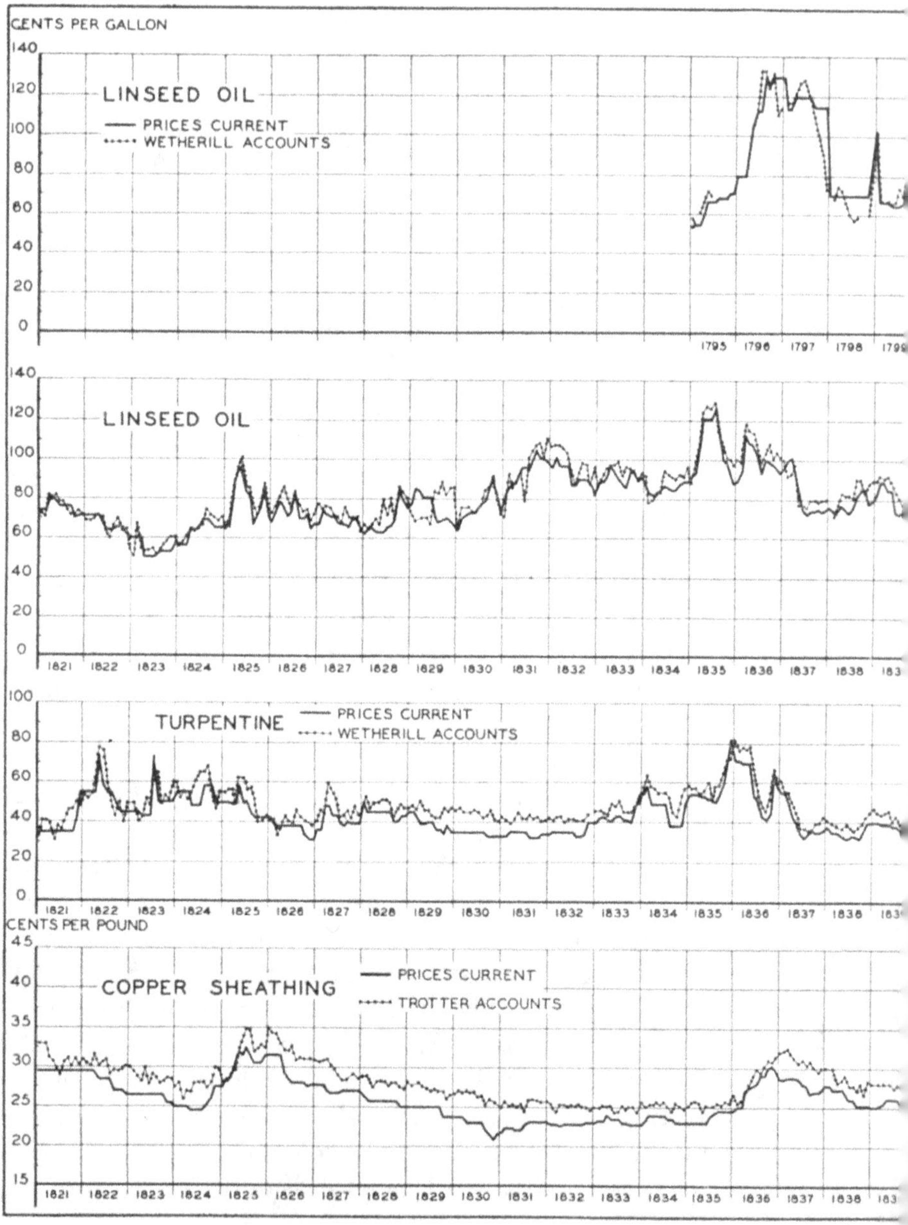

CHART XIV—COMPARISON OF AVERAGE MONTHLY WHO

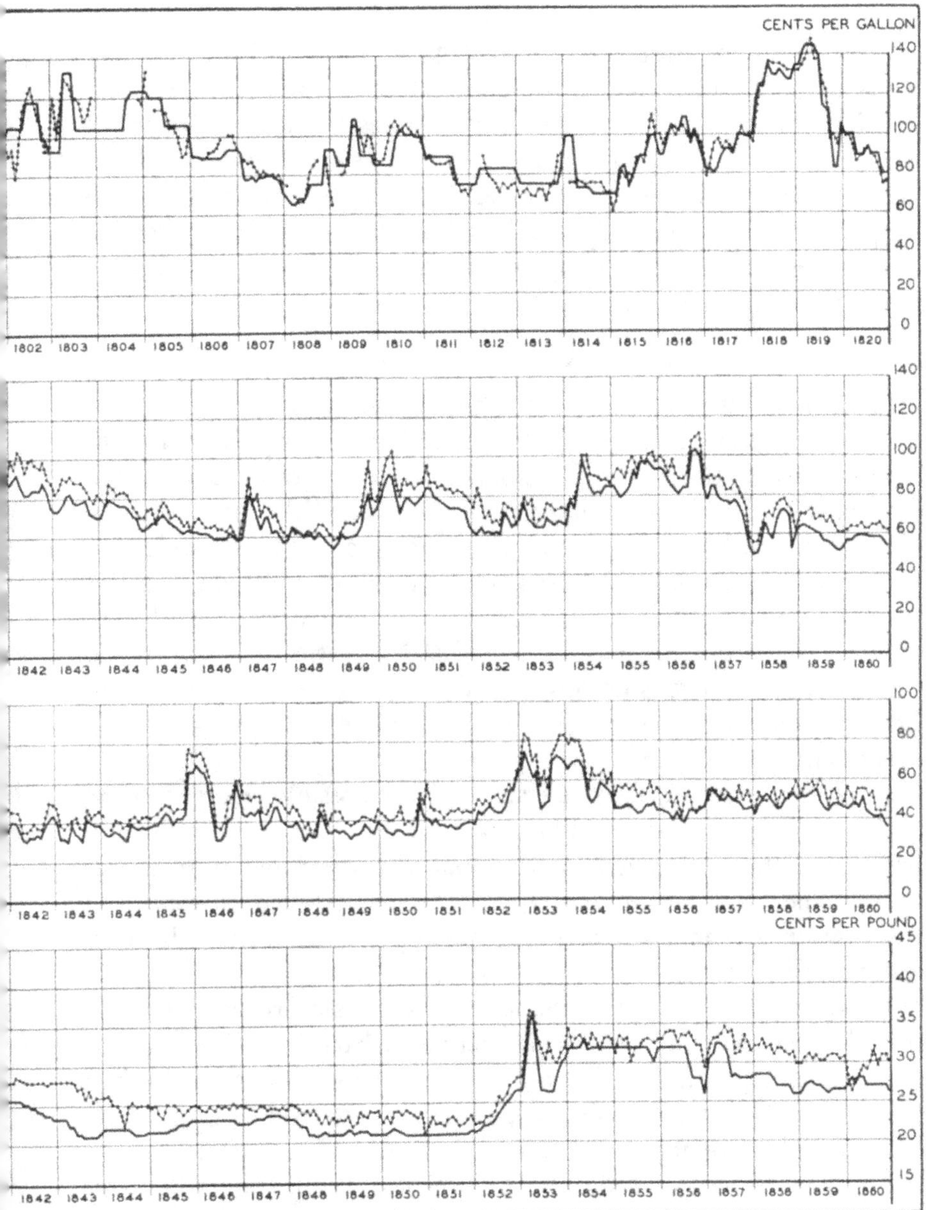

ces from Merchants' Accounts and from Prices Current

be analyzed in detail. The close approximation of the prices from the two sources for linseed oil from 1795 to 1860 and for spirits of turpentine and copper sheathing from 1821 to 1860 indicates that the filling in of gaps in the newspaper prices by use of quotations from merchants is justified (by use of the range) and that the editors of the Philadelphia newspapers carefully collected the prices which they published and changed their listed prices promptly. These conclusions are further verified by many other comparisons which we have made in the course of this study.

Construction of Index Numbers

Not until we were satisfied with the accuracy and completeness of the absolute prices did we begin the task of combining them into indices of prices. As the first step, all of the original data were converted into relative prices by dividing the average monthly prices of each series by its monthly average price from 1821 to 1825 inclusive.

Many adjustments had to be made. The most frequent one was the conversion of prices quoted in Pennsylvania pounds, shillings, and pence into equivalent dollar values. The ratio of 7 shillings 6 pence to one dollar was used. Generally the conversion was simply made by expressing the average of the base period, 1821-1825, in pounds, shillings, or pence.

In addition every series was examined for possible changes in the unit in which it was quoted. This involved not only obvious changes such as from pipe to gallon for wine but also variations in measures and containers arising out of modifications of trading customs and laws. The most important of these two types of alterations in units are described below.

On March 12, 1789 the Pennsylvania legislature repealed the act of August 18, 1727, which had defined a barrel of either beef or pork as a cask gauging 31½ gallons wine measure, and established instead a uniform weight of 200 pounds for a barrel of either beef or pork. This new unit was equivalent to 28 gallons wine measure for beef and 29 gallons for pork. The act was to take effect November 1, 1789,[3] but from the newspaper prices and the records of merchants it is apparent that the change was actually made in March.

[3] March 21, 1789, *Pennsylvania Mercury and Universal Advertiser.*

Among the wines there was no problem in the series of Marseilles Madeira, Sicily Madeira, and Teneriffe Particular, which were always quoted by the gallon, nor in that of claret, which was clearly specified "cask of 60 gallons." In the other six series, however, the quotations shifted from pipes to gallons. In order to secure an accurate method of adjusting for this change, many merchants' accounts as well as various studies of weights and measures, notably Homans' *Cyclopaedia of Commerce and Commercial Navigation,* were examined. The following relationships were ascertained and verified:

Madeira	Pipe =	110 gallons
Malaga	Pipe =	114 gallons
Teneriffe Cargo	Pipe =	120 gallons
Sherry	Pipe =	130 gallons
Port	Pipe =	138 gallons
Lisbon	Pipe =	140 gallons

In many other series there were individual changes in units. Each required a large amount of detailed work in order to determine to our satisfaction what the proper relationship was. The results of our investigations are as follows:

Coal, Lehigh Coal, Schuylkill	28 bus. of 80 lbs. =	1 ton of 2240 lbs.
Cornmeal	1¾ cwt. of 112 lbs. =	1 bbl. of 196 lbs.
Flaxseed	7 bus. =	1 hogshead
Hemp	2240 lbs. =	1 ton
Honey	5 gals. =	1 demijohn
Peas	8 bus. =	1 cask
Steel, Am.	2000 lbs. =	1 ton
Timothy seed	8 bus. =	1 cask

The most frequently appearing change in unit was in the definition of the number of pounds constituting a hundredweight. In the early years most commodities sold by weight were quoted in units of 112 pounds. On July 13, 1824 the Chamber of Commerce of Philadelphia adopted a general revision of trading customs to take effect on the following August 2. Among other changes was the requirement "that sugar, rice, cocoa, copperas, alum, brimstone, shot, lead and all other articles heretofore sold by the cwt. (112 lbs.) shall hereafter be sold by the decimal hundred (100 lbs.)."[4] Subsequent comments in all of the market reports clearly indicate that this revision was accomplished. The final result was that many series that had been quoted by the hundredweight of 112 pounds appeared with a price per pound and then later shifted to a price per 100 pounds.

Whenever any of these various changes occurred in the base period it was necessary to recompute the prices on a uniform basis in order to secure an average that could be used in computing the relative prices. If the change in unit appeared at any other time, however, it was possible to convert merely the base average to its equivalent in the other unit.

When all of the absolute prices had been expressed as comparable relative prices, we attacked the problem of combining them into groups and into a total. A method of weighting and the type of average had to be determined.

Despite a thorough search, no adequate basis for weighting which would add to the measures devised by others or would fully suit our series could be found. It was clear that variable rather than constant weights were needed since shifts occurred in the relative importance of specific commodities between 1784 and 1861. For this reason alone the census data, which cover only the latter part of this period, could not be used. In addition there was the question whether the weights should represent the importance of the commodity in the United States as a whole, in Pennsylvania, or in Philadelphia alone. The use of quantities of specific articles imported into and exported from Philadelphia was also considered, but these data are not complete and do not include the coastwise or overland trade. In addition, there is no method of combining these figures, since the amount exported may be considered as a surplus that was not consumed at home while the imports represent more closely the total consumption. We therefore decided to use an unweighted average, with the hope that we may later find sufficient materials supplementing the present data to warrant the development of weights.

Two types of averages were considered: arithmetic and geometric.

[4] July 19, 1824, *Grotjan's Philadelphia Public Sale Report.*

Although the geometric average involved more work, its advantages dictated its use.[5]

Before starting to compute any unweighted geometric indices of prices, however, it was necessary to eliminate any chance weighting which might result from having two or more grades of some commodities and only one of others. Accordingly the relative prices of the various grades were arithmetically averaged. For example, the grades of mess and prime beef were combined into one beef "commodity-group." The other combinations which reduced the 205 series to 157 commodities and commodity-groups are indicated on Table 2, pp. 13 ff. Most of these series covered the entire period 1784-1861. In order to have continuous data for as many as 140 commodities and commodity-groups, however, it was necessary in a few cases to substitute for part of the period the relative prices of a related commodity. For example, yellow beeswax was used for white beeswax in the early years as well as by itself for the entire period. In the combination of the grades of a commodity and in the substitution of one commodity to complete another, the series were carefully inspected to insure that no undue change in prices was introduced and that the series did tend to move in a similar fashion. Seventeen commodities and commodity-groups could not be extended in this manner. It is these series which are included in the index of 157 commodities and commodity-groups and not in the index of 140.

The annual relatives and indices were computed in a comparable manner. Usually the 12 monthly prices were averaged, divided by the appropriate base, and combined into unweighted geometric averages. Only in years for which the data for a particular series were not complete was it necessary to deviate from the general method. In such cases quarterly averages were secured by averaging two or three monthly prices or allowing the price of one month to represent the quarter. When a quarter had no price at all, estimates were made on the basis of the closest months before and after.

In the construction of the unweighted geometric average of the relatives of 20 commodities from 1731 to 1861 the series were first inspected to insure that the particular grades and qualities before the

[5] Fisher, Irving, *The Making of Index Numbers*, pp. 206-212.

Revolution were comparable with those in the later period. The absolute prices were then converted into relative ones by dividing them by the average of 1821-1825 expressed as pounds, shillings, or pence in the ratio of 7 shillings 6 pence to one dollar. The unweighted geometric average of the relatives was then constructed.

The unweighted index of 12 commodities from 1720 to 1861 differs markedly in construction from all other indices presented in this study: first, it is an arithmetic instead of a geometric average of relatives; second, the relatives are based on the average of 1741-1745 instead of that of 1821-1825. The same adjustments for the change from Pennsylvania pounds, shillings, and pence to dollars and cents and for changes in units and containers that were made in the preliminary steps of the construction of the other indices also had to be effected in the computation of the relatives from which the index of 12 commodities was derived.

All of the statistical analyses in this study were based on the prices of the commodities expressed as relatives to the average of 1821-1825 or on the various unweighted sub-group, group, and general geometric indices of the adjusted relatives.

Cyclical Analysis

The cyclical analysis of the monthly relatives and indices of prices follows closely the method used by Professor F. C. Mills.[6] The least definite part of such an analysis is the location of the critical turning points, yet the amount of disagreement among those who independently scanned the series was actually less than was anticipated. From monthly charts of all of the group indices and of many of the relatives of the individual commodities, supplemented by annual charts of all of the indices and relatives, we selected the successive points at which the cyclical swings ended their expansion and contraction. The sub-group of miscellaneous articles was omitted from this analysis. The original location was made by a team of two persons and checked by another pair. All differences were ironed out by conferences. In certain places a moving average was used to determine whether or not there was a noticable oscillation. When the peak or low extended over several months, the first and last months were

[6] Mills, Frederick C., *Behavior of Prices*, pp. 76-82.

both noted. Account was also taken when the high or low price reappeared unless it recurred for a single month after two or more months with a different price following a peak or low of long duration. It was felt that, when prices had held a peak or low for several months, it was more significant that they started to fall or rise than that they momentarily returned to the peak or low after departing from it for two months or more.

The second step in the cyclical analysis consisted of relating the cycles in the indices of the groups and sub-groups and in the relatives of the 140 commodities to the total index. In some cases it was necessary to combine two or more swings, especially from 1789 to 1798, in order to have a movement comparable to the cycle in the general index. At other times the swing in the prices of a particular commodity or in the index of a group extended over more than one cycle in the composite index. For these cases the swings were placed with the general cycle with whose peak they corresponded most closely.

With the swings in the prices of the various commodities and in the indices of the groups related to the 17 cycles in the general curve, the various measurements could easily be computed. The only adjustment which had to be made was in the cases where the low or peak extended over more than a month: the last month of low or high prices was considered as the real low or peak since it was followed by a rise or decline.

The first measure of the cycles was the relation of the timing of the appearance of the successive lows and highs in the relatives of the specific commodities and in the indices of the groups to the corresponding turning points of the composite curve. The purpose of this was to ascertain how much earlier or later the cycles appeared in the 140 commodities and in the groups than they did in the general index.

The other measures did not involve a direct comparison of the relatives and group indices with the total. Instead, the computations were made in the same manner for all relatives and indices and the results compared for the same series in different cycles and for various series in the same cycle.

1. Number of months of rise—the elapsed time from the last low month at the beginning to the last high month of each cycle.

2. Number of months of fall—the elapsed time from the last high month to the last low month at the end of each cycle.

3. Number of months in the total cycle—the elapsed time from the last low month at the beginning to the last low month at the end of each cycle, or the sum of the number of months of rise and the number of months of fall.

4. Percentage of rise—the difference between the peak relative or index and the preceding low relative or index divided by the preceding low relative or index.

5. Percentage of fall—the difference between the peak relative or index and the succeeding low relative or index divided by the peak relative or index.

6. Index of cyclical variability—100 per cent minus the average of the preceding low relative or index expressed as a percentage of the peak relative or index and the succeeding low relative or index also expressed as a percentage of the peak relative or index.

Analysis of Distribution of Annual Relatives

The annual relative prices of the 140 commodities and commodity-groups were selected for detailed analysis in Chapter II. As a preliminary step the 140 relatives for each year were arrayed. The medians were selected by averaging the 70th and 71st items, the quartiles by averaging the 35th and 36th items for the lower quartiles and the 105th and 106th for the upper quartiles, and the deciles by averaging the 14th and 15th, 28th and 29th, etc.

These measures of the distribution, given in Appendix Table 46, are the bases from which the relative semi-interdecile and semi-interquartile ranges found in Table 3 and the skewness shown in Table 4 and Appendix Table 47 were derived. The relative semi-interdecile ranges were computed by dividing the distance between deciles in a corresponding position on either side of the median (deciles 4 and 6, 3 and 7, 2 and 8) by 2, dividing this semi-interdecile range by the median, and multiplying the result by 100. The relative semi-interquartile ranges were computed in a similar manner.

All of the measures of skewness used in this study were computed on a logarithmic base—in other words, the skewness indicates the divergence from a normal geometric distribution rather than from a

Gaussian curve. For example, the difference between the logarithm of the median and the logarithm of the third decile was subtracted from the difference between the logarithm of the seventh decile and the logarithm of the median and the result was divided by the sum of these two differences. A similar process yielded the skewness between the eighth and second deciles and between the quartiles.

Year-to-Year Variability

A brief description of the method by which the measure of year-to-year variability was computed has been given on page 51 in Chapter IV. It is essential here to point out how and why it differs from the measure used by Professor F. C. Mills.[7] The annual relatives of each of the 140 series were converted to link relatives, thus expressing the yearly prices as a percentage of the average price of the previous year. The average link relative of each commodity in each of the four yeriods—1785-1808, 1809-1821, 1822-1843, and 1844-1860—was then found. The next step involved the determination of the mean deviation of the link relatives of each commodity in these periods from the appropriate average link relative. Professor Mills used this mean deviation as the measurement of year-to-year variability. Because of the variation in the size of the various average link relatives for the same commodity in successive periods and among different commodities in the same period, we preferred a more refined measure. In his text on statistical methods, Professor Mills points out: "A measure of absolute variation is significant only in relation to the average from which the deviations are measured. Its use, apart from this average, is meaningless."[8] Accordingly we adopted as a measure of relative year-to-year variability of each commodity the absolute mean deviation of its link relatives from its average link relative in each period divided by the average link relative from which the deviation was measured and multiplied by 100.

Seasonality

Seasonal Patterns

The measurement of seasonality in Chapter VI is based on the method followed by Professor Simon Kuznets in *Seasonal Variations*

[7] Mills, Frederick C., *op. cit.*, pp. 49-50.
[8] Mills, Frederick C., *Statistical Methods*, p. 165.

in Industry and Trade.[9] As the first step, a two-item moving total of a 12-month moving total was computed from the monthly relatives of the selected series and divided by 24. This average is equivalent to a 13-month moving average with only half of the usual weight given to the first and the last month. The first total for any series would include January 1784 and January 1785 each with a weight of one and the intervening months of February to December 1784 inclusive each with a weight of two. Such a total and its average secured by dividing it by 24 are correctly centered at the seventh month—in the example given above at July 1784. The second step in the process consisted of dividing each of the original relatives of the series by the appropriate moving average and multiplying the result by 100. Thus the relative price of corn in July 1784 was divided by the first moving average and the quotient was multiplied by 100. In this way the relative deviation of the specific monthly relative prices from the moving average was secured. For dairy products the computations were based on the geometric index of that sub-group. The entire period from 1784 to 1860 was then sub-divided into eight sections: 1784 to 1790 and the seven decades from 1791 to 1860. Since the monthly data did not begin until January 1784 and since the data for 1861 were not then available, the deviations of the data from the moving averages covered only the period from July 1784 to June 1860 inclusive. Accordingly the first and last periods were shortened to cover only 1785 to 1790 and 1851 to 1859 respectively. It is in the remaining steps that we departed from the procedure devised by Professor Kuznets. The relative deviations of all the Januaries in each sub-period, for example, were ranked and the center-most items averaged: 1785-1790 the four central items, 1851-1859 the five central items, and for the other decades the six central items, except that in the decade 1791-1800, when there were gaps in the relative prices of some series, four central items were used for Georgia cotton and dairy products and five for James River tobacco, Hyson skin tea, pepper, and tar. As a result of this process an average relative deviation in each period was secured for the twelve months. The average seasonal indices were derived from these average relative deviations by centering them around 100.

[9] Pp. 27-30.

Index of Similarity

The index of similarity which was used to measure the persistence of any seasonal pattern in adjoining decades is also based on a measure used by Professor Kuznets.[10] The seasonal indices were first expressed as deviations from their arithmetic mean—100. Then these deviations were adjusted so that their total regardless of signs equaled 100. As the next step the difference between the corresponding months in adjoining decades was computed. For this it was necessary to take account of the direction of deviation. Thus the difference between — 13 and — 5 is 8 and the difference between + 3 and — 9 is 12. No sign was given to the difference because it did not matter whether any month in the second decade was considered as being more or less than the same month in the previous one and in the summation of the differences the signs were to be disregarded. The index of similarity was derived by dividing the total of the differences by 100 and subtracting the quotient from 1. Thus when the differences between two seasonal patterns exceed 100 the index of similarity is negative and when the differences are less than 100 the index is positive.

[10] Kuznets, Simon, *op. cit.*, pp. 281-283.

TABLES

TABLES

Geometric Indices of Average Monthly Wholesale Prices in Philadelphia

Table 1 .... 140 Commodities 1784-1861
Table 2 .... 157 Commodities 1818-1861
Table 3 .... 69 Domestic Commodities 1784-1861
Table 4 .... 59 Imported Commodities 1784-1861
Table 5 .... 26 Agricultural Commodities 1784-1861
Table 6 .... 67 Industrial Commodities 1784-1861
Tables 7-15 .... Major Groups 1784-1861
Tables 16-38 .... Sub-Groups 1784-1861
Table 39 .... 20 Commodities 1731-1861

(Base—Monthly average, 1821-1825)

Arithmetic Index of Average Monthly Wholesale Prices in Philadelphia

Table 40 .... 12 Commodities 1720-1861

(Base—Monthly Average, 1741-1745)

Geometric Indices of Average Annual Wholesale Prices in Philadelphia

Table 41 .... Summaries 1784-1861
Table 42 .... Major Groups 1784-1861
Table 43 .... Sub-Groups 1784-1861
Table 44 .... 20 Commodities 1731-1861

(Base—Monthly Average, 1821-1825)

Arithmetic Index of Average Annual Wholesale Prices in Philadelphia

Table 45 .... 12 Commodities 1720-1861

(Base—Monthly Average, 1741-1745)

Comparative Summaries

Tables 45-61

The monthly relatives of the individual commodities and commodity-groups are published in a separate volume. (Part II—*Series of Relative Monthly Prices*)

TABLE 1—140 COMMODITIES

Year	Jan.	Feb.	Mar.	Apr.	May	June	July	Aug.	Sept.	Oct.	Nov.	Dec.
1784	101.9	101.6	100.4	98.7	97.8	98.5	99.2	98.6	99.6	100.3	99.0	98.1
1785	96.4	95.8	96.0	94.2	92.7	91.2	92.0	92.2	91.8	92.9	93.6	93.7
1786	93.5	93.3	92.4	91.1	88.8	89.4	90.3	89.8	90.1	89.5	89.7	89.7
1787	89.7	90.0	89.8	89.6	88.3	88.4	88.4	87.6	86.9	86.4	87.0	86.2
1788	85.4	85.0	84.8	83.7	83.8	83.6	83.1	82.2	81.6	81.3	81.7	81.3
1789	81.3	81.1	80.8	80.2	82.0	82.3	82.7	82.4	82.4	82.7	83.4	84.8
1790	84.6	85.1	85.6	84.9	85.3	85.9	85.6	86.1	85.7	86.7	88.7	89.9
1791	90.4	90.1	88.8	88.1	88.0	88.1	88.2	88.2	88.8	91.6	91.3	91.1
1792	89.7	89.9	90.4	90.7	90.7	90.9	90.9	90.9	90.9	91.9	94.0	95.1
1793	95.4	95.5	96.0	95.8	95.7	96.3	96.3	96.3	96.2	95.9	96.4	96.5
1794	98.0	98.0	102.1	102.2								
1795	123.7	124.6	125.4	126.8	128.5	128.7	130.6	131.4	132.9	134.9	135.2	136.6
1796	139.6	138.0	138.9	137.8	138.6	138.5	137.7	136.5	136.7	139.7	138.1	138.9
1797	140.7	140.7	137.5	133.6	134.3	131.3	131.3	130.5	129.1	129.9	129.2	128.8
1798	125.6	125.3	125.9	124.8	125.4	125.6	126.9	127.2	127.4	127.6	128.7	
1799					125.4	126.9	126.8	125.9				
1800						126.3	125.5	125.0	127.5	129.2	130.6	130.6
1801	129.7	131.8	131.9	131.2	130.5	131.4	131.7	131.5	130.7	131.4	133.6	131.9
1802	129.1	127.8	124.8	122.9	121.2	120.4	119.4	119.4	120.0	121.0	121.1	119.3
1803	120.0	119.4	118.3	118.6	119.0	118.7	118.5	119.6	120.0	121.0	122.7	123.7
1804	124.5	125.6	126.3	127.3	126.9	126.9	127.7	126.9	127.8	128.6	130.7	132.7
1805	132.7	133.5	133.0	133.1	132.4	131.4	131.1	129.6	129.3	129.3	129.3	130.1
1806	131.0	129.8	129.4	127.9	128.1	127.2	127.4	127.3	126.7	126.6	126.8	126.1
1807	126.4	126.1	125.6	123.9	122.5	122.4	121.6	120.8	122.3	122.0	124.1	123.5
1808	122.3	122.2	122.1	121.1	120.7	120.6	120.6	120.8	121.5	122.6	125.1	131.7
1809	134.6	135.4	139.0	140.6	138.0	132.4	128.9	129.0	131.8	133.6	136.6	137.4
1810	136.8	136.0	136.6	136.5	139.2	137.1	139.3	138.8	139.2	140.4	139.7	138.5
1811	140.0	139.2	137.5	135.7	134.3	134.5	133.5	133.9	133.5	132.5	130.6	131.2
1812	132.4	133.2	132.5	131.7	132.5	134.3	148.7	150.5	151.4	150.5	150.3	150.0
1813	151.0	152.0	152.9	156.3	157.5	159.1	160.0	160.7	161.3	161.7	168.5	182.4
1814	197.8	194.1	192.1	186.6	181.2	182.3	180.1	181.0	181.9	190.9	198.8	197.3
1815	196.9	197.0	167.8	160.1	157.5	156.6	162.0	163.7	169.2	172.8	174.4	168.5
1816	167.2	165.4	158.9	156.9	151.6	151.5	149.6	146.9	143.4	140.8	139.0	138.8
1817	137.9	137.8	139.1	137.6	135.7	130.0	127.6	127.5	127.1	126.4	127.1	129.1
1818	129.9	131.3	131.1	131.3	131.2	130.0	128.9	128.2	128.6	130.1	130.2	129.7
1819	130.5	129.0	127.9	124.7	120.3	116.8	113.7	112.9	111.8	111.8	112.9	113.2
1820	112.1	111.8	109.6	107.2	106.7	104.9	104.5	104.1	104.0	103.9	103.8	103.9
1821	103.0	102.6	101.9	99.5	100.4	99.8	100.0	100.4	100.6	102.1	104.5	105.0
1822	105.3	105.5	105.8	105.7	105.4	105.1	103.9	102.9	102.7	102.1	102.0	100.9
1823	100.8	100.5	99.4	98.6	98.8	98.6	98.8	97.6	96.9	97.0	96.5	96.2
1824	96.0	95.7	94.8	94.6	94.0	94.0	94.1	93.8	93.0	93.2	93.1	93.1
1825	93.9	94.8	95.2	97.8	100.9	99.7	99.3	97.7	98.9	100.1	99.9	100.0
1826	99.4	98.5	97.5	96.7	95.8	95.3	94.8	93.9	93.9	93.8	94.0	94.0
1827	94.7	94.7	93.8	94.6	93.7	92.3	91.1	90.6	91.3	92.0	91.7	91.9
1828	91.7	90.7	90.3	89.3	89.3	89.1	89.3	90.1	91.0	91.4	93.4	92.6
1829	92.6	91.9	91.4	90.7	89.2	88.6	86.9	86.4	86.4	86.8	86.4	85.7
1830	84.4	84.0	83.4	82.8	82.2	82.3	81.9	83.3	83.6	84.1	83.9	84.3
1831	84.4	85.1	85.8	86.1	87.5	87.4	87.1	87.7	88.6	89.8	90.2	90.4
1832	90.5	89.9	88.9	87.9	88.4	88.4	88.2	88.2	88.6	89.4	90.2	90.0
1833	88.7	88.1	87.1	87.2	87.2	86.9	86.8	87.3	88.7	88.8	88.4	88.7
1834	88.1	87.3	86.4	85.1	84.8	84.6	84.7	84.8	84.6	84.8	85.6	86.0
1835	86.4	86.6	88.2	89.5	90.9	91.8	91.9	91.8	91.1	91.9	92.3	93.3
1836	94.0	94.2	95.7	98.4	98.4	96.3	95.5	96.5	98.1	99.1	100.6	100.2
1837	101.0	101.3	100.3	97.5	94.9	93.2	92.1	91.1	90.6	91.2	93.3	92.9
1838	92.4	91.6	90.5	89.4	89.2	89.0	88.8	91.3	92.3	94.3	94.6	95.0
1839	95.4	95.6	96.8	97.8	97.8	97.2	96.4	95.3	94.9	94.0	93.8	92.9
1840	92.2	90.9	88.5	88.2	86.2	85.5	85.2	84.9	85.6	86.1	86.3	86.0
1841	85.9	85.4	85.2	84.8	84.3	84.5	84.1	84.7	84.9	86.9	85.4	84.4
1842	84.1	83.2	82.5	80.0	78.2	77.4	76.9	77.0	77.0	77.5	76.9	76.3
1843	75.6	74.6	74.1	74.3	74.6	75.6	76.4	76.0	75.5	75.4	75.1	74.3
1844	74.6	75.4	75.7	77.3	77.2	76.9	76.9	76.9	77.1	77.6	77.5	76.9
1845	76.0	76.5	77.2	79.0	79.1	78.9	79.0	79.7	80.8	81.3	82.9	83.0
1846	82.1	81.9	82.3	81.5	80.1	78.8	77.9	77.2	77.3	79.1	80.8	79.6
1847	79.5	81.7	83.2	84.3	84.2	85.6	83.2	82.9	83.1	83.7	84.3	82.5
1848	82.2	80.8	80.8	80.0	78.6	77.6	76.7	76.6	77.3	77.2	76.4	76.0
1849	76.2	76.1	76.0	75.6	74.5	74.7	74.8	76.1	77.4	77.8	78.0	77.6
1850	77.6	78.7	79.1	78.8	79.5	79.0	79.0	79.7	80.2	81.2	81.6	81.5
1851	81.9	81.8	81.2	81.0	80.4	79.8	79.8	79.8	79.6	79.8	78.3	77.9
1852	77.9	78.4	78.4	78.1	79.1	79.5	79.6	79.8	81.5	82.4	82.8	84.3
1853	85.0	86.6	87.2	87.3	86.9	85.5	85.6	85.9	88.2	90.0	90.7	90.7
1854	91.1	93.5	94.2	94.2	96.0	95.9	95.2	96.1	97.4	97.4	97.9	97.3
1855	97.4	97.1	97.5	98.2	98.5	98.5	97.4	98.5	99.6	101.0	101.1	101.3
1856	100.8	100.0	99.0	98.6	97.1	96.5	97.4	97.3	97.7	99.1	100.0	99.5
1857	100.2	100.5	101.0	101.7	104.1	104.7	102.6	102.3	102.3	99.3	94.5	91.8
1858	88.8	87.4	88.8	89.9	90.2	89.4	89.3	90.4	90.9	90.7	88.9	88.5
1859	88.9	90.4	90.8	90.8	91.3	90.3	88.7	88.2	87.3	88.0	87.8	88.1
1860	87.5	88.0	88.5	88.5	88.2	88.1	88.5	89.5	89.7	89.9	88.7	86.8
1861	86.2	85.5	84.9	85.0	85.1	84.3	83.0	86.6	88.3	90.6	92.8	95.7

Table 2—157 Commodities

Year	Jan.	Feb.	Mar.	Apr.	May	June	July	Aug.	Sept.	Oct.	Nov.	Dec.
1818												130.6
1819	131.0	129.6	128.6	125.3	121.0	117.6	114.4	113.4	112.3	112.5	113.3	113.6
1820	112.5	112.2	110.0	107.3	106.6	105.2	104.8	104.2	104.4	103.6	103.8	103.8
1821	102.9	102.6	101.7	99.6	100.3	99.6	99.8	100.2	100.4	102.1	104.6	104.9
1822	105.1	105.3	105.8	105.6	105.3	104.9	103.7	102.8	102.3	101.8	102.2	101.2
1823	101.0	100.7	99.5	98.6	99.0	98.8	99.0	97.8	97.1	97.4	96.8	96.4
1824	96.1	96.0	95.1	94.9	94.3	93.0	94.4	94.2	92.8	92.4	92.0	92.0
1825	92.8	93.7	93.9	96.6	100.1	99.2	98.9	97.4	98.9	100.1	100.1	100.1
1826	99.2	98.3	97.3	96.4	95.4	94.7	94.0	93.7	93.6	93.1	93.3	93.4
1827	93.9	94.1	93.3	94.1	93.3	91.8	90.4	90.2	90.7	91.1	90.6	90.7
1828	90.2	89.3	88.6	87.5	87.3	87.2	87.3	87.9	88.7	89.5	91.3	90.6
1829	90.6	90.0	89.5	88.5	87.2	86.5	85.0	84.3	84.3	84.8	84.6	84.1
1830	82.8	82.5	81.9	81.4	80.8	81.0	80.5	82.1	82.3	82.7	82.6	82.9
1831	83.3	83.9	84.4	84.7	85.9	85.8	85.4	86.2	87.4	88.4	88.6	88.7
1832	88.8	88.3	87.3	86.7	87.0	86.7	86.6	86.6	87.2	88.1	88.9	88.8
1833	87.6	87.1	86.5	86.7	86.7	86.4	86.2	86.9	88.1	87.9	87.3	87.5
1834	86.8	85.9	85.0	83.7	83.2	83.0	83.0	83.1	83.0	83.4	84.1	84.9
1835	85.1	85.3	87.0	88.3	89.6	90.5	90.4	90.4	89.8	90.8	91.1	92.2
1836	93.1	93.5	94.7	97.3	97.0	94.9	94.3	95.3	97.1	98.2	99.5	99.0
1837	99.6	99.9	99.1	96.2	93.6	91.9	90.5	89.7	89.8	90.1	91.7	91.4
1838	90.5	89.8	88.7	87.8	87.7	87.5	87.2	90.0	91.8	94.1	94.3	94.8
1839	95.0	95.4	96.6	97.5	97.6	97.0	96.1	95.0	94.6	93.4	93.1	92.0
1840	91.4	90.3	88.0	87.6	85.8	85.3	84.9	84.7	85.3	85.7	85.7	85.3
1841	85.0	84.5	84.3	83.8	83.2	83.5	83.0	83.6	83.9	86.1	84.9	84.1
1842	83.4	82.3	81.6	78.9	77.3	76.5	76.1	76.3	76.3	76.8	76.0	75.5
1843	74.8	73.5	73.2	73.5	73.7	74.6	75.1	75.0	74.7	74.7	74.3	73.5
1844	74.0	74.9	75.2	76.7	76.4	76.1	76.0	76.3	76.3	76.7	76.6	76.0
1845	75.2	75.6	76.0	77.6	77.7	77.5	77.6	78.5	79.7	80.3	82.5	82.7
1846	81.9	81.4	81.6	80.8	79.4	78.1	77.4	76.8	76.7	78.4	79.8	78.6
1847	78.6	81.0	82.4	83.3	83.2	85.0	82.6	82.3	82.3	82.8	83.3	81.4
1848	80.9	79.6	79.8	78.9	77.5	76.5	75.7	75.6	76.2	76.3	75.4	74.7
1849	75.0	75.3	75.2	74.5	73.6	73.7	73.9	75.2	76.4	77.1	77.2	77.1
1850	77.2	78.2	78.6	78.5	79.0	78.6	78.6	79.4	79.8	80.8	81.3	81.9
1851	82.3	82.3	81.8	81.6	81.0	80.5	80.7	80.8	80.2	80.1	78.8	78.4
1852	78.5	79.0	78.9	78.5	79.3	79.9	80.2	80.3	81.7	81.9	82.5	83.8
1853	84.4	86.1	86.6	86.6	86.0	84.9	85.1	85.9	88.2	89.7	90.6	90.5
1854	90.9	93.2	93.9	93.6	95.0	95.0	94.4	95.4	97.2	97.1	98.0	97.4
1855	97.3	97.3	97.7	98.6	98.9	99.1	98.3	99.2	100.1	101.2	100.9	101.3
1856	101.6	99.6	98.8	98.5	96.7	96.1	97.5	97.8	98.0	99.1	99.8	99.2
1857	99.6	100.2	100.7	101.2	103.6	104.3	102.1	102.0	101.4	98.3	93.5	91.0
1858	88.2	86.9	87.9	88.8	89.2	88.2	88.1	89.5	90.1	90.4	88.7	88.1
1859	88.6	90.2	90.6	90.4	90.8	89.9	88.3	87.9	87.1	87.7	87.5	87.6
1860	87.5	88.3	88.6	88.6	88.2	88.1	88.5	89.2	89.4	90.3	89.2	87.1
1861	86.5	85.8	85.4	85.3	85.0	84.3	82.9	86.7	88.3	90.7	92.9	95.5

TABLE 3—69 DOMESTIC COMMODITIES

Year	Jan.	Feb.	Mar.	Apr.	May	June	July	Aug.	Sept.	Oct.	Nov.	Dec.
1784	105.7	104.8	104.1	102.3	102.5	103.2	103.9	103.4	105.3	106.8	104.3	103.4
1785	102.0	101.0	100.8	98.0	96.6	94.4	94.2	93.6	92.5	93.9	94.5	94.6
1786	94.0	93.5	92.8	90.8	87.3	88.1	89.0	88.1	88.6	87.6	88.1	87.4
1787	87.2	87.4	87.3	87.4	85.9	86.2	85.9	84.2	83.3	82.7	82.7	81.5
1788	80.5	80.1	79.7	77.8	78.3	78.3	77.7	76.7	76.0	76.3	77.3	76.3
1789	76.5	76.2	75.1	74.0	75.4	75.9	76.5	76.5	76.5	76.7	77.6	79.5
1790	79.6	80.6	81.9	81.7	82.3	83.0	82.8	84.3	83.3	83.9	85.9	86.9
1791	87.0	86.2	84.8	84.2	82.9	82.7	82.6	82.6	83.8	85.8	85.5	85.3
1792	83.8	83.9	84.2	84.8	84.9	85.0	84.9	84.8	84.0	86.1	88.3	89.6
1793	90.1	90.5	90.8	91.3	91.2	91.1	91 2	90.7	90.9	91.2	91.6	92.1
1794	92.4	92.3	94.6	95.0								
1795	116.3	117.5	118.3	120.4	122.9	122.9	125.3	125.7	127.3	131.4	132.3	133.8
1796	138.4	138.5	141.5	140.4	140.7	141.7	139.7	137.8	137.0	141.9	140.7	141.9
1797	144.1	144.2	140.8	134.3	134.3	130.7	130.9	129.0	128.5	129.6	129.4	130.8
1798	125.7	125.6	126.5	124.3	123.6	123.2	120.7	120.5	120.7	120.9	121.9	
1799					113.2	113.7	113.9	114.0				
1800						119.6	120.5	120.0	123.0	124.2	124.6	125.5
1801	125.7	128.1	128.9	128.6	128.6	129.5	129.6	130.1	130.2	129.6	132.2	127.9
1802	125.0	124.3	121.5	119.3	116.5	115.2	113.8	113.8	114.8	116.5	116.9	115.8
1803	116.9	116.1	116.5	115.1	114.9	114.7	114.1	114.7	114.7	115.8	117.5	117.6
1804	118.1	118.5	119.6	121.7	121.9	122.1	124.0	124.1	125.7	126.6	128.6	131.6
1805	132.0	134.1	134.8	134.9	134.2	132.7	132.1	128.8	127.5	127.1	127.2	128.1
1806	128.3	127.7	127.3	125.7	124.8	124.8	125.0	125.3	123.9	124.4	124.9	124.8
1807	125.3	125.3	124.6	123.6	121.3	120.3	120.1	118.8	118.8	119.6	121.7	121.2
1808	118.2	115.7	114.3	112.2	110.7	110.6	109.4	108.3	109.5	111.1	112.7	113.1
1809	114.2	115.0	118.6	123.1	124.8	123.7	122.1	121.1	120.4	122.4	125.8	126.2
1810	127.6	128.8	130.7	130.0	132.8	130.5	131.8	132.1	132.3	132.8	133.2	133.0
1811	137.4	136.3	136.2	134.7	131.7	131.7	129.8	129.0	127.6	126.0	124.4	124.9
1812	126.1	126.1	124.6	123.3	122.2	122.6	124.4	123.9	127.5	127.2	128.2	127.0
1813	128.0	128.8	129.0	132.0	134.0	134.3	135.8	135.7	135.9	136.1	139.2	149.3
1814	160.5	160.1	160.3	158.8	156.4	155.4	152.2	153.9	154.2	159.5	164.4	166.2
1815	165.9	166.5	158.5	149.5	145.6	147.4	155.4	155.8	159.3	165.2	168.2	167.3
1816	168.0	166.9	163.0	161.8	157.2	160.0	159.3	157.3	153.5	151.9	151.9	152.5
1817	152.8	153.6	155.5	153.2	150.9	142.8	139.5	138.8	138.1	135.3	135.8	136.8
1818	137.3	138.0	138.7	139.0	139.8	138.4	136.7	136.6	137.2	138.8	138.0	138.1
1819	138.5	137.1	135.3	131.5	124.5	119.9	116.3	114.5	113.5	114.1	115.7	116.3
1820	114.7	114.5	112.6	109.7	109.7	108.4	107.3	106.1	105.7	105.1	103.8	103.0
1821	101.7	101.1	100.4	96.6	97.7	96.8	97.3	98.4	99.8	101.5	105.1	104.3
1822	105.1	105.4	106.5	105.8	107.1	106.4	105.6	104.8	104.3	103.9	103.7	102.7
1823	102.8	102.3	101.4	99.6	100.0	100.2	100.8	97.8	96.2	97.0	97.6	97.3
1824	97.4	97.2	95.5	95.2	94.9	94.6	94.6	94.0	91.4	92.3	92.1	92.0
1825	92.8	93.6	94.4	96.5	99.2	97.9	97.2	96.2	98.2	99.6	99.1	99.4
1826	99.0	98.3	97.8	96.4	95.4	95.6	96.1	94.5	94.5	94.3	95.1	95.3
1827	95.9	95.7	95.4	95.8	93.8	91.9	90.0	89.6	90.5	91.9	91.9	91.6
1828	91.5	90.2	89.5	88.4	88.4	88.5	88.3	89.1	90.0	92.0	95.4	94.8
1829	94.6	94.6	93.9	93.4	91.4	90.5	87.5	86.6	86.7	86.9	87.4	86.1
1830	85.2	84.9	84.2	82.4	81.8	82.3	81.8	82.9	84.2	85.7	85.3	85.1
1831	86.5	87.5	88.6	89.2	89.6	89.1	88.4	88.5	90.5	91.8	92.3	92.0
1832	92.3	92.1	91.1	89.7	90.2	91.3	90.6	91.0	91.5	92.3	93.8	93.3
1833	93.1	92.9	92.4	92.5	92.9	93.6	93.0	93.4	94.4	94.7	95.2	94.8
1834	93.8	92.5	91.5	90.0	89.9	90.4	91.0	90.9	91.1	91.4	92.3	92.3
1835	91.6	93.0	94.5	96.4	99.2	101.7	102.4	102.0	101.2	102.8	103.9	106.2
1836	107.2	107.5	109.8	113.9	114.2	111.1	109.4	110.5	114.0	115.4	119.1	118.7
1837	119.6	123.0	118.5	113.0	108.8	105.7	104.2	102.6	102.6	104.1	106.4	105.7
1838	104.3	103.3	100.9	98.9	98.7	99.8	99.1	101.9	103.8	107.0	107.7	108.9
1839	109.5	109.9	111.9	114.3	114.3	113.5	112.1	109.7	108.8	108.0	107.1	105.8
1840	104.7	102.7	98.5	97.9	94.7	93.7	93.9	93.9	94.4	95.3	94.9	93.6
1841	94.2	93.6	93.2	92.1	92.3	92.6	92.3	93.5	94.3	98.0	93.9	93.1
1842	93.0	91.8	91.0	87.7	84.3	83.2	82.4	82.6	81.2	81.1	80.0	79.8
1843	78.6	76.2	75.8	76.3	76.2	78.4	78.6	77.8	77.7	77.0	76.3	74.8
1844	75.3	76.2	76.1	78.1	77.4	77.6	77.1	77.3	77.5	78.1	78.4	77.4
1845	77.3	78.4	78.9	81.0	81.4	81.1	81.0	81.6	82.9	84.3	87.4	88.7
1846	86.6	85.8	85.9	85.5	83.1	81.2	79.7	78.5	79.0	82.7	85.5	84.1
1847	83.9	87.9	89.8	92.7	92.8	95.5	90.0	89.2	89.2	91.1	91.8	89.5
1848	88.2	86.7	87.0	85.6	83.9	82.9	81.3	81.3	83.4	82.8	81.7	81.6
1849	82.0	81.6	81.0	80.5	78.9	79.0	79.4	81.8	82.9	83.2	83.4	82.5
1850	82.7	83.8	83.6	83.4	84.8	84.1	83.8	84.6	85.6	87.2	88.1	88.6
1851	89.1	88.9	88.1	87.6	86.7	85.7	85.3	84.9	84.4	85.0	84.5	84.5
1852	84.8	86.0	86.5	87.1	88.6	88.3	88.7	89.0	91.1	92.4	93.4	95.0
1853	96.2	96.7	96.4	96.0	94.7	92.9	93.5	94.6	97.5	99.7	101.0	99.8
1854	100.0	103.4	102.3	102.9	105.4	106.1	104.8	105.3	109.1	108.3	107.9	103.6
1855	108.2	106.5	106.4	108.2	108.8	108.6	106.4	105.9	105.7	106.4	108.0	108.5
1856	107.1	104.9	103.4	102.8	100.6	99.5	100.7	100.8	101.9	103.8	105.4	104.5
1857	104.5	105.0	105.6	105.1	109.3	111.7	109.5	108.9	107.9	104.3	100.0	96.4
1858	93.3	92.1	93.2	94.7	94.9	94.0	93.5	95.1	96.1	96.4	95.6	96.1
1859	97.3	100.5	101.0	101.1	102.0	100.2	97.5	96.7	95.8	96.8	96.6	96.4
1860	96.6	97.0	97.2	97.0	96.4	94.7	94.4	95.2	95.2	95.6	94.8	92.4
1861	91.4	91.3	91.1	90.7	92.3	91.7	89.3	92.7	93.4	96.3	98.8	101.8

Table 4—59 Imported Commodities

Year	Jan.	Feb.	Mar.	Apr.	May	June	July	Aug.	Sept.	Oct.	Nov.	Dec.
1784	99.3	99.9	98.7	97.4	95.7	96.0	96.5	96.3	96.5	96.9	96.6	95.9
1785	93.5	92.4	93.2	92.9	91.1	90.3	91.6	92.7	93.1	94.1	94.7	94.4
1786	94.6	94.5	93.7	93.0	92.2	92.3	93.1	93.6	93.6	93.3	93.2	93.8
1787	93.9	94.0	93.6	93.1	92 0	91.5	92.1	91.8	91.8	91.9	92.9	92.0
1788	91.6	91.3	91.3	90.7	90.7	90.2	89.5	88.9	88.6	86.9	86.6	86.8
1789	86.8	86.9	87.4	86.9	89.1	88.9	89.3	88.6	88.8	89.5	89.8	90.2
1790	90.1	89.8	89.3	88.0	87.9	88.6	88.8	88.3	88.1	89.7	91.9	93.8
1791	95.1	95.7	94.9	93.4	94.1	95.3	96.1	96.3	96.0	98.8	98.9	98.6
1792	97.1	97.6	98.0	98.4	98.3	98.7	98.9	99.0	99.9	99.4	101.0	102.3
1793	101.9	101.9	102.7	101.7	102.0	103.3	103.1	103.3	102.9	102.6	103.5	103.0
1794	106.8	106.9	112.0	111.3								
1795	135.5	135.8	137.0	137.9	138.8	140.1	141.0	142.0	143.5	143.4	143.6	145.3
1796	147.5	143.0	141.6	139.5	141.5	139.4	140.0	139.7	141.4	142.7	140.5	141.0
1797	142.4	141.6	138.2	136.7	138.3	135.1	135.0	134.8	131.7	132.3	130.8	128.4
1798	126.7	125.8	126.3	126.4	128.2	129.3	134.5	134.7	135.0	135.3	136.6	
1799					139.7	143.6	143.2	141.7				
1800						134.1	132.3	142.2	134.2	136.9	140.0	138.9
1801	136.5	138.5	138.1	137.0	135.2	136.2	136.9	135.6	134.6	136.7	138.7	139.7
1802	136.4	134.6	130.8	129.1	128.4	128.2	127.7	127.7	127.7	127.6	127.1	124.2
1803	124.3	123.8	120.3	122 3	123.8	123.4	123.5	125.0	126.0	126.8	127.4	129.3
1804	130.9	132.8	133.4	133.2	132.1	132.0	131.5	129.5	129.2	130.6	132.9	134.4
1805	133.6	132.7	131.2	131.3	130.2	129.3	129.2	129.0	129.9	130.3	130.1	131.0
1806	132.4	130.3	129.8	128.1	130.0	128.2	128.5	127.7	128.0	126.9	126.5	125.3
1807	125.5	124.7	125.2	122.7	122.1	122.4	121.4	121.6	123.8	122.9	124.5	124.4
1808	125.4	128.3	129.3	129.1	129.6	129.1	131.7	133.2	133.4	134.2	138.4	154.2
1809	158.6	159.2	163.2	161.2	154.1	142.0	135.1	137.1	144.4	146.2	148.9	150.4
1810	146.5	143.1	143.2	143.8	147.2	145.1	149.1	147.6	148.4	150.3	148.5	145.8
1811	144.3	143.6	139.7	137.8	138.0	137.6	137.1	137.5	138.3	137.7	135.3	136.2
1812	137.9	139.8	140.1	139.6	142.1	143.7	173.8	177.9	175.9	174.9	172.9	173.8
1813	174.4	175.7	177.3	181.1	181.5	185.3	185.4	187.1	187.9	189.1	201.7	217.8
1814	239.1	231.4	226.5	215.9	206.5	210.2	210.7	210.7	212.9	227.3	239.0	231.4
1815	230.7	230.5	178.3	171.1	170.2	167.0	169.0	172.1	181.1	181.6	183.5	172.5
1816	169.2	167.3	158.2	154.8	147.4	145.2	142.2	138.1	135.5	131.7	128.5	127.6
1817	125.9	125.0	126.7	125.6	123.8	120.8	118.7	119.0	118.7	119.5	120.5	123.8
1818	125.2	127.2	125.6	126.1	124.8	123.8	123.0	121.6	122.6	124.5	125.6	124.5
1819	125.5	123.5	123.2	120.5	118.0	115.1	111.5	111.8	110.5	110.0	110.8	110.7
1820	110.1	109.8	106.9	104.7	103.5	101.5	101.7	101.5	101.8	102.1	103.6	104.7
1821	104.6	104.3	103.7	102.8	103.4	103.2	102.9	102.6	101.8	103.2	104.4	106.0
1822	105.9	105.9	105.5	106.1	103.9	103.8	102.1	100.6	100.4	99.8	99.9	98.7
1823	98.2	98.2	97.1	97.5	97.2	96.9	96.5	97.4	97.6	97.2	95.4	94.9
1824	94.5	94.1	93.9	93.7	92.9	92.9	93.0	93.5	93.8	93.2	93.2	93.3
1825	94.3	95.6	95.8	99.2	103.2	102.3	102.2	99.9	99.9	100.8	100.8	100.5
1826	99.5	98.5	97.0	96.5	95.8	94.1	92.3	92.3	92.1	92.3	91.9	91.6
1827	92.6	92.8	91.4	94.6	93.0	92.3	91.8	91.3	91.7	91.8	91.2	92.1
1828	91.7	91.3	91.5	90.3	90.2	89.6	90.4	91.5	92.5	91.7	92.2	91.6
1829	91.4	89.9	89.6	88.9	88.2	87.8	87.4	87.2	88.2	88.6	87.0	87.1
1830	85.5	85.1	84.5	85.1	84.4	84.5	84.3	86.2	85.6	85.0	84.7	85.5
1831	84.5	84.8	84.9	84.5	87.3	88.0	87.3	87.5	87.4	88.5	88.7	89.3
1832	89.2	87.9	86.8	85.7	86.3	85.4	85.5	84.8	85.2	86.2	86.4	86.5
1833	83.8	82.8	81.1	81.1	80.6	79.6	79.8	80.4	82.2	82.0	80.7	81.9
1834	81.3	81.2	80.7	79.3	78.7	77.9	77.4	77.7	77.2	77.2	78.1	78.8
1835	80.7	79.8	81.5	82.1	82.5	82.0	81.3	81.3	80.6	80.7	80.4	80.4
1836	80.9	81.2	82.2	83.1	82.9	81.1	81.3	82.1	82.4	83.2	83.0	82.6
1837	83.3	83.6	82.6	81.8	80.0	79.5	79.1	78.7	77.9	77.6	79.8	79.6
1838	79.7	79.3	79.4	79.2	78.9	77.5	77.5	80.2	80.6	81.9	82.0	82.0
1839	82.1	82.3	83.0	82.9	82.9	82.2	81.9	81.9	81.8	80.8	81.0	80.3
1840	80.2	79.3	78.3	78.3	77.4	76.8	76.5	76.2	77.5	77.8	78.4	79.3
1841	78.4	78.0	77.9	78.1	77.2	77.5	76.8	76.7	76.4	77.1	77.7	76.6
1842	76.0	75.5	74.8	73.2	72.8	72.3	71.9	72.2	73.8	75.1	74.8	74.1
1843	73.7	73.9	73.3	72.9	73.7	74.0	75.3	75.3	74.4	75.2	75.3	75.0
1844	75.2	75.7	76.5	77.7	78.3	77.4	77.9	77.7	77.7	77.7	76.9	76.7
1845	75.8	75.7	76.4	78.0	77.8	77.8	78.2	79.2	80.3	79.9	80.4	79.4
1846	79.3	79.7	80.3	79.0	78.4	77.7	77.3	77.1	77.5	77.4	78.4	76.7
1847	76.7	77.2	78.6	78.0	77.7	78.1	78.4	78.5	78.9	78.5	79.0	77.8
1848	78.3	77.0	76.6	76.6	75.7	74.4	74.1	73.9	73.0	73.4	72.7	71.6
1849	72.0	72.2	72.5	72.0	71.7	71.3	71.4	72.0	73.6	74.4	74.4	74.4
1850	74.3	75.5	76.4	76.2	76.2	75.7	76.2	77.3	77.3	77.8	77.7	77.1
1851	77.0	77.1	76.7	76.7	76.3	76.2	76.4	77.0	77.0	77.0	75.1	73.9
1852	74.1	73.9	73.4	72.6	73.2	74.3	74.1	74.1	75.8	76.2	76.2	77.4
1853	77.7	79.7	81.0	82.0	82.3	81.3	81.0	80.9	82.8	84.6	84.9	85.6
1854	86.3	88.5	90.9	90.5	91.9	91.2	91.0	92.3	91.4	92.1	93.9	93.1
1855	92.2	93.2	94.2	93.9	93.5	94.0	93.5	96.0	98.7	101.4	99.7	99.2
1856	99.6	100.3	99.5	99.4	98.3	98.2	98.4	98.1	97.7	98.8	98.9	98.6
1857	99.8	99.7	100.2	102.2	102.9	102.1	99.7	99.8	101.3	99.6	93.8	91.6
1858	88.2	86.6	88.5	88.9	89.2	88.1	88.4	88.7	88.9	88.5	85.4	83.8
1859	83.5	83.4	83.6	83.6	83.6	83.5	82.8	82.4	81.5	82.4	82.2	82.3
1860	81.2	81.5	82.6	82.7	82.7	84.0	85.3	86.9	87.7	87.5	85.5	84.2
1861	84.0	82.4	81.3	81.9	80.8	79.8	79.4	83.7	86.5	88.2	90.1	93.7

TABLE 5—26 AGRICULTURAL COMMODITIES

Year	Jan.	Feb.	Mar.	Apr.	May	June	July	Aug.	Sept.	Oct.	Nov.	Dec.
1784	105.3	103.7	105.2	102.2	106.3	107.6	108.1	106.2	107.3	109.8	108.3	106.7
1785	104.3	104.2	104.1	100.4	97.8	99.2	98.9	98.5	97.9	100.9	103.8	104.9
1786	102.7	100.8	99.9	98.0	98.7	103.5	105.5	102.6	103.4	100.6	102.2	98.7
1787	99.0	98.6	98.6	100.2	100.0	99.7	101.1	96.7	95.0	94.1	92.4	90.3
1788	87.9	87.3	87.3	85.8	86.5	86.1	84.7	82.8	80.9	81.8	81.8	78.0
1789	78.6	78.2	77.3	75.7	78.5	79.0	80.9	82.2	81.0	81.7	84.2	86.9
1790	86.7	89.5	93.3	94.5	95.8	96.1	95.0	94.5	90.7	89.6	95.5	94.4
1791	94.4	92.1	87.5	87.2	86.4	85.4	84.3	84.0	86.3	90.5	89.5	88.7
1792	86.6	86.8	87.4	87.9	87.8	86.8	87.0	86.7	85.4	87.3	91.3	93.5
1793	95.1	96.0	94.9	97.5	97.8	97.5	98.1	96.3	98.4	99.2	99.4	100.2
1794	101.2	100.9	101.9	102.0								
1795	117.5	121.1	123.0	124.1	129.3	131.6	137.3	130.2	130.6	134.1	134.9	136.7
1796	141.4	141.2	147.4	145.9	146.5	146.3	141.9	138.0	140.3	145.9	144.0	143.5
1797	144.6	147.0	139.7	132.7	132.3	130.0	130.3	131.2	131.7	134.4	134.1	136.9
1798	135.3	134.7	134.8	129.6	128.4	124.8	123.6	124.7	125.7	126.0	126.2	
1799					118.5	121.5	122.1	123.6				
1800						126.6	129.6	130.3	132.1	134.6	138.4	137.3
1801	137.6	142.2	146.7	145.9	146.0	145.2	146.9	146.0	143.4	141.6	144.2	133.1
1802	124.8	125.0	120.9	120.9	119.9	119.9	120.4	120.5	119.6	117.6	115.8	116.8
1803	116.8	114.2	113.7	111.2	111.1	111.4	110.7	113.0	113.3	116.1	119.8	120.9
1804	120.1	120.7	122.4	121.8	122.0	122.4	125.2	125.0	128.5	130.0	133.9	143.2
1805	143.3	144.9	147.1	149.8	149.1	148.1	146.1	136.6	132.8	131.0	131.7	133.1
1806	138.2	137.6	138.2	135.6	134.5	137.3	137.3	137.2	132.5	133.2	131.5	129.3
1807	129.5	130.2	130.0	127.7	125.9	125.8	125.5	122.8	124.1	122.7	123.4	122.4
1808	115.4	112.7	112.0	110.7	107.7	108.1	107.3	105.5	105.3	107.7	109.6	108.1
1809	109.9	110.5	114.7	120.5	125.5	122.4	120.6	119.0	118.0	118.6	123.3	122.3
1810	124.7	126.0	129.4	129.3	135.4	132.9	135.3	137.0	136.5	138.0	136.0	135.4
1811	137.0	135.1	135.7	133.2	130.1	130.9	128.2	127.9	124.8	123.0	120.4	121.2
1812	125.8	126.8	126.0	123.1	122.1	122.6	125.5	123.8	127.4	129.0	129.7	129.0
1813	129.9	132.4	132.8	129.8	132.3	131.7	132.2	132.1	132.2	132.3	133.9	142.5
1814	151.5	150.5	148.5	151.1	147.6	148.6	146.4	148.5	148.5	153.5	157.8	158.6
1815	155.3	154.5	144.9	141.1	143.0	147.6	159.7	165.0	168.8	179.6	181.1	176.2
1816	174.4	173.5	169.3	169.7	169.3	175.6	181.3	184.5	179.4	177.0	181.2	185.3
1817	187.2	192.5	198.4	198.3	195.9	178.3	169.0	167.7	160.9	156.6	156.4	160.1
1818	159.2	161.5	162.1	162.1	162.2	159.2	156.9	158.4	159.1	161.4	158.3	157.8
1819	156.0	150.3	147.7	139.5	129.6	123.2	122.4	122.0	122.8	124.4	124.1	122.8
1820	119.3	118.9	115.3	109.9	110.9	108.5	106.1	105.3	105.2	104.4	101.5	99.9
1821	98.2	97.0	94.7	92.2	93.7	91.9	92.1	93.7	97.7	101.4	104.9	102.8
1822	104.2	104.8	107.6	109.2	111.9	111.8	109.7	107.4	105.8	105.5	106.9	104.9
1823	105.2	104.6	103.8	102.0	102.4	103.5	103.9	98.4	95.8	97.5	98.6	97.3
1824	96.8	95.2	92.7	92.1	92.7	92.8	92.5	91.7	88.6	90.9	91.4	91.6
1825	91.3	93.0	93.5	95.9	98.7	97.0	95.5	94.2	98.8	100.9	99.2	100.6
1826	100.4	100.6	101.1	98.8	96.9	99.4	102.3	98.9	99.6	98.8	101.5	101.1
1827	101.2	101.2	100.3	99.7	96.2	92.9	89.6	89.4	91.2	91.7	90.8	90.4
1828	89.7	87.0	85.8	84.4	84.4	84.4	84.8	86.8	89.4	93.1	101.2	98.4
1829	96.9	96.3	94.9	95.1	93.0	91.8	87.7	85.8	86.2	86.4	87.4	85.4
1830	83.2	83.1	82.3	81.2	81.7	83.3	82.8	85.7	88.1	90.9	90.1	89.0
1831	92.8	93.9	96.4	97.1	97.2	95.6	95.3	96.0	99.9	100.2	98.9	98.2
1832	98.1	96.5	94.4	95.6	96.7	101.4	100.4	102.6	100.0	101.3	104.1	102.1
1833	101.2	100.9	100.1	101.5	101.7	102.5	101.9	100.9	102.6	103.5	102.7	100.3
1834	98.9	96.8	95.8	94.8	95.8	97.0	97.8	98.0	98.0	98.6	98.8	99.6
1835	98.8	103.1	104.2	107.9	115.2	119.9	121.7	119.8	118.4	121.5	122.6	126.9
1836	125.3	125.1	127.7	135.5	134.8	130.8	130.9	133.6	142.3	142.8	147.2	145.6
1837	144.2	145.7	142.3	133.0	127.4	123.9	125.4	122.4	121.5	124.2	129.8	126.1
1838	120.9	119.5	114.0	115.1	115.9	118.0	113.9	121.8	127.3	136.0	136.5	137.7
1839	139.4	140.5	142.4	144.1	145.4	142.8	138.8	131.8	130.8	126.8	126.3	122.9
1840	119.6	113.9	106.1	106.7	102.7	102.4	105.4	105.3	106.9	108.4	107.4	102.0
1841	102.2	100.0	99.3	98.0	98.2	100.8	100.8	103.2	106.6	104.8	104.0	102.2
1842	100.7	97.9	97.1	93.9	88.0	86.9	85.7	85.1	83.1	83.2	80.5	80.7
1843	78.7	77.1	76.6	78.9	79.7	84.0	84.9	83.0	83.5	82.8	81.2	79.5
1844	79.7	82.5	82.5	83.7	82.4	80.6	79.8	79.2	79.9	81.3	80.3	79.3
1845	79.8	82.3	84.0	86.6	87.3	87.4	87.7	89.7	92.9	95.2	100.5	102.6
1846	97.8	94.9	95.3	94.3	91.9	88.2	86.2	84.6	87.7	97.0	99.9	96.3
1847	95.9	107.7	111.0	118.5	122.7	129.0	110.9	110.0	109.0	112.5	111.6	107.3
1848	104.1	101.1	101.9	100.7	97.8	94.7	92.1	91.7	97.6	95.9	94.2	92.1
1849	94.7	93.5	93.4	91.0	89.8	90.1	91.0	95.4	96.5	97.1	96.2	94.9
1850	95.5	95.6	95.1	95.7	98.3	97.9	97.6	99.6	98.9	100.3	103.3	103.2
1851	104.5	106.2	104.5	106.7	106.4	103.0	100.8	98.3	98.0	98.4	97.6	97.9
1852	99.5	101.7	102.1	103.8	106.5	106.5	107.5	107.4	111.1	112.5	113.8	116.7
1853	117.7	116.1	115.1	115.5	113.9	112.4	113.6	114.9	118.3	122.2	124.4	120.9
1854	123.7	131.9	126.4	126.7	133.6	132.8	129.5	130.0	137.1	134.6	136.4	135.5
1855	137.0	134.7	137.4	144.9	147.0	148.3	143.4	141.5	139.0	141.6	144.8	144.2
1856	140.5	133.3	129.2	129.6	121.4	118.6	123.0	124.4	126.4	129.5	132.7	131.0
1857	131.1	131.1	133.2	134.5	142.3	145.8	143.2	143.0	137.0	130.2	124.2	117.3
1858	113.1	108.1	110.3	114.4	114.8	113.4	113.1	117.1	120.6	120.4	118.6	117.6
1859	121.6	124.1	127.8	126.8	130.1	128.3	121.6	118.4	116.5	119.9	120.4	120.0
1860	120.3	120.8	119.3	120.8	119.1	116.6	115.9	117.3	118.6	118.6	115.7	110.5
1861	111.7	110.2	109.9	111.1	111.7	109.2	104.1	106.1	106.5	112.0	117.3	117.1

Table 6—67 Industrial Commodities

Year	Jan.	Feb.	Mar.	Apr.	May	June	July	Aug.	Sept.	Oct.	Nov.	Dec.
1784	98.9	99.9	98.7	97.3	94.2	95.0	96.3	96.4	96.0	96.5	93.9	92.6
1785	91.9	91.2	91.8	91.3	90.1	89.3	90.2	90.1	89.7	89.8	89.3	89.3
1786	89.7	89.8	89.4	88.2	88.1	87.7	87.7	87.5	88.1	88.3	88.1	88.4
1787	88.6	89.2	89.3	89.1	88.6	87.9	88.1	88.1	86.9	86.7	87.8	87.5
1788	87.0	86.6	86.7	85.9	85.4	85.5	85.4	84.6	84.0	83.7	83.9	83.7
1789	83.9	83.8	84.0	84.0	85.3	85.3	86.0	85.7	85.6	85.5	85.7	86.2
1790	85.9	86.2	86.3	85.6	85.3	85.2	84.3	84.3	83.8	84.9	85.9	85.7
1791	85.5	86.8	86.2	85.9	86.0	86.6	87.1	87.8	87.7	87.9	87.5	87.5
1792	87.6	87.5	88.0	88.5	88.5	89.2	89.4	89.3	90.1	89.8	90.9	92.4
1793	91.8	91.8	92.3	91.5	91.5	92.4	92.4	92.7	93.2	93.4	94.2	94.1
1794	96.8	97.0	102.4	103.0								
1795	123.9	123.8	124.8	127.2	128.6	127.9	129.4	131.6	133.4	134.4	134.3	134.6
1796	137.2	135.7	137.8	135.3	135.1	134.6	134.2	133.5	134.7	135.7	134.4	134.5
1797	134.8	134.7	133.0	130.3	131.3	128.6	128.4	128.4	127.1	127.8	126.4	125.5
1798	124.3	124.4	124.7	124.5	126.3	127.7	130.2	130.8	131.0	131.5	133.2	
1799					134.5	134.0	133.7	131.2				
1800						129.3	127.0	126.3	127.3	129.3	131.7	131.8
1801	130.5	131.8	131.8	131.8	130.1	131.3	131.9	131.3	130.3	130.7	132.5	132.0
1802	130.3	129.1	126.2	123.4	123.1	122.2	121.3	121.5	122.3	122.4	123.0	118.9
1803	120.2	120.1	119.3	121.5	122.8	122.5	122.8	124.6	125.4	125.7	126.1	125.2
1804	127.3	129.9	129.4	130.1	129.2	128.9	128.6	126.8	127.4	128.9	130.6	131.7
1805	132.0	133.3	132.2	132.4	131.5	130.9	130.9	131.2	131.6	131.6	131.5	132.1
1806	134.4	133.8	133.8	132.9	132.0	129.9	130.6	130.0	130.4	129.4	130.0	130.9
1807	130.5	130.4	130.7	129.3	127.9	126.9	126.6	126.2	128.1	127.2	128.2	127.8
1808	128.4	130.1	130.1	130.2	129.8	129.7	130.7	131.5	131.7	132.2	135.0	145.7
1809	149.5	150.1	152.8	152.8	146.0	139.3	134.6	135.1	140.9	143.4	146.2	149.0
1810	147.8	146.0	146.1	145.7	147.6	144.6	145.6	145.4	144.6	146.5	145.5	144.1
1811	144.0	143.7	142.1	141.3	140.7	139.7	139.7	141.4	142.1	140.9	139.0	139.9
1812	139.1	139.0	139.6	139.6	142.0	145.0	165.1	168.8	165.8	164.0	162.9	163.2
1813	164.9	164.9	166.0	172.2	172.0	173.9	174.7	175.3	176.1	176.7	183.9	200.3
1814	221.1	213.6	210.4	201.7	191.9	193.9	192.0	191.4	194.0	205.2	219.5	215.3
1815	216.0	214.1	176.9	167.7	164.0	155.5	157.0	157.3	161.2	164.6	166.9	160.6
1816	159.6	158.2	154.7	152.1	146.2	142.4	139.3	136.4	133.4	130.7	128.7	127.8
1817	127.7	126.7	126.8	124.1	122.3	118.9	118.4	118.5	118.5	117.7	118.3	120.4
1818	120.4	122.2	123.4	123.1	122.3	120.9	120.1	119.2	119.4	120.7	121.1	120.8
1819	121.6	120.7	119.5	117.3	114.6	113.6	109.6	109.4	107.3	106.3	107.2	108.0
1820	107.7	107.6	106.7	105.7	105.2	104.4	104.7	105.0	105.0	105.3	105.1	105.1
1821	105.1	104.8	105.4	104.0	104.2	104.1	104.1	104.5	104.0	104.5	105.3	105.8
1822	105.7	105.9	105.5	104.4	103.2	102.9	102.4	102.0	102.6	101.9	100.8	100.1
1823	100.0	99.7	98.7	97.9	98.4	98.0	97.8	98.0	97.7	97.8	96.4	96.1
1824	95.9	96.1	95.6	95.5	94.8	95.2	95.3	94.4	93.8	93.5	93.4	93.2
1825	93.6	93.9	94.2	96.6	98.9	97.9	97.9	96.8	97.6	97.8	98.0	98.0
1826	98.0	97.4	96.4	95.9	94.6	93.4	92.9	91.9	91.5	91.2	91.4	91.6
1827	92.6	92.9	92.7	92.9	92.4	91.7	91.3	90.9	90.9	91.9	91.9	92.1
1828	91.8	91.2	91.1	90.0	89.4	89.1	89.4	89.6	89.5	89.6	90.1	90.7
1829	91.1	91.4	91.1	89.5	88.3	88.0	87.0	87.0	86.7	87.9	87.6	87.3
1830	86.3	86.3	85.8	84.5	83.4	83.4	83.0	82.8	82.6	83.2	83.5	84.9
1831	84.3	85.2	85.3	85.4	87.6	86.9	86.8	87.6	87.5	88.7	88.9	89.3
1832	89.7	89.3	88.5	87.7	87.7	87.3	87.2	87.2	87.9	88.5	88.2	88.3
1833	88.3	88.0	88.6	87.9	87.2	87.2	87.3	87.8	88.8	88.8	88.6	88.7
1834	88.2	88.0	87.0	86.1	86.0	85.6	85.6	85.3	85.4	85.6	86.3	86.7
1835	86.4	85.7	86.7	87.5	87.4	87.3	87.1	87.5	87.0	86.9	87.8	88.3
1836	90.2	90.4	91.5	93.3	93.7	92.9	92.4	93.4	94.9	96.1	96.6	97.2
1837	99.0	98.9	99.3	98.3	96.3	95.0	93.3	92.2	91.7	91.7	92.4	92.4
1838	92.8	92.6	92.0	91.5	90.8	90.0	89.6	91.9	92.3	94.3	94.6	95.3
1839	95.6	95.4	96.4	96.8	96.5	96.2	95.8	95.8	95.3	94.4	94.3	94.0
1840	93.3	93.0	91.3	91.2	90.1	89.6	89.0	88.1	87.8	87.8	87.8	87.8
1841	88.0	87.9	87.8	87.3	86.3	86.3	86.1	86.2	86.4	87.3	86.9	87.2
1842	87.5	86.9	86.2	83.8	82.6	81.8	81.4	81.7	82.0	81.3	80.9	80.7
1843	80.4	80.0	79.5	79.1	78.6	78.3	78.3	78.3	77.0	77.3	77.7	78.1
1844	78.2	78.4	78.9	79.4	79.0	78.3	78.4	79.0	79.2	79.6	79.5	78.9
1845	78.0	77.6	77.8	79.2	78.9	78.4	78.2	78.0	78.2	79.0	79.6	79.8
1846	79.8	79.7	79.9	80.1	79.4	78.9	78.2	77.8	77.2	77.2	78.9	78.6
1847	78.9	79.6	80.9	80.2	79.9	80.4	79.9	79.9	80.7	81.4	81.8	81.3
1848	81.8	81.0	80.5	79.9	79.0	77.6	77.5	77.3	77.5	77.0	77.1	76.6
1849	76.5	76.7	76.5	76.2	75.0	75.5	75.3	75.6	76.2	75.9	76.0	76.1
1850	76.2	76.9	77.0	77.1	77.1	76.7	76.9	76.7	76.6	77.2	77.6	77.6
1851	77.5	77.3	76.7	76.7	76.0	75.3	75.2	75.6	75.0	74.8	74.5	74.6
1852	74.3	74.4	74.6	74.6	74.6	73.6	73.8	73.9	74.6	76.1	76.8	78.4
1853	79.2	82.5	82.9	83.3	83.2	81.7	81.4	81.9	82.4	83.7	84.2	85.4
1854	85.9	88.1	88.7	89.2	91.0	91.1	91.2	91.6	92.3	92.3	92.6	92.4
1855	92.5	92.9	92.7	91.1	91.0	90.7	90.8	91.4	92.8	95.2	95.0	95.3
1856	95.3	94.8	93.9	94.5	93.8	93.4	92.7	92.3	92.2	92.4	92.8	91.7
1857	91.9	92.7	92.9	93.6	94.0	93.3	92.8	93.3	93.1	91.6	90.0	88.1
1858	85.8	85.1	85.5	85.9	85.8	84.6	84.8	85.2	85.2	85.2	84.4	84.2
1859	84.1	84.8	85.2	85.4	85.4	84.8	83.9	83.4	82.5	82.3	82.0	82.6
1860	82.1	82.7	83.5	83.1	82.6	82.6	83.1	83.5	83.8	83.6	83.7	82.8
1861	81.4	80.3	80.0	80.2	78.9	77.6	77.3	78.5	78.8	79.7	81.1	82.8

TABLE 7—FARM CROPS

Year	Jan.	Feb.	Mar.	Apr.	May	June	July	Aug.	Sept.	Oct.	Nov.	Dec.
1784	98.4	97.3	97.2	94.4	98.5	100.5	100.5	98.5	103.0	108.3	107.6	109.3
1785	108.1	109.6	109.3	104.0	100.1	103.6	101.4	99.9	97.5	103.9	110.5	112.8
1786	107.6	104.0	103.3	99.2	99.4	109.8	113.3	107.2	108.8	103.9	108.6	104.7
1787	105.0	104.8	105.0	106.9	110.7	108.4	108.7	103.5	99.9	99.1	97.9	95.2
1788	93.4	92.6	91.4	90.6	92.4	91.5	89.4	87.8	84.3	87.8	85.5	81.8
1789	81.5	81.1	79.6	78.2	83.2	83.0	84.7	86.6	85.7	88.1	89.5	90.4
1790	90.1	94.7	98.0	101.4	101.3	102.3	98.1	94.7	90.9	87.6	97.6	96.5
1791	96.9	92.5	87.3	88.5	87.5	84.8	82.6	81.8	85.7	91.1	89.6	86.9
1792	85.7	85.7	86.5	87.5	87.5	86.4	87.7	88.0	85.2	89.4	91.5	96.5
1793	96.7	97.1	95.2	97.5	98.2	96.8	98.0	97.7	99.8	101.7	102.0	102.8
1794	101.3	100.6	100.1	100.6								
1795	110.2	114.5	115.0	115.8	123.7	126.8	132.5	123.8	124.1	131.1	131.3	134.7
1796	144.4	140.8	146.4	148.8	153.1	150.2	146.5	138.7	142.8	148.7	149.2	149.5
1797	150.0	155.0	146.2	136.6	135.8	137.1	137.7	140.2	139.0	144.3	142.9	141.3
1798	141.4	140.0	141.7	135.5	134.4	134.1	134.6	135.1	135.6	136.0	134.6	
1799					120.3	126.2	126.4	127.4				
1800						128.8	130.6	129.8	130.4	131.0	136.5	137.4
1801	136.5	143.7	149.9	146.1	146.4	144.4	146.0	142.7	138.7	133.7	142.8	133.7
1802	126.9	127.6	121.4	122.5	121.6	121.8	121.2	120.0	120.5	116.6	116.5	121.0
1803	121.7	121.6	120.8	118.1	116.8	117.2	115.2	115.6	115.6	121.9	127.1	129.6
1804	128.1	129.7	129.2	127.9	126.1	126.1	127.1	127.1	130.8	131.5	134.7	148.4
1805	148.7	148.7	150.6	155.5	155.8	153.9	149.2	141.4	134.7	130.6	131.9	135.0
1806	137.5	137.7	137.1	133.8	132.4	133.3	133.1	133.8	126.3	128.8	125.4	124.9
1807	126.3	128.3	128.2	127.4	127.1	128.6	128.0	124.7	124.1	121.9	121.9	122.5
1808	114.6	111.1	110.1	110.4	107.9	109.5	107.0	104.7	105.2	107.2	108.2	105.0
1809	109.5	108.3	116.9	116.0	121.3	116.5	116.4	113.8	111.9	111.6	119.8	119.4
1810	122.2	122.2	125.4	125.8	134.8	130.9	133.7	135.5	131.6	134.6	132.6	129.5
1811	133.8	132.3	132.2	126.8	122.8	124.7	122.3	118.7	114.4	113.3	108.9	109.2
1812	118.4	120.2	119.6	118.0	117.5	118.6	123.8	117.0	118.9	124.4	122.0	121.5
1813	123.2	128.0	129.6	125.4	132.8	130.7	133.6	133.6	132.6	132.6	135.7	149.1
1814	149.5	149.6	143.8	144.0	146.8	149.7	146.1	144.6	143.7	146.0	151.6	150.7
1815	148.5	148.5	133.8	124.1	128.5	138.8	156.6	158.7	160.3	178.7	180.7	174.6
1816	173.3	172.9	172.4	174.7	175.4	185.3	195.4	198.1	189.4	182.8	189.2	195.9
1817	196.7	207.0	211.0	209.1	207.7	179.0	168.9	167.9	161.8	155.9	153.9	162.0
1818	159.8	160.3	165.1	164.9	162.5	161.8	158.8	162.0	161.1	165.0	160.9	163.2
1819	163.2	155.8	153.9	148.6	134.8	126.8	122.0	120.8	125.0	123.8	126.1	127.2
1820	125.3	125.6	122.7	114.9	117.1	113.4	110.4	107.5	108.6	106.3	99.5	97.5
1821	97.6	96.9	93.5	89.5	92.8	88.3	88.8	89.9	94.6	95.1	102.7	102.7
1822	102.8	102.9	108.5	110.9	114.9	114.0	110.2	106.0	103.8	102.0	105.5	104.5
1823	104.8	105.9	107.0	104.7	104.1	106.2	106.7	95.9	92.4	94.4	97.2	96.2
1824	95.1	94.6	91.2	90.8	91.0	91.1	92.0	90.9	87.4	90.3	89.8	90.3
1825	89.5	90.4	91.9	98.0	105.0	104.9	102.1	98.6	104.1	106.1	102.7	105.0
1826	105.4	106.8	108.3	107.6	103.4	106.0	112.3	105.2	103.3	101.6	106.7	107.7
1827	106.4	107.9	106.6	106.3	101.4	95.3	87.3	87.6	88.1	89.0	89.8	90.4
1828	89.0	86.6	84.7	82.7	82.5	82.0	81.8	82.6	84.2	87.8	95.9	94.4
1829	93.7	94.7	93.9	94.6	94.2	92.1	89.0	86.3	86.3	87.1	88.9	87.7
1830	85.8	86.0	83.9	81.5	82.2	82.6	80.4	81.9	82.6	87.0	87.2	86.6
1831	89.6	90.7	92.9	94.0	93.0	92.3	92.1	92.8	98.1	98.0	97.8	97.7
1832	97.1	95.5	93.0	95.9	97.0	102.1	102.1	103.9	98.5	100.2	104.6	101.6
1833	100.0	99.9	99.6	102.3	101.0	102.9	101.1	100.7	102.6	105.1	103.8	102.4
1834	100.1	97.7	97.0	95.4	99.4	101.1	103.5	102.7	103.4	103.8	104.0	105.2
1835	104.1	113.5	114.9	119.0	125.6	131.9	133.3	130.8	129.5	134.3	136.5	138.2
1836	133.5	135.1	137.2	143.3	143.5	138.6	137.5	142.0	148.2	146.7	150.4	149.6
1837	149.5	150.1	143.7	132.4	127.8	126.6	127.2	121.1	118.7	121.7	130.3	125.6
1838	121.5	118.9	113.3	115.8	115.5	118.7	113.5	124.1	129.2	135.0	137.5	140.5
1839	145.8	152.2	152.9	157.9	159.7	156.0	151.5	142.1	138.5	133.3	132.4	129.1
1840	126.5	118.4	110.0	108.7	101.2	101.5	105.7	107.0	107.3	109.6	109.8	105.3
1841	106.3	105.5	104.4	105.7	106.8	110.5	113.3	115.8	119.3	117.0	116.9	112.6
1842	112.2	108.7	107.6	105.5	96.7	95.4	94.2	90.6	87.0	88.7	84.9	87.8
1843	85.7	84.0	84.5	88.0	87.7	90.7	91.1	88.3	88.9	89.3	88.9	86.2
1844	86.8	90.0	89.3	90.2	89.1	88.0	87.1	86.6	85.7	87.2	85.9	84.3
1845	83.6	84.3	87.5	87.2	88.7	91.3	91.8	95.6	99.3	100.8	106.2	108.5
1846	103.7	101.0	103.2	102.8	101.8	96.8	95.5	91.9	97.3	106.1	110.5	106.2
1847	106.8	121.4	121.5	129.8	132.7	141.2	121.0	121.7	118.2	122.5	118.8	113.1
1848	113.7	110.4	109.6	108.7	106.1	102.1	94.8	93.9	101.7	102.0	98.7	95.7
1849	99.1	97.1	98.8	97.6	97.0	96.3	97.2	101.1	101.9	103.4	102.9	101.6
1850	103.4	104.0	103.7	106.2	109.0	109.9	110.2	111.0	109.1	110.5	115.2	116.3
1851	118.7	119.9	115.4	118.0	115.2	109.9	107.0	102.2	103.6	102.4	101.5	102.0
1852	103.5	104.6	103.7	104.3	106.9	107.1	108.6	106.4	109.2	110.0	112.2	112.0
1853	113.5	113.4	114.1	114.4	115.0	114.4	114.5	115.2	117.6	120.4	122.2	119.7
1854	123.3	134.4	128.0	131.0	139.0	139.4	136.1	134.2	138.0	139.3	140.4	139.9
1855	141.2	140.3	141.2	151.7	156.8	160.7	152.2	146.8	142.0	143.4	144.5	144.7
1856	145.6	132.5	130.9	129.4	120.2	119.1	123.3	124.3	125.6	131.1	135.7	134.0
1857	133.9	134.2	136.0	137.4	147.7	150.8	147.0	145.8	133.7	129.5	124.1	116.7
1858	114.4	107.2	108.5	114.6	114.5	112.8	115.5	119.1	120.8	120.0	119.1	117.7
1859	122.6	125.1	129.1	127.6	131.7	128.0	122.8	119.4	117.4	121.0	122.2	121.5
1860	117.3	119.7	117.3	118.7	116.4	112.6	111.2	111.6	112.0	111.8	109.0	105.8
1861	108.0	107.1	105.9	108.4	112.5	111.3	107.7	116.0	118.3	125.2	138.2	142.4

Table 8—Farm Derivatives

Year	Jan.	Feb.	Mar.	Apr.	May	June	July	Aug.	Sept.	Oct.	Nov.	Dec.
1784	111.6	109.6	112.5	109.4	113.4	114.0	115.1	113.4	111.2	111.2	109.0	104.5
1785	101.1	99.8	99.9	97.4	95.8	95.5	96.9	97.4	98.3	98.5	98.4	98.5
1786	98.7	98.2	97.0	97.0	98.2	98.5	99.3	98.7	99.0	97.8	97.1	93.8
1787	94.0	93.5	93.4	94.7	91.7	92.8	95.0	91.2	91.0	90.0	88.0	86.3
1788	83.4	83.1	83.9	81.8	81.7	81.8	81.0	78.7	78.1	76.9	78.8	74.9
1789	76.2	75.8	75.4	73.6	74.7	75.7	77.8	78.7	77.2	76.6	79.9	84.1
1790	83.9	85.3	89.5	89.0	91.2	91.2	92.5	94.2	90.5	91.4	93.8	92.6
1791	92.4	91.7	87.6	86.1	85.4	85.9	85.8	86.0	86.8	90.0	89.5	90.3
1792	87.3	87.7	88.2	88.2	88.1	87.2	86.3	85.6	85.7	85.6	91.2	91.0
1793	93.8	95.1	94.7	97.5	97.4	98.1	98.3	95.2	97.2	97.1	97.3	98.0
1794	101.1	101.2	103.5	103.2								
1795	124.2	127.0	130.3	131.7	134.4	135.9	141.5	135.9	136.5	136.7	138.0	138.4
1796	138.9	141.6	148.2	143.5	141.1	143.1	138.0	137.3	138.1	143.6	139.7	138.6
1797	140.1	140.5	134.3	129.5	129.4	124.2	124.3	124.0	125.7	126.4	127.1	133.3
1798	130.4	130.4	129.1	124.7	123.5	117.4	115.0	116.4	117.9	118.0	119.4	
1799					116.9	117.7	118.4	120.4				
1800						124.7	128.7	130.7	133.6	137.7	140.1	137.2
1801	138.6	141.0	144.0	145.8	145.6	145.9	147.6	149.0	147.6	148.7	145.3	132.6
1802	123.0	122.9	120.4	119.6	118.6	118.4	119.8	120.9	118.9	118.4	115.3	113.4
1803	112.8	108.2	107.9	105.5	106.4	106.7	106.9	110.9	111.4	111.3	113.9	113.9
1804	113.7	113.5	116.8	116.8	118.6	119.4	123.6	123.1	126.5	128.7	133.3	138.9
1805	138.9	141.8	144.3	145.0	143.6	143.4	143.4	132.7	131.2	131.2	131.5	131.5
1806	138.8	137.6	139.1	137.1	136.4	140.9	140.9	140.1	138.1	137.1	136.9	133.3
1807	132.2	131.9	131.5	128.0	124.8	123.4	123.4	121.2	124.1	123.4	124.7	122.3
1808	116.1	114.2	113.8	110.9	107.6	106.9	107.5	106.2	105.4	108.1	110.9	110.7
1809	110.3	112.4	112.8	124.6	129.3	127.8	124.3	123.5	123.4	124.9	126.4	124.9
1810	126.9	129.5	132.9	132.5	135.8	134.6	136.6	138.4	140.8	141.0	139.0	140.7
1811	139.8	137.5	138.7	139.1	136.8	136.5	133.6	136.4	134.3	132.0	131.2	132.5
1812	132.6	132.7	131.7	127.7	126.2	126.1	127.1	129.9	135.2	133.1	136.8	135.8
1813	135.9	136.3	135.6	133.8	131.8	132.6	131.0	130.7	131.7	132.0	132.3	137.1
1814	153.3	151.2	152.7	157.4	148.2	147.7	146.6	151.9	152.7	160.1	163.3	165.7
1815	161.4	159.8	155.2	157.6	156.7	155.6	162.4	170.6	176.5	180.3	181.3	177.5
1816	175.4	173.9	166.8	165.6	164.3	167.7	170.0	173.5	171.2	172.3	174.6	176.6
1817	179.5	180.8	188.1	189.4	186.3	177.7	169.1	167.5	160.1	157.2	158.5	158.5
1818	158.6	162.6	159.6	159.8	162.0	156.9	155.4	155.3	157.5	158.3	156.1	153.4
1819	150.1	145.8	142.6	132.2	125.4	120.3	122.7	123.1	120.9	124.8	122.4	119.1
1820	114.4	113.4	109.3	105.7	105.7	104.4	102.6	103.4	102.4	102.9	103.3	102.0
1821	98.7	97.0	95.6	94.5	94.4	95.0	95.0	97.1	100.5	107.2	106.7	102.9
1822	105.5	106.5	106.7	107.7	109.5	109.9	109.3	108.5	107.6	108.6	108.1	105.3
1823	105.6	103.5	101.1	99.7	100.9	101.1	101.5	100.6	98.8	100.2	99.9	98.4
1824	98.2	95.7	94.0	93.3	94.1	94.2	93.0	92.5	89.7	91.4	92.7	92.7
1825	92.9	95.3	94.8	94.1	93.6	90.8	90.2	90.6	94.5	96.7	96.3	97.0
1826	96.3	95.5	95.4	91.9	91.7	94.1	94.5	93.7	96.5	96.4	97.1	95.7
1827	97.1	95.8	95.2	94.3	92.0	90.8	91.7	90.9	94.0	94.1	91.7	90.4
1828	90.3	87.4	86.8	86.0	86.2	86.6	87.5	90.5	94.1	97.9	105.9	102.0
1829	99.6	97.7	95.8	95.4	91.9	91.6	86.5	85.3	86.2	85.7	86.1	83.4
1830	81.0	80.6	81.0	81.0	81.3	83.8	84.9	89.0	93.2	94.3	92.7	91.1
1831	95.5	96.7	99.5	99.8	100.8	98.4	98.2	98.7	101.5	102.1	99.8	98.7
1832	99.1	97.3	95.5	95.4	96.5	100.8	98.9	101.4	101.4	102.2	103.6	102.5
1833	102.2	101.8	100.5	100.8	102.4	102.2	102.6	101.1	102.6	102.3	101.8	98.6
1834	97.9	96.0	94.8	94.2	92.8	93.7	93.1	94.1	93.5	94.4	94.6	95.0
1835	94.4	94.9	95.8	99.2	106.9	110.5	112.5	111.1	109.7	111.4	111.8	117.9
1836	118.6	117.1	120.0	129.2	127.7	124.5	125.4	126.8	137.4	139.7	144.5	142.4
1837	139.7	142.0	141.1	133.5	127.0	121.6	123.8	123.5	123.9	126.3	129.4	126.4
1838	120.5	120.0	114.6	114.6	116.3	117.4	114.2	119.9	125.7	136.9	135.6	135.4
1839	134.1	131.2	133.9	133.3	134.2	132.4	128.8	123.5	124.6	121.6	121.3	117.7
1840	114.0	110.1	102.9	105.1	104.0	103.2	105.1	103.9	106.6	107.3	105.3	99.2
1841	98.8	95.5	95.1	91.9	91.4	93.1	91.2	93.5	96.7	95.3	94.2	94.0
1842	91.8	89.6	88.9	85.0	81.1	80.2	79.1	80.6	80.0	78.8	76.9	75.1
1843	73.1	71.6	70.4	71.9	73.4	78.7	80.0	78.8	79.2	77.6	75.2	74.2
1844	72.9	76.5	77.1	78.5	77.1	74.7	74.1	73.4	75.2	76.6	75.8	75.3
1845	76.6	80.7	81.1	86.1	86.2	84.1	84.3	84.9	87.7	90.7	96.0	97.7
1846	93.0	89.9	89.1	87.6	84.2	81.5	79.0	78.7	80.2	89.9	91.6	88.6
1847	87.3	97.2	102.7	109.5	114.7	119.3	103.0	100.9	101.7	104.6	105.7	102.6
1848	96.5	93.7	95.7	94.4	91.2	88.7	89.9	89.8	94.2	91.0	90.4	89.1
1849	91.1	90.6	89.0	85.7	84.0	85.1	86.0	90.7	92.0	92.0	90.8	89.4
1850	89.2	89.0	88.3	87.5	90.0	88.6	88.0	90.8	90.9	92.2	94.2	93.1
1851	93.7	95.7	96.0	97.9	99.4	97.4	95.8	95.1	93.4	95.1	94.5	94.6
1852	96.2	99.3	100.8	103.4	106.1	105.9	106.5	108.3	112.8	114.8	115.2	120.9
1853	121.5	118.5	115.9	116.4	113.0	110.7	112.7	114.7	118.8	123.7	126.3	122.0
1854	123.9	129.8	125.0	123.2	129.2	127.4	124.1	126.6	136.3	130.8	133.1	131.8
1855	133.4	130.0	134.2	139.2	139.1	138.5	136.3	137.1	136.5	140.1	145.1	143.7
1856	136.3	133.9	127.8	129.8	122.4	118.1	122.7	124.4	127.1	128.2	130.2	128.5
1857	128.8	128.4	130.8	132.0	137.7	141.6	140.0	140.6	140.0	130.9	124.3	117.8
1858	112.0	108.8	111.8	114.1	115.1	113.9	111.0	115.5	120.4	120.7	118.2	117.6
1859	120.7	123.3	126.6	126.2	128.8	128.6	120.7	117.6	115.8	119.0	118.9	118.7
1860	122.9	121.8	121.0	122.7	121.5	120.1	120.1	122.3	124.5	124.7	121.8	114.6
1861	115.0	112.8	113.5	113.5	110.9	107.5	101.0	98.3	97.4	101.9	101.9	99.0

Table 9—Imported Foods

Year	Jan.	Feb.	Mar.	Apr.	May	June	July	Aug.	Sept.	Oct.	Nov.	Dec.
1784	129.9	127.7	122.2	119.6	119.1	119.1	121.0	119.2	119.7	119.6	119.1	118.4
1785	112.2	111.4	110.1	106.5	105.2	102.6	106.0	110.0	109.7	112.3	114.0	114.6
1786	114.7	115.4	111.1	109.8	107.6	109.5	113.2	114.0	112.8	111.7	112.3	113.7
1787	113.6	114.0	112.0	110.3	106.2	110.1	109.2	108.6	110.9	109.9	111.7	110.7
1788	110.9	110.5	109.8	107.3	108.6	107.8	106.9	105.7	105.5	104.4	103.8	104.4
1789	102.8	101.4	99.8	99.6	103.7	104.0	102.2	101.1	101.4	102.6	103.8	106.4
1790	106.9	105.7	103.6	100.4	102.0	106.0	107.3	107.5	109.3	112.7	115.9	124.4
1791	129.8	127.9	123.8	121.7	126.3	126.0	123.2	121.0	122.4	138.2	136.2	135.3
1792	130.3	132.3	133.9	133.4	132.6	133.4	133.0	130.4	129.3	129.8	134.5	134.8
1793	133.2	133.3	138.3	133.7	133.0	132.2	132.2	133.9	135.0	129.6	129.9	129.3
1794	129.9	129.7	139.9	139.6								
1795	159.6	161.5	161.8	163.6	165.0	170.2	174.2	179.1	181.2	178.0	180.7	189.1
1796	190.3	181.7	175.5	182.3	178.4	174.2	174.0	172.3	171.3	176.6	171.1	175.1
1797	180.7	176.5	170.6	169.1	171.8	171.8	170.3	168.4	162.7	162.0	162.2	158.2
1798	153.4	151.0	151.3	150.5	150.3	149.8	153.2	153.0	152.4	152.2	152.0	
1799					156.1	159.8	159.8	154.8				
1800						154.2	154.3	149.7	152.9	154.2	151.9	147.2
1801	145.0	145.8	143.4	141.1	140.7	141.4	140.3	140.9	140.8	146.4	146.2	150.2
1802	146.8	143.6	137.9	138.6	134.6	135.4	133.0	132.9	133.0	137.0	136.5	134.8
1803	131.9	132.0	129.7	130.6	129.9	127.5	126.1	126.7	126.7	128.0	133.0	142.3
1804	142.0	139.6	140.9	140.6	139.4	139.1	141.9	142.1	141.8	141.0	144.1	145.7
1805	145.9	143.7	140.9	140.1	140.8	140.9	141.0	140.9	142.2	143.3	144.2	146.4
1806	145.2	138.2	135.9	132.6	139.3	138.9	139.1	136.5	137.2	138.9	138.1	133.1
1807	134.3	131.7	129.0	123.2	124.0	129.2	125.4	123.6	128.3	127.4	132.8	130.4
1808	129.6	129.4	131.3	132.1	134.3	134.6	135.1	135.7	135.5	135.9	138.6	152.8
1809	158.6	159.6	159.1	156.1	147.5	137.9	133.5	132.9	138.8	141.5	142.8	142.0
1810	137.7	135.3	129.5	130.4	129.0	128.6	133.6	130.4	135.8	137.2	134.3	135.2
1811	136.2	137.5	129.4	124.4	127.0	128.5	125.0	123.7	122.7	121.4	119.6	118.2
1812	122.4	124.0	122.2	121.5	124.8	127.1	158.1	163.8	166.4	163.6	160.4	159.5
1813	160.6	163.6	166.0	173.6	175.1	179.5	178.7	182.4	183.8	184.9	203.3	225.0
1814	222.4	222.7	217.4	204.5	205.3	213.7	212.9	208.3	206.7	227.6	231.5	226.7
1815	224.7	227.1	172.2	170.5	171.9	185.7	192.7	197.1	203.0	199.8	199.9	185.4
1816	184.4	182.3	160.3	159.0	155.4	155.4	152.8	148.2	145.6	147.6	141.5	140.0
1817	135.7	135.3	135.3	136.9	135.7	129.6	124.9	125.1	125.6	129.5	130.9	133.3
1818	137.6	137.1	135.3	133.9	136.7	135.7	134.3	134.0	135.0	138.2	136.8	136.2
1819	137.7	135.5	136.6	130.9	128.8	122.0	118.4	119.0	118.6	119.6	121.1	120.6
1820	119.9	118.9	112.5	106.3	104.9	101.2	101.7	101.3	102.0	102.2	106.3	109.3
1821	106.7	106.5	103.3	101.7	102.9	102.2	101.2	100.5	98.7	101.8	104.3	107.3
1822	105.1	105.1	104.9	106.4	102.7	103.9	102.1	101.7	101.3	100.4	103.5	100.9
1823	100.1	99.8	96.2	96.0	94.3	93.8	93.0	94.3	94.3	92.8	92.3	92.3
1824	91.8	90.7	90.9	91.6	90.3	90.3	90.2	91.7	94.3	92.9	93.2	93.4
1825	95.0	97.1	97.0	103.3	106.6	105.1	105.1	101.0	100.8	103.4	104.1	104.0
1826	100.9	98.7	95.9	95.7	97.3	95.2	91.8	94.0	95.4	96.4	94.4	93.8
1827	94.4	94.5	89.5	90.5	90.7	90.1	90.8	90.6	91.6	91.5	91.5	91.7
1828	91.0	89.5	88.2	87.0	86.5	85.7	86.9	89.6	93.3	91.6	93.2	89.1
1829	88.9	84.5	84.7	85.3	85.6	84.3	84.0	83.7	85.5	84.8	82.3	81.5
1830	78.8	77.4	76.0	78.8	78.5	78.3	78.7	84.8	84.0	82.2	81.2	80.2
1831	78.5	78.0	77.6	77.2	79.4	80.6	80.0	80.6	81.9	84.6	86.1	87.5
1832	86.8	85.5	85.0	83.3	85.7	82.8	83.7	80.4	81.8	83.3	84.4	84.7
1833	77.2	74.7	69.6	70.9	71.1	68.0	68.5	69.3	72.4	72.6	69.6	72.3
1834	71.4	70.6	70.2	67.7	67.1	66.5	65.8	67.3	65.9	65.9	66.5	67.1
1835	71.9	69.9	72.9	74.6	76.5	76.1	76.7	76.2	74.4	75.2	74.0	74.3
1836	74.3	74.8	76.1	77.4	76.3	73.9	74.3	74.9	74.4	74.7	73.8	72.0
1837	71.7	71.8	70.8	69.6	67.3	67.0	66.7	66.2	65.2	65.1	68.8	69.0
1838	68.3	67.3	67.5	66.3	66.5	65.7	66.8	68.2	68.3	68.1	67.4	66.4
1839	66.1	66.4	67.5	68.0	68.6	67.7	67.3	67.6	67.7	66.7	66.5	65.3
1840	65.4	63.9	62.5	62.9	62.1	61.0	60.2	60.7	63.8	64.3	65.4	67.5
1841	65.6	65.5	65.3	65.7	64.7	64.1	63.8	64.0	63.3	65.2	67.1	63.7
1842	62.5	61.5	60.5	58.9	58.7	58.6	58.1	58.3	59.6	64.4	63.8	61.8
1843	61.3	61.1	59.8	60.0	61.6	62.8	65.4	66.0	66.4	67.7	67.3	65.3
1844	66.1	66.5	66.5	67.7	69.3	68.8	69.9	69.1	69.4	69.5	68.8	69.2
1845	66.6	66.7	68.7	72.5	71.5	72.0	73.4	76.3	78.5	76.2	76.2	73.8
1846	73.0	72.9	74.1	72.6	71.5	70.5	70.3	69.7	70.7	71.3	72.6	69.9
1847	69.8	70.2	71.5	72.3	71.4	72.0	73.9	74.1	73.0	71.6	72.9	68.8
1848	68.7	67.4	67.1	66.5	65.0	64.5	63.8	63.6	62.0	63.6	61.8	60.6
1849	62.0	61.9	62.0	61.9	61.5	61.5	62.5	63.8	65.7	68.7	68.9	68.2
1850	68.2	69.9	71.2	69.3	69.5	69.4	70.1	72.6	74.9	75.2	73.5	71.2
1851	72.5	71.9	71.5	70.6	69.7	70.5	71.7	72.8	73.1	72.9	66.8	64.1
1852	63.9	63.8	62.2	60.0	61.4	66.0	65.7	65.5	68.9	68.9	67.1	68.2
1853	67.9	66.6	68.9	70.7	71.2	70.5	70.6	68.9	73.7	75.7	75.6	75.7
1854	76.2	76.4	76.5	74.5	74.8	74.3	73.2	76.3	75.0	77.3	71.7	70.5
1855	69.0	67.9	69.0	71.7	71.7	73.2	72.8	78.1	81.8	81.4	78.2	79.3
1856	79.5	80.5	81.0	79.5	78.7	79.8	83.7	83.4	83.4	85.9	87.4	88.5
1857	90.1	88.8	89.7	92.1	92.2	92.0	87.7	85.9	88.3	82.7	69.7	68.0
1858	63.9	61.9	64.7	65.9	66.5	66.9	67.2	68.4	68.5	66.8	65.3	62.9
1859	63.1	63.3	63.0	62.7	63.6	62.5	62.4	62.7	61.7	63.0	63.2	63.6
1860	61.4	61.3	62.0	61.0	61.6	64.2	65.8	68.3	68.5	68.5	64.5	61.6
1861	62.2	61.9	60.4	60.5	59.3	58.9	58.3	65.5	71.7	76.0	79.3	84.5

TABLE 10—LUMBER PRODUCTS AND NAVAL STORES

Year	Jan.	Feb.	Mar.	Apr.	May	June	July	Aug.	Sept.	Oct.	Nov.	Dec.
1784	109.5	106.9	105.0	102.2	101.5	101.1	98.9	98.9	104.7	105.9	106.1	104.8
1785	105.4	104.2	103.4	99.4	98.1	87.4	86.3	84.9	83.3	84.4	84.3	83.8
1786	83.4	83.2	83.2	80.5	63.5	61.6	62.1	62.1	62.5	61.8	61.6	63.5
1787	62.4	62.4	62.7	63.9	59.8	60.3	58.0	57.9	58.0	57.1	57.7	56.1
1788	56.9	56.9	55.5	54.2	54.2	54.1	53.7	54.7	55.4	57.9	60.4	63.3
1789	63.3	63.1	62.5	60.3	60.2	60.2	60.1	58.1	58.1	58.1	58.2	62.7
1790	62.2	62.2	62.2	60.7	61.3	61.7	62.8	69.2	70.9	73.1	73.7	78.3
1791	78.3	76.2	78.5	74.2	69.1	69.7	72.4	72.3	72.1	73.3	74.5	73.9
1792	69.6	69.6	69.6	70.3	70.3	70.5	71.0	71.2	70.0	76.0	78.7	78.7
1793	78.5	78.5	77.7	79.9	79.9	79.9	79.9	79.9	77.7	78.2	78.7	79.1
1794	79.1	79.1	79.1	79.1								
1795	110.3	110.3	110.3	110.3	110.3	102.6	102.6	111.6	114.7	126.9	125.9	125.9
1796	128.6	130.3	130.3	123.5	126.8	127.3	130.1	129.6	124.8	135.1	135.1	140.7
1797	144.1	152.7	150.4	137.5	137.1	122.1	127.4	124.8	124.8	124.8	124.8	124.8
1798	122.7	122.7	122.7	122.7	122.7	122.7	122.7	122.7	122.7	122.7	122.7	122.7
1799					102.6	102.3	102.3	102.3				
1800						117.3	115.3	112.9	116.5	116.4	114.3	120.9
1801	120.9	124.1	119.5	115.4	118.4	118.4	118.3	118.2	118.2	118.1	124.9	125.6
1802	125.1	122.0	121.9	118.4	109.6	104.0	104.0	104.0	106.6	118.9	121.4	122.7
1803	130.4	130.9	128.8	123.8	123.0	123.0	123.0	123.0	123.0	123.0	123.0	123.0
1804	123.0	123.0	123.0	125.8	127.5	127.7	127.7	127.7	128.9	128.6	128.6	126.4
1805	127.4	126.9	127.3	124.0	122.9	122.9	123.2	123.4	123.4	125.4	123.2	125.2
1806	118.6	118.2	117.0	115.0	115.0	112.0	111.5	112.0	112.0	112.0	117.0	116.1
1807	118.8	118.8	116.1	116.5	109.4	108.7	108.7	110.2	108.6	112.2	119.1	119.2
1808	119.2	117.4	114.7	114.7	114.6	114.6	108.2	107.4	110.1	112.2	115.0	115.0
1809	115.0	115.0	123.8	132.9	138.1	136.0	132.9	134.2	130.5	132.6	139.0	139.7
1810	139.6	140.4	142.9	140.9	144.0	138.5	137.4	134.9	135.1	132.9	133.8	135.8
1811	146.9	142.0	139.5	138.3	128.6	130.6	126.6	126.6	127.3	125.6	124.7	127.1
1812	126.7	128.8	123.3	121.7	116.5	116.5	112.3	112.3	121.1	119.4	124.5	121.1
1813	120.6	120.6	120.6	122.4	127.6	130.4	135.4	135.4	135.4	135.4	141.3	159.1
1814	186.1	177.3	189.8	188.9	188.0	173.7	167.1	167.1	167.1	171.5	168.9	176.5
1815	180.4	181.2	182.9	162.6	146.8	149.8	161.5	157.7	161.3	161.3	161.3	162.6
1816	164.7	164.6	164.2	156.9	139.0	148.4	143.0	140.9	130.6	130.6	131.3	131.8
1817	131.8	129.2	129.2	124.2	121.5	119.4	114.5	116.5	122.0	122.0	123.2	123.2
1818	127.0	127.6	123.7	123.4	124.7	125.8	123.8	126.6	128.0	125.9	129.4	128.5
1819	133.7	134.4	132.9	129.8	122.3	118.9	116.0	110.8	108.4	110.2	115.9	116.8
1820	116.3	116.3	113.9	113.9	111.5	110.2	109.4	105.5	105.0	102.9	101.8	101.1
1821	100.5	100.5	99.4	89.5	92.0	91.6	94.5	95.0	94.1	94.1	95.1	98.2
1822	100.9	100.9	102.0	101.7	108.6	103.8	104.3	104.3	101.4	100.2	99.7	100.2
1823	100.2	100.2	100.5	100.0	100.9	99.1	102.5	99.1	99.1	99.1	99.1	99.1
1824	99.9	100.9	99.3	99.5	96.9	95.5	95.7	97.2	97.2	97.2	96.8	96.8
1825	100.8	100.3	101.0	101.3	104.9	103.0	102.7	102.3	101.8	104.5	104.7	103.4
1826	102.1	101.7	99.5	98.8	97.3	97.0	96.3	97.5	97.0	95.7	95.3	96.3
1827	97.9	96.0	96.9	98.7	97.3	96.4	93.2	89.7	91.5	93.3	94.5	94.7
1828	95.6	95.4	95.3	95.3	97.4	97.9	97.1	96.6	95.4	95.4	95.9	96.8
1829	96.6	96.0	95.5	93.7	89.9	90.1	88.4	87.0	85.4	85.2	84.4	83.9
1830	84.1	82.2	82.8	82.2	79.6	79.5	79.5	79.9	79.8	80.0	80.2	80.2
1831	80.2	80.2	82.8	85.1	84.4	84.5	83.1	82.5	86.2	86.7	89.5	89.5
1832	89.5	89.9	89.8	85.9	86.5	85.5	85.5	85.1	85.3	86.2	89.0	89.5
1833	90.4	90.6	87.6	88.1	88.5	90.0	89.3	91.8	92.7	92.9	96.4	98.3
1834	98.7	97.4	95.5	93.5	90.9	92.5	92.5	91.4	91.4	90.7	94.1	95.3
1835	91.7	92.6	97.0	96.1	95.9	99.9	98.9	98.6	99.6	102.6	103.9	106.6
1836	105.4	105.4	105.3	107.1	109.2	105.2	100.1	99.1	99.2	100.3	109.7	109.8
1837	107.3	107.3	106.4	100.2	97.4	92.6	88.2	89.5	91.1	92.8	96.4	97.9
1838	98.1	95.2	94.2	91.2	89.9	90.6	93.0	93.3	93.8	95.9	94.8	96.6
1839	96.4	95.3	95.5	96.1	93.5	93.4	93.9	94.4	92.5	95.5	95.6	95.5
1840	95.5	95.5	94.7	92.1	89.5	88.1	87.8	87.3	87.0	86.5	87.1	88.7
1841	89.7	88.8	88.0	87.6	89.5	89.1	87.5	88.8	85.9	88.4	89.2	87.2
1842	88.2	88.0	87.4	82.5	82.6	80.9	81.0	81.9	80.7	79.9	80.6	80.5
1843	80.1	78.3	77.7	77.6	76.8	77.3	78.3	76.4	74.9	72.8	70.5	65.9
1844	66.2	65.1	65.1	73.5	70.5	71.6	70.9	71.0	71.0	70.6	73.4	70.6
1845	70.1	72.0	73.7	72.6	73.8	73.6	72.8	72.8	74.6	76.9	84.1	85.1
1846	83.7	85.7	85.7	83.9	79.2	76.7	74.6	73.1	70.7	72.7	75.5	74.4
1847	73.3	73.1	74.2	77.5	73.0	76.6	76.1	73.6	73.4	75.7	77.9	75.7
1848	75.2	73.2	74.2	71.4	69.4	70.9	68.5	69.0	73.5	74.1	73.3	76.0
1849	74.0	73.0	72.4	76.0	72.1	70.6	70.4	72.7	74.7	75.3	73.9	70.7
1850	70.6	73.8	77.2	76.3	78.8	77.5	76.5	76.5	79.3	84.8	84.7	88.3
1851	88.1	87.3	88.2	84.8	84.8	86.5	87.7	87.5	87.6	91.6	89.7	89.7
1852	89.1	90.3	90.0	88.5	91.0	91.2	90.9	93.0	96.3	96.9	97.4	98.5
1853	99.1	99.9	101.1	98.7	97.2	94.5	95.0	97.3	106.9	107.0	108.0	105.6
1854	103.9	106.5	109.0	109.9	112.6	113.2	112.3	112.6	113.9	112.3	108.2	107.4
1855	109.7	104.9	103.3	103.4	103.6	101.6	96.0	95.5	95.7	95.2	95.4	95.2
1856	94.6	94.8	94.6	92.5	92.0	90.4	90.0	91.7	90.4	92.0	93.0	92.7
1857	94.0	93.9	93.2	95.0	104.7	108.4	103.3	101.7	104.1	102.3	96.1	93.9
1858	92.1	93.1	95.1	96.5	98.0	97.6	98.5	99.4	96.3	97.7	99.9	100.0
1859	99.9	105.1	104.4	105.1	103.2	104.2	103.3	102.9	103.6	103.9	102.4	102.2
1860	100.2	101.2	101.4	101.0	101.1	100.2	99.9	99.3	99.3	99.5	98.4	97.8
1861	95.4	96.4	95.3	94.9	111.6	117.0	115.3	135.4	141.9	142.7	143.7	158.7

TABLE 11—INDUSTRIAL RAW AND SEMI-FINISHED COMMODITIES

Year	Jan.	Feb.	Mar.	Apr.	May	June	July	Aug.	Sept.	Oct.	Nov.	Dec.
1784	106.2	107.0	105.1	103.8	101.9	102.6	103.5	103.2	103.0	102.5	99.8	100.0
1785	99.5	100.2	100.4	99.8	100.3	99.4	100.5	100.9	100.5	99.8	98.3	98.2
1786	98.2	98.0	97.3	96.4	95.3	95.4	95.3	95.1	95.1	94.9	94.4	94.4
1787	94.3	94.6	94.4	94.1	94.3	93.6	94.1	93.6	92.6	91.8	93.0	92.7
1788	92.1	92.0	92.2	92.8	91.7	92.2	92.1	91.1	90.0	90.0	90.7	90.9
1789	91.3	91.4	90.5	90.4	90.8	90.9	91.7	91.3	91.1	90.7	91.1	91.2
1790	90.5	90.9	91.2	91.6	91.1	90.2	88.7	89.5	88.7	88.5	89.0	88.0
1791	87.8	87.6	87.4	87.2	86.6	86.8	87.3	87.7	88.0	87.3	86.8	86.8
1792	87.4	87.4	87.4	87.7	87.8	88.8	88.9	88.8	89.3	89.5	90.0	90.5
1793	90.3	90.3	90.4	91.2	90.8	91.2	91.6	91.9	92.4	92.5	93.3	92.6
1794	91.0	91.2	94.6	95.4								
1795	120.2	119.4	121.4	121.6	122.8	121.1	123.3	127.7	130.6	128.5	126.0	124.3
1796	126.1	123.6	126.1	124.5	124.4	121.6	122.6	122.7	126.3	127.9	128.2	128.3
1797	128.3	128.7	126.9	126.0	126.6	123.8	123.7	124.7	124.0	123.9	123.1	122.3
1798	119.5	119.3	119.5	118.8	121.4	122.0	126.6	127.8	128.4	129.3	132.2	
1799					133.8	133.8	133.6	131.0				
1800						130.6	127.7	127.7	127.5	130.6	131.8	131.7
1801	130.0	130.9	130.7	131.3	129.3	131.3	132.6	132.8	131.6	131.9	135.1	133.8
1802	132.7	131.3	130.0	126.2	124.6	123.1	122.3	122.4	123.2	124.5	125.2	119.2
1803	121.4	121.9	121.6	124.1	125.9	125.9	126.5	129.2	129.3	129.3	129.2	128.4
1804	128.8	131.5	131.3	133.2	132.8	132.6	131.8	128.6	128.7	129.7	131.5	131.6
1805	131.2	132.2	131.5	131.6	130.4	129.6	129.4	130.2	130.9	130.7	130.8	131.5
1806	137.6	137.0	137.0	136.2	134.2	132.1	133.9	133.8	134.1	133.4	135.2	137.0
1807	136.3	136.1	137.0	135.1	133.8	132.3	131.1	131.3	133.4	132.2	133.9	133.1
1808	131.4	133.2	133.3	134.6	134.5	134.0	135.1	135.5	136.2	135.6	139.1	146.5
1809	153.4	152.9	155.1	157.0	146.9	144.8	134.6	136.1	140.8	143.8	148.5	150.5
1810	149.8	151.3	151.9	152.3	154.2	149.2	150.5	149.7	149.2	151.3	151.0	149.9
1811	149.2	148.7	147.8	147.5	146.3	143.8	143.3	146.2	144.3	142.9	142.4	143.4
1812	141.2	141.2	142.1	142.0	144.4	149.5	172.7	175.9	171.2	169.6	169.1	169.1
1813	170.5	170.5	172.2	172.8	172.6	174.2	174.4	175.0	176.0	176.5	183.1	201.8
1814	225.2	219.2	217.0	209.2	199.6	199.7	195.8	196.7	197.3	205.4	218.7	214.3
1815	215.3	213.8	176.1	169.1	165.1	152.5	155.4	156.9	160.8	164.6	169.0	163.0
1816	159.8	157.9	155.5	152.7	146.0	141.2	136.5	133.9	129.7	128.2	125.0	124.3
1817	123.7	123.4	122.0	118.1	117.7	114.0	113.1	113.4	114.4	113.8	113.8	116.5
1818	116.4	118.3	120.1	119.3	118.2	117.1	117.1	116.0	115.7	116.7	117.2	117.3
1819	117.2	116.4	115.8	114.1	110.7	109.0	106.6	106.2	103.8	102.1	102.2	103.3
1820	103.0	103.1	102.1	101.7	101.6	100.7	100.9	101.6	101.6	101.5	101.5	101.6
1821	102.1	101.5	102.4	100.7	101.0	100.9	100.8	101.7	101.2	101.7	102.9	103.1
1822	103.3	103.4	103.1	102.2	102.1	102.2	102.0	101.6	102.9	102.0	100.3	99.7
1823	99.3	99.0	98.3	97.2	97.8	97.4	97.3	97.7	97.2	97.2	95.2	95.2
1824	95.2	95.8	95.6	95.3	94.8	95.8	95.9	95.2	95.1	95.5	95.2	95.3
1825	96.7	97.0	97.9	100.4	103.3	102.4	102.4	100.6	101.5	101.7	102.5	102.1
1826	102.1	101.1	99.9	99.6	98.3	96.2	96.0	94.6	94.0	94.0	94.6	94.6
1827	95.8	96.3	95.7	95.2	93.8	93.0	92.9	92.5	92.6	94.2	94.0	94.0
1828	93.7	93.2	93.2	92.1	91.2	90.3	90.8	90.9	90.7	91.0	91.1	91.8
1829	92.7	93.3	92.7	91.3	89.2	88.9	88.0	88.1	87.8	88.5	88.2	88.3
1830	86.7	86.9	86.7	85.4	84.1	84.4	83.9	84.3	83.9	84.5	84.9	86.6
1831	86.3	86.4	86.7	86.3	89.4	88.7	89.0	90.2	89.2	89.5	89.5	90.1
1832	90.6	90.5	89.3	88.6	88.1	87.7	87.5	87.5	88.3	88.6	88.4	88.1
1833	88.7	88.8	89.4	88.4	88.6	88.8	89.0	89.9	91.8	91.4	91.2	91.9
1834	91.1	90.8	90.0	89.8	89.8	89.7	89.7	89.0	89.0	89.2	90.3	90.7
1835	89.1	88.6	89.8	90.7	89.8	90.0	89.3	89.7	88.6	88.9	90.6	91.1
1836	93.2	93.8	95.7	97.0	97.2	96.1	95.3	96.8	97.8	100.0	101.1	101.3
1837	102.0	102.2	102.7	100.6	97.8	97.0	94.8	93.8	93.4	93.2	93.2	93.0
1838	93.7	93.7	93.3	92.5	91.8	90.9	90.5	94.2	95.3	98.0	98.5	99.2
1839	99.7	99.8	101.4	101.2	100.7	99.6	99.0	99.0	98.1	97.1	97.2	96.9
1840	96.2	95.9	94.8	94.2	92.7	92.5	92.3	91.4	91.7	91.3	91.5	91.6
1841	91.4	91.6	91.4	90.7	89.7	89.8	89.9	90.0	90.3	91.4	91.1	91.0
1842	91.2	91.1	90.3	88.5	87.8	86.4	85.4	86.1	85.7	84.8	84.4	84.0
1843	84.0	83.6	83.1	82.5	81.6	81.0	81.1	81.3	79.8	80.0	80.7	81.1
1844	81.4	81.7	81.8	82.3	81.9	81.4	81.6	83.1	82.9	83.6	83.2	82.3
1845	80.7	80.4	80.6	82.3	81.8	81.3	81.3	80.8	80.9	81.4	82.3	81.8
1846	81.7	81.8	82.0	82.6	81.6	81.0	80.4	80.0	79.1	78.7	79.8	80.2
1847	81.1	81.4	82.9	82.1	82.3	82.3	81.8	82.2	82.6	83.4	83.8	83.3
1848	83.6	83.0	82.5	82.1	81.3	79.4	79.5	79.5	79.3	78.5	78.6	78.1
1849	77.8	78.5	78.1	78.5	76.9	77.7	77.6	77.7	78.6	78.0	78.2	78.2
1850	78.4	79.2	79.9	80.6	80.8	80.1	80.3	79.8	79.6	80.2	80.4	80.5
1851	80.5	80.1	79.7	80.0	79.0	77.9	77.7	78.0	78.1	78.2	77.9	78.0
1852	77.8	77.8	78.3	77.9	77.9	76.1	76.4	76.9	77.3	79.1	79.8	81.6
1853	83.0	86.8	87.7	87.5	87.5	85.5	85.5	85.9	86.1	87.3	88.0	89.0
1854	89.4	90.8	91.7	92.2	93.1	91.7	91.8	92.1	92.4	92.3	93.1	92.6
1855	91.8	92.2	91.9	89.4	89.4	89.5	90.0	90.6	92.7	95.8	96.0	95.3
1856	96.1	95.4	93.7	94.4	93.7	93.0	92.4	91.8	92.6	92.8	92.9	92.3
1857	92.0	92.9	93.2	94.5	96.2	94.7	94.5	95.5	95.3	93.6	90.9	89.5
1858	86.9	85.8	86.4	87.3	87.2	85.8	86.6	87.3	87.2	87.3	86.5	86.6
1859	86.3	87.2	88.0	88.6	89.2	88.6	87.4	86.5	85.9	85.2	85.3	86.0
1860	85.2	86.7	87.5	87.4	86.7	86.6	86.8	87.5	87.4	87.3	87.3	86.6
1861	84.9	83.1	83.3	83.5	82.3	80.6	79.9	80.3	80.5	81.0	82.8	85.1

Table 12—Industrial Commodities Ready for Consumption

Year	Jan.	Feb.	Mar.	Apr.	May	June	July	Aug.	Sept.	Oct.	Nov.	Dec.
1784	89.0	90.2	90.0	88.3	83.9	84.8	86.6	87.2	86.6	88.2	85.8	82.6
1785	81.7	79.4	80.4	79.9	76.9	76.2	76.9	76.2	75.9	76.9	77.4	77.6
1786	78.4	79.0	78.8	77.4	78.4	77.4	77.6	77.5	78.7	79.4	79.5	80.3
1787	80.9	81.8	82.2	82.1	80.9	80.1	79.9	80.5	79.2	79.7	80.5	80.4
1788	79.8	79.2	79.2	76.6	76.8	76.6	76.2	75.9	75.8	75.3	74.7	74.0
1789	74.0	73.6	75.2	75.3	77.8	77.7	78.1	78.0	78.0	78.3	78.3	79.2
1790	79.5	79.6	79.5	77.5	77.4	78.3	78.2	77.2	77.0	79.9	81.5	82.4
1791	82.2	85.7	84.5	83.9	85.0	86.4	86.7	88.0	87.4	88.9	88.7	88.5
1792	88.0	87.8	88.8	89.6	89.6	89.9	90.3	90.1	91.4	90.3	92.4	95.3
1793	93.9	93.9	95.2	91.9	92.4	94.1	93.6	93.7	94.5	94.8	95.7	96.5
1794	106.2	106.3	115.2	115.2								
1795	129.7	130.6	130.0	135.9	137.7	138.6	139.0	137.6	137.7	143.6	147.6	151.6
1796	155.3	155.7	157.3	153.1	152.7	156.6	153.4	151.1	148.0	148.1	144.2	144.2
1797	144.9	144.1	142.6	136.9	138.6	136.2	135.6	133.9	132.0	133.7	131.5	130.5
1798	131.7	132.2	132.9	133.6	134.0	136.8	135.9	135.3	134.8	134.8	134.8	
1799					135.6	134.3	133.8	131.4				
1800						127.3	126.1	124.4	127.1	127.5	131.5	131.8
1801	131.3	133.2	133.5	132.6	131.3	131.3	130.9	129.2	128.5	129.0	128.6	129.2
1802	126.9	125.8	120.8	119.3	120.8	121.0	120.0	120.1	121.0	119.4	119.8	118.6
1803	118.5	117.6	116.0	117.6	118.3	117.7	117.6	118.2	119.9	120.6	121.6	120.6
1804	125.1	127.5	126.7	125.6	123.9	123.6	124.0	124.1	125.6	127.8	129.3	131.9
1805	133.1	134.8	133.3	133.5	133.2	132.9	133.1	132.6	132.6	133.0	132.5	133.0
1806	129.7	129.2	129.4	128.1	128.9	126.7	125.8	124.6	125.1	123.8	122.5	122.5
1807	122.5	122.3	122.0	121.1	119.7	119.3	120.2	119.2	120.5	120.1	120.3	120.4
1808	124.1	125.6	125.6	124.1	123.3	123.5	124.5	125.8	125.3	127.4	129.2	144.6
1809	143.9	146.1	149.5	146.7	144.7	131.6	134.5	133.7	141.0	142.8	142.8	146.7
1810	145.0	138.6	138.0	136.6	138.3	138.0	138.6	139.2	138.0	139.8	137.8	135.9
1811	136.6	136.6	134.0	132.7	132.9	134.0	134.6	134.6	138.8	138.0	134.1	134.8
1812	135.9	135.9	135.9	136.3	138.5	138.7	154.4	158.8	158.2	156.1	154.2	154.8
1813	156.8	157.0	157.3	171.3	171.1	173.5	175.1	175.9	176.2	177.2	185.1	198.0
1814	215.1	205.6	201.1	191.0	180.9	185.6	186.5	183.9	189.3	205.0	220.7	216.9
1815	217.0	214.7	178.1	165.7	162.4	160.0	159.4	158.0	161.8	164.8	164.0	157.1
1816	159.2	158.6	153.5	151.2	146.6	144.2	143.4	140.1	139.2	134.6	134.3	133.4
1817	133.7	131.8	134.3	133.7	129.5	126.6	126.7	126.4	124.8	123.7	125.2	126.5
1818	126.5	128.3	128.5	128.8	128.6	126.7	124.8	124.2	124.9	127.0	127.0	126.1
1819	128.3	127.4	125.2	122.2	120.7	120.8	114.3	114.4	112.8	112.7	115.1	115.4
1820	115.0	114.6	113.8	112.0	110.9	110.3	110.6	110.4	110.4	111.2	110.8	110.4
1821	109.8	109.9	110.1	108.9	109.2	108.9	109.1	108.8	108.3	108.9	108.9	109.9
1822	109.5	109.7	109.3	107.8	104.9	103.9	103.1	102.6	102.1	101.9	101.5	100.7
1823	101.0	100.8	99.2	99.1	99.3	99.0	98.7	98.4	98.4	98.7	98.1	97.3
1824	97.0	96.6	95.6	95.7	94.7	94.3	94.3	93.1	91.8	90.6	90.9	90.2
1825	89.3	89.5	89.0	91.3	92.7	91.7	91.6	91.5	92.0	92.4	91.7	92.2
1826	92.3	92.0	91.3	90.5	89.3	89.4	88.6	88.1	87.9	87.3	87.0	87.4
1827	88.1	88.0	88.5	89.6	90.5	89.8	89.0	88.5	88.4	88.5	88.8	89.4
1828	89.1	88.4	87.9	86.8	86.8	87.3	87.3	87.8	87.7	87.5	88.6	88.9
1829	88.8	88.7	88.7	87.1	87.0	86.6	85.6	85.4	85.1	87.0	86.8	85.8
1830	85.6	85.4	84.5	83.0	82.5	81.9	81.6	80.6	80.8	81.4	81.4	82.4
1831	81.4	83.4	83.2	84.0	85.1	84.4	83.6	83.9	84.9	87.5	88.1	88.0
1832	88.4	87.5	87.3	86.4	87.1	86.8	86.6	86.8	87.3	88.4	87.8	88.5
1833	87.6	86.8	87.4	87.0	85.2	84.9	84.9	84.8	84.6	85.0	84.9	84.2
1834	84.1	84.0	82.7	80.8	80.5	79.9	80.0	80.0	80.5	80.7	80.8	81.2
1835	82.5	81.7	82.3	82.9	84.1	83.6	83.9	84.4	84.6	84.0	83.7	84.3
1836	85.9	85.5	85.7	88.1	88.8	88.4	88.3	88.6	90.7	90.7	90.3	91.3
1837	94.7	94.2	94.6	95.1	94.0	92.1	91.1	90.0	89.2	89.7	91.3	91.6
1838	91.5	91.1	90.1	90.0	89.5	88.7	88.3	88.6	88.1	89.0	89.2	89.7
1839	89.7	89.4	89.4	90.7	90.6	91.3	91.3	91.3	91.2	90.4	90.3	89.8
1840	89.2	88.7	86.4	87.0	86.3	85.3	84.2	83.5	82.4	82.9	82.6	82.6
1841	83.3	82.8	82.7	82.6	81.6	81.2	80.7	81.0	81.0	81.5	80.9	81.9
1842	82.2	81.0	80.4	77.3	75.4	75.4	75.8	75.6	76.7	76.4	76.1	76.1
1843	75.3	75.0	74.5	74.2	74.3	74.4	74.3	74.1	73.0	73.4	73.5	73.8
1844	73.8	73.7	74.7	75.3	74.8	74.0	73.9	73.4	73.9	74.1	74.2	74.2
1845	74.1	73.7	73.7	75.0	74.7	74.2	73.8	74.0	74.3	75.5	75.8	76.9
1846	77.1	76.6	77.0	76.5	76.2	75.8	75.0	74.8	74.4	75.0	77.5	76.3
1847	75.9	76.9	78.0	77.4	76.6	77.6	77.2	76.6	78.0	78.5	79.0	78.5
1848	79.2	78.0	77.5	76.7	75.6	75.1	74.5	74.2	74.9	74.9	74.9	74.6
1849	74.5	74.2	74.0	72.8	72.3	72.4	72.0	72.5	72.9	72.9	72.8	73.2
1850	72.9	73.6	72.8	72.2	71.9	71.8	72.2	72.3	72.5	73.0	73.5	73.5
1851	73.4	73.3	72.5	71.9	71.7	71.6	71.5	72.3	70.6	70.1	69.6	69.7
1852	69.4	69.7	69.5	69.9	70.0	70.0	70.2	69.7	70.7	71.9	72.5	73.8
1853	73.9	76.5	76.3	77.4	77.2	76.5	75.8	76.4	77.1	78.6	78.9	80.4
1854	81.0	84.2	84.5	85.0	87.9	90.1	90.4	90.8	92.2	92.3	92.0	92.2
1855	93.5	93.9	93.9	93.6	93.5	92.5	91.9	92.5	93.1	94.2	93.5	95.2
1856	94.2	94.1	94.2	94.5	94.0	94.0	93.2	93.2	91.6	91.8	92.5	90.7
1857	91.8	92.4	92.4	92.3	90.9	91.3	90.2	90.0	89.8	88.7	88.7	86.0
1858	84.1	84.2	84.2	83.7	83.9	82.7	82.2	82.2	82.3	82.1	81.4	80.8
1859	81.0	81.4	81.3	80.7	80.2	79.5	79.0	79.0	77.7	78.1	77.4	77.8
1860	77.9	77.0	77.8	77.2	76.9	76.9	78.0	77.9	78.7	78.5	78.6	77.4
1861	76.4	76.3	75.3	75.6	74.2	73.4	73.7	76.0	76.3	77.9	78.6	79.4

TABLE 13—FISH

Year	Jan.	Feb.	Mar.	Apr.	May	June	July	Aug.	Sept.	Oct.	Nov.	Dec.
1784	125.7	126.3	135.1	136.6	124.2	128.7	127.5	126.2	126.1	126.0	125.3	123.5
1785	121.9	122.6	123.1	121.2	119.0	123.0	123.0	123.0	123.0	123.0	123.0	116.2
1786	116.2	116.2	116.2	116.2	118.6	118.6	118.6	118.6	118.6	118.6	118.6	118.6
1787	118.6	118.6	118.6	118.6	118.6	118.6	118.6	118.6	111.1	111.1	111.1	111.1
1788	111.1	111.1	111.1	110.2	111.1	107.1	103.0	93.7	93.7	93.7	95.1	99.4
1789	99.4	99.4	99.3	99.3	99.3	108.9	108.9	105.6	105.6	105.6	104.5	105.2
1790	105.2	105.1	105.1	105.1	105.1	105.1	105.1	102.4	105.8	108.0	105.9	107.4
1791	109.8	113.3	114.2	123.4	123.4	118.6	112.1	110.6	118.5	116.9	117.1	123.8
1792	120.7	120.7	120.7	120.7	120.7	120.7	110.5	110.5	108.1	113.5	113.1	113.1
1793	113.1	113.1	113.1	113.4	113.4	113.4	113.4	110.8	115.3	115.3	115.3	115.3
1794	115.3	115.3	115.3	115.3								
1795	217.8	217.1	214.7	214.0	208.9	206.7	194.3	182.7	182.7	187.8	187.4	186.0
1796	192.0	192.0	192.0	211.6	211.6	222.7	223.6	223.6	212.4	220.9	220.9	199.8
1797	246.2	246.2	252.0	248.7	248.7	248.7	226.9	198.3	198.3	198.9	199.5	200.1
1798	178.7	178.5	214.1	209.8	209.4	189.4	181.5	173.0	172.7	172.4	187.8	
1799					131.5	131.3	131.1	164.8				
1800						103.9	103.9	103.9	141.3	148.4	148.4	152.4
1801	152.4	155.1	155.1	159.6	159.5	168.4	162.9	170.2	186.5	189.2	181.1	185.4
1802	189.5	189.4	189.2	174.0	173.9	173.8	150.4	150.3	152.7	151.4	153.6	145.4
1803	145.3	145.2	145.1	145.0	144.9	144.8	142.2	128.2	128.3	128.2	128.1	128.0
1804	127.9	133.6	146.2	146.1	146.0	145.9	159.7	159.6	151.0	148.2	153.3	153.3
1805	153.3	163.9	163.9	163.9	163.9	163.9	163.9	163.9	163.9	163.9	163.9	163.9
1806	161.8	167.6	167.6	167.6	164.5	164.7	164.9	184.3	181.4	181.4	176.9	176.9
1807	179.5	181.1	181.1	175.7	176.0	162.5	160.7	155.7	153.6	161.7	162.2	159.9
1808	158.5	140.3	139.7	114.8	114.3	113.8	113.3	112.8	121.8	130.3	134.0	134.0
1809	133.8	133.8	133.8	139.9	137.4	137.4	135.8	135.8	137.9	138.8	138.8	138.8
1810	138.8	138.8	138.8	138.8	138.8	138.8	138.8	138.8	138.8	138.8	144.9	149.1
1811	161.6	161.5	164.2	164.2	164.2	158.9	158.9	150.2	142.8	144.6	157.2	157.2
1812	160.6	161.4	161.4	161.4	160.0	161.4	161.4	163.8	163.8	175.2	175.7	170.3
1813	170.7	170.7	170.7	176.0	176.0	176.0	176.0	176.0	176.0	176.0	176.0	176.0
1814	229.0	230.5	220.6	200.9	188.0	193.9	193.9	267.7	261.2	244.8	244.8	244.5
1815	244.1	243.7	211.9	205.7	195.2	195.2	208.9	189.1	207.1	240.7	247.1	247.1
1816	228.3	228.3	205.8	218.1	218.1	212.6	200.8	180.9	185.6	165.1	161.0	153.5
1817	154.7	153.0	162.6	169.8	169.8	154.6	154.6	143.1	143.8	149.1	150.5	150.5
1818	150.5	154.0	162.5	172.8	166.7	166.7	166.7	161.4	159.4	170.0	169.0	169.5
1819	168.0	176.8	171.6	165.0	147.4	133.8	123.4	111.3	110.8	113.2	112.0	116.7
1820	113.3	113.3	113.3	112.6	111.9	112.6	105.5	103.8	105.1	105.1	102.4	102.4
1821	97.5	97.5	96.7	96.7	96.7	96.4	96.4	94.8	95.4	100.1	113.6	106.7
1822	108.3	108.3	108.2	104.5	104.5	107.7	104.5	103.5	109.2	110.3	104.5	104.5
1823	102.2	103.4	103.1	103.4	106.2	112.0	112.0	105.0	99.2	101.3	103.0	106.4
1824	106.9	109.6	106.6	105.6	105.0	103.4	102.7	98.8	87.0	88.8	87.8	89.4
1825	89.4	90.1	94.2	98.0	96.6	91.8	86.4	79.6	82.8	85.9	88.3	85.5
1826	85.1	84.7	85.2	84.4	85.2	81.5	82.1	81.6	80.8	85.2	85.6	85.7
1827	85.2	86.5	89.6	104.5	102.3	94.0	93.6	97.6	94.7	97.8	98.3	96.8
1828	97.5	98.8	97.8	96.9	99.1	102.0	96.8	92.9	91.7	93.1	93.5	95.2
1829	95.8	97.7	98.4	99.3	92.7	91.7	84.4	86.2	84.5	87.9	88.6	87.3
1830	87.1	87.8	88.0	86.0	88.2	86.2	83.9	81.8	86.2	93.0	92.7	93.5
1831	97.2	98.0	98.2	103.0	102.7	99.6	99.4	100.2	90.8	91.5	92.3	91.9
1832	91.9	93.2	90.9	86.3	86.6	81.9	77.7	75.3	85.1	83.6	89.7	91.7
1833	90.1	91.3	92.1	92.1	93.1	97.2	92.2	93.3	93.8	91.1	92.9	94.9
1834	93.1	88.7	88.4	88.3	91.0	88.9	89.3	90.7	90.0	91.5	97.5	101.5
1835	103.7	104.4	108.4	112.6	109.2	112.0	109.8	113.3	114.9	115.9	115.1	116.2
1836	116.2	122.6	135.8	144.8	141.2	127.1	110.5	111.1	108.0	114.7	131.7	127.4
1837	127.8	129.3	130.7	130.7	119.8	117.8	117.2	110.8	110.5	116.7	113.7	117.1
1838	118.5	118.7	118.7	116.0	118.0	124.8	132.2	138.4	136.1	138.4	150.6	152.9
1839	156.0	157.3	187.4	187.7	186.3	190.1	183.2	168.7	170.9	179.2	178.4	178.7
1840	179.1	179.1	168.1	154.3	128.2	124.5	106.8	110.0	113.3	130.2	133.7	135.6
1841	134.3	135.3	135.3	134.7	134.9	129.3	125.5	123.2	136.9	138.2	125.5	125.6
1842	122.4	121.5	121.3	114.9	110.0	107.4	105.0	101.2	101.2	104.2	103.5	95.1
1843	93.2	93.2	96.0	96.0	102.9	110.9	111.9	110.8	122.4	115.1	117.4	119.3
1844	124.9	128.6	128.4	128.4	127.9	125.8	122.8	126.1	123.5	123.3	128.2	129.8
1845	131.3	131.6	129.8	131.3	130.6	129.3	129.4	131.7	127.7	121.9	115.8	120.8
1846	126.3	127.5	123.8	118.4	122.3	114.4	118.3	121.0	118.2	117.3	117.4	114.7
1847	114.7	118.8	124.4	124.1	125.4	124.6	120.7	120.9	130.5	122.0	123.5	124.0
1848	126.6	126.5	129.8	129.4	125.3	129.5	125.0	128.5	101.1	104.2	94.1	97.1
1849	90.0	97.4	103.5	92.1	94.9	100.0	100.2	103.6	102.9	101.8	125.0	132.2
1850	129.8	134.0	125.8	127.5	128.2	121.4	117.5	120.8	126.6	124.8	126.9	128.3
1851	125.0	124.0	123.8	117.6	112.5	113.2	114.9	114.9	122.7	119.2	117.6	115.0
1852	116.8	118.3	126.7	132.2	148.7	146.8	141.0	143.2	137.4	126.2	142.5	142.3
1853	142.3	153.9	154.2	137.1	138.8	138.0	138.2	138.1	135.9	151.9	162.0	162.5
1854	160.8	155.2	157.3	157.1	151.8	154.2	152.4	151.1	163.1	162.8	155.7	155.7
1855	152.4	156.4	154.2	152.6	154.8	146.6	142.3	145.5	145.7	147.3	169.0	166.7
1856	166.7	181.9	180.1	160.5	152.3	153.4	146.0	133.2	154.8	152.8	145.2	152.0
1857	152.1	167.5	166.0	148.3	163.5	182.5	163.6	157.6	173.1	167.1	155.7	139.2
1858	132.7	132.9	139.3	137.2	141.0	134.1	115.9	116.8	138.4	139.6	143.4	162.3
1859	152.0	151.2	155.5	147.5	152.7	154.0	143.3	157.7	153.1	156.9	153.0	148.8
1860	148.7	156.3	165.7	156.8	164.2	145.9	138.5	149.7	139.8	145.2	147.3	145.0
1861	143.8	145.4	144.5	130.2	116.4	112.7	102.5	100.6	100.3	102.6	101.8	111.9

TABLE 14—FURS

Year	Jan.	Feb.	Mar.	Apr.	May	June	July	Aug.	Sept.	Oct.	Nov.	Dec.
1784	78.9	78.9	71.2	72.8	73.9	75.0	76.1	77.2	78.3	79.4	80.4	80.4
1785	80.4	80.4	80.4	73.6	68.7	68.7	68.7	66.7	66.7	71.2	71.2	71.2
1786	71.2	70.8	70.0	70.0	63.4	63.1	62.9	62.6	62.6	62.5	62.5	62.5
1787	62.5	62.4	62.4	52.2	52.1	52.1	52.1	52.0	52.0	52.0	55.2	55.2
1788	52.2	51.5	52.6	52.7	52.8	52.9	53.0	53.0	53.0	53.2	53.2	53.2
1789	53.2	53.2	53.1	53.1	53.1	53.1	53.1	53.1	61.9	61.9	61.9	55.6
1790	55.6	55.6	55.6	55.6	58.9	58.9	61.1	61.1	61.1	61.1	60.1	60.1
1791	60.1	55.8	55.8	57.7	57.7	57.7	57.7	57.7	57.7	57.7	57.7	57.7
1792	62.2	62.2	62.2	62.2	62.2	62.2	62.2	62.2	62.2	62.2	62.2	62.2
1793	64.5	64.5	64.5	64.5	64.5	64.5	64.5	64.5	56.4	56.4	56.4	56.4
1794	56.4	56.4	56.4	56.1								
1795	67.1	67.1	67.1	67.1	67.1	75.4	75.4	67.1	67.1	72.3	72.3	72.3
1796	78.9	78.9	78.3	78.3	77.6	90.9	91.1	91.1	91.1	86.9	88.3	92.8
1797	92.8	74.6	74.6	74.6	74.6	74.6	74.6	74.6	71.2	71.2	71.2	71.2
1798	56.4	56.4	56.4	56.4	56.4	67.9	56.3	56.3	56.3	56.3	56.3	
1799					58.9	59.9	59.9	59.9				
1800						78.9	78.9	76.8	76.8	76.8	76.8	76.8
1801	76.8	76.8	76.8	78.3	78.3	78.3	78.3	78.3	78.3	78.3	78.3	73.7
1802	73.7	73.7	73.7	73.7	70.6	70.6	70.6	70.6	70.6	73.7	73.7	72.9
1803	72.9	72.9	72.9	72.9	72.9	72.9	72.9	72.9	72.9	72.9	72.9	72.9
1804	72.9	72.9	72.9	89.1	89.1	89.1	89.1	89.1	89.1	89.1	89.1	89.1
1805	89.1	89.1	89.1	89.1	89.1	75.5	75.5	75.5	75.5	75.5	75.5	75.5
1806	74.3	74.3	74.3	74.3	74.3	74.3	74.3	74.3	76.3	76.3	76.3	76.3
1807	76.3	76.3	76.3	84.9	84.9	83.1	83.1	83.1	83.1	86.1	86.1	86.1
1808	86.1	86.1	86.1	74.1	74.1	74.1	74.1	74.1	77.4	77.4	77.4	77.4
1809	77.4	84.8	84.8	84.8	84.8	84.8	84.8	84.8	83.5	83.5	83.5	83.5
1810	83.5	83.5	89.2	89.2	89.2	89.2	94.4	94.4	94.4	93.1	93.1	93.1
1811	93.1	93.1	97.9	97.9	95.3	100.3	100.3	100.3	100.3	100.3	97.1	95.5
1812	95.5	96.7	96.7	96.7	96.7	96.7	90.0	90.0	90.7	90.7	90.7	90.7
1813	90.7	90.7	90.7	90.7	90.7	90.7	90.7	90.7	90.7	90.7	90.7	90.7
1814	85.6	87.9	87.9	87.9	90.1	90.1	87.6	87.6	87.6	87.6	97.5	95.8
1815	95.8	110.9	110.9	108.3	108.3	108.3	108.3	114.6	116.6	116.6	116.6	116.6
1816	116.6	110.3	110.3	110.3	110.3	110.3	106.4	106.4	106.4	106.4	95.2	92.6
1817	92.6	92.6	92.6	92.6	92.6	92.6	100.9	100.9	100.9	87.9	87.9	87.9
1818	87.9	87.9	87.9	88.7	88.7	88.7	88.7	71.7	71.7	71.7	71.7	71.7
1819	71.7	71.7	71.7	81.2	81.2	73.8	73.8	73.8	73.8	73.8	73.8	73.8
1820	73.8	73.8	73.8	73.8	73.8	73.8	73.8	73.8	68.9	68.9	74.8	74.8
1821	74.8	74.8	77.3	77.3	77.3	77.3	77.3	77.3	77.3	77.3	109.3	109.3
1822	109.3	109.3	109.3	109.3	101.0	101.0	101.0	101.0	101.0	101.0	101.0	101.0
1823	101.0	101.0	101.0	101.0	101.0	101.0	101.0	101.0	101.0	101.0	101.0	101.0
1824	101.0	101.0	101.0	101.0	101.0	101.0	101.0	101.0	97.9	97.9	92.1	92.1
1825	92.1	98.3	98.3	98.3	116.7	116.7	115.0	120.4	120.4	120.3	120.2	120.1
1826	120.0	105.2	109.8	106.4	105.5	105.4	94.7	88.5	90.5	93.5	93.0	92.9
1827	92.8	92.8	92.7	92.6	97.6	96.5	89.1	89.1	89.1	89.1	96.7	96.7
1828	98.1	98.1	98.1	96.0	101.2	101.2	101.2	105.6	105.6	103.2	103.2	103.2
1829	103.2	103.2	103.2	103.2	103.2	99.0	93.8	93.8	93.8	90.6	90.6	90.6
1830	90.6	90.6	90.6	84.9	84.9	84.9	84.9	84.9	84.9	79.8	79.8	79.8
1831	79.8	79.8	79.8	82.9	82.9	90.1	90.1	90.1	90.1	91.9	91.9	91.9
1832	91.9	91.9	91.9	83.0	83.0	83.0	83.0	83.0	83.0	83.0	80.5	80.5
1833	80.5	80.4	80.4	80.4	87.8	87.8	87.8	87.8	87.8	87.8	87.8	86.6
1834	89.3	89.3	89.3	89.3	89.3	89.3	89.3	89.3	89.3	89.3	89.3	78.2
1835	79.4	81.2	81.2	81.6	84.1	84.4	84.4	84.4	84.4	84.4	84.4	84.1
1836	85.7	85.7	90.2	92.3	94.0	94.0	94.0	94.0	94.0	94.0	94.0	94.0
1837	94.0	95.5	96.1	88.1	90.4	86.4	86.4	86.4	86.4	84.6	84.6	84.6
1838	84.6	84.6	84.6	59.9	60.1	60.1	60.1	60.1	60.1	54.2	56.7	56.7
1839	56.7	56.7	56.7	71.5	75.9	77.3	77.3	77.3	77.3	77.3	77.3	77.3
1840	77.3	78.3	78.3	78.3	72.7	71.9	72.2	72.2	72.2	72.2	72.2	72.2
1841	72.2	72.2	72.2	72.2	72.2	74.0	73.5	73.0	65.0	65.0	65.0	65.0
1842	65.0	65.0	65.0	65.0	60.5	59.3	59.3	59.3	59.3	58.3	58.3	58.3
1843	58.3	45.0	45.0	45.0	43.4	44.0	44.0	43.8	43.8	43.8	43.8	43.8
1844	44.9	44.9	44.9	44.9	49.8	63.1	63.1	63.1	63.1	63.1	63.1	63.1
1845	62.3	62.3	60.7	65.0	66.9	66.9	66.9	66.9	66.9	66.9	66.9	66.9
1846	66.9	66.9	66.9	66.9	66.0	65.7	63.8	62.1	62.1	62.1	62.1	62.1
1847	62.1	62.1	55.7	55.7	56.8	56.3	56.0	56.0	56.0	56.0	56.0	56.0
1848	56.0	56.0	56.0	56.0	56.0	56.0	56.0	56.0	56.0	56.0	56.0	56.0
1849	56.0	56.0	56.0	56.0	56.0	56.0	56.0	56.0	56.0	56.0	56.0	56.0
1850	56.0	56.0	56.0	56.0	56.0	56.0	56.0	56.0	56.0	56.0	56.0	56.0
1851	56.0	56.0	56.0	56.0	56.0	56.0	56.0	56.0	56.0	56.0	56.0	56.0
1852	56.0	56.0	56.0	56.0	55.5	57.8	57.8	57.8	57.8	57.8	57.8	57.6
1853	57.6	57.6	57.6	57.6	53.5	52.9	52.9	52.9	52.9	52.9	52.9	52.9
1854	48.1	48.9	48.9	48.9	43.6	43.6	43.6	43.6	43.6	43.6	43.6	43.6
1855	43.6	43.6	43.6	43.6	44.3	44.3	44.9	45.0	45.0	45.0	45.0	45.0
1856	44.6	44.6	44.6	44.6	51.1	51.1	51.1	51.1	51.1	58.5	58.5	58.5
1857	58.5	58.5	58.5	52.8	52.8	52.8	52.8	52.8	52.8	52.8	52.8	52.8
1858	49.9	49.9	49.9	49.9	49.9	49.9	49.9	49.9	49.9	49.9	47.2	47.2
1859	47.2	57.6	50.5	56.8	55.3	46.3	46.3	46.3	46.3	46.3	46.3	46.3
1860	46.3	46.7	46.7	46.7	46.7	46.7	46.7	46.7	46.7	49.3	50.8	50.8
1861	50.1	50.1	50.1	50.1	50.1	50.1	49.3	49.3	49.3	52.0	52.0	55.1

TABLE 15—WINES

Year	Jan.	Feb.	Mar.	Apr.	May	June	July	Aug.	Sept.	Oct.	Nov.	Dec.
1784	56.6	57.0	56.7	56.4	58.1	58.3	57.6	56.7	60.9	60.3	63.7	66.4
1785	63.9	62.8	65.3	66.7	66.5	65.0	64.9	64.9	65.6	65.6	69.1	69.1
1786	69.1	69.1	69.1	69.1	69.1	69.1	69.1	69.1	69.1	69.1	69.1	69.1
1787	69.1	69.1	69.1	69.1	69.1	69.1	69.1	69.1	69.1	69.1	69.1	69.1
1788	66.8	66.8	66.8	66.8	66.8	66.8	66.8	66.8	66.8	60.2	60.2	59.4
1789	59.4	61.4	61.4	61.4	63.5	63.5	63.5	63.5	63.5	63.5	63.5	64.0
1790	64.0	64.0	64.0	64.0	64.0	64.0	63.3	63.3	63.3	63.3	65.0	65.0
1791	65.0	64.1	65.1	64.4	65.4	65.6	67.7	67.7	67.7	69.5	70.9	70.9
1792	68.4	68.4	68.4	68.4	68.4	68.4	68.9	73.5	75.7	75.2	75.2	75.2
1793	80.1	80.1	80.1	78.9	78.9	82.1	80.8	80.8	74.8	74.8	74.8	74.8
1794	74.8	74.8	76.4	74.8								
1795	88.4	89.4	89.4	87.6	86.7	87.1	85.5	86.4	86.4	83.6	83.6	83.6
1796	86.1	84.7	79.5	79.5	88.8	89.3	89.2	90.4	89.0	88.9	88.7	88.7
1797	87.7	87.7	86.1	86.1	86.1	86.1	86.1	84.5	84.5	84.5	84.5	84.7
1798	78.3	78.3	78.0	78.0	78.0	78.0	84.1	84.1	84.1	84.1	84.1	87.6
1799	87.3	86.9	86.3	84.7	82.7	90.9	90.9	90.3	91.3	93.1	95.1	95.9
1800	95.5	95.2	94.7	94.5	92.1	87.3	86.7	93.1	95.3	95.4	96.8	97.5
1801	97.0	99.5	100.1	100.7	99.9	102.1	102.1	101.8	100.9	100.4	106.5	106.5
1802	106.5	106.5	105.2	102.4	104.2	104.2	104.2	104.2	104.2	98.7	98.7	102.0
1803	98.8	98.8	97.3	97.3	97.3	97.3	98.3	98.3	98.5	100.6	101.3	100.6
1804	101.1	100.9	104.2	104.2	104.2	105.1	102.1	103.5	104.2	104.2	104.9	102.3
1805	99.0	99.0	99.8	98.9	96.4	95.9	95.9	95.4	95.4	95.4	95.4	93.3
1806	90.3	91.6	90.5	90.5	89.3	88.2	88.2	89.6	89.0	88.4	88.2	88.5
1807	88.7	88.7	88.1	89.1	89.1	89.0	88.6	89.3	89.2	88.1	89.3	90.2
1808	90.4	93.5	93.5	93.3	94.5	92.7	97.2	100.0	101.9	101.3	102.7	108.3
1809	108.9	108.9	120.3	115.8	118.4	111.6	111.3	113.3	112.4	111.4	112.0	109.2
1810	109.7	110.0	115.6	117.4	128.8	132.2	139.4	140.2	139.9	140.4	137.5	132.8
1811	131.0	129.9	132.3	131.3	130.6	131.7	138.4	139.6	143.3	146.7	141.9	143.4
1812	143.4	145.5	144.5	144.5	143.3	142.6	162.5	158.7	158.7	157.6	157.6	162.7
1813	162.7	162.7	162.7	162.7	163.4	163.4	163.4	163.4	163.4	163.4	169.2	172.8
1814	193.7	199.9	192.7	192.7	190.6	190.6	190.6	190.6	190.6	190.6	190.6	190.6
1815	190.6	193.6	153.0	142.2	143.2	146.5	148.6	157.0	181.6	176.8	178.0	178.5
1816	174.3	166.4	156.3	153.3	150.8	151.5	151.1	142.5	141.2	128.9	127.2	127.2
1817	121.1	121.1	126.2	125.7	122.1	119.9	121.3	121.3	121.3	121.9	124.1	124.1
1818	124.1	124.1	116.7	123.9	122.2	121.5	121.5	121.7	122.0	123.0	127.9	125.8
1819	125.8	124.9	125.4	126.9	124.2	121.4	120.6	120.6	121.5	121.1	121.1	119.7
1820	117.7	117.7	117.7	116.6	116.9	111.0	111.0	111.2	111.2	111.2	111.0	111.0
1821	110.2	110.2	110.2	109.4	109.4	109.4	109.4	109.4	108.9	108.9	107.8	108.3
1822	109.9	109.9	108.3	108.3	108.3	108.3	103.2	98.5	97.1	97.1	96.0	95.5
1823	95.8	96.3	96.3	96.3	96.0	95.5	95.5	95.5	95.2	93.8	93.8	93.8
1824	93.8	93.3	92.0	90.0	90.0	90.0	91.9	91.9	92.5	92.5	92.5	92.5
1825	93.8	95.2	95.2	95.2	101.5	101.6	103.7	101.4	100.7	100.6	98.6	98.0
1826	98.0	98.7	97.8	97.8	97.4	97.9	97.6	96.7	94.1	93.9	93.4	92.8
1827	91.7	91.7	91.5	94.8	95.0	93.8	92.2	92.2	93.6	92.5	85.6	88.5
1828	88.5	88.5	92.3	92.2	92.2	92.2	91.6	90.8	90.8	90.4	90.4	90.4
1829	90.4	90.4	89.3	88.6	87.6	87.6	86.9	86.9	87.0	85.6	85.0	85.0
1830	84.7	84.7	84.7	83.4	83.4	83.4	81.0	81.0	81.0	81.0	79.7	80.4
1831	79.9	81.2	82.9	81.1	81.0	84.5	84.5	85.0	84.2	84.2	84.5	84.5
1832	84.5	84.5	82.8	82.8	82.2	82.2	82.6	86.3	86.8	86.8	86.8	86.4
1833	86.7	86.7	86.4	85.6	85.6	85.6	85.6	85.6	85.6	85.6	85.6	85.6
1834	84.7	84.7	84.7	83.0	81.4	78.4	78.9	79.4	79.3	79.3	79.5	79.5
1835	80.0	80.8	80.1	81.0	80.9	81.1	80.5	80.5	80.2	80.0	79.3	77.7
1836	77.6	76.8	76.8	79.3	78.5	77.2	78.0	78.4	77.2	77.3	75.3	74.8
1837	79.1	79.7	72.9	72.1	71.2	71.2	70.9	70.7	70.7	69.8	69.7	69.4
1838	69.7	69.4	69.4	72.8	72.8	71.6	71.4	71.0	70.8	70.7	70.6	70.6
1839	71.0	73.2	71.8	71.1	71.1	70.4	70.2	70.1	70.1	69.8	69.2	69.2
1840	69.2	69.1	69.4	69.1	69.0	69.1	69.1	68.0	68.0	68.1	68.3	67.9
1841	68.2	68.8	68.8	68.8	68.8	68.6	68.3	68.8	68.8	66.1	66.1	65.7
1842	65.3	65.6	65.6	64.1	64.1	63.4	63.4	63.4	65.2	63.6	64.8	64.8
1843	64.8	65.5	65.5	65.5	66.0	67.5	67.5	67.5	67.5	66.7	66.7	66.7
1844	66.8	70.6	71.9	74.7	76.2	76.2	75.9	74.8	74.3	74.1	73.9	73.6
1845	73.6	73.6	72.0	72.0	74.2	74.2	74.2	74.2	74.3	73.3	72.3	72.3
1846	72.3	74.2	74.2	71.8	70.3	70.3	70.3	70.3	70.0	70.0	70.0	70.0
1847	70.0	70.0	72.4	72.4	72.7	72.7	72.7	72.7	72.0	72.0	71.6	71.6
1848	70.6	70.4	70.2	70.2	69.7	69.7	69.8	69.7	69.7	69.7	69.7	69.7
1849	69.7	68.4	68.2	68.2	68.2	66.5	66.5	66.5	70.8	70.0	70.0	70.0
1850	70.0	70.9	71.0	70.5	70.5	70.5	70.5	70.5	70.5	70.5	70.5	70.5
1851	70.5	70.5	70.3	70.3	70.3	70.3	70.3	70.3	70.3	70.3	70.3	70.3
1852	70.3	70.3	70.3	70.3	70.3	70.3	70.3	70.3	70.3	70.3	70.3	70.3
1853	71.8	75.5	75.5	74.3	74.3	74.1	74.1	74.1	74.1	74.1	74.1	74.1
1854	74.1	74.1	87.4	87.4	87.4	87.4	87.4	87.4	87.4	87.4	117.2	117.2
1855	117.2	126.4	126.4	126.4	126.4	126.4	126.4	126.4	126.4	126.4	126.4	126.4
1856	126.4	126.4	126.4	126.4	126.4	126.4	126.4	126.4	126.4	126.4	126.4	126.4
1857	130.8	130.8	130.8	130.8	130.8	130.8	130.8	130.8	130.8	130.8	130.8	130.8
1858	130.8	130.8	130.8	130.8	130.8	130.8	130.3	130.3	130.3	130.3	108.8	108.8
1859	108.8	108.5	108.5	108.5	108.5	108.5	108.5	108.5	108.5	108.5	108.5	108.4
1860	113.9	113.9	113.9	121.9	121.9	121.9	121.9	121.9	121.9	121.9	121.9	121.9
1861	124.2	124.2	124.2	124.2	124.2	124.2	125.5	125.5	125.5	125.5	125.5	126.9

Table 16—Grains

Year	Jan.	Feb.	Mar.	Apr.	May	June	July	Aug.	Sept.	Oct.	Nov.	Dec.
1784	98.2	95.1	94.0	96.5	104.9	107.8	109.2	107.2	116.6	115.5	108.8	110.9
1785	104.7	105.7	105.0	104.1	102.9	104.5	102.1	99.2	94.9	98.2	99.2	101.9
1786	96.3	97.0	96.4	92.3	91.3	112.9	120.7	106.9	105.9	99.1	90.6	90.7
1787	92.1	91.7	90.7	92.0	94.1	94.9	98.0	91.8	85.4	84.4	83.7	79.9
1788	76.1	75.6	75.8	76.8	77.9	80.0	75.7	72.6	69.2	76.8	75.4	72.3
1789	72.8	72.0	68.7	67.0	77.7	77.3	81.1	84.5	82.3	84.9	86.0	87.8
1790	88.7	96.9	108.3	117.4	117.2	115.5	106.6	102.4	96.1	87.9	102.8	102.0
1791	102.9	101.9	90.6	88.7	89.5	85.4	81.8	79.8	86.9	92.5	87.8	88.2
1792	85.4	85.4	85.4	85.7	85.7	86.5	85.3	85.9	79.5	90.8	89.9	101.8
1793	100.6	101.7	105.0	106.5	108.4	104.7	107.6	107.0	104.0	108.9	108.1	109.1
1794	107.6	107.6	106.2	107.6	108.7	113.7	113.8	118.7	122.1	127.1	129.0	140.5
1795	130.0	137.6	141.7	138.7	150.1	154.5	166.9	152.9	156.1	166.3	160.2	163.8
1796	179.7	179.7	193.6	195.5	193.9	186.2	179.4	151.8	155.2	164.0	150.1	146.6
1797	149.1	162.6	144.6	131.5	130.3	135.8	132.2	131.3	130.3	142.6	139.3	138.2
1798	128.1	128.1	128.1	113.6	110.4	108.8	107.6	107.6	107.6	107.6	107.6	110.1
1799	113.0	109.5	107.7	109.7	110.0	109.9	109.6	113.4	119.7	127.5	128.2	128.9
1800	126.7	133.3	135.7	136.4	149.4	148.2	150.1	149.5	144.4	144.2	139.4	140.1
1801	141.2	152.6	168.8	161.2	166.8	162.4	162.7	154.5	147.3	144.9	160.5	134.4
1802	128.4	126.2	115.3	120.2	120.2	120.2	122.4	122.4	126.6	114.6	118.0	124.7
1803	124.7	124.7	124.7	117.1	114.2	115.3	110.6	110.6	110.6	124.4	136.6	142.0
1804	140.2	139.0	137.7	137.7	129.8	129.8	132.4	132.4	141.9	144.8	147.8	177.7
1805	187.7	187.7	191.6	198.7	199.5	193.8	183.9	161.6	144.0	144.0	143.7	142.1
1806	152.2	152.2	151.2	145.6	141.8	144.6	143.9	143.2	125.7	129.0	121.8	121.8
1807	125.1	129.0	129.0	131.7	129.4	131.6	130.9	122.3	123.1	124.7	125.6	125.0
1808	107.3	98.7	98.7	99.6	95.8	98.6	93.8	90.2	91.9	95.0	94.1	88.9
1809	99.7	96.8	107.8	104.9	117.4	115.1	117.2	115.3	112.3	112.1	124.9	126.9
1810	137.7	137.7	135.2	134.3	144.6	140.9	148.3	154.7	145.0	149.2	145.1	141.3
1811	150.8	152.6	152.7	141.9	142.5	149.6	147.8	150.1	138.3	139.8	145.0	146.8
1812	153.5	153.5	150.0	145.3	145.3	148.9	156.7	135.6	139.4	153.4	160.8	160.8
1813	162.5	162.5	162.5	146.8	147.0	147.0	155.2	155.2	149.1	149.1	149.1	179.0
1814	173.3	173.3	165.5	165.2	169.5	178.5	169.8	168.4	164.0	164.4	168.4	167.2
1815	162.2	162.2	140.2	121.2	131.0	146.9	166.6	165.0	166.8	180.7	184.7	177.0
1816	167.7	162.6	158.4	159.4	162.3	179.3	202.6	209.4	191.9	192.9	237.4	241.2
1817	243.3	255.9	264.1	263.5	274.7	216.5	206.4	206.6	176.3	161.6	153.6	164.2
1818	167.7	167.7	178.1	177.8	169.8	172.8	171.3	173.7	167.2	171.2	165.1	169.1
1819	168.4	156.1	153.0	141.0	124.6	116.3	117.1	119.2	124.6	120.4	120.7	118.4
1820	116.9	116.9	111.3	104.2	106.3	102.2	97.1	90.8	91.5	88.4	80.7	76.1
1821	76.6	75.4	74.5	68.2	74.6	75.7	76.1	78.9	89.1	94.5	106.9	107.7
1822	107.7	111.5	115.3	121.6	132.9	132.3	126.0	117.5	117.1	120.0	121.8	118.6
1823	119.3	121.0	121.6	126.4	125.3	121.1	122.4	105.3	96.2	96.7	97.2	96.7
1824	97.1	96.5	88.4	87.4	86.6	86.7	84.5	82.6	80.5	84.2	84.1	85.2
1825	82.1	82.1	82.7	85.7	95.9	93.8	89.8	88.0	102.7	105.1	101.9	102.8
1826	104.1	106.5	112.7	114.9	114.9	128.9	122.9	116.2	116.6	116.6	123.9	125.0
1827	123.1	126.7	121.9	116.6	107.0	105.2	92.4	90.8	94.0	95.8	97.9	97.8
1828	94.2	90.3	87.8	85.4	87.0	83.8	82.9	85.2	89.4	96.0	119.1	112.1
1829	112.5	113.9	111.9	108.1	109.0	108.1	100.6	97.5	94.2	94.5	96.5	92.5
1830	86.2	86.4	82.6	83.2	85.8	86.8	87.3	90.5	92.2	100.8	100.6	100.7
1831	106.8	110.8	116.4	120.3	116.9	114.6	114.3	115.7	119.0	117.8	122.9	123.2
1832	122.4	115.6	106.2	109.9	113.0	128.0	127.7	133.4	123.3	125.3	131.8	122.4
1833	124.9	124.7	117.0	123.5	120.3	120.6	117.3	114.6	115.2	119.7	117.5	110.9
1834	107.2	101.9	101.0	98.8	106.6	107.9	113.2	109.8	111.9	113.9	113.8	108.9
1835	114.8	113.8	114.8	122.7	136.8	145.4	156.8	142.5	137.9	143.7	144.6	151.0
1836	140.2	141.1	142.6	149.8	145.9	141.2	140.8	150.5	171.2	169.6	180.5	182.1
1837	185.2	185.4	183.9	172.2	170.2	173.5	175.9	160.3	152.5	163.0	180.4	164.7
1838	153.7	149.1	137.0	143.5	142.7	153.0	135.3	161.8	162.1	168.8	163.6	161.6
1839	166.2	166.6	162.7	167.9	170.6	163.1	153.5	137.6	136.3	125.6	127.5	121.6
1840	118.6	109.2	97.0	99.6	95.4	95.9	103.4	107.0	105.0	105.6	103.6	100.1
1841	100.8	98.5	95.6	98.2	100.5	111.1	118.1	125.0	132.7	125.1	127.3	125.1
1842	122.6	122.5	120.2	120.9	116.8	114.1	110.2	102.1	91.4	93.8	86.5	86.8
1843	84.8	81.9	83.4	95.5	92.5	102.2	103.7	96.0	93.8	94.8	97.1	94.1
1844	94.7	99.3	97.6	101.0	98.0	96.2	93.9	92.5	92.5	97.8	98.3	96.6
1845	95.0	96.1	96.9	97.7	96.2	99.6	99.6	101.3	109.6	120.0	135.3	141.4
1846	131.0	119.5	124.0	124.7	118.5	106.0	103.2	98.7	109.0	119.2	127.1	114.6
1847	116.7	146.5	140.2	157.2	172.6	202.7	142.4	146.3	137.7	148.6	141.3	130.1
1848	135.2	125.9	123.7	123.0	121.1	114.0	110.3	108.4	120.6	118.1	113.8	103.7
1849	111.4	107.1	105.9	98.3	106.0	104.9	104.6	113.1	113.1	112.2	110.4	107.3
1850	109.8	109.1	107.5	108.4	114.7	120.5	120.6	121.2	116.0	115.9	122.5	115.9
1851	117.6	119.3	112.3	118.5	115.0	115.5	113.4	104.4	105.1	105.8	106.2	107.4
1852	111.6	113.3	111.3	114.2	121.9	122.1	126.8	120.6	125.1	128.5	134.5	130.4
1853	131.0	127.2	125.6	126.8	128.4	127.4	128.0	130.5	138.1	145.6	149.5	141.0
1854	145.8	168.8	150.1	155.8	170.0	171.5	161.5	156.1	169.2	173.3	177.3	175.2
1855	183.7	182.4	183.8	216.5	227.2	228.4	204.1	186.0	170.5	175.8	171.2	171.3
1856	170.7	152.3	143.3	135.9	118.0	118.4	128.5	130.0	131.9	135.2	139.3	137.4
1857	140.4	139.7	141.1	143.8	171.1	180.5	174.2	168.6	136.9	132.9	129.4	119.9
1858	111.7	110.1	112.9	120.9	119.4	115.6	123.6	132.2	135.4	135.7	131.2	127.3
1859	135.2	144.1	155.8	150.5	167.7	158.3	142.5	133.8	128.5	140.8	144.6	142.3
1860	140.5	141.6	143.6	143.3	143.3	135.1	130.5	131.5	136.9	135.1	124.5	119.1
1861	122.4	118.6	114.5	117.1	126.4	118.6	110.2	115.3	115.1	129.4	138.5	140.0

Table 17—Leaf Tobacco

Year	Jan.	Feb.	Mar.	Apr.	May	June	July	Aug.	Sept.	Oct.	Nov.	Dec.
1784	104.5	105.9	119.2	105.1	109.2	119.1	117.0	114.8	89.7	115.5	95.9	108.0
1785	105.1	105.1	105.6	105.6	102.8	102.8	102.8	99.9	99.9	99.9	89.4	89.4
1786	88.6	86.4	86.4	77.3	71.6	71.6	71.6	71.6	74.8	74.8	82.0	81.0
1787	80.0	80.0	83.3	81.6	87.7	82.0	82.0	85.4	84.3	84.3	84.3	84.3
1788	84.3	84.3	84.3	84.3	84.3	84.3	84.3	84.3	84.3	84.3	84.3	84.3
1789	84.3	84.3	84.3	84.3	84.3	84.3	84.3	84.3	84.3	84.3	84.3	84.3
1790	84.3	84.3	84.3	84.3	84.3	84.3	84.3	84.3	84.3	84.3	84.3	84.3
1791	84.3	67.0	67.0	67.0	60.6	60.6	57.4	54.3	54.3	54.3	54.3	51.3
1792	56.4	56.4	56.4	56.4	56.4	56.4	56.4	56.4	56.4	56.4	61.1	61.1
1793	61.1	61.1	61.1	61.1	61.1	61.1	61.1	61.1	61.1	61.1	61.1	61.1
1794	61.1	61.1	61.1	61.1	62.3	63.8	65.0	66.3	67.2	67.9	68.7	69.5
1795	74.2	74.2	74.2	81.6	84.9	91.6	94.7	82.7	79.6	77.5	79.6	79.6
1796	84.3	84.3	84.3	83.1	96.5	96.5	91.6	92.5	98.8	106.7	111.3	111.3
1797	111.3	114.6	124.0	124.0	122.5	116.2	124.1	140.8	140.8	140.8	140.8	140.8
1798	156.3	156.3	173.2	173.2	173.2	173.2	177.5	177.5	177.5	177.5	177.5	
1799					169.9	169.9	169.9	160.8				
1800						81.2	81.2	81.2	81.2	83.8	85.6	85.6
1801	85.6	85.6	85.6	85.6	85.6	85.6	85.6	85.6	85.6	85.6	93.7	92.3
1802	92.3	99.5	99.5	99.5	97.2	97.2	97.2	97.2	97.2	94.4	94.4	95.1
1803	95.1	95.1	95.1	95.1	95.1	95.1	95.1	95.1	95.1	95.1	95.1	95.1
1804	95.1	101.9	101.9	101.9	101.9	101.9	101.9	101.9	101.9	99.9	99.9	99.9
1805	99.9	99.9	99.9	99.9	99.9	99.9	99.9	99.9	99.9	99.9	99.9	99.9
1806	98.5	98.5	98.5	98.5	98.5	98.5	98.5	98.5	98.5	98.5	98.5	98.5
1807	103.5	105.1	105.1	100.2	100.2	105.1	105.1	107.3	111.3	100.6	100.6	100.6
1808	100.6	100.6	100.6	100.6	100.6	100.6	100.6	100.6	100.6	100.6	100.6	98.8
1809	98.8	98.8	98.8	98.8	98.8	98.8	98.8	98.8	98.8	98.8	100.6	100.5
1810	91.5	91.5	102.5	102.5	102.5	102.5	102.5	100.5	98.8	98.8	95.2	95.2
1811	95.2	95.2	95.2	95.2	95.2	95.2	95.2	75.0	75.0	75.0	70.2	70.2
1812	70.2	74.5	74.5	74.5	74.5	74.5	74.5	74.5	74.5	74.5	74.5	74.5
1813	74.5	84.1	84.1	85.9	109.6	102.2	102.2	102.2	102.2	102.2	102.2	102.2
1814	102.5	102.5	102.5	102.5	102.5	102.5	102.5	102.5	102.5	102.5	131.8	131.8
1815	131.8	131.8	131.8	131.8	131.8	131.8	175.7	190.4	190.4	231.9	231.9	231.9
1816	260.6	280.0	280.0	273.7	273.7	273.7	277.3	277.3	277.3	277.3	221.8	221.8
1817	221.8	221.8	221.8	221.8	197.1	146.2	122.5	117.1	138.3	138.3	153.1	153.1
1818	136.0	136.0	140.4	140.4	156.4	153.1	142.8	153.1	160.9	175.5	164.7	168.2
1819	168.2	168.2	160.9	160.9	149.0	121.6	100.1	94.2	98.5	98.5	109.3	109.3
1820	109.3	109.3	109.3	109.3	109.3	99.8	99.8	99.8	105.1	107.3	107.3	107.3
1821	107.3	107.3	107.3	107.3	107.3	107.3	107.3	107.3	107.3	107.3	107.3	96.4
1822	96.4	96.4	96.4	96.4	96.4	96.4	96.4	96.4	96.4	96.4	96.4	96.4
1823	96.4	96.4	96.4	96.4	96.4	96.4	96.4	96.4	96.4	98.6	98.6	98.6
1824	98.6	98.6	98.6	98.6	98.6	98.6	98.6	98.6	98.6	98.6	90.8	90.8
1825	90.8	90.8	90.8	98.2	103.5	103.5	103.5	105.6	109.6	115.3	107.6	107.6
1826	111.5	111.5	103.5	96.8	89.8	79.6	88.9	75.8	75.8	78.7	78.7	78.7
1827	77.8	79.6	77.8	77.8	74.8	73.1	73.1	73.1	71.2	71.2	69.2	69.2
1828	71.2	71.2	71.2	71.2	71.2	73.1	73.1	73.1	73.1	73.1	73.1	73.1
1829	67.7	67.7	67.7	82.3	82.3	75.5	75.5	75.5	82.3	82.3	86.0	86.0
1830	86.0	86.0	86.0	74.8	74.8	74.8	62.2	62.2	62.2	63.0	63.8	63.8
1831	63.8	63.8	63.8	63.8	63.8	63.8	63.8	63.8	69.5	69.5	61.2	61.2
1832	61.2	61.2	65.5	69.5	69.5	69.5	69.5	69.5	68.5	68.5	76.8	76.8
1833	68.5	68.5	76.8	76.8	78.5	86.0	86.0	86.0	97.0	99.7	97.8	104.2
1834	111.5	111.5	111.5	115.3	115.3	115.3	115.3	117.1	117.1	117.1	117.1	117.1
1835	109.8	109.8	109.8	108.0	108.0	118.6	118.6	120.3	120.3	136.6	136.6	135.0
1836	135.0	135.0	128.0	128.0	139.1	139.1	139.1	139.1	135.3	127.3	127.3	127.3
1837	127.3	127.3	102.4	92.9	87.6	87.6	87.6	85.6	85.6	87.6	93.3	97.0
1838	97.0	91.5	91.5	93.3	93.3	98.8	98.8	106.1	130.0	130.0	138.9	142.6
1839	151.9	190.4	194.0	194.0	197.7	208.6	208.6	201.3	195.6	195.6	173.9	166.5
1840	162.9	148.1	140.9	133.5	108.0	106.1	105.9	105.9	106.9	111.7	115.3	115.3
1841	120.8	122.5	122.5	124.3	124.3	108.0	106.1	102.2	106.1	105.2	105.2	100.2
1842	100.2	84.2	84.2	80.5	67.7	65.8	65.8	65.8	67.7	67.7	71.2	72.3
1843	69.4	69.4	69.4	69.4	70.4	75.1	75.1	74.1	74.1	70.4	67.7	65.9
1844	65.9	65.9	65.9	65.9	68.6	66.8	66.8	67.7	67.7	68.6	68.6	65.9
1845	67.7	67.7	82.9	76.9	84.3	92.6	92.6	109.6	109.6	97.9	93.9	93.9
1846	90.8	92.9	96.8	96.8	110.7	109.8	109.8	102.2	102.2	102.2	102.2	98.2
1847	93.0	93.0	96.2	102.2	87.6	88.4	88.4	89.2	90.0	94.1	98.8	101.6
1848	101.6	101.6	101.6	101.6	95.9	95.9	68.5	68.5	70.2	71.8	71.8	72.9
1849	72.9	72.9	83.0	92.6	91.9	88.8	96.0	96.9	96.9	103.6	100.6	100.6
1850	100.6	100.6	99.7	104.0	104.0	104.0	104.0	108.9	110.5	113.6	123.6	146.0
1851	146.0	146.0	144.0	144.0	144.0	109.6	106.1	106.1	106.1	97.0	98.8	98.6
1852	94.9	95.1	95.1	95.1	91.5	90.6	90.6	90.6	90.6	88.8	88.8	91.5
1853	91.5	91.5	102.2	102.2	102.2	102.2	102.2	102.2	103.2	104.2	104.2	104.2
1854	104.2	109.8	109.8	109.8	109.8	106.2	106.2	106.2	108.0	108.0	106.1	106.1
1855	106.1	106.1	112.9	120.3	120.3	120.3	120.3	120.3	120.3	120.3	120.3	120.3
1856	120.3	120.3	120.3	120.3	120.3	120.3	120.3	120.3	120.3	140.5	140.5	146.5
1857	141.9	138.3	138.3	138.3	138.3	138.3	138.3	138.3	138.3	138.3	138.3	134.2
1858	130.0	108.9	108.9	108.9	108.9	108.9	108.9	108.9	108.9	108.9	108.9	108.9
1859	108.9	108.9	108.9	108.9	108.9	108.9	108.9	108.9	108.9	108.9	108.9	108.9
1860	93.3	93.3	93.3	93.3	93.3	93.3	93.3	93.3	93.3	93.3	99.7	99.7
1861	99.7	99.7	98.8	106.1	106.1	116.2	122.5	145.0	145.0	145.0	168.9	171.0

TABLE 18—MINOR FARM PRODUCTS

Year	Jan.	Feb.	Mar.	Apr.	May	June	July	Aug.	Sept.	Oct.	Nov.	Dec.
1784	99.0	99.0	96.7	96.7	96.7	95.8	97.3	94.8	110.6	110.0	114.6	115.2
1785	126.7	126.7	126.7	107.7	101.7	102.5	100.5	101.6	97.9	112.5	139.8	139.7
1786	129.9	116.2	113.6	110.4	115.7	118.0	120.2	115.0	127.1	116.1	125.5	126.2
1787	125.1	125.1	125.1	134.3	134.3	134.3	121.3	102.1	100.1	100.1	100.1	95.1
1788	96.0	96.0	91.7	91.7	91.7	91.7	91.7	91.7	84.9	83.3	81.9	73.6
1789	71.1	71.1	71.1	71.1	71.1	71.1	71.1	73.6	73.6	80.6	86.1	86.4
1790	86.4	86.4	80.6	80.6	80.6	80.6	80.6	80.6	80.6	80.6	93.1	88.1
1791	88.1	89.5	84.9	89.5	88.0	88.0	88.0	88.0	89.5	102.7	100.1	87.8
1792	87.8	87.8	87.8	87.8	87.8	87.8	87.8	87.8	87.8	84.0	91.5	93.9
1793	93.9	93.9	91.5	89.1	89.1	89.1	89.1	89.1	106.9	106.9	106.9	106.9
1794	101.1	101.1	101.1	101.1								
1795	96.5	96.5	96.5	96.5	96.5	96.5	96.5	96.5	96.5	102.5	110.4	121.7
1796	144.5	124.4	130.5	130.0	133.2	131.3	130.8	130.4	129.9	129.5	162.4	169.6
1797	165.8	160.6	160.6	137.5	137.5	137.5	137.5	137.5	137.5	137.5	137.5	131.1
1798	140.5	140.5	146.6	146.6	146.6	146.6	146.6	146.6	146.6	146.6	146.6	126.7
1799	94.3	92.2	90.0	85.4	85.4	99.1	99.1	99.1	103.4	107.5	107.5	107.5
1800	111.0	110.4	113.7	115.5	122.6	127.9	127.9	127.9	135.1	135.1	147.9	136.7
1801	138.3	150.2	150.2	150.2	146.6	146.6	146.6	153.5	153.5	130.8	130.0	138.4
1802	122.4	122.4	122.4	122.4	122.4	123.8	125.3	126.7	128.1	129.5	130.8	136.9
1803	138.2	137.5	137.5	119.4	119.4	119.4	119.4	119.4	119.4	121.9	124.4	126.8
1804	129.2	129.2	129.2	129.2	129.2	129.2	129.2	129.2	129.2	129.2	129.2	144.1
1805	130.3	130.3	130.3	130.3	130.3	130.3	130.3	130.3	130.3	108.3	115.4	136.5
1806	115.4	119.8	124.1	124.9	125.7	126.5	127.2	128.0	128.7	129.4	129.4	129.4
1807	125.1	125.1	125.1	122.9	120.9	118.7	116.5	114.3	112.0	109.7	118.9	120.2
1808	120.2	120.2	120.2	118.9	117.5	116.1	114.8	113.4	112.0	110.6	109.2	107.7
1809	107.7	107.7	107.7	109.7	104.5	101.1	95.7	95.7	95.7	94.4	101.9	92.0
1810	93.7	94.1	102.4	102.4	123.1	118.7	118.7	113.0	119.5	121.1	121.1	121.1
1811	119.9	120.7	121.4	116.7	116.7	115.6	115.6	115.6	115.6	110.8	96.0	96.6
1812	134.5	134.5	139.8	139.8	139.8	139.8	148.3	139.8	135.2	135.2	106.1	98.1
1813	103.8	103.8	103.8	103.8	103.8	98.1	98.1	98.1	98.1	98.1	108.1	111.9
1814	109.7	111.0	111.0	111.0	111.0	111.0	111.0	111.0	111.0	111.0	111.0	111.0
1815	109.7	109.7	109.7	109.7	109.7	128.7	134.4	134.4	139.0	160.5	167.1	164.4
1816	160.1	160.1	171.3	171.3	171.3	171.3	171.3	171.3	171.3	147.9	139.1	164.6
1817	173.4	192.0	198.8	198.8	198.8	198.8	198.8	198.8	184.0	184.0	184.0	186.5
1818	183.4	161.5	158.6	158.6	166.0	166.0	166.0	166.0	166.0	166.0	166.0	166.0
1819	165.8	164.5	164.5	164.5	157.8	157.8	157.8	150.2	150.2	150.2	150.2	161.5
1820	155.7	155.7	157.5	127.5	127.5	127.5	124.4	124.4	124.4	119.6	119.6	119.6
1821	119.6	119.6	118.0	118.0	118.0	83.4	83.4	83.4	83.4	74.2	87.0	90.9
1822	90.9	90.9	107.9	107.9	107.9	107.9	107.9	107.9	107.9	94.8	97.4	98.3
1823	98.3	101.1	101.1	101.1	101.1	101.1	101.1	92.2	92.2	97.4	109.5	104.0
1824	97.1	95.6	95.6	95.6	95.6	95.6	95.6	94.1	88.5	88.5	97.9	97.9
1825	97.9	96.3	96.3	107.7	109.1	107.7	104.1	98.1	98.1	98.1	103.3	107.3
1826	111.1	120.6	123.9	124.8	112.8	112.8	162.8	142.8	131.9	115.4	109.5	109.5
1827	109.5	109.5	109.5	109.5	109.5	85.6	85.6	87.0	82.9	82.9	81.6	84.2
1828	82.9	82.3	78.0	78.0	73.6	73.6	73.6	73.6	76.2	83.1	82.7	81.4
1829	84.7	90.1	90.1	84.7	85.4	85.4	85.4	78.0	78.0	78.3	79.8	80.2
1830	83.4	83.9	83.5	83.5	82.7	82.7	82.7	82.7	79.8	84.3	84.2	83.5
1831	89.3	88.6	90.1	89.8	89.8	89.8	89.8	91.8	93.8	95.9	98.0	98.0
1832	95.9	100.3	98.0	95.1	94.9	95.6	95.6	95.6	89.3	93.0	93.8	93.3
1833	94.8	94.8	96.6	97.3	94.2	93.8	93.8	93.8	91.9	93.9	92.8	92.6
1834	92.6	93.0	89.3	83.1	84.0	90.1	90.1	90.1	90.1	90.1	90.1	97.3
1835	97.7	158.2	158.6	166.9	169.1	164.8	145.4	163.5	165.1	166.4	167.7	169.7
1836	166.4	175.6	186.2	201.9	201.3	174.9	168.9	171.7	170.4	177.3	178.8	180.3
1837	179.6	179.2	177.2	150.6	143.7	137.7	136.4	136.4	134.6	134.6	139.1	137.9
1838	139.1	138.4	134.0	133.3	133.3	129.3	130.2	133.2	134.8	155.6	171.6	191.3
1839	202.6	206.4	205.7	202.9	200.1	187.0	185.5	177.7	167.9	164.6	162.9	164.6
1840	167.0	169.6	166.2	158.2	158.2	162.1	161.3	161.3	162.1	167.0	170.6	145.2
1841	146.0	141.8	143.7	141.0	143.0	153.8	153.8	158.0	162.1	170.7	163.0	144.5
1842	149.4	150.2	150.2	144.0	115.3	114.4	116.5	111.0	107.9	112.2	103.7	133.3
1843	132.6	132.8	134.2	133.3	136.1	120.9	119.4	122.9	125.0	121.8	117.4	107.0
1844	106.7	110.7	111.1	112.0	112.0	114.4	114.2	114.6	111.3	110.1	101.0	102.8
1845	104.7	108.9	108.7	108.5	110.0	108.5	111.2	114.1	113.0	106.8	110.7	113.8
1846	112.0	112.9	111.8	100.4	100.6	102.7	102.5	101.6	100.8	127.2	134.7	134.7
1847	133.4	146.7	158.3	160.4	159.4	153.5	151.4	154.1	150.9	153.5	154.1	139.4
1848	122.9	124.2	127.5	128.1	122.5	122.5	121.4	120.7	148.0	146.6	137.9	137.9
1849	137.9	137.9	128.9	128.7	102.9	102.7	102.7	102.7	104.1	108.5	110.0	110.4
1850	110.4	111.4	111.4	118.6	117.0	110.5	113.9	114.3	114.3	115.2	115.5	116.5
1851	126.8	130.8	130.4	130.0	128.4	128.4	125.4	125.4	122.9	120.3	120.3	120.3
1852	120.3	122.5	122.5	120.3	117.9	117.9	117.9	114.4	121.9	123.1	126.4	132.7
1853	135.9	140.2	133.7	129.3	130.1	130.1	130.1	128.2	131.8	132.9	137.5	137.5
1854	137.5	141.6	141.6	143.7	169.8	171.0	171.0	171.0	169.8	168.6	169.8	171.0
1855	165.7	167.2	164.5	154.3	165.7	167.9	166.8	166.8	166.8	171.3	199.0	199.0
1856	203.2	149.6	146.9	156.0	147.6	140.0	140.0	140.0	151.8	152.4	176.4	160.6
1857	157.1	166.3	166.3	167.3	167.3	168.5	169.6	170.6	169.6	158.3	136.1	129.9
1858	151.2	128.2	129.4	146.8	146.8	148.1	142.2	143.3	145.5	145.5	157.3	158.5
1859	162.1	156.8	156.8	155.7	144.4	144.4	144.4	144.4	142.2	137.7	137.7	136.8
1860	137.7	150.0	150.4	151.3	146.0	146.0	146.0	146.6	139.8	139.8	137.9	129.6
1861	128.1	125.9	129.2	129.2	128.1	128.5	120.3	119.8	122.7	132.5	165.7	172.3

TABLE 19—GRAIN PRODUCTS

Year	Jan.	Feb.	Mar.	Apr.	May	June	July	Aug.	Sept.	Oct.	Nov.	Dec.
1784	104.8	104.0	108.9	101.3	112.6	117.0	122.2	119.5	117.9	118.7	117.9	111.9
1785	106.5	103.8	101.4	99.5	102.6	101.2	102.0	102.0	101.9	103.6	102.9	101.6
1786	101.6	100.9	98.3	97.6	96.9	100.5	103.4	102.0	103.1	102.2	101.5	93.3
1787	92.0	92.7	91.4	90.0	89.2	90.7	92.1	85.6	78.4	78.4	75.8	73.8
1788	72.6	73.9	79.0	79.2	80.5	80.4	78.0	77.7	78.7	77.2	75.7	76.8
1789	76.5	75.5	76.2	74.7	79.9	82.8	84.5	88.4	87.5	85.0	86.9	94.0
1790	96.3	102.1	121.7	118.4	123.7	122.0	120.3	115.1	105.3	100.8	100.1	98.8
1791	101.7	102.7	90.7	90.7	88.3	85.7	81.8	78.4	78.4	83.4	84.3	84.3
1792	87.4	88.6	88.6	88.6	88.1	84.4	84.4	82.2	83.0	82.7	91.1	91.1
1793	98.0	98.0	98.0	98.2	97.1	99.7	100.6	88.7	88.9	88.9	88.9	88.9
1794	92.8	92.8	98.0	98.0								
1795	136.7	145.6	154.0	153.7	162.5	166.8	176.4	172.9	179.2	182.7	185.0	186.4
1796	187.9	195.3	225.7	215.5	216.2	204.3	181.3	175.9	182.3	194.3	194.1	191.2
1797	188.0	188.0	169.6	158.1	159.2	152.5	152.8	152.8	152.8	155.9	155.9	155.9
1798	151.7	146.1	140.3	124.6	120.5	114.7	106.3	110.4	115.0	115.0	121.3	130.5
1799	130.7	128.5	126.5	129.8	127.3	126.1	128.1	133.6	133.1	146.7	147.2	150.4
1800	153.5	155.5	152.4	146.9	149.0	150.0	158.8	161.8	162.8	161.3	167.5	168.3
1801	172.3	181.1	184.0	190.2	191.0	186.3	181.9	179.1	166.4	163.8	160.3	136.0
1802	128.8	128.8	121.5	121.5	116.4	117.4	124.8	124.8	122.6	126.5	126.5	126.0
1803	126.0	120.0	121.1	113.5	113.2	111.5	113.5	118.9	121.0	120.5	126.9	123.7
1804	123.7	123.7	121.6	121.6	119.4	122.2	135.3	136.8	162.7	167.3	175.6	183.9
1805	183.9	191.6	204.6	202.5	201.4	193.9	186.9	142.5	140.3	140.3	141.4	141.4
1806	147.3	141.7	143.3	135.8	133.6	141.6	141.6	137.6	133.4	132.2	134.5	139.3
1807	139.3	137.9	136.8	136.8	130.8	130.3	129.7	129.2	134.1	134.8	134.8	131.4
1808	121.7	121.5	121.1	117.0	113.3	113.3	115.4	114.9	111.8	115.0	115.8	116.6
1809	113.8	121.7	121.7	128.2	138.8	136.8	139.6	138.7	138.7	139.9	147.1	141.1
1810	147.1	151.7	152.9	157.4	160.8	158.4	168.1	177.6	183.2	186.1	182.3	190.4
1811	182.2	176.3	178.2	180.1	177.2	176.6	174.4	171.3	162.5	161.2	161.5	165.7
1812	166.0	168.6	167.7	154.3	149.6	149.4	148.7	149.2	171.8	176.8	194.4	189.8
1813	185.4	184.4	178.1	170.0	158.7	160.5	153.7	152.7	156.7	157.8	160.6	150.7
1814	165.7	154.5	154.6	167.8	157.4	154.2	152.2	158.7	161.8	169.4	169.4	162.7
1815	159.5	159.5	163.5	154.9	159.3	173.0	178.1	181.5	179.7	188.9	190.0	190.2
1816	183.8	177.8	165.0	162.7	158.6	169.9	190.4	200.9	198.0	200.8	233.1	239.7
1817	247.7	251.6	277.1	270.9	269.3	234.3	219.5	217.6	202.9	188.5	181.8	180.0
1818	179.6	188.9	183.5	174.1	164.0	167.0	156.3	159.1	164.7	164.1	160.0	152.8
1819	150.7	145.8	137.1	127.1	119.3	111.3	117.0	124.8	123.6	126.3	127.6	126.1
1820	123.7	119.8	103.2	100.4	99.7	99.7	92.3	91.2	89.3	88.0	85.9	84.0
1821	78.4	73.9	73.5	74.5	74.1	75.0	76.2	82.1	95.4	101.7	108.4	105.2
1822	103.7	107.3	112.9	117.8	124.4	124.7	121.2	122.1	127.3	122.1	121.2	118.2
1823	119.3	120.4	121.5	120.8	119.3	117.4	113.5	109.0	100.2	103.4	102.9	100.9
1824	101.7	92.1	91.7	88.1	90.9	90.5	85.4	84.9	85.7	88.9	88.2	86.6
1825	87.7	89.9	89.6	88.0	96.7	87.0	82.1	84.9	95.6	99.8	100.3	100.2
1826	97.7	97.9	100.1	99.2	97.5	104.7	105.9	103.3	107.3	108.6	111.1	106.6
1827	107.7	110.6	106.2	102.8	99.2	98.2	94.7	91.2	94.0	96.7	92.2	90.2
1828	90.2	86.9	85.6	82.3	84.0	82.0	81.8	86.0	94.7	106.5	137.9	127.3
1829	127.9	125.0	117.8	109.3	104.6	107.4	93.9	92.1	98.0	98.3	96.8	94.8
1830	86.6	86.3	85.8	87.5	90.3	90.8	91.0	97.5	103.6	102.2	99.4	98.1
1831	111.4	112.2	121.1	122.4	115.2	105.5	101.9	102.7	111.3	112.8	113.4	108.6
1832	110.2	105.7	100.5	104.2	107.0	123.4	118.6	123.5	120.4	117.9	122.2	116.3
1833	118.3	114.8	108.8	111.1	111.5	114.3	118.2	112.1	111.4	111.9	110.7	105.6
1834	103.7	100.4	96.2	97.4	103.4	105.8	106.1	109.0	107.7	111.9	111.6	107.1
1835	104.2	104.9	105.8	108.0	127.9	125.8	132.4	127.3	122.8	123.8	127.0	138.9
1836	137.3	136.2	138.4	139.1	132.8	132.9	143.1	146.2	171.8	170.9	188.9	193.6
1837	192.2	194.9	195.9	173.6	166.2	166.2	172.4	166.3	163.6	169.4	183.3	177.2
1838	151.5	146.6	138.1	139.6	138.9	136.0	122.7	134.7	139.8	155.9	150.7	148.9
1839	148.8	151.2	145.9	146.1	145.5	135.8	127.6	118.4	127.9	120.1	123.1	123.5
1840	115.8	114.6	101.0	97.7	96.3	92.7	96.6	97.5	99.1	99.5	97.5	91.0
1841	91.9	92.9	91.8	90.4	90.5	98.5	99.2	106.9	117.1	110.5	111.4	116.8
1842	115.2	113.2	111.0	107.1	105.3	102.0	103.8	105.7	97.2	95.3	88.4	85.6
1843	83.6	81.2	79.9	84.4	87.3	95.8	99.1	95.2	89.5	89.2	87.8	88.5
1844	89.4	92.3	93.0	93.8	90.1	87.0	83.9	82.5	83.7	86.5	88.0	87.2
1845	85.4	85.6	86.5	89.5	85.4	83.6	85.0	83.1	87.9	97.6	120.0	122.5
1846	112.9	104.2	101.3	101.8	97.4	87.2	85.4	85.3	88.8	112.0	113.2	107.2
1847	107.1	135.4	130.1	141.9	153.5	173.1	113.5	108.5	107.2	122.0	124.3	123.3
1848	116.5	103.3	103.6	105.0	104.3	98.4	99.6	101.3	111.9	108.5	105.3	98.0
1849	97.9	95.7	94.2	88.5	92.8	92.6	93.2	100.4	99.2	99.3	97.4	93.9
1850	93.8	92.7	91.7	91.6	100.5	98.1	94.1	97.9	96.8	97.3	99.9	97.2
1851	97.9	96.9	95.6	97.7	93.3	91.9	91.7	91.6	87.2	90.3	91.2	92.1
1852	93.1	95.5	94.5	91.3	92.2	94.9	94.0	95.9	99.5	98.8	102.9	106.6
1853	108.2	106.3	99.9	103.3	102.0	99.7	98.4	102.2	114.2	128.8	132.2	124.4
1854	127.7	144.4	131.9	132.1	148.4	149.2	139.6	143.8	162.4	152.5	166.0	163.5
1855	168.5	164.0	162.0	181.5	191.1	191.2	174.6	167.8	151.2	159.6	168.9	161.9
1856	152.0	140.3	126.7	126.8	104.0	100.8	108.8	115.3	113.1	114.9	117.2	114.3
1857	106.9	105.3	103.6	108.5	121.7	133.0	128.7	125.2	120.8	104.5	110.4	106.8
1858	101.0	93.1	94.5	97.6	97.8	98.5	98.9	109.4	115.0	118.5	107.7	106.8
1859	111.1	116.3	115.5	121.7	135.6	129.7	119.1	110.2	105.5	109.6	112.5	112.3
1860	116.0	112.8	113.0	117.0	113.8	109.4	106.8	107.5	114.9	115.2	107.5	96.7
1861	101.9	96.9	100.4	106.6	102.3	100.8	94.9	90.8	93.6	103.8	104.5	104.6

Table 20—Meats and Meat Products

Year	Jan.	Feb.	Mar.	Apr.	May	June	July	Aug.	Sept.	Oct.	Nov.	Dec.
1784	93.5	93.2	95.1	91.8	94.9	98.3	102.8	105.6	106.3	110.3	108.5	99.4
1785	99.2	97.2	95.8	95.1	95.5	96.0	98.1	99.9	102.3	100.4	100.0	94.0
1786	94.0	92.1	90.1	89.1	93.8	97.4	97.4	97.4	98.0	97.9	99.6	96.8
1787	97.6	93.7	93.6	92.4	89.8	92.1	95.7	91.9	96.7	93.1	93.3	91.2
1788	88.9	87.0	85.2	81.4	80.4	80.3	80.3	73.5	70.7	72.8	72.8	68.7
1789	70.0	70.0	67.5	63.2	61.8	62.1	62.1	61.8	62.1	62.1	69.2	68.4
1790	64.3	64.3	63.8	63.8	66.2	66.2	68.1	76.7	73.4	80.1	85.0	83.4
1791	78.4	78.3	75.1	74.0	74.0	78.2	82.8	85.0	87.0	87.9	86.1	86.5
1792	80.1	80.3	81.6	81.8	81.8	82.5	82.5	82.4	81.8	81.8	88.4	87.6
1793	88.7	93.3	89.7	98.9	100.2	100.2	99.9	101.3	104.1	100.8	103.7	106.5
1794	107.1	107.3	107.7	109.0								
1795	127.2	128.3	128.3	130.2	131.9	132.8	133.1	132.1	133.4	134.7	135.5	137.4
1796	145.1	146.4	148.6	140.9	139.6	142.3	146.3	143.3	151.2	157.8	148.6	149.7
1797	146.6	146.6	141.7	136.5	136.5	136.9	136.8	135.5	139.0	139.0	141.6	152.3
1798	144.0	144.0	138.1	138.1	138.1	121.7	123.2	124.6	126.0	127.4	128.7	
1799					108.3	108.8	109.3	111.5				
1800						110.4	111.9	116.0	126.7	142.0	144.8	134.4
1801	136.3	137.7	143.4	145.0	143.6	147.3	158.2	168.5	174.3	177.2	165.7	141.7
1802	119.7	119.1	122.0	119.2	119.2	120.0	117.6	121.5	123.5	124.7	126.7	120.1
1803	116.7	106.0	106.0	106.0	109.5	112.1	110.9	117.0	117.0	117.0	117.0	119.9
1804	119.0	119.9	119.9	119.9	117.0	117.0	122.7	122.7	115.8	115.8	120.6	119.0
1805	119.0	122.9	122.9	122.9	120.5	120.5	129.6	129.6	129.6	129.6	129.6	129.6
1806	151.6	152.7	152.7	155.9	154.6	163.0	163.0	171.1	167.7	168.6	167.7	154.8
1807	150.5	150.5	150.5	136.7	132.3	129.7	130.6	128.0	130.6	127.6	133.7	128.2
1808	114.2	109.0	110.5	104.6	102.1	102.1	102.1	98.5	98.5	102.1	108.8	107.5
1809	106.1	106.1	109.7	120.1	123.1	123.1	122.1	121.6	127.5	127.6	126.5	126.5
1810	128.4	129.5	135.5	133.8	139.0	135.6	139.3	137.0	138.9	138.9	140.4	140.4
1811	143.5	143.5	143.5	143.5	137.6	133.9	133.0	133.0	133.0	133.0	133.0	133.0
1812	133.0	130.7	128.2	124.8	123.6	123.6	123.6	123.6	123.6	124.7	124.7	125.3
1813	125.3	125.3	125.3	125.3	125.3	125.3	125.3	125.3	125.3	125.3	125.3	139.5
1814	143.3	144.6	155.0	159.2	168.5	168.1	165.7	179.7	179.7	179.8	192.5	192.5
1815	184.7	184.3	176.0	173.4	167.2	177.2	205.5	209.6	219.0	213.5	208.2	191.8
1816	184.4	174.0	170.0	170.0	166.8	174.6	174.5	176.2	176.7	173.6	168.9	168.9
1817	173.1	173.1	177.2	177.2	177.7	177.7	172.9	172.9	172.9	180.8	184.0	184.0
1818	183.2	183.2	176.4	182.2	178.5	173.0	175.0	176.0	179.2	185.4	180.1	174.9
1819	167.0	155.3	146.8	139.3	135.8	133.7	129.0	125.8	125.5	134.6	135.5	132.0
1820	119.4	119.4	118.7	115.4	115.4	112.4	112.9	112.9	112.9	116.6	120.6	117.8
1821	112.5	112.5	102.0	94.7	94.7	94.7	94.7	94.7	94.7	101.6	105.2	98.7
1822	98.7	98.7	97.5	94.9	95.8	96.3	96.3	98.3	98.9	105.2	105.1	101.1
1823	99.0	97.6	94.6	94.6	92.8	96.5	98.8	98.8	100.9	102.9	102.4	101.8
1824	100.3	99.6	98.6	98.4	100.1	100.8	102.0	104.0	107.2	107.2	109.5	107.3
1825	104.2	104.2	102.3	102.8	97.7	98.1	98.1	96.2	96.8	95.5	95.1	94.5
1826	94.5	93.5	90.2	86.9	86.1	86.1	86.7	86.7	92.6	91.7	91.7	90.9
1827	89.6	87.5	90.3	91.1	89.5	89.8	90.8	95.4	101.3	100.9	101.3	100.9
1828	101.3	94.2	92.7	92.7	92.2	92.9	96.8	100.6	105.0	104.4	103.3	100.0
1829	99.0	94.1	94.1	93.4	92.7	89.9	89.1	90.5	89.5	87.2	85.3	80.3
1830	79.2	79.2	81.4	82.0	84.3	91.8	96.5	106.3	106.4	107.9	106.0	99.5
1831	98.6	99.9	97.5	96.7	99.7	102.1	103.8	103.8	103.7	100.1	96.2	95.5
1832	94.4	95.5	95.5	91.8	91.8	93.2	97.1	100.6	101.3	106.5	102.0	101.4
1833	100.6	100.6	98.4	93.8	97.4	96.9	97.3	97.3	107.5	105.8	104.0	98.1
1834	98.0	97.6	97.6	94.7	91.8	94.2	93.8	94.9	94.5	93.9	92.9	92.3
1835	92.6	92.5	91.8	98.6	105.9	118.4	119.3	118.9	116.0	117.4	114.4	115.7
1836	115.5	117.1	121.6	143.7	143.2	133.1	132.9	132.4	138.9	145.5	144.0	136.9
1837	132.9	137.1	133.2	127.3	116.1	112.6	118.3	124.8	121.7	115.8	115.0	112.1
1838	110.7	111.9	102.8	105.0	108.7	116.3	117.1	123.5	134.2	143.2	140.3	137.9
1839	134.9	128.8	133.5	133.9	135.0	133.9	129.3	120.7	114.5	113.8	112.3	110.0
1840	105.5	100.0	94.1	109.2	111.6	113.0	113.7	114.1	121.0	123.9	116.5	105.5
1841	103.0	92.9	92.7	87.6	85.6	82.8	76.5	75.8	76.7	73.5	70.3	64.9
1842	64.4	63.4	63.2	63.0	58.9	58.0	58.8	62.3	65.1	65.5	64.3	65.5
1843	64.8	66.8	62.6	64.5	66.1	75.5	75.5	72.2	70.2	68.7	66.5	65.3
1844	64.1	66.4	64.5	62.7	60.1	57.5	61.0	63.8	64.4	64.2	61.4	61.7
1845	64.9	74.3	75.8	84.7	83.8	84.9	85.3	86.1	88.9	86.3	83.1	83.2
1846	79.7	78.4	77.1	72.6	70.6	72.2	65.2	64.9	67.1	77.0	79.3	75.4
1847	74.0	88.9	103.7	108.8	111.5	114.4	108.7	108.3	108.3	107.6	105.6	98.8
1848	85.6	86.4	85.0	80.9	73.3	75.1	81.4	86.2	91.6	92.1	88.6	87.8
1849	94.4	90.7	86.5	83.0	83.1	87.7	89.3	92.2	92.2	89.5	85.7	84.4
1850	85.4	87.1	86.9	83.0	83.6	86.1	86.0	84.1	83.3	86.0	86.4	86.3
1851	89.6	95.2	97.5	99.6	108.3	105.6	103.3	103.2	105.7	107.1	103.3	99.3
1852	102.6	108.0	112.5	118.2	124.2	121.2	127.6	132.0	134.5	133.6	128.9	133.5
1853	132.6	126.6	124.1	119.1	116.7	116.9	119.6	118.4	119.5	126.0	125.4	115.3
1854	115.5	118.7	116.4	112.8	116.7	111.5	112.2	113.8	121.1	117.3	113.5	113.3
1855	112.6	114.1	118.2	122.9	123.2	127.7	129.6	132.7	140.9	144.7	145.2	141.3
1856	126.8	126.9	125.3	122.0	124.4	124.4	133.9	131.4	133.5	131.8	131.1	128.1
1857	130.3	132.2	143.9	144.2	144.6	150.8	148.5	154.8	157.3	159.5	140.1	120.9
1858	108.2	113.8	118.2	120.1	123.5	120.3	115.2	119.4	119.4	118.4	117.2	116.6
1859	116.4	121.0	119.2	115.3	115.1	118.5	117.9	111.7	111.1	113.7	110.9	109.6
1860	107.2	110.9	110.0	110.1	113.2	113.8	119.1	121.8	121.2	119.8	119.3	110.2
1861	109.5	109.7	110.8	107.8	107.7	106.3	98.5	96.0	94.9	95.0	91.6	82.8

TABLE 21—DAIRY PRODUCTS

Year	Jan.	Feb.	Mar.	Apr.	May	June	July	Aug.	Sept.	Oct.	Nov.	Dec.
1784	146.7	135.0	143.9	143.9	148.8	142.7	136.8	130.9	124.9	118.7	112.4	117.4
1785	103.4	103.4	105.8	105.8	101.1	101.1	105.2	105.2	105.2	105.2	105.2	108.9
1786	108.9	108.9	108.9	110.7	112.5	97.4	96.2	95.0	93.8	92.6	91.4	90.1
1787	92.6	95.0	97.4	94.5	86.3	86.3	86.3	86.3	86.3	91.2	93.8	90.1
1788	82.3	82.3	82.3	82.3	78.8	80.6	80.6	80.6	80.6	73.3	82.3	67.2
1789	73.6	73.2	72.9	72.5	72.1	69.7	67.2	67.2	67.2	67.2	73.6	92.6
1790	92.6	92.6	92.6	93.9	95.2	96.4	103.6	101.8	100.1	98.2	108.1	108.1
1791	108.1	108.1	98.2	97.4	97.4	96.0	96.0	99.4	99.4	101.4	100.1	105.2
1792	109.8	109.8	109.8	109.8	109.8	109.8	102.1	102.1	102.1	102.1	112.3	112.3
1793	117.1	117.1	117.1	126.5	126.5	126.5	126.5	126.5	126.5	134.6	133.1	131.5
1794	148.8	148.8	155.4	148.8							142.5	142.5
1795	140.2	140.2	147.2	151.7	156.2	160.4	170.0	157.6	150.2	138.9	145.2	144.4
1796	139.5	144.2	144.2	144.0	139.3	160.0	154.6	154.6	134.6	132.0	129.0	123.9
1797	126.5	129.0	123.9	138.6	138.6	113.1	113.1	113.1	118.6	118.6	118.6	143.1
1798	145.2	147.2	147.2	147.2	147.2	147.2	147.2	147.2	147.2	147.2	143.6	139.7
1799	142.3	144.7	147.2	147.2	147.2	147.2	147.2	144.9				
1800						135.3	145.7	145.7	140.8	140.8	142.0	140.8
1801	140.3	140.3	145.3	145.3	145.3	147.2	145.3	140.8	143.1	150.6	142.6	142.6
1802	142.6	142.6	132.4	132.4	132.4	127.0	127.0	127.0	121.3	121.3	104.9	104.9
1803	99.3	99.3	95.2	95.2	95.2	95.2	95.2	100.7	100.7	100.7	106.9	106.9
1804	106.9	111.1	131.8	131.8	159.7	159.7	151.0	144.0	137.5	137.5	156.2	178.0
1805	178.0	178.0	176.3	186.4	186.4	186.4	173.7	173.7	173.7	173.7	173.7	173.7
1806	164.1	164.1	173.3	167.3	169.7	167.3	167.3	161.0	161.0	153.7	159.7	145.0
1807	145.0	145.0	145.0	145.0	145.0	140.1	140.1	132.4	132.4	132.4	129.5	129.5
1808	132.5	132.5	126.9	126.9	114.7	109.8	109.8	109.8	109.8	109.8	109.8	109.8
1809	109.8	109.8	109.8	121.7	128.3	121.7	121.7	121.7	109.8	117.1	117.1	117.1
1810	117.1	121.7	128.3	121.7	144.2	146.5	137.0	141.9	141.9	138.6	138.6	138.6
1811	138.6	138.6	135.2	135.2	135.2	141.9	139.5	151.6	151.6	136.2	126.5	129.0
1812	129.0	126.5	126.5	126.5	126.5	126.5	131.0	144.8	144.8	120.4	120.4	119.1
1813	125.2	125.2	125.2	125.2	129.6	129.6	129.6	129.6	129.6	129.6	129.6	150.4
1814	176.5	189.5	176.9	175.8	151.0	151.0	141.9	141.9	141.9	180.1	180.1	200.3
1815	189.3	177.6	171.7	173.2	187.0	180.1	191.3	159.3	183.7	188.1	190.3	190.3
1816	196.7	196.7	188.1	191.6	189.3	192.5	173.7	176.5	162.3	164.8	176.9	181.5
1817	181.5	181.5	178.0	201.5	195.9	195.9	168.2	168.2	155.3	144.6	159.2	162.3
1818	165.3	162.3	154.5	160.1	151.8	154.5	158.7	154.5	151.6	145.7	145.0	136.1
1819	136.1	138.6	147.5	125.1	120.4	106.9	125.5	121.5	124.2	126.9	112.7	110.1
1820	108.0	108.0	108.0	95.6	95.6	85.5	88.2	93.2	93.2	93.2	93.2	93.2
1821	88.2	88.2	88.2	93.2	93.2	93.2	93.2	93.2	90.1	102.3	99.1	106.4
1822	130.2	130.2	130.2	135.0	135.0	137.9	137.9	137.9	117.8	125.1	129.6	122.7
1823	122.7	107.6	102.1	102.1	102.1	102.1	102.1	98.0	98.0	98.0	98.0	93.7
1824	93.7	93.7	85.5	88.3	88.3	88.3	88.3	82.6	69.8	69.8	69.8	75.3
1825	78.9	90.1	90.7	90.7	84.4	84.4	84.4	84.4	84.4	93.7	93.7	98.7
1826	103.6	103.6	101.2	96.3	100.7	105.8	105.8	105.8	105.8	105.8	105.8	105.8
1827	104.3	101.2	98.7	93.7	96.6	87.7	95.6	90.1	93.2	89.4	88.2	88.2
1828	85.2	85.2	84.0	80.9	77.1	79.6	79.6	82.6	80.0	82.6	82.6	82.6
1829	83.6	83.6	83.6	92.0	80.9	80.9	78.4	78.4	78.4	78.4	84.4	79.6
1830	79.6	79.6	79.6	77.1	71.8	74.5	77.1	77.1	77.1	84.0	81.3	82.6
1831	86.4	86.4	94.7	94.7	96.4	96.4	96.4	96.4	95.2	95.2	93.6	93.6
1832	93.6	96.9	96.9	101.2	101.2	101.2	94.7	95.8	97.5	97.5	100.2	104.3
1833	104.3	104.3	109.8	113.9	115.1	110.8	105.2	105.2	102.8	102.8	105.2	105.2
1834	105.2	102.8	102.8	102.8	92.5	92.5	92.5	92.5	92.5	92.5	92.5	105.2
1835	105.1	106.3	105.1	104.3	105.8	111.8	114.3	114.3	120.0	125.6	124.5	143.5
1836	147.4	138.3	144.4	157.1	148.1	143.1	138.6	141.9	147.4	149.6	158.0	149.6
1837	145.3	144.8	141.3	141.3	138.9	124.2	122.8	115.9	126.7	130.2	125.5	123.1
1838	123.1	122.7	121.6	115.9	121.7	114.7	116.1	118.3	122.2	144.4	140.5	142.5
1839	138.6	126.2	134.0	133.5	138.6	138.6	138.6	138.6	140.8	140.8	131.5	119.4
1840	119.4	113.5	109.8	103.1	95.2	97.9	100.8	91.7	93.7	96.0	97.2	93.5
1841	94.7	90.5	90.5	84.0	84.0	84.0	84.0	84.6	86.7	91.7	89.2	93.5
1842	91.0	91.0	96.3	96.0	92.9	91.7	85.5	85.5	92.4	84.2	84.2	74.5
1843	73.1	65.5	69.0	67.0	70.4	71.1	71.8	77.8	76.1	72.9	68.3	67.0
1844	68.9	72.3	72.3	73.6	79.7	85.1	76.3	71.5	73.2	76.1	76.5	78.1
1845	82.4	89.4	86.4	90.7	99.6	89.5	87.2	93.2	93.6	100.8	109.9	118.7
1846	107.9	104.4	109.6	108.0	93.9	89.7	91.1	90.5	86.7	93.7	96.6	94.4
1847	93.1	97.0	103.2	114.7	118.0	115.2	106.5	108.2	109.1	103.9	106.3	114.3
1848	113.1	112.2	114.9	116.8	118.3	108.7	108.7	94.0	95.2	80.0	86.8	98.0
1849	99.2	99.7	99.7	98.6	80.0	80.0	82.6	93.9	95.8	97.0	100.0	104.0
1850	102.4	100.7	96.6	95.2	91.6	88.3	89.1	102.0	105.1	103.9	103.6	100.5
1851	97.9	98.3	98.3	98.3	97.7	95.2	95.2	96.4	92.8	96.4	95.2	100.8
1852	104.0	107.9	114.1	120.1	118.1	107.9	106.8	103.0	111.8	130.8	135.5	148.4
1853	148.4	139.4	137.1	139.4	129.8	111.9	113.2	124.8	124.8	123.7	130.7	128.3
1854	124.7	135.0	132.4	127.0	129.7	135.0	124.2	132.4	152.1	142.6	140.1	137.6
1855	140.1	129.7	151.4	150.6	145.0	145.0	147.4	147.4	147.4	145.0	152.1	148.8
1856	148.8	151.0	149.3	149.3	147.5	131.5	127.4	121.7	128.3	129.6	131.8	136.2
1857	135.2	133.0	133.0	133.0	142.6	140.1	142.6	142.6	142.6	125.9	109.8	118.3
1858	109.8	109.8	109.8	113.9	113.9	111.3	103.6	103.6	110.4	108.2	105.9	105.9
1859	109.2	109.2	127.0	121.3	109.0	109.0	109.0	115.4	110.3	116.9	122.8	122.8
1860	128.4	125.6	122.6	122.6	115.4	114.2	109.0	114.6	114.6	116.5	115.1	112.3
1861	109.7	110.3	107.0	100.7	102.1	90.5	86.7	87.4	86.0	87.4	88.2	93.0

Table 22—Fruit

Year	Jan.	Feb.	Mar.	Apr.	May	June	July	Aug.	Sept.	Oct.	Nov.	Dec.
1784	85.6	85.6	86.9	87.3	85.3	83.1	80.5	80.6	80.5	80.4	80.0	78.8
1785	77.0	77.0	76.8	76.5	76.4	76.1	81.4	79.9	78.3	76.6	74.9	73.1
1786	72.6	71.9	70.9	64.5	65.0	65.8	72.4	78.5	78.5	77.0	75.5	75.4
1787	75.0	70.4	65.4	62.9	60.1	60.6	61.1	61.6	63.8	63.8	63.8	64.8
1788	65.7	65.5	65.3	65.0	64.7	64.5	64.1	63.8	63.4	63.0	61.2	59.4
1789	57.5	55.6	53.6	51.7	51.7	51.7	51.7	53.8	55.9	58.3	60.8	63.2
1790	63.3	60.0	60.0	60.2	59.0	64.7	64.7	69.0	70.7	70.3	73.9	99.6
1791	112.7	111.6	118.9	104.2	104.5	109.6	109.9	95.7	93.9	99.8	100.9	98.2
1792	86.3	86.5	86.7	86.9	87.2	88.0	89.5	84.8	85.0	77.3	82.6	80.9
1793	81.6	81.8	82.0	80.1	80.3	80.5	85.9	86.1	86.3	86.5	86.6	86.8
1794	87.0	87.3	87.5	87.8								
1795	97.9	93.4	93.6	93.9	94.1	94.4	103.7	108.4	108.7	109.0	119.3	134.3
1796	132.7	131.4	119.2	118.6	136.2	115.6	115.3	118.1	120.6	109.8	111.0	111.6
1797	121.8	121.8	109.9	109.9	120.2	120.2	117.0	106.0	106.0	106.0	106.7	108.2
1798	115.2	118.7	114.6	114.0	113.4	114.7	114.0	113.4	110.9	110.2	109.5	108.2
1799	108.4	108.6	105.6	101.3	101.3	113.9	113.9	113.9				
1800						136.2	136.0	114.3	114.2	114.0	113.9	101.1
1801	98.7	98.6	96.2	102.1	99.9	105.3	109.4	109.3	114.1	114.1	107.7	111.1
1802	106.9	106.5	100.8	106.5	97.5	100.5	100.7	100.3	99.8	102.9	102.4	97.0
1803	82.2	82.2	80.9	81.0	81.0	81.1	76.2	76.3	76.4	76.4	76.5	101.0
1804	99.9	92.2	94.3	94.4	96.8	96.9	102.2	102.2	102.3	102.4	106.4	117.9
1805	117.1	115.9	110.5	108.8	104.7	104.7	104.7	104.7	110.1	114.8	119.0	122.8
1806	130.2	110.2	110.3	101.0	142.5	149.4	142.6	138.9	131.6	133.6	126.4	110.6
1807	110.1	109.8	107.2	92.6	91.7	101.4	94.6	95.1	95.1	95.8	96.0	97.3
1808	102.6	100.5	95.7	92.6	97.7	100.8	100.8	101.2	101.2	101.0	103.0	103.0
1809	105.1	105.1	108.4	115.2	115.2	113.9	93.0	94.1	95.8	94.6	98.7	93.0
1810	91.7	91.7	85.6	85.8	83.9	81.6	103.9	102.1	119.2	119.4	118.7	124.4
1811	137.4	137.4	114.4	109.0	110.5	101.6	101.6	96.0	96.0	96.0	111.5	111.5
1812	126.1	129.3	121.1	114.1	114.1	114.1	127.4	120.0	121.3	122.5	123.8	125.0
1813	126.2	127.3	129.1	129.1	129.1	128.6	128.6	128.6	128.6	128.6	128.6	128.6
1814	148.8	155.8	153.7	158.3	157.0	157.0	157.0	157.0	157.0	157.0	157.0	157.0
1815	157.0	157.0	131.4	130.0	130.0	140.3	156.3	152.5	154.9	143.8	145.0	157.3
1816	142.8	143.1	99.9	100.3	98.9	98.7	99.1	91.6	89.2	93.7	93.7	91.2
1817	80.0	80.0	82.5	111.1	111.1	89.1	89.1	88.6	89.2	101.0	101.0	101.0
1818	109.1	110.4	116.9	116.9	126.0	126.0	123.1	123.6	126.2	123.2	124.5	125.5
1819	128.8	122.2	132.1	127.9	126.8	109.2	109.8	116.5	114.4	112.6	117.0	115.9
1820	118.7	116.5	103.7	99.0	86.0	80.1	79.3	79.5	79.5	79.5	93.1	99.9
1821	96.7	96.7	82.0	83.8	84.0	84.0	87.5	87.5	87.7	95.2	97.7	111.5
1822	105.5	105.5	105.5	107.5	102.2	101.9	99.6	102.0	103.2	103.2	113.3	108.1
1823	106.6	106.1	96.1	92.3	82.1	82.1	78.5	85.1	85.1	87.7	89.1	89.2
1824	90.8	89.0	89.4	91.7	92.0	92.0	89.9	89.9	105.3	107.1	107.6	107.6
1825	113.6	113.6	113.6	102.9	112.3	111.7	113.4	98.1	95.7	107.2	112.0	111.8
1826	100.4	100.8	92.7	88.2	93.5	85.1	77.0	87.9	94.6	100.7	85.2	82.3
1827	85.7	85.5	70.1	71.2	64.9	62.9	66.1	69.0	70.4	70.4	71.3	73.0
1828	72.3	74.2	74.1	73.8	69.7	68.9	75.5	82.5	103.5	97.4	101.7	98.1
1829	96.4	77.4	77.4	78.7	84.9	83.0	84.1	83.5	95.1	94.8	81.1	81.0
1830	72.1	67.9	59.6	70.9	69.8	72.4	73.4	93.5	92.7	76.1	71.2	64.2
1831	64.2	62.3	62.2	63.7	69.5	76.3	72.9	71.0	71.0	72.1	75.3	81.2
1832	81.2	76.3	72.1	71.5	78.2	78.2	76.2	55.3	55.3	62.2	70.9	70.9
1833	64.3	60.3	54.0	62.2	62.2	52.3	54.3	55.0	65.8	64.2	52.3	66.1
1834	61.8	61.8	59.9	51.9	48.8	49.3	49.3	57.4	57.4	57.4	62.1	64.5
1835	75.1	65.8	68.8	68.7	75.9	78.4	79.0	77.7	65.5	72.8	70.5	69.6
1836	62.7	63.2	63.8	67.4	65.2	61.8	63.9	64.7	66.4	68.1	68.6	66.0
1837	64.5	63.6	58.3	57.5	52.5	54.0	51.5	53.8	51.6	51.4	68.0	65.7
1838	63.9	60.3	60.3	58.3	59.5	59.5	65.1	71.7	64.0	64.0	56.9	53.1
1839	53.1	53.1	54.7	58.6	61.3	58.9	58.9	61.6	61.6	55.7	54.4	51.9
1840	51.9	52.4	52.3	54.8	54.1	53.8	51.3	41.4	63.2	63.0	69.1	73.5
1841	68.4	66.5	66.5	64.4	64.4	61.6	61.6	59.9	59.6	65.4	70.5	60.7
1842	55.8	53.4	53.0	49.4	50.4	49.4	47.5	49.0	49.0	66.2	62.0	55.8
1843	54.3	54.4	53.4	52.8	58.3	61.1	75.4	71.3	71.8	82.0	82.8	68.1
1844	70.6	65.6	63.5	66.1	71.3	64.2	68.3	65.2	67.3	69.8	69.7	74.5
1845	70.7	69.4	68.6	68.9	69.2	70.1	78.4	85.8	89.4	82.5	83.8	71.9
1846	70.2	70.0	74.3	70.5	70.2	68.2	66.1	67.8	65.2	68.4	75.1	67.5
1847	69.6	67.0	64.1	66.3	59.8	60.4	70.5	72.1	71.0	66.4	76.7	67.4
1848	68.8	61.2	60.7	60.1	65.7	63.0	61.1	61.7	62.2	66.1	57.9	54.9
1849	54.9	57.0	56.3	53.6	52.6	54.4	59.7	62.0	66.7	71.1	69.1	69.0
1850	70.0	71.0	74.7	74.3	74.9	74.2	76.7	91.2	90.8	85.0	77.9	74.7
1851	75.0	72.0	70.9	67.5	66.0	73.3	86.3	91.7	97.8	97.1	72.4	63.2
1852	63.6	63.6	58.1	51.4	54.6	56.1	55.6	55.0	74.4	75.8	66.5	72.7
1853	72.7	66.7	70.4	76.3	79.9	77.6	79.3	73.8	96.7	110.5	109.8	105.5
1854	108.3	110.3	107.4	105.8	107.4	107.4	104.1	125.2	120.0	135.0	95.7	83.7
1855	76.3	75.3	80.2	83.9	81.2	84.5	80.2	99.5	112.3	118.2	96.1	93.0
1856	93.4	92.7	92.7	89.8	87.1	90.5	105.6	103.5	107.6	117.6	118.0	117.7
1857	119.9	107.0	113.8	112.4	109.0	109.0	109.0	102.3	135.4	135.8	92.4	82.1
1858	62.2	64.2	66.6	67.6	70.3	73.9	76.8	75.4	74.7	73.7	71.5	60.6
1859	62.1	59.1	57.8	57.5	57.4	56.4	57.2	60.0	60.0	70.6	71.5	68.9
1860	55.6	56.0	61.5	53.6	56.6	67.6	62.7	84.6	89.2	91.0	67.9	64.9
1861	65.7	66.5	56.8	56.9	53.2	52.4	51.0	71.1	91.9	103.9	104.4	118.4

TABLE 23—BEVERAGES

Year	Jan.	Feb.	Mar.	Apr.	May	June	July	Aug.	Sept.	Oct.	Nov.	Dec.
1784	102.5	104.2	99.6	95.1	98.0	98.0	100.9	101.7	101.8	105.1	107.3	109.1
1785	105.3	107.7	109.1	102.4	100.2	100.9	106.9	102.8	102.1	111.8	111.5	111.5
1786	111.6	111.3	109.1	110.7	99.6	101.7	101.7	100.7	100.7	101.7	105.8	107.7
1787	107.7	107.7	107.7	98.1	93.4	95.7	97.7	97.5	98.0	97.3	105.0	105.0
1788	105.0	101.0	96.5	92.6	92.4	92.4	92.5	93.8	98.7	100.5	102.1	105.9
1789	104.7	101.7	101.5	108.8	113.4	115.4	109.8	107.6	106.9	104.4	104.5	102.1
1790	101.1	101.1	93.9	95.7	95.7	96.7	92.5	84.6	84.6	87.2	85.9	83.5
1791	82.4	81.4	82.4	81.8	81.8	82.0	81.2	80.7	79.1	80.0	88.9	88.9
1792	94.5	103.5	102.5	104.4	103.7	107.4	105.5	104.5	103.1	103.1	101.2	101.4
1793	99.4	99.4	100.4	99.4	95.2	86.6	86.1	86.1	88.0	88.0	88.0	88.0
1794	88.0	88.0	93.0	90.3	98.2	101.7	104.6	103.5	110.1	111.0	106.5	117.1
1795	116.7	124.1	124.1	124.1	126.3	130.7	132.1	135.3	137.7	139.3	134.3	133.3
1796	125.5	143.2	136.4	139.5	133.9	133.6	133.6	131.3	130.5	132.2	135.5	135.5
1797	139.1	139.1	132.7	132.7	131.0	131.0	129.2	134.0	130.8	127.5	127.5	135.2
1798	136.7	137.3	136.8	136.8	136.8	136.8	148.9	148.9	148.9	148.9	148.9	164.1
1799					162.6	161.7	161.7	153.1				
1800						148.0	145.7	147.8	146.9	147.4	147.1	142.8
1801	139.2	144.7	140.7	137.6	136.9	134.4	133.6	133.9	134.2	141.8	127.8	129.9
1802	123.7	123.7	124.8	126.3	116.8	116.8	112.7	112.7	112.7	117.2	117.2	116.6
1803	116.6	116.6	118.6	121.9	127.3	127.9	127.3	130.5	130.5	136.0	138.4	139.0
1804	138.4	139.9	143.4	140.7	142.3	145.3	146.4	145.3	147.3	144.4	148.9	147.4
1805	147.0	147.0	145.3	143.5	144.0	144.7	142.2	141.5	141.0	141.0	143.4	140.6
1806	143.3	138.7	136.0	134.1	131.3	131.6	134.1	128.3	126.0	122.5	121.2	124.9
1807	124.0	121.4	120.7	117.8	118.8	121.8	119.2	117.0	116.4	115.4	115.3	114.9
1808	115.6	109.7	108.3	109.6	107.0	108.5	107.7	108.6	110.4	110.4	111.7	127.9
1809	131.8	132.9	128.9	125.6	117.9	115.2	111.2	107.7	110.8	112.0	111.6	110.2
1810	110.7	106.6	106.7	108.8	105.6	101.8	98.4	98.7	96.0	97.4	99.0	91.6
1811	90.0	91.9	91.1	87.6	84.8	84.6	73.4	78.0	76.4	71.7	61.9	59.1
1812	61.1	62.4	65.0	65.1	68.0	69.5	82.5	96.1	94.2	98.5	98.0	98.7
1813	100.5	104.7	105.6	110.0	107.9	112.2	112.1	113.2	114.0	116.6	128.0	145.8
1814	163.7	144.8	141.1	135.7	136.8	139.3	138.5	138.5	137.9	175.8	171.9	162.5
1815	161.4	164.8	135.6	134.0	131.7	140.7	157.4	159.3	155.9	151.2	161.8	138.0
1816	138.6	154.0	149.1	137.7	134.0	140.8	136.2	133.6	122.5	120.3	118.9	116.3
1817	114.3	115.2	111.2	107.7	105.2	105.1	103.2	103.2	105.8	110.9	112.3	111.9
1818	115.2	115.0	109.4	111.7	112.9	114.2	112.3	115.3	118.9	120.6	120.9	116.2
1819	118.7	117.9	117.8	114.1	110.4	108.8	108.0	107.0	105.3	104.5	104.3	103.6
1820	103.6	103.9	101.3	101.3	101.0	102.0	102.3	102.9	106.4	106.8	106.8	106.9
1821	107.2	106.8	106.5	106.5	107.9	108.0	108.0	107.8	107.8	108.1	107.2	106.9
1822	106.3	106.3	106.6	106.8	107.5	107.3	102.3	102.3	102.2	102.1	103.5	102.3
1823	102.1	101.3	100.7	100.7	101.4	96.9	96.0	96.3	96.8	95.7	99.1	99.7
1824	98.6	98.0	98.2	97.3	94.8	92.4	92.7	93.5	93.1	91.1	90.2	89.4
1825	91.0	91.3	91.0	94.8	95.6	96.3	96.5	93.6	92.5	91.2	90.6	89.6
1826	89.8	88.9	88.1	89.1	87.8	85.0	81.4	81.1	80.6	80.8	80.1	80.0
1827	80.0	80.6	80.6	80.5	79.1	79.1	79.2	78.7	78.2	78.1	78.1	77.8
1828	77.5	76.6	75.7	75.2	74.5	74.3	74.3	75.5	76.0	75.8	75.8	74.6
1829	72.8	72.8	73.3	73.7	73.1	73.4	73.2	72.7	71.8	71.7	71.8	72.2
1830	72.1	71.9	72.0	71.1	70.3	69.8	69.0	69.6	66.9	67.6	68.0	66.1
1831	60.0	60.8	61.3	61.8	63.0	63.2	63.1	64.4	65.9	68.1	68.1	68.3
1832	65.2	64.3	63.0	60.6	60.7	61.2	61.5	61.7	63.1	64.4	65.5	65.2
1833	65.0	65.5	58.5	57.8	57.8	57.2	57.4	57.8	59.7	58.2	58.1	57.6
1834	57.6	57.0	57.0	56.8	57.2	56.9	56.7	56.6	54.2	54.3	54.3	54.9
1835	52.7	52.7	55.6	63.2	63.2	61.5	62.7	62.7	63.8	60.2	57.5	57.9
1836	58.8	58.7	59.8	58.4	58.4	57.8	57.8	58.2	58.2	58.1	58.1	59.2
1837	58.7	59.2	58.7	58.5	57.6	57.5	57.6	54.6	54.3	52.4	52.7	53.2
1838	53.2	53.1	52.9	52.3	52.0	50.6	50.6	51.2	51.3	51.3	51.5	51.4
1839	51.4	51.6	52.5	52.5	52.6	52.3	52.3	52.3	53.1	54.6	56.8	56.7
1840	57.0	56.9	56.8	57.6	57.3	57.4	56.9	57.9	60.0	61.1	61.6	72.9
1841	73.0	74.8	74.9	74.6	74.5	71.9	71.9	74.0	69.5	69.3	69.2	68.4
1842	67.6	67.3	63.1	61.8	61.0	60.8	60.5	60.6	60.6	60.2	60.1	58.4
1843	58.3	57.8	55.9	56.0	57.2	54.7	54.8	54.9	54.9	54.6	53.8	53.8
1844	54.2	56.4	56.4	56.6	55.8	55.5	55.5	55.8	55.2	55.3	55.1	54.1
1845	54.2	53.3	53.5	55.5	55.2	54.8	54.7	55.7	56.2	56.2	56.2	56.3
1846	56.5	56.8	56.9	57.0	55.4	54.8	55.3	55.0	54.8	55.0	55.0	55.4
1847	55.6	55.4	55.8	56.0	55.7	55.4	55.4	55.4	55.5	55.5	55.6	55.6
1848	55.3	55.2	55.3	55.1	55.0	54.9	53.7	53.1	53.0	53.2	53.1	53.2
1849	53.1	53.0	54.0	54.0	53.9	54.5	54.8	56.1	57.7	60.8	61.4	62.2
1850	63.3	69.0	66.6	59.5	59.8	59.0	60.0	60.3	61.3	63.7	63.0	62.1
1851	61.7	62.3	61.5	60.7	58.7	58.0	57.3	56.9	56.4	55.6	50.7	50.5
1852	50.6	50.5	50.5	49.8	47.8	47.0	47.1	46.9	46.8	46.9	46.8	46.9
1853	46.9	47.4	47.4	50.0	49.4	50.1	50.8	50.8	53.8	53.7	53.4	54.7
1854	55.0	55.0	57.1	56.7	56.6	55.7	55.1	55.1	55.2	55.7	55.5	55.3
1855	56.1	55.3	56.5	56.6	56.5	56.0	56.1	57.7	58.5	58.4	57.5	57.8
1856	57.7	57.9	58.2	58.2	57.7	57.3	57.5	57.4	54.5	54.5	54.5	54.0
1857	57.9	58.4	60.6	66.4	66.4	68.1	69.5	70.8	70.8	70.8	67.1	67.1
1858	66.8	66.8	66.9	68.3	68.3	68.3	66.8	66.8	66.8	66.8	64.7	61.8
1859	61.8	62.1	62.1	62.1	62.5	62.5	62.5	62.5	60.8	61.3	61.3	61.3
1860	59.8	59.0	59.6	60.1	59.9	60.5	61.1	62.3	63.5	63.6	63.7	60.5
1861	61.5	60.5	66.7	67.9	67.9	67.8	68.9	72.3	72.5	74.7	76.4	78.3

TABLE 24—CONDIMENTS

Year	Jan.	Feb.	Mar.	Apr.	May	June	July	Aug.	Sept.	Oct.	Nov.	Dec.
1784	148.1	145.9	142.6	142.4	143.8	144.5	148.9	152.9	150.8	157.1	152.7	155.0
1785	142.5	143.8	140.5	135.4	123.9	117.3	121.4	131.7	133.2	134.1	134.7	135.8
1786	131.6	130.4	128.2	128.8	126.6	125.5	125.7	127.5	124.6	123.6	124.2	126.5
1787	128.1	129.4	130.2	127.5	126.8	126.3	127.8	125.6	127.1	127.4	132.4	130.1
1788	130.7	130.8	130.8	127.1	129.7	126.8	123.4	121.8	120.0	116.5	115.9	114.9
1789	114.4	113.7	115.3	115.7	119.1	119.1	117.0	114.1	114.5	115.7	116.4	115.0
1790	118.3	118.0	118.2	112.2	112.2	112.6	118.9	117.8	118.7	124.1	131.2	132.2
1791	137.8	134.8	123.9	125.1	126.1	130.3	129.6	128.9	129.7	141.0	136.8	136.8
1792	132.5	132.3	132.1	130.4	130.4	129.3	128.5	127.1	127.1	132.1	142.1	151.8
1793	141.2	141.2	152.4	142.0	142.0	143.9	143.1	143.1	142.5	142.5	143.1	143.7
1794	174.2	173.6	179.9	179.9								
1795	195.9	199.8	200.3	203.0	204.9	212.3	213.8	217.5	221.0	218.9	219.1	227.5
1796	239.5	211.9	208.2	214.1	199.5	198.6	195.6	190.8	189.2	199.4	188.9	193.8
1797	197.7	187.1	186.4	183.6	183.9	183.9	183.9	179.7	170.4	170.4	170.4	164.4
1798	158.9	152.8	155.3	154.2	154.1	156.5	155.3	155.3	155.3	155.3	155.3	
1799					163.3	163.3	163.3	162.0				
1800						153.0	151.1	151.6	158.9	161.8	165.1	162.6
1801	159.5	157.1	156.6	152.4	153.0	151.8	149.4	147.8	146.3	156.4	163.3	169.3
1802	163.3	155.3	155.5	152.4	150.9	152.6	153.8	153.8	154.5	156.4	156.7	155.7
1803	158.5	153.8	147.8	146.4	143.4	140.2	140.6	141.3	141.3	142.0	144.8	147.1
1804	150.1	146.8	148.4	148.4	146.6	145.3	144.7	145.6	146.5	150.1	157.0	154.8
1805	155.5	151.8	148.1	152.2	153.6	153.6	154.4	154.0	154.0	153.9	154.3	157.8
1806	149.9	148.1	145.7	142.4	141.6	138.5	140.5	137.6	143.0	144.8	144.2	141.8
1807	142.4	138.5	139.9	138.6	137.0	141.6	141.8	140.7	146.3	146.2	152.5	150.7
1808	152.5	154.9	155.9	152.3	154.9	155.0	157.3	159.4	157.9	159.6	164.0	193.9
1809	194.3	193.6	193.0	189.7	179.8	144.6	146.3	149.0	161.1	165.2	158.5	161.0
1810	155.0	141.9	138.8	139.2	140.2	140.2	140.0	132.3	133.0	135.1	134.8	131.2
1811	131.7	133.0	131.1	125.4	128.4	131.1	129.3	128.8	134.5	135.0	127.4	125.2
1812	126.5	128.9	129.1	131.0	133.8	138.5	181.8	191.1	194.6	186.5	179.9	180.1
1813	179.7	180.9	182.5	190.6	193.3	201.3	200.9	205.5	207.1	207.1	238.2	269.4
1814	277.2	252.9	241.8	229.7	226.4	231.5	233.6	232.2	238.5	267.7	282.8	260.0
1815	252.5	247.7	187.9	184.6	183.2	193.9	195.1	200.1	210.5	208.1	211.5	191.7
1816	192.1	185.6	177.3	176.3	171.3	166.9	167.2	161.8	161.4	163.5	152.7	152.1
1817	151.1	149.7	149.7	140.4	138.0	137.4	130.2	130.7	130.4	130.6	131.1	133.6
1818	135.6	135.6	137.3	134.9	132.0	130.7	128.0	125.7	125.2	130.2	129.9	130.3
1819	131.2	130.1	129.3	125.5	126.5	122.3	111.9	112.3	111.7	115.5	119.0	119.9
1820	119.1	118.3	117.0	108.3	109.9	106.8	108.5	107.0	107.2	107.4	109.5	111.6
1821	112.2	112.6	113.9	110.3	112.0	110.4	107.1	105.0	101.5	103.7	104.8	105.3
1822	104.3	104.3	103.9	105.8	101.6	102.1	101.1	98.6	97.8	98.1	101.5	100.7
1823	99.3	98.9	96.8	98.4	97.2	99.5	99.4	99.0	99.0	94.7	91.0	90.9
1824	90.3	89.1	89.6	89.5	88.0	87.8	89.8	92.3	92.2	90.1	90.3	90.4
1825	90.1	93.6	93.4	103.5	105.2	102.6	101.4	98.4	98.7	100.4	101.1	101.8
1826	99.8	99.2	97.7	96.7	96.0	95.7	94.2	94.7	93.7	93.4	95.5	95.5
1827	97.1	97.2	96.4	97.0	100.6	100.4	99.8	97.2	96.8	97.3	97.9	98.7
1828	98.0	96.2	94.2	91.4	91.3	89.7	88.9	90.4	91.2	90.9	93.0	90.4
1829	91.4	90.6	90.5	88.7	86.6	85.7	85.5	84.6	84.5	84.2	83.3	81.5
1830	79.7	79.2	79.1	79.6	79.3	79.3	80.7	83.9	83.6	86.5	86.6	86.6
1831	85.4	85.4	85.4	83.4	87.0	86.5	86.9	87.4	88.6	90.7	92.9	92.8
1832	92.4	90.8	91.9	90.8	92.2	86.8	88.1	90.2	92.4	92.4	88.8	89.4
1833	78.1	75.1	70.7	70.0	70.1	68.6	67.7	68.6	68.4	69.5	69.7	69.4
1834	69.3	69.1	67.4	67.4	66.5	66.5	65.5	64.3	62.7	63.7	63.2	63.3
1835	68.3	68.1	70.5	70.9	71.1	70.4	70.0	69.9	71.0	71.6	70.7	70.5
1836	71.4	71.2	72.2	71.6	71.4	69.7	69.7	69.7	69.0	69.1	69.2	67.9
1837	68.8	68.8	70.0	69.6	67.6	67.3	67.5	66.0	64.2	63.8	63.4	64.1
1838	63.4	63.9	64.7	64.7	64.7	63.7	63.2	61.9	62.4	62.2	63.9	64.6
1839	64.4	64.9	65.7	65.1	64.8	64.0	64.4	64.1	64.1	63.2	63.1	62.7
1840	63.0	61.6	59.9	60.0	59.0	57.2	57.0	56.7	56.5	56.7	56.3	56.5
1841	56.1	56.7	56.4	58.9	56.6	57.1	56.6	57.4	57.2	58.8	60.2	59.2
1842	59.2	59.4	59.0	57.0	56.0	56.7	57.2	57.2	59.1	60.8	60.7	60.5
1843	60.2	59.7	58.3	58.9	59.0	59.2	59.1	59.6	59.1	59.6	59.7	60.4
1844	60.6	61.2	61.3	62.5	64.5	65.4	65.3	64.2	64.4	64.0	63.2	62.4
1845	62.2	62.4	63.4	65.7	65.7	65.6	64.7	66.3	68.5	69.7	69.8	71.7
1846	72.0	72.1	72.5	70.0	69.6	67.6	67.5	66.9	69.7	69.9	71.4	68.2
1847	66.3	67.2	68.1	67.4	68.4	69.1	68.8	68.1	66.9	67.9	67.6	66.1
1848	65.7	66.3	66.2	65.6	61.7	61.6	61.7	61.2	58.3	58.6	59.6	58.5
1849	60.8	58.7	58.6	58.1	58.1	58.1	57.3	58.0	58.9	61.1	61.9	61.1
1850	61.0	61.5	63.5	64.0	63.5	62.3	62.1	62.1	63.3	64.1	66.0	64.3
1851	65.7	65.5	65.1	64.7	64.7	64.7	63.5	64.0	62.4	62.2	60.9	59.5
1852	59.9	59.5	58.6	58.0	57.9	64.5	64.6	64.6	64.3	64.2	65.7	66.4
1853	66.0	68.2	69.4	69.7	71.1	70.5	69.4	70.3	69.5	69.8	69.8	69.6
1854	69.5	74.9	75.1	74.4	75.2	75.7	74.8	74.3	73.0	73.0	73.0	72.9
1855	72.8	71.4	71.8	73.8	72.1	71.8	70.2	70.9	72.3	73.8	74.6	74.4
1856	71.1	73.4	73.8	73.8	73.3	73.0	71.7	71.4	72.0	71.8	71.3	68.9
1857	69.0	69.5	68.3	69.6	67.8	68.1	62.2	61.8	61.8	61.2	55.6	56.1
1858	55.5	52.3	54.5	54.0	54.4	53.9	53.5	52.3	52.3	51.1	51.1	50.9
1859	50.4	50.9	51.1	51.1	50.6	50.6	50.6	50.2	49.2	49.3	49.3	49.7
1860	49.0	49.0	48.8	48.4	48.4	49.4	53.8	52.4	52.7	52.2	51.8	51.4
1861	51.4	50.2	50.3	50.3	50.3	50.0	49.3	53.2	54.7	55.5	58.3	61.0

TABLE 25—SUGAR AND MOLASSES

Year	Jan.	Feb.	Mar.	Apr.	May	June	July	Aug.	Sept.	Oct.	Nov.	Dec.
1784	99.9	95.2	89.0	84.4	81.9	86.0	90.8	83.3	85.2	81.4	80.8	76.9
1785	77.1	75.4	78.0	75.4	74.8	72.5	73.3	73.2	71.4	74.8	75.3	77.3
1786	82.0	85.7	77.5	77.0	77.7	78.6	82.4	77.7	77.7	77.9	78.6	81.3
1787	81.2	84.6	84.6	88.6	81.3	87.6	81.9	81.9	83.9	80.7	80.7	80.1
1788	80.4	80.2	80.3	80.2	80.0	80.3	80.0	78.5	78.6	77.0	77.0	79.3
1789	77.8	77.8	77.8	76.1	87.1	87.1	87.1	86.5	84.8	85.0	85.0	91.2
1790	88.6	88.3	84.8	83.5	88.3	91.8	88.5	91.2	93.5	101.7	104.9	110.0
1791	108.9	114.5	112.4	106.7	123.8	116.2	108.2	112.2	113.2	156.0	146.1	145.7
1792	142.8	143.7	151.3	154.3	151.4	153.3	155.0	154.1	150.2	150.2	158.0	156.0
1793	162.0	162.0	157.3	146.9	146.9	146.9	136.4	142.3	149.8	129.5	127.7	123.0
1794	120.1	120.1	141.7	142.3	145.2	141.9	147.0	163.7	150.6	154.9	160.9	165.4
1795	157.1	157.1	157.1	158.8	158.8	162.0	160.2	161.4	161.1	161.1	161.1	161.1
1796	154.0	161.9	161.9	169.9	165.4	167.7	172.5	173.3	168.8	177.2	173.5	178.9
1797	182.3	188.4	181.6	184.8	185.8	185.8	184.9	182.5	182.5	181.4	181.4	171.0
1798	171.5	171.5	171.5	171.5	171.5	171.0	179.0	179.0	178.5	178.5	178.5	178.0
1799	177.7	177.5	179.5	178.5	178.5	177.9	177.9	164.5	171.8	171.0	171.6	171.6
1800	170.8	164.2	158.2	158.1	160.0	159.0	155.7	154.9	154.6	155.0	154.7	156.7
1801	155.7	152.4	149.1	147.0	147.3	148.7	146.8	148.1	145.1	147.4	146.5	143.8
1802	143.2	143.2	125.6	130.1	129.8	129.8	124.3	124.3	124.7	132.4	131.1	129.0
1803	133.7	133.7	127.8	130.4	136.6	134.3	132.4	132.7	132.7	133.3	148.2	150.9
1804	154.7	160.0	156.5	157.0	151.3	151.3	157.3	156.8	152.2	152.5	153.9	152.7
1805	152.9	152.2	147.6	144.7	144.4	144.5	144.5	144.5	144.5	144.5	140.2	140.2
1806	143.6	137.7	135.5	136.9	134.7	131.9	131.1	129.7	130.9	130.6	130.4	128.3
1807	127.8	127.1	118.2	112.5	113.0	112.6	112.6	106.6	117.6	112.3	118.7	114.5
1808	110.2	110.0	117.6	118.0	117.8	120.3	120.1	121.2	118.4	116.4	116.1	142.5
1809	139.0	143.3	137.5	125.3	118.3	116.8	119.5	117.2	126.5	129.9	136.8	145.6
1810	140.2	138.4	124.5	127.0	128.3	131.2	130.1	137.5	139.4	146.8	145.8	146.1
1811	143.8	145.4	133.5	130.9	135.0	141.9	139.0	138.5	138.0	136.4	140.3	139.8
1812	139.8	140.4	137.2	137.2	142.7	142.8	183.8	180.3	178.7	179.7	179.5	174.0
1813	175.6	179.8	182.5	203.4	205.5	212.7	221.4	231.6	235.7	241.9	262.0	341.1
1814	271.8	286.7	284.9	230.6	236.4	282.3	281.7	269.2	264.0	305.4	313.4	305.0
1815	305.8	316.4	182.4	186.4	199.8	226.0	216.7	228.7	256.8	267.0	247.6	211.7
1816	217.7	206.3	184.7	189.1	182.4	179.4	171.5	173.1	173.0	171.9	169.0	169.0
1817	169.0	163.5	158.4	156.3	158.9	156.1	152.9	152.0	153.7	154.8	159.3	164.7
1818	167.1	164.1	146.3	144.3	155.5	151.6	153.6	156.8	157.1	162.6	158.1	153.9
1819	156.0	155.2	153.1	145.3	141.4	139.2	140.5	137.3	139.6	139.1	140.2	138.1
1820	134.5	134.1	121.8	115.3	117.3	112.7	111.9	111.3	112.2	112.5	111.6	111.6
1821	103.5	101.8	99.9	98.5	98.7	97.5	96.1	97.6	98.3	99.8	105.1	107.5
1822	106.0	106.0	105.7	104.3	103.5	104.6	103.6	105.8	106.6	105.2	102.7	98.1
1823	98.9	98.6	94.3	93.9	97.6	93.7	93.9	93.9	93.9	95.5	96.0	95.7
1824	94.7	94.7	94.2	95.4	92.7	92.8	91.6	92.1	91.7	91.3	92.5	92.5
1825	94.7	94.7	94.2	100.5	105.2	104.3	106.4	111.2	115.8	117.2	114.0	111.6
1826	110.8	103.8	102.2	104.0	107.2	108.0	105.5	105.2	106.8	106.4	106.5	105.8
1827	105.2	105.0	102.0	104.3	104.6	104.4	103.4	104.8	109.3	109.3	107.6	107.5
1828	105.6	101.7	100.5	101.0	102.6	104.2	104.8	107.1	104.5	104.2	104.2	100.4
1829	99.3	97.8	98.2	97.7	98.5	96.6	95.1	97.0	97.5	97.4	97.6	96.1
1830	96.1	93.6	94.9	94.0	94.3	91.5	89.8	89.3	89.6	89.6	89.1	91.9
1831	89.8	88.4	84.7	84.0	82.6	81.3	80.9	81.9	84.8	91.1	89.6	90.0
1832	90.0	88.6	89.9	88.4	91.3	91.0	93.1	94.5	94.5	95.5	95.5	95.8
1833	96.1	94.8	93.6	93.0	93.8	93.7	96.4	97.2	99.8	101.3	99.6	98.4
1834	98.4	95.2	96.1	93.3	93.3	89.7	89.7	91.1	90.1	90.1	90.6	91.3
1835	92.0	90.9	94.1	96.4	96.9	95.7	98.5	99.8	99.5	100.1	101.1	102.1
1836	106.9	110.0	112.5	121.5	118.2	114.8	113.9	115.8	117.1	116.5	114.0	109.3
1837	105.0	106.5	103.5	99.2	96.5	94.3	93.8	95.1	97.5	102.7	107.3	108.6
1838	107.5	104.0	102.4	100.6	98.9	97.7	98.8	103.3	107.2	106.9	105.2	101.9
1839	101.3	99.9	99.5	99.0	100.9	101.2	100.3	100.4	99.7	99.5	99.3	96.4
1840	95.8	91.4	88.6	87.6	85.5	83.6	83.5	85.4	86.8	88.9	88.2	86.4
1841	83.1	80.8	80.6	80.5	80.1	80.2	80.7	80.5	80.0	79.8	79.8	76.0
1842	77.3	71.7	70.4	68.5	67.3	66.2	65.7	65.1	66.7	68.4	68.6	69.0
1843	68.9	69.5	70.0	67.3	68.6	72.9	72.9	77.6	79.6	77.3	74.7	75.1
1844	76.0	78.5	80.1	80.7	79.5	79.8	81.0	81.6	81.4	80.1	79.6	80.2
1845	73.1	74.5	80.8	92.2	87.9	88.8	88.7	90.3	89.7	84.0	83.3	82.4
1846	80.1	79.6	80.8	78.9	77.2	77.6	78.4	76.0	76.6	77.0	77.2	76.0
1847	77.1	79.6	84.1	83.9	81.7	82.1	80.9	80.9	81.4	76.9	74.8	68.6
1848	67.1	66.3	66.0	65.9	62.3	62.8	62.7	62.4	63.3	66.8	64.0	64.0
1849	64.2	65.2	66.1	69.1	68.4	66.8	66.3	67.0	67.9	68.8	68.6	68.0
1850	65.8	67.9	67.1	63.0	64.1	67.1	69.7	70.7	74.8	76.5	72.9	71.7
1851	71.1	71.7	72.3	73.2	71.7	71.1	70.4	70.6	70.0	69.7	67.4	65.6
1852	63.1	63.1	63.0	61.8	66.4	69.0	68.1	68.0	67.0	66.7	66.7	67.1
1853	67.1	66.7	68.2	68.5	68.6	68.3	66.6	64.8	68.0	68.4	67.9	69.7
1854	70.1	67.7	67.6	63.8	62.9	60.8	60.8	63.1	63.8	65.0	62.2	63.8
1855	63.1	63.2	62.6	66.6	71.3	72.5	73.8	82.8	88.6	85.6	81.3	91.2
1856	96.5	95.1	96.7	92.7	92.2	97.3	107.1	110.4	107.3	114.3	123.3	126.6
1857	129.5	131.2	129.7	132.8	138.2	134.7	134.3	129.0	117.1	91.6	80.8	76.6
1858	74.3	72.6	76.7	81.2	81.2	81.4	81.3	93.5	94.1	91.3	85.4	86.0
1859	87.6	90.6	90.0	88.5	91.0	85.1	85.1	85.4	84.6	82.1	82.4	87.5
1860	88.2	87.3	85.4	87.6	86.4	86.6	87.1	85.2	82.2	80.8	81.8	70.4
1861	71.5	71.5	67.8	67.2	65.7	63.5	62.7	71.1	80.2	90.5	93.4	92.6

Table 26—Foods*

Year	Jan.	Feb.	Mar.	Apr.	May	June	July	Aug.	Sept.	Oct.	Nov.	Dec.
1784	115.7	113.8	113.3	110.8	111.6	113.3	116.0	115.1	114.7	115.8	114.1	112.2
1785	107.3	107.0	106.5	103.8	100.6	98.5	101.5	103.8	103.7	105.2	105.1	104.4
1786	104.3	104.3	101.3	100.3	99.9	100.1	102.1	102.2	101.6	101.1	101.5	101.5
1787	101.9	102.0	101.4	99.8	96.6	98.4	98.5	96.8	97.1	96.4	98.0	96.8
1788	96.2	95.9	96.0	94.2	94.7	93.8	92.3	90.1	89.8	88.4	88.5	87.6
1789	87.5	86.6	86.4	85.5	88.8	89.8	89.0	88.6	88.7	89.0	91.1	93.8
1790	93.8	93.7	94.3	92.5	94.0	95.6	96.9	97.5	97.2	100.6	104.2	108.1
1791	110.5	110.8	106.0	104.4	106.8	107.3	105.5	104.3	105.0	115.2	113.8	114.3
1792	111.3	112.4	113.4	113.5	113.1	113.0	111.8	110.3	109.6	110.2	117.0	118.9
1793	118.1	118.8	120.7	118.2	117.8	117.8	117.0	116.2	118.0	115.3	115.5	115.3
1794	123.5	123.4	129.8	129.5								
1795	153.9	156.0	157.3	158.7	160.6	164.0	166.6	166.8	168.3	168.2	170.0	174.4
1796	176.2	173.6	173.1	175.7	172.6	171.0	169.0	167.1	166.0	170.8	166.6	167.0
1797	172.8	170.9	164.8	163.4	165.2	162.7	160.8	156.3	154.2	154.1	154.5	155.0
1798	152.0	150.2	151.2	148.7	148.0	144.9	145.1	145.2	145.6	145.6	147.3	
1799					143.6	145.2	145.4	146.1				
1800						140.9	141.3	139.7	146.4	149.5	151.3	147.8
1801	146.7	147.1	146.8	146.9	146.7	147.9	147.6	148.3	148.6	153.4	150.8	148.0
1802	141.9	139.5	135.0	134.6	131.5	132.3	130.4	130.8	130.8	133.9	133.1	130.3
1803	128.7	125.6	122.9	122.4	123.3	122.2	121.1	122.3	122.5	123.1	127.3	132.1
1804	133.2	132.8	135.2	135.1	135.0	135.2	139.5	139.4	139.9	141.0	146.9	149.1
1805	149.2	149.7	147.9	148.6	148.0	147.5	147.6	143.2	143.7	144.3	144.6	145.9
1806	147.7	143.2	142.4	139.4	143.2	144.1	144.1	143.3	143.2	143.3	142.3	138.2
1807	137.9	136.2	134.6	129.2	130.8	129.3	128.1	125.6	129.7	129.0	132.4	130.3
1808	128.2	126.1	126.8	122.5	122.1	122.8	123.5	123.7	123.4	125.0	127.6	140.4
1809	140.0	141.6	141.2	142.3	139.7	129.2	127.1	127.1	132.5	134.8	135.2	135.7
1810	133.9	130.4	127.5	128.0	129.9	129.2	132.7	132.0	135.0	137.0	137.2	136.9
1811	138.5	138.9	133.9	130.7	131.3	131.6	128.8	128.0	128.4	130.0	126.1	125.4
1812	128.0	129.3	128.1	126.4	127.9	129.6	150.9	154.7	157.7	156.3	156.2	155.0
1813	155.5	157.0	157.6	162.6	162.5	166.1	166.3	168.7	170.1	171.3	182.9	202.9
1814	211.1	205.3	201.6	192.5	189.7	196.7	195.9	201.8	202.8	222.1	228.2	220.5
1815	216.4	215.8	172.6	170.3	171.4	182.6	190.6	190.8	201.1	202.7	202.8	189.4
1816	186.2	182.4	166.2	166.2	162.3	162.9	161.8	158.8	156.5	156.2	154.5	153.7
1817	152.1	151.1	152.9	155.0	154.0	146.6	140.9	139.9	138.8	140.8	142.3	143.9
1818	146.5	147.1	144.6	144.4	144.3	143.3	141.5	141.3	142.4	145.6	144.1	141.7
1819	142.0	139.8	138.7	132.1	128.8	122.2	119.3	119.0	118.8	121.1	122.3	121.8
1820	119.5	118.5	112.9	107.3	106.3	103.2	102.3	101.9	102.2	102.5	104.6	105.6
1821	102.2	101.4	98.5	97.2	97.8	97.3	96.7	97.0	97.4	101.7	105.0	105.8
1822	105.7	106.1	106.4	107.0	105.8	106.5	104.8	104.8	104.9	105.4	107.0	104.3
1823	103.5	102.5	99.5	99.5	98.4	98.8	98.2	97.8	96.7	96.5	95.9	95.6
1824	95.3	93.8	93.1	93.1	92.5	92.2	91.9	92.4	92.5	92.2	92.5	92.6
1825	93.6	95.7	95.7	99.3	101.5	99.1	98.2	95.7	97.7	100.4	101.0	100.7
1826	98.8	97.5	95.6	94.4	95.1	94.6	92.7	93.8	95.4	96.3	95.5	94.5
1827	95.2	95.2	92.6	93.9	93.5	91.9	92.2	92.2	93.6	94.1	93.7	93.7
1828	93.1	91.2	89.8	88.4	88.0	87.9	88.5	91.0	94.2	94.8	98.5	95.6
1829	95.5	92.2	91.8	91.1	89.6	88.7	86.5	86.5	87.9	87.8	86.2	84.3
1830	81.8	80.8	80.0	81.4	81.5	82.2	82.9	87.4	87.9	88.0	86.8	85.6
1831	85.7	85.6	85.9	85.8	87.4	87.1	86.6	86.9	87.9	89.8	90.4	90.6
1832	90.2	88.8	88.0	86.9	88.9	88.3	88.1	86.6	88.2	89.7	90.5	90.6
1833	85.9	83.9	80.1	80.8	81.4	79.6	79.8	80.0	82.7	82.7	80.7	81.6
1834	80.8	79.5	78.3	76.6	75.9	75.7	75.3	76.6	75.5	76.2	77.0	77.9
1835	80.8	79.6	81.9	84.2	87.3	88.2	89.2	89.0	87.7	89.0	88.1	89.8
1836	89.9	90.5	92.9	96.8	94.9	91.5	91.3	92.0	94.2	95.3	97.3	95.1
1837	94.1	94.8	93.7	91.1	87.0	85.9	86.1	85.2	84.5	85.0	88.4	88.2
1838	86.0	85.1	83.8	83.1	83.6	83.4	83.7	86.4	87.2	89.6	89.0	88.1
1839	87.8	87.2	89.3	89.7	90.4	89.2	88.0	86.4	86.8	85.4	85.1	83.5
1840	82.7	80.8	77.7	78.2	75.9	74.6	73.7	73.8	76.7	78.3	78.4	78.3
1841	77.0	75.9	75.6	75.5	74.3	74.1	73.3	73.9	74.9	75.8	75.9	73.6
1842	72.7	71.2	70.5	68.3	66.8	66.2	65.9	66.4	67.3	70.1	68.8	66.9
1843	66.2	65.7	64.8	65.0	67.0	69.8	71.7	71.8	71.8	71.8	71.0	69.9
1844	70.7	71.8	71.6	72.4	73.1	72.1	72.4	71.9	72.3	72.6	72.2	72.5
1845	71.5	73.0	74.2	78.3	77.6	77.2	77.8	79.8	81.6	81.1	82.7	82.7
1846	81.1	80.2	80.6	78.2	76.4	74.4	73.6	73.3	74.3	78.0	79.9	76.6
1847	76.1	80.3	82.6	84.2	84.4	86.0	82.3	81.9	81.8	81.3	82.3	79.2
1848	77.3	75.5	75.5	74.9	72.6	71.9	72.1	72.0	71.1	71.6	69.7	68.9
1849	69.9	69.6	69.6	68.1	67.6	68.3	68.9	71.2	72.3	73.9	74.8	74.6
1850	74.3	75.7	75.8	74.2	75.0	74.5	74.7	77.1	78.6	79.1	78.8	77.2
1851	77.7	77.8	77.7	77.2	76.6	76.8	77.4	78.1	77.9	78.0	73.9	71.9
1852	72.2	72.8	72.5	71.7	73.7	76.4	76.3	76.6	79.3	79.4	79.8	81.9
1853	81.8	81.6	82.0	82.5	82.8	81.5	81.2	81.2	85.3	89.0	89.7	88.3
1854	88.7	92.1	91.1	89.3	90.8	90.3	88.6	91.3	93.6	93.8	90.0	88.7
1855	87.9	86.9	88.5	91.9	92.4	92.8	91.0	95.3	97.8	99.3	98.5	99.0
1856	96.7	97.3	96.5	94.4	91.6	91.7	95.1	94.7	95.9	97.7	98.5	97.8
1857	98.4	98.3	99.2	100.4	102.3	104.4	100.3	98.8	100.7	94.1	84.1	80.6
1858	75.7	74.1	76.7	77.9	78.8	78.4	76.9	79.1	80.9	79.9	77.8	76.9
1859	77.1	78.0	78.4	77.8	78.6	77.6	76.5	76.5	75.0	76.9	77.1	77.4
1860	75.6	75.7	76.3	75.3	75.6	76.6	77.9	80.5	80.9	80.8	77.7	73.5
1861	74.1	73.2	72.2	71.6	70.0	68.5	66.4	71.5	75.6	79.7	81.2	83.6

* Includes all commodities classified in the sub-groups presented in Appendix Tables 19 to 25 inclusive and the major group, fish, in Table 13.

Table 27—Chemicals

Year	Jan.	Feb.	Mar.	Apr.	May	June	July	Aug.	Sept.	Oct.	Nov.	Dec.
1784	114.5	114.5	112.9	111.2	110.6	113.7	116.2	118.3	119.8	121.0	118.9	117.8
1785	116.6	119.2	121.4	123.4	125.4	127.2	129.1	131.9	129.5	126.9	124.2	121.3
1786	121.3	121.3	121.2	122.2	121.7	124.8	124.5	124.2	123.9	123.7	123.0	122.9
1787	122.8	122.7	124.2	124.1	123.6	123.6	123.6	121.2	118.7	117.2	117.6	118.8
1788	122.5	121.3	119.9	119.5	112.9	112.5	111.7	109.9	107.9	105.9	109.6	110.2
1789	110.8	111.7	109.4	110.2	113.4	113.0	112.2	110.0	110.0	110.3	110.6	110.9
1790	111.7	112.5	113.3	114.1	114.5	108.0	101.5	103.3	98.9	98.9	98.9	96.7
1791	96.3	97.8	100.1	101.4	98.7	98.7	102.0	101.0	101.0	98.9	98.9	98.9
1792	93.4	94.2	93.4	95.6	95.6	95.6	95.6	95.6	96.6	96.6	93.2	93.2
1793	93.2	93.2	92.0	95.7	95.7	95.7	95.7	95.7	95.5	95.5	95.5	95.5
1794	89.5	89.5	102.9	102.9								
1795	204.0	202.1	217.1	212.3	211.7	209.9	215.3	239.4	252.4	260.2	257.9	245.8
1796	250.7	226.5	245.5	222.0	221.3	197.7	193.3	189.3	210.8	210.8	199.5	197.1
1797	198.6	197.1	193.8	186.8	190.4	184.7	183.5	180.4	172.3	174.3	172.4	167.4
1798	162.5	162.8	162.2	156.0	159.8	163.2	192.9	188.7	188.8	189.7	196.3	200.2
1799	198.4	193.0	193.6	194.8	197.7	191.3	193.3	195.2				
1800						185.8	168.8	169.7	168.1	167.8	177.2	178.6
1801	170.5	172.7	172.1	172.0	172.8	170.0	173.4	172.7	168.5	168.1	167.3	164.4
1802	161.5	160.6	155.0	152.2	149.7	143.0	140.0	139.6	141.7	142.9	143.3	143.6
1803	145.7	147.4	146.5	153.0	153.0	153.0	155.6	157.5	157.5	157.5	157.5	154.5
1804	154.5	154.1	154.1	154.1	155.3	155.3	151.0	153.2	152.0	154.9	157.0	153.3
1805	153.3	153.3	153.8	154.8	149.1	148.6	147.2	147.6	149.1	148.7	147.8	151.4
1806	157.4	158.6	162.6	162.0	161.6	160.2	161.9	164.7	164.4	159.5	164.5	167.4
1807	158.6	158.6	164.4	161.3	157.9	156.3	153.3	157.6	166.0	162.7	164.0	165.3
1808	160.5	169.8	178.4	188.3	191.0	190.3	192.2	197.0	200.9	199.4	207.5	256.0
1809	264.5	264.5	259.1	253.9	212.3	200.8	172.2	180.2	198.5	219.6	228.1	238.5
1810	234.7	238.2	244.8	247.8	240.6	224.6	227.2	220.9	216.4	220.3	222.4	222.4
1811	229.8	228.8	229.8	226.7	222.4	227.5	227.8	231.7	231.8	234.5	220.4	227.4
1812	223.8	217.6	219.1	222.1	233.7	248.6	332.4	346.6	311.9	291.6	291.7	284.3
1813	293.0	292.2	297.0	301.4	302.2	302.3	299.8	297.2	300.5	299.2	291.3	343.7
1814	398.5	377.4	352.0	324.3	311.0	301.7	300.1	308.0	296.7	313.6	382.8	346.3
1815	336.3	333.9	198.1	201.2	201.0	184.8	187.7	190.2	212.0	214.6	220.5	204.9
1816	196.3	196.9	196.3	197.6	183.4	175.1	161.7	160.2	156.5	155.8	155.8	155.8
1817	155.8	155.8	151.0	139.9	139.7	134.5	132.2	132.2	132.2	132.2	132.2	131.1
1818	133.4	140.3	139.7	136.9	135.1	128.8	130.8	131.8	133.1	133.6	135.3	133.0
1819	133.0	127.8	127.8	124.5	113.3	107.2	102.3	101.0	96.1	95.9	95.4	94.9
1820	95.8	96.2	96.2	98.7	98.9	98.2	98.2	98.9	98.9	98.9	99.9	99.9
1821	100.1	100.1	100.1	99.9	99.9	99.7	100.5	102.0	101.2	101.7	104.7	103.5
1822	102.8	102.8	102.8	101.8	101.8	101.8	100.5	101.0	105.0	105.0	98.0	96.3
1823	96.4	96.4	95.0	97.0	99.8	98.5	98.5	97.5	97.5	97.0	96.9	96.9
1824	96.9	96.9	96.9	96.9	94.5	98.8	98.8	96.6	98.8	99.3	99.3	99.3
1825	99.2	99.2	99.2	101.0	99.2	101.5	100.6	100.3	101.5	101.0	100.9	100.6
1826	100.5	99.6	96.8	96.8	95.1	91.7	90.2	91.5	90.4	90.4	92.6	92.0
1827	92.3	92.7	90.0	89.7	87.7	87.6	88.0	88.8	88.8	88.4	89.5	89.5
1828	89.1	89.4	90.3	90.1	89.4	89.0	90.1	90.3	90.6	91.5	93.3	96.1
1829	97.3	97.9	97.0	95.1	89.4	88.4	87.9	88.8	88.3	92.4	93.7	92.0
1830	91.1	91.6	90.8	87.5	85.8	86.8	87.3	87.5	86.2	87.0	88.5	93.3
1831	93.3	91.9	92.1	90.1	104.4	102.0	99.5	96.5	94.0	95.0	95.1	93.6
1832	93.6	93.6	90.3	90.0	89.0	88.9	88.1	89.7	90.9	90.9	89.5	89.7
1833	91.4	91.6	92.4	91.9	93.0	95.8	96.5	101.8	103.8	102.4	102.6	103.6
1834	103.5	103.5	101.0	101.0	101.6	101.6	101.6	102.8	104.3	104.7	107.3	106.3
1835	108.2	106.5	111.0	109.8	103.9	103.1	100.5	102.7	98.7	97.4	106.2	110.2
1836	114.8	113.5	111.7	105.7	103.4	99.5	96.4	102.1	100.6	105.2	103.6	100.1
1837	101.4	101.9	100.9	96.8	90.9	94.2	93.6	92.4	94.5	95.0	95.6	94.7
1838	96.6	96.7	96.1	96.1	94.5	92.3	92.3	103.0	104.6	109.0	109.5	110.3
1839	110.5	109.0	111.5	109.2	106.3	103.3	104.1	104.6	103.3	100.7	99.8	101.0
1840	100.8	101.8	102.1	102.4	100.1	98.5	98.8	98.1	97.5	97.9	98.6	99.4
1841	99.6	100.2	100.3	97.6	94.9	94.1	93.4	95.4	95.5	97.8	97.6	98.5
1842	99.6	100.1	98.5	97.1	94.9	93.8	92.4	92.6	91.3	91.3	90.6	91.2
1843	90.8	91.3	91.5	88.7	85.5	85.4	84.9	85.0	83.2	82.1	83.5	84.9
1844	84.9	84.7	84.4	86.4	85.0	84.1	83.7	84.3	84.0	83.8	83.2	80.9
1845	80.3	78.8	78.6	80.3	79.2	78.0	78.5	77.3	78.0	77.9	77.9	75.5
1846	76.6	76.2	76.8	78.8	78.0	75.0	74.6	74.3	73.8	74.7	76.8	78.0
1847	79.0	78.7	79.4	80.2	80.5	80.1	79.6	81.8	82.2	83.6	84.5	83.0
1848	85.4	85.0	84.6	81.3	79.8	78.7	80.1	81.2	81.1	81.3	81.4	83.1
1849	84.0	83.8	81.3	82.1	79.7	82.6	82.7	82.3	83.6	83.4	84.6	83.1
1850	83.5	84.1	84.4	87.4	87.9	87.4	88.7	89.3	87.4	87.0	86.9	85.8
1851	86.7	85.0	83.5	83.6	83.5	84.2	84.0	83.6	84.6	86.5	85.1	89.8
1852	89.3	89.1	86.8	84.1	84.1	80.3	80.0	80.3	80.7	82.7	82.6	82.9
1853	82.7	82.0	81.5	79.7	82.2	82.0	82.1	82.2	82.4	83.1	82.9	82.7
1854	83.3	85.3	85.7	85.2	85.6	89.5	88.8	89.5	90.4	90.4	90.4	91.2
1855	91.1	93.0	91.9	88.1	87.2	84.7	86.4	88.9	96.9	108.9	109.5	105.1
1856	109.4	108.5	101.4	101.7	96.5	94.9	96.9	94.1	93.8	95.2	96.0	95.5
1857	94.8	98.4	99.8	102.0	102.3	102.9	101.8	104.4	106.7	105.8	103.8	100.9
1858	96.6	95.5	92.0	95.9	94.7	95.0	96.1	98.3	98.1	101.1	99.9	97.6
1859	97.9	96.7	96.7	98.1	100.2	105.6	105.2	99.5	96.7	94.4	95.1	97.6
1860	93.2	99.8	101.0	103.9	104.0	106.4	106.6	107.5	107.8	107.8	108.0	106.3
1861	104.1	98.1	97.8	98.4	98.8	99.3	101.8	101.5	95.3	94.9	96.6	105.7

Table 28—Dyes

Year	Jan.	Feb.	Mar.	Apr.	May	June	July	Aug.	Sept.	Oct.	Nov.	Dec.
1784	98.1	100.1	98.1	97.5	97.8	98.0	98.1	98.3	98.2	98.2	98.0	98.5
1785	98.9	98.0	96.5	94.8	92.9	90.7	92.1	98.2	99.2	99.2	99.2	99.2
1786	99.2	99.2	99.2	99.2	104.4	104.4	104.4	104.4	104.4	104.4	104.4	104.4
1787	104.4	104.4	104.4	97.4	97.4	97.4	101.9	101.9	101.9	101.9	104.4	104.4
1788	104.4	102.1	99.7	97.3	94.8	92.4	89.8	87.2	84.6	87.2	82.0	82.0
1789	85.2	84.9	84.6	84.3	84.0	83.8	88.2	88.0	87.8	87.6	87.4	84.1
1790	80.7	80.7	80.7	80.7	80.7	80.7	80.7	80.7	80.7	80.7	78.7	78.7
1791	78.7	78.7	78.0	78.0	76.3	76.3	77.5	77.5	77.5	74.8	74.8	74.8
1792	84.6	84.6	84.6	84.6	84.6	84.6	84.6	84.6	84.6	84.6	91.1	86.4
1793	92.6	92.6	92.6	92.6	92.6	92.6	94.1	94.1	94.1	94.1	105.2	99.0
1794	99.0	99.0	99.0	99.0								
1795	139.5	139.5	139.5	139.5	139.5	139.5	139.5	139.5	139.5	139.5	121.6	100.8
1796	100.8	100.8	102.2	103.5	104.9	107.8	112.4	119.3	125.9	125.9	125.0	112.3
1797	112.3	112.3	106.4	106.4	106.4	106.4	106.4	110.4	110.4	110.4	110.4	106.4
1798	117.7	114.5	110.3	110.3	110.3	110.3	110.3	120.2	128.7	136.2	168.6	169.3
1799				228.8	228.0	228.0	229.5	237.0				
1800						157.2	140.7	145.7	145.1	151.9	143.4	143.4
1801	134.3	140.7	140.7	138.9	136.2	140.5	139.1	139.1	135.0	135.0	143.9	149.6
1802	141.0	144.7	138.4	137.4	137.4	137.4	137.4	137.4	141.2	145.6	145.6	106.8
1803	125.8	125.8	112.2	108.3	131.8	132.2	132.5	142.7	142.2	142.2	142.2	138.3
1804	136.9	190.3	188.3	186.3	177.8	175.5	175.5	137.6	135.0	144.0	146.1	146.1
1805	146.1	146.1	146.1	146.1	153.2	149.4	149.4	149.4	149.4	149.4	149.4	149.4
1806	173.2	172.4	173.6	173.6	163.8	154.1	155.0	147.8	148.3	148.3	148.0	148.0
1807	148.2	153.2	149.9	145.3	144.8	139.9	135.2	135.2	140.6	138.9	137.7	128.6
1808	121.0	124.7	124.7	124.7	117.3	120.2	120.2	120.2	120.2	120.2	120.2	122.8
1809	121.3	121.3	121.3	124.7	126.3	126.3	122.0	140.0	139.2	134.4	136.4	137.3
1810	137.3	137.3	138.6	142.3	141.4	141.4	140.5	140.1	140.1	154.3	154.2	154.0
1811	144.2	132.9	131.3	145.0	134.4	133.1	133.9	131.1	109.1	109.0	117.2	117.1
1812	107.1	114.4	123.5	115.8	115.8	115.8	133.3	117.5	117.5	117.5	117.5	120.2
1813	120.2	120.2	120.2	120.2	120.2	135.5	139.5	146.1	146.2	146.2	146.3	169.6
1814	190.2	181.4	182.5	173.1	163.1	181.6	164.6	164.6	164.7	169.9	169.9	170.0
1815	165.8	168.5	160.6	151.0	149.6	150.5	140.1	142.0	140.8	175.0	173.6	148.0
1816	140.6	135.1	133.7	133.8	108.9	111.0	111.0	107.6	99.5	99.5	96.6	94.2
1817	94.7	92.8	92.9	93.6	91.8	90.0	90.0	90.1	89.9	90.0	98.2	110.8
1818	110.8	110.9	109.4	109.4	104.8	104.1	105.1	105.1	105.1	106.6	109.1	109.1
1819	109.1	105.6	106.7	106.8	104.5	104.5	100.6	99.9	91.6	89.4	83.7	83.8
1820	82.5	82.5	75.7	78.5	78.5	81.1	81.1	82.1	82.1	82.1	82.1	82.1
1821	83.2	79.7	82.3	85.4	85.4	86.5	86.5	87.0	87.0	89.6	86.1	100.8
1822	100.8	100.8	100.8	101.8	101.8	101.8	101.8	97.6	97.9	97.9	102.2	102.2
1823	102.2	102.2	102.2	102.2	102.2	102.2	102.2	102.2	107.2	107.2	107.2	107.2
1824	107.0	104.9	104.9	104.0	99.5	99.5	101.2	101.2	103.3	100.3	100.3	101.2
1825	100.9	101.5	103.1	110.2	108.4	106.5	106.0	103.4	101.1	102.0	102.1	102.1
1826	101.8	99.6	100.1	100.0	96.5	95.5	90.9	86.7	86.9	88.7	89.1	89.8
1827	88.7	90.1	92.0	93.8	95.7	93.1	93.1	94.1	94.0	93.8	93.5	93.5
1828	91.6	91.3	91.0	91.0	91.0	84.6	86.7	86.5	85.3	83.1	82.9	82.3
1829	82.3	83.4	83.4	84.1	83.5	84.0	84.0	81.6	81.4	79.8	74.1	77.9
1830	75.0	74.4	73.3	72.7	73.2	72.0	72.0	71.8	70.2	69.6	69.6	68.7
1831	66.9	66.9	66.9	67.3	67.3	67.0	67.4	70.8	71.1	71.5	71.5	71.5
1832	71.5	71.5	71.5	71.0	70.7	69.5	69.5	69.5	69.5	69.7	69.7	71.0
1833	71.0	70.5	70.5	68.1	69.2	69.2	69.2	69.6	78.7	78.5	77.8	81.5
1834	81.5	81.5	81.5	80.5	80.5	80.5	78.1	78.1	78.1	77.4	76.7	76.7
1835	69.8	67.1	68.3	66.6	68.3	67.3	65.8	65.8	66.5	65.1	64.4	64.8
1836	66.4	66.1	66.1	66.8	65.6	65.6	65.6	65.6	68.0	73.9	74.1	80.2
1837	80.7	81.5	80.9	81.4	80.3	80.3	79.5	79.3	78.1	78.7	79.2	80.0
1838	80.2	76.5	77.2	72.1	70.2	73.0	68.8	77.8	86.5	106.8	107.0	106.3
1839	106.1	105.2	103.1	100.7	100.9	103.5	105.2	101.3	100.0	100.0	96.4	97.5
1840	97.5	97.3	86.6	87.2	87.0	87.0	90.3	84.9	85.5	81.6	81.6	80.9
1841	80.7	80.3	80.3	80.3	80.2	78.8	78.8	76.2	75.0	74.8	74.0	73.3
1842	73.3	73.3	73.3	71.3	71.3	70.9	70.9	70.9	70.2	68.7	68.7	68.9
1843	68.3	65.6	65.3	65.2	64.9	66.8	70.7	70.7	70.1	69.3	69.0	69.0
1844	66.0	66.4	67.4	66.3	65.8	66.3	66.6	79.5	79.1	78.2	62.2	60.5
1845	60.4	59.9	59.5	60.4	61.4	61.4	61.5	60.7	61.1	60.4	60.8	59.4
1846	62.4	62.8	62.8	61.7	61.8	61.8	60.6	61.1	61.1	61.5	62.1	61.6
1847	63.0	64.1	68.8	71.7	71.7	70.7	70.3	70.4	70.3	68.8	70.6	71.6
1848	71.6	69.3	70.3	70.1	67.4	59.4	59.4	59.1	58.4	58.1	58.1	57.8
1849	57.5	58.2	59.8	57.8	57.4	55.5	55.5	55.2	55.2	56.7	56.9	57.1
1850	57.3	57.6	57.6	59.5	61.9	62.8	63.6	63.6	64.6	64.9	67.2	67.5
1851	66.7	66.7	66.7	66.4	66.4	66.2	65.9	65.9	65.9	65.5	58.7	58.5
1852	58.8	57.1	57.7	57.9	58.1	58.3	58.0	58.4	58.4	58.4	58.4	58.9
1853	58.9	59.1	59.1	62.8	63.5	64.0	69.4	69.3	70.0	69.8	69.5	75.9
1854	75.6	75.8	75.3	75.3	75.3	75.4	75.2	75.1	75.0	74.4	78.3	76.8
1855	74.8	75.1	74.8	68.6	68.4	69.2	71.3	71.3	70.8	70.8	70.4	71.4
1856	71.4	70.5	71.7	71.8	71.6	72.6	73.0	72.7	72.7	71.6	71.6	72.1
1857	72.2	70.2	67.7	67.7	78.4	79.4	83.3	84.2	84.2	76.4	68.4	68.4
1858	59.6	59.6	60.0	60.4	62.8	62.8	65.1	66.4	69.0	68.4	68.9	68.9
1859	66.3	66.3	66.3	66.3	65.9	68.4	64.7	63.3	63.5	66.3	66.3	66.3
1860	66.1	67.3	68.0	64.4	64.4	64.7	69.0	69.4	68.6	68.8	67.2	66.4
1861	62.9	62.7	62.7	67.8	67.8	63.3	63.3	64.9	68.7	68.7	72.9	73.6

TABLE 29—FUEL AND LIGHTING MATERIALS

Year	Jan.	Feb.	Mar.	Apr.	May	June	July	Aug.	Sept.	Oct.	Nov.	Dec.
1784	117.4	118.2	111.3	110.0	106.2	102.5	100.3	98.0	97.1	96.5	92.2	90.0
1785	88.4	84.9	88.0	87.1	86.1	88.6	87.6	87.8	85.0	85.2	88.8	92.3
1786	91.9	91.3	90.7	88.9	87.7	88.9	88.9	90.0	90.5	91.0	91.4	93.0
1787	93.0	95.2	95.2	95.2	95.7	96.7	95.2	95.4	95.2	95.9	95.2	95.2
1788	94.6	90.3	89.8	79.6	81.5	82.7	83.8	83.6	83.2	81.9	80.1	76.8
1789	76.8	75.8	75.1	75.3	75.7	77.8	77.8	77.8	77.4	76.9	75.7	78.3
1790	79.6	80.5	80.5	76.7	76.7	81.0	81.0	81.0	81.0	83.6	84.0	85.1
1791	85.6	87.8	87.2	83.5	84.9	84.6	85.7	85.8	86.1	85.9	84.4	84.4
1792	83.2	82.9	83.2	83.2	83.9	83.9	83.2	82.3	82.3	82.3	83.9	85.3
1793	87.6	87.6	87.6	87.6	86.1	86.1	87.2	88.1	92.4	92.0	96.1	99.6
1794	99.0	99.0	100.4	100.4								
1795	121.6	122.2	123.1	125.1	125.7	125.2	133.2	137.5	136.5	134.0	139.2	139.4
1796	139.5	149.9	144.0	145.2	140.4	142.9	139.3	137.1	136.3	136.5	129.8	137.9
1797	137.3	131.3	131.5	123.3	122.6	125.8	125.8	124.0	124.0	124.0	124.3	124.3
1798	131.8	134.3	134.2	134.1	133.4	133.3	125.7	125.5	125.4	125.2	125.1	
1799					119.4	119.6	120.2	110.3				
1800						124.0	123.2	121.1	122.8	125.9	126.8	126.8
1801	126.4	129.1	129.1	131.3	127.4	130.8	129.5	129.5	129.5	131.2	135.1	132.7
1802	129.3	129.3	126.1	120.2	120.2	118.8	118.8	118.8	118.9	120.7	119.9	115.2
1803	117.8	117.8	117.8	117.9	117.3	117.3	118.1	118.6	118.6	119.4	121.1	121.1
1804	126.0	125.3	125.3	131.6	131.6	131.8	134.0	130.9	134.6	134.5	136.6	144.5
1805	142.4	154.8	154.5	154.5	150.7	155.4	155.4	155.4	153.3	153.3	153.3	153.3
1806	144.7	144.2	140.4	138.3	136.0	127.6	129.6	129.0	128.5	130.0	130.4	129.8
1807	129.3	129.5	129.5	126.2	122.6	122.6	122.2	119.1	120.1	119.5	123.0	123.2
1808	122.8	121.4	120.7	119.6	116.3	115.7	115.1	114.5	113.9	112.5	114.0	114.3
1809	114.7	114.9	115.3	117.7	114.9	114.9	115.6	113.9	114.4	115.8	117.5	118.5
1810	127.9	130.5	132.5	130.1	128.1	126.1	124.5	127.1	126.2	127.8	130.4	127.4
1811	138.3	138.6	137.1	135.2	133.7	135.7	138.5	141.2	141.3	142.4	144.2	143.1
1812	145.6	142.7	142.7	142.7	142.7	142.7	147.0	151.6	158.7	153.9	152.5	152.5
1813	159.2	159.2	162.0	203.6	203.6	203.6	203.6	203.6	201.2	201.2	224.7	246.0
1814	246.0	248.3	249.8	240.6	222.8	225.7	222.6	213.2	214.0	227.2	227.2	248.2
1815	254.0	247.9	239.0	189.9	174.9	168.3	170.1	164.6	170.4	177.6	186.6	186.6
1816	205.5	206.0	188.2	183.5	181.0	174.3	164.1	158.8	158.3	156.5	149.3	149.5
1817	150.6	151.8	153.6	141.0	132.8	127.1	126.4	126.1	127.1	131.1	130.4	137.0
1818	136.1	135.9	134.9	132.1	136.4	129.9	127.3	129.6	131.7	133.2	133.9	138.8
1819	145.4	143.9	144.5	138.4	135.0	134.8	123.3	121.4	120.2	121.1	126.6	130.8
1820	129.4	129.2	126.9	122.7	123.6	123.6	123.6	123.6	122.6	122.2	122.2	123.2
1821	122.2	121.4	123.6	110.5	112.7	112.7	113.2	116.6	115.8	118.1	118.1	116.2
1822	118.1	118.9	116.9	109.3	107.8	108.6	108.4	108.4	111.9	110.2	105.3	104.4
1823	105.5	103.4	102.5	91.3	91.1	92.4	90.8	89.8	90.9	90.8	90.8	89.5
1824	90.4	90.4	89.9	87.1	86.4	86.4	86.5	85.6	83.1	85.6	85.2	83.3
1825	83.3	84.4	84.6	88.2	90.5	89.4	89.4	89.4	89.7	89.8	90.5	95.5
1826	95.5	93.5	90.2	88.8	90.7	90.9	89.7	89.0	89.0	89.3	91.7	92.6
1827	96.4	93.9	91.3	90.6	87.6	87.8	88.3	88.9	88.4	94.9	94.4	93.7
1828	91.6	89.3	88.7	86.6	83.1	82.7	82.1	81.9	84.3	85.1	83.3	82.6
1829	82.6	82.9	81.9	81.4	78.9	78.9	78.4	78.9	81.9	83.7	83.7	81.9
1830	82.4	82.4	80.2	77.9	77.6	77.0	77.0	78.0	78.7	80.0	79.0	81.1
1831	83.4	86.2	85.2	83.5	83.5	84.1	82.5	83.9	85.2	89.4	91.9	93.8
1832	94.0	94.1	94.6	91.4	91.5	91.5	91.4	89.3	94.4	97.4	101.6	101.9
1833	98.1	97.2	98.1	97.0	94.0	93.6	93.2	96.5	96.8	95.9	96.1	94.8
1834	94.6	93.3	92.7	90.4	88.5	88.1	89.4	89.4	89.6	89.4	89.5	89.5
1835	88.2	86.7	87.2	90.5	94.0	93.3	94.1	94.8	94.9	94.8	95.3	97.1
1836	107.5	106.3	105.2	106.2	104.0	104.0	102.4	102.9	107.2	108.0	109.3	114.8
1837	118.8	119.4	120.1	112.2	109.4	103.5	100.7	94.4	94.6	98.2	98.8	101.3
1838	103.0	102.7	100.2	98.8	97.9	98.6	98.8	99.0	99.8	101.6	106.5	107.1
1839	107.3	107.9	109.1	113.3	112.2	114.0	114.0	113.6	113.6	113.3	113.9	110.5
1840	109.1	108.1	105.4	103.4	104.2	103.3	102.9	101.6	100.9	102.0	102.2	102.5
1841	105.9	105.9	105.0	102.0	101.7	98.8	97.5	97.5	99.1	100.6	101.1	102.0
1842	101.8	98.6	96.3	91.5	87.9	85.5	82.4	84.5	82.8	81.1	81.5	79.9
1843	78.5	75.9	75.0	74.8	74.6	75.6	75.8	77.1	79.2	79.7	80.6	79.9
1844	79.9	80.2	80.3	79.5	77.3	76.9	76.6	78.3	78.2	78.7	78.9	79.2
1845	78.7	77.5	75.7	76.8	76.7	76.1	76.3	76.6	77.7	82.0	81.5	81.7
1846	81.6	82.2	81.7	83.1	82.2	82.7	79.6	78.6	77.6	77.9	84.7	87.2
1847	85.7	85.4	90.3	91.0	88.1	89.1	89.3	89.8	91.8	95.1	97.3	91.9
1848	91.1	91.5	91.4	88.9	85.5	84.3	83.0	83.3	84.4	84.8	86.9	88.4
1849	88.6	85.9	86.5	84.6	85.4	86.1	86.6	89.1	91.1	91.8	92.1	92.3
1850	92.9	93.9	90.3	88.6	91.1	89.3	89.0	89.3	94.1	98.5	100.0	100.7
1851	99.5	94.7	93.1	90.7	90.8	88.7	88.6	92.4	90.6	90.6	92.0	95.2
1852	94.6	96.9	97.1	100.3	100.6	99.9	100.2	100.1	103.0	104.9	101.5	101.0
1853	100.4	99.4	99.9	100.0	97.4	94.9	96.7	96.9	100.1	102.0	103.3	105.3
1854	109.7	112.6	112.0	111.7	112.9	112.2	113.6	116.9	117.8	118.3	121.2	117.4
1855	121.2	118.5	118.1	117.7	117.2	117.8	119.3	118.1	119.5	122.9	122.6	124.6
1856	124.5	123.7	121.4	120.9	121.9	121.9	119.0	116.7	119.5	120.6	124.5	122.5
1857	122.1	122.1	123.3	121.1	118.4	117.0	114.3	114.7	115.4	114.4	108.9	109.0
1858	110.4	109.0	109.5	105.9	102.9	102.9	101.3	101.5	101.6	102.1	101.8	101.2
1859	103.1	105.2	104.5	101.7	104.9	103.7	102.2	104.0	99.8	100.0	101.0	100.9
1860	101.2	100.4	102.8	102.0	100.4	100.0	100.0	103.3	103.9	103.9	104.9	102.2
1861	99.1	101.7	99.7	98.3	95.0	91.7	91.2	91.4	91.9	94.0	96.0	95.8

Table 30—Ferrous Metals and Metal Products

Year	Jan.	Feb.	Mar.	Apr.	May	June	July	Aug.	Sept.	Oct.	Nov.	Dec.
1784	98.7	100.3	98.9	96.7	95.1	95.9	97.4	94.9	95.0	94.6	91.7	91.1
1785	90.3	90.6	90.1	88.9	88.3	84.8	83.8	81.5	82.1	82.1	82.1	82.1
1786	82.1	82.1	80.5	81.0	78.8	77.7	77.4	77.1	76.7	76.5	76.3	76.3
1787	76.3	76.7	76.3	76.3	75.0	75.5	76.1	75.2	75.6	75.0	76.0	76.0
1788	75.5	75.5	76.4	75.7	75.7	76.5	76.4	76.2	76.0	75.6	75.6	75.2
1789	75.6	75.6	76.0	76.0	76.0	76.0	76.0	76.8	76.8	76.8	76.6	77.1
1790	76.7	76.7	77.0	77.0	77.0	77.0	77.0	76.1	76.1	76.1	78.8	79.5
1791	79.1	79.5	79.5	77.9	78.1	78.2	77.8	78.0	78.0	78.0	78.0	78.0
1792	80.4	80.4	81.2	81.2	81.2	82.6	83.6	83.6	83.6	83.6	83.6	84.9
1793	84.5	84.5	84.8	82.1	82.1	82.1	81.7	81.7	79.9	79.9	79.6	78.7
1794	79.0	79.0	79.0	79.0								
1795	88.3	88.3	88.3	89.0	91.7	91.4	91.2	93.4	98.0	97.4	95.6	95.7
1796	97.7	98.4	98.5	100.4	98.4	99.0	98.9	99.7	99.7	102.4	103.4	104.5
1797	103.5	103.6	103.3	104.6	104.7	105.4	105.4	103.4	103.4	103.3	103.3	103.3
1798	105.7	105.7	105.9	105.9	105.9	105.9	107.2	107.2	107.2	107.2	107.2	
1799					103.7	105.5	105.5	105.4				
1800						107.9	107.9	107.7	107.2	107.5	107.7	108.2
1801	108.4	108.4	108.8	108.8	108.8	111.2	111.6	113.3	113.3	113.3	120.6	120.3
1802	120.3	120.3	120.3	117.6	113.1	110.9	109.3	109.3	109.3	109.6	109.6	108.3
1803	108.3	108.3	106.2	106.2	106.2	106.2	106.2	106.2	106.2	106.2	106.2	105.4
1804	105.4	105.4	105.4	105.4	105.4	105.4	105.4	105.4	105.4	105.4	105.4	105.0
1805	105.0	106.2	106.2	106.2	106.4	106.4	106.4	106.4	106.4	105.9	106.5	106.5
1806	109.3	109.3	109.3	109.3	109.3	109.3	109.1	109.4	110.1	110.6	112.0	112.0
1807	112.3	112.6	112.6	112.9	113.0	113.0	113.0	112.6	112.2	112.1	111.9	111.2
1808	111.2	111.2	111.2	111.2	111.2	111.2	112.5	112.5	111.9	111.9	111.9	111.9
1809	123.9	123.9	123.9	128.3	128.2	127.3	119.8	119.5	119.7	119.7	119.7	120.3
1810	120.3	120.3	120.3	120.3	120.3	120.3	122.5	122.6	121.6	122.6	121.9	121.9
1811	115.9	116.0	116.0	116.5	116.5	116.5	116.8	119.8	121.0	121.1	120.9	119.7
1812	121.8	120.6	121.0	121.0	121.0	121.1	123.8	123.9	123.9	123.9	126.1	130.7
1813	130.8	130.8	130.8	130.8	130.3	130.3	130.1	130.1	130.1	130.2	134.2	136.5
1814	142.9	141.2	144.6	148.2	144.9	141.1	137.4	137.9	138.1	148.2	151.6	152.9
1815	153.8	157.6	156.2	141.8	141.7	137.2	136.8	134.5	132.8	132.8	134.1	134.8
1816	136.0	135.7	137.3	135.2	133.4	129.3	129.3	124.5	123.8	123.5	123.2	123.2
1817	121.4	121.4	121.4	119.1	116.3	116.1	116.2	115.8	115.6	110.1	107.6	108.6
1818	109.2	109.2	108.9	109.1	108.3	108.1	108.1	108.3	108.3	108.3	106.6	106.6
1819	105.0	106.9	104.5	104.5	103.8	103.6	104.3	104.1	104.0	104.5	104.5	104.5
1820	104.5	104.5	104.5	104.5	104.5	104.4	104.2	104.2	104.2	104.2	104.2	104.2
1821	104.2	104.2	104.2	104.2	104.2	104.2	104.2	104.2	104.2	104.2	104.2	104.2
1822	100.7	101.0	101.0	101.0	101.0	101.0	101.2	101.2	100.8	100.2	100.2	100.2
1823	100.2	100.2	100.2	100.6	100.6	100.6	100.5	100.5	97.3	97.3	97.3	97.3
1824	97.3	97.3	97.3	97.6	97.8	97.8	97.8	97.8	94.3	94.5	93.4	93.5
1825	92.9	92.9	93.0	93.1	99.7	100.9	101.6	101.2	100.7	100.5	100.5	100.4
1826	100.4	100.4	100.2	100.7	100.9	100.6	100.0	99.0	97.8	97.7	98.4	98.4
1827	98.8	98.8	98.8	98.7	97.5	97.3	96.5	96.4	96.3	96.6	97.2	97.6
1828	97.6	97.6	96.6	96.3	96.1	95.6	95.6	95.6	95.6	95.6	95.0	94.9
1829	94.9	94.8	94.8	94.7	94.7	94.7	94.1	94.1	93.9	92.6	91.5	90.8
1830	90.6	90.5	89.0	89.0	87.9	87.9	86.4	86.3	86.0	86.0	86.0	86.0
1831	86.0	85.5	85.5	85.9	85.8	85.8	85.9	85.4	86.1	87.0	86.9	86.9
1832	88.4	88.7	88.7	88.0	88.4	87.5	86.9	87.2	87.5	87.5	86.6	86.6
1833	86.9	86.7	89.1	87.4	88.7	88.7	88.7	88.6	88.6	90.1	90.3	90.9
1834	87.5	87.5	86.6	86.6	86.3	85.9	85.9	85.9	86.9	86.9	88.2	86.2
1835	85.2	84.2	84.0	87.3	87.8	86.5	85.5	85.5	85.3	85.4	85.7	86.8
1836	86.9	87.0	91.9	96.9	99.7	99.6	99.6	99.5	100.9	100.6	101.9	102.1
1837	102.5	102.5	103.9	103.9	102.3	102.5	99.6	99.5	97.6	97.2	96.3	96.4
1838	94.6	95.3	95.3	94.6	93.5	93.6	93.7	92.8	92.1	91.8	92.7	92.8
1839	93.0	94.5	97.3	97.2	97.3	96.8	94.9	94.3	93.1	92.2	92.2	92.0
1840	92.0	90.3	90.0	89.0	86.8	86.8	86.3	86.3	85.7	85.7	85.2	85.2
1841	85.1	85.1	85.1	85.1	84.9	84.6	84.7	84.7	84.7	84.4	84.4	85.0
1842	85.0	85.0	83.5	83.7	83.7	83.6	83.5	83.0	82.2	80.9	80.9	80.9
1843	80.6	79.3	78.3	78.0	77.7	77.6	77.3	77.1	74.5	75.3	76.2	76.2
1844	76.2	76.4	76.2	76.1	77.3	78.1	78.0	79.0	79.1	79.9	80.1	80.2
1845	80.0	79.8	81.7	85.4	86.2	86.4	84.9	83.9	83.3	83.5	84.1	85.7
1846	84.2	83.5	83.5	83.5	83.2	83.2	83.0	82.7	81.7	80.5	80.6	80.8
1847	81.0	81.0	81.3	81.4	81.8	81.9	81.5	80.8	81.9	82.2	82.9	82.8
1848	82.6	80.9	80.6	80.6	82.4	82.1	82.1	81.4	80.3	77.3	77.2	77.3
1849	77.3	77.4	74.4	74.6	72.1	72.9	72.9	71.7	71.9	71.2	71.4	71.4
1850	71.4	71.4	70.7	70.9	70.5	70.4	70.4	68.5	68.4	68.1	67.8	67.8
1851	68.1	68.1	68.1	68.1	65.3	65.1	65.1	64.9	64.0	63.8	64.9	63.9
1852	63.8	63.8	63.7	63.7	63.0	63.0	63.8	63.7	65.5	69.7	71.7	74.5
1853	79.0	81.9	82.8	82.3	80.9	78.7	78.6	79.2	79.0	79.2	79.1	79.0
1854	79.7	79.9	80.6	80.4	80.2	80.7	80.9	80.9	81.9	81.9	81.2	79.6
1855	80.1	79.7	79.0	79.0	78.2	77.3	77.1	77.1	77.9	77.9	77.9	77.4
1856	76.9	76.9	76.6	76.9	77.5	76.8	76.8	76.7	76.7	76.9	75.8	75.2
1857	74.6	75.1	74.6	75.0	74.6	74.6	74.6	74.4	74.4	73.2	71.2	71.2
1858	70.4	68.9	68.8	68.4	68.2	67.9	68.9	68.8	68.6	67.6	66.8	67.1
1859	67.7	68.6	68.5	68.5	68.0	67.6	67.5	67.0	67.5	67.5	67.5	67.5
1860	67.8	67.8	67.8	66.9	66.6	66.6	66.4	66.2	65.7	65.6	65.6	65.6
1861	64.9	64.6	64.1	63.9	62.5	62.5	62.1	61.9	62.1	62.1	62.1	62.2

TABLE 31—NON-FERROUS METALS AND METAL PRODUCTS

Year	Jan.	Feb.	Mar.	Apr.	May	June	July	Aug.	Sept.	Oct.	Nov.	Dec.
1784	87.1	87.4	87.4	87.1	74.1	74.7	75.2	74.2	73.0	71.9	70.7	72.9
1785	73.6	76.7	77.6	80.0	82.3	83.2	83.2	83.7	82.0	82.8	85.1	84.0
1786	84.4	84.4	84.4	84.4	84.6	83.9	83.9	83.9	85.3	85.3	85.3	85.3
1787	85.3	85.3	85.3	86.9	89.3	86.9	88.4	94.5	91.0	91.0	91.0	87.8
1788	87.8	87.8	87.8	87.8	87.8	87.8	87.8	87.8	86.7	97.0	97.0	96.8
1789	96.8	96.8	96.8	96.8	96.8	96.8	96.8	96.8	96.8	96.8	96.8	96.8
1790	96.8	96.8	96.8	96.8	96.8	95.0	95.0	95.0	95.0	95.0	95.0	90.9
1791	90.9	90.9	89.9	88.8	90.5	90.5	90.2	89.7	91.0	91.0	91.0	91.0
1792	90.4	90.6	90.7	90.9	91.0	91.1	91.3	91.4	91.6	91.7	91.8	92.0
1793	92.1	92.3	92.4	92.5	92.7	95.5	95.6	95.8	93.5	93.6	93.7	93.9
1794	94.0	94.1	94.3	94.3								
1795	104.8	104.9	105.1	105.2	105.3	105.5	105.6	105.8	105.9	106.0	106.2	107.3
1796	106.2	106.2	106.2	108.5	106.6	112.5	108.3	103.5	105.3	104.2	114.8	111.7
1797	111.7	112.0	112.0	109.0	113.9	103.5	103.5	115.3	118.2	118.2	118.2	119.4
1798	115.9	115.9	116.8	116.8	129.3	129.8	132.6	136.9	136.9	136.9	135.5	138.3
1799	139.6	140.8	139.3	139.3	139.3	143.5	136.4	138.6	138.6	138.0	138.3	134.6
1800	134.6	134.6	136.3	137.0	136.6	127.5	125.9	125.9	125.9	138.9	139.0	139.0
1801	139.9	139.9	139.9	139.9	124.2	123.7	127.9	127.9	129.3	130.5	130.5	130.5
1802	130.5	125.1	125.1	125.1	125.1	125.1	124.1	124.1	127.3	130.6	133.2	130.8
1803	130.7	131.2	131.7	134.0	132.6	133.2	135.8	142.5	143.1	145.4	147.4	150.3
1804	149.9	151.1	151.1	152.0	150.7	149.8	148.9	148.0	149.0	148.7	149.5	147.0
1805	147.0	147.0	147.0	147.0	143.8	144.9	144.9	147.2	149.5	149.5	147.8	147.8
1806	149.3	149.3	149.8	145.7	142.0	142.0	142.5	142.7	143.8	143.3	142.6	142.6
1807	142.6	142.0	141.9	140.4	139.3	139.3	137.8	137.2	137.9	138.9	140.9	140.6
1808	141.0	140.6	140.6	140.6	140.9	140.9	138.5	138.5	137.5	132.2	135.1	139.4
1809	151.3	152.4	152.4	152.4	136.6	134.1	130.3	130.3	130.4	130.4	131.9	137.9
1810	137.9	137.9	137.9	140.8	137.4	134.7	134.7	134.7	134.9	133.1	133.1	131.9
1811	126.6	127.4	128.2	125.8	122.4	121.4	124.0	123.0	128.6	128.6	128.7	128.7
1812	129.7	131.4	129.7	130.9	134.2	134.1	174.3	190.4	191.3	191.1	180.9	174.8
1813	174.7	174.5	178.0	177.0	176.8	176.7	177.9	179.3	185.3	189.4	228.6	240.1
1814	260.6	250.0	248.3	235.3	214.0	237.2	235.0	235.0	244.1	248.6	261.6	262.3
1815	291.5	278.2	186.4	183.1	171.3	143.9	144.5	146.2	158.2	157.6	173.9	172.4
1816	170.5	170.5	155.8	138.8	138.5	127.5	127.5	121.3	119.9	110.7	103.0	103.0
1817	103.0	100.5	100.4	99.4	99.4	99.2	99.8	99.1	101.2	100.5	102.0	106.6
1818	105.8	109.3	108.8	108.6	106.0	108.1	107.8	105.0	104.0	104.7	104.5	103.2
1819	103.2	103.6	103.6	102.4	102.1	102.1	100.7	103.8	103.7	103.7	101.6	101.6
1820	101.6	101.6	101.6	101.6	101.6	98.6	99.1	99.1	99.1	99.1	99.6	99.6
1821	99.6	99.6	99.6	99.6	99.6	99.6	99.6	99.6	97.4	97.4	97.4	99.1
1822	98.1	98.1	98.1	98.1	97.6	100.9	100.6	100.4	100.1	99.7	99.9	99.5
1823	100.1	100.1	100.1	100.1	100.1	99.8	99.8	95.4	95.4	94.6	94.0	94.0
1824	93.0	93.0	93.0	93.0	91.3	91.3	91.3	92.4	96.3	97.2	98.5	98.5
1825	98.5	99.1	97.0	101.7	114.5	113.4	114.9	113.3	113.6	113.0	113.0	113.5
1826	113.0	109.0	108.5	106.9	105.2	103.3	102.9	102.3	103.1	102.9	102.3	101.9
1827	104.1	104.0	104.9	101.4	104.9	100.2	101.1	96.7	97.5	97.5	96.9	96.6
1828	95.8	93.7	93.4	93.4	93.3	92.8	92.6	92.7	91.6	90.9	90.3	90.3
1829	89.0	88.8	88.8	85.1	85.0	85.4	84.2	84.7	82.8	83.7	83.5	83.5
1830	81.4	81.6	81.6	78.9	79.4	77.7	76.3	75.1	74.2	74.2	72.7	73.9
1831	74.0	74.3	76.9	77.5	77.1	76.4	79.9	82.6	82.2	83.4	82.8	83.2
1832	83.8	83.1	82.8	82.4	83.5	84.1	84.2	84.0	83.3	83.3	83.5	83.7
1833	83.5	83.1	82.8	82.8	81.4	81.6	81.8	81.1	81.6	81.5	81.6	81.1
1834	80.9	81.3	81.9	81.9	82.1	81.4	80.7	82.4	82.4	82.1	82.4	83.0
1835	80.9	82.4	83.3	83.8	84.0	85.6	87.0	87.1	89.3	89.2	89.7	89.0
1836	90.0	90.3	92.5	100.9	103.8	104.6	104.7	106.4	107.4	108.0	110.5	109.7
1837	110.6	110.0	110.9	113.2	112.1	111.5	107.0	100.7	95.7	90.4	91.3	91.3
1838	91.0	91.2	89.8	89.9	90.1	89.6	89.2	87.9	86.1	85.0	85.2	86.5
1839	87.4	87.9	88.5	89.3	87.9	88.1	88.1	89.6	90.3	90.3	91.6	91.5
1840	90.0	89.7	89.7	89.7	89.4	89.3	86.6	85.4	86.1	85.9	85.6	86.0
1841	85.7	86.0	85.9	86.4	86.4	85.3	85.1	85.5	82.6	83.5	83.3	83.3
1842	83.3	83.1	83.2	81.6	81.1	81.0	81.1	80.8	80.7	77.0	76.9	76.8
1843	77.1	79.3	76.4	75.9	75.1	74.2	74.0	72.2	69.3	68.8	69.1	70.9
1844	71.2	70.9	71.5	72.1	71.8	72.5	72.5	72.5	73.2	74.2	74.8	74.8
1845	74.6	74.8	75.1	74.9	74.3	75.1	76.0	76.0	79.2	79.2	81.5	82.7
1846	82.6	82.4	81.7	83.5	83.5	83.8	83.9	83.0	83.5	83.3	83.4	83.4
1847	83.4	83.1	83.2	83.3	83.6	84.4	84.3	83.9	83.8	85.5	85.2	85.1
1848	85.4	86.4	84.7	82.9	80.6	79.6	79.8	80.0	82.6	82.6	82.5	80.4
1849	80.4	82.8	84.0	85.0	84.6	83.6	82.4	82.3	82.1	77.5	77.3	77.7
1850	77.6	79.8	81.4	81.8	80.4	79.6	78.5	79.1	79.3	80.2	80.3	80.2
1851	80.3	81.4	81.2	81.3	80.6	80.6	80.6	81.0	80.9	80.4	80.3	80.3
1852	80.4	80.4	81.7	81.5	81.7	81.5	82.0	82.3	83.5	83.7	84.3	91.6
1853	91.9	114.4	119.5	117.5	110.6	101.4	99.4	98.0	99.1	103.7	106.9	109.9
1854	112.6	112.6	115.1	115.1	113.8	112.1	112.0	113.1	112.0	112.7	111.8	111.5
1855	105.4	104.1	104.1	104.6	104.2	104.3	105.2	105.5	105.2	106.1	106.6	108.7
1856	108.3	108.3	108.0	107.7	107.8	107.6	106.2	105.0	104.1	102.8	102.8	101.0
1857	105.3	106.4	109.8	114.9	114.7	108.0	106.5	106.4	104.9	105.7	105.7	104.2
1858	101.2	96.9	100.6	101.5	103.4	98.3	97.4	96.3	95.1	94.1	93.5	92.4
1859	92.4	94.3	96.7	98.8	100.5	97.9	97.6	98.8	99.5	99.5	99.4	99.4
1860	99.4	98.7	98.1	98.8	99.1	98.3	98.3	98.2	98.2	98.3	98.0	97.2
1861	95.7	92.9	89.4	89.6	89.7	88.6	88.8	86.3	91.9	93.0	94.1	95.1

TABLE 32—WOOD

Year	Jan.	Feb.	Mar.	Apr.	May	June	July	Aug.	Sept.	Oct.	Nov.	Dec.
1784	85.7	85.8	84.6	84.2	80.1	79.1	78.1	79.2	83.9	84.7	86.4	86.7
1785	86.5	85.2	84.5	81.3	79.4	75.0	73.8	71.1	66.8	68.2	68.4	68.2
1786	68.0	67.6	67.4	67.7	55.0	54.7	54.7	54.7	55.2	54.3	54.1	54.0
1787	53.5	53.4	53.6	55.8	52.9	52.7	51.4	52.1	52.0	51.3	52.0	52.0
1788	50.4	50.6	49.0	49.3	49.5	49.6	49.2	49.5	50.5	51.9	54.7	54.9
1789	55.1	55.3	55.5	55.3	55.4	55.4	55.3	52.5	52.5	52.5	52.6	52.8
1790	52.5	52.5	52.5	52.1	52.9	53.3	53.3	57.4	57.4	57.4	54.6	61.0
1791	61.0	61.1	63.0	61.2	60.6	61.4	65.0	65.4	64.8	65.3	69.4	68.6
1792	64.8	64.8	64.8	65.7	65.8	66.0	66.7	67.0	67.1	76.0	79.0	79.0
1793	78.8	78.8	75.7	75.7	75.7	75.7	75.7	75.7	75.9	75.9	75.9	75.9
1794	75.9	75.9	75.9	75.9								
1795	94.9	94.9	94.9	94.9	94.9	95.9	95.9	91.7	95.6	95.6	96.7	96.7
1796	99.9	102.0	102.0	102.0	107.4	109.2	110.7	110.1	110.4	113.3	119.2	122.0
1797	123.8	123.8	119.4	119.4	119.4	108.0	108.0	108.0	107.3	107.3	107.3	107.3
1798	107.7	107.7	105.0	105.0	105.0	105.0	105.0	105.0	105.0	105.0	105.0	
1799					106.5	106.0	106.0	106.2				
1800						117.2	114.4	113.4	113.4	113.4	113.4	110.7
1801	110.7	114.1	114.1	114.1	114.1	113.7	113.0	113.0	113.0	113.0	113.8	113.8
1802	113.2	113.2	113.2	108.7	103.8	100.4	100.0	100.0	100.5	107.3	108.7	109.7
1803	109.7	110.4	110.4	110.4	108.7	108.7	108.7	108.7	108.7	108.7	108.7	108.7
1804	108.7	108.7	108.7	112.4	114.7	115.0	115.0	115.0	116.6	116.6	116.6	116.5
1805	116.6	115.8	115.8	114.0	114.0	114.0	114.0	114.2	114.2	114.2	114.2	114.2
1806	114.4	114.4	115.0	115.0	115.0	106.2	106.2	106.9	106.9	106.9	112.4	112.8
1807	116.2	116.2	116.2	115.2	114.9	114.9	114.9	114.2	111.8	113.3	113.3	113.6
1808	113.6	113.6	113.6	113.6	113.5	109.1	109.1	109.0	109.0	109.0	110.2	110.2
1809	110.2	110.2	114.3	114.2	114.7	115.6	116.9	115.4	114.4	114.4	120.8	120.8
1810	120.8	120.8	120.8	120.8	126.8	126.8	126.8	129.1	129.0	129.0	129.0	129.0
1811	129.0	129.0	127.2	125.5	126.0	126.6	126.6	126.6	122.3	122.9	122.9	122.9
1812	122.9	122.9	122.9	122.9	122.3	122.3	122.3	122.3	122.3	122.3	122.3	122.3
1813	121.5	121.5	121.5	121.5	124.5	124.5	124.1	124.1	124.1	124.1	124.1	131.0
1814	137.9	137.9	140.8	140.8	140.8	140.8	140.8	140.8	140.8	143.9	149.6	149.6
1815	154.6	156.5	162.5	160.4	150.0	152.9	146.8	144.3	144.3	144.3	144.3	144.3
1816	146.0	146.0	146.0	146.0	130.6	144.0	139.0	138.3	136.1	133.2	133.2	133.2
1817	133.2	129.6	129.6	129.6	128.4	123.9	116.3	117.7	125.8	125.8	125.8	125.8
1818	125.8	126.7	121.0	121.0	121.3	123.3	114.4	114.0	119.2	120.1	126.3	126.8
1819	126.8	127.8	127.8	127.8	122.6	121.1	120.1	120.1	120.1	114.3	114.3	114.3
1820	112.9	112.9	112.9	112.6	110.2	107.6	107.6	101.9	101.9	98.9	98.9	98.9
1821	98.9	98.9	98.9	86.1	90.1	90.1	91.6	91.6	91.6	91.6	91.6	91.6
1822	101.8	101.8	101.8	101.8	101.8	101.8	103.2	103.2	103.2	103.2	103.1	103.2
1823	103.2	103.2	102.1	102.1	102.1	98.3	98.3	98.3	98.3	98.3	98.3	98.3
1824	98.3	99.4	99.4	100.0	98.3	98.3	98.6	98.6	98.4	98.4	98.4	98.4
1825	100.9	100.9	102.2	104.0	106.5	106.4	106.4	106.4	106.4	106.4	106.4	104.5
1826	104.5	105.9	105.9	106.6	104.1	104.1	105.7	104.7	104.5	104.5	104.5	104.5
1827	105.3	100.8	100.8	104.9	107.6	106.0	104.5	99.6	98.6	98.3	100.1	100.1
1828	100.1	100.4	101.2	101.2	102.6	102.1	102.1	102.1	102.1	102.1	102.1	102.1
1829	101.2	101.2	101.2	99.6	93.4	93.4	93.4	90.7	88.2	88.2	88.2	88.2
1830	88.5	85.5	85.5	85.5	82.9	82.9	82.9	82.9	82.9	82.9	82.9	82.9
1831	82.9	85.5	88.2	91.7	91.4	91.7	91.7	91.7	97.4	96.7	98.7	98.7
1832	98.7	98.7	98.7	94.3	93.8	91.2	91.2	91.2	91.2	91.2	91.2	91.2
1833	94.2	94.2	91.2	91.2	91.2	91.2	91.2	95.8	95.8	95.8	95.8	95.8
1834	94.5	94.5	94.5	92.4	92.4	92.4	92.4	92.4	92.4	92.4	92.4	92.4
1835	86.9	88.5	94.2	92.9	93.1	97.2	98.6	99.7	99.7	100.7	97.4	94.3
1836	94.3	94.3	95.3	99.4	101.0	101.0	101.0	98.9	98.9	98.9	99.5	99.5
1837	99.5	99.5	99.5	98.1	96.7	95.8	90.6	91.4	91.4	91.8	93.6	91.3
1838	94.5	94.5	94.5	93.3	92.2	92.2	92.6	92.6	92.4	91.7	90.5	90.6
1839	90.6	90.6	90.7	92.0	92.0	92.2	91.8	91.9	91.9	95.4	95.4	95.5
1840	95.5	95.6	94.9	94.2	89.4	87.8	87.9	87.9	87.9	87.7	87.8	87.8
1841	87.8	87.8	87.9	88.1	91.8	93.0	94.0	94.0	87.2	87.2	86.9	86.5
1842	86.5	86.3	86.4	85.6	85.8	81.5	82.0	82.0	80.5	77.2	77.2	77.7
1843	78.7	79.9	80.3	79.3	77.8	78.2	78.2	76.6	73.3	72.1	70.1	63.2
1844	65.2	65.2	65.2	75.8	74.5	76.8	76.8	74.1	74.2	74.2	74.2	73.7
1845	72.8	73.6	73.6	72.6	73.9	73.5	73.5	73.1	73.1	73.7	78.9	77.9
1846	78.1	77.8	77.8	79.8	79.0	80.7	78.0	76.3	71.9	71.9	72.2	70.9
1847	70.4	70.4	71.6	77.8	71.2	74.9	74.1	72.7	73.6	77.8	80.0	78.0
1848	78.3	77.3	78.1	75.9	74.9	72.9	69.2	69.6	69.6	70.2	70.2	72.2
1849	72.2	72.2	72.4	74.6	71.6	70.7	71.8	71.9	71.6	71.8	70.8	73.5
1850	74.2	74.2	74.5	76.1	78.9	78.3	77.6	80.2	80.2	81.3	81.5	90.9
1851	90.3	89.4	89.1	89.7	90.3	91.2	90.8	90.4	88.6	87.4	87.4	87.4
1852	86.7	86.7	86.7	87.3	88.1	87.2	86.7	86.7	88.5	88.3	88.9	90.5
1853	90.5	90.5	90.7	91.0	91.3	91.7	91.7	91.9	91.9	91.9	91.7	91.2
1854	91.2	91.2	93.6	96.7	96.9	97.2	98.0	98.0	97.0	97.0	97.0	97.0
1855	97.0	97.0	97.0	97.0	92.4	91.5	86.0	86.1	86.1	85.5	87.0	87.0
1856	87.0	87.4	87.4	87.4	87.6	87.6	87.6	87.3	85.7	85.7	85.7	84.9
1857	87.3	87.3	87.3	89.1	103.3	103.3	96.9	96.9	96.9	96.1	92.0	92.0
1858	90.0	90.0	90.0	92.6	92.6	92.8	92.8	92.8	88.3	88.3	88.3	90.8
1859	90.5	96.7	96.7	97.1	97.5	97.9	97.9	97.1	97.1	97.1	96.3	96.3
1860	96.6	97.5	97.5	96.9	95.8	96.6	96.0	95.1	95.1	94.9	95.2	95.2
1861	94.4	94.4	94.4	93.8	91.2	90.7	89.9	88.0	86.7	87.3	87.3	90.0

TABLE 33—BUILDING MATERIALS OTHER THAN WOOD

Year	Jan.	Feb.	Mar.	Apr.	May	June	July	Aug.	Sept.	Oct.	Nov.	Dec.
1784	147.3	145.8	141.4	136.4	141.4	141.8	140.4	139.4	139.8	138.3	135.0	133.4
1785	133.1	132.9	132.0	126.8	126.8	118.1	121.1	122.3	124.6	123.5	120.1	121.2
1786	121.2	121.2	121.2	114.0	103.2	100.1	101.1	100.6	101.1	100.3	99.1	101.7
1787	100.7	100.1	99.8	99.2	98.6	98.3	95.5	94.6	93.2	92.0	93.9	91.4
1788	92.1	92.2	92.6	93.1	93.4	94.2	94.7	95.0	94.4	96.5	95.9	100.2
1789	100.0	99.4	98.4	94.7	94.2	94.7	94.8	94.0	93.8	92.5	93.5	99.9
1790	97.8	98.1	98.2	96.9	95.1	95.9	96.7	102.6	104.8	106.9	111.1	109.2
1791	109.2	105.6	105.0	102.0	96.0	96.3	96.1	96.4	96.6	97.5	94.8	94.8
1792	94.4	93.6	93.2	92.6	92.5	94.3	93.9	94.2	93.0	93.5	95.5	94.9
1793	94.5	94.5	96.4	100.6	100.2	101.1	102.2	103.2	103.1	104.2	105.4	106.3
1794	105.2	105.8	109.3	113.2								
1795	134.7	133.6	133.3	135.3	136.2	123.8	127.1	140.6	140.2	145.8	144.2	151.7
1796	153.0	153.6	153.5	146.6	147.1	148.4	154.1	152.6	146.7	156.5	151.6	158.6
1797	161.7	171.0	168.8	155.0	153.7	146.1	152.2	149.8	150.4	149.3	147.4	147.8
1798	140.5	140.7	140.5	141.9	142.1	142.3	143.6	145.5	145.6	146.1	146.0	
1799					126.3	124.9	124.2	118.5				
1800						130.6	130.1	128.5	132.2	131.9	130.1	137.3
1801	138.3	140.2	135.3	131.3	135.0	137.8	138.4	138.3	137.7	138.1	144.2	142.0
1802	142.2	137.2	138.6	134.0	129.5	127.5	127.8	128.6	130.3	135.3	137.6	135.5
1803	143.0	143.5	142.3	142.0	142.2	142.1	140.3	142.8	142.6	143.0	143.0	143.3
1804	145.0	145.8	145.5	145.1	144.7	144.4	144.6	144.0	144.0	143.9	145.8	146.4
1805	147.0	147.5	145.4	142.7	142.1	139.9	140.4	141.8	142.0	144.1	143.6	145.6
1806	139.1	138.8	136.3	134.5	132.4	132.5	133.7	134.7	134.8	134.7	138.2	137.5
1807	140.3	138.4	135.1	135.6	128.4	127.3	127.6	129.5	129.8	131.7	139.9	140.0
1808	139.9	139.2	135.6	135.9	136.6	137.7	134.0	135.1	136.5	140.1	147.1	148.2
1809	149.9	149.9	162.6	174.3	179.7	176.9	167.3	166.0	165.9	168.2	179.8	179.5
1810	178.6	181.2	181.2	175.6	185.6	172.3	171.7	168.9	170.2	169.1	166.8	167.6
1811	178.0	174.2	169.6	167.4	159.7	154.9	150.8	155.2	155.0	150.9	150.9	154.3
1812	153.4	156.2	150.8	148.7	144.6	153.2	154.9	160.8	169.4	167.4	174.5	169.5
1813	170.6	171.0	171.3	174.3	178.0	181.4	187.7	187.9	188.4	188.5	196.4	221.8
1814	280.6	267.5	281.1	268.1	260.7	236.6	226.0	225.8	228.8	236.3	227.9	235.6
1815	234.8	230.7	216.1	192.5	175.0	161.9	181.5	179.8	178.8	182.4	182.6	176.6
1816	173.5	169.0	167.7	162.1	153.6	152.7	149.4	147.8	133.4	133.8	131.1	130.0
1817	128.8	128.9	127.9	124.9	123.4	117.0	117.5	120.0	121.6	123.7	122.9	123.6
1818	125.6	126.3	129.1	129.4	130.7	130.0	133.1	133.7	127.7	125.3	126.5	126.3
1819	132.0	133.2	132.0	129.1	121.2	118.6	114.4	109.8	106.9	106.2	112.3	115.4
1820	115.0	115.0	112.9	110.9	109.5	108.5	108.0	109.3	108.9	108.9	106.7	106.2
1821	105.8	105.8	104.9	103.6	103.1	102.4	103.7	103.9	102.1	101.6	102.7	105.5
1822	105.0	105.0	105.0	105.0	108.5	102.7	102.3	102.3	100.1	97.7	96.3	96.9
1823	96.9	96.9	97.1	95.5	96.2	96.4	99.3	100.7	100.3	100.3	95.2	95.7
1824	96.4	98.3	96.6	97.5	97.4	96.2	96.4	96.0	93.9	93.3	93.0	93.0
1825	98.2	97.6	99.9	99.6	100.3	94.7	94.0	90.7	92.3	95.4	98.4	97.3
1826	96.7	96.3	93.8	92.7	90.8	89.1	89.7	88.5	87.6	86.6	85.9	87.0
1827	88.9	90.5	91.0	90.3	87.2	86.2	84.6	83.9	85.6	88.3	88.1	88.3
1828	88.8	88.3	88.1	86.8	87.4	87.9	87.6	87.4	85.6	86.1	86.3	87.8
1829	88.9	89.9	89.1	86.6	85.2	85.2	82.8	83.0	81.4	81.2	80.4	80.6
1830	78.3	78.9	80.6	80.3	77.1	77.8	77.7	78.4	78.1	78.9	79.8	80.5
1831	80.4	80.8	82.2	82.5	82.5	82.1	82.0	85.3	84.5	84.7	86.1	88.3
1832	88.0	88.6	88.2	86.3	85.8	85.2	85.2	85.0	85.3	86.0	89.4	89.3
1833	89.0	89.7	89.0	89.8	89.3	89.2	88.7	87.7	89.2	88.5	90.6	92.2
1834	93.9	91.6	89.9	89.4	87.6	88.9	88.9	84.9	84.0	84.0	87.4	90.5
1835	90.4	90.3	91.3	92.3	90.5	93.2	91.7	90.3	89.3	92.5	94.4	97.5
1836	97.3	99.1	100.6	99.3	98.5	94.3	89.8	91.0	91.3	92.8	101.6	102.9
1837	101.8	102.1	101.1	95.2	92.3	86.3	83.9	85.3	86.7	88.7	90.1	91.5
1838	92.0	89.8	88.5	86.4	86.1	85.2	87.1	89.8	91.4	94.4	93.8	95.9
1839	96.3	95.7	96.2	95.9	93.5	92.1	91.6	92.3	90.0	89.9	90.2	89.6
1840	88.5	88.8	87.8	85.3	84.4	84.4	83.2	82.3	82.9	82.0	83.0	84.2
1841	85.1	84.2	83.5	82.5	81.0	82.0	80.6	81.2	84.1	87.5	87.7	84.5
1842	85.4	85.0	84.7	77.7	77.8	76.8	76.1	77.8	78.4	79.7	79.4	77.9
1843	77.6	75.6	75.2	76.7	77.0	74.8	75.6	75.5	76.1	75.3	74.3	74.0
1844	74.3	74.0	73.9	75.9	73.3	71.3	71.3	71.5	71.5	72.3	77.6	75.2
1845	72.1	73.9	75.4	75.5	74.5	73.6	73.2	73.5	74.6	77.3	81.7	82.1
1846	80.2	82.4	83.8	80.4	76.2	73.5	72.4	72.1	70.9	72.0	74.7	74.2
1847	74.2	75.3	77.9	73.8	73.5	75.1	74.5	73.4	73.3	73.0	73.3	72.7
1848	72.0	71.4	71.8	71.6	69.5	70.3	70.4	70.4	74.2	74.3	73.6	73.4
1849	70.8	70.2	70.4	72.9	70.8	70.6	69.8	72.8	75.5	76.4	75.0	71.0
1850	70.6	73.8	77.8	75.5	75.7	73.4	73.2	71.3	73.6	77.9	77.8	76.7
1851	76.2	76.8	77.3	75.3	74.9	72.7	73.8	74.6	75.8	78.5	76.3	74.8
1852	74.6	75.6	77.7	75.5	77.5	75.1	75.1	78.0	79.2	80.6	81.0	82.6
1853	83.8	88.5	90.1	87.8	86.9	83.4	82.6	85.4	92.2	92.9	94.6	93.7
1854	91.7	95.3	96.8	97.8	102.2	99.2	98.6	99.0	100.4	99.2	96.4	94.9
1855	96.1	93.7	93.8	90.8	94.8	95.8	93.7	93.5	93.8	94.0	93.0	92.8
1856	92.4	91.6	90.6	90.1	89.9	87.5	85.7	87.8	89.8	91.1	91.8	91.8
1857	89.8	90.3	89.8	90.2	92.5	93.2	93.0	92.9	93.2	91.7	88.5	86.0
1858	85.2	86.5	90.7	90.8	91.4	88.7	89.7	91.2	91.1	92.0	91.9	91.4
1859	90.7	90.6	91.4	92.4	90.9	89.2	87.1	87.3	87.4	87.1	86.3	86.6
1860	85.4	85.4	87.0	87.1	86.9	84.8	84.3	84.8	84.8	85.0	83.5	83.2
1861	81.4	81.8	83.5	82.8	92.7	94.9	93.3	110.5	116.0	116.8	120.5	130.3

Table 34—Textile Fibers

Year	Jan.	Feb.	Mar.	Apr.	May	June	July	Aug.	Sept.	Oct.	Nov.	Dec.
1784	94.3	94.3	89.9	83.5	83.8	82.4	80.9	79.2	87.5	92.3	109.1	103.6
1785	104.1	108.6	108.4	100.4	93.1	103.3	100.0	99.8	100.0	111.2	130.1	135.4
1786	130.0	122.6	122.6	123.0	128.7	132.7	132.9	134.9	131.6	130.0	137.9	139.4
1787	139.4	139.4	139.4	141.3	149.4	141.3	145.0	145.0	145.0	143.7	138.1	138.1
1788	138.1	134.9	131.5	124.2	131.2	120.5	120.5	120.5	116.7	116.7	109.3	105.5
1789	105.5	105.5	105.5	102.5	102.5	102.5	102.5	102.5	102.5	102.5	102.5	102.5
1790	99.4	104.6	104.6	104.6	104.6	111.3	107.6	100.3	94.6	94.6	101.9	102.2
1791	102.2	99.6	99.6	105.2	107.0	102.3	102.3	106.5	110.5	116.1	120.1	120.1
1792	112.1	112.1	116.5	121.2	121.2	113.4	123.3	123.3	123.3	123.3	123.3	122.1
1793	125.2	125.2	111.3	122.1	122.1	122.1	122.1	122.1	123.3	123.3	125.9	128.4
1794	128.4	124.9	124.9	124.9								
1795	118.9	126.1	122.2	122.2	136.1	136.1	139.4	134.4	134.4	147.8	147.8	147.8
1796	143.5	143.3	143.2	152.3	154.4	154.2	154.2	163.0	169.3	172.9	169.6	172.9
1797	172.9	171.0	156.4	154.4	154.4	155.4	158.2	158.2	154.4	154.4	154.4	154.4
1798	156.3	150.2	143.5	146.2	148.7	151.2	153.6	155.9	158.1	160.3	153.7	
1799					139.6	153.0	154.8	156.6				
1800						139.0	144.0	141.7	147.4	147.4	170.7	183.3
1801	174.5	178.5	178.5	173.7	168.6	166.4	173.7	167.5	161.7	160.0	165.8	165.8
1802	157.5	157.5	150.3	145.2	143.1	143.1	135.2	129.0	122.7	128.6	121.3	124.4
1803	126.5	126.5	123.3	137.6	136.9	136.9	136.9	138.8	138.8	138.8	138.8	138.8
1804	133.6	136.2	136.2	130.9	136.2	136.2	136.2	136.2	136.2	136.2	144.8	145.9
1805	143.6	143.6	145.9	156.1	156.1	156.1	150.5	150.5	150.5	150.5	150.5	150.5
1806	162.7	159.5	155.1	149.2	148.8	147.2	147.2	151.1	148.3	153.3	151.3	151.3
1807	147.7	147.7	147.1	144.8	149.5	149.5	149.5	150.7	144.7	143.3	134.0	136.8
1808	135.2	136.9	132.1	132.5	130.3	132.8	132.4	130.6	130.3	134.0	142.4	142.0
1809	138.4	139.5	158.0	158.4	162.3	145.8	146.2	137.5	134.3	134.6	139.7	143.9
1810	145.0	144.4	145.0	148.3	153.0	145.6	145.5	149.3	144.7	149.4	151.2	143.8
1811	148.1	138.0	137.0	134.3	117.3	115.8	109.4	111.0	109.9	106.8	91.4	97.1
1812	99.8	102.0	101.2	101.2	99.4	99.3	103.9	109.6	114.5	116.9	117.2	121.6
1813	121.7	130.9	137.6	140.6	149.9	153.0	153.0	153.0	158.9	158.9	163.3	171.1
1814	184.9	183.9	169.5	170.8	176.8	175.2	173.1	168.3	171.6	182.2	172.1	170.0
1815	169.9	169.9	142.6	134.4	136.1	137.4	144.8	147.1	147.1	158.5	155.5	147.1
1816	147.1	146.2	144.3	152.9	150.8	159.1	159.1	159.1	153.9	145.8	143.2	143.2
1817	138.4	146.1	146.1	141.5	139.0	139.1	134.3	135.1	142.9	142.3	137.5	149.9
1818	149.8	164.8	166.5	166.1	152.7	147.9	146.0	147.2	148.4	148.4	148.6	149.2
1819	150.2	142.1	144.2	143.9	129.4	130.0	125.5	126.0	130.5	132.9	132.9	135.3
1820	133.3	134.7	132.0	130.7	136.3	136.0	135.0	135.8	134.8	132.7	118.4	120.5
1821	119.6	119.6	106.8	103.9	103.5	104.3	105.4	104.6	104.6	104.6	104.4	107.4
1822	107.8	102.1	106.6	106.4	105.5	103.0	97.5	94.0	86.7	84.3	93.0	93.0
1823	93.1	93.1	96.3	82.8	82.2	94.2	94.2	83.8	84.1	86.3	88.7	88.9
1824	88.6	88.4	88.4	88.4	90.5	91.0	98.5	98.5	91.7	97.1	93.9	93.9
1825	96.2	101.2	107.1	114.6	120.2	125.2	124.0	114.4	107.1	107.6	100.3	105.3
1826	100.1	96.2	95.3	93.8	90.2	88.7	88.3	90.5	88.0	88.0	100.3	102.6
1827	100.7	100.0	103.3	110.1	107.8	103.5	90.5	93.8	94.8	95.9	98.7	99.6
1828	98.7	95.1	94.7	89.9	89.7	91.7	92.3	92.0	89.5	88.5	88.5	92.7
1829	91.9	90.1	89.5	89.5	86.3	84.5	83.3	82.4	82.4	84.7	85.2	86.4
1830	86.9	86.8	85.1	82.0	81.1	81.1	81.8	82.8	84.9	86.3	86.6	84.7
1831	84.1	83.4	83.5	83.1	83.7	83.9	83.3	83.1	92.2	92.0	91.2	90.3
1832	90.3	90.3	90.9	95.2	95.2	94.5	94.9	94.9	92.1	93.5	94.0	95.1
1833	92.2	92.2	92.6	93.7	93.6	94.6	92.5	94.7	94.8	94.3	94.8	94.8
1834	87.6	86.0	87.1	87.1	89.7	89.7	91.0	92.0	91.6	90.3	91.1	97.3
1835	89.0	92.4	95.6	96.2	98.8	103.6	103.8	103.3	104.2	102.9	107.8	105.6
1836	105.4	105.6	110.1	114.2	113.9	114.7	114.3	115.2	112.7	111.5	110.5	105.9
1837	103.2	104.7	103.9	99.4	94.3	90.5	90.7	88.5	89.4	87.2	90.6	89.3
1838	87.1	87.6	85.2	85.1	85.0	83.0	84.7	84.4	85.7	86.8	88.1	89.7
1839	91.5	92.1	96.6	105.0	106.9	105.9	104.6	102.4	99.3	98.9	102.3	102.6
1840	98.9	91.8	87.4	85.2	79.3	79.3	82.7	82.0	84.8	87.1	87.3	87.1
1841	86.5	87.8	87.8	88.5	88.0	89.2	90.1	90.1	88.1	87.6	87.1	86.6
1842	86.3	85.2	84.3	81.9	79.7	80.3	80.0	80.3	82.0	82.8	81.1	77.2
1843	75.0	73.1	72.5	68.1	69.4	69.7	69.7	69.2	73.0	76.9	76.6	77.0
1844	78.8	82.0	81.5	79.6	77.5	76.6	76.6	75.9	74.2	72.3	71.6	69.2
1845	66.9	66.0	66.3	67.8	69.6	69.7	70.2	70.4	72.3	73.9	74.7	74.5
1846	72.9	74.7	75.2	75.7	75.5	73.5	72.8	71.1	76.0	79.5	80.8	84.1
1847	87.2	93.6	93.9	96.1	100.1	100.0	97.9	94.1	93.2	91.0	84.6	83.8
1848	87.1	86.6	85.1	83.0	82.8	78.6	77.7	77.1	76.4	79.2	77.1	78.8
1849	80.5	79.1	82.8	83.2	83.4	84.7	83.7	85.5	87.5	87.2	89.0	88.4
1850	91.0	93.6	95.6	96.7	98.5	97.4	96.5	95.0	94.7	97.6	98.9	100.5
1851	100.5	100.2	96.1	96.2	92.6	91.3	87.8	84.0	88.8	90.1	85.4	85.7
1852	87.4	87.9	87.3	86.8	89.3	90.4	89.6	91.5	91.6	90.8	89.7	88.8
1853	91.4	93.7	94.0	95.7	95.2	94.4	94.2	94.4	91.0	90.6	89.7	91.0
1854	97.1	101.5	101.5	103.9	101.6	103.4	103.8	103.8	100.8	101.0	101.1	101.0
1855	99.1	97.1	95.4	96.8	97.1	105.3	102.6	103.9	105.0	102.1	99.6	99.9
1856	101.5	103.4	110.2	110.4	108.1	107.5	107.5	108.9	105.1	107.6	106.5	107.4
1857	107.0	106.7	110.6	111.1	111.1	110.0	104.9	106.6	107.1	103.7	101.4	94.7
1858	90.7	90.2	90.2	92.1	93.6	92.5	93.5	94.0	94.7	91.9	89.3	89.3
1859	93.6	93.3	92.8	94.4	93.9	92.3	93.1	92.4	93.5	92.4	92.1	92.7
1860	90.9	91.9	82.6	86.7	81.9	79.2	79.8	79.8	78.0	79.2	79.2	78.9
1861	82.4	85.1	85.3	85.9	88.3	88.3	88.3	99.0	105.4	103.4	106.7	114.1

Table 35—Textile Fabrics

Year	Jan.	Feb.	Mar.	Apr.	May	June	July	Aug.	Sept.	Oct.	Nov.	Dec.
1784	83.6	87.5	91.3	91.3	91.3	91.3	91.3	91.3	91.3	91.3	91.3	85.4
1785	86.2	79.8	81.3	82.6	84.0	85.2	85.2	83.9	86.4	87.8	88.3	88.7
1786	89.8	89.7	89.7	89.6	88.6	91.4	90.3	89.2	91.4	93.6	94.0	94.2
1787	94.0	93.7	93.4	94.0	92.8	93.9	93.9	95.0	93.4	93.4	92.6	91.6
1788	88.0	87.6	88.3	88.3	88.3	88.3	88.3	88.3	88.3	88.0	88.0	88.0
1789	88.0	88.0	88.0	88.9	88.9	87.9	87.1	88.6	88.6	88.6	88.6	90.0
1790	90.0	90.0	90.0	90.0	90.0	90.0	89.4	85.6	85.6	85.6	87.2	87.3
1791	86.1	86.4	87.3	87.1	86.8	86.8	86.8	86.4	86.4	86.4	86.4	85.9
1792	85.9	85.9	85.9	85.9	85.9	85.9	85.9	85.9	85.9	85.9	85.9	92.5
1793	92.5	92.5	92.5	93.7	96.8	97.8	97.8	97.8	99.9	101.1	101.6	102.0
1794	106.4	107.2	107.7	108.2								
1795	112.2	116.6	113.8	114.6	117.5	117.4	120.1	119.2	119.1	126.8	126.6	126.9
1796	126.9	126.9	126.9	123.1	129.3	129.3	129.3	131.0	131.3	131.3	131.3	130.6
1797	130.6	134.6	134.6	129.0	133.8	133.9	130.0	137.6	134.5	134.5	130.7	130.7
1798	116.2	117.8	120.8	123.2	129.1	133.0	131.6	131.0	131.0	131.0	131.0	131.0
1799	131.0	126.9	125.5	122.5	122.9	122.9	122.9	127.0	124.4	125.4	121.9	121.4
1800	116.1	115.8	115.8	121.8	120.3	118.4	119.0	120.2	122.8	124.6	130.2	130.6
1801	131.2	139.1	139.1	139.1	144.0	144.0	143.1	140.2	133.9	129.0	127.8	127.8
1802	121.4	121.4	114.8	113.9	113.9	113.9	113.9	113.9	114.8	112.0	112.0	112.0
1803	111.0	111.0	111.0	120.5	119.6	119.6	119.6	119.6	125.9	124.5	123.0	121.3
1804	119.1	127.2	124.6	124.6	124.6	124.6	124.6	124.6	124.6	125.7	125.7	135.9
1805	136.1	136.1	137.3	137.3	138.6	136.8	138.6	138.6	138.6	139.0	138.0	140.2
1806	137.4	137.4	137.4	136.0	139.3	143.5	141.8	141.8	140.3	136.8	136.2	136.6
1807	142.3	143.0	143.0	146.3	144.5	144.5	144.5	144.5	144.5	142.3	142.3	142.3
1808	142.3	146.3	146.0	146.0	146.0	146.0	146.0	147.4	150.5	157.1	169.5	169.5
1809	175.9	182.8	204.7	206.3	206.3	192.1	183.6	179.5	188.5	188.5	188.5	183.5
1810	167.3	159.0	163.9	159.2	159.2	157.4	157.4	157.4	157.4	155.6	152.9	149.2
1811	150.2	147.3	139.6	137.5	131.5	128.9	128.9	128.9	128.9	123.6	119.7	118.1
1812	118.9	118.9	119.9	117.2	117.2	118.1	142.9	148.9	145.7	150.9	150.9	157.2
1813	161.3	161.3	161.3	161.3	161.3	161.3	161.3	161.3	161.3	161.3	161.3	163.4
1814	172.3	163.0	164.6	160.2	154.2	154.4	154.2	153.9	153.6	164.6	164.6	167.3
1815	165.9	165.9	159.2	143.3	142.6	142.6	145.6	147.2	143.0	141.4	141.1	139.6
1816	139.6	139.6	139.6	139.6	137.7	137.6	138.8	134.6	133.5	125.5	123.5	120.9
1817	120.9	120.9	119.8	119.8	120.1	118.3	120.5	121.0	113.0	106.9	106.9	108.6
1818	108.5	110.6	110.5	112.8	114.1	113.6	113.0	112.7	113.9	114.3	114.0	114.0
1819	114.0	113.9	113.9	113.9	114.3	113.6	113.6	113.6	111.0	111.0	111.0	111.0
1820	111.0	111.0	111.0	111.0	111.0	109.6	109.6	109.6	109.6	109.6	107.7	107.7
1821	107.7	107.7	107.7	107.7	107.7	107.7	109.3	108.7	109.1	109.1	109.1	111.5
1822	111.0	111.0	111.5	111.5	105.6	105.6	104.9	104.9	103.4	103.4	102.6	102.6
1823	102.3	102.3	101.9	101.9	101.9	101.9	101.5	101.5	101.5	101.5	101.5	98.9
1824	97.2	95.5	94.8	94.8	94.8	94.8	93.4	90.3	89.8	87.8	87.8	87.8
1825	87.8	87.8	87.8	92.5	92.5	93.6	90.9	88.3	88.5	88.5	86.6	86.6
1826	86.8	87.8	88.3	88.3	83.7	83.7	83.0	83.0	83.0	81.4	79.6	80.9
1827	80.5	80.5	82.2	86.7	87.8	88.1	86.6	84.9	84.9	84.7	83.8	83.8
1828	83.8	84.5	84.5	82.5	82.5	84.6	84.6	84.6	84.6	82.9	84.3	83.2
1829	83.2	83.2	83.2	83.2	83.4	83.3	83.3	83.3	83.3	89.8	89.8	90.7
1830	90.7	90.7	90.2	90.2	90.2	90.2	90.3	89.5	88.7	88.3	88.3	88.3
1831	87.7	87.7	87.7	91.2	91.2	91.2	91.2	88.5	90.9	91.1	91.1	91.1
1832	91.1	91.9	91.9	91.3	91.3	90.6	90.6	90.7	90.7	90.7	90.3	90.3
1833	89.3	88.3	87.0	86.4	84.2	83.9	83.9	82.3	82.3	82.9	82.9	80.8
1834	80.3	80.3	79.7	78.6	78.6	78.6	78.6	78.6	78.3	76.9	76.9	75.9
1835	75.4	75.8	76.6	76.8	78.1	77.8	77.8	77.8	76.8	76.2	75.1	75.3
1836	75.5	76.1	76.2	78.7	82.2	82.8	82.8	82.8	83.5	83.2	83.2	83.5
1837	83.6	84.0	84.9	87.1	87.6	87.6	87.6	87.8	88.8	86.2	91.8	91.8
1838	91.8	91.4	91.5	91.1	91.1	88.1	88.1	87.0	87.1	89.4	89.0	89.0
1839	89.1	86.8	86.8	88.0	87.8	88.4	88.4	88.4	88.4	88.4	88.4	88.4
1840	88.4	87.1	87.1	87.1	87.1	87.1	86.8	86.4	84.1	84.1	84.1	83.0
1841	83.0	83.0	83.0	83.0	81.8	81.8	81.3	82.2	82.2	82.2	82.2	82.2
1842	82.2	82.2	81.5	81.1	81.1	81.1	81.1	81.1	81.1	81.1	81.1	80.4
1843	80.4	80.4	80.4	80.4	80.4	78.7	78.7	80.2	80.2	78.7	78.7	78.7
1844	78.7	78.7	78.7	79.0	77.0	77.0	77.0	77.0	77.8	77.8	77.8	77.5
1845	77.5	77.2	77.2	77.2	77.2	77.2	77.2	77.2	77.2	77.8	77.8	77.8
1846	77.8	77.8	77.8	77.8	77.8	78.0	78.0	78.0	78.0	78.0	78.0	78.0
1847	78.0	78.0	78.0	78.0	78.0	78.0	78.6	78.9	78.9	78.9	78.9	78.9
1848	78.9	78.9	78.9	78.9	78.9	78.9	78.9	78.9	78.9	78.3	78.3	78.3
1849	77.5	77.5	77.5	79.4	77.9	77.9	77.9	77.9	77.9	77.9	76.2	76.2
1850	76.2	76.2	76.2	76.2	76.2	76.2	76.2	76.2	76.2	76.7	76.7	76.7
1851	76.7	76.7	76.7	76.7	76.7	76.7	76.7	76.7	76.7	76.7	76.7	76.7
1852	76.7	76.7	76.7	76.7	76.4	76.1	76.1	76.1	75.8	75.8	75.8	75.8
1853	75.1	75.1	75.1	75.5	75.5	75.5	75.5	75.5	75.5	75.8	75.9	78.0
1854	77.5	81.0	82.3	85.3	89.4	90.5	90.5	89.8	89.8	89.8	88.6	92.2
1855	92.4	92.0	92.0	92.0	93.4	93.4	93.4	93.4	92.6	92.6	93.4	93.4
1856	93.4	93.4	93.4	93.4	93.2	92.8	89.9	85.9	86.2	86.7	86.7	88.1
1857	86.8	86.5	86.8	86.8	87.0	87.5	88.2	88.7	88.7	89.0	87.4	87.4
1858	87.4	87.6	87.6	87.6	87.6	87.6	87.6	86.7	86.7	86.7	86.7	86.7
1859	86.7	87.9	87.9	87.9	87.6	84.4	84.4	84.4	82.9	82.9	83.8	83.8
1860	83.8	83.8	83.8	83.8	83.8	83.8	85.2	84.9	84.9	84.9	84.9	85.5
1861	85.5	85.5	85.5	85.5	85.5	85.5	85.5	85.5	84.5	85.2	85.2	91.6

Table 36—Hides and Leather

Year	Jan.	Feb.	Mar.	Apr.	May	June	July	Aug.	Sept.	Oct.	Nov.	Dec.
1784	75.4	74.5	74.5	73.6	72.6	71.6	70.7	69.6	68.0	66.4	64.7	64.7
1785	64.7	64.7	64.7	64.7	64.7	64.7	64.7	64.7	66.0	67.2	68.4	69.6
1786	70.7	71.9	73.0	72.2	73.2	72.3	73.3	73.3	75.3	71.5	67.4	67.4
1787	67.4	70.3	68.3	68.3	63.4	63.4	63.4	63.4	63.4	63.4	63.4	65.1
1788	66.5	66.2	65.6	65.2	64.6	64.2	63.6	63.2	61.7	60.2	60.2	60.2
1789	60.2	60.2	54.7	54.7	54.7	54.7	72.4	72.4	72.4	72.4	72.4	72.4
1790	72.4	72.4	72.4	72.4	72.4	72.4	72.4	72.4	72.4	72.4	72.4	72.4
1791	72.4	67.1	67.1	68.1	68.1	70.4	70.4	70.4	70.4	70.4	70.4	70.4
1792	66.9	66.9	66.9	66.9	66.9	66.9	66.9	66.9	68.8	68.8	68.8	68.8
1793	65.9	65.9	65.9	68.8	68.8	68.8	68.8	68.8	68.8	68.8	67.0	65.2
1794	65.2	65.2	65.2	65.2	69.8	70.5	71.2	71.9	72.6	73.3	74.0	77.2
1795	81.4	79.5	79.5	79.5	76.5	76.5	76.5	75.4	75.4	75.4	75.4	75.4
1796	62.8	62.8	62.8	62.8	62.8	56.8	55.2	56.0	56.0	56.0	56.0	55.6
1797	55.2	55.2	55.2	55.2	55.2	55.2	55.2	55.2	55.2	55.2	55.2	55.2
1798	56.8	56.8	67.8	67.8	67.8	67.8	67.8	67.8	67.8	67.8	67.8	67.8
1799	67.8	67.8	67.8	67.8	67.8	67.8	67.8	67.8	68.0	68.2	68.4	68.6
1800	68.8	68.9	69.1	69.3	69.5	69.7	69.7	69.7	69.7	69.7	69.7	69.7
1801	69.7	69.7	69.7	69.7	69.7	69.7	69.7	69.7	69.7	69.7	74.8	74.8
1802	74.8	74.8	74.8	74.8	74.8	74.8	74.8	74.8	74.8	73.9	73.9	73.9
1803	73.9	73.9	73.9	75.6	75.6	75.6	75.6	75.6	75.6	75.6	75.6	75.6
1804	75.6	75.6	75.6	75.6	75.6	75.6	75.6	75.6	75.6	75.6	75.6	75.6
1805	75.6	75.6	75.6	75.6	75.6	75.6	75.6	75.6	75.6	75.6	75.6	75.6
1806	75.6	75.6	75.6	75.6	75.6	77.1	77.1	77.1	77.1	77.1	77.1	77.1
1807	77.1	77.1	77.1	77.1	77.1	77.1	77.1	75.1	75.1	75.1	75.1	75.1
1808	75.1	73.3	73.3	73.3	74.1	74.1	74.1	70.8	70.8	74.1	77.1	77.1
1809	77.1	77.1	77.1	76.2	76.2	76.2	75.3	73.7	73.7	73.7	73.7	73.7
1810	73.7	75.3	77.0	77.0	84.0	84.0	84.0	77.1	79.7	78.8	72.7	72.7
1811	72.7	68.9	67.0	67.0	67.0	67.0	55.6	61.3	65.4	67.0	66.5	66.5
1812	66.5	68.3	68.3	68.3	68.3	68.3	72.7	76.2	76.2	76.2	76.2	76.2
1813	75.3	77.9	80.3	80.3	80.3	81.9	81.9	81.9	81.9	81.9	81.9	82.6
1814	124.2	123.2	117.1	124.2	92.4	94.5	96.5	96.5	96.5	96.5	101.5	103.5
1815	103.5	103.5	81.1	81.9	81.9	81.9	85.0	98.2	100.9	103.1	103.1	104.6
1816	104.6	104.6	104.6	104.6	98.8	98.8	98.8	98.8	98.8	102.2	104.2	104.2
1817	104.2	104.2	103.0	99.8	93.6	91.8	90.8	92.6	92.6	90.9	90.9	90.9
1818	90.9	90.9	94.4	94.8	93.2	94.4	95.9	92.7	95.6	95.6	95.2	102.0
1819	101.1	100.6	100.6	93.5	93.9	90.5	89.7	87.2	87.2	87.2	86.5	83.0
1820	83.5	83.5	79.6	79.6	77.8	84.1	84.1	86.1	86.1	86.1	86.9	86.9
1821	91.8	91.8	91.8	91.8	91.8	93.6	93.6	93.6	93.6	98.9	105.6	105.6
1822	105.6	105.6	99.2	99.2	102.1	101.3	103.4	103.4	103.4	100.0	100.0	100.0
1823	100.0	100.0	100.0	100.0	101.7	101.7	101.7	101.7	101.7	101.7	100.3	99.8
1824	99.8	99.8	99.8	99.8	99.8	99.8	99.8	100.0	99.4	99.8	98.9	98.9
1825	97.0	97.0	97.9	100.8	100.8	101.6	102.7	102.7	105.8	105.1	106.1	106.1
1826	106.1	98.2	98.2	98.9	98.1	90.8	90.1	89.6	89.0	89.0	89.6	89.6
1827	92.8	92.8	92.8	95.7	93.5	93.5	92.0	92.0	93.7	93.7	93.7	91.9
1828	91.9	91.9	92.5	93.7	93.7	93.7	92.9	92.9	92.9	92.9	92.9	88.9
1829	88.9	88.9	88.9	88.9	88.9	87.6	87.1	86.7	89.7	89.7	89.7	89.7
1830	89.7	89.7	89.7	89.7	88.6	89.0	89.4	89.4	91.3	91.3	91.3	93.6
1831	93.6	93.6	93.6	93.6	95.9	95.9	95.9	95.5	97.5	97.5	99.5	99.5
1832	99.5	92.8	92.8	92.8	92.2	91.5	89.7	89.7	89.7	89.7	89.7	90.5
1833	89.7	89.7	89.7	83.2	83.6	82.7	82.7	82.7	82.7	82.7	82.7	82.7
1834	82.7	82.7	82.7	82.7	82.7	82.7	79.5	79.5	78.6	78.6	81.8	81.5
1835	76.2	77.5	80.1	82.7	81.3	79.9	75.8	75.8	78.8	80.0	78.8	79.1
1836	77.4	75.2	76.0	78.1	80.0	80.0	80.0	80.0	86.1	88.0	88.0	87.7
1837	87.3	87.3	87.5	83.4	80.5	77.2	76.4	76.9	75.6	79.9	81.0	80.1
1838	80.1	79.6	79.2	79.2	79.2	77.8	78.2	80.9	81.7	88.8	89.6	89.6
1839	89.6	90.0	89.7	88.7	86.8	86.4	86.7	86.2	86.5	86.5	89.3	84.6
1840	84.6	81.5	81.5	82.5	82.5	82.5	82.5	82.5	83.9	88.4	89.2	88.4
1841	85.7	81.3	81.3	79.7	79.7	83.0	84.4	87.5	88.5	88.9	89.2	87.6
1842	81.1	80.2	79.8	75.0	73.2	74.5	75.0	75.0	73.8	73.8	75.4	73.6
1843	71.1	70.2	70.2	70.0	67.7	68.1	70.6	71.9	76.6	72.4	72.0	71.6
1844	71.4	71.6	72.4	72.8	72.0	70.0	70.5	69.8	69.8	69.6	69.6	68.6
1845	69.0	68.8	69.6	69.8	70.2	69.1	69.7	70.3	70.3	69.9	69.3	69.5
1846	68.9	68.9	69.1	68.4	68.9	68.7	69.3	69.0	68.6	66.8	63.1	62.8
1847	63.7	66.3	67.0	67.0	67.0	67.0	68.6	69.6	74.1	72.4	73.3	73.1
1848	72.4	71.5	74.3	70.9	70.4	70.4	66.0	65.2	61.3	60.0	58.8	58.8
1849	58.8	65.7	68.0	62.7	60.6	58.9	59.2	60.2	67.1	68.5	69.8	69.8
1850	69.8	70.1	69.7	72.0	72.0	71.8	71.8	73.6	74.9	76.9	76.9	76.9
1851	76.9	76.9	76.9	77.6	77.6	77.7	77.7	77.7	77.7	74.2	73.7	73.4
1852	73.0	73.8	73.0	72.2	72.8	79.6	80.1	83.1	84.7	84.7	83.4	83.4
1853	83.4	83.2	85.3	87.2	87.2	87.4	89.2	91.3	91.3	95.7	97.0	97.0
1854	105.6	114.1	114.1	113.7	113.7	114.1	114.9	111.1	108.9	100.8	103.4	105.1
1855	105.1	107.4	107.4	109.4	109.4	108.6	108.6	110.5	111.2	112.1	115.9	115.9
1856	119.0	123.5	123.5	131.9	134.1	128.0	128.0	130.6	133.6	133.6	145.2	145.9
1857	151.8	151.8	151.8	172.5	169.6	163.4	163.4	163.4	163.4	163.4	155.9	134.7
1858	134.7	114.6	115.6	116.7	116.4	116.3	116.3	116.3	123.5	121.3	121.3	137.3
1859	138.1	139.5	139.5	139.5	142.1	142.1	142.1	143.2	133.7	132.6	132.0	131.5
1860	126.6	125.0	125.0	125.0	125.0	125.0	125.0	124.3	126.0	126.0	127.5	124.5
1861	123.1	115.2	115.2	114.5	114.5	114.5	113.1	111.4	108.4	117.4	119.6	114.5

TABLE 37—SPIRITS

Year	Jan.	Feb.	Mar.	Apr.	May	June	July	Aug.	Sept.	Oct.	Nov.	Dec.
1784	72.6	74.8	72.9	69.3	57.5	59.0	62.2	64.7	65.3	70.5	70.8	64.6
1785	64.7	60.7	60.1	59.4	57.7	56.1	57.4	55.8	55.6	57.4	57.0	57.0
1786	58.9	61.4	62.3	58.5	59.1	57.5	59.2	59.3	61.2	61.0	60.7	60.9
1787	61.1	64.0	64.0	64.0	61.2	58.6	60.1	59.4	56.9	58.5	58.8	58.8
1788	58.8	58.8	59.1	59.1	59.1	59.1	59.1	57.0	57.0	57.6	57.6	57.5
1789	57.6	57.6	59.3	60.0	64.8	64.4	67.7	67.1	67.1	69.6	70.0	73.3
1790	73.7	74.4	74.4	70.2	70.6	74.0	75.2	76.4	75.8	80.6	79.5	78.9
1791	78.9	82.8	83.1	85.3	89.2	92.7	94.6	107.2	106.6	103.2	103.2	103.2
1792	112.8	112.8	120.2	123.3	123.3	125.2	127.0	125.1	124.6	116.9	116.2	111.7
1793	109.3	109.3	110.8	109.3	108.5	108.9	109.7	108.8	110.5	110.5	110.2	109.8
1794	116.2	116.2	127.7	128.6								
1795	130.5	128.2	128.8	128.8	134.1	137.1	138.4	137.6	137.1	145.9	156.7	167.8
1796	200.7	196.0	198.7	179.9	191.6	199.5	197.0	195.3	185.5	188.2	177.5	168.9
1797	169.5	169.5	167.3	162.4	162.4	162.4	166.3	161.3	152.9	155.0	146.1	141.8
1798	141.6	141.6	141.6	141.6	141.6	142.5	141.5	141.5	138.9	138.9	138.9	142.3
1799	142.8	140.8	137.5	140.2	136.8	135.7	133.5	124.9				
1800				131.1	133.0	127.1	135.7	129.3	136.6	137.0	137.5	138.6
1801	136.7	142.2	144.0	139.1	138.4	139.0	137.4	134.6	136.9	136.9	136.0	141.2
1802	143.9	142.0	129.5	120.3	130.7	130.5	125.1	125.3	125.4	125.8	126.0	125.1
1803	125.5	125.7	127.3	124.0	123.9	124.4	124.4	124.6	127.7	128.6	127.9	123.0
1804	127.2	123.3	123.3	120.1	115.9	114.9	114.6	112.3	113.9	112.3	110.4	109.7
1805	110.6	110.2	108.9	105.8	106.3	105.7	104.8	103.3	103.3	104.6	104.1	103.7
1806	105.2	105.9	106.5	105.8	106.5	104.0	101.4	99.9	100.6	101.4	100.2	99.8
1807	99.6	99.4	99.3	96.7	97.0	94.9	94.0	94.5	95.3	96.9	97.1	96.1
1808	109.5	116.5	118.3	120.2	119.6	115.7	117.6	119.6	121.5	123.4	123.4	155.6
1809	161.7	160.0	158.4	144.6	135.6	121.3	140.7	138.0	146.5	143.1	146.5	155.2
1810	150.1	148.9	147.4	146.0	153.8	158.5	161.9	162.4	157.3	159.3	155.2	152.5
1811	147.4	149.0	148.6	150.1	163.1	166.9	170.5	163.3	166.8	165.8	166.5	168.3
1812	172.7	172.7	169.8	174.5	188.3	183.4	202.8	201.5	199.9	194.1	181.8	181.3
1813	178.9	179.8	181.5	193.6	192.6	197.4	195.9	194.5	193.1	195.4	201.2	214.8
1814	264.8	265.1	241.7	226.1	214.4	218.0	229.7	229.7	250.6	269.9	317.2	309.3
1815	309.7	309.7	215.7	219.4	237.1	223.6	219.9	223.0	220.9	213.8	201.0	185.7
1816	183.4	189.5	182.4	177.5	164.3	157.7	150.2	147.2	145.5	143.4	144.0	142.2
1817	144.9	143.6	165.1	164.4	154.8	152.2	145.8	145.8	146.3	146.3	159.5	161.2
1818	161.2	161.2	172.7	171.5	160.9	156.4	152.8	143.6	147.5	152.9	154.8	146.6
1819	147.7	138.9	133.6	120.3	116.6	120.7	115.6	113.7	114.3	111.6	115.9	116.2
1820	114.7	112.6	110.3	106.4	101.4	102.0	104.0	104.3	104.0	108.4	108.5	108.2
1821	107.2	107.2	108.4	105.0	106.3	106.7	106.7	106.7	105.7	107.6	107.2	112.7
1822	111.7	111.7	111.7	109.3	106.4	104.4	102.8	104.6	101.4	97.5	100.0	99.1
1823	97.5	97.5	94.1	95.2	96.1	97.0	97.0	96.2	96.2	99.4	99.4	97.8
1824	97.8	97.7	96.7	97.7	96.3	95.5	94.5	94.5	92.8	92.5	93.0	93.3
1825	87.7	88.5	88.5	94.1	97.7	95.8	95.7	97.4	96.2	95.0	95.2	93.1
1826	94.6	94.1	93.8	94.8	95.1	96.5	95.6	95.1	95.6	95.2	95.0	95.0
1827	94.8	96.3	97.3	99.5	102.7	102.9	103.2	103.0	102.2	103.3	102.6	103.1
1828	104.0	103.1	102.1	100.9	104.0	103.9	104.4	105.1	104.5	103.7	103.7	102.4
1829	102.9	103.1	102.7	103.1	103.1	103.6	103.2	100.6	100.0	101.6	101.8	101.6
1830	100.7	100.7	100.7	97.7	97.7	97.7	97.3	97.6	101.4	102.1	104.1	109.6
1831	108.5	111.2	108.8	111.2	111.2	111.2	107.9	108.2	109.4	111.9	110.0	109.7
1832	111.2	109.8	106.8	103.6	104.4	104.5	105.2	105.9	106.8	107.1	106.8	107.6
1833	106.6	106.6	113.0	113.0	110.5	110.5	110.4	109.1	108.3	108.3	108.3	109.3
1834	109.3	109.3	107.5	105.5	105.5	103.2	103.5	103.3	105.2	105.6	105.3	107.4
1835	112.2	109.7	112.1	109.4	111.2	109.7	110.8	111.9	111.3	108.5	109.5	112.6
1836	114.1	113.1	112.4	114.4	112.9	111.2	111.2	112.6	118.2	117.9	117.0	117.2
1837	119.0	120.5	124.3	123.0	120.8	118.4	115.8	117.3	117.9	120.4	122.2	122.9
1838	123.5	121.8	118.1	115.0	115.8	114.7	114.9	118.6	119.5	121.7	121.1	121.3
1839	121.2	120.9	119.6	119.0	121.0	121.9	119.2	118.3	118.9	118.9	118.9	117.3
1840	116.5	116.0	114.7	114.0	113.1	113.0	113.0	111.7	109.7	113.4	112.2	113.3
1841	113.3	110.6	110.3	107.8	107.0	106.3	104.9	103.8	104.6	106.4	102.9	110.5
1842	110.5	108.9	108.9	104.2	104.0	105.5	106.5	106.5	118.3	120.8	119.8	119.7
1843	120.2	120.1	120.0	120.2	122.0	124.9	123.9	119.2	109.1	118.3	120.1	121.7
1844	120.8	119.4	134.5	137.5	137.5	135.0	135.0	134.6	134.7	133.8	134.2	135.0
1845	134.2	133.8	134.5	137.6	136.8	136.0	135.6	135.4	136.1	135.0	137.0	137.9
1846	137.6	135.2	133.9	137.2	136.1	135.3	132.8	132.2	131.6	134.7	136.7	133.1
1847	132.4	136.0	141.2	137.7	136.3	142.0	137.2	137.6	136.1	136.1	138.5	139.4
1848	149.7	142.4	134.5	133.5	133.1	129.4	123.6	122.9	125.2	125.7	124.8	123.9
1849	124.8	129.4	129.1	119.4	117.1	117.1	117.1	119.0	121.0	120.6	121.0	121.7
1850	122.1	124.6	125.0	124.5	121.1	120.6	120.4	121.3	113.9	114.7	115.6	115.1
1851	116.7	115.9	112.4	113.5	113.1	113.1	112.7	113.2	112.2	112.2	112.2	112.2
1852	111.8	112.2	111.8	117.4	117.4	116.1	117.0	113.2	113.6	121.1	122.0	123.0
1853	123.2	122.0	122.0	130.8	127.7	127.7	127.3	127.3	129.5	140.3	144.5	144.2
1854	143.8	142.3	143.1	141.1	154.5	153.6	153.1	155.4	164.8	164.8	169.5	176.3
1855	186.0	189.9	189.9	184.2	180.1	179.2	180.1	178.4	178.4	178.4	178.4	185.0
1856	184.7	184.0	184.0	178.5	175.8	174.2	175.0	188.7	179.7	179.7	179.7	179.7
1857	196.7	199.6	199.6	198.0	191.7	195.5	185.0	184.6	183.2	176.7	181.7	162.2
1858	157.2	158.5	158.8	158.8	158.8	148.6	148.6	148.6	149.4	149.8	146.0	143.3
1859	143.0	142.6	142.6	142.6	139.4	138.6	133.3	132.9	132.9	133.3	123.4	123.4
1860	125.1	125.1	125.1	123.4	123.4	123.4	123.4	123.1	127.4	129.2	129.2	129.2
1861	127.7	127.3	122.9	128.8	128.8	128.0	125.0	125.0	125.0	127.6	127.6	129.6

TABLE 38—MISCELLANEOUS COMMODITIES

Year	Jan.	Feb.	Mar.	Apr.	May	June	July	Aug.	Sept.	Oct.	Nov.	Dec.
1784	103.7	101.2	101.1	101.6	101.0	100.3	99.6	99.4	97.9	96.8	90.8	90.4
1785	88.6	87.9	87.4	85.5	83.2	82.6	82.6	82.6	82.6	82.6	82.6	82.6
1786	83.1	83.2	83.3	83.3	86.7	86.6	86.6	86.7	86.7	87.5	87.5	86.2
1787	86.4	86.4	86.4	90.4	88.7	88.7	89.7	87.9	89.7	87.9	85.7	85.7
1788	82.7	84.9	84.7	82.8	83.1	83.2	83.3	83.4	83.5	80.8	84.4	84.4
1789	83.6	83.6	84.6	84.1	84.1	84.1	84.1	83.1	80.6	80.6	80.8	79.9
1790	80.7	80.7	80.7	80.7	80.7	80.9	79.5	78.3	78.3	78.3	77.1	78.9
1791	79.4	82.2	81.8	84.1	82.0	81.4	80.6	80.3	82.0	83.8	83.8	83.8
1792	75.5	75.5	75.5	75.5	75.5	75.5	75.5	75.5	79.4	79.4	79.4	81.3
1793	79.9	79.9	83.7	79.3	79.1	82.0	82.0	82.0	81.9	81.7	81.2	81.5
1794	81.5	81.5	95.9	93.8								
1795	117.9	118.1	118.2	134.7	134.8	135.0	132.5	124.7	125.0	127.0	127.4	127.7
1796	129.8	129.7	130.3	129.8	125.0	127.6	127.0	129.5	126.2	130.2	126.6	127.4
1797	131.5	131.6	130.5	123.1	121.5	111.8	110.8	109.3	109.3	113.5	113.5	113.4
1798	105.2	105.2	107.5	107.5	105.6	105.6	105.1	103.0	102.7	102.4	102.1	101.8
1799	101.5	105.0	108.8	109.1	109.9	110.3	112.4	111.3				
1800						115.6	118.3	115.1	116.1	116.1	115.4	115.4
1801	115.4	113.9	113.9	113.9	110.8	110.8	110.8	110.8	110.8	110.8	110.8	112.2
1802	112.2	112.2	110.7	110.7	111.4	111.4	111.4	111.4	110.7	106.1	105.3	100.6
1803	99.4	100.9	105.6	105.6	105.6	103.2	104.4	104.4	104.4	104.4	104.4	104.4
1804	107.9	106.8	108.6	110.8	109.5	109.5	109.5	109.5	112.1	115.0	114.5	115.7
1805	118.3	118.3	118.3	118.3	118.9	118.9	118.9	118.9	118.9	118.9	118.9	118.9
1806	126.9	123.3	123.3	123.3	122.5	122.5	125.1	121.0	121.0	120.3	119.5	120.9
1807	120.9	120.9	120.9	119.1	119.9	116.9	116.1	115.4	116.3	116.3	117.8	117.4
1808	115.0	112.6	108.2	108.2	108.2	108.2	108.2	105.6	108.3	111.2	110.0	111.1
1809	112.4	112.4	116.0	126.5	121.1	120.1	112.2	112.2	117.8	123.7	123.7	124.6
1810	123.5	123.5	123.5	124.3	118.5	118.5	119.8	118.5	121.3	120.6	120.0	118.5
1811	121.3	121.3	125.1	124.8	124.5	123.2	121.4	122.1	122.0	117.4	110.7	116.4
1812	110.1	110.1	109.8	109.8	110.0	110.1	112.4	112.8	112.1	111.6	111.6	110.4
1813	110.4	110.4	110.4	110.4	110.4	110.4	110.4	110.4	110.4	110.4	109.9	113.3
1814	121.1	121.1	121.1	120.3	114.5	114.5	114.5	110.8	110.8	110.8	120.5	120.5
1815	119.4	119.4	118.5	126.1	118.5	110.1	112.0	122.1	122.1	128.5	130.6	134.9
1816	132.8	135.2	132.2	129.1	129.1	129.8	128.3	129.0	129.0	126.7	123.8	123.8
1817	124.3	123.4	123.4	123.4	123.4	121.1	120.2	118.3	115.5	115.5	115.5	115.0
1818	115.0	120.3	126.3	126.3	136.0	132.3	130.5	130.5	132.4	137.0	134.6	137.2
1819	136.7	137.3	133.1	130.7	127.2	125.7	120.1	120.7	113.3	113.9	112.6	111.2
1820	110.5	110.5	113.4	113.4	113.7	113.7	113.7	113.7	113.7	113.7	113.7	113.7
1821	114.3	114.3	118.9	118.5	118.5	118.7	116.9	116.9	117.1	117.1	109.9	103.4
1822	103.4	103.4	103.4	103.4	103.4	103.4	103.4	97.4	97.2	97.2	97.2	95.0
1823	95.0	95.0	92.8	92.8	95.8	94.4	94.4	95.2	95.2	95.2	95.2	95.7
1824	95.7	97.1	94.9	94.3	94.1	94.1	94.1	94.1	92.3	91.2	92.9	92.9
1825	95.8	95.8	95.0	94.7	91.9	90.3	93.0	92.4	93.7	93.7	91.0	91.0
1826	89.5	89.5	90.2	86.5	86.0	85.7	85.7	84.1	84.1	83.6	82.1	82.1
1827	83.2	83.1	83.0	82.5	79.4	80.1	79.4	79.0	79.0	78.6	77.2	77.2
1828	78.7	78.3	78.9	78.6	78.5	79.1	79.7	80.3	79.9	80.9	84.9	85.7
1829	84.6	83.8	83.1	83.6	84.1	82.4	78.1	76.5	75.2	74.3	76.0	76.0
1830	76.0	75.9	75.8	74.0	73.6	72.9	71.5	71.1	74.3	75.0	75.6	75.4
1831	74.0	77.5	77.5	78.1	82.1	79.5	79.1	80.5	78.9	81.3	80.9	80.1
1832	81.1	80.0	78.0	78.0	78.8	79.2	78.3	78.4	78.8	78.8	77.8	77.8
1833	78.8	79.0	78.1	79.2	78.6	79.0	79.0	78.9	77.7	78.0	78.1	78.1
1834	78.1	78.1	77.9	74.8	75.2	74.6	74.6	74.6	74.6	74.6	74.4	76.4
1835	78.9	78.6	78.5	78.1	80.6	80.8	81.7	81.6	81.3	80.9	81.9	81.2
1836	81.7	81.8	82.0	85.6	89.5	89.2	89.2	88.2	89.7	90.7	88.1	88.0
1837	95.7	92.3	93.2	95.5	95.6	90.0	90.0	90.4	89.8	90.5	90.6	89.4
1838	89.4	90.1	90.5	91.8	90.9	92.3	90.8	90.5	91.5	91.2	91.6	94.1
1839	94.3	94.3	98.1	100.1	101.1	103.0	103.0	103.0	102.8	101.9	101.7	101.7
1840	100.3	100.0	93.4	95.5	95.3	94.2	92.5	92.2	92.2	89.4	89.9	88.8
1841	89.2	90.5	90.5	90.6	90.8	91.5	91.5	91.3	91.6	91.8	92.1	93.2
1842	92.5	91.9	90.6	86.9	82.1	82.0	80.2	79.8	77.9	78.0	77.8	77.9
1843	75.1	74.1	73.7	74.0	73.8	74.2	74.2	73.6	76.6	76.0	75.0	74.9
1844	74.4	75.1	74.6	77.5	77.7	75.2	75.2	74.1	76.1	77.7	77.0	75.1
1845	74.5	74.5	74.0	75.8	76.2	75.1	74.8	75.5	76.0	76.1	75.5	75.6
1846	75.8	75.5	75.1	75.4	73.9	73.8	74.1	73.4	73.7	72.8	75.5	74.9
1847	75.0	73.3	73.4	75.0	78.1	78.3	78.2	75.2	77.4	78.1	78.7	77.9
1848	77.7	75.4	78.3	78.3	79.3	78.7	77.6	76.9	77.6	76.9	76.4	73.3
1849	72.9	73.8	73.6	73.4	73.4	73.1	72.8	73.4	73.6	73.8	74.8	75.1
1850	74.8	74.7	75.3	75.8	76.3	76.4	76.3	76.9	77.3	77.2	78.6	77.8
1851	78.5	79.5	80.1	80.2	80.9	80.1	78.2	77.2	75.0	75.5	76.3	76.1
1852	76.1	76.9	76.2	77.4	78.6	78.9	78.6	78.3	77.8	78.0	78.5	80.0
1853	80.6	81.3	81.6	82.7	83.3	84.1	85.5	84.1	84.1	82.0	82.2	85.5
1854	85.1	83.1	83.0	83.0	85.5	85.8	86.4	85.6	85.9	86.7	86.9	86.5
1855	86.3	85.2	85.2	84.1	82.9	81.2	81.8	82.7	83.5	83.7	85.5	86.4
1856	85.5	84.8	84.0	90.0	88.0	88.0	87.8	87.8	86.9	87.4	87.9	88.0
1857	88.6	88.5	89.2	86.6	87.3	87.4	87.7	87.7	87.9	86.7	85.4	84.1
1858	81.2	82.6	83.5	84.1	85.5	85.7	85.5	85.3	86.2	86.6	90.4	88.4
1859	89.6	90.9	93.1	92.0	92.5	91.9	85.9	86.3	87.7	86.7	85.3	86.2
1860	92.6	90.7	92.1	92.7	91.7	90.1	90.2	90.7	90.4	90.5	90.2	90.0
1861	86.9	86.8	87.4	86.6	84.0	82.2	79.3	80.5	79.5	81.2	84.3	84.9

TABLE 39—20 COMMODITIES

Year	Jan.	Feb.	Mar.	Apr.	May	June	July	Aug.	Sept.	Oct.	Nov.	Dec.
1731	53.2	51.6	47.9	47.0	48.1	48.0	48.1	49.7	48.4	49.1	50.3	48.9
1732	48.2	47.5	47.6	48.3	46.8	47.0	47.4	47.9	49.3	50.1	49.6	49.6
1733	49.4	49.2	49.0	48.1	48.0	48.5	49.5	52.1	52.0	53.0	53.0	51.7
1734	51.6	51.2	51.3	51.7	50.8	49.7	53.5	50.3	50.1	50.4	52.3	54.4
1735	54.6	54.4	54.6	52.1	49.9	51.1	52.9	50.1	50.8	50.0	49.4	48.8
1736	49.3	49.7	48.9	48.6	48.1	49.2	49.8	48.9	48.9	49.5	51.7	50.2
1737	50.2	50.9	50.7	45.7	47.5	50.8	53.4	53.7	53.0	54.1	55.0	54.4
1738	54.2	54.2	53.7	52.1	50.8	50.8	51.7	50.0	50.7	49.3	50.3	51.2
1739	48.6	49.4	48.1	47.7	47.2	47.1	48.8	48.0	50.9	52.7	50.8	50.3
1740	49.7	49.1	47.8	47.9	47.0	47.8	48.7	52.6	55.1	52.3	54.5	54.7
1741	56.1	58.2	59.9	58.6	60.9	63.7	65.0	65.2	64.3	63.2	64.4	64.5
1742	62.8	65.0	63.7	61.2	60.8	61.2	60.4	59.9	59.6	59.8	58.2	56.5
1743	56.6	56.3	53.4	50.2	52.5	53.0	52.4	53.1	51.9	53.0	51.2	51.2
1744	50.9	50.3	49.9	49.0	47.4	50.5	52.7	51.7	52.3	53.0	53.0	52.4
1745	52.3	52.3	50.8	49.3	47.4	49.8	51.1	53.0	55.2	54.2	54.0	51.5
1746	50.8	51.3	51.3	51.2	51.5	53.2	54.9	56.0	55.0	54.1	55.9	56.7
1747	56.7	54.1	53.7	57.0	57.3	59.5	59.9	62.6	64.8	64.8	63.3	62.5
1748	62.0	62.0	63.5	65.2	65.3	64.9	67.0	66.2	65.1	66.0	68.1	68.4
1749	68.5	68.8	67.1	65.7	65.7	64.0	65.4	63.5	63.4	62.6	63.6	66.0
1750	66.4	66.0	64.5	65.3	63.2	64.0	67.1	65.1	65.7	65.2	64.7	64.0
1751	63.7	63.3	63.5	63.4	64.1	65.7	67.6	67.4	67.4	65.1	64.8	65.1
1752	64.8	64.4	63.7	63.8	65.4	65.0	65.8	64.6	65.6	66.1	66.8	66.2
1753	65.4	64.8	64.2	64.1	65.2	65.3	64.7	64.7	64.7	64.4	63.4	61.8
1754	62.4	62.5	62.7	64.4	63.3	62.3	64.9	62.6	61.9	62.2	61.3	60.8
1755	60.3	60.8	60.7	59.4	59.9	61.3	61.9	62.2	61.8	62.8	62.2	61.5
1756	61.9	61.2	61.8	62.0	61.7	61.9	61.6	61.6	61.0	62.8		
1757						60.3	63.1	62.2	63.0	64.9	63.7	62.2
1758	60.7						65.6	65.6	65.4	65.4	64.9	67.1
1759	67.8	67.6	67.4	68.2	69.9	70.6	70.9	70.7	72.0	72.9	73.5	72.4
1760	69.7	69.5	69.1	68.9	70.9	71.3	70.4	70.1	69.3	71.7	71.2	72.0
1761	71.7	71.5	73.3	69.2	66.2	68.8	66.0	64.6	68.6	70.1	71.4	70.3
1762	70.3	70.7	70.0	70.1	74.1	77.1	77.5	78.9	78.7	77.6	78.9	78.9
1763	79.5	79.2	76.8	74.6	73.6	70.1	70.6	70.0	74.3	75.4	74.7	73.8
1764	71.7	70.9	68.4	66.8	66.0	65.2	65.0	67.4	67.6	68.0	69.4	68.8
1765	68.1	65.1	64.9	65.7	64.5	64.1	67.7	68.1	69.2	71.8	72.8	73.3
1766	70.2	69.6	67.9	65.7	71.9	72.7	73.5	74.7	74.1	72.9	74.9	73.6
1767	73.7	74.0	73.0	72.5	71.4	71.2	71.3	70.1	69.9	68.9	69.5	69.3
1768	69.4	70.3	67.6	67.2	68.3	68.5	69.0	66.6	66.4	65.8	68.4	65.4
1769	65.2	63.0	65.4	61.9	63.0	65.2	66.2	67.9	68.5	67.7	67.0	66.7
1770	66.1	67.2	67.9	66.3	67.0	70.4	67.7	69.7	69.5	71.2	70.6	69.7
1771	68.8	68.1	69.9	70.1	70.2	70.3	71.4	71.8	71.5	70.8	71.1	71.5
1772	73.8	73.8	73.7	73.1	75.4	76.5	79.0	79.2	78.9	80.9	81.2	80.0
1773	78.0	77.9	75.5	75.8	75.5	73.6	74.2	74.2	74.4	75.8	73.7	73.4
1774	73.7	74.6	73.1	72.3	73.6	74.0	72.4	72.9	72.3	72.2	73.6	75.8
1775	72.8	73.9	71.6	74.7	73.7	73.6	78.4	80.0	79.3			
1784	97.8	96.1	98.5	94.6	96.1	100.7	102.4	101.6	101.2	103.2	102.6	98.0
1785	97.3	96.3	95.8	93.6	90.9	85.4	85.4	85.4	87.4	87.9	87.3	86.4
1786	85.9	86.4	84.4	81.6	78.1	79.4	81.3	80.6	80.7	79.6	79.7	80.2
1787	80.3	81.0	81.5	80.4	78.7	80.1	79.9	77.7	77.4	76.3	75.8	73.7
1788	75.0	74.8	74.5	73.9	73.9	73.9	73.2	72.2	71.9	72.3	72.4	72.9
1789	73.1	72.6	72.5	70.3	74.3	75.3	75.3	75.2	75.2	75.9	76.5	81.4
1790	81.0	82.6	85.3	84.9	85.6	85.3	84.0	83.7	81.6	83.7	87.4	86.5
1791	86.8	84.4	82.0	79.8	78.0	77.5	76.8	76.7	77.7	81.9	81.0	80.6
1792	80.3	80.4	81.9	83.0	82.8	82.5	82.7	82.8	84.1	84.5	86.2	88.8
1793	88.2	89.7	91.2	92.9	92.7	92.4	93.5	94.5	92.2	90.9	92.9	92.9
1794	97.4	97.0	101.9	102.6								
1795	123.2	126.1	128.0	129.0	134.3	130.4	135.0	139.7	142.8	150.7	151.2	153.1
1796	154.6	156.0	161.0	155.4	159.3	156.7	153.2	149.6	150.0	157.5	149.7	149.3
1797	151.8	157.5	150.3	137.4	139.4	132.8	136.0	133.4	132.6	136.4	135.9	134.4
1798	132.4	132.5	133.1	128.9	128.2	124.6	125.1	126.4	126.3	126.3	126.7	
1799					124.0	123.9	123.5	121.7				
1800						128.7	127.2	126.7	126.5	128.5	130.7	137.6
1801	136.2	142.5	141.8	137.8	138.1	137.9	140.1	138.1	136.2	135.9	138.7	133.0
1802	127.3	123.7	117.7	118.2	115.9	114.8	113.6	113.1	116.3	119.5	121.6	124.7
1803	126.1	123.9	121.8	117.7	119.6	120.3	120.5	123.7	124.1	125.0	129.2	130.3
1804	130.6	132.0	130.3	129.3	125.8	125.9	127.5	128.6	130.0	132.5	135.8	138.9
1805	140.2	140.2	140.2	140.1	139.1	136.2	135.4	131.9	131.1	132.2	132.3	133.4
1806	132.6	129.7	127.4	123.8	122.8	124.6	124.4	124.4	122.6	123.6	124.0	124.0
1807	124.7	125.8	124.2	121.9	115.1	115.3	115.4	115.9	116.7	115.3	119.9	120.2
1808	114.7	111.7	110.8	110.4	107.1	107.4	103.7	102.9	103.9	107.4	108.4	117.9
1809	117.0	119.5	126.0	122.6	129.1	120.3	119.5	120.6	122.1	123.6	128.4	134.1
1810	132.2	130.2	129.5	127.7	130.7	127.9	130.6	133.6	133.9	135.5	134.5	135.4
1811	141.4	142.1	138.4	136.3	129.7	133.2	129.6	128.6	128.4	127.8	127.5	129.5
1812	132.0	132.0	128.0	122.5	120.9	121.3	131.8	128.3	135.6	137.9	140.8	138.4
1813	139.9	141.2	141.7	142.6	144.5	148.2	152.7	154.7	157.6	156.9	166.2	185.5
1814	196.1	189.4	191.9	187.4	186.0	187.4	181.7	181.2	184.0	205.1	204.5	200.2
1815	197.1	197.9	163.3	155.4	153.9	160.3	170.8	177.0	180.9	188.4	185.3	177.0

TABLE 39 (*Concluded*)

Year	Jan.	Feb.	Mar.	Apr.	May	June	July	Aug.	Sept.	Oct.	Nov.	Dec.
1816	174.9	170.8	165.7	164.2	151.7	154.8	157.9	157.7	154.3	155.0	158.6	159.3
1817	157.7	160.0	164.8	161.1	160.2	149.1	143.8	144.0	142.1	139.9	141.4	143.5
1818	147.0	147.4	147.2	144.4	145.2	143.6	143.8	148.8	146.1	149.3	147.9	147.1
1819	148.2	143.4	139.0	132.7	122.4	119.1	113.9	110.6	112.2	114.8	118.4	118.1
1820	115.2	114.8	109.3	107.5	107.1	104.5	102.7	102.3	102.4	102.2	100.1	98.9
1821	96.8	96.7	95.1	90.1	91.2	91.8	93.3	95.4	96.7	98.5	102.0	103.7
1822	103.8	104.4	104.4	104.6	107.7	106.1	103.1	102.8	100.5	100.2	100.4	100.5
1823	100.3	100.7	100.3	101.6	102.8	102.6	102.7	100.0	99.7	100.5	100.8	99.6
1824	99.3	99.3	97.1	96.8	97.4	95.6	95.0	94.6	95.4	94.9	94.8	94.1
1825	95.6	95.6	96.3	100.1	103.7	102.7	100.6	99.1	100.4	102.0	101.3	101.5
1826	99.5	97.1	96.3	94.8	93.0	91.6	92.7	90.8	91.4	91.6	92.4	92.7
1827	93.1	93.8	92.7	91.4	91.8	91.4	89.0	89.3	92.1	94.2	94.7	94.0
1828	92.3	90.2	89.6	89.0	90.6	89.8	89.5	91.8	92.6	93.9	99.3	97.7
1829	96.4	95.7	94.4	93.4	92.0	91.3	86.6	86.7	87.1	87.5	84.3	82.6
1830	81.2	80.7	80.4	79.5	79.4	78.6	78.2	80.4	80.7	81.8	81.0	81.3
1831	82.7	82.5	84.2	84.5	84.5	82.0	81.7	81.9	84.9	85.6	85.5	84.3
1832	84.7	83.1	83.3	83.9	84.4	87.1	87.5	89.3	88.4	90.4	92.1	89.6
1833	89.8	88.9	86.6	86.4	87.8	91.4	92.5	91.8	95.7	96.6	97.8	97.1
1834	93.5	91.8	90.2	89.6	89.1	89.6	90.3	91.5	90.7	91.3	93.7	92.7
1835	91.7	90.4	91.7	94.5	98.4	100.2	103.0	102.8	102.6	105.3	105.5	106.4
1836	106.4	107.7	109.1	111.9	111.7	109.5	106.6	110.3	115.4	117.0	121.5	121.2
1837	120.5	122.6	120.0	112.4	106.5	103.9	104.5	104.3	105.0	105.1	111.0	109.3
1838	106.7	106.0	100.7	101.0	101.0	104.0	101.7	104.8	109.9	114.4	111.2	112.1
1839	112.7	112.6	112.4	113.2	111.9	110.2	108.4	107.2	106.5	104.8	105.5	102.3
1840	101.2	97.2	93.2	92.1	88.9	88.2	89.7	89.3	89.2	89.6	88.2	87.5
1841	86.7	84.6	84.4	84.1	83.4	84.7	84.3	86.0	88.2	87.2	87.0	83.5
1842	83.4	80.9	80.7	76.5	74.9	74.3	74.3	73.8	72.6	73.0	71.4	70.9
1843	69.8	69.4	68.6	70.0	69.8	74.5	75.6	75.1	73.8	73.6	71.9	71.7
1844	71.6	72.5	72.7	74.0	72.8	71.8	71.2	71.0	71.1	70.8	70.5	69.8
1845	69.6	70.3	72.4	75.6	74.2	74.5	74.3	76.9	80.1	80.2	84.9	86.6
1846	84.3	81.8	83.3	81.3	79.0	75.4	74.1	72.6	73.8	79.6	82.9	78.4
1847	79.8	87.9	89.0	90.9	90.3	95.0	87.3	85.1	84.1	86.2	84.9	82.1
1848	80.9	77.8	77.2	75.8	73.4	72.5	70.8	71.2	75.4	76.3	75.2	75.1
1849	75.5	73.9	73.5	73.9	73.8	73.3	73.7	77.7	78.5	78.9	77.8	76.4
1850	77.4	76.8	78.1	76.8	78.6	77.9	78.0	78.3	79.4	83.1	82.7	83.0
1851	82.9	83.1	82.6	81.8	79.9	79.0	78.3	78.0	78.1	80.1	77.6	77.2
1852	77.7	77.9	77.5	76.7	79.2	81.1	81.7	83.0	85.1	83.9	84.9	85.2
1853	85.7	86.4	87.8	88.0	88.0	87.9	89.3	89.5	95.0	97.8	98.7	96.0
1854	96.8	103.5	102.2	101.2	105.0	105.9	104.2	105.2	107.1	107.8	107.2	106.0
1855	110.2	107.7	106.7	112.9	114.0	113.7	110.5	109.9	109.7	110.4	109.4	110.6
1856	108.5	106.2	103.8	100.1	95.3	95.3	98.3	99.9	98.1	99.6	100.7	99.1
1857	102.7	103.5	104.9	105.2	110.4	113.0	111.4	111.1	108.9	103.1	97.3	91.7
1858	88.3	88.1	88.5	90.6	92.1	90.7	91.4	95.5	94.8	94.3	92.9	91.4
1859	93.1	95.5	95.9	96.2	98.1	97.6	95.0	93.4	90.7	91.8	92.2	90.5
1860	89.2	89.6	89.8	88.6	87.9	86.7	89.8	90.5	91.3	90.6	88.1	84.8
1861	87.3	85.9	85.4	87.2	93.3	93.9	91.9	106.2	114.2	117.0	118.7	121.4

TABLE 40—ARITHMETIC INDEX—12 COMMODITIES

Year	Jan.	Feb.	Mar.	Apr.	May	June	July	Aug.	Sept.	Oct.	Nov.	Dec.
1720	95.9	93.1	93.0	91.1	84.7	84.4	83.9	82.2	82.3	82.5	82.1	79.9
1721	81.8	83.2	81.8	80.5	77.2	76.6	76.5	75.9	75.8	76.0	78.4	79.1
1722	79.6	79.6	78.5	77.9	78.0	78.6	82.3	82.3	85.7	85.3	85.6	85.4
1723	87.2	83.5	82.8	79.5	79.9	79.4	78.3	83.2	87.4	89.5	90.7	90.4
1724	92.7	91.7	87.5	85.2	80.6	87.9	89.1	88.9	89.1	89.1	92.4	92.6
1725	94.4	94.5	95.7	94.6	92.5	93.1	96.0	98.5	98.7	100.0	100.1	100.7
1726	99.8	100.0	99.8	103.1	100.0	100.0	100.4	99.6	101.2	100.1	102.8	105.7
1727	103.4	101.3	100.0	96.9	95.9	94.7	95.8	95.6	95.4	97.1	97.7	97.6
1728	99.7	98.6	91.7	86.9	89.9	92.2	93.3	91.9	89.9	90.9	93.0	96.0
1729	92.0	90.3	90.7	87.7	87.4	92.8	92.6	93.2	93.8	93.3	97.5	98.8
1730	102.9	103.8	97.1	98.6	96.4	97.3	96.3	97.3	94.3	96.5	99.8	96.3
1731	96.5	92.7	85.0	82.5	85.0	84.7	84.1	87.5	84.7	85.8	90.1	86.5
1732	84.9	83.5	83.9	84.2	82.6	80.1	79.6	80.5	83.0	85.8	87.4	87.6
1733	88.2	88.4	86.6	84.7	85.1	87.1	91.1	95.0	92.6	94.7	94.6	92.2
1734	91.2	89.3	87.9	87.5	85.4	84.9	89.5	84.4	81.6	83.2	89.4	92.5
1735	92.9	92.9	94.9	88.5	85.1	87.3	91.9	85.3	85.4	84.9	83.4	81.5
1736	82.6	84.2	82.8	82.3	81.5	82.6	83.5	81.5	83.4	84.3	89.2	85.8
1737	85.8	86.1	85.6	77.7	81.9	89.5	96.1	99.2	95.4	97.8	99.5	98.7
1738	99.1	99.1	100.3	95.9	92.9	90.7	91.5	85.9	85.1	82.3	84.2	86.0
1739	83.5	84.7	80.6	79.2	78.1	77.2	81.9	79.6	85.9	88.1	83.7	83.4
1740	82.7	83.6	83.3	79.7	79.7	81.7	83.5	92.3	98.8	91.5	95.3	95.3
1741	98.5	105.7	110.8	108.3	110.8	119.0	116.6	119.3	117.2	111.4	115.9	117.2
1742	115.2	117.2	114.5	108.0	105.5	106.5	110.5	108.5	107.5	105.1	101.8	99.5
1743	100.5	98.7	92.5	87.1	95.2	97.8	98.9	100.6	96.1	96.0	91.7	91.6
1744	90.4	89.1	89.5	87.9	84.8	90.9	96.4	91.8	92.2	91.9	92.9	92.4
1745	91.4	92.5	91.1	88.7	85.0	89.7	92.5	95.5	101.2	97.2	96.2	91.6
1746	91.5	92.5	93.4	94.7	94.2	96.7	100.9	104.8	101.8	100.5	106.8	118.1
1747	118.1	100.3	99.2	103.1	105.2	108.8	110.9	117.1	118.3	117.6	115.2	114.0
1748	116.9	116.3	116.5	121.3	120.9	119.0	126.9	126.6	128.2	131.5	134.2	138.1
1749	139.3	137.6	132.2	128.4	124.2	114.1	117.8	111.2	111.2	109.6	113.3	118.9
1750	118.9	113.6	111.8	114.7	109.8	108.7	115.3	111.6	112.7	113.3	113.2	113.0
1751	112.2	111.4	111.8	112.5	112.4	113.4	114.8	116.1	117.2	109.7	109.9	111.8
1752	111.3	110.7	108.9	109.3	113.0	111.6	114.1	110.9	111.7	111.9	113.9	115.3
1753	112.2	111.2	109.3	109.5	108.5	110.7	109.5	109.8	110.0	112.1	108.9	107.3
1754	109.9	106.6	106.6	112.7	109.8	109.3	113.6	109.2	108.6	108.1	108.2	106.7
1755	105.8	106.1	104.8	101.5	105.0	107.5	108.5	110.5	109.0	112.0	110.3	106.6
1756	107.9	109.3	112.5	112.4	111.4	111.8	109.6	110.1	109.7	107.5		
1757						104.2	108.8	108.1	107.7	111.3	107.2	104.7
1758	103.3					110.7	112.8	113.3	111.9	110.0	110.0	116.1
1759	119.2	119.3	118.1	119.0	121.6	124.8	126.6	127.3	129.6	131.8	132.8	130.3
1760	126.7	126.9	123.2	123.2	126.0	124.7	124.4	124.8	125.8	126.3	128.3	128.2
1761	124.5	125.8	125.5	122.6	120.2	119.7	116.9	115.1	118.9	119.7	122.7	122.4
1762	122.8	123.9	124.0	128.5	128.5	132.0	137.0	142.3	140.7	136.4	143.1	142.1
1763	145.8	143.9	139.5	141.3	138.2	132.0	130.9	127.2	134.2	136.7	134.4	132.4
1764	127.8	126.0	121.2	119.1	116.5	114.0	114.3	117.4	117.7	118.3	121.1	119.7
1765	117.6	110.1	109.0	114.2	113.8	113.3	117.5	118.4	123.1	125.5	127.5	130.4
1766	124.2	123.0	120.3	115.5	124.6	126.8	128.5	125.6	125.9	124.9	131.7	125.6
1767	125.2	127.0	124.5	123.4	122.9	125.6	126.1	123.0	121.7	119.7	122.6	122.8
1768	121.5	123.6	119.5	119.2	121.1	122.2	123.8	115.4	114.6	116.1	122.0	117.4
1769	117.0	113.3	114.7	109.5	110.5	112.5	117.4	120.0	121.7	119.7	117.5	117.4
1770	117.3	115.7	117.0	116.2	118.0	123.9	123.6	128.9	125.9	126.4	125.3	121.6
1771	120.7	119.7	125.0	126.1	126.3	127.3	128.6	127.9	129.5	129.4	129.3	130.7
1772	135.6	135.1	134.6	134.3	139.5	143.6	145.9	142.6	143.1	146.7	146.5	144.9
1773	142.7	142.7	138.7	136.4	134.5	129.4	130.5	131.9	131.2	130.9	126.7	129.4
1774	130.2	131.0	129.7	127.8	130.5	127.0	124.3	124.7	125.7	124.2	126.1	128.7
1775	124.6	125.7	120.7	122.8	118.9	118.7	127.9	131.2	128.7			
1784	166.7	160.1	163.8	157.7	163.2	174.5	182.6	182.0	180.4	187.8	182.5	170.2
1785	166.8	166.2	166.1	160.8	158.0	150.3	152.2	152.2	156.8	157.2	156.9	152.6
1786	147.5	148.7	146.3	141.3	139.6	146.3	150.3	148.3	148.8	143.3	140.7	138.9
1787	138.9	140.2	140.9	140.0	138.7	143.5	142.7	134.6	131.9	131.3	127.2	120.3
1788	122.4	122.1	121.7	121.6	123.2	123.2	120.5	117.7	117.5	119.1	117.9	119.6
1789	119.9	118.5	117.8	116.5	127.8	132.2	132.1	131.4	131.9	134.7	135.9	144.4
1790	145.4	153.2	166.7	170.3	173.3	166.9	161.5	159.2	150.0	152.1	164.8	159.9
1791	160.6	158.5	149.8	143.1	144.7	143.6	141.6	140.2	143.6	156.9	153.9	154.2
1792	149.1	150.1	154.3	156.6	156.0	157.6	156.2	156.9	156.0	155.8	159.6	170.3
1793	166.5	171.2	176.1	176.9	176.5	174.8	175.9	180.0	177.5	172.8	174.0	177.1
1794	189.5	189.5	201.7	203.0								
1795	231.6	240.3	247.5	245.8	253.9	252.0	253.8	260.1	267.5	284.5	279.2	277.7
1796	292.7	303.0	319.9	301.9	304.9	299.3	292.7	284.9	286.1	304.5	280.9	278.5
1797	283.6	296.5	285.9	257.1	257.3	249.3	256.1	253.9	254.5	269.7	269.7	266.4
1798	248.9	248.9	247.7	234.5	231.2	219.3	225.9	230.9	230.8	230.8	232.5	
1799					232.7	233.0	233.2	229.3				

TABLE 40 (*Concluded*)

Year	Jan.	Feb.	Mar.	Apr.	May	June	July	Aug.	Sept.	Oct.	Nov.	Dec.
1800						249.3	250.7	251.4	246.7	251.2	256.8	271.8
1801	271.1	285.5	285.9	275.2	282.4	284.3	286.2	281.2	270.3	269.1	261.1	240.2
1802	221.9	214.8	205.8	205.8	203.8	207.2	209.0	209.9	212.3	211.2	214.2	218.2
1803	217.8	211.1	209.8	201.3	203.0	205.8	207.0	210.8	212.6	212.3	223.8	229.7
1804	237.5	238.6	235.1	236.0	226.5	228.6	233.6	234.5	243.1	249.5	255.4	273.7
1805	278.1	278.7	276.1	278.3	275.8	269.6	264.3	247.7	244.1	246.2	246.6	249.3
1806	245.8	238.7	234.2	228.0	228.0	235.5	235.5	236.4	227.5	227.2	230.8	229.6
1807	232.3	232.6	224.9	223.3	213.2	212.1	211.1	208.0	213.0	210.8	217.9	216.1
1808	199.9	198.0	197.5	191.1	187.3	189.5	183.4	183.7	184.5	188.6	192.7	215.2
1809	211.3	217.9	229.9	220.4	234.2	210.7	211.9	215.9	224.7	226.8	238.6	245.7
1810	244.8	239.5	235.7	233.0	241.9	240.8	250.7	262.6	264.2	261.8	258.1	262.6
1811	275.1	276.7	268.9	269.1	253.1	260.5	257.2	255.6	249.2	249.9	251.5	255.7
1812	260.6	263.3	254.2	237.8	237.3	238.9	255.2	247.9	263.4	274.2	279.8	275.3
1813	280.5	278.2	275.1	266.4	264.1	268.8	275.9	283.1	284.5	287.5	314.6	357.3
1814	386.4	350.0	356.7	354.8	353.5	355.8	343.8	344.9	360.6	409.0	435.3	404.3
1815	397.6	391.3	315.2	296.6	300.1	315.6	326.6	337.8	346.4	349.5	341.6	326.6
1816	315.2	308.2	294.9	284.3	268.8	278.9	296.6	298.8	289.6	293.9	321.8	328.3
1817	323.8	330.0	351.1	343.9	348.3	308.5	304.2	296.1	274.8	267.6	267.3	275.1
1818	280.4	283.0	278.8	273.6	273.6	273.6	272.7	283.2	274.4	280.7	274.1	266.8
1819	267.8	257.2	244.0	234.2	220.8	214.7	208.8	202.0	200.4	205.7	211.9	210.9
1820	204.8	203.6	190.9	186.0	186.3	180.3	173.3	171.3	170.2	170.9	165.9	164.9
1821	160.0	159.6	155.2	150.2	151.5	151.4	154.7	160.1	163.1	169.5	176.6	171.1
1822	176.7	178.7	179.2	185.0	190.0	190.7	185.9	184.5	182.3	184.1	181.7	181.5
1823	180.0	182.2	182.0	182.7	185.7	185.4	185.1	175.2	173.9	175.3	173.8	169.9
1824	168.8	168.7	168.7	168.2	168.2	164.6	158.1	159.4	158.7	156.9	159.1	156.7
1825	159.2	159.4	157.5	161.0	168.5	163.7	158.6	159.4	166.5	170.2	170.1	168.6
1826	164.0	161.4	161.1	160.2	158.4	159.3	159.3	158.6	160.8	162.6	159.4	159.5
1827	162.7	166.7	162.3	159.5	157.5	158.3	155.6	156.2	161.1	165.0	167.2	165.6
1828	161.8	155.9	152.6	152.3	155.3	154.6	155.4	165.0	168.0	173.8	196.2	193.5
1829	193.3	191.6	188.2	181.2	176.6	175.0	159.8	161.3	165.1	165.6	158.4	152.2
1830	146.3	144.9	143.4	145.2	147.5	147.3	148.5	154.4	157.8	157.3	154.4	155.9
1831	164.1	164.7	172.5	172.3	172.0	161.8	159.3	160.3	165.1	164.7	164.5	161.1
1832	162.7	157.9	156.3	157.8	159.8	171.1	168.7	175.0	171.1	175.4	177.4	167.1
1833	168.6	165.2	162.6	162.2	165.8	176.8	180.5	171.9	175.8	176.5	176.8	171.5
1834	167.6	162.0	158.4	157.0	160.6	161.9	162.1	166.5	163.8	165.1	167.9	162.6
1835	160.2	158.3	160.9	170.0	184.2	187.0	197.5	191.7	189.0	193.6	193.9	196.3
1836	193.8	198.1	202.1	210.1	207.6	202.4	204.9	217.4	237.0	237.6	249.5	251.2
1837	253.8	255.6	252.0	235.1	225.8	225.4	230.4	225.1	220.1	218.3	237.3	226.9
1838	210.8	207.8	200.6	204.6	204.9	207.0	197.2	207.7	218.4	233.9	221.3	222.8
1839	222.0	219.6	214.9	217.8	214.8	204.7	198.9	194.8	195.1	187.6	190.8	183.9
1840	182.2	178.1	169.4	168.0	162.4	160.1	161.5	163.1	164.2	163.8	158.5	153.7
1841	151.2	145.3	143.9	145.5	144.2	148.9	152.4	158.7	166.2	159.7	161.1	150.8
1842	149.0	147.2	146.2	138.4	138.8	136.0	136.6	132.2	127.1	129.2	123.2	124.3
1843	121.0	121.0	120.6	126.7	126.5	140.8	144.3	142.0	136.2	134.7	132.0	130.5
1844	130.3	132.8	132.6	136.4	133.1	129.0	126.3	126.5	126.5	127.1	126.7	124.7
1845	126.8	129.4	132.3	144.6	137.8	138.1	137.4	139.0	146.8	149.2	164.1	164.8
1846	155.5	151.1	153.9	150.1	142.4	133.4	130.8	128.1	134.7	149.4	155.7	144.1
1847	147.3	176.9	175.2	189.6	200.6	215.8	173.6	171.2	164.3	177.0	172.3	166.3
1848	160.8	152.0	151.7	148.3	145.9	141.8	141.6	141.4	152.4	153.6	151.8	149.8
1849	154.2	149.7	143.8	142.1	145.8	143.9	141.7	149.9	150.4	150.3	147.4	142.2
1850	145.7	141.5	142.4	143.2	150.3	148.4	147.9	149.0	147.7	152.3	151.1	147.6
1851	148.1	148.4	148.6	150.1	146.5	144.7	142.7	143.5	141.6	144.3	139.3	139.4
1852	143.1	145.6	144.2	146.3	151.5	152.3	155.4	156.0	159.4	157.4	159.8	162.4
1853	163.3	162.3	161.6	160.7	161.2	161.5	160.6	168.0	184.3	195.4	197.2	186.7
1854	192.1	212.2	201.1	202.6	224.9	220.7	208.9	210.5	218.8	212.1	218.2	217.3
1855	232.1	226.6	226.5	252.1	256.2	249.3	236.7	226.1	219.4	232.4	230.3	230.8
1856	221.6	207.8	200.4	191.3	178.6	178.6	190.4	193.6	189.4	194.2	195.3	194.0
1857	194.2	196.7	198.9	199.7	215.0	222.2	215.7	211.0	198.4	186.3	178.5	164.7
1858	158.7	155.4	157.9	162.1	164.4	159.9	161.5	174.5	176.2	174.0	172.6	166.6
1859	173.4	179.8	183.3	183.4	197.2	189.0	177.5	169.1	163.8	169.3	168.5	164.1
1860	163.3	163.6	165.0	169.5	167.0	161.5	162.2	164.9	169.5	167.8	162.7	154.1
1861	157.7	151.8	150.1	154.8	163.2	159.1	147.8	171.1	179.2	182.4	187.2	205.5

TABLE 41—SUMMARIES

Year	140	157	69 Domestic	59 Imported	26 Agricultural	67 Industrial
1784	100.1		104.8	97.7	107.0	96.9
1785	94.1		97.0	93.5	101.8	90.9
1786	91.0		90.0	93.8	101.6	88.6
1787	88.4		85.4	92.7	97.5	88.3
1788	83.3		78.1	89.7	84.5	85.4
1789	82.4		76.5	88.8	80.7	85.2
1790	86.5		83.4	89.9	93.5	85.4
1791	89.7		84.7	96.5	88.4	87.0
1792	91.5		85.5	99.3	88.0	89.4
1793	96.3		91.2	103.0	97.8	92.8
1794	109.6		101.6	120.7	108.7	110.7
1795	130.7		125.3	141.3	129.6	130.4
1796	139.1		140.7	142.6	144.6	136.0
1797	133.5		134.4	135.8	135.9	130.0
1798	127.1		123.4	131.9	128.8	129.0
1799	127.3		115.6	142.2	123.3	133.4
1800	128.3		121.1	138.0	129.6	130.5
1801	131.9		129.5	137.4	143.8	131.6
1802	122.5		118.1	129.5	120.5	124.0
1803	120.2		115.9	124.9	114.7	123.1
1804	128.1		123.9	132.6	126.9	129.5
1805	131.5		131.6	130.8	142.0	131.9
1806	128.1		125.8	128.8	135.5	131.7
1807	123.7		121.9	123.7	126.0	128.4
1808	123.1		112.4	133.6	109.4	132.6
1809	135.6		121.9	151.1	119.3	145.9
1810	138.7		131.6	147.3	133.4	146.2
1811	135.3		134.2	139.4	129.4	141.8
1812	142.3		125.6	158.6	126.3	153.7
1813	161.0		135.5	187.8	133.4	175.9
1814	189.7		159.0	223.4	151.5	205.6
1815	173.1		160.8	186.4	161.1	175.1
1816	151.9		159.5	146.6	177.8	143.2
1817	132.6		145.1	122.9	178.0	121.8
1818	130.6		138.8	125.0	160.3	121.8
1819	119.4	120.0	123.8	116.4	132.9	113.5
1820	106.6	106.9	108.6	104.7	109.2	105.7
1821	102.0	101.9	100.5	103.8	97.5	104.7
1822	104.2	104.1	105.4	102.9	107.9	103.3
1823	98.6	98.8	99.7	97.3	101.5	98.2
1824	94.3	94.3	94.4	93.8	92.6	94.9
1825	98.5	98.0	97.4	99.9	97.0	97.0
1826	95.9	95.5	96.3	94.7	100.3	94.0
1827	93.0	92.4	93.2	92.3	95.0	92.2
1828	91.0	89.1	90.7	91.6	89.5	90.2
1829	88.8	86.8	90.2	88.6	90.9	88.7
1830	84.0	82.6	84.7	85.4	87.3	84.2
1831	87.7	86.2	89.7	87.1	97.0	87.1
1832	89.3	87.8	91.8	86.6	99.7	88.2
1833	88.1	87.3	93.8	81.6	101.9	88.3
1834	85.8	84.3	91.6	79.1	97.6	86.4
1835	90.7	89.5	99.9	81.4	115.4	87.3
1836	97.6	96.6	113.0	82.4	135.7	93.8
1837	95.3	93.9	109.7	80.5	131.0	95.3
1838	91.9	90.8	103.2	80.2	123.3	92.6
1839	95.9	95.5	110.8	82.0	136.6	95.6
1840	87.4	86.9	96.8	78.2	107.6	89.8
1841	85.2	84.3	93.6	77.5	102.2	87.1
1842	79.1	78.3	85.1	74.1	89.0	83.2
1843	75.4	74.5	77.2	74.6	81.1	78.7
1844	76.9	76.1	77.4	77.3	81.1	79.0
1845	79.7	78.7	82.3	78.4	90.1	78.6
1846	80.1	79.5	83.4	78.3	93.2	78.9
1847	83.5	82.6	90.7	78.4	112.8	80.6
1848	78.5	77.5	84.2	74.9	97.4	78.7
1849	76.5	75.6	81.6	72.9	94.0	76.1
1850	79.9	79.5	85.2	76.7	98.6	77.1
1851	80.3	81.0	86.4	76.7	102.2	75.9
1852	80.4	80.6	89.5	74.8	107.7	75.1
1853	87.7	87.4	96.8	82.3	117.4	82.8
1854	95.8	95.5	105.6	91.5	131.8	90.7
1855	99.3	99.6	107.6	96.5	142.5	93.1
1856	99.1	99.0	103.7	99.2	128.8	93.9
1857	100.9	100.3	106.1	99.9	134.8	92.5
1858	89.7	88.9	94.8	88.0	115.4	85.3
1859	89.4	89.0	98.7	83.0	123.3	84.0
1860	88.8	89.0	95.7	84.9	118.0	83.2
1861	88.2	88.3	94.7	85.3	111.6	79.9

Table 42—Major Groups

Year	Farm		Imported Foods	Lumber Products and Naval Stores	Industrial		Fish	Furs	Wines
	Crops	Derivatives			Raw	Consumption			
1784	101.7	111.8	122.0	104.3	103.9	87.4	127.9	76.9	59.1
1785	105.9	98.4	110.7	92.4	100.6	78.3	121.9	72.4	66.0
1786	106.1	97.9	113.0	69.6	95.9	78.7	117.8	65.4	69.1
1787	104.2	92.1	110.9	59.9	93.7	80.8	116.2	55.3	69.1
1788	89.3	80.6	107.5	56.5	91.7	76.8	103.5	52.8	65.2
1789	84.6	77.4	102.7	60.5	91.1	77.1	103.5	55.8	62.7
1790	96.6	90.8	109.3	67.0	89.9	79.2	105.5	58.9	64.0
1791	88.3	88.4	128.7	74.2	87.3	86.5	117.1	57.7	67.1
1792	88.4	87.7	132.5	72.4	88.7	90.6	116.5	62.2	71.3
1793	98.8	96.9	133.3	79.1	91.7	94.4	113.8	61.9	78.6
1794	104.6	112.3	143.7	86.6	104.2	121.0	141.9	59.3	83.3
1795	124.1	134.6	173.3	114.2	124.9	138.9	200.3	70.1	86.5
1796	147.8	141.8	178.3	130.7	126.1	152.0	211.0	85.7	87.1
1797	142.8	130.2	169.3	133.9	125.4	137.1	226.3	75.1	85.7
1798	136.6	122.4	152.3	122.7	125.4	134.6	189.5	58.1	81.5
1799	127.4	120.0	158.7	104.8	132.9	134.2	146.2	60.5	89.9
1800	129.0	130.1	155.3	116.2	131.5	129.1	124.6	74.4	93.9
1801	142.7	144.8	144.2	120.5	132.1	130.9	169.4	77.6	101.7
1802	121.7	119.4	137.3	115.2	125.7	121.4	167.1	72.4	103.6
1803	120.6	109.9	130.8	125.0	126.1	118.9	138.2	72.9	98.7
1804	130.9	123.4	142.2	126.6	131.6	126.5	147.9	85.3	103.5
1805	145.5	139.0	142.8	124.7	130.9	133.3	163.0	81.7	96.7
1806	132.3	138.2	138.3	114.8	135.3	126.4	171.7	75.0	89.4
1807	125.9	126.0	128.8	114.3	133.9	120.7	167.6	82.7	89.1
1808	108.7	110.0	135.7	113.9	136.3	127.4	128.1	78.5	97.7
1809	115.7	122.5	146.8	131.3	148.1	142.6	136.9	83.8	113.0
1810	130.3	136.1	134.2	138.6	151.3	138.9	140.2	90.7	128.9
1811	122.2	135.9	127.0	132.5	146.1	135.7	157.7	97.6	137.0
1812	120.5	131.6	143.8	120.7	158.3	147.0	165.0	93.5	151.9
1813	133.2	133.7	182.4	132.9	177.0	174.2	174.7	90.7	164.5
1814	147.5	154.9	217.7	176.6	209.5	199.9	227.8	89.6	192.0
1815	154.1	167.3	194.8	165.8	175.1	175.0	220.5	111.5	167.1
1816	185.0	171.8	157.8	146.3	141.8	145.1	196.8	107.0	147.9
1817	183.5	173.5	133.0	123.4	117.2	128.8	155.1	93.7	122.7
1818	162.5	158.4	136.6	126.9	118.3	127.0	164.4	80.3	123.0
1819	136.7	129.6	126.1	121.5	109.6	119.4	137.9	75.0	122.8
1820	112.9	106.2	107.7	109.1	101.8	111.8	108.5	73.4	114.0
1821	95.3	99.4	103.5	95.6	101.8	109.3	99.2	82.6	109.3
1822	107.7	108.1	103.6	102.5	102.2	104.9	106.8	103.8	103.4
1823	101.8	101.3	95.3	100.1	97.6	99.1	105.0	101.0	95.4
1824	91.4	93.7	92.3	97.8	95.5	93.9	99.4	99.0	92.1
1825	100.5	94.1	102.4	102.8	101.0	91.4	89.3	111.8	99.1
1826	106.7	95.1	96.1	98.0	97.2	89.4	84.1	101.0	96.4
1827	96.8	93.4	91.9	95.5	94.4	89.0	95.4	93.1	92.2
1828	86.5	92.2	90.1	96.2	91.8	87.9	96.4	101.4	90.9
1829	91.1	90.7	84.9	89.8	89.9	87.0	91.4	97.6	87.6
1830	84.3	89.9	80.7	80.9	85.3	82.7	88.0	85.2	82.5
1831	94.3	99.4	81.2	84.7	88.6	84.9	97.1	86.8	83.3
1832	99.6	99.8	84.4	87.4	88.7	87.5	86.3	84.9	84.8
1833	102.2	101.7	71.7	91.6	90.1	85.7	92.8	85.4	85.9
1834	101.3	94.6	68.0	94.1	90.1	81.3	91.8	88.4	81.6
1835	126.6	106.5	74.8	99.0	89.9	83.6	111.5	83.2	80.2
1836	142.8	129.8	75.0	105.2	97.4	88.6	124.9	92.2	77.3
1837	132.0	130.3	68.5	97.6	97.2	92.6	120.3	88.8	72.4
1838	123.9	122.9	67.4	94.0	94.7	89.6	130.7	66.1	71.2
1839	146.7	128.5	67.2	95.0	99.3	90.5	177.5	72.0	70.6
1840	109.5	106.0	63.7	90.1	93.1	85.2	139.7	74.3	68.7
1841	111.8	94.6	65.0	88.6	90.9	81.8	131.8	70.2	68.0
1842	97.1	82.6	60.8	83.0	87.2	77.5	109.3	61.1	64.7
1843	88.0	75.5	64.3	75.7	81.7	74.3	107.7	45.4	66.5
1844	87.7	75.9	68.6	70.2	82.4	74.2	126.5	56.6	73.6
1845	94.2	86.6	73.1	75.5	81.4	74.7	128.3	65.5	73.4
1846	101.7	86.4	71.7	78.4	80.9	76.1	119.6	64.5	71.1
1847	123.1	104.6	72.2	75.3	82.6	77.7	123.1	57.3	71.9
1848	103.7	92.4	64.8	72.6	80.6	75.9	118.4	56.0	69.9
1849	100.1	89.1	64.3	73.2	78.1	73.1	104.0	56.0	68.7
1850	109.2	90.3	71.5	79.1	80.1	72.8	126.1	56.0	70.6
1851	110.0	95.9	71.3	87.9	78.9	71.6	118.7	56.0	70.3
1852	107.6	107.7	65.4	92.9	78.2	70.7	135.7	57.1	70.3
1853	116.4	118.3	71.8	101.2	86.8	77.2	146.5	54.5	74.2
1854	135.5	128.7	75.1	111.0	92.1	88.8	156.7	45.4	90.4
1855	147.7	138.2	75.1	100.2	92.7	93.6	153.4	44.4	125.6
1856	129.9	127.9	83.0	92.5	94.3	93.4	156.8	51.4	126.4
1857	136.8	133.1	86.5	99.9	93.8	90.5	161.9	54.3	130.8
1858	115.6	115.2	66.0	97.2	86.9	82.9	136.5	49.4	127.2
1859	124.3	122.4	63.1	103.3	87.1	79.6	152.4	49.9	108.5
1860	113.8	121.7	64.7	100.0	87.0	77.8	150.8	47.6	122.2
1861	117.9	106.4	67.3	125.0	82.5	76.2	118.5	50.6	125.0

TABLE 43

Year	Farm Products			Foods							
	Grains	Tobacco	Minor	Grain Products	Meats and Meat Products	Dairy Products	Fruit	Beverages	Condiments	Sugar and Molasses	Total
1784	105.8	108.8	102.8	113.5	100.2	133.9	83.6	102.6	150.2	86.5	114
1785	102.2	100.7	116.8	102.5	98.1	104.7	77.1	106.3	135.7	75.0	104
1786	100.7	78.3	119.7	100.2	95.5	100.6	72.7	105.4	128.5	79.5	102
1787	90.1	83.4	117.4	86.2	93.5	90.6	64.6	101.0	128.8	83.2	99
1788	75.6	84.3	89.0	77.5	78.7	79.5	63.9	98.1	124.6	79.3	92
1789	78.9	84.3	75.0	82.7	65.1	72.5	55.5	107.0	116.1	83.7	89
1790	104.1	84.3	83.4	110.7	71.5	98.6	69.1	92.1	119.9	93.1	98
1791	89.9	61.0	90.6	87.7	81.2	100.7	106.1	82.7	132.6	122.4	109
1792	87.6	57.2	88.4	86.7	82.8	107.7	85.2	102.9	133.6	151.9	113
1793	106.1	61.1	96.4	94.8	99.3	125.9	83.7	92.3	144.0	144.6	117
1794	117.2	64.6	99.2	111.4	116.1	150.1	89.3	101.1	181.2	146.0	136
1795	152.2	81.3	100.5	167.2	132.2	150.3	104.4	129.9	213.8	159.8	164
1796	174.1	95.1	137.9	196.7	147.0	144.4	121.4	134.7	204.1	168.9	172
1797	139.6	128.6	143.6	162.0	141.0	125.0	113.2	132.7	180.8	182.9	161
1798	114.2	172.6	144.0	125.3	131.9	146.2	113.2	144.2	156.0	175.1	148
1799	116.0	167.7	98.0	134.3	111.4	146.3	113.8	157.6	163.6	174.9	147
1800	141.9	83.3	126.2	157.4	119.7	144.0	124.4	148.7	159.2	158.6	145
1801	155.6	86.8	145.0	174.7	153.6	144.3	105.7	136.3	156.3	148.2	148
1802	121.5	96.8	126.2	124.0	121.3	126.5	101.9	118.7	155.5	130.9	134
1803	121.7	95.1	125.5	119.3	113.1	99.8	81.3	127.7	146.0	135.7	124
1804	141.6	100.9	130.4	141.3	119.4	142.7	100.8	144.2	150.0	154.7	139
1805	174.6	99.9	128.0	173.5	125.8	178.2	112.2	143.5	153.9	145.5	147
1806	139.6	98.5	125.7	138.6	160.6	162.8	129.8	131.1	143.0	133.5	14
1807	127.4	103.9	119.2	133.9	135.8	138.5	99.2	118.6	143.8	116.2	13
1808	96.4	100.5	115.1	116.6	105.1	117.0	100.1	111.4	160.6	119.3	12
1809	113.0	99.1	101.6	134.6	120.1	117.3	103.4	118.0	171.1	129.9	13
1810	143.4	98.7	112.7	168.2	136.6	134.7	102.0	101.8	138.9	136.4	13
1811	147.3	86.2	113.5	172.5	137.1	138.5	111.7	79.5	130.6	138.6	13
1812	150.8	74.1	132.9	165.9	125.8	128.7	121.8	80.2	159.4	159.8	14
1813	156.8	96.2	102.6	164.4	126.5	130.0	128.5	114.5	206.4	224.6	16
1814	169.3	107.4	110.9	160.9	169.8	167.6	156.6	149.3	250.6	278.2	20
1815	159.9	170.3	132.5	173.6	193.7	182.3	147.9	150.0	208.0	234.4	19
1816	189.5	266.4	164.5	190.5	173.3	183.2	109.2	133.9	168.9	182.5	16
1817	216.6	171.2	191.7	229.0	177.1	175.2	95.4	109.2	139.1	158.5	14
1818	171.2	152.6	166.0	168.2	179.1	153.5	122.5	115.4	131.8	156.0	14
1819	132.3	128.7	158.2	128.5	138.7	125.2	120.0	110.0	121.6	143.9	12
1820	98.8	106.1	132.5	98.3	116.2	96.6	93.4	103.8	111.3	117.5	10
1821	83.4	106.4	99.4	85.2	100.2	94.3	91.5	107.4	108.6	100.5	10
1822	120.7	96.4	102.7	118.7	99.0	131.3	105.8	104.7	101.8	104.7	10
1823	113.0	97.0	100.0	112.6	98.5	102.4	90.7	99.0	97.3	95.6	9
1824	87.1	97.4	94.8	89.7	103.0	83.2	98.1	94.2	90.1	93.1	9
1825	93.4	102.3	102.2	92.3	98.9	88.2	110.2	92.8	99.6	105.8	9
1826	117.4	88.4	123.5	103.7	89.9	103.9	91.7	84.4	96.1	106.1	9
1827	106.3	74.1	95.8	99.0	94.2	94.0	72.8	79.2	98.2	105.6	9
1828	93.0	72.3	78.3	95.6	98.1	81.8	85.3	75.6	92.3	103.4	9
1829	103.8	77.7	83.5	105.7	90.5	81.9	85.8	72.7	86.6	97.4	8
1830	90.5	71.6	83.1	107.2	93.9	78.5	76.4	69.6	82.3	92.0	8
1831	116.9	64.4	92.1	111.8	99.9	93.8	70.6	64.1	87.8	85.9	8
1832	121.9	69.1	95.1	114.4	97.8	98.5	71.9	63.1	90.7	92.3	8
1833	119.1	85.5	94.2	112.5	99.9	107.3	60.0	59.3	70.8	96.4	8
1834	108.1	115.2	90.1	105.1	94.7	97.4	57.7	56.2	65.9	92.4	7
1835	135.8	119.5	159.5	120.8	108.6	115.3	73.4	59.7	70.4	97.3	8
1836	155.3	133.6	179.8	153.0	133.9	147.3	66.1	58.5	70.3	114.3	9
1837	173.4	96.9	149.0	177.3	122.6	132.3	58.2	56.3	66.8	101.0	8
1838	153.0	109.4	142.7	142.1	121.2	125.7	61.8	51.8	63.7	102.9	8
1839	150.7	189.9	186.4	134.8	125.4	135.1	57.2	53.2	64.3	99.8	8
1840	103.5	121.7	162.6	100.0	111.3	101.1	58.3	59.8	58.4	87.7	7
1841	113.7	112.4	152.4	101.6	81.9	88.0	64.6	72.5	57.7	80.1	7
1842	107.7	74.2	126.3	102.5	62.8	89.0	54.0	61.8	58.7	68.8	6
1843	93.5	70.9	125.6	88.5	68.5	70.9	66.3	56.2	59.7	72.9	6
1844	96.8	67.1	110.2	88.1	62.9	75.3	68.2	55.6	63.4	79.9	7
1845	107.6	89.7	110.0	92.8	81.9	95.2	77.0	55.2	66.5	84.7	7
1846	116.7	101.3	112.2	99.9	73.5	97.5	69.8	55.7	69.9	77.9	7
1847	149.3	94.1	151.3	128.7	103.4	107.6	68.7	55.6	67.9	79.4	8
1848	118.5	85.4	130.8	104.8	84.6	104.0	62.2	54.2	62.3	64.5	7
1849	108.0	91.6	115.9	95.5	88.5	94.5	61.0	56.4	59.5	67.2	7
1850	115.3	110.0	114.1	96.1	85.4	98.6	79.0	62.4	63.2	69.3	7
1851	111.9	120.6	126.1	93.2	101.6	96.9	80.0	57.6	63.7	70.4	7
1852	122.0	92.0	121.5	96.6	123.2	117.5	62.8	48.2	62.5	65.9	7
1853	133.4	101.1	133.3	110.3	121.8	129.4	86.3	51.2	69.5	67.7	8
1854	164.9	107.6	160.7	147.0	115.3	134.6	110.9	55.7	73.9	64.3	9
1855	192.3	117.4	171.4	170.3	129.7	146.0	92.1	56.9	72.7	75.3	9
1856	137.0	126.0	156.1	119.8	128.5	137.7	102.7	56.7	72.3	105.0	9
1857	148.6	138.3	160.7	115.0	143.7	133.3	112.5	66.3	64.4	119.7	9
1858	123.3	110.6	145.5	103.4	117.6	109.0	70.3	66.6	53.1	83.4	[illegible]
1859	145.8	108.9	147.0	116.8	115.1	115.4	62.0	61.9	50.3	86.5	[illegible]
1860	135.7	94.5	143.5	111.0	114.8	117.6	69.3	61.2	50.8	84.1	[illegible]
1861	122.9	128.3	133.6	100.3	101.0	95.9	76.3	69.8	53.1	74.9	[illegible]

* For indices of fish, furs, and wines see Appendix Table 42.

ub-Groups*

Chem-icals	Dyes	Fuel and Lighting	Metals		Building Materials		Textiles		Hides and Leather	Spirit	Miscel-laneous	Year
			Ferrous	Non-Ferrous	Wood	Other	Fibers	Fabrics				
117.8	98.6	103.5	96.2	78.0	83.7	140.4	90.5	89.8	70.5	67.4	98.8	1784
127.1	96.9	87.6	85.7	81.3	75.9	125.9	108.9	85.0	65.8	58.3	84.4	1785
123.0	102.8	90.4	78.6	84.6	59.4	107.5	130.7	91.0	72.0	60.2	85.8	1786
121.6	101.9	95.3	75.8	88.6	52.8	96.7	142.1	93.5	65.3	60.5	80.0	1787
114.0	91.7	84.3	75.9	90.2	50.9	94.8	122.7	88.1	63.4	58.4	83.5	1788
111.2	85.8	76.7	76.3	96.8	54.3	96.0	103.3	88.4	64.7	65.3	82.9	1789
106.2	80.3	81.0	77.1	95.5	54.9	101.8	103.0	88.4	72.4	75.4	79.6	1790
99.6	76.9	85.5	78.4	90.5	64.1	99.6	107.9	86.6	69.8	94.3	82.3	1791
95.0	85.4	83.3	82.5	91.2	69.1	93.9	119.7	86.5	67.5	120.2	77.1	1792
95.0	94.8	90.0	81.8	93.7	76.3	101.4	122.9	97.2	67.7	109.7	81.3	1793
135.7	122.6	107.7	82.0	100.3	80.5	119.0	123.9	109.9	69.8	126.3	100.9	1794
231.2	135.2	130.5	93.3	105.6	95.2	138.4	134.6	119.5	77.4	139.9	127.2	1795
217.3	112.1	139.3	100.2	108.0	109.4	152.6	158.1	129.0	58.8	190.2	128.4	1796
183.9	108.8	126.7	104.0	113.0	113.8	155.3	158.3	132.6	55.2	160.0	118.9	1797
178.0	127.1	129.5	106.5	128.8	105.5	143.6	152.2	127.3	66.1	141.1	104.6	1798
195.6	214.9	117.4	104.7	139.0	105.7	127.4	147.9	124.7	68.0	135.4	110.4	1799
184.9	146.0	124.1	107.9	133.6	114.0	132.6	149.7	121.5	69.4	135.4	116.2	1800
170.7	139.6	130.5	112.3	132.3	113.5	138.7	170.1	136.6	70.5	138.8	112.1	1801
148.0	138.1	121.6	113.3	127.5	106.7	134.2	138.6	114.9	74.7	129.5	109.5	1802
153.4	128.9	118.6	106.5	138.3	109.2	142.9	135.4	119.0	75.2	125.8	104.0	1803
154.2	168.7	132.6	105.4	149.7	113.8	145.1	137.2	125.6	75.6	116.5	110.9	1804
150.6	148.6	153.2	106.2	147.1	114.6	143.8	150.4	138.0	75.6	105.9	118.7	1805
162.0	159.1	134.3	109.9	144.7	111.2	135.8	152.2	138.8	76.5	103.2	122.5	1806
160.3	141.6	124.0	112.5	139.9	114.6	134.1	145.5	143.7	76.3	96.8	118.2	1807
195.5	121.4	116.8	111.7	139.3	111.3	139.5	134.7	151.2	74.1	122.0	109.6	1808
226.6	130.0	115.9	123.3	139.5	115.4	169.1	145.4	190.4	75.3	146.2	119.1	1809
230.5	143.6	128.5	121.4	136.0	125.9	175.1	147.3	158.1	78.1	154.8	121.0	1810
229.3	128.7	139.5	118.3	126.3	125.7	161.1	118.8	132.2	66.0	160.9	121.2	1811
271.2	118.4	148.6	123.4	158.2	122.5	159.7	107.4	134.2	71.8	185.7	110.9	1812
302.3	136.1	200.0	131.3	188.6	124.0	185.9	149.9	161.5	80.7	193.8	110.6	1813
337.0	173.5	232.8	144.6	245.9	142.1	247.9	175.1	160.8	105.6	254.1	117.2	1814
228.3	155.9	202.3	141.7	187.4	151.8	194.7	149.8	148.4	94.1	232.6	122.6	1815
175.7	114.9	174.2	129.6	133.7	139.8	151.0	150.7	134.3	102.0	160.9	129.2	1816
139.7	91.5	137.0	115.9	101.1	126.3	123.8	141.5	116.4	95.6	152.8	120.1	1817
134.5	107.6	133.5	110.5	106.4	122.1	129.2	153.1	112.7	94.7	157.4	130.1	1818
110.6	101.7	132.4	104.6	102.7	121.7	120.0	136.5	112.9	91.8	122.4	124.1	1819
98.4	81.0	124.5	104.3	100.2	106.6	110.1	132.0	109.9	83.8	107.2	113.1	1820
101.2	87.5	116.9	104.2	99.0	92.9	103.9	107.6	108.6	95.4	107.4	115.7	1821
101.8	100.7	110.8	100.8	99.4	102.5	102.5	99.1	106.6	102.0	105.1	100.8	1822
97.4	104.1	94.1	99.4	97.9	100.1	97.9	89.4	101.6	100.9	97.1	94.8	1823
98.0	102.4	87.0	96.5	94.2	98.7	95.8	92.6	92.5	99.6	95.2	94.1	1824
100.5	104.0	88.9	98.2	109.0	104.9	96.9	110.9	89.4	101.9	93.8	93.3	1825
94.1	94.1	91.0	99.6	105.1	105.0	90.6	93.8	84.2	94.0	95.1	85.9	1826
89.6	93.0	91.5	98.0	100.6	102.6	88.0	99.8	84.6	93.2	101.0	80.2	1827
91.0	87.4	85.2	96.0	92.6	101.6	87.4	92.1	83.9	92.6	103.5	80.6	1828
92.5	81.7	81.3	93.8	85.4	94.1	84.8	86.4	85.1	88.7	102.3	80.1	1829
88.8	72.0	79.4	87.7	77.3	84.1	79.0	84.3	89.7	90.2	100.7	74.4	1830
95.8	68.9	86.2	86.1	79.0	92.3	83.7	86.5	90.2	96.0	110.0	79.3	1831
90.5	70.4	94.5	87.7	83.5	93.6	87.0	93.6	90.9	91.7	106.7	78.8	1832
97.8	73.1	96.0	88.8	82.0	93.7	89.7	94.1	84.6	84.6	109.6	78.6	1833
103.5	79.3	90.4	86.7	81.9	92.9	88.9	90.2	78.5	81.3	105.9	75.8	1834
105.6	66.7	92.7	85.8	86.0	95.4	92.3	100.4	76.7	78.7	110.9	80.5	1835
105.1	68.9	106.6	97.3	102.5	98.7	97.0	111.3	80.9	81.4	114.5	87.1	1836
96.3	80.0	106.3	100.5	103.9	95.0	92.4	94.8	87.7	81.1	120.5	92.1	1837
100.9	84.1	101.3	93.6	88.5	92.7	90.2	86.1	89.6	82.1	118.9	91.3	1838
105.4	101.8	112.0	94.6	89.2	92.6	92.9	100.8	88.1	87.6	119.7	100.6	1839
99.8	87.4	103.8	87.3	87.8	90.5	84.9	86.1	86.1	84.2	113.5	93.7	1840
97.4	77.8	101.5	84.8	85.0	89.4	84.0	88.2	82.3	84.7	107.5	91.2	1841
94.6	71.0	88.1	83.0	80.6	82.4	79.9	82.0	81.3	75.9	111.4	83.4	1842
86.6	67.3	77.7	77.5	73.4	75.7	75.8	72.6	79.7	71.1	120.6	74.7	1843
84.2	69.2	78.7	78.0	72.7	72.7	73.7	76.5	77.8	70.7	132.8	75.9	1844
78.4	60.5	78.2	83.8	77.0	74.3	75.9	70.4	77.4	69.7	135.8	75.3	1845
76.3	61.8	81.7	82.6	83.2	76.3	76.5	76.0	77.9	67.8	134.8	74.5	1846
81.2	69.6	90.5	81.8	84.1	74.7	74.4	93.2	78.4	69.1	137.7	76.7	1847
82.2	63.3	87.2	80.5	82.3	73.3	72.1	80.9	78.8	66.7	130.9	77.3	1848
82.9	56.9	88.5	73.4	81.7	72.2	72.4	85.1	77.7	64.2	121.5	73.7	1849
86.7	62.4	93.3	69.7	79.9	79.3	75.1	96.4	76.3	73.0	120.0	76.5	1850
85.1	65.1	92.4	65.9	80.7	89.4	75.8	91.8	76.7	76.5	113.3	78.2	1851
83.8	58.2	100.3	66.0	83.0	87.8	77.9	89.3	76.2	78.8	117.1	78.0	1852
82.2	66.1	99.8	80.1	106.2	91.4	88.8	93.0	75.7	89.7	131.0	83.2	1853
88.3	75.7	115.0	80.7	112.8	95.9	98.4	101.8	87.4	110.0	155.5	85.3	1854
96.5	71.4	120.0	78.3	105.4	91.0	94.0	100.4	92.9	110.2	182.5	84.2	1855
99.2	72.0	121.6	78.6	105.8	86.8	90.2	107.3	90.5	131.5	180.6	87.3	1856
102.4	75.2	116.9	74.0	107.8	94.8	91.2	106.4	87.6	158.8	188.3	87.4	1857
96.9	64.7	104.3	68.4	97.7	90.9	90.3	91.9	87.2	121.0	152.4	85.5	1858
98.8	65.5	102.7	67.8	98.0	96.6	89.0	93.1	85.5	138.0	136.2	89.2	1859
104.6	67.1	102.2	66.5	98.4	96.1	85.3	82.5	84.4	125.5	125.7	91.1	1860
99.6	67.2	95.5	63.0	91.4	90.8	103.7	95.8	85.9	115.1	127.1	83.9	1861

TABLE 44—20 COMMODITIES

Decade	0	1	2	3	4	5	6	7	8	9
1730		49.4	48.4	50.4	51.8	51.7	49.6	51.9	51.8	49.3
1740	51.0	62.4	61.0	53.1	51.4	52.0	53.8	60.2	65.8	65.7
1750	65.4	65.3	65.5	64.6	62.8	61.4	62.1	62.5	64.2	70.5
1760	70.5	69.5	75.7	74.8	68.2	68.1	72.1	71.3	67.8	65.8
1770	68.8	70.5	77.3	75.3	73.5					
1780					100.0	90.4	81.9	78.7	73.6	75.0
1790	84.8	80.7	83.5	92.3	109.1	138.5	155.3	140.5	128.8	125.4
1800	129.1	138.6	119.4	123.9	131.3	137.6	125.6	119.6	109.4	124.3
1810	132.4	133.3	131.5	153.9	191.8	177.8	161.8	151.5	146.7	125.0
1820	105.8	96.2	103.6	101.1	96.3	100.3	93.8	92.5	92.6	90.1
1830	80.5	83.9	87.2	92.2	92.0	100.1	112.9	111.4	106.9	110.0
1840	92.7	87.4	78.0	73.8	73.2	78.5	81.1	89.2	77.5	77.7
1850	81.0	81.6	83.2	92.3	106.5	112.3	102.0	106.9	92.8	95.3
1860	90.8	101.9								

TABLE 45—ARITHMETIC INDEX—12 COMMODITIES

Decade	0	1	2	3	4	5	6	7	8	9
1720	86.2	78.6	81.6	84.3	88.9	96.6	101.0	97.6	92.8	92.5
1730	98.0	87.1	83.6	90.0	87.2	87.8	83.6	91.1	91.1	82.2
1740	87.3	112.6	108.3	95.6	90.9	92.7	99.7	110.6	124.7	121.5
1750	113.0	112.8	111.9	109.9	109.1	107.3	109.6	107.1	109.6	125.0
1760	125.7	121.2	133.4	136.4	119.4	118.4	124.7	123.7	119.7	115.9
1770	121.6	126.7	141.0	133.7	127.5					
1780					172.6	158.0	145.0	135.8	120.5	128.6
1790	160.3	149.2	156.5	174.9		257.8	295.8	266.7		
1800		274.4	211.2	212.1	241.0	262.9	233.1	217.9	192.6	224.0
1810	249.6	260.2	257.3	286.3	371.3	337.1	298.3	307.6	276.2	223.2
1820	180.7	160.2	183.4	179.3	163.0	163.6	160.4	161.5	165.4	172.4
1830	150.2	165.2	166.7	171.2	163.0	181.9	217.7	233.8	211.4	203.8
1840	165.4	152.3	135.7	131.4	129.3	142.5	144.1	177.5	149.3	146.8
1850	147.3	144.8	152.8	171.9	211.6	234.9	194.6	198.4	165.3	176.5
1860	164.3	167.5								

Table 46—Minima, Maxima, Deciles, Quartiles, and Medians of Relatives of Average Annual Wholesale Prices of 140 Commodities

Year	Minimum	Decile 1	Decile 2	Quartile 1	Decile 3	Decile 4	Median	Decile 6	Decile 7	Quartile 3	Decile 8	Decile 9	Maximum
1784	38.3	63.4	71.5	76.2	81.0	90.9	96.1	102.8	115.8	125.4	133.9	165.5	388.8
1785	31.1	60.3	66.0	72.0	76.4	87.2	91.5	99.1	110.7	113.4	119.5	157.0	313.0
1786	32.7	56.8	65.3	70.8	73.2	82.2	89.7	96.7	105.5	111.8	121.3	144.0	495.5
1787	24.5	56.5	63.4	69.3	71.7	81.2	88.7	92.1	103.9	108.4	114.5	138.5	699.6
1788	21.0	52.1	61.0	67.4	71.7	77.0	80.9	87.7	96.0	101.9	105.9	129.6	585.7
1789	18.1	53.5	62.7	66.9	70.4	74.9	80.6	89.8	93.0	98.3	106.1	130.4	394.2
1790	32.2	55.5	67.4	70.2	72.5	77.9	86.4	93.1	101.6	106.0	113.7	134.0	457.0
1791	32.6	60.7	67.9	71.4	73.9	80.3	87.7	94.5	104.6	107.8	115.8	134.7	569.9
1792	39.9	61.9	68.7	69.8	72.2	82.2	89.8	96.6	106.7	113.4	120.6	137.8	459.5
1793	37.2	66.1	71.9	73.8	77.6	87.1	96.4	100.8	110.6	115.9	124.9	148.5	451.9
1794	32.3	69.5	81.6	83.7	85.3	95.6	107.1	116.7	128.2	134.3	140.4	175.1	528.9
1795	37.2	81.0	91.2	95.8	101.4	115.5	122.7	131.9	149.3	163.6	172.9	215.7	1128.7
1796	44.8	79.5	100.8	106.7	114.7	126.6	133.7	144.3	156.7	165.9	177.8	212.7	876.5
1797	42.5	77.9	103.9	106.8	114.5	123.2	129.6	139.2	150.3	158.5	166.3	223.8	590.1
1798	41.2	74.9	100.2	108.2	112.6	118.0	125.9	135.6	142.0	148.1	157.1	203.9	480.4
1799	47.8	81.6	98.3	101.8	105.3	116.3	125.6	134.1	140.1	150.3	158.7	200.8	532.1
1800	47.8	81.5	99.6	109.3	112.4	118.1	129.8	138.0	148.9	153.5	160.3	193.6	391.7
1801	46.2	89.9	103.4	109.9	113.4	122.6	130.2	144.6	158.9	165.8	170.3	187.3	326.4
1802	38.9	89.9	99.5	103.7	107.7	114.9	119.9	128.2	139.0	142.3	145.7	164.0	395.4
1803	24.3	90.1	100.0	103.8	107.7	113.4	117.9	124.5	135.2	139.4	143.2	155.3	366.8
1804	36.0	93.3	103.1	107.1	109.7	116.8	125.1	137.4	143.7	149.1	155.1	186.7	309.3
1805	40.2	90.4	104.0	109.0	113.8	121.9	130.9	143.5	154.7	163.5	168.0	185.3	320.0
1806	62.6	88.1	101.3	107.3	112.1	120.4	130.7	139.3	149.5	153.3	156.3	181.9	293.6
1807	57.4	87.7	97.4	100.8	111.7	119.8	125.6	132.1	138.7	141.8	148.2	172.0	280.8
1808	56.0	89.2	96.5	100.7	104.7	114.2	119.0	127.9	138.8	143.2	148.7	165.9	451.9
1809	47.6	96.0	104.8	110.1	112.4	120.7	128.4	137.7	151.6	163.5	167.8	208.9	558.6
1810	43.4	93.2	108.3	113.5	119.4	124.5	132.2	142.3	154.1	160.4	172.0	200.1	635.9
1811	47.8	87.2	108.3	112.8	116.9	125.6	130.5	139.3	150.3	167.4	175.3	188.5	638.2
1812	58.0	89.4	110.9	115.9	121.3	129.8	135.8	145.3	162.3	167.4	181.3	240.5	636.7
1813	58.9	101.3	116.9	122.2	124.8	140.0	152.4	167.8	181.8	193.5	217.2	301.3	593.3
1814	70.0	114.7	126.9	134.4	142.4	162.7	179.8	197.4	232.0	250.0	266.4	371.9	1207.6
1815	65.4	125.4	136.2	139.4	142.7	156.9	171.8	181.2	197.3	207.5	213.0	267.0	620.6
1816	45.0	113.0	124.4	127.9	130.3	136.7	145.0	156.1	171.1	182.7	194.1	209.5	566.9
1817	37.1	96.8	105.6	108.0	111.9	120.0	124.6	135.9	154.1	163.5	174.9	197.2	413.8
1818	57.9	99.3	106.4	108.5	111.9	118.4	131.7	139.4	149.4	159.7	163.3	176.3	241.5
1819	57.9	97.9	104.0	105.7	110.1	115.2	120.5	124.5	130.5	133.6	136.5	150.9	181.3
1820	60.6	90.6	97.5	100.1	101.8	103.0	107.6	111.9	115.3	116.5	118.4	127.8	166.9
1821	70.3	88.0	92.8	95.8	97.6	100.4	102.7	105.4	107.7	110.0	112.3	119.0	139.6
1822	86.1	95.6	98.1	98.9	100.3	101.2	103.0	104.6	106.9	108.6	109.3	113.9	140.6
1823	76.9	90.2	92.6	93.6	94.6	96.8	98.4	100.7	102.1	103.7	105.1	109.0	121.2
1824	69.2	84.3	89.4	90.5	91.8	93.7	95.1	97.3	99.1	100.1	100.6	103.1	113.2
1825	74.5	85.3	89.0	90.5	92.9	96.2	98.4	100.9	104.5	105.3	107.4	112.8	143.7
1826	67.9	78.6	82.7	86.2	87.8	91.0	96.0	99.0	103.1	105.4	106.7	116.8	157.4
1827	58.5	72.7	81.0	84.2	86.8	89.7	94.3	97.1	99.9	103.8	105.4	113.4	197.7
1828	51.8	72.1	80.8	82.7	84.8	87.4	90.5	94.2	98.5	99.8	102.7	109.4	183.9
1829	48.0	68.9	76.0	78.2	80.1	85.2	89.1	92.1	97.8	101.3	105.2	110.1	181.1
1830	45.6	63.3	70.2	72.6	74.4	79.8	85.4	88.1	92.2	93.8	97.3	108.9	177.1
1831	43.4	63.7	73.9	77.4	79.5	83.7	88.1	90.7	96.8	100.3	103.1	123.0	202.3
1832	48.2	65.1	75.4	77.7	80.8	84.9	88.8	94.0	99.7	101.3	103.1	118.5	222.9
1833	24.9	63.5	73.2	78.1	81.8	84.9	90.1	96.0	100.7	104.4	106.7	122.6	220.9
1834	21.5	61.3	67.0	74.2	78.3	85.4	88.7	92.0	97.5	100.1	104.9	120.9	179.0
1835	21.2	60.1	70.0	76.4	79.5	86.0	93.5	101.1	105.4	110.4	115.3	137.9	201.9
1836	22.2	61.6	78.0	79.5	85.3	94.1	100.4	104.9	115.3	122.8	131.1	151.9	221.9
1837	24.4	62.6	75.8	79.6	83.7	89.3	99.0	107.6	111.0	114.7	121.6	136.2	216.0
1838	23.4	60.0	72.1	76.6	80.1	88.3	94.0	103.1	112.3	115.1	121.0	135.4	193.1
1839	24.7	59.4	73.0	78.8	85.8	90.4	97.9	106.6	117.1	125.6	130.8	146.1	265.2
1840	22.7	58.7	68.7	71.3	81.8	85.6	89.1	96.1	101.6	104.9	111.1	124.3	259.2
1841	21.8	56.7	69.9	73.9	77.4	81.4	87.3	94.0	100.5	105.8	110.3	125.7	211.2
1842	25.6	52.7	61.8	67.1	68.4	75.8	81.7	86.5	95.2	98.8	102.7	118.1	159.8
1843	19.2	51.4	62.0	64.9	67.9	71.8	75.8	80.3	86.1	89.9	97.6	108.8	164.0
1844	25.8	52.0	60.6	64.2	67.8	72.8	76.3	83.5	89.0	90.3	96.7	113.1	173.1
1845	27.7	51.6	62.8	66.3	69.8	75.2	80.9	86.9	91.7	96.3	102.0	116.8	184.3
1846	28.4	52.9	63.7	66.4	69.6	73.9	80.1	84.5	91.3	99.5	106.9	123.5	174.8
1847	23.5	51.8	63.9	67.2	70.4	74.9	82.8	92.4	100.9	103.4	113.0	138.6	197.7
1848	20.6	48.3	57.3	63.9	66.4	73.3	79.5	89.2	97.3	101.6	106.0	121.6	193.1
1849	19.8	48.9	58.3	62.8	64.9	71.8	77.9	84.8	93.1	97.5	99.0	118.9	377.0
1850	19.0	52.6	60.5	65.7	68.8	73.6	78.2	85.7	97.3	101.6	107.1	124.3	381.6
1851	18.1	50.1	61.7	66.0	68.0	74.9	79.1	88.9	98.5	102.3	107.9	125.2	377.5
1852	18.4	46.3	56.7	63.7	67.0	72.9	77.9	91.6	102.1	106.2	113.5	132.2	414.5
1853	17.5	52.9	63.1	59.0	74.5	79.3	85.8	98.3	110.1	118.1	122.8	139.9	441.3
1854	16.6	55.5	67.9	74.6	79.0	86.2	96.5	108.4	120.1	127.3	132.1	166.1	441.3
1855	14.0	54.9	69.3	75.3	80.0	91.2	100.0	113.5	126.6	138.3	146.6	180.5	441.3
1856	13.1	54.9	69.0	74.9	79.5	91.2	106.8	119.3	132.1	136.2	141.9	157.3	449.8
1857	10.9	53.7	71.4	74.5	80.9	93.8	107.5	125.0	134.0	141.1	147.7	166.2	419.8
1858	7.3	52.4	64.6	72.1	76.1	84.1	95.5	106.4	118.4	122.0	128.1	150.6	367.8
1859	7.3	47.5	65.9	68.5	73.8	84.4	96.7	105.6	120.6	124.8	131.7	149.4	367.8
1860	8.0	47.6	63.4	67.3	73.0	83.5	95.9	105.7	118.2	126.0	132.0	148.5	367.8
1861	9.0	47.6	63.4	66.7	73.1	86.3	90.9	101.4	112.9	120.0	129.3	152.6	425.3

TABLE 47—SKEWNESS OF DISTRIBUTIONS OF RELATIVES OF AVERAGE ANNUAL WHOLESALE PRICES OF 140 COMMODITIES

Year	$d_7 - d_3$	$q_3 - q_1$	$d_8 - d_2$	Year	$d_7 - d_3$	$q_3 - q_1$	$d_8 - d_2$
1784	+.044	+.068	+.057	1823	−.033	+.024	+.040
1785	+.027	−.055	−.101	1824	+.077	+.016	−.047
1786	−.112	−.036	−.025	1825	+.022	−.105	−.069
1787	−.147	−.103	−.136	1826	−.112	−.071	−.171
1788	+.173	+.117	−.024	1827	−.179	−.083	−.155
1789	+.028	+.032	+.045	1828	+.131	+.041	+.055
1790	−.040	−.008	+.050	1829	−.067	−.008	+.022
1791	+.014	+.002	+.041	1830	−.286	−.268	−.201
1792	−.117	−.038	+.048	1831	−.043	+.001	−.056
1793	−.224	−.184	−.062	1832	+.102	−.007	−.046
1794	−.117	−.043	−.002	1833	+.070	+.015	−.102
1795	+.014	+.075	+.072	1834	−.137	−.192	−.252
1796	+.017	−.022	+.005	1835	−.150	−.097	−.160
1797	+.089	+.020	+.060	1836	−.082	−.074	+.028
1798	+.037	+.035	−.015	1837	−.189	−.194	−.130
1799	−.235	−.078	−.023	1838	+.053	−.005	−.025
1800	−.024	−.012	−.113	1839	+.152	+.069	−.006
1801	+.181	+.176	+.076	1840	+.211	−.154	−.082
1802	+.159	+.083	+.022	1841	+.078	+.071	+.025
1803	+.204	+.136	+.083	1842	−.075	−.018	−.099
1804	+.027	+.061	+.053	1843	+.073	+.047	+.114
1805	+.088	+.097	+.041	1844	+.132	−.012	+.014
1806	−.066	−.106	−.175	1845	−.082	−.066	−.044
1807	−.076	−.289	−.208	1846	−.035	+.072	+.115
1808	+.092	+.051	+.031	1847	+.099	+.031	+.091
1809	+.110	+.222	+.137	1848	+.057	+.058	−.065
1810	+.202	+.118	+.138	1849	−.012	+.020	−.095
1811	+.124	+.262	+.226	1850	+.261	+.201	+.101
1812	+.224	+.138	+.176	1851	+.184	+.174	+.111
1813	−.062	+.039	+.144	1852	+.284	+.213	+.085
1814	+.044	+.062	+.060	1853	+.277	+.189	+.077
1815	−.146	−.051	−.039	1854	+.045	+.037	−.056
1816	+.215	+.296	+.311	1855	+.028	+.067	+.021
1817	+.328	+.310	+.344	1856	−.163	−.187	−.212
1818	−.127	−.003	+.004	1857	−.127	−.148	−.126
1819	−.062	−.119	−.083	1858	−.027	−.069	−.142
1820	+.110	+.048	−.015	1859	−.101	−.150	−.108
1821	−.034	−.006	−.063	1860	−.132	−.129	−.129
1822	+.166	+.132	+.098	1861	−.003	−.054	−.011

Table 48—Percentage of Commodities which Increased in Price over the Previous Year

Year	Farm		Imported Foods	Lumber Products and Naval Stores	Industrial		Total
	Crops	Derivatives			Raw	Consumption	
1785	58.3	14.3	38.1	25.0	37.5	11.1	32.9
1786	50.0	42.9	61.9		37.5	74.1	46.4
1787	41.7	14.3	61.9	8.3	42.5	59.3	40.7
1788	8.3	7.1	38.1	16.7	50.0	18.5	27.1
1789	25.0	35.7	42.9	66.7	50.0	48.1	45.0
1790	58.3	78.6	52.4	66.7	32.5	51.9	52.1
1791	33.3	42.9	66.7	66.7	32.5	74.1	52.9
1792	41.7	35.7	52.4	66.7	62.5	63.0	59.3
1793	83.3	85.7	38.1	83.3	55.0	55.6	62.1
1794	66.7	92.9	66.7	91.7	80.0	92.6	81.4
1795	83.3	78.6	85.7	100.0	82.5	81.5	84.3
1796	91.7	71.4	57.1	83.3	60.0	66.7	67.1
1797	41.7	14.3	47.6	66.7	57.5	29.6	43.6
1798	33.3	35.7	28.6	33.3	60.0	37.0	40.7
1799	33.3	42.9	76.2	25.0	60.0	33.3	52.1
1800	66.7	64.3	47.6	75.0	52.5	25.9	52.1
1801	75.0	85.7	23.8	50.0	57.5	40.7	55.0
1802	33.3	21.4	19.0	25.0	27.5	14.8	25.7
1803	33.3	21.4	47.6	66.7	55.0	22.2	41.4
1804	66.7	85.7	71.4	41.7	52.5	77.8	66.4
1805	75.0	78.6	38.1	50.0	45.0	51.9	52.1
1806	33.3	42.9	28.6	25.0	67.5	22.2	40.0
1807	33.3	14.3	28.6	50.0	35.0	14.8	29.3
1808	16.7	7.1	47.6	33.3	40.0	55.6	39.3
1809	50.0	92.9	81.0	83.3	60.0	74.1	72.9
1810	66.7	85.7	28.6	83.3	57.5	48.1	59.3
1811	33.3	57.1	23.8	41.7	30.0	40.7	40.0
1812	50.0	14.3	81.0	25.0	57.5	66.7	55.0
1813	58.3	42.9	85.7	58.3	82.5	70.4	69.3
1814	75.0	71.4	71.4	75.0	80.0	74.1	76.4
1815	50.0	78.6	28.6	58.3	22.5	22.2	35.0
1816	83.3	64.3	9.5	25.0	27.5	22.2	31.4
1817	58.3	50.0	4.8		2.5	11.1	15.0
1818	33.3	21.4	52.4	58.3	47.5	51.9	45.7
1819	33.3		23.8	33.3	30.0	33.3	27.9
1820	16.7		9.5	8.3	25.0	18.5	17.1
1821	8.3	21.4	47.6	8.3	40.0	25.9	30.7
1822	50.0	64.3	47.6	58.3	40.0	29.6	44.3
1823	41.7	28.6	4.8	16.7	27.5	18.5	21.4
1824	33.3	42.9	28.6	16.7	32.5	25.9	29.3
1825	75.0	50.0	81.0	58.3	67.5	40.7	61.4
1826	41.7	35.7	28.6	41.7	35.0	40.7	35.0
1827	33.3	57.1	28.6	41.7	27.5	44.4	35.7
1828	16.7	50.0	28.6	58.3	22.5	40.7	34.3
1829	58.3	42.9	28.6	8.3	25.0	33.3	30.0
1830	8.3	42.9	23.8		27.5	18.5	20.7
1831	66.7	92.9	61.9	75.0	55.0	51.9	61.4
1832	58.3	50.0	76.2	83.3	45.0	51.9	55.0
1833	33.3	64.3	28.6	58.3	32.5	22.2	35.7
1834	25.0	14.3	23.8	58.3	40.0	25.9	32.9
1835	83.3	100.0	71.4	58.3	42.5	63.0	62.1
1836	91.7	92.9	52.4	66.7	70.0	66.7	68.6
1837	50.0	57.1	9.5	25.0	55.0	74.1	47.1
1838	33.3	42.9	47.6	16.7	30.0	37.0	35.7
1839	83.3	64.3	47.6	58.3	65.0	48.1	60.7
1840			28.6	33.3	15.0	18.5	15.7
1841	58.3	14.3	47.6	33.3	40.0	18.5	35.0
1842	25.0	21.4	42.9	16.7	30.0	25.9	25.7
1843	8.3	21.4	76.2		17.5	22.2	25.7
1844	50.0	42.9	66.7	25.0	47.5	33.3	47.9
1845	75.0	78.6	66.7	66.7	42.5	40.7	55.0
1846	75.0	42.9	47.6	66.7	40.0	44.4	46.4
1847	83.3	85.7	57.1	33.3	45.0	63.0	55.7
1848	8.3	14.3	28.6	33.3	25.0	40.7	25.7
1849	33.3	42.9	57.1	41.7	25.0	18.5	32.1
1850	75.0	50.0	66.7	91.7	52.5	37.0	57.1
1851	66.7	71.4	42.9	91.7	37.5	25.9	43.6
1852	58.3	92.9	23.8	66.7	40.0	29.6	44.3
1853	100.0	78.6	71.4	66.7	67.5	66.7	71.4
1854	83.3	57.1	47.6	75.0	72.5	74.1	69.3
1855	75.0	85.7	52.4	16.7	40.0	59.3	54.3
1856	33.3	42.9	61.9	8.3	45.0	33.3	40.7
1857	75.0	57.1	61.9	58.3	37.5	44.4	48.6
1858		14.3	14.3	33.3	17.5	18.5	15.0
1859	58.3	78.6	33.3	75.0	45.0	18.5	44.3
1860	8.3	35.7	38.1	16.7	35.0	25.9	32.9
1861	33.3		66.7	41.7	20.0	51.9	37.1

TABLE 49—PERCENTAGE OF COMMODITIES WHICH HELD SAME PRICE AS IN THE PREVIOUS YEAR

Year	Farm		Imported Foods	Lumber Products and Naval Stores	Industrial		Total
	Crops	Derivatives			Raw	Con-sumption	
1785			4.8		2.5	3.7	2.1
1786			9.5		2.5		2.9
1787		14.3		8.3	2.5	18.5	10.0
1788				8.3	2.5	3.7	4.3
1789	25.0		4.8	8.3	17.5	11.1	13.6
1790	25.0	7.1	4.8	16.7	17.5	7.4	12.1
1791			4.8		7.5	7.4	4.3
1792							0.7
1793	8.3	7.1	9.5		22.5	11.1	12.1
1794							
1795							
1796			4.8		2.5		1.4
1797	8.3	7.1			2.5	3.7	2.9
1798						3.7	0.7
1799		7.1			5.0	7.4	3.6
1800		7.1		8.3		3.7	2.9
1801		7.1		8.3	2.5	7.4	3.6
1802	8.3	7.1			7.5	3.7	5.0
1803	16.7	7.1			7.5	14.8	8.6
1804	8.3	7.1		16.7	22.5		10.0
1805		7.1	4.8	8.3	22.5	7.4	10.7
1806		7.1	4.8		7.5		3.6
1807			4.8		20.0	7.4	7.9
1808	8.3		4.8	8.3	15.0	3.7	8.6
1809					10.0	7.4	5.0
1810						7.4	2.9
1811		7.1			2.5	3.7	2.9
1812		21.4		8.3	5.0	3.7	5.7
1813		21.4	4.8	41.7	10.0	3.7	12.1
1814			4.8	25.0			2.9
1815					2.5		0.7
1816					2.5	3.7	1.4
1817					5.0		1.4
1818		7.1					0.7
1819						3.7	1.4
1820					5.0		2.9
1821	8.3			8.3	35.0	18.5	16.4
1822	8.3			8.3	17.5	14.8	10.0
1823	8.3	7.1	4.8	33.3	10.0	18.5	12.1
1824			4.8	41.7	12.5	3.7	10.0
1825				8.3			0.7
1826					5.0		1.4
1827					2.5		1.4
1828					2.5		1.4
1829					15.0	7.4	7.1
1830	16.7			8.3	12.5	14.8	9.3
1831	8.3			8.3	12.5	11.1	7.9
1832	8.3				10.0	14.8	7.9
1833	8.3			16.7	10.0	7.4	9.3
1834	8.3			8.3	15.0	7.4	8.6
1835				8.3	5.0	3.7	3.6
1836			4.8	8.3	2.5	7.4	3.6
1837				8.3	5.0	3.7	2.9
1838			4.8		12.5	7.4	7.1
1839			9.5		12.5	11.1	7.1
1840					12.5	7.4	7.9
1841				8.3	15.0	7.4	8.6
1842					12.5	7.4	7.9
1843					10.0	11.1	7.1
1844					10.0	18.5	7.9
1845					5.0	18.5	5.7
1846					2.5	18.5	5.7
1847			4.8		10.0	14.8	7.9
1848					12.5	22.2	10.7
1849			9.5	8.3	15.0	22.2	13.6
1850			9.5		15.0	22.2	12.9
1851					5.0	22.2	12.9
1852				8.3	2.5	22.2	10.7
1853				8.3	5.0	18.5	5.7
1854			4.8	16.7	5.0	14.8	7.1
1855			14.3		10.0	18.5	8.6
1856			9.5	8.3	12.5	14.8	12.1
1857					10.0		8.6
1858					7.5	7.4	5.7
1859			4.8	8.3	7.5	22.2	8.6
1860	8.3	7.1	4.8	33.3	5.0	29.6	12.1
1861					7.5	3.7	4.3

TABLE 50—PERCENTAGE OF COMMODITIES WHICH DECREASED IN PRICE FROM THE PREVIOUS YEAR

Year	Farm		Imported Foods	Lumber Products and Naval Stores	Industrial		Total
	Crops	Derivatives			Raw	Con-sumption	
1785	41.7	85.7	57.1	75.0	60.0	85.2	65.0
1786	50.0	57.1	28.6	100.0	60.0	25.9	50.7
1787	58.3	71.4	38.1	83.3	55.0	22.2	49.3
1788	91.7	92.9	61.9	75.0	47.5	77.8	68.6
1789	50.0	64.3	52.4	25.0	32.5	40.7	41.4
1790	16.7	14.3	42.9	16.7	50.0	40.7	35.7
1791	66.7	57.1	28.6	33.3	60.0	18.5	42.9
1792	58.3	64.3	47.6	33.3	37.5	37.0	40.0
1793	8.3	7.1	52.4	16.7	22.5	33.3	25.7
1794	33.3	7.1	33.3	8.3	20.0	7.4	18.6
1795	16.7	21.4	14.3		17.5	18.5	15.7
1796	8.3	28.6	38.1	16.7	37.5	33.3	31.4
1797	50.0	78.6	52.4	33.3	40.0	66.7	53.6
1798	66.7	64.3	71.4	66.7	40.0	59.3	58.6
1799	66.7	50.0	23.8	75.0	35.0	59.3	44.3
1800	33.3	28.6	52.4	16.7	47.5	70.4	45.0
1801	25.0	7.1	76.2	41.7	40.0	51.9	41.4
1802	58.3	71.4	81.0	75.0	65.0	81.5	69.3
1803	50.0	71.4	52.4	33.3	37.5	63.0	50.0
1804	25.0	7.1	28.6	41.7	25.0	22.2	23.6
1805	25.0	14.3	57.1	41.7	32.5	40.7	37.1
1806	66.7	50.0	66.7	75.0	25.0	77.8	56.4
1807	66.7	85.7	66.7	50.0	45.0	77.8	62.9
1808	75.0	85.7	47.6	58.3	45.0	40.7	52.1
1809	50.0	7.1	19.0	16.7	30.0	18.5	22.1
1810	33.3	14.3	71.4	16.7	42.5	44.4	37.9
1811	66.7	35.7	76.2	58.3	67.5	55.6	57.1
1812	50.0	64.3	19.0	66.7	37.5	29.6	39.3
1813	41.7	35.7	9.5		7.5	25.9	18.6
1814	25.0	28.6	23.8		20.0	25.9	20.7
1815	50.0	21.4	71.4	41.7	75.0	77.8	64.3
1816	16.7	35.7	90.5	75.0	70.0	74.1	67.1
1817	41.7	50.0	95.2	100.0	92.5	88.9	83.6
1818	66.7	71.4	47.6	41.7	52.5	48.1	53.6
1819	66.7	100.0	76.2	66.7	70.0	63.0	70.7
1820	83.3	100.0	90.5	91.7	70.0	81.5	80.0
1821	83.3	78.6	52.4	83.3	25.0	55.6	52.9
1822	41.7	35.7	52.4	33.3	42.5	55.6	45.7
1823	50.0	64.3	90.5	50.0	62.5	63.0	66.4
1824	66.7	57.1	66.7	41.7	55.0	70.4	60.7
1825	25.0	50.0	19.0	33.3	32.5	59.3	37.9
1826	58.3	64.3	71.4	58.3	60.0	59.3	63.6
1827	66.7	42.9	71.4	58.3	70.0	55.6	62.9
1828	83.3	50.0	71.4	41.7	75.0	59.3	64.3
1829	41.7	57.1	71.4	91.7	60.0	59.3	62.9
1830	75.0	57.1	76.2	91.7	60.0	66.7	70.0
1831	25.0	7.1	38.1	16.7	32.5	37.0	30.7
1832	33.3	50.0	23.8	16.7	45.0	33.3	37.1
1833	58.3	35.7	71.4	25.0	57.5	70.4	55.0
1834	66.7	85.7	76.2	33.3	45.0	66.7	58.6
1835	16.7		28.6	33.3	52.5	33.3	34.3
1836	8.3	7.1	42.9	25.0	27.5	25.9	27.9
1837	50.0	42.9	90.5	66.7	40.0	22.2	50.0
1838	66.7	57.1	47.6	83.3	57.5	55.6	57.1
1839	16.7	35.7	42.9	41.7	22.5	40.7	32.1
1840	100.0	100.0	71.4	66.7	72.5	74.1	76.4
1841	41.7	85.7	52.4	58.3	45.0	74.1	56.4
1842	75.0	78.6	57.1	83.3	57.5	66.7	66.4
1843	91.7	78.6	23.8	100.0	72.5	66.7	67.1
1844	50.0	57.1	33.3	75.0	42.5	48.1	44.3
1845	25.0	21.4	33.3	33.3	52.5	40.7	39.3
1846	25.0	57.1	52.4	33.3	57.5	37.0	47.9
1847	16.7	14.3	38.1	66.7	45.0	22.2	36.4
1848	91.7	85.7	71.4	66.7	62.5	37.0	63.6
1849	66.7	57.1	33.3	50.0	60.0	59.3	54.3
1850	25.0	50.0	23.8	8.3	32.5	40.7	30.0
1851	33.3	28.6	57.1	8.3	57.5	51.9	43.6
1852	41.7	7.1	76.2	25.0	57.5	48.1	45.0
1853		21.4	28.6	25.0	27.5	14.8	22.9
1854	16.7	42.9	47.6	8.3	22.5	11.1	23.6
1855	25.0	14.3	33.3	83.3	50.0	22.2	37.1
1856	66.7	57.1	28.6	83.3	42.5	51.9	47.1
1857	25.0	42.9	38.1	41.7	52.5	55.6	42.9
1858	100.0	85.7	85.7	66.7	75.0	74.1	79.3
1859	41.7	21.4	61.9	16.7	47.5	59.3	47.1
1860	83.3	57.1	57.1	50.0	60.0	44.4	55.0
1861	66.7	100.0	33.3	58.3	72.5	44.4	58.6

Table 51—Percentage of Commodities which Increased in Price 2.5 Per Cent or More over the Previous Year

Year	Farm		Imported Foods	Lumber Products and Naval Stores	Industrial		Total
	Crops	Derivatives			Raw	Con-sumption	
1785	58.3		38.1	16.7	37.5	11.1	30.0
1786	50.0	35.7	57.1		27.5	51.9	37.1
1787	33.3	14.3	52.4	8.3	27.5	44.4	30.7
1788	8.3		23.8	16.7	32.5	14.8	18.6
1789	16.7	35.7	33.3	66.7	25.0	37.0	32.1
1790	58.3	78.6	42.9	50.0	27.5	33.3	42.1
1791	25.0	42.9	66.7	58.3	32.5	70.4	49.3
1792	33.3	35.7	47.6	50.0	37.5	44.4	43.6
1793	75.0	71.4	38.1	66.7	45.0	48.1	52.1
1794	66.7	78.6	66.7	83.3	75.0	88.9	75.0
1795	83.3	78.6	81.0	100.0	80.0	66.7	77.9
1796	91.7	64.3	52.4	83.3	50.0	63.0	60.7
1797	41.7	14.3	38.1	50.0	47.5	22.2	36.4
1798	16.7	35.7	23.8	16.7	47.5	33.3	31.4
1799	33.3	35.7	47.6	25.0	45.0	25.9	40.7
1800	58.3	50.0	42.9	75.0	50.0	18.5	46.4
1801	66.7	78.6	19.0	41.7	37.5	37.0	45.0
1802	33.3	14.3	19.0	25.0	22.5	14.8	22.9
1803	33.3	21.4	28.6	66.7	40.0	14.8	30.7
1804	58.3	64.3	71.4	33.3	35.0	59.3	53.6
1805	66.7	71.4	38.1	25.0	42.5	44.4	44.3
1806	25.0	35.7	23.8	16.7	60.0	14.8	33.6
1807	25.0	7.1	28.6	41.7	27.5	3.7	21.4
1808	16.7	7.1	47.6	25.0	37.5	48.1	36.4
1809	50.0	85.7	76.2	75.0	57.5	74.1	70.0
1810	66.7	85.7	28.6	66.7	47.5	40.7	52.9
1811	33.3	42.9	23.8	25.0	25.0	29.6	33.6
1812	33.3	14.3	71.4		55.0	63.0	47.9
1813	58.3	21.4	85.7	50.0	70.0	66.7	62.1
1814	66.7	64.3	66.7	75.0	80.0	63.0	72.1
1815	50.0	57.1	19.0	50.0	22.5	22.2	30.0
1816	75.0	64.3	9.5	16.7	22.5	18.5	26.4
1817	58.3	50.0				7.4	12.9
1818	25.0	21.4	47.6	58.3	42.5	33.3	38.6
1819	25.0		14.3	16.7	15.0	22.2	16.4
1820	8.3		4.8	8.3	10.0	3.7	6.4
1821		14.3	33.3	8.3	27.5	14.8	19.3
1822	50.0	64.3	38.1	50.0	32.5	25.9	39.3
1823	33.3	21.4	4.8	16.7	22.5	18.5	17.9
1824	33.3	28.6	23.8	16.7	22.5	11.1	21.4
1825	75.0	35.7	66.7	58.3	52.5	37.0	52.9
1826	41.7	35.7	28.6	33.3	20.0	22.2	25.7
1827	33.3	35.7	28.6	25.0	17.5	29.6	25.0
1828	8.3	42.9	23.8	41.7	17.5	33.3	27.9
1829	58.3	35.7	23.8		22.5	29.6	26.4
1830	8.3	21.4	9.5		20.0	18.5	14.3
1831	66.7	92.9	47.6	66.7	47.5	44.4	55.0
1832	58.3	35.7	61.9	50.0	30.0	44.4	42.1
1833	33.3	42.9	28.6	50.0	20.0	11.1	27.1
1834	16.7		9.5	50.0	25.0	7.4	19.3
1835	83.3	85.7	57.1	41.7	32.5	44.4	50.0
1836	75.0	85.7	47.6	66.7	57.5	55.6	59.3
1837	50.0	42.9	9.5	16.7	45.0	51.9	37.1
1838	25.0	35.7	28.6	8.3	27.5	22.2	25.7
1839	66.7	64.3	33.3	41.7	45.0	33.3	46.4
1840			28.6	16.7	7.5	7.4	10.0
1841	50.0	14.3	38.1	16.7	17.5	7.4	21.4
1842	25.0	14.3	28.6	8.3	10.0	22.2	15.7
1843	8.3	14.3	61.9		7.5	18.5	19.3
1844	33.3	28.6	57.1		37.5	25.9	37.1
1845	75.0	78.6	42.9	66.7	35.0	37.0	47.9
1846	58.3	35.7	23.8	66.7	25.0	33.3	32.9
1847	83.3	78.6	42.9	25.0	27.5	40.7	41.4
1848	8.3	7.1	4.8	16.7	20.0	25.9	15.7
1849	25.0	28.6	33.3	33.3	22.5	11.1	23.6
1850	75.0	35.7	47.6	66.7	37.5	22.2	42.9
1851	41.7	50.0	38.1	91.7	20.0	14.8	31.4
1852	50.0	85.7	19.0	50.0	30.0	25.9	36.4
1853	75.0	64.3	47.6	58.3	62.5	55.6	57.9
1854	75.0	57.1	33.3	58.3	57.5	66.7	59.3
1855	66.7	71.4	33.3		30.0	55.6	44.3
1856	33.3	28.6	52.4		25.0	18.5	25.7
1857	58.3	57.1	52.4	58.3	32.5	44.4	44.3
1858		14.3		25.0	15.0	7.4	9.3
1859	58.3	71.4	19.0	50.0	35.0	7.4	33.6
1860	8.3	35.7	38.1	16.7	27.5	18.5	27.9
1861	33.3		57.1	41.7	10.0	33.3	27.1

TABLE 52—PERCENTAGE OF COMMODITIES WHICH CHANGED IN PRICE LESS THAN 2.5 PER CENT OVER THE PREVIOUS YEAR

Year	Farm		Imported Foods	Lumber Products and Naval Stores	Industrial		Total
	Crops	Derivatives			Raw	Con-sumption	
1785	16.7	21.4	4.8	8.3	15.0	7.4	12.1
1786		7.1	14.3		22.5	33.3	17.1
1787	25.0	14.3	9.5	8.3	25.0	44.4	25.7
1788	16.7	7.1	14.3	16.7	32.5	22.2	21.4
1789	41.7	21.4	23.8	25.0	50.0	37.0	37.1
1790	25.0	14.3	23.8	50.0	45.0	40.7	37.1
1791	25.0	21.4	14.3	8.3	20.0	18.5	17.9
1792	16.7	21.4	4.8	16.7	40.0	25.9	25.0
1793	25.0	28.6	33.3	16.7	45.0	25.9	32.1
1794		14.3	4.8	16.7	5.0	7.4	8.6
1795		7.1	4.8		10.0	18.5	10.0
1796		7.1	9.5		22.5	3.7	12.1
1797	16.7	14.3	14.3	16.7	25.0	14.8	18.6
1798	33.3		9.5	25.0	12.5	22.2	16.4
1799		21.4	33.3		37.5	37.0	25.7
1800	8.3	42.9	4.8	8.3	12.5	40.7	19.3
1801	25.0	14.3	4.8	25.0	37.5	40.7	27.1
1802	8.3	14.3	4.8	25.0	30.0	11.1	17.1
1803	25.0	21.4	28.6		30.0	37.0	27.9
1804	25.0	28.6	9.5	41.7	50.0	25.9	30.7
1805	8.3	14.3	9.5	41.7	25.0	33.3	25.7
1806	16.7	14.3	14.3	25.0	17.5	29.6	18.6
1807	8.3	28.6	9.5	16.7	32.5	37.0	27.9
1808	8.3	14.3	23.8	41.7	30.0	18.5	22.9
1809	25.0	7.1	9.5	16.7	27.5	11.1	16.4
1810	8.3	7.1	4.8	25.0	22.5	18.5	17.1
1811	8.3	35.7	23.8	25.0	12.5	25.9	20.0
1812	25.0	35.7	14.3	50.0	15.0	25.9	23.6
1813		64.3	9.5	50.0	22.5	14.8	24.3
1814	16.7	7.1	14.3	25.0		18.5	10.0
1815		28.6	9.5	8.3	10.0	18.5	13.6
1816	8.3		4.8	8.3	7.5	18.5	10.7
1817		7.1	14.3	8.3	10.0	7.4	7.9
1818	8.3	14.3	9.5		15.0	29.6	15.0
1819	8.3	14.3	23.8	25.0	30.0	29.6	25.0
1820	8.3		9.5	16.7	37.5	25.9	22.9
1821	16.7	21.4	23.8	16.7	52.5	55.6	38.6
1822	16.7		14.3	41.7	35.0	25.9	23.6
1823	16.7	28.6	14.3	41.7	25.0	25.9	24.3
1824	8.3	28.6	19.0	41.7	30.0	40.7	28.6
1825	8.3	21.4	19.0	16.7	25.0	22.2	18.6
1826				8.3	30.0	29.6	17.9
1827		28.6	33.3	16.7	32.5	25.9	25.7
1828	25.0	7.1	19.0	16.7	35.0	22.2	22.9
1829	8.3	7.1	14.3	33.3	37.5	25.9	24.3
1830	33.3	35.7	23.8	16.7	22.5	18.5	25.0
1831	8.3	7.1	14.3	25.0	30.0	33.3	22.9
1832	16.7	28.6	19.0	33.3	37.5	44.4	32.1
1833	33.3	35.7	14.3	33.3	50.0	55.6	40.0
1834	16.7	28.6	28.6	25.0	42.5	44.4	34.3
1835	8.3	14.3	23.8	25.0	30.0	29.6	24.3
1836	16.7	14.3	9.5	16.7	25.0	22.2	19.3
1837		14.3	4.8	41.7	25.0	33.3	22.1
1838	8.3	14.3	23.8	41.7	25.0	29.6	25.0
1839	16.7		28.6	25.0	37.5	37.0	26.4
1840	16.7	7.1	4.8	16.7	30.0	25.9	22.1
1841	16.7	14.3	28.6	33.3	47.5	33.3	35.0
1842		7.1	19.0	8.3	45.0	18.5	24.3
1843	8.3	14.3	14.3	16.7	35.0	18.5	22.9
1844	33.3	28.6	19.0	50.0	30.0	37.0	30.0
1845		21.4	38.1		32.5	44.4	28.6
1846	25.0	14.3	42.9	8.3	47.5	48.1	37.1
1847	8.3	14.3	23.8	16.7	40.0	37.0	30.7
1848		7.1	23.8	25.0	27.5	37.0	26.4
1849	33.3	14.3	33.3	16.7	30.0	40.7	31.4
1850	16.7	35.7	42.9	25.0	35.0	48.1	36.4
1851	33.3	21.4	14.3	8.3	45.0	55.6	39.3
1852	16.7	7.1	23.8	25.0	32.5	37.0	31.4
1853	25.0	28.6	28.6	33.3	17.5	29.6	26.4
1854	8.3		38.1	33.3	27.5	25.9	22.9
1855	25.0	14.3	38.1	16.7	32.5	33.3	26.4
1856		21.4	23.8	25.0	42.5	51.9	37.9
1857	25.0	14.3	14.3	8.3	22.5	7.4	20.7
1858		7.1	23.8	33.3	20.0	29.6	23.6
1859	33.3	7.1	23.8	33.3	32.5	44.4	29.3
1860	25.0	14.3	28.6	58.3	27.5	48.1	32.1
1861	8.3	7.1	9.5	41.7	32.5	33.3	27.1

TABLE 53—PERCENTAGE OF COMMODITIES WHICH DECREASED IN PRICE 2.5 PER CENT OR MORE FROM THE PREVIOUS YEAR

Year	Farm		Imported Foods	Lumber Products and Naval Stores	Industrial		Total
	Crops	Derivatives			Raw	Con-sumption	
1785	25.0	78.6	57.1	75.0	47.5	81.5	57.9
1786	50.0	57.1	28.6	100.0	50.0	14.8	45.7
1787	41.7	71.4	38.1	83.3	47.5	11.1	43.6
1788	75.0	92.9	61.9	66.7	35.0	63.0	60.0
1789	41.7	42.9	42.9	8.3	25.0	25.9	30.7
1790	16.7	7.1	33.3		27.5	25.9	20.7
1791	50.0	35.7	19.0	33.3	47.5	11.1	32.9
1792	50.0	42.9	47.6	33.3	22.5	49.6	31.4
1793			28.6	16.7	10.0	25.9	15.7
1794	33.3	7.1	28.6		20.0	3.7	16.4
1795	16.7	14.3	14.3		10.0	14.8	12.1
1796	8.3	28.6	38.1	16.7	27.5	33.3	27.1
1797	41.7	71.4	47.6	33.3	27.5	63.0	45.0
1798	50.0	64.3	66.7	58.3	40.0	44.4	52.1
1799	66.7	42.9	19.0	75.0	17.5	37.0	33.6
1800	33.3	7.1	52.4	16.7	37.5	40.7	34.3
1801	8.3	7.1	76.2	33.3	25.0	22.2	27.9
1802	58.3	71.4	76.2	50.0	47.5	74.1	60.0
1803	41.7	57.1	42.9	33.3	30.0	48.1	41.4
1804	16.7	7.1	19.0	25.0	15.0	14.8	15.7
1805	25.0	14.3	52.4	33.3	32.5	22.2	30.0
1806	58.3	50.0	61.9	58.3	22.5	55.6	47.9
1807	66.7	64.3	61.9	41.7	40.0	59.3	50.7
1808	75.0	78.6	28.6	33.3	32.5	33.3	40.7
1809	25.0	7.1	14.3	8.3	15.0	14.8	13.6
1810	25.0	7.1	66.7	8.3	30.0	40.7	30.0
1811	58.3	21.4	52.4	50.0	62.5	44.4	46.4
1812	41.7	50.0	14.3	50.0	30.0	11.1	28.6
1813	41.7	14.3	4.8		7.5	18.5	13.6
1814	16.7	28.6	19.0		20.0	18.5	17.9
1815	50.0	14.3	71.4	41.7	67.5	59.3	56.4
1816	16.7	35.7	85.7	75.0	70.0	63.0	62.9
1817	41.7	42.9	85.7	91.7	90.0	85.2	79.3
1818	66.7	64.3	42.9	41.7	42.5	37.0	46.4
1819	66.7	85.7	61.9	58.3	55.0	48.1	58.6
1820	83.3	100.0	85.7	75.0	52.5	70.4	70.7
1821	83.3	64.3	42.9	75.0	20.0	29.6	42.1
1822	33.3	35.7	47.6	8.3	32.5	48.1	37.1
1823	50.0	50.0	81.0	41.7	52.5	55.6	57.9
1824	58.3	42.9	57.1	41.7	47.5	48.1	50.0
1825	16.7	42.9	14.3	25.0	22.5	40.7	28.6
1826	58.3	64.3	71.4	58.3	50.0	48.1	56.4
1827	66.7	35.7	38.1	58.3	50.0	44.4	49.3
1828	66.7	50.0	57.1	41.7	47.5	44.4	49.3
1829	33.3	57.1	61.9	66.7	40.0	44.4	49.3
1830	58.3	42.9	66.7	83.3	57.5	63.0	60.7
1831	25.0		38.1	8.3	22.5	22.2	22.1
1832	25.0	35.7	19.0	16.7	32.5	11.1	25.7
1833	33.3	21.4	57.1	16.7	30.0	33.3	32.9
1834	66.7	71.4	61.9	25.0	32.5	48.1	46.4
1835	8.3		19.0	33.3	37.5	25.9	25.7
1836	8.3		42.9	16.7	17.5	22.2	21.4
1837	50.0	42.9	85.7	41.7	30.0	14.8	40.7
1838	66.7	50.0	47.6	50.0	47.5	48.1	49.3
1839	16.7	35.7	38.1	33.3	17.5	29.6	27.1
1840	83.3	92.9	66.7	66.7	62.5	66.7	67.9
1841	33.3	71.4	33.3	50.0	35.0	59.3	43.6
1842	75.0	78.6	52.4	83.3	45.0	59.3	60.0
1843	83.3	71.4	23.8	83.3	57.5	63.0	57.9
1844	33.3	42.9	23.8	50.0	32.5	37.0	32.9
1845	25.0		19.0	33.3	32.5	18.5	23.6
1846	16.7	50.0	33.3	25.0	27.5	18.5	30.0
1847	8.3	7.1	33.3	58.3	32.5	22.2	27.9
1848	91.7	85.7	71.4	58.3	52.5	37.0	57.9
1849	41.7	57.1	33.3	50.0	47.5	48.1	45.0
1850	8.3	28.6	9.5	8.3	27.5	29.6	20.7
1851	25.0	28.6	47.6		35.0	29.6	29.3
1852	33.3	7.1	57.1	25.0	37.5	37.0	32.1
1853		7.1	23.8	8.3	20.0	14.8	15.7
1854	16.7	42.9	28.6	8.3	15.0	7.4	17.9
1855	8.3	14.3	28.6	83.3	37.5	11.1	29.3
1856	66.7	50.0	23.8	75.0	32.5	29.6	36.4
1857	16.7	28.6	33.3	33.3	45.0	48.1	35.0
1858	100.0	78.6	76.2	41.7	65.0	63.0	67.1
1859	8.3	21.4	57.1	16.7	32.5	48.1	37.1
1860	66.7	50.0	33.3	25.0	45.0	33.3	40.0
1861	58.3	92.9	33.3	16.7	57.5	33.3	45.7

Table 54—Percentage of Years in which Price of Each Commodity Changed Less than 2.5 Per Cent from Previous Year by Periods 1785–1861

Group and Commodity	1785–1808	1809–1821	1822–1843	1844–1861
Farm Crops				
Corn	0.0	15.4	4.5	11.1
Cotton	29.2	0.0	13.6	5.6
Flax	20.8	7.7	9.1	27.8
Flaxseed	16.7	0.0	13.6	22.2
Hemp	20.8	15.4	22.7	38.9
Oats	12.5	23.1	0.0	22.2
Peas	33.3	15.4	31.8	5.6
Rice	4.2	15.4	22.7	11.1
Rye	4.2	0.0	0.0	5.6
Tobacco				
James River	25.0	15.4	18.2	27.8
Kentucky	20.8	15.4	9.1	22.2
Wheat	0.0	0.0	9.1	11.1
Farm Derivatives				
Beef	12.5	23.1	31.8	16.7
Bread	12.5	7.7	27.3	16.7
Butter	12.5	23.1	4.5	27.8
Cheese	8.3	30.8	22.7	22.2
Corn meal	8.3	7.7	4.5	16.7
Feathers	37.5	38.5	22.7	22.2
Flour	8.3	7.7	9.1	5.6
Ginseng	25.0	15.4	18.2	5.6
Hams	8.3	7.7	18.2	16.7
Hides	37.5	7.7	31.8	16.7
Lard	16.7	7.7	13.6	11.1
Pork	25.0	23.1	13.6	5.6
Rye meal	4.2	7.7	0.0	22.2
Tallow	25.0	53.8	9.1	11.1
Imported Foods				
Almonds	16.7	15.4	9.1	0.0
Chocolate	25.0	61.5	18.2	61.1
Cloves	4.2	15.4	9.1	11.1
Cocoa	12.5	7.7	27.3	61.1
Coffee	4.2	15.4	22.7	33.3
Currants	8.3	15.4	13.6	0.0
Ginger				
ground	12.5	7.7	36.4	55.6
race	12.5	0.0	13.6	22.2
Honey	29.2	15.4	18.2	27.8
Lemons	12.5	0.0	9.1	11.1
Mace	16.7	7.7	13.6	38.9
Molasses	8.3	7.7	18.2	27.8
Nutmegs	12.5	7.7	27.3	5.6
Oil, sweet	20.8	15.4	36.4	38.9
Pepper	12.5	15.4	27.3	38.9
Pimento	12.5	15.4	0.0	22.2
Raisins	12.5	30.8	0.0	5.6
Sugar, Havana brown	8.3	7.7	18.2	22.2
Tea	29.2	0.0	18.2	33.3

Group and Commodity	1785–1808	1809–1821	1822–1843	1844–1861
Industrial Raw and Semi-Finished				
Alum	12.5	7.7	31.8	27.8
Ashes				
pearl	33.3	15.4	36.4	16.7
pot	25.0	15.4	18.2	16.7
Beeswax				
white	37.5	30.8	27.3	33.3
yellow	37.5	30.8	45.5	22.2
Brimstone				
crude	25.0	15.4	9.1	16.7
rolls	25.0	7.7	22.7	22.2
Copper				
old	25.0	7.7	31.8	27.8
sheathing	25.0	15.4	40.9	50.0
Copperas	8.3	0.0	27.3	33.3
Fustic	8.3	7.7	22.7	5.6
Indigo	25.0	15.4	22.7	11.1
Iron				
bar domestic	29.2	53.8	31.8	16.7
bar foreign	37.5	30.8	40.9	22.2
hop	33.3	46.2	45.5	38.9
nail rod	33.3	53.8	31.8	38.9
pig	20.8	23.1	27.3	22.2
sheet	41.7	46.2	27.3	38.9
Lead	25.0	30.8	0.0	38.9
Lead				
red	37.5	7.7	40.9	33.3
white dry	41.7	7.7	50.0	38.9
white ground in oil	45.8	46.2	40.9	38.9
Leather	37.5	30.8	36.4	33.3
Logwood	12.5	7.7	27.3	22.2
Mahogany	20.8	7.7	31.8	33.3
Oil				
linseed	8.3	0.0	18.2	11.1
sperm	12.5	0.0	31.8	33.3
whale	0.0	7.7	13.6	11.1
Plaster of Paris	4.2	0.0	9.1	22.2
Saltpeter				
refined	8.3	15.4	4.5	33.3
rough	8.3	15.4	13.6	11.1
Spanish brown				
dry	33.3	23.1	59.1	66.7
ground in oil	45.8	23.1	40.9	44.4
Steel				
country	41.7	46.2	50.0	88.9
English				
blistered	45.8	15.4	90.9	77.8
German	37.5	15.4	72.7	61.1
Crowley and Trieste	62.5	38.5	72.7	38.9
Tin				
block	41.7	23.1	27.3	11.1
plate	45.8	15.4	40.9	61.1
Verdigris	20.8	7.7	18.2	5.6

TABLE 54 (*Concluded*)

Group and Commodity	1785-1808	1809-1821	1822-1843	1844-1861
LUMBER PRODUCTS AND NAVAL STORES				
Pine boards				
heart	37.5	7.7	27.3	22.2
sap	16.7	46.2	45.5	27.8
white	8.3	23.1	22.7	27.8
Pitch	8.3	7.7	27.3	11.1
Rosin	12.5	7.7	27.3	16.7
Shingles	29.2	23.1	50.0	44.4
Staves				
barrel	20.8	38.5	22.7	27.8
hogshead	20.8	53.8	31.8	33.3
pipe	20.8	38.5	22.7	38.9
Tar	20.8	0.0	18.2	11.1
Turpentine				
spirits	8.3	7.7	9.1	16.7
unspecified	12.5	0.0	9.1	27.8
FISH				
Cod	20.8	7.7	18.2	5.6
Herring	8.3	30.8	9.1	16.7
Mackerel	12.5	0.0	9.1	5.6
FURS				
Beaver	20.8	15.4	31.8	55.6
Deer	20.8	38.5	4.5	38.9
Muskrat	12.5	15.4	9.1	55.6
WINES				
Claret	20.8	7.7	31.8	33.3
Lisbon	41.7	30.8	36.4	72.2
Madeira	37.5	30.8	50.0	66.7
Malaga	33.3	15.4	4.5	55.6
Port	37.5	15.4	27.3	50.0
Sherry	29.2	38.5	40.9	44.4
Teneriffe				
cargo	20.8	23.1	40.9	27.8
particular	33.3	23.1	45.5	38.9

Group and Commodity	1785-1808	1809-1821	1822-1843	1844-1861
INDUSTRIAL READY FOR CONSUMPTION				
Brandy	12.5	0.0	27.3	11.1
Candles				
sperm	41.7	38.5	13.6	22.2
tallow	4.2	23.1	9.1	16.7
Coal				
anthracite	25.0	15.4	9.1	22.2
bituminous	25.0	7.7	27.3	5.6
Cordage				
American	41.7	38.5	13.6	50.0
foreign	37.5	23.1	31.8	50.0
Duck				
bear ravens	37.5	23.1	22.7	94.4
ravens	33.3	23.1	36.4	83.3
Gin	16.7	15.4	40.9	50.0
Glass	37.5	53.8	45.5	77.8
Gunpowder	16.7	23.1	81.8	55.6
Nails	58.3	53.8	31.8	11.1
Rum				
Jamaica	16.7	0.0	45.5	16.7
New England	8.3	7.7	18.2	38.9
West India	25.0	15.4	45.5	16.7
Salt				
coarse	12.5	7.7	4.5	5.6
fine	4.2	7.7	22.7	16.7
Soap				
castile	20.8	23.1	36.4	38.9
white	29.2	38.5	18.2	44.4
yellow	29.2	30.8	36.4	50.0
Sheeting				
Russian brown	41.7	15.4	31.8	72.2
Russian white	54.2	30.8	31.8	88.9
Shot	25.0	30.8	27.3	33.3
Starch	12.5	38.5	40.9	27.8
Sugar				
loaf and lump	33.3	15.4	45.5	11.1
Havana white	12.5	23.1	18.2	22.2

TABLE 55—PERCENTAGE OF ANNUAL FREQUENCY OF MONTHLY PRICE CHANGES OF 135 COMMODITIES 1791–1860

Decade	0	1	2	3	4	5	6	7	8	9
1790		31.0	17.2	18.0	35.5	34.0	43.2	22.7	23.9	39.2
1800	40.5	27.9	25.0	16.8	20.2	13.4	31.7	28.5	27.3	36.8
1810	31.4	30.7	27.0	18.7	39.7	44.4	36.0	27.4	40.1	37.6
1820	21.3	23.5	23.5	18.9	22.6	38.0	34.9	36.1	32.7	31.5
1830	29.7	34.3	29.5	33.1	20.4	47.6	41.3	42.5	39.0	35.2
1840	36.8	37.0	38.1	39.1	41.7	43.5	43.1	45.7	42.7	43.1
1850	42.2	37.6	39.5	40.8	35.7	38.8	38.1	39.9	33.8	33.5
1860	34.1									

Table 56—Percentage of Frequency of Monthly Price Changes of 135 Commodities by 20-Year Periods 1791–1860

1791–1810	1811–1830	1821–1840	1841–1860
	Farm Crops		
15.0 hops	18.8 peas	15.0 peas	18.4 tobacco, James River
18.6 peas	19.2 tobacco, James River	18.8 tobacco, James River	27.1 peas
19.0 tobacco, Kentucky	19.2 flax	22.5 flax	34.6 flax
23.3 flax	26.7 tobacco, Kentucky	33.3 tobacco, Kentucky	36.3 hemp
23.6 tobacco, James River	37.9 flaxseed	49.2 rice	38.4 tobacco, Kentucky
25.9 cloverseed	40.9 hops	56.7 hemp	74.2 hops
31.3 oats	46.3 cloverseed	59.2 hops	76.7 rice
31.7 rye	47.5 rye	61.7 cloverseed	78.4 flaxseed
32.4 hemp	47.9 cotton, Georgia	62.5 cotton, Georgia	83.8 rye
39.6 flaxseed	51.7 rice	64.2 flaxseed	84.2 cotton, Georgia
45.9 cotton, Georgia	54.6 hemp	70.8 rye	89.6 cloverseed
51.3 rice	56.3 oats	72.1 oats	90.9 oats
52.5 wheat	62.9 wheat	76.3 wheat	95.0 corn, Indian
65.0 corn, Indian	67.5 corn, Indian	82.5 corn, Indian	96.3 wheat
	Farm Derivatives		
10.7 hides, raw	15.0 beef, prime	16.3 beef, mess	32.1 bread, pilot
12.6 ginseng	15.4 beef, mess	20.4 beef, prime	32.9 bread, small water
14.2 feathers	15.4 feathers	28.3 hides, raw	44.2 beef, prime
17.7 bread, small water	22.5 hides, raw	28.8 cheese	48.4 cheese
20.2 bread, pilot	24.6 ginseng	30.5 bread, small water	52.5 beef, mess
20.8 tallow	27.1 tallow	32.5 bread, pilot	57.5 tallow
24.1 beef, prime	27.9 bread, pilot	32.9 feathers	58.4 hides, raw
26.4 beef, mess	28.8 bread, small water	32.9 ginseng	61.7 ginseng
27.6 cheese	32.5 hams	37.1 hams	70.8 hams
34.6 pork, prime	33.4 cheese	38.0 tallow	74.2 butter
37.3 butter	40.9 lard, hogs	50.9 butter	77.9 feathers
40.5 pork, Burlington	42.5 pork, prime	53.4 lard, hogs	82.9 corn meal
40.9 lard, hogs	42.9 butter	53.8 pork, prime	83.9 pork, prime
41.4 hams	47.1 pork, Burlington	63.4 pork, Burlington	85.0 lard, hogs
45.8 corn meal	60.4 corn meal	72.9 corn meal	86.3 rye meal
55.5 rye meal	75.0 rye meal	77.9 rye meal	91.3 pork, Burlington
65.9 flour	81.3 flour	85.4 flour	97.5 flour
	Imported Foods		
10.4 honey	17.5 ginger, ground	13.8 cocoa, Island	5.4 cocoa, Island
16.9 ginger, race	17.5 cocoa, Island	14.2 ginger, ground	8.8 ginger, ground
18.2 oil, sweet	18.4 mace	17.9 mace	16.3 tea, Hyson skin
20.4 currants	22.1 almonds	20.4 tea, Souchong	16.7 tea, Souchong
20.5 ginger, ground	22.9 oil, sweet	20.9 almonds	16.7 tea, Hyson
24.9 lemons	27.5 honey	22.5 oil, sweet	20.0 oil, sweet
26.0 mace	30.0 ginger, race	23.8 tea, Hyson skin	20.4 almonds
27.5 cloves	30.0 currants	26.7 tea, Hyson	25.4 mace
27.8 cocoa, Island	30.9 tea, Souchong	28.4 currants	26.3 ginger, race
29.4 almonds	37.1 tea, Hyson	34.2 cloves	28.8 molasses, Sugar House
32.9 tea, Souchong	40.8 cloves	38.4 honey	34.2 currants
33.8 tea, Hyson	43.8 tea, Hyson skin	39.6 ginger, race	35.4 cloves
37.3 nutmegs	45.4 nutmegs	40.9 molasses, Sugar House	44.2 pimento
40.8 pimento	51.3 pepper	43.8 nutmegs	49.2 pepper
41.7 sugar, Havana brown	51.3 lemons	49.6 molasses, West India	49.6 nutmegs
43.6 pepper	55.4 pimento	50.8 pimento	55.4 honey
45.9 molasses, Sugar House	57.1 sugar, Havana brown	53.8 sugar, Havana brown	56.7 sugar, Havana brown
48.8 tea, Hyson skin	57.1 molasses, West India	54.6 pepper	58.4 coffee, St. Domingo
49.2 molasses, West India	59.2 coffee, St. Domingo	57.1 coffee, St. Domingo	72.9 molasses, West India
60.0 coffee, St. Domingo	59.8 molasses, Sugar House	63.8 lemons	73.8 lemons

TABLE 56 (*Continued*)

1791-1810	1811-1830	1821-1840	1841-1860
	LUMBER PRODUCTS AND NAVAL STORES		
9.9 pine boards, heart	8.3 pine boards, heart	7.5 shingles, long	10.0 staves, pipe
10.1 shingles, long	9.6 pine boards, sap	7.9 pine boards, sap	11.3 staves, white oak hogshead
11.7 pine boards, white	10.0 pine boards, white	8.8 pine boards, white	11.7 staves, barrel
15.5 staves, white oak hogshead	10.0 staves, pipe	10.5 staves, pipe	12.9 shingles, long
17.4 staves, pipe	10.9 staves, white oak hogshead	12.9 pine boards, heart	32.9 pine boards, heart
19.2 staves, barrel	11.3 shingles, long	13.4 staves, white oak hogshead	34.2 turpentine
19.4 pine boards, sap	11.7 staves, barrel	15.0 staves, barrel	34.2 pine boards, sap
25.8 turpentine	23.4 pitch	18.8 pitch	38.4 pine boards, white
26.0 rosin	24.2 rosin	19.2 rosin	48.4 pitch
27.0 spirits of turpentine	37.1 spirits of turpentine	49.2 tar	64.2 tar
33.1 pitch	40.0 turpentine	49.6 spirits of turpentine	71.3 rosin
39.3 tar	50.4 tar	52.1 turpentine	92.1 spirits of turpentine
	INDUSTRIAL RAW AND SEMI-FINISHED COMMODITIES		
9.0 iron, sheet	5.0 steel, Crowley	2.1 steel, English blistered	2.1 steel, English blistered
9.5 steel, English blistered	6.7 steel, American	3.4 steel, Crowley	2.5 steel, German
10.0 steel, German	10.0 steel, German	4.6 steel, German	2.9 steel, American
10.6 steel, Crowley	10.4 iron, sheet	5.4 iron, hoop	5.4 mahogany, St. Domingo
11.4 steel, American	10.8 iron, hoop	6.3 steel, American	8.4 iron, hoop
12.2 leather, sole	10.9 steel, English blistered	7.5 mahogany, St. Domingo	14.6 mahogany, Bay
12.3 iron, pig	12.1 mahogany, St. Domingo	10.4 mahogany, Bay	15.0 tin plate
12.9 mahogany, Bay	12.9 mahogany, Bay	11.3 logwood, chipt	16.3 fustic
13.9 indigo, French	15.4 iron, bar, American	12.9 leather, sole	17.1 brimstone, rolls
15.0 lead, pig	17.1 leather, sole	12.9 iron, sheet	17.9 iron, sheet
15.4 mahogany, St. Domingo	18.8 iron, pig	14.2 tin plate	18.0 copperas
16.8 tin plate	19.2 logwood, chipt	16.7 indigo, French	18.4 steel, Crowley
18.4 iron, bar, Swedish	21.3 indigo, French	19.6 lead, bar	19.2 leather, sole
19.2 copper sheathing	22.5 lead, bar	20.0 iron, bar, American	19.2 verdigris
19.3 lead, bar	22.9 fustic	21.3 fustic	19.6 saltpeter, refined
20.3 fustic	22.9 verdigris	21.7 copperas	22.5 logwood, Campeachy
20.5 verdigris	27.1 saltpeter, refined	22.1 verdigris	22.9 lead, bar
20.8 alum	27.9 brimstone, rolls	23.8 logwood, Campeachy	24.6 iron, bar, American
24.0 logwood, chipt	28.8 iron, bar, Swedish	23.8 iron, pig	25.0 indigo, French
24.6 iron, bar, American	29.6 alum	24.2 alum	30.0 alum
28.8 oil, sperm	29.6 tin plate	25.8 brimstone, rolls	34.2 iron, bar, Swedish
29.4 iron, hoop	30.0 copper sheathing	25.8 saltpeter, refined	34.6 logwood, chipt
31.7 copperas	31.3 logwood, Campeachy	30.0 iron, bar, Swedish	40.4 copper sheathing
31.8 ashes, pearl	33.4 ashes, pearl	38.0 copper sheathing	40.9 oil, sperm
33.1 brimstone, rolls	35.0 ashes, pot	40.8 oil, sperm	51.3 iron, pig
35.2 oil, whale	36.3 beeswax, yellow	45.4 beeswax, yellow	59.6 ashes, pot
36.3 beeswax, yellow	37.1 copperas	45.4 oil, whale	72.1 beeswax, yellow
36.4 logwood, Campeachy	41.7 oil, sperm	48.8 ashes, pearl	72.9 ashes, pearl
38.4 ashes, pot	42.9 lead, pig	49.6 ashes, pot	74.2 oil, whale
39.1 saltpeter, refined	46.3 oil, whale	59.6 lead, pig	76.3 lead, pig
41.3 oil, linseed	60.0 oil, linseed	68.4 plaster of Paris	84.2 plaster of Paris
50.4 plaster of Paris	61.7 plaster of Paris	81.3 oil, linseed	91.7 oil, linseed

TABLE 56 (*Concluded*)

1791–1810	1811–1830	1821–1840	1841–1860
INDUSTRIAL COMMODITIES READY FOR CONSUMPTION			
6.1 nails	7.9 soap, white	4.6 gunpowder	2.1 duck, ravens
10.0 soap, white	9.6 glass	6.7 glass	2.5 duck, bear ravens
12.6 soap, yellow	10.0 soap, yellow	9.6 cordage, foreign	2.9 glass
19.3 candles, sperm	11.3 nails	11.3 soap, Castile	3.3 gunpowder
19.3 coal, bituminous	12.1 soap, Castile	12.5 cordage, American	3.8 sheeting, Russian brown
20.0 starch	13.8 cordage, foreign	13.4 coal, bituminous	6.3 soap, white
21.0 soap, Castile	14.6 gunpowder	13.8 soap, white	7.1 cordage, American
21.1 cordage, American	17.1 candles, tallow dipt	14.2 soap, yellow	8.3 soap, yellow
21.7 sugar, loaf	17.5 cordage, American	16.3 gin, Holland	10.4 gin, Holland
22.4 cordage, foreign	18.4 duck, bear ravens	16.7 duck, bear ravens	15.0 rum, Jamaica
23.8 duck, bear ravens	20.9 starch	17.5 duck, ravens	17.5 soap, Castile
26.9 candles, tallow mold	21.3 shot	18.8 shot	17.5 candles, tallow dipt
26.9 candles, tallow dipt	21.7 duck, ravens	21.3 candles, tallow dipt	17.9 shot
27.1 glass	23.8 candles, tallow mold	22.5 nails	19.6 cordage, foreign
27.9 sheeting, Russian brown	23.8 coal, bituminous	22.5 starch	21.3 candles, tallow mold
28.4 duck, ravens	24.2 sugar, loaf	22.5 sugar, loaf	21.7 nails
29.6 shot	27.1 sheeting, Russian brown	25.0 rum, Jamaica	26.3 starch
35.0 gunpowder	34.2 gin, Holland	25.4 candles, tallow mold	29.2 salt, fine
37.8 salt, fine	35.5 candles, sperm	30.9 sheeting, Russian brown	33.8 brandy, French
45.7 whiskey, apple	44.6 sugar, Havana white	40.0 sugar, Havana white	45.4 whiskey, apple
45.9 sugar, Havana white	48.8 rum, Jamaica	43.8 candles, sperm	46.3 sugar, loaf
47.2 gin, Holland	53.4 salt, fine	57.1 salt, fine	46.7 candles, sperm
50.7 brandy, French	55.9 rum, New England	57.5 brandy, French	50.0 sugar, Havana white
53.3 rum, Jamaica	56.7 whiskey, apple	59.2 whiskey, apple	63.3 coal, bituminous
60.5 rum, New England	58.8 brandy, French	67.9 rum, New England	73.3 rum, New England
FISH			
26.3 herring	28.8 herring	30.0 herring	49.2 herring
28.3 mackerel, #1	28.8 codfish	35.5 codfish	57.1 codfish
32.0 codfish	53.0 mackerel, #3	64.6 mackerel, #3	80.4 mackerel, #3
36.0 mackerel, #2	59.6 mackerel, #1	75.0 mackerel, #1	82.1 mackerel, #2
38.3 mackerel, #3	68.8 mackerel, #2	80.5 mackerel, #2	83.3 mackerel, #1
FURS			
10.0 beaver	8.8 deer	11.7 beaver	4.6 beaver
11.9 muskrat	12.1 beaver	13.8 muskrat	7.5 muskrat
12.5 deer	13.8 muskrat	17.1 deer	15.0 deer
WINES			
17.2 Madeira	10.0 Madeira	5.0 Madeira	3.4 Madeira
20.4 Teneriffe cargo	12.9 claret	8.8 sherry	4.2 Lisbon
23.8 Lisbon	13.3 sherry	9.2 claret	5.0 claret
25.5 claret	16.3 Teneriffe cargo	10.0 Teneriffe cargo	6.7 Teneriffe cargo
31.7 sherry	17.1 port	10.0 port	8.8 sherry
32.7 Malaga	21.3 Lisbon	15.0 Lisbon	8.8 port
36.7 port	31.7 Malaga	43.8 Malaga	22.1 Malaga

Table 57—Seasonal Patterns of Selected Commodities by Decades 1785–1859

Month	1785–1790	1791–1800	1801–1810	1811–1820	1821–1830	1831–1840	1841–1850	1851–1859
				Corn				
January	84	100	101	103	99	93	98	98
February	87	98	103	103	99	92	97	96
March	91	99	104	101	95	92	94	92
April	94	94	95	96	97	98	98	97
May	103	96	96	91	99	98	102	102
June	108	96	96	95	98	99	100	100
July	110	99	98	98	99	103	98	101
August	106	96	99	103	99	109	105	102
September	107	103	104	98	104	108	103	106
October	109	109	101	102	105	111	105	107
November	108	105	106	105	104	105	105	103
December	93	105	97	105	102	92	95	96
				Wheat				
January	100	98	96	103	99	101	99	102
February	96	100	97	103	100	100	100	103
March	103	101	105	105	101	97	100	101
April	99	100	105	100	101	96	103	102
May	106	103	106	102	105	100	105	109
June	110	100	105	98	105	101	104	108
July	106	100	107	99	98	98	99	99
August	95	100	99	98	96	100	96	94
September	92	98	93	92	96	100	95	93
October	96	102	93	97	98	101	100	95
November	98	94	93	101	100	102	100	98
December	99	104	101	102	101	104	99	96
				Rice				
January	105	103	99	100	105	104	98	95
February	104	104	100	104	105	99	97	95
March	98	102	101	99	104	93	98	98
April	97	103	103	96	98	92	97	100
May	95	103	99	94	95	93	95	100
June	97	101	98	94	94	96	98	102
July	102	98	97	100	94	99	100	104
August	100	95	95	100	93	101	102	104
September	99	96	95	103	97	104	107	103
October	99	97	99	104	101	107	106	100
November	100	98	106	104	107	108	103	102
December	104	100	108	102	107	104	99	97
				Tobacco, James River				
January	101	100	99	102	99	99	102	100
February	101	98	100	102	100	101	100	99
March	100	99	101	101	100	100	101	100
April	99	102	100	102	100	99	101	101
May	98	104	100	104	101	99	99	101
June	98	102	101	101	100	99	98	100
July	98	101	101	97	100	98	96	100
August	100	100	101	96	100	99	99	100
September	100	100	101	95	100	102	99	100
October	101	99	98	99	100	102	98	100
November	102	98	99	100	100	101	103	100
December	102	97	99	101	100	101	104	99
				Cotton, Georgia				
January	100	100	102	106	100	101	100	96
February	100	97	102	102	98	96	99	96
March	100	97	100	102	98	98	102	98
April	98	100	96	102	98	99	99	101
May	100	99	98	98	99	98	98	100
June	102	97	98	97	101	98	98	100
July	102	100	96	96	101	102	98	101
August	103	101	98	95	101	103	102	105
September	98	101	97	96	101	100	102	104
October	98	103	103	101	101	100	103	104
November	100	103	104	101	100	101	101	98
December	99	102	106	104	102	104	98	97

TABLE 57 (*Continued*)

Month	1785–1790	1791–1800	1801–1810	1811–1820	1821–1830	1831–1840	1841–1850	1851–1859
				FLOUR				
January	96	99	100	105	100	103	100	102
February	97	103	101	104	100	100	101	100
March	100	101	98	99	100	97	99	99
April	100	98	95	98	99	95	101	99
May	105	99	99	93	100	99	101	103
June	108	99	100	96	100	98	99	102
July	103	100	102	97	96	99	96	99
August	102	99	100	98	97	99	100	97
September	99	99	102	99	101	101	98	98
October	98	99	100	101	102	101	102	99
November	96	101	101	104	105	105	102	101
December	96	103	102	106	100	103	101	101
				CORN MEAL				
January	98	106	101	101	100	98	99	98
February	101	106	101	101	99	97	98	99
March	99	103	103	99	100	95	97	94
April	96	100	100	97	100	95	96	96
May	97	100	97	96	97	97	101	99
June	97	99	96	96	97	97	100	100
July	104	96	96	97	96	100	96	97
August	103	94	97	101	95	102	101	101
September	103	94	100	102	102	107	103	107
October	101	99	103	103	107	108	106	106
November	101	101	105	106	106	105	104	106
December	100	102	101	101	101	99	99	97
				PORK				
January	99	97	96	101	101	96	103	93
February	97	97	95	99	99	97	101	96
March	96	99	96	100	97	98	99	100
April	95	100	95	99	97	98	98	101
May	97	99	97	98	97	100	99	102
June	99	100	100	99	99	101	98	102
July	101	100	104	99	99	100	99	102
August	103	101	105	98	101	101	101	102
September	105	102	104	99	102	103	102	105
October	105	102	104	102	104	104	100	102
November	104	102	104	104	104	103	100	99
December	99	101	100	102	100	99	100	96
				DAIRY PRODUCTS				
January	100	103	98	102	102	102	101	100
February	101	104	98	102	102	100	101	101
March	102	101	101	100	100	101	102	104
April	102	103	101	100	100	102	104	104
May	99	102	104	100	99	101	101	102
June	97	100	102	99	99	99	98	98
July	99	98	101	100	100	97	96	95
August	99	98	99	100	99	96	97	98
September	98	97	99	99	96	98	99	98
October	97	98	99	99	101	101	100	99
November	103	97	99	99	101	101	100	101
December	103	99	99	100	101	102	101	100
				MACKEREL, #1				
January	102		100	102	98	100	98	97
February	102		102	104	102	100	101	100
March	102		102	104	102	102	103	100
April	100		102	102	100	101	101	101
May	100		103	100	102	101	100	104
June	100		102	99	107	100	98	100
July	100		100	98	101	99	98	96
August	99		98	96	98	99	104	100
September	98		96	96	94	99	105	107
October	98		96	101	99	100	97	100
November	99		99	99	99	100	98	97
December	100		100	99	98	99	97	98

TABLE 57 (*Continued*)

Month	1785–1790	1791–1800	1801–1810	1811–1820	1821–1830	1831–1840	1841–1850	1851–1859
				COFFEE, ST. DOMINGO				
January	104	100	103	102	99	100	100	102
February	100	100	100	103	99	100	101	102
March	95	99	100	99	99	98	101	102
April	91	100	100	97	100	97	100	101
May	93	99	100	99	101	99	99	100
June	102	102	100	101	100	99	99	97
July	97	101	99	98	98	99	98	97
August	96	99	97	99	99	101	99	98
September	101	101	99	98	101	102	100	100
October	106	100	98	99	102	102	101	100
November	109	98	101	104	102	101	102	99
December	106	101	103	101	100	102	100	102
				TEA, HYSON SKIN				
January		102	102	105	100	102	100	99
February		101	101	106	100	101	101	99
March		100	101	96	101	101	100	99
April		98	98	94	100	101	100	100
May		97	97	91	101	100	100	101
June		97	98	94	101	98	99	101
July		100	98	99	101	98	100	101
August		100	100	100	99	99	100	101
September		100	101	100	99	99	101	100
October		101	102	106	99	99	100	100
November		102	101	105	100	100	100	99
December		102	101	104	99	102	99	100
				PEPPER				
January	105	101	100	101	97	100	99	99
February	103	101	99	100	98	100	101	98
March	102	100	100	97	100	99	100	99
April	99	100	100	98	101	99	101	100
May	97	100	102	101	103	100	101	101
June	97	99	99	99	103	100	101	101
July	98	98	97	101	103	101	100	101
August	97	96	100	100	101	101	99	101
September	102	99	100	101	99	100	100	101
October	99	103	101	102	98	99	100	101
November	100	100	100	102	98	100	100	99
December	101	103	102	98	99	101	98	99
				MOLASSES, WEST INDIA				
January	102	100	108	105	100	104	96	99
February	103	100	106	106	98	104	96	101
March	101	100	100	92	98	102	99	99
April	98	100	95	91	102	98	99	99
May	100	100	94	97	103	96	97	101
June	103	98	95	97	99	93	100	101
July	100	99	96	98	96	94	101	99
August	98	101	97	99	99	99	101	101
September	98	99	99	100	102	100	106	101
October	97	101	101	104	101	104	105	100
November	97	102	103	105	101	105	101	99
December	103	100	106	106	101	101	99	100
				SUGAR, HAVANA BROWN				
January	97	97	100	102	100	100	98	99
February	98	100	98	102	98	99	97	99
March	99	101	98	97	98	100	97	100
April	100	101	99	96	98	100	98	100
May	100	99	100	97	98	100	97	99
June	101	100	101	97	99	97	100	98
July	101	101	100	99	99	98	101	99
August	101	101	101	101	102	100	103	102
September	101	98	100	101	102	102	103	102
October	100	99	101	103	101	103	104	101
November	103	101	101	103	103	102	103	101
December	99	102	101	102	102	99	99	100

TABLE 57 (*Concluded*)

Month	1785–1790	1791–1800	1801–1810	1811–1820	1821–1830	1831–1840	1841–1850	1851–1859
				RUM, NEW ENGLAND				
January	98	100	105	108	102	105	104	106
February	101	99	106	109	101	103	100	104
March	100	100	104	100	98	97	100	103
April	98	99	99	97	98	96	98	100
May	102	103	99	94	99	98	96	97
June	104	103	99	94	99	95	97	95
July	104	101	97	96	99	96	96	96
August	100	101	97	97	99	97	98	98
September	99	100	97	99	99	102	100	98
October	99	98	98	101	101	104	104	100
November	98	98	98	102	102	103	104	100
December	97	98	101	103	103	104	103	103
				TAR				
January	111	113	118	115	103	105	98	100
February	111	110	116	114	100	101	96	99
March	112	111	112	115	101	98	97	98
April	99	98	98	93	97	95	96	89
May	94	98	93	83	95	93	94	97
June	89	87	92	85	96	94	95	98
July	89	89	86	93	96	95	95	97
August	87	99	89	94	101	99	101	99
September	95	95	89	100	100	103	108	106
October	101	98	93	100	105	105	109	106
November	100	97	104	102	102	104	109	107
December	112	105	110	106	104	108	102	104
				OIL, LINSEED				
January	96	96	99	95	96	98	94	98
February	94	92	95	99	100	100	102	101
March	94	90	94	104	103	102	104	99
April	99	95	96	101	103	104	103	100
May	97	96	98	101	101	103	101	98
June	98	100	103	102	100	98	100	99
July	106	101	102	101	100	98	101	99
August	116	107	102	101	99	101	101	101
September	108	108	103	100	100	101	101	106
October	103	108	101	99	101	101	101	104
November	95	104	104	97	100	98	97	98
December	94	103	103	100	97	96	95	97
				OIL, WHALE				
January	102		101	107	105	103	103	103
February	101		102	106	104	102	102	101
March	99		100	105	104	101	100	102
April	100		101	103	101	99	98	102
May	100		98	101	94	99	99	100
June	100		101	97	95	99	98	98
July	101		98	94	93	98	96	98
August	100		97	93	94	99	97	98
September	100		101	94	97	100	99	97
October	99		100	97	104	100	101	98
November	98		101	99	104	100	103	101
December	100		100	104	105	100	104	102
				LEAD, PIG				
January	98	100	102	98	100	101	105	98
February	100	100	102	98	99	100	101	99
March	100	100	101	98	99	99	102	102
April	99	99	102	100	99	101	100	103
May	102	99	100	100	99	100	97	102
June	99	99	99	97	100	97	97	101
July	99	99	99	100	100	98	97	100
August	101	101	97	102	100	99	95	99
September	99	101	98	102	100	99	98	99
October	102	100	98	101	101	99	101	99
November	103	101	101	102	102	103	104	100
December	98	101	101	102	101	104	103	98

Table 58—Summary of Cyclical Movements of 24 Sub-groups 1789–1861

Group	End of Preceding Recession	Peak	End of Succeeding Low	Number of Months			Index of Cyclical Variability
				Rise	Fall	Total Cycle	
Farm Products							
Grains	Apr. 1789	Apr. 1796	Nov. 1798	84	31	115	55.3
Tobacco	Dec. 1791	Nov. 1798	Sept. 1800	83	22	105	62.7
Minor	July 1789	Dec. 1796	May 1799	89	29	118	53.8
Foods							
Grain Products	Jan. 1788	Mar. 1796	July 1798	98	28	126	60.3
Meats and Meat Products	Aug. 1789	Oct. 1796	May 1799	86	31	117	46.1
Dairy Products	Oct. 1789	July 1795	Aug. 1797	69	25	94	47.0
Fish	Oct. 1788	Mar. 1797	Aug. 1800	101	41	142	60.8
Fruit	July 1789	May 1796	May 1799	82	36	118	43.8
Beverages	Sept. 1791	Feb. 1796	Nov. 1797	53	21	74	27.9
Condiments	May 1790	Jan. 1796	Sept. 1801	68	68	136	46.0
Sugar and Molasses	Apr. 1789	Feb. 1797	Aug. 1802	94	66	160	46.8
Chemicals and Dyes							
Chemicals	Oct. 1788	Oct. 1795	Apr. 1798	84	30	114	49.6
Dyes	Dec. 1791	Oct. 1795	Feb. 1796	46	4	50	37.0
Fuel and Lighting	Mar. 1789	Feb. 1796	Aug. 1799	83	42	125	38.1
Metals and Metal Products							
Ferrous							
Non-Ferrous	Apr. 1791	June 1799	Sept. 1800	98	15	113	25.2
Building Materials							
Wood	Mar. 1788	Feb. 1797	Nov. 1798	107	21	128	37.8
Other	Dec. 1787	Feb. 1797	Aug. 1799	110	30	140	38.6
Furs	Feb. 1788	Jan. 1797	Nov. 1798	107	22	129	41.9
Textiles							
Fibers	Oct. 1790	Jan. 1797	June 1800	75	41	116	32.4
Fabrics	Oct. 1790	Aug. 1797	Mar. 1800	82	31	113	26.8
Hides and Leather	June 1789	Jan. 1795	Dec. 1797	67	35	102	32.5
Spirits and Wines							
Spirits	Sept. 1788	Jan. 1796	Aug. 1799	88	43	131	54.7
Wines	Jan. 1789	Aug. 1796	June 1798	91	22	113	24.0
Farm Products							
Grains	Nov. 1798	Mar. 1801	Sept. 1803	28	30	58	35.4
Tobacco	Sept. 1800	Apr. 1802	Nov. 1802	19	7	26	11.7
Minor	May 1799	Sept. 1801	Sept. 1803	28	24	52	33.3
Foods							
Grain Products	July 1798	May 1801	June 1803	34	25	59	42.9
Meats and Meat Products	May 1799	Oct. 1801	Apr. 1803	29	18	47	39.5
Dairy Products	Aug. 1797	Oct. 1801	July 1803	50	21	71	30.8
Fish	Aug. 1800	Jan. 1802	Jan. 1804	17	24	41	38.8
Fruit	May 1799	June 1800	July 1803	13	37	50	34.8
Beverages	Nov. 1797	Dec. 1798	Sept. 1802	13	45	58	26.8
Condiments	Sept. 1801	Dec. 1801	June 1803	3	18	21	15.4
Sugar, Molasses							
Chemicals and Dyes							
Chemicals	Apr. 1798	Dec. 1798	Aug. 1802	8	44	52	26.2
Dyes	Feb. 1796	Aug. 1799	Dec. 1802	42	40	82	56.2
Fuel and Lighting	Aug. 1799	Nov. 1801	Dec. 1802	27	13	40	16.5
Metals and Metal Products							
Ferrous	Oct. 1787	Nov. 1801	Jan. 1805	169	38	207	25.3
Non-Ferrous	Sept. 1800	Apr. 1801	Aug. 1802	7	16	23	10.6
Building Materials							
Wood	Nov. 1798	June 1800	Aug. 1802	19	26	45	12.5
Other	Aug. 1799	Nov. 1801	June 1802	27	7	34	14.7
Furs	Nov. 1798	July 1800	Sept. 1802	20	26	46	19.5
Textiles							
Fibers	June 1800	Dec. 1800	Nov. 1802	6	23	29	29.0
Fabrics	Mar. 1800	June 1801	Mar. 1803	15	21	36	21.2
Hides and Leather							
Spirits and Wines							
Spirits	Aug. 1799	Mar. 1801	July 1807	19	76	95	24.0
Wines	June 1798	Feb. 1802	June 1803	44	16	60	17.7

TABLE 58 (*Continued*)

Group	End of Preceding Recession	Peak	End of Succeeding Low	Number of Months			Index of Cyclical Variability
				Rise	Fall	Total Cycle	
Farm Products							
Grains	Sept. 1803	May 1805	Dec. 1808	20	43	63	50.0
Tobacco	Nov. 1802	Sept. 1807	Jan. 1812	58	52	110	26.0
Minor	Sept. 1803	Dec. 1804	Dec. 1809	15	60	75	26.6
Foods							
Grain Products	June 1803	Mar. 1805	Sept. 1808	21	42	63	45.4
Meats and Meat Products	Apr. 1803	Aug. 1806	Sept. 1808	40	25	65	40.2
Dairy Products	July 1803	June 1805	Mar. 1809	23	45	68	45.0
Fish	Jan. 1804	Aug. 1806	Aug. 1808	31	24	55	34.7
Fruit	July 1803	June 1806	May 1807	35	11	46	43.8
Beverages	Sept. 1802	Nov. 1804	May 1808	26	42	68	26.2
Condiments	June 1803	Dec. 1805	May 1807	30	17	47	12.2
Sugar and Molasses	Aug. 1802	Feb. 1804	Aug. 1807	18	42	60	27.8
Chemicals and Dyes							
Chemicals	Aug. 1802	Dec. 1806	July 1807	52	7	59	12.5
Dyes	Dec. 1802	Feb. 1804	May 1808	14	51	65	41.1
Fuel and Lighting	Dec. 1802	Aug. 1805	Oct. 1808	32	38	70	26.7
Metals and Metal Products							
Ferrous							
Non-Ferrous	Aug. 1802	Apr. 1804	Oct. 1808	20	54	74	15.7
Building Materials							
Wood	Aug. 1802	Jan. 1805	Oct. 1808	29	45	74	10.3
Other	June 1802	Feb. 1805	June 1807	32	28	60	13.6
Furs	Sept. 1802	May 1805	Aug. 1808	32	39	71	18.8
Textiles							
Fibers	Nov. 1802	Jan. 1806	Sept. 1808	38	32	70	22.6
Fabrics							
Hides and Leather							
Spirits and Wines							
Spirits							
Wines	June 1803	June 1804	Oct. 1807	12	40	52	11.8
Farm Products							
Grains							
Tobacco							
Minor	Dec. 1809	July 1812	Oct. 1813	31	15	46	35.9
Foods							
Grain Products	Sept. 1808	Dec. 1810	July 1812	27	19	46	31.6
Meats and Meat Products	Sept. 1808	Apr. 1811	Sept. 1812	31	17	48	22.6
Dairy Products	Mar. 1809	Sept. 1811	Dec. 1812	30	15	45	24.5
Fish	Aug. 1808	May 1811	Sept. 1811	33	4	37	22.1
Fruit	May 1807	May 1809	June 1810	24	13	37	24.8
Beverages	May 1808	Feb. 1809	Dec. 1811	9	34	43	37.5
Condiments	May 1807	Jan. 1809	Dec. 1811	20	35	55	32.5
Sugar and Molasses	Aug. 1807	Oct. 1810	Apr. 1811	38	6	44	19.1
Chemicals and Dyes							
Chemicals	July 1807	Feb. 1809	July 1809	19	5	24	38.4
Dyes	May 1808	Oct. 1810	Jan. 1812	29	15	44	27.3
Fuel and Lighting							
Metals and Metal Products							
Ferrous	Jan. 1805	Apr. 1809	Jan. 1811	51	21	72	13.9
Non-Ferrous	Oct. 1808	Apr. 1809	June 1811	6	26	32	16.8
Building Materials							
Wood	Oct. 1808	Aug. 1810	Apr. 1813	22	32	54	10.7
Other	June 1807	May 1810	May 1812	35	24	59	26.7
Furs	Aug. 1808	Oct. 1811	Jan. 1814	38	27	65	20.4
Textiles							
Fibers	Sept. 1808	May 1809	Nov. 1811	8	30	38	31.7
Fabrics	Mar. 1803	May 1809	May 1812	74	36	110	44.7
Hides and Leather	Dec. 1797	July 1810	July 1811	151	12	163	34.0
Spirits and Wines							
Spirits	July 1807	Jan. 1809	June 1809	18	5	23	33.4
Wines	Oct. 1807	Oct. 1810	Feb. 1811	36	4	40	22.4

TABLE 58 (*Continued*)

Group	End of Preceding Recession	Peak	End of Succeeding Low	Number of Months: Rise	Number of Months: Fall	Number of Months: Total Cycle	Index of Cyclical Variability
Farm Products							
Grains	Dec. 1808	May 1817	Apr. 1821	101	47	148	71.4
Tobacco	Jan. 1812	Mar. 1816	Mar. 1825	50	108	158	71.2
Minor	Oct. 1813	Aug. 1817	Oct. 1821	46	50	96	56.7
Foods							
Grain Products	July 1812	Mar. 1817	Mar. 1821	56	48	104	59.9
Meats and Meat Products	Sept. 1812	Sept. 1815	May 1823	36	92	128	50.6
Dairy Products	Dec. 1812	Apr. 1817	June 1820	52	38	90	49.2
Fish	Sept. 1811	Aug. 1814	Aug. 1821	35	84	119	55.6
Fruit	June 1810	Apr. 1814	July 1820	46	75	121	49.2
Beverages	Dec. 1811	Oct. 1814	May 1820	34	67	101	54.4
Condiments	Dec. 1811	Nov. 1814	June 1824	35	115	150	62.3
Sugar and Molasses	Apr. 1811	Dec. 1813	July 1821	32	91	123	66.7
Chemicals and Dyes							
Chemicals	July 1809	Jan. 1814	Dec. 1819	54	71	125	66.5
Dyes	Jan. 1812	Jan. 1814	Mar. 1820	24	74	98	51.9
Fuel and Lighting	Oct. 1808	Jan. 1815	Sept. 1824	75	116	191	61.5
Metals and Metal Products							
Ferrous	Jan. 1811	Feb. 1815	Feb. 1825	49	120	169	33.8
Non-Ferrous	June 1811	Jan. 1815	Nov. 1821	43	82	125	62.5
Building Materials							
Wood	Apr. 1813	Mar. 1815	Apr. 1821	23	73	96	36.1
Other	May 1812	Mar. 1814	Oct. 1821	22	91	113	56.2
Furs	Jan. 1814	Jan. 1816	Mar. 1819	24	38	62	32.5
Textiles							
Fibers	Nov. 1811	Jan. 1814	May 1823	26	112	138	53.0
Fabrics	May 1812	Jan. 1814	Nov. 1826	20	154	174	42.9
Hides and Leather	July 1811	Apr. 1814	May 1820	33	73	106	46.3
Spirits and Wines							
Spirits	June 1809	Nov. 1814	May 1820	65	66	131	64.9
Wines	Feb. 1811	Feb. 1814	June 1824	36	124	160	45.0
Farm Products							
Grains	Apr. 1821	May 1822	Sept. 1824	13	28	41	44.0
Tobacco							
Minor	Oct. 1821	Nov. 1823	Oct. 1824	25	11	36	25.7
Foods							
Grain Products	Mar. 1821	Sept. 1822	July 1825	18	34	52	38.9
Meats and Meat Products							
Dairy Products	June 1820	Aug. 1822	Nov. 1824	26	27	53	43.7
Fish	Aug. 1821	Nov. 1821	Sept. 1824	3	34	37	19.9
Fruit	July 1820	Nov. 1822	July 1823	28	8	36	30.3
Beverages	May 1820	Oct. 1821	Dec. 1824	17	38	55	11.9
Condiments							
Sugar and Molasses	July 1821	Dec. 1821	Oct. 1824	5	34	39	12.8
Chemicals and Dyes							
Chemicals	Dec. 1819	Oct. 1822	Mar. 1823	34	5	39	9.5
Dyes	Mar. 1820	Dec. 1823	June 1824	45	6	51	18.3
Fuel and Lighting							
Metals and Metal Products							
Ferrous							
Non-Ferrous	Nov. 1821	July 1822	July 1824	8	24	32	6.2
Building Materials							
Wood	Apr. 1821	Feb. 1823	June 1824	22	16	38	10.6
Other	Oct. 1821	May 1822	Dec. 1824	7	31	38	10.3
Furs	Mar. 1819	Apr. 1822	Jan. 1825	37	33	70	25.0
Textiles							
Fibers							
Fabrics							
Hides and Leather	May 1820	Feb. 1822	Feb. 1825	21	36	57	17.2
Spirits and Wines							
Spirits	May 1820	Dec. 1821	Jan. 1825	19	37	56	16.1
Wines							

TABLE 58 (*Continued*)

Group	End of Preceding Recession	Peak	End of Succeeding Low	Number of Months			Index of Cyclical Variability
				Rise	Fall	Total Cycle	
Farm Products							
Grains	Sept. 1824	June 1826	July 1828	21	25	46	36.6
Tobacco	Mar. 1825	Oct. 1825	Mar. 1829	7	41	48	31.2
Minor	Oct. 1824	July 1826	Aug. 1828	21	25	46	50.2
Foods							
Grain Products	July 1825	Nov. 1826	July 1828	16	20	36	26.2
Meats and Meat Products	May 1823	Nov. 1824	June 1826	18	19	37	18.3
Dairy Products	Nov. 1824	Dec. 1826	May 1828	25	17	42	30.5
Fish	Sept. 1824	Apr. 1825	Sept. 1826	7	17	24	14.4
Fruit	July 1823	Mar. 1825	June 1827	20	27	47	37.7
Beverages	Dec. 1824	July 1825	Jan. 1831	7	66	73	22.6
Condiments	June 1824	May 1825	Oct. 1826	11	17	28	13.8
Sugar and Molasses	Oct. 1824	Oct. 1825	July 1831	12	69	81	26.5
Chemicals and Dyes							
Chemicals	Mar. 1823	Sept. 1825	June 1827	30	21	51	10.0
Dyes	June 1824	Apr. 1825	Aug. 1826	10	16	26	15.5
Fuel and Lighting	Sept. 1824	Jan. 1827	July 1830	28	42	70	16.9
Metals and Metal Products							
Ferrous	Feb. 1825	July 1825	Aug. 1831	5	73	78	12.2
Non-Ferrous	July 1824	July 1825	Nov. 1830	12	64	76	28.6
Building Materials							
Wood							
Other	Dec. 1824	May 1825	Aug. 1827	5	27	32	11.8
Furs	Jan. 1825	Sept. 1825	Aug. 1826	8	11	19	25.0
Textiles							
Fibers	May 1823	June 1825	Oct. 1826	25	16	41	32.0
Fabrics							
Hides and Leather	Feb. 1825	Jan. 1826	Oct. 1826	11	9	20	12.3
Spirits and Wines							
Spirits							
Wines	June 1824	July 1825	Nov. 1827	13	28	41	15.3
Farm Products							
Grains	July 1828	Nov. 1828	Mar. 1830	4	16	20	30.5
Tobacco	Mar. 1829	Mar. 1830	Feb. 1832	12	23	35	25.0
Minor	Aug. 1828	Mar. 1829	Sept. 1829	7	6	13	15.8
Foods							
Grain Products	July 1828	Nov. 1828	Mar. 1830	4	16	20	39.2
Meats and Meat Products	June 1826	Sept. 1828	Feb. 1830	27	17	44	21.3
Dairy Products	May 1828	Apr. 1829	May 1830	11	13	24	19.1
Fish	Sept. 1826	Apr. 1827	Aug. 1830	7	40	47	22.2
Fruit	June 1827	Sept. 1828	Mar. 1831	15	30	45	39.5
Beverages							
Condiments	Oct. 1826	May 1827	Mar. 1830	7	34	41	14.3
Sugar and Molasses							
Chemicals and Dyes							
Chemicals	June 1827	Feb. 1829	May 1830	20	15	35	11.4
Dyes	Aug. 1826	May 1827	Mar. 1831	9	46	55	19.7
Fuel and Lighting							
Metals and Metal Products							
Ferrous							
Non-Ferrous							
Building Materials							
Wood	June 1824	May 1827	Jan. 1831	35	44	79	15.8
Other	Aug. 1827	Feb. 1829	May 1830	18	15	33	10.4
Furs	Aug. 1826	Sept. 1828	Mar. 1831	25	30	55	20.3
Textiles							
Fibers	Oct. 1826	Apr. 1827	June 1830	6	38	44	23.2
Fabrics							
Hides and Leather	Oct. 1826	Apr. 1827	Aug. 1829	6	28	34	8.2
Spirits and Wines							
Spirits	Jan. 1825	Aug. 1828	July 1830	43	23	66	12.0
Wines	Nov. 1827	Mar 1828	Nov. 1830	4	32	36	10.5

Table 58 (*Continued*)

Group	End of Preceding Recession	Peak	End of Succeeding Low	Number of Months: Rise	Number of Months: Fall	Number of Months: Total Cycle	Index of Cyclical Variability
Farm Products							
Grains	Mar. 1830	Aug. 1832	Apr. 1834	29	20	49	32.0
Tobacco							
Minor	Sept. 1829	Feb. 1832	Apr. 1834	29	26	55	19.6
Foods							
Grain Products	Mar. 1830	Aug. 1832	Mar. 1834	29	19	48	26.3
Meats and Meat Products	Feb. 1830	Oct. 1830	May 1834	8	43	51	20.7
Dairy Products	May 1830	May 1833	Nov. 1834	36	18	54	28.6
Fish	Aug. 1830	Apr. 1831	Aug. 1832	8	16	24	23.7
Fruit	Mar. 1831	Jan. 1832	May 1834	10	28	38	31.6
Beverages	Jan. 1831	Dec. 1831	Feb. 1835	11	38	49	17.5
Condiments	Mar. 1830	Nov. 1831	Sept. 1834	20	34	54	23.7
Sugar and Molasses	July 1831	Oct. 1833	July 1834	27	9	36	15.8
Chemicals and Dyes							
Chemicals	May 1830	May 1831	July 1832	12	14	26	16.7
Dyes	Mar. 1831	Mar. 1834	Nov. 1835	36	20	56	19.4
Fuel and Lighting	July 1830	Dec. 1832	Feb. 1835	29	26	55	19.6
Metals and Metal Products							
Ferrous	Aug. 1831	Dec. 1833	Mar. 1835	28	15	43	6.8
Non-Ferrous							
Building Materials							
Wood	Jan. 1831	Mar. 1832	Jan. 1835	14	34	48	14.0
Other	May 1830	Jan. 1834	Oct. 1834	44	9	53	14.2
Furs	Mar. 1831	Mar. 1832	Dec. 1834	12	33	45	14.0
Textiles							
Fibers	June 1830	May 1832	Feb. 1834	23	21	44	12.2
Fabrics	Nov. 1826	Mar. 1832	Nov. 1835	64	44	108	15.8
Hides and Leather	Aug. 1829	Jan. 1832	Feb. 1836	29	49	78	18.6
Spirits and Wines							
Spirits	July 1830	Apr. 1833	June 1834	33	14	47	11.3
Wines	Nov. 1830	Nov. 1832	Aug. 1842	24	117	141	17.6
Farm Products							
Grains	Apr. 1834	Feb. 1837	May 1840	34	39	73	47.6
Tobacco	Feb. 1832	Aug. 1836	Sept. 1837	54	13	67	47.2
Minor	Apr. 1834	Apr. 1836	June 1838	24	26	50	47.4
Foods							
Grain Products	Mar. 1834	Mar. 1837	July 1838	36	16	52	44.1
Meats and Meat Products	May 1834	Oct. 1836	Mar. 1838	29	17	46	33.1
Dairy Products	Nov. 1834	Nov. 1836	June 1838	24	19	43	34.4
Fish	Aug. 1832	Apr. 1836	Sept. 1837	44	17	61	35.8
Fruit	May 1834	July 1835	Oct. 1837	14	27	41	36.5
Beverages	Feb. 1835	Sept. 1835	July 1838	7	34	41	19.0
Condiments	Sept. 1834	Mar. 1836	Aug. 1838	18	29	47	13.7
Sugar and Molasses	July 1834	Apr. 1836	July 1837	21	15	36	24.5
Chemicals and Dyes							
Chemicals	July 1832	Jan. 1836	May 1837	42	16	58	22.0
Dyes	Nov. 1835	Feb. 1837	July 1838	15	17	32	18.3
Fuel and Lighting	Feb. 1835	Mar. 1837	Aug. 1837	25	5	30	24.6
Metals and Metal Products							
Ferrous	Mar. 1835	Apr. 1837	Oct. 1838	25	18	43	15.4
Non-Ferrous	Nov. 1830	Apr. 1837	Oct. 1838	77	18	95	30.3
Building Materials							
Wood	Jan. 1835	July 1836	Dec. 1843	18	89	107	25.7
Other	Oct. 1834	Dec. 1836	July 1837	26	7	33	18.4
Furs	Dec. 1834	Mar. 1837	Oct. 1838	27	19	46	31.1
Textiles							
Fibers	Feb. 1834	Aug. 1836	June 1838	30	22	52	26.6
Fabrics	Nov. 1835	Jan. 1838	Aug. 1844	26	79	105	17.1
Hides and Leather	Feb. 1836	Nov. 1836	Sept. 1837	9	10	19	14.3
Spirits and Wines							
Spirits	June 1834	Mar. 1837	June 1838	33	15	48	12.3
Wines							

TABLE 58 (*Continued*)

Group	End of Preceding Recession	Peak	End of Succeeding Low	Number of Months: Rise	Number of Months: Fall	Number of Months: Total Cycle	Index of Cyclical Variability
Farm Products							
Grains	May 1840	Sept. 1841	Feb. 1843	16	17	33	33.2
Tobacco	Sept. 1837	July 1839	Aug. 1842	22	37	59	63.7
Minor	June 1838	Feb. 1839	Nov. 1844	8	69	77	44.2
Foods							
Grain Products	July 1838	Oct. 1838	Mar. 1843	3	53	56	35.0
Meats and Meat Products	Mar. 1838	Oct. 1838	June 1844	7	68	75	44.0
Dairy Products	June 1838	Oct. 1838	Feb. 1843	4	52	56	37.6
Fish	Sept. 1837	June 1839	Feb. 1843	21	44	65	46.4
Fruit	Oct. 1837	Dec. 1840	July 1842	38	19	57	32.7
Beverages	July 1838	Mar. 1841	Feb. 1849	32	95	127	30.8
Condiments	Aug. 1838	Mar. 1839	May 1842	7	38	45	10.3
Sugar and Molasses	July 1837	Dec. 1837	Aug. 1842	5	56	61	26.8
Chemicals and Dyes							
Chemicals	May 1837	Mar. 1839	Sept. 1846	22	90	112	26.1
Dyes	July 1838	Nov. 1838	May 1843	4	54	58	37.5
Fuel and Lighting	Aug. 1837	July 1839	May 1843	23	46	69	25.9
Metals and Metal Products							
Ferrous	Oct. 1838	May 1839	Sept. 1843	7	52	59	14.5
Non-Ferrous	Oct. 1838	Nov. 1839	Oct. 1843	13	47	60	16.0
Building Materials							
Wood							
Other	July 1837	Jan. 1839	July 1844	18	66	84	19.4
Furs	Oct. 1838	Apr. 1840	May 1843	18	37	55	37.7
Textiles							
Fibers	June 1838	May 1839	Apr. 1843	11	47	58	29.3
Fabrics							
Hides and Leather	Sept. 1837	Feb. 1839	May 1843	17	51	68	20.4
Spirits and Wines							
Spirits	June 1838	June 1839	Nov. 1841	12	29	41	10.7
Wines							
Farm Products							
Grains	Feb. 1843	Dec. 1845	Aug. 1846	34	8	42	36.1
Tobacco	Aug. 1842	Sept. 1845	Jan. 1846	37	4	41	28.6
Minor	Nov. 1844	Aug. 1845	Apr. 1846	9	8	17	11.7
Foods							
Grain Products	Mar. 1843	Dec. 1845	Aug. 1846	33	8	41	32.6
Meats and Meat Products	June 1844	Sept. 1845	Aug. 1846	15	11	26	31.1
Dairy Products	Feb. 1843	Dec. 1845	Sept. 1846	34	9	43	35.9
Fish	Feb. 1843	Aug. 1845	June 1846	30	10	40	21.1
Fruit	July 1842	Sept. 1845	May 1849	38	44	82	44.0
Beverages							
Condiments	May 1842	Mar. 1846	July 1849	46	40	86	21.9
Sugar and Molasses	Aug. 1842	Apr. 1845	Dec. 1846	32	20	52	23.5
Chemicals and Dyes							
Chemicals							
Dyes	May 1843	Aug. 1844	Dec. 1845	15	16	31	21.8
Fuel and Lighting							
Metals and Metal Products							
Ferrous	Sept. 1843	June 1845	June 1852	21	84	105	20.4
Non-Ferrous							
Building Materials							
Wood	Dec. 1843	June 1846	Feb. 1847	30	8	38	17.2
Other	July 1844	Mar. 1846	May 1848	20	26	46	16.0
Furs	May 1843	Apr. 1846	Apr. 1855	35	108	143	34.9
Textiles							
Fibers	Apr. 1843	Feb. 1844	Feb. 1845	10	12	22	18.2
Fabrics							
Hides and Leather	May 1843	Sept. 1843	Dec. 1846	4	39	43	14.8
Spirits and Wines							
Spirits	Nov. 1841	Dec. 1845	Sept. 1846	49	9	58	15.0
Wines	Aug. 1842	June 1844	Feb. 1847	22	32	54	12.4

Table 58 (*Continued*)

Group	End of Preceding Recession	Peak	End of Succeeding Low	Number of Months: Rise	Number of Months: Fall	Number of Months: Total Cycle	Index of Cyclical Variability
Farm Products							
Grains	Aug. 1846	June 1847	Apr. 1849	10	22	32	51.4
Tobacco	Jan. 1846	May 1846	Aug. 1848	4	27	31	28.0
Minor	Apr. 1846	Apr. 1847	Aug. 1849	12	28	40	36.7
Foods							
Grain Products	Aug. 1846	June 1847	Apr. 1849	10	22	32	49.8
Meats and Meat Products	Aug. 1846	June 1847	May 1848	10	11	21	39.6
Dairy Products	Sept. 1846	May 1848	June 1849	20	13	33	29.5
Fish	June 1846	Sept. 1847	Jan. 1849	15	16	31	21.6
Fruit							
Beverages							
Condiments							
Sugar and Molasses	Dec. 1846	Mar. 1847	May 1848	3	14	17	17.7
Chemicals and Dyes							
Chemicals	Sept. 1846	Jan. 1848	June 1848	16	5	21	10.7
Dyes	Dec. 1845	May 1847	Sept. 1849	17	28	45	20.1
Fuel and Lighting	May 1843	Nov. 1847	July 1848	54	8	62	19.0
Metals and Metal Products							
Ferrous							
Non-Ferrous	Oct. 1843	Feb. 1848	Nov. 1849	52	21	73	15.4
Building Materials							
Wood	Feb. 1847	Nov. 1847	July 1848	9	8	17	12.7
Other							
Furs							
Textiles							
Fibers	Feb. 1845	May 1847	Sept. 1848	27	16	43	28.9
Fabrics							
Hides and Leather	Dec. 1846	Mar. 1848	Jan. 1849	15	10	25	18.2
Spirits and Wines							
Spirits	Sept. 1846	Jan. 1848	July 1849	16	18	34	16.9
Wines	Feb. 1847	Aug. 1847	Aug. 1849	6	24	30	6.1
Farm Products							
Grains	Apr. 1849	Nov. 1850	Aug. 1851	19	9	28	17.3
Tobacco	Aug. 1848	Feb. 1851	Nov. 1852	30	21	51	46.1
Minor	Aug. 1849	Feb. 1851	Aug. 1852	18	18	36	17.0
Foods							
Grain Products	Apr. 1849	May 1850	Sept. 1851	13	16	29	12.5
Meats and Meat Products	May 1848	Sept. 1852	June 1854	52	21	73	31.3
Dairy Products	June 1849	Sept. 1850	Sept. 1851	15	12	27	17.8
Fish	Jan. 1849	Feb. 1850	May 1851	13	15	28	24.4
Fruit	May 1849	Sept. 1851	Apr. 1852	28	7	35	46.8
Beverages	Feb. 1849	Feb. 1850	Nov. 1852	12	33	45	27.7
Condiments	July 1849	Nov. 1850	May 1852	16	18	34	12.7
Sugar and Molasses	May 1848	Oct. 1850	Apr. 1852	29	18	47	18.9
Chemicals and Dyes							
Chemicals	June 1848	Dec. 1851	July 1852	42	7	49	11.6
Dyes	Sept. 1849	Dec. 1850	Feb. 1852	15	14	29	16.8
Fuel and Lighting	July 1848	Dec. 1850	July 1851	29	7	36	14.8
Metals and Metal Products							
Ferrous							
Non-Ferrous	Nov. 1849	Mar. 1853	Aug. 1853	40	5	45	26.6
Building Materials							
Wood							
Other							
Furs							
Textiles							
Fibers	Sept. 1848	Jan. 1851	Aug. 1851	28	7	35	20.2
Fabrics							
Hides and Leather	Jan. 1849	Sept. 1851	Apr. 1852	32	7	39	15.7
Spirits and Wines							
Spirits	July 1849	Mar. 1850	Mar. 1852	8	24	32	8.4
Wines							

TABLE 58 (*Continued*)

Group	End of Preceding Recession	Peak	End of Succeeding Low	Number of Months			Index of Cyclical Variability
				Rise	Fall	Total Cycle	
Farm Products							
Grains	Aug. 1851	June 1855	May 1856	46	11	57	51.3
Tobacco							
Minor	Aug. 1852	Jan. 1856	Aug. 1856	41	7	48	37.4
Foods							
Grain Products	Sept. 1851	June 1855	June 1856	45	12	57	50.8
Meats and Meat Products	June 1854	Nov. 1855	Apr. 1856	17	5	22	19.6
Dairy Products	Sept. 1851	Nov. 1855	Aug. 1856	50	9	59	29.5
Fish	May 1851	Feb. 1856	Aug. 1856	57	6	63	32.5
Fruit	Apr. 1852	Oct. 1854	May 1856	30	19	49	48.7
Beverages	Nov. 1852	Sept. 1855	Dec. 1856	34	15	49	13.8
Condiments	May 1852	June 1854	May 1860	25	71	96	29.8
Sugar and Molasses							
Chemicals and Dyes							
Chemicals	July 1852	Nov. 1855	Sept. 1856	40	10	50	20.6
Dyes	Feb. 1852	Nov. 1854	Apr. 1857	33	29	62	20.3
Fuel and Lighting	July 1851	Dec. 1855	July 1861	53	67	120	27.8
Metals and Metal Products							
Ferrous	June 1852	Mar. 1853	Aug. 1861	9	101	110	29.5
Non-Ferrous	Aug. 1853	Apr. 1854	Dec. 1856	8	32	40	13.6
Building Materials							
Wood	July 1848	Aug. 1854	Dec. 1856	73	28	101	21.4
Other	May 1848	May 1854	July 1856	72	26	98	24.0
Furs							
Textiles							
Fibers	Aug. 1851	Apr. 1854	Mar. 1855	32	11	43	13.7
Fabrics	Mar. 1853	Apr. 1856	Oct. 1859	37	42	79	15.4
Hides and Leather	Apr. 1852	July 1854	Oct. 1854	27	3	30	24.7
Spirits and Wines							
Spirits	Mar. 1852	Mar. 1855	June 1856	36	15	51	24.7
Wines							
Farm Products							
Grains	May 1856	June 1857	Feb. 1858	13	8	21	36.8
Tobacco	Nov. 1852	Dec. 1856	Oct. 1860	49	46	95	37.8
Minor	Aug. 1856	Nov. 1856	Feb. 1858	3	15	18	23.9
Foods							
Grain Products	June 1856	June 1857	Feb. 1858	12	8	20	27.1
Meats and Meat Products	Apr. 1856	Sept. 1857	Dec. 1861	17	51	68	34.9
Dairy Products	Aug. 1856	Sept. 1857	Aug. 1858	13	11	24	21.0
Fish	Aug. 1856	June 1857	July 1858	10	13	23	31.7
Fruit	May 1856	Oct. 1857	Jan. 1858	17	3	20	45.0
Beverages	Dec. 1856	Oct. 1857	Feb. 1860	10	28	38	20.2
Condiments							
Sugar and Molasses	Apr. 1852	May 1857	Feb. 1858	61	9	70	51.4
Chemicals and Dyes							
Chemicals	Sept. 1856	Sept. 1857	Mar. 1858	12	6	18	12.9
Dyes	Apr. 1857	Sept. 1857	Feb. 1858	5	5	10	24.4
Fuel and Lighting							
Metals and Metal Products							
Ferrous							
Non-Ferrous	Dec. 1856	Apr. 1857	Jan. 1859	4	21	25	15.8
Building Materials							
Wood	Dec. 1856	June 1857	Nov. 1858	6	17	23	16.1
Other	July 1856	Sept. 1857	Jan. 1858	14	4	18	8.3
Furs	Apr. 1855	Mar. 1857	Jan. 1859	23	22	45	22.4
Textiles							
Fibers	Mar. 1855	May 1857	Mar. 1858	26	10	36	16.4
Fabrics							
Hides and Leather	Oct. 1854	Apr. 1857	Feb. 1858	30	10	40	37.6
Spirits and Wines							
Spirits	June 1856	Mar. 1857	Mar. 1861	9	48	57	25.5
Wines							

TABLE 58 (*Concluded*)

Group	End of Preceding Recession	Peak	End of Succeeding Low	Number of Months: Rise	Number of Months: Fall	Number of Months: Total Cycle	Index of Cyclical Variability
Farm Products							
Grains	Feb. 1858	May 1859	July 1861	15	26	41	34.3
Tobacco							
Minor	Feb. 1858	Jan. 1859	Aug. 1861	11	31	42	23.5
Foods							
Grain Products	Feb. 1858	May 1859	Aug. 1861	15	27	42	32.1
Meats and Meat Products							
Dairy Products	Aug. 1858	Jan. 1860	Sept. 1861	17	20	37	26.1
Fish	July 1858	Mar. 1860	Sept. 1861	20	18	38	34.8
Fruit	Jan. 1858	July 1858	July 1861	6	36	42	26.3
Beverages							
Condiments							
Sugar and Molasses	Feb. 1858	Sept. 1858	July 1861	7	34	41	28.1
Chemicals and Dyes							
Chemicals	Mar. 1858	June 1859	Oct. 1861	15	28	43	11.5
Dyes	Feb. 1858	Aug. 1860	Mar. 1861	30	7	37	11.9
Fuel and Lighting							
Metals and Metal Products							
Ferrous							
Non-Ferrous	Jan. 1859	May 1859	Aug. 1861	4	27	31	11.1
Building Materials							
Wood	Nov. 1858	July 1859	Sept. 1861	8	26	34	10.6
Other	Jan. 1858	Apr. 1859	Jan. 1861	15	21	36	9.8
Furs	Jan. 1859	Feb. 1859	Jan. 1860	1	11	12	18.8
Textiles							
Fibers	Mar. 1858	Sept. 1858	Sept. 1860	6	24	30	11.2
Fabrics							
Hides and Leather	Feb. 1858	Aug. 1859	Sept. 1861	18	25	43	22.1
Spirits and Wines							
Spirits							
Wines	Aug. 1849	June 1858	Dec. 1859	106	18	124	33.1

TABLE 59—ANNUAL PERCENTAGE OF CHA

Year	Farm Products			Foods								Chemicals
	Grains	Tobacco	Minor	Grain Products	Meats and Meat Products	Dairy Products	Fish	Fruit	Beverages	Condiments	Sugar and Molasses	
1785	− 3.4	− 7.4	+13.6	− 9.7	− 2.1	−21.8	− 4.7	− 7.8	+ 3.6	− 9.7	−13.3	+ 7.9
1786	− 1.5	−22.2	+ 2.5	− 2.2	− 2.7	− 3.9	− 3.4	− 5.7	− 0.8	− 5.3	+ 6.0	− 3.2
1787	−10.5	+ 6.5	− 1.9	−14.0	− 2.1	− 9.9	− 1.4	−11.1	− 4.2	+ 0.2	+ 4.7	− 1.1
1788	−16.1	+ 1.1	−24.2	−10.1	−15.8	−12.3	−10.9	− 1.1	− 2.9	− 3.3	− 4.7	− 6.2
1789	+ 4.4	0.0	−15.7	+ 6.7	−17.3	− 8.8	0.0	−13.1	+ 9.1	− 6.8	+ 5.5	− 2.5
1790	+31.9	0.0	+11.2	+33.9	+ 9.8	+36.0	+ 1.9	+24.5	−13.9	+ 3.3	+11.2	− 4.5
1791	−13.6	−27.6	+ 8.6	−20.8	+13.6	+ 2.1	+11.0	+53.5	−10.2	+10.6	+31.5	− 6.2
1792	− 2.6	− 6.2	− 2.4	− 1.1	+ 2.0	+ 7.0	− 0.5	−19.7	+24.4	+ 0.8	+24.1	− 4.6
1793	+21.1	+ 6.8	+ 9.0	+ 9.3	+19.9	+16.9	− 2.3	− 1.8	−10.3	+ 7.8	− 4.8	0.0
1794	+10.5	+ 5.7	+ 2.9	+17.5	+16.9	+19.2	+24.7	+ 6.7	+ 9.5	+25.8	+ 1.0	+42.8
1795	+29.9	+25.9	+ 1.3	+50.1	+13.9	+ 0.1	+41.2	+16.9	+28.5	+18.0	+ 9.5	+70.4
1796	+14.4	+17.0	+37.2	+17.6	+11.2	− 3.9	+ 5.3	+16.3	+ 3.7	− 4.5	+ 5.7	− 6.0
1797	−19.8	+35.2	+ 4.1	−17.6	− 4.1	−13.4	+ 7.3	− 6.8	− 1.5	−11.4	+ 8.3	−15.4
1798	−18.2	+34.2	+ 0.3	−22.7	− 6.5	+17.0	−16.3	0.0	+ 8.7	−13.7	− 4.3	− 3.2
1799	+ 1.6	− 2.8	−31.9	+ 7.2	−15.5	+ 0.1	−22.8	+ 0.5	+ 9.3	+ 4.9	− 0.1	+ 9.9
1800	+22.3	−50.3	+28.8	+17.2	+ 7.5	− 1.6	−14.8	+ 9.3	− 5.6	− 2.7	− 9.3	− 5.5
1801	+ 9.7	+ 4.2	+14.9	+11.0	+28.3	+ 0.2	+36.0	−15.0	− 8.3	− 1.8	− 6.6	− 7.7
1802	−21.9	+11.5	−13.0	−29.0	−21.0	−12.3	− 1.4	− 3.6	−12.9	− 0.5	−11.7	−13.3
1803	+ 0.2	− 1.8	− 0.6	− 3.8	− 6.8	−21.1	−17.3	−20.2	+ 7.6	− 6.1	+ 3.7	+ 3.6
1804	+16.4	+ 6.1	+ 3.9	+18.4	+ 5.6	+43.0	+ 7.0	+24.0	+12.9	+ 2.7	+14.0	+ 0.5
1805	+23.3	− 1.0	− 1.8	+22.8	+ 5.4	+24.9	+10.2	+11.3	− 0.5	+ 2.6	− 5.9	− 2.3
1806	−20.0	− 1.4	− 1.8	−20.1	+27.7	− 8.6	+ 5.3	+15.7	− 8.6	− 7.1	− 8.2	+ 7.6
1807	− 8.7	+ 5.5	− 5.2	− 3.4	−15.4	−14.9	− 2.4	−23.6	− 9.5	+ 0.6	−13.0	− 1.0
1808	−24.3	− 3.3	− 3.4	−12.9	−22.6	−15.5	−23.6	+ 0.9	− 6.1	+11.7	+ 2.7	+22.0
1809	+17.2	− 1.4	−11.7	+15.4	+14.3	+ 0.3	+ 6.9	+ 3.3	+ 5.9	+ 6.5	+ 8.9	+15.9
1810	+26.9	− 0.4	+10.9	+25.0	+13.7	+14.8	+ 2.4	− 1.4	−13.7	−18.8	+ 5.0	+ 1.7
1811	+ 2.7	−12.7	+ 0.7	+ 2.6	+ 0.4	+ 2.8	+12.5	+ 9.5	−21.9	− 6.0	+ 1.6	− 0.5
1812	+ 2.4	−14.0	+17.1	− 3.8	− 8.2	− 7.1	+ 4.6	+ 9.0	+ 0.9	+22.1	+15.3	+18.3
1813	+ 4.0	+29.8	−22.8	− 0.9	+ 0.6	+ 1.0	+ 5.9	+ 5.5	+42.8	+29.5	+40.6	+11.5
1814	+ 8.0	+11.6	+ 8.1	− 2.1	+34.2	+28.9	+30.4	+21.9	+30.4	+21.4	+23.9	+11.5
1815	− 5.6	+58.6	+19.5	+ 7.9	+14.1	+ 8.8	− 3.2	− 5.6	+ 0.5	−17.0	−15.7	−32.3
1816	+18.5	+56.4	+24.2	+ 9.7	−10.5	+ 0.5	−10.7	−26.2	−10.7	−18.8	−22.1	−23.0
1817	+14.3	−35.7	+16.5	+20.2	+ 2.2	− 4.4	−21.2	−12.6	−18.4	−17.6	−13.2	−20.5
1818	−21.0	−10.9	−13.4	−26.6	+ 1.1	−12.4	+ 6.0	+28.4	+ 5.7	− 5.2	− 1.6	− 3.7
1819	−22.7	−15.7	− 4.7	−23.6	−22.6	−18.4	−16.1	− 2.0	− 4.7	− 7.7	− 7.8	−17.8
1820	−25.3	−17.6	−16.2	−23.5	−16.2	−22.8	−21.3	−22.2	− 5.6	− 8.5	−18.3	−11.0
1821	−15.6	+ 0.3	−25.0	−13.3	−13.8	− 2.4	− 8.6	− 2.0	+ 3.5	− 2.4	−14.5	+ 2.8
1822	+44.7	− 9.4	+ 3.3	+39.3	− 1.2	+39.2	+ 7.7	+15.6	− 2.5	− 6.3	+ 4.2	+ 0.6
1823	− 6.4	+ 0.6	− 2.6	− 5.1	− 0.5	−22.0	− 1.7	−14.3	− 5.4	− 4.4	− 8.7	− 4.3
1824	−22.9	+ 0.4	− 5.2	−20.3	+ 4.6	−18.7	− 5.3	+ 8.2	− 4.8	− 7.4	− 2.6	+ 0.6
1825	+ 7.2	+ 5.0	+ 7.8	+ 2.9	− 4.0	+ 6.0	−10.2	+12.3	− 1.5	+10.5	+13.6	+ 2.6
1826	+25.7	−13.6	+20.8	+12.4	− 9.1	+17.8	− 5.8	−16.8	− 9.1	− 3.5	+ 0.3	− 6.4
1827	− 9.5	−16.2	−22.4	− 4.5	+ 4.8	− 9.5	+13.4	−20.6	− 6.2	+ 2.2	− 0.5	− 4.8
1828	−12.5	− 2.4	−18.3	− 3.4	+ 4.1	−13.0	+ 1.0	+17.2	− 4.5	− 6.0	− 2.1	+ 1.6
1829	+11.6	+ 7.5	+ 6.6	+10.6	− 7.7	+ 0.1	− 5.2	+ 0.6	− 3.8	− 6.2	− 5.8	+ 1.6
1830	−12.8	− 7.9	− 0.5	+ 1.4	+ 3.8	− 4.2	− 3.7	−11.0	− 4.3	− 5.0	− 5.5	− 4.0
1831	+29.2	−10.1	+10.8	+ 4.3	+ 6.4	+19.5	+10.3	− 7.6	− 7.9	+ 6.7	− 6.6	+ 7.9
1832	+ 4.3	+ 7.3	+ 3.3	+ 2.3	− 2.1	+ 5.0	−11.1	+ 1.8	− 1.6	+ 3.3	+ 7.5	− 5.5
1833	− 2.3	+23.7	− 0.9	− 1.7	+ 2.2	+ 8.9	+ 7.5	−16.6	− 6.0	−21.9	+ 4.4	+ 8.1
1834	− 9.2	+34.7	− 4.4	− 6.6	− 5.2	− 9.2	− 1.1	− 3.8	− 5.2	− 6.9	− 4.1	+ 5.8
1835	+25.6	+ 3.7	+77.0	+14.9	+14.7	+18.4	+21.5	+27.2	+ 6.2	+ 6.8	+ 5.3	+ 2.0
1836	+14.4	+11.8	+12.7	+26.7	+23.3	+27.8	+12.0	− 9.9	− 2.0	− 0.1	+17.5	− 0.5
1837	+11.7	−27.5	−17.1	+15.9	− 8.4	−10.2	− 3.7	−12.0	− 3.8	− 5.0	−11.6	− 8.4
1838	−11.8	+12.9	− 4.2	−19.9	− 1.1	− 5.0	+ 8.6	+ 6.2	− 8.0	− 4.6	+ 1.9	+ 4.8
1839	− 1.5	+73.6	+30.6	− 5.1	+ 3.5	+ 7.5	+35.8	− 7.4	+ 2.7	+ 0.9	− 3.0	+ 4.5
1840	−31.3	−35.9	−12.8	−25.8	−11.2	−25.2	−21.3	+ 1.9	+12.4	− 9.2	−12.1	− 5.3
1841	+ 9.9	− 7.6	− 6.3	+ 1.6	−26.4	−13.0	− 5.7	+10.8	+21.2	− 1.2	− 8.7	− 2.4
1842	− 5.3	−34.0	−17.1	+ 0.9	−23.3	+ 1.1	−17.1	−16.4	−14.8	+ 1.7	−14.1	− 2.9
1843	−13.2	− 4.4	− 0.5	−13.7	+ 9.1	−20.3	− 1.5	+22.8	− 9.1	+ 1.7	+ 6.0	− 8.5
1844	+ 3.5	− 5.4	−12.3	− 0.5	− 8.2	+ 6.2	+17.5	+ 2.9	− 1.1	+ 6.2	+ 9.6	− 2.8
1845	+11.2	+33.7	− 0.2	+ 5.3	+30.2	+26.4	+ 1.4	+12.9	− 0.7	+ 4.9	+ 6.0	− 6.9
1846	+ 8.5	+12.9	+ 2.0	+ 7.7	−10.3	+ 2.4	− 6.8	− 9.4	+ 0.9	+ 5.1	− 8.0	− 2.7
1847	+27.9	− 7.1	+34.8	+28.8	+40.7	+10.4	+ 2.9	− 1.6	− 0.2	− 2.9	+ 1.9	+ 6.4
1848	−20.6	− 9.2	−13.5	−18.6	−18.2	− 3.3	− 3.8	− 9.5	− 2.5	− 8.2	−18.8	+ 1.2
1849	− 8.9	+ 7.3	−11.4	− 8.9	+ 4.6	− 9.1	−12.2	− 1.9	+ 4.1	− 4.5	+ 4.2	+ 0.9
1850	+ 6.8	+20.1	− 1.6	+ 0.6	− 3.5	+ 4.3	+21.3	+29.5	+10.6	+ 6.2	+ 3.1	+ 4.6
1851	− 2.9	+ 9.6	+10.5	− 3.0	+19.0	− 1.7	− 5.9	+ 1.3	− 7.7	+ 0.8	+ 1.6	− 1.8
1852	+ 9.0	−23.7	− 3.6	+ 3.6	+21.3	+21.3	+14.3	−21.5	−16.3	− 1.9	− 6.4	− 1.5
1853	+ 9.3	+ 9.9	+ 9.7	+14.2	− 1.1	+10.1	+ 8.0	+37.4	+ 6.2	+11.2	+ 2.7	− 1.9
1854	+23.6	+ 6.4	+20.6	+33.3	− 5.3	+ 4.0	+ 7.0	+28.5	+ 8.8	+ 6.3	− 5.0	+ 7.4
1855	+16.6	+ 9.1	+ 6.7	+15.9	+12.5	+ 8.5	− 2.1	−17.0	+ 2.2	− 1.6	+17.1	+ 9.3
1856	−28.8	+ 7.3	− 8.9	−29.7	− 0.9	− 5.7	+ 2.2	+11.5	− 0.4	− 0.6	+39.4	+ 2.8
1857	+ 8.5	+ 9.8	+ 2.9	− 4.0	+11.8	− 3.2	+ 3.3	+ 9.6	+16.9	−10.9	+14.0	+ 3.2
1858	−17.0	−20.0	− 9.5	−10.1	−18.2	−18.2	−15.7	−37.5	+ 0.5	−17.5	−30.3	− 5.4
1859	+18.2	− 1.5	+ 1.0	+13.0	− 2.1	+ 5.9	+11.6	−11.8	− 7.1	− 5.3	+ 3.7	+ 2.0
1860	− 6.9	−13.2	− 2.4	− 5.0	− 0.3	+ 1.9	− 1.0	+11.8	− 1.1	+ 1.0	− 2.8	+ 5.9
1861	− 9.4	+35.8	− 6.9	− 9.6	−12.0	−18.5	−21.4	+10.1	+14.1	+ 4.5	−10.9	− 4.8

THE INDICES OF THE 25 SUB-GROUPS

Fuel and Lighting	Metals		Building Materials		Furs	Textiles		Hides and Leather	Spirits	Wines	Miscellaneous	Year
	Ferrous	Non-Ferrous	Wood	Other		Fibers	Fabrics					
−15.4	−10.9	+ 4.2	− 9.3	−10.3	− 5.9	+20.3	− 5.3	− 6.7	−13.5	+11.7	−14.6	1785
+ 3.2	− 8.3	+ 4.1	−21.7	−14.6	− 9.7	+20.0	+ 7.1	+ 9.4	+ 3.3	+ 4.7	+ 1.7	1786
+ 5.4	− 3.6	+ 4.7	−11.1	−10.0	−15.4	+ 8.7	+ 2.7	− 9.3	+ 0.5	0.0	− 6.8	1787
−11.5	+ 0.1	+ 1.8	− 3.6	− 2.0	− 4.5	−13.7	− 5.8	− 2.9	− 3.5	− 5.6	+ 4.4	1788
− 9.0	+ 0.5	+ 7.3	+ 6.7	+ 1.3	+ 5.7	−15.8	+ 0.3	+ 2.1	+11.8	− 3.8	− 0.7	1789
+ 5.6	+ 1.0	− 1.3	+ 1.1	+ 6.0	+ 5.6	− 0.3	0.0	+11.9	+15.5	+ 2.1	− 4.0	1790
+ 5.6	+ 1.7	− 5.2	+16.8	− 2.2	− 2.0	+ 4.8	− 2.0	− 3.6	+25.1	+ 4.8	+ 3.4	1791
− 2.6	+ 5.2	+ 0.8	+ 7.8	− 5.7	+ 7.8	+10.9	− 0.1	− 3.3	+27.5	+ 6.3	− 6.3	1792
+ 8.0	− 0.8	+ 2.7	+10.4	+ 8.0	− 0.5	+ 2.7	+12.4	+ 0.3	− 8.7	+10.2	+ 5.4	1793
+19.7	+ 0.2	+ 7.0	+ 5.5	+17.4	− 4.2	+ 0.8	+13.1	+ 3.1	+15.1	+ 6.0	+24.1	1794
+21.2	+13.8	+ 5.3	+18.3	+16.3	+18.2	+ 8.6	+ 8.7	+10.9	+10.8	+ 3.8	+26.1	1795
+ 6.7	+ 7.4	+ 2.3	+14.9	+10.3	+22.3	+17.5	+ 7.9	−24.0	+36.0	+ 0.7	+ 0.9	1796
− 9.0	+ 3.8	+ 4.6	+ 4.0	+ 1.8	−12.4	+ 0.1	+ 2.8	− 6.1	−15.9	− 1.6	− 7.4	1797
+ 2.2	+ 2.4	+14.0	− 7.3	− 7.5	−22.6	− 3.9	− 4.0	+19.7	−11.8	− 4.9	−12.0	1798
− 9.3	− 1.7	+ 7.9	+ 0.2	−11.3	+ 4.1	− 2.8	− 2.0	+ 2.9	− 4.0	+10.3	+ 5.5	1799
+ 5.7	+ 3.1	− 3.9	+ 7.9	+ 4.1	+23.0	+ 1.2	− 2.6	+ 2.1	0.0	+ 4.4	+ 5.3	1800
+ 5.2	+ 4.1	− 1.0	− 0.4	+ 4.6	+ 4.3	+13.6	+12.4	+ 1.6	+ 2.5	+ 8.3	− 3.5	1801
− 6.8	+ 0.9	− 3.6	− 6.0	− 3.2	− 6.7	−18.5	−15.9	+ 6.0	− 6.7	+ 1.9	− 2.3	1802
− 2.5	− 6.0	+ 8.5	+ 2.3	+ 6.5	+ 0.7	− 2.3	+ 3.6	+ 0.7	− 2.9	− 4.7	− 5.0	1803
+11.8	− 1.0	+ 8.2	+ 4.2	+ 1.5	+17.0	+ 1.3	+ 5.5	+ 0.5	− 7.4	+ 4.9	+ 6.6	1804
+15.5	+ 0.8	− 1.7	+ 0.7	− 0.9	− 4.2	+ 9.6	+ 9.9	0.0	− 9.1	− 6.6	+ 7.0	1805
−12.3	+ 3.5	− 1.6	− 3.0	− 5.6	− 8.2	+ 1.2	+ 0.6	+ 1.2	− 2.5	− 7.5	+ 3.2	1806
− 7.7	+ 2.4	− 3.3	+ 3.1	− 1.3	+10.3	− 4.4	+ 3.5	− 0.3	− 6.2	− 0.3	− 3.5	1807
− 5.8	− 0.7	− 0.4	− 2.9	+ 4.0	− 5.1	− 7.4	+ 5.2	− 2.9	+26.0	+ 9.7	− 7.3	1808
− 0.8	+10.4	+ 0.1	+ 3.7	+21.2	+ 6.8	+ 7.9	+25.9	+ 1.6	+19.8	+15.7	+ 8.7	1809
+10.9	− 1.5	− 2.5	+ 9.1	+ 3.5	+ 8.2	+ 1.3	−17.0	+ 3.7	+ 5.9	+14.1	+ 1.6	1810
+ 8.6	− 2.6	− 7.1	− 0.2	− 8.0	+ 7.6	−19.3	−16.4	−15.5	+ 3.9	+ 6.3	+ 0.2	1811
+ 6.5	+ 4.3	+25.3	− 2.5	− 0.9	− 4.2	− 9.6	+ 1.5	+ 8.8	+15.4	+10.9	− 8.5	1812
+34.6	+ 6.4	+19.2	+ 1.2	+16.4	− 3.0	+39.6	+20.3	+12.4	+ 4.4	+ 8.3	− 0.3	1813
+16.4	+10.1	+30.4	+14.6	+33.4	− 1.2	+16.8	− 0.4	+30.9	+31.1	+16.7	+ 6.0	1814
−13.1	− 2.0	−23.8	+ 6.8	−21.5	+24.4	−14.4	− 7.7	−10.9	− 8.5	−13.0	+ 4.6	1815
−13.9	− 8.5	−28.7	− 7.9	−22.4	− 4.0	+ 0.6	− 9.5	+ 8.4	−30.8	−11.5	+ 5.4	1816
−21.4	−10.6	−24.4	− 9.7	−18.0	−12.4	− 6.1	−13.3	− 6.3	− 5.0	−17.0	− 7.0	1817
− 2.6	− 4.7	+ 5.2	− 3.3	+ 4.4	−14.3	+ 8.2	− 3.2	− 0.9	+ 3.0	+ 0.2	+ 8.3	1818
− 0.8	− 5.3	− 3.5	− 0.3	− 7.1	− 6.6	−10.8	+ 0.2	− 3.1	−22.2	− 0.2	− 4.6	1819
− 6.0	− 0.3	− 2.4	−12.4	− 8.2	− 2.1	− 3.3	− 2.7	− 8.7	−12.4	− 7.2	− 8.9	1820
− 6.1	− 0.1	− 1.2	−12.9	− 5.6	+12.5	−18.5	− 1.2	+13.8	+ 0.2	− 4.1	+ 2.3	1821
− 5.2	− 3.3	+ 0.4	+10.3	− 1.3	+25.7	− 7.9	− 1.8	+ 6.9	− 2.1	− 5.4	−12.9	1822
−15.1	− 1.4	− 1.5	− 2.3	− 4.5	− 2.7	− 9.8	− 4.7	− 1.1	− 7.6	− 7.7	− 6.0	1823
− 7.5	− 2.9	− 3.8	− 1.4	− 2.1	− 2.0	+ 3.6	− 9.0	− 1.3	− 2.0	− 3.5	− 0.7	1824
+ 2.2	+ 1.8	+15.7	+ 6.3	+ 1.1	+12.9	+19.8	− 3.4	+ 2.3	− 1.5	+ 7.6	− 0.9	1825
+ 2.4	+ 1.4	− 3.6	+ 0.1	− 6.5	− 9.7	−15.4	− 5.8	− 7.8	+ 1.4	− 2.7	− 7.9	1826
+ 0.5	− 1.6	− 4.3	− 2.3	− 2.9	− 7.8	+ 6.4	+ 0.5	− 0.9	+ 6.2	− 4.4	− 6.6	1827
− 6.9	− 2.0	− 8.0	− 1.0	− 0.7	+ 8.9	− 7.7	− 0.8	− 0.6	+ 2.5	− 1.4	+ 0.5	1828
− 4.6	− 2.3	− 7.8	− 7.4	− 3.0	− 3.7	− 6.2	+ 1.4	− 4.2	− 1.2	− 3.6	− 0.6	1829
− 2.3	− 6.5	− 9.5	−10.6	− 6.8	−12.7	− 2.4	+ 5.4	+ 1.7	− 1.6	− 5.8	− 7.1	1830
+ 8.6	− 1.8	+ 2.2	+ 9.8	+ 5.9	+ 1.9	+ 2.6	+ 0.6	+ 6.4	+ 9.2	+ 1.0	+ 6.6	1831
+ 9.6	+ 1.9	+ 5.7	+ 1.4	+ 3.9	− 2.2	+ 8.2	+ 0.8	− 4.5	− 3.0	+ 1.8	− 0.6	1832
+ 1.6	+ 1.3	− 1.8	+ 0.1	+ 3.1	+ 0.6	+ 0.5	− 6.9	− 7.7	+ 2.7	+ 1.3	− 0.3	1833
− 5.8	− 2.4	− 0.1	− 0.9	− 0.9	+ 3.5	− 4.1	− 7.2	− 3.9	− 3.4	− 5.0	− 3.6	1834
+ 2.5	− 1.0	+ 5.0	+ 2.7	+ 3.8	− 5.9	+11.3	− 2.3	− 3.2	+ 4.7	− 1.7	+ 6.2	1835
+15.0	+13.4	+19.2	+ 3.5	+ 5.1	+10.8	+10.9	+ 5.5	+ 3.4	+ 3.2	− 3.6	+ 8.2	1836
− 0.3	+ 3.3	+ 1.4	− 3.7	− 4.7	− 3.7	−14.8	+ 8.4	− 0.4	+ 5.2	− 6.3	+ 5.7	1837
− 4.7	− 6.9	−14.8	− 2.4	− 2.4	−25.6	− 9.2	+ 2.2	+ 1.2	− 1.3	− 1.7	− 0.9	1838
+10.6	+ 1.1	+ 0.8	− 0.1	+ 3.0	+ 8.9	+17.1	− 1.7	+ 6.7	+ 0.7	− 0.8	+10.2	1839
− 7.3	− 7.7	− 1.6	− 2.3	− 8.6	+ 3.2	−14.6	− 2.3	− 3.9	− 5.2	− 2.7	− 6.9	1840
− 2.2	− 2.9	− 3.2	− 1.2	− 1.1	− 5.5	+ 2.4	− 4.4	+ 0.6	− 5.3	− 1.0	− 2.7	1841
−13.2	− 2.1	− 5.2	− 7.8	− 4.9	−13.0	− 7.0	− 1.2	−10.4	+ 3.6	− 4.9	− 8.6	1842
−11.8	− 6.6	− 8.9	− 8.1	− 5.1	−25.7	−11.5	− 2.0	− 6.3	+ 8.3	+ 2.8	−10.4	1843
+ 1.3	+ 0.6	− 1.0	− 4.0	− 2.8	+24.7	+ 5.4	− 2.4	− 0.6	+10.1	+10.7	+ 1.6	1844
− 0.6	+ 7.4	+ 5.9	+ 2.2	+ 3.0	+15.7	− 8.0	− 0.5	− 1.4	+ 2.3	− 0.3	− 0.8	1845
+ 4.5	− 1.4	+ 8.1	+ 2.7	+ 0.8	− 1.5	+ 8.0	+ 0.6	− 2.7	− 0.7	− 3.1	− 1.1	1846
+10.8	− 1.0	+ 1.1	− 2.1	− 2.7	−11.2	+22.6	+ 0.6	+ 1.9	+ 2.2	+ 1.1	+ 3.0	1847
− 3.6	− 1.6	− 2.1	− 1.9	− 3.1	− 2.3	−13.2	+ 0.5	− 3.5	− 4.9	− 2.8	+ 0.8	1848
+ 1.5	− 8.8	− 0.7	− 1.5	+ 0.4	0.0	+ 5.2	− 1.4	− 3.7	− 7.2	− 1.7	− 4.7	1849
+ 5.4	− 5.0	− 2.2	+ 9.8	+ 3.7	0.0	+13.3	− 1.8	+13.7	− 1.2	+ 2.8	+ 3.8	1850
− 1.0	− 5.5	+ 1.0	+12.7	+ 0.9	0.0	− 4.8	+ 0.5	+ 4.8	− 5.6	− 0.4	+ 2.2	1851
+ 8.5	+ 0.2	+ 2.9	− 1.8	+ 2.8	+ 2.0	− 2.7	− 0.7	+ 3.0	+ 3.4	0.0	− 0.3	1852
− 0.5	+21.4	+28.0	+ 4.1	+14.0	− 4.6	+ 4.1	− 0.7	+13.8	+11.9	+ 5.5	+ 6.7	1853
+15.2	+ 0.7	+ 6.2	+ 4.9	+10.8	−16.7	+ 9.5	+15.5	+22.6	+18.7	+21.8	+ 2.5	1854
+ 4.3	− 3.0	− 6.6	− 5.1	− 4.5	− 2.2	− 1.4	+ 6.3	+ 0.2	+17.4	+38.9	− 1.3	1855
+ 1.3	+ 0.4	+ 0.4	− 4.6	− 4.0	+15.8	+ 6.9	− 2.6	+19.3	− 1.0	+ 0.6	+ 3.7	1856
− 3.9	− 5.9	+ 1.9	+ 9.2	+ 1.1	+ 5.6	− 0.8	− 3.2	+20.8	+ 4.3	+ 3.5	+ 0.1	1857
−10.8	− 7.6	− 9.4	− 4.1	− 1.0	− 9.0	−13.6	− 0.5	−23.8	−19.1	− 2.8	− 2.2	1858
− 1.5	− 0.9	+ 0.3	+ 6.3	− 1.4	+ 1.0	+ 1.3	− 1.9	+14.0	−10.6	−14.7	+ 4.3	1859
− 0.5	− 1.9	+ 0.4	− 0.5	− 4.2	− 4.6	−11.4	− 1.3	− 9.1	− 7.7	+12.6	+ 2.1	1860
− 6.6	− 5.3	− 8.1	− 5.5	+21.6	+ 6.3	+16.1	+ 1.8	− 8.3	+ 1.1	+ 2.3	− 7.9	1861

Table 60—Percentage of Commodities in Six Largest Major Groups which Declined Before or With the General Index

Year of Peak	Farm		Imported Foods	Lumber Products and Naval Stores	Industrial		Domestic	Imported
	Crops	Derivatives			Raw	Consumption		
1797	66.7	78.6	61.9	33.3	55.0	66.7	63.8	64.4
1801	66.7	71.4	81.0	58.3	55.0	77.8	58.0	69.5
1805	25.0	21.4	52.4	41.7	37.5	40.7	30.4	44.1
1809	8.3	0.0	47.6	8.3	40.0	22.2	8.7	44.1
1814	50.0	28.6	71.4	25.0	42.5	40.7	29.0	59.3
1822	33.3	42.9	47.6	25.0	40.0	55.6	40.6	42.4
1825	25.0	57.1	33.3	25.0	42.5	37.0	42.0	35.6
1828	58.3	57.1	81.0	66.7	55.0	51.9	56.5	61.0
1832	25.0	57.1	23.8	0.0	42.5	48.1	37.7	42.4
1837	58.3	50.0	90.5	50.0	52.5	37.0	47.8	66.1
1839	33.3	71.4	66.7	58.3	40.0	51.9	49.3	52.5
1845	83.3	71.4	52.4	33.3	72.5	37.0	60.9	54.2
1847	75.0	71.4	42.9	50.0	42.5	22.2	46.4	35.6
1851	41.7	28.6	66.7	8.3	55.0	48.1	40.6	45.8
1855	50.0	64.3	38.1	83.3	50.0	40.7	53.6	39.0
1857	58.3	42.9	57.1	33.3	65.0	55.6	55.1	45.8
1859	75.0	42.9	61.9	25.0	62.5	44.4	47.8	61.0

Table 61—Percentage of Commodities in Six Largest Major Groups which Rose Before or With the General Index

Year of Low	Farm		Imported Foods	Lumber Products and Naval Stores	Industrial		Domestic	Imported
	Crops	Derivatives			Raw	Consumption		
1789	33.3	42.9	52.4	66.7	42.5	29.6	46.4	37.3
1798	16.7	21.4	42.9	8.3	52.5	44.4	20.3	47.5
1803	33.3	28.6	52.4	75.0	65.0	37.0	42.0	55.9
1808	16.7	21.4	71.4	58.3	47.5	48.1	26.1	66.1
1811	25.0	21.4	42.9	25.0	55.0	44.4	24.6	59.3
1821	50.0	35.7	61.9	33.3	40.0	29.6	31.9	52.5
1824	58.3	64.3	57.1	33.3	47.5	37.0	39.1	50.8
1828	66.7	71.4	57.1	66.7	30.0	44.4	52.2	55.9
1830	75.0	78.6	28.6	25.0	30.0	18.5	42.0	30.5
1834	75.0	35.7	38.1	50.0	40.0	29.6	44.9	35.6
1838	66.7	85.7	71.4	41.7	52.5	44.4	63.8	52.5
1843	58.3	42.9	57.1	0.0	22.5	33.3	30.4	32.2
1846	91.7	71.4	33.3	25.0	22.5	29.6	43.5	22.0
1849	66.7	57.1	38.1	58.3	45.0	22.2	53.6	28.8
1852	58.3	50.0	19.0	58.3	30.0	22.2	43.5	33.9
1856	83.3	42.9	57.1	16.7	42.5	33.3	47.8	47.5
1858	41.7	64.3	33.3	25.0	27.5	7.4	30.4	33.9
1861	58.3	7.1	95.2	58.3	30.0	59.3	40.6	64.4

BIBLIOGRAPHY

Newspaper Sources

American Sentinel, 1818-1819, 1822, 1824-1829, 1832-1834, 1838.

Atkinson's Saturday Evening Post, 1823-1825, 1827-1829, 1835-1836.

Aurora, see *General Advertiser*

Carey's Pennsylvania Evening Herald, 1785.

Carey's Pennsylvania Evening Herald, and American Monitor, 1785.

Pennsylvania Herald, and General Advertiser, 1787-1788.

Columbian Magazine, 1788-1791.

Columbian Observer, 1825.

Commercial List and Philadelphia Price Current, 1833-1848, 1853-1855.

Commercial List and Trade and Statistical Register, 1849-1850.

Commercial List and Trade Statistical Register, 1851.

Philadelphia Commercial and Trade and Statistical Register, 1852-1853.

Philadelphia Commercial List and Price Current, 1856-1861.

Complete Counting House Companion (Supplement to *Pennsylvania Evening Herald* until 1788), 1785-1789.

Democratic Press, 1810, 1823-1826.

The Federal Gazette, and Philadelphia Evening Post, 1788-1790.

Federal Gazette and Philadelphia Daily Advertiser, 1790-1793.

Philadelphia Gazette and Universal Daily Advertiser, 1795, 1797-1799.

Relfs Philadelphia Gazette, And Daily Advertiser, 1803-1807.

Relf's Philadelphia Gazette, and Daily Advertiser, 1818-1826, 1832.

Finlay's American Naval and Commercial Register, 1795-1797.

Freeman's Journal; or the North American Intelligencer, 1786.

Freeman's Journal and Philadelphia Daily Advertiser, 1805.

Gazette of the United States, 1789-1793, 1801-1804.

Gazette of the United States and Evening Advertiser, 1793-1794.
Gazette of the United States and Daily Evening Advertiser, 1794.
Gazette of the United States, & Philadelphia Daily Advertiser, 1796, 1798.
Gazette of the United States & Daily Advertiser, 1801.
– *United States Gazette*, 1804-1810, 1823-1827, 1832-1835, 1838.
The Union United States Gazette and True American, 1819, 1821-1823.
North American and United States Gazette, 1853-1861.
Gemeinnutzige Philadelphische Correspondenz, 1788.
General Advertiser, and Political, Commercial, Agricultural and Literary Journal, 1790.
General Advertiser and Political, Comercial and Literary Journal, 1791.
General Advertiser, 1791-1793.
Aurora. General Advertiser, 1803, 1806-1807, 1821-1827.
Grotjan's Philadelphia Public Sale Report, 1812-1825.
Philadelphia Public Sale Report, 1825-1827.
·*Hope's Philadelphia Price-Current*, 1804-1813.
Independent Gazetteer; or, the Chronicle of Freedom, 1785-1786.
Independent Gazetteer, 1794.
McPherson's Philadelphia Price Current, 1784.
Moore's Philadelphia Price Current or Trade, News, and Shipping List, 1833-1834.
National Gazette, 1792-1793.
The Pennsylvanian, 1833-1834, 1841-1845.
Pennsylvania Inquirer and Daily Courier, 1836-1837.
Pennsylvania Journal, 1856.
Pennsylvania Mercury and Universal Advertiser, 1784-1791.
Pennsylvania Mercury, and Philadelphia Price-Current, 1791.
Pennsylvania Packet and Daily Advertiser, 1784-1785, 1788-1790.
Philadelphia Liberalist, 1833.
Philadelphia Price Current, 1827-1829.
Philadelphia Price Current and Commercial Advertiser, 1829-1835.
Saturday Courier, 1831-1843.
United States Gazette, see *Gazette of the United States*.
Universal Gazette, 1799-1800.

Baltimore and New York Prices

Baltimore Weekly Price Current, 1810, 1819.
Ming and Young's New York Price Current, 1804-1805.
Ming's New York Price Current, 1805-1813, 1815-1817.
New York Price Current, 1786.
New York Prices Current, 1797.
Oram's New York Price Current and Marine Register, 1798-1804.
New York Shipping List and Commercial Advertiser, 1813-1814.
Shipping and Commercial List and New York Price Current, 1815-1819, 1823-1861.
Shipping and Commercial List and New York New Price Current, 1820-1823.

MANUSCRIPT SOURCES OF PRICES AND COMMENTS[1]

Biddle, Clement, letter book, 1790.
Biddle, Nicholas, letters, Vols. I and II, 1825, 1834.
Bond, Dr. Phineas, receipt book, 1790.
Chaloner and White, papers, 1784.
Clifford Correspondence, 1784, 1786-1790.
Coates, George M., letter book, 1832.
Collins, Stephen (Library of Congress), 1784.
Cooke, Jay, correspondence, 1854, 1855, 1857, 1859.
Devitt, Peter, letter book, 1798-1799.
Evans, Thomas, ledger, 1784.
Fearson, Joseph, waste book, 1784.
Fisher, Thomas, ledger, 1793.
Fisher, Samuel and Miers, letter book (Lippincott Library, Wharton School, University of Pennsylvania), 1796-1800.
Fisher, Thomas, Samuel, and Miers, ledgers, 1792-1795.
Fuller, Benjamin, letter book, 1784, 1786, 1788.
Girard, Stephen, memorandum and waste books (Library of Girard College), 1784, 1785, 1790, 1794, 1799, 1800, 1811.
Hamilton, John, letter book, 1810, 1813.

[1] All manuscripts are in the possession of the Historical Society of Pennsylvania unless otherwise noted. The dates in this list refer to the period for which data were used in this book and not to the entire period covered by the collections.

Hand, Edward, letters, 1811.
Henderson, Robert, letter book, 1784, 1785, 1789, 1790-1792.
Hildeburn, Samuel, letter book, 1816.
Hollingsworth, Levi, or Levi and Son, letters and account books, 1784, 1786-1803, 1805, 1810.
Hewes and Anthony (John Carter Brown Library, Providence), 1785-1786.
Kuhl, Frederick, waste book, 1784.
Landenberger, Matthias, receipt book, 1784, 1787.
Lippincott and Company, account books, 1798-1805, 1808-1819.
L'Orrange, Louis, receipt book, 1799-1800.
Marshall, John, receipt book, 1784.
McCurrack, James and Company, letter book, 1794-1795.
Meade, George, receipt book, 1785-1788.
Morris and Miercken, ledger, 1784-1788.
Philadelphia merchant, unknown, Am. 3081, day book, 1784-1787.
Redwood, William, 1788-1790, 1794.
Reed and Forde, correspondence, 1788-1790, 1793-1794, 1796-1797, 1801-1802, 1805-1806.
Robeson and Paul, letter book, 1815.
Trotter, Nathan, and Company, account books (Baker Library, Harvard University), 1821-1860.
Warder and Brothers, 1834-1837, 1842.
Webster, Peletiah, correspondence, 1788.
Weems, James N., letter book, 1811, 1812, 1814.
Wetherill and Brother, account books (Mr. A. P. Wetherill), 1784-1860.
Wetherill, Samuel, correspondence book (Mr. A. P. Wetherill), 1793, 1799, 1808-1812, 1816, 1819.
Wetmore Papers (Boston Historical Society), 1784.
Wharton, Charles, day book and invoice books, 1784-1785, 1788-1789.
Wynkoop and Siemen, receipt book, 1784.

Published Sources

Adams, Henry
The Life of Albert Gallatin, Philadelphia, J. B. Lippincott Company, 1879.

Bezanson, Anne, Gray, Robert D., and Hussey, Miriam
Prices in Colonial Pennsylvania, Philadelphia, University of Pennsylvania Press, 1935.

Carey, Mathew
Letters to The Bank Directors, on the Pernicious Consequences of the Prevailing System of Banking Operations, Philadelphia, Carey, 1816.

Catterall, Ralph C. H.
The Second Bank of the United States, Chicago, University of Chicago Press, 1903.

Channing, Edward
A History of the United States, Vols. III and IV, New York, The Macmillan Company, 1930 and 1917.

Coxe, Tench
A View of the United States of America, London, 1795.

Dunaway, Wayland Fuller
A History of Pennsylvania, New York, Prentice-Hall, Inc., 1935.

Edwards, Bryan
The History, Civil and Commercial, of the British West Indies, London, 1819.

Fisher, Irving
The Making of Index Numbers—A Study of Their Varieties, Tests, and Reliability, Boston, Houghton Mifflin Co., 1922.

Gray, Lewis Cecil
History of Agriculture in the Southern United States to 1860, Vol. II, Washington, The Carnegie Institution of Washington, 1933.

Holdsworth, J. T.
Financing an Empire—History of Banking in Pennsylvania, Vol. I, Philadelphia, the S. J. Clarke Publishing Company, 1928.

Homans, J. Smith and J. Smith, Jr., editors.
A Cyclopedia of Commerce and Commercial Navigation, New York, Harper and Brothers, 1858.

Jevons, W. Stanley
Investigations in Currency and Finance, London, Macmillan and Company, 1884.

Kuznets, Simon S.
Seasonal Variations in Industry and Trade, New York, National Bureau of Economic Research, 1933.

Laughlin, J. Laurence
A New Exposition of Money, Credit, and Prices, Vol. I, Chicago, University of Chicago Press, 1931.

McMaster, John Bach
A History of the People of the United States (from the Revolution to the Civil War), Vol. VIII, 1850-1861, New York, D. Appleton and Company, 1913.
The Life and Times of Stephen Girard, Vol. II, Philadelphia, J. B. Lippincott Company, 1918.

Mahan, Alfred T.
Sea Power in Its Relations to the War of 1812, Vol. I, Boston, Little, Brown and Company, 1905.

Mills, Frederick C.
Behavior of Prices, New York, National Bureau of Economic Research, 1927.
Statistical Methods Applied to Economics and Business, New York, Henry Holt and Company, 1924.

Oberholtzer, Ellis Paxson
Jay Cooke, Financier of the Civil War, Philadelphia, George W. Jacobs and Company, 1907.

Phillips, Henry, Jr.
Historical Sketches of the Paper Currency of the American Colonies, Roxbury, Massachusetts, W. Elliott Woodward, 1865.

Scharf, J. Thomas and Westcott, Thompson
History of Philadelphia, 1609-1884, Vol. I, Philadelphia, L. H. Everts and Company, 1884.

Smith, Walter Buckingham and Cole, Arthur Harrison
Fluctuations in American Business, 1790-1860, Cambridge, Harvard University Press, 1935.

Webster, Pelatiah
Political Essays on the Nature and Operation of Money, Public Finances and Other Subjects, Philadelphia, Joseph Crukshank, 1791.

INDEX

INDEX

Acts of Assembly of Pennsylvania, 96
Adams, Henry, 113 note
Agriculture, 96, 173-174, 245
Agricultural commodities:
—annual price index, 392
—commodities included, 11, 21
—monthly price index, facing 4, 354
——fluctuations of, 21-25
Almonds, 42, 44, 61
Alum, 337
Ashes, pearl, 60, 64, 307

Bank failures, 147, 208-209, 239-241
Bank, Girard, 209
Bank of North America, 96
Bank of the United States:
—First, 146-147
—Second, 172, 191-192, 202-204
Bank, Schuylkill, 209
Banking:
—policies, 191-193, 202-205
—situation, 8, 10, 172-173, 176, 192, 202-210, 239-241
Banks:
—specie payment by:
——resumption of, 208-210
——suspension of, 6, 10, 151, 168, 179, 206-207, 247
Base period, selection of, 336
Beaver, 43, 60, 62
Beef, 42, 119, 336
—prime, 294-296, 328
Beeswax, yellow, 64
Beverages (see also Sub-groups):
—annual price index, 394
—commodities included, 13-16
—monthly price index, 372
Biddle, Clement, 110, 111
Biddle, Nicholas, 191, 192, 203-205
Blockades, 162, 164, 166, 168, 309
Bowley, Arthur L., 30
Brandy, 43, 47
Bread, 42, 292, 294-296, 327-328
—small water, 59
Brimstone, 337
—crude, 47
—rolls, 60
British dry goods, 163
British Orders in Council, 125, 128, 146, 152
Building materials other than wood (see also Sub-groups):
—annual price index, 395
—commodities included, 13-16
—monthly price index, 382
Business conditions (see also Banking situation and Trade, conditions of), 8, 10, 104-106, 112, 119, 123-124, 144-147, 153-154, 164-167, 172-174, 176, 207-208, 210-211, 235-236, 239-241, 244-245
Business failures, 112, 119, 173, 202, 203, 205, 206, 209, 236, 239
Butter, 47, 59, 63, 174, 244
Candles, sperm, 61, 307
Carey, Mathew, 173, 331
Catterall, Ralph C. H., 192 note
Channing, Edward, 95 note, 104
Cheese, 42
Chemicals and drugs (see also Sub-groups):
—annual price index, 395
—commodities included, 13-16
—monthly price index, 376
Chocolate, 42
Clark, E. W., 239-240, 241
Clark, E. W. and Company, 239, 240
Clifford, John, 95 note, 96 note, 109, 110-111
Clifford, Thomas, 105
Cloverseed, 59, 63
Coal:
—Lehigh, 337
—Schuylkill, 337
Coates, George M., 202 note
Cocoa, 42, 337
—Island, 61, 62
Codfish, 59
Coffee, 44, 162, 168, 171
—St. Domingo, 61, 67, 72-73, 84, 86, 90-92, 308, 413
Coinage Acts, 2
Cole, Arthur H., ix, x, 120 note, 238 note
Colonial period:
—comparison of prices and price move-

ments in, with those in period *1784-1861*, 292-304
Comments of merchants, see Merchants' comments
Commercial List and Philadelphia Price Current, 206 note, 207, 208 and note, 209-211, 217 note, 231 note, 235 note, 236 note, 242 note
Commodities:
—classification of, 11-16, 37-39, 309, 315
—classified by Grotjan, 164-166
—in Colonial period, vii, 292-293
—identical, *1720-1861*, 292-293
—number of, vii, 2, 339
Commodities, 135 individual:
—frequency of monthly price change, 53-65, 307-308, 315-317, 326, 407-410
Commodities, 140 individual:
—annual price relatives:
——distribution around general average, 27-33, 324-325, 342-343, 397-398
——percentage increasing, decreasing, and unchanging, 132-134, 184-186, 223-224, 256-257, 325-326
——stability, 34-44, 399-406
——variability, 45-52, 307, 315, 326, 343
Commodity-groups, 2, 339
Condiments (see also Sub-groups):
—annual price index, 394
—commodities included, 13-16
—monthly price index, 373
Cooke, Jay, 239-240
Cooke, Pitt, 239
Copper sheathing, 60, 307, 333-336
Copperas, 42, 337
Cordage, American, 49, 61-62, 306
Corn, viii, 41, 47, 67, 70-71, 74-75, 79, 81, 89-92, 97, 123, 307-308, 411
—Indian, 59, 63, 153, 174, 294-297, 327-328
Corn meal, 49, 59, 63, 67, 68, 70-71, 80-81, 89-92, 102, 306, 308, 337, 412
Cotton, viii, 41, 47, 97, 121, 191, 265
—Georgia, 59, 63, 67, 70-71, 78-79, 90-92, 294-296, 308, 327-328, 411
Coxe, Tench, 104
Credit terms, 96, 124
Crops:
—failure of, abroad, viii, 9, 123, 174, 236
—failure of, at home, 96, 174, 265
—plentiful harvests of, abroad, 120-121, 236
—plentiful harvests of, at home, 174, 210, 240
Currants, 42, 47
Currency, Pennsylvania, 2, 336
Cycles:
—in general index, 4-11, 261-263, 269, 271, 273-275, 297-304
——in relation to cycles in indices of major groups, 277-291
——length of, 273-275
——variability of, 262-263
—in indices of major groups, 273-275
——in relation to cycles in general index, 277-291
——length of, 273-277
——percentage of commodities which influenced rise or decline, 426
——percentage of decline, 270-272
——percentage of rise, 268-270
——process of decline, 277-284, 319-321, 426
——process of rise, 284-291, 317-319, 426
——variability of, 272-276, 321-322
—in indices of sub-groups, 415-425
——percentage of decline, 266-267
——percentage of rise, 264-266, 309
——variability of, 267-268, 312
—in 20-commodity index, 299
——in relation to cycles in general index, 297-304
——length of, 303-304
——percentage of decline, 299-300, 301
——percentage of rise, 299-300, 301
——variability of, 298-299, 303-304
—method of analyzing, 340-342

Dairy products (see also Sub-groups):
—annual price index, 394
—commodities included, 13-16
—monthly price index, 370
—seasonality of prices, 70-71, 82, 90-92, 412
Data:
—collection of, 331-336
—sources of, 1, 331-333, 427-430
Deciles of 140 commodities, 27-33, 342, 397
Decline in indices of major groups, process of:
—proportion of commodities contributing to, 280-284, 426
—relation to start in general index, 278-280, 319-321
—timing of start, 280-284, 291
Deer skins, 43, 60

Demand, European:
—for American foodstuffs, vii, viii, 7, 9, 18, 96, 109, 112, 119-120, 123, 171, 174, 231, 236, 243, 253, 265
—for cotton, 191
—for naval stores, 112
—for West India products, vii
Discount on paper currency, 172-173
Domestic commodities:
—annual price index, 392
—commodities included, 11, 13-16
—monthly price index, facing 4, 352
——fluctuations of, 17-20, 24-25, 97, 106, 114, 118, 119-120, 122, 125-126, 142-148, 152-156, 190-193, 201-211, 230-231, 234, 237-242
Drugs, 171
Duck, bear ravens, 61-62
—ravens, 61-62
Dunaway, Wayland Fuller, 333 note
Duties, see Tariff
Dyes (see also Sub-groups):
—annual prices, 395
—commodities included, 13-16
—monthly price index, 377

Embargo Acts, viii, 17, 22, 125, 128, 132, 143, 145, 149, 176, 298, 309
Embargoes, 17, 113, 157, 166, 176-177
Employment, 111, 177
Exchange on London, 119, 191
Exchange rates between New York and other cities, 203
Exports (see also Demand and Trade), 109, 111, 119

Factors affecting prices (see also Banking situation, Crops, Gold, Embargoes, Tariff, Trade, War):
—approach of winter, 153
—bounties, viii
—building activity, 110-111, 254
—buying habits, 75, 78, 308
—cessation of sales for supply of western country, 153
—changes in standards of living, 69
—changing importance of commodity, 44, 65, 84
—character of commodity, 44, 64-65, 317
—demand, vii, viii, 7, 9, 18, 64-65, 69, 84, 96, 109, 110-111, 119-120, 123, 142, 171, 174, 231, 236, 243, 253, 265, 307
—expeditions against China, 10, 217, 255
—famine in Ireland, 9, 231
—importations of foreign goods, 153, 170-171, 176
—improved means of communication and transportation, viii, 10, 54, 65, 305, 326
—peace, 5, 6, 17, 22, 53, 119, 120-121, 123, 155, 169, 171, 179, 290
—railroad construction, 9
—rumors of peace, 123, 162-163, 169
—rumors of war, 205
—shift in unit of sale, 65
—supply, 69, 77, 78, 84, 85, 109-110, 142, 153-154, 170-171, 172, 174, 176, 191, 242, 254, 308, 316
—technical improvements, 69
—uncertainty as to government action, 202, 207-208, 235
—weather, 174, 208
—yellow fever, 5, 17, 113, 116, 120
Factors affecting seasonality of prices, 66-93, 308
Factors affecting sensitivity of prices, 44, 64-65, 316-317
Farm crops (see also Major groups):
—annual price index, 393
—commodities included, 11, 13-16, 37-38
—monthly price index, 98-99, 158-159, 194-195, 232-233, 356
Farm derivatives (see also Major groups):
—annual price index, 393
—commodities included, 11, 13-16, 37-38
—monthly price index, 98-99, 158-159, 194-195, 232-233, 357
Farm products (see also Grains, Tobacco, and Minor farm products), 109
Feathers, 42, 49, 59, 63
Ferrous metals and metal products (see also Sub-groups), 43-44
—annual price index, 395
—commodities included, 13-16
—monthly price index, 379
Financial situation, see Banking situation
Fish (see also Major groups and Sub-groups), 242, 245
—annual price index, 393
—commodities included, 12-16, 38
—monthly price index, 100-101, 160-161, 194-195, 234-235, 362
Fisher, Irving, 339
Fisher, Samuel and Miers, 116 and note, 117 note, 119 note
Flax, 41, 49, 97, 306
Flaxseed, 41, 59, 63, 97, 337

Flour, 47, 59, 63, 67, 68, 70-71, 79-80, 89-92, 97, 104, 109, 113, 119, 123, 124, 153, 244, 294-297, 307-308, 327-328, 412
Foods, 109, 115, 121
—annual price index, 394
—commodities included, 13-16
—monthly price index, 375
—sub-groups included, 375 note
Foods, imported, see Imported foods
Foreign commodities, see Imported commodities
French Revolution, 5, 52, 106, 112
Frequency of monthly price changes, 53-65, 67-68, 307-308, 315-317, 326, 407-410
Fruit (see also Sub-groups):
—annual price index, 394
—commodities included, 13-16
—monthly price index, 371
Fuel and lighting (see also Sub-groups):
—annual price index, 395
—commodities included, 13-16
—monthly price index, 378
Funding Acts, 96, 111
Furs (see also Major groups and Sub-groups):
—annual price index, 393
—commodities included, 12-16, 38
—monthly price index, 100-101, 160-161, 194-195, 234-235, 363
Fustic, 47

General index (140 commodities):
—annual, 3, 392
——distribution of 140 commodities around, 27-33, 324-325, 342-343, 397-398
——moving average of, 3
——percentage change, 112-113, 128-131, 181-183, 219-221, 249-252
——proportion of 140 commodities influencing, 112-113, 132-134, 184-186, 223-224, 256-257, 325-326
—monthly, facing 4, facing 300, 350
——cycles in, 4-11, 261-263, 269, 271, 273-275, 297-304
——fluctuations of, 2-11, 24-25, 97, 106, 107, 109, 117, 118, 121, 124, 142, 151-152, 190, 230
Gin, Holland, 43, 49, 61, 306
Ginger, ground, 42, 61
—race, 42, 47
Ginseng, 42, 59
Girard, Stephen, 113 and note, 145, 147, 332
Glass, 43, 47, 61-62, 105, 110, 147
Gold:
—discovery of, in California, 9, 238
—value of, 1-2
Grain, 109
Grain products (see also Sub-groups):
—annual price index, 394
—commodities included, 13-16
—monthly price index, 368
Grains (see also Sub-groups):
—annual price index, 394
—commodities included, 13-16
—monthly price index, 365
Gray, Lewis C., 78 note, 191 note
Grotjan's Philadelphia Public Sale Report, 153-154, 162-163, 164-166, 167, 168 note, 169, 170, 171, 174, 176, 338 note
Gunpowder, 43, 61-62, 293-296, 327-328

Hamilton, Alexander, 2
Hamilton, John, 146, 162
Hams, 42, 63
Hand, Edward, 147 note
Harris, Samuel, and Sons, 241 note
Hemp, 41, 97, 337
Henderson, Robert, 78 note, 96, 109, 111 note, 112
Herring, 43
Hides, 42, 59
Hides and Leather (see also Sub-groups):
—annual price index, 395
—commodities included, 13-16
—monthly price index, 385
Hildeburn, Samuel, 172
Hollingsworth, Levi, 97 note, 104, 109 note, 110, 113 and note, 116, 120-121, 123, 124 note, 146
Holdsworth, J. T., 146-147
Homans, J. Smith and J. Smith, Jr., 337
Honey, 61, 307, 337
Hops, 59, 63
Hundredweight, 337-338

Imported commodities:
—annual price index, 392
—commodities included, 11, 13-16
—monthly price index, facing 4, 353
——fluctuations of, 17-20, 24-25, 97, 106, 114, 118, 119-120, 122, 125-126, 142-148, 152-156, 190-193, 201-211, 230-231, 234, 237-242
Imported foods (see also Major groups):
—annual price index, 393

—commodities included, 12-16, 37-38
—monthly price index, 100-101, 160-161, 196-197, 232-233, 358
Imports (see also Trade), 153, 170-171, 176
Index numbers, construction of, 336-340
Index of cyclical variability, 262-263, 267-268, 272-276, 298-299, 303-304, 312, 321-322, 415-425
—method of computing, 262, 342
Index of 140 commodities, see General index
Index of similarity, see Seasonality and Similarity
India goods, 171
Indices, price, see Price indices
Indigo, French, 294-296, 328
Industrial commodities:
—annual price index, 392
—commodities included, 12, 21
—monthly price index, facing 4, 355
——fluctuations of, 21-25
Industrial commodities ready for consumption (see also Major groups)
—annual price index, 393
—commodities included, 12-16, 38-39
—monthly price index, 98-99, 158-159, 194-195, 232-233, 361
Industrial raw and semi-finished commodities (see also Major groups):
—annual price index, 393
—commodities included, 12-16, 38-39
—monthly price index, 98-99, 158-159, 194-195, 232-233, 360
International Scientific Committee on Price History, ix, 12
Iron:
—bar, 110
——Swedish, 60, 307
—hoop, 62
—nail rod, 47, 110
—pig, 49, 60, 307
—sheet, 60, 307

Kuznets, Simon S., 66, 89, 343, 345

Labor:
—disturbances, 206
—supply, 95, 244-245
Lard, 49, 63, 306
Laughlin, J. Laurence, 2 note
Lead:
—pig, 60, 64, 67, 72-73, 88-92, 307-308, 337, 414
—red, 144, 148, 177
—white, 144, 148, 177
——ground in oil, 110
Leather, see Hides and leather
Lemons, 42, 47, 61, 64, 307
Lewis, John, 109 note
Logwood, 49, 306-307
—Campeachy, 60
Lumber, 110
Lumber products, 42, 44, 110, 306
Lumber products and naval stores (see also Major groups):
—annual price index, 393
—commodities included, 12-16, 38-39
—monthly price index, 98-99, 158-159, 194-195, 232-233, 359

Macaulay, F. R., 66
Mace, 42
Mackerel, 43
—#1, 63, 67, 70-71, 82-83, 90-92, 308, 412
—#2, 63
—#3, 63
Mahan, Alfred T., 116
Mahogany, St. Domingo, 60, 62
Major groups (see also Farm crops, Farm derivatives, Fish, Furs, Imported foods, Industrial commodities ready for consumption, Industrial raw and semi-finished commodities, Lumber products and naval stores, and Wines):
—annual price indices, 393
——deviation from general index, 139-141, 188-189, 228-229, 259-260, 322-324
——percentage change, 128-131, 181-183, 219-221, 249-252
——proportion of commodities increasing, decreasing, and unchanging, 134-139, 186-188, 224-228, 257-259, 399-404
——stability of, 39-44, 306, 315
——variability of, 50-52, 315
—commodities included, 11-16, 37-39
—monthly price indices, 356-364
——cycles in, 268-291, 317-322
——fluctuations of, *1784-1808*, 97-103, 105-108, 114-115, 118-119, 120, 122, 124, 126-127; *1808-1821*, 148, 156-178, 180-181; *1821-1843*, 193-198, 211-214, 218-219; *1843-1861*, 232-236, 242-247, 248-249

—frequency of change, 58-64, 307-308, 315-317
Manufacturing, viii, 105, 127-128, 144-145, 147, 165, 177, 305
Marks, S., 241
McCurrach, James and Company, 113 note
McMaster, John Bach, 145 note, 168 note, 171 note, 240 note
Meats and meat products (see also Sub-groups):
—annual price index, 394
—commodities included, 13-16
—monthly price index, 369
Medians of 140 commodities, 27-33, 342, 397
Merchants' accounts, x, xi, 1, 332-336, 429-430
Merchants' comments:
—sources of, 429-430
—use of, ix, 1
Metals and metal products, see Ferrous metals and metal products and Non-ferrous metals and metal products
Method, 331-345
Migration, 9, 245
Mills, Frederick C., 262 note, 340, 343
Minor farm products (see also Sub-groups):
—annual price index, 394
—commodities included, 13-16
—monthly price index, 367
Miscellaneous commodities:
—annual price index, 395
—commodities included, 13-16
—monthly price index, 387
Molasses (see also Sugar and molasses), 153, 171
—West India, 64, 67, 72-73, 85, 86, 90-92, 294-296, 327-328, 413
Muskrat, 43, 47, 60, 62

Nails, 44, 49, 61-62, 105
Naval stores (see also Lumber products and naval stores), 42, 60, 306-307
Napoleonic wars, see Wars
Newspapers, 1, 331, 427-429
Non-ferrous metals and metal products (see also Sub-groups):
—annual price index, 395
—commodities included, 13-16
—monthly price index, 380
Non-Intercourse Acts, viii, 143-144, 145-146, 149, 150

Oats, 41, 59, 63, 97, 307
Oberholtzer, Ellis Paxson, 241 note
Oil:
—linseed, 42, 49, 60, 63, 67, 72-73, 87-88, 89-92, 110, 306-308, 333-336, 414
—sperm, 42
—sweet, 42, 49, 306-307
—whale, 42, 47, 64, 67, 68, 72-73, 88, 89-92, 308, 414
157-commodity index:
—annual, 392
—commodities included, 12-16
—monthly, 3, facing 4, 351
Oregon, dispute over boundary of, 8, 235
Other farm products, see Minor farm products

Panic:
—of *1819*, 7, 176, 181
—of *1825*, 191, 204
—of *1837*, 8, 18, 206-207, 222
—of *1857*, 9, 20, 24, 239-241, 246
Paper currency, 96, 97, 172-173
Paul, Joseph N., 171 note
Peace of Amiens, 119, 120
Peas, 97, 337
Pennsylvania Mercury and Universal Daily Advertiser, 336 note
Pepper, 42, 44, 67, 68, 72-73, 84-85, 86, 89-93, 413
Periods:
—defined, 3, 45, 55
—20-year, 55-65
—*1784-1808*, 5-6, 21-22, 34-37, 39-44, 45-52, 94-141
—*1808-1821*, 6-7, 22-23, 35-37, 39-44, 45-52, 142-189
—*1821-1843*, 7-8, 23, 35-37, 39-44, 45-52, 190-229
—*1843-1861*, 8-10, 24, 35-37, 39-44, 45-52, 230-260
Price indices, annual:
—agricultural commodities, 392
—computation of, 339
—domestic commodities, 392
—general, 392
—imported commodities, 392
—industrial commodities, 392
—major groups, 393
—sub-groups, 394-395
—12-commodity, 396
—20-commodity, 396
—157-commodity, 392
Price indices, monthly:

—agricultural commodities, 354
—domestic commodities, 352
—general, 350
—imported commodities, 353
—industrial commodities, 355
—major groups, 356-364
—sub-groups, 365-387
—12-commodity, 390-391
—20-commodity, 388-389
—157-commodity, 351
Philadelphia Gazette and Universal Daily Advertiser, 2
Phillips, Henry, Jr., 96 note
Pimento, 42
Pine:
—boards, 60, 110
——sap, 49, 62, 306
——white, 42, 49, 306
Pitch, 293-296, 327-328
Plaster of Paris, 42, 47, 60, 63, 307-308
Pork, 42, 44, 47, 67, 70-71, 81-82, 89-92, 119, 174, 308, 336, 412
—Burlington, 59, 63, 294-295, 327-328
—prime, 59, 63
Potatoes, 244

Quartiles of 140 commodities, 27-33, 342, 397

Raisins, 42, 47
Reed and Forde, 112 note, 113 note, 119 note
Recovery in indices of major groups, process of:
—proportion of commodities contributing, 288-290, 426
—relation to start in general index, 284-286, 317-319
—timing of start, 286-288, 291
Rice, 41, 59, 63, 67, 70-71, 75-77, 79, 90-92, 97, 153, 293-297, 327-328, 337, 411
Robeson and Paul, 171 note
Rosin, 64
Rum:
—Jamaica, 43, 61
—New England, 61, 64, 67, 72-73, 86, 89-92, 294-296, 308, 327-328, 414
—West India, 294-297, 327-328
Rye, 41, 47, 59, 63, 97, 174
Rye meal, 42, 47, 59, 63, 109, 153, 307

Sail cloth, Russian, 254
Salt, 171, 293-296, 327-328
—coarse, 47
Saltpeter, refined, 60
Scharf, J. Thomas, 168 note
Seasonality, 66-93, 308, 343-345, 411-414
—amplitude of variation, 90-93
—causes of, 69, 74
—commodities selected for study of, 66
—construction of indices, 343-344
—indices of similarity of, 89-90, 345
—relation to frequency of monthly price change, 67-69, 308
Secession of southern states, 10, 247
Semi-interdecile range, 29-30, 342
Semi-interquartile range, 29-33, 342
Sensitivity of prices, see Factors affecting prices and Frequency of monthly price changes
Severity, see Index of cyclical variability
Sheeting, Russian:
—brown, 47, 62
—white, 47
Shingles, long, 62
Shot, 61, 177, 337
Similarity, indices of, 89-90
—construction of, 345
Skewness, 27-33, 325, 342-343, 398
Smith, Walter B., 120 note, 238 note
Soap:
—Castile, 44
—white, 61-62
—yellow, 43, 44, 49, 306
Sources of data, see Data
Spanish brown ground in oil, 47
Specie Circular, 206
Specie payment, see Banks
Spices, see Condiments
Spirits (see also Sub-groups):
—annual price index, 395
—commodities included, 13-16
—monthly price index, 386
Spirits of turpentine, 47, 60, 64, 307-308, 333-336
Starch, 49, 61, 306, 307
Staves, white oak, 60, 292, 294-297, 327-328
Steel:
—country (American), 44, 47, 60, 62, 337
—Crowley, 62
—English blistered, 62
—German, 62
Sub-groups (see also Beverages, Building materials other than wood, Chemicals and drugs, Condiments, Dairy products, Dyes, Ferrous metals and metal products, Fish, Furs, Fruit, Fuel and lighting,

Grain products, Grains, Hides and leather, Meats and meat products, Minor farm products, Miscellaneous, Non-ferrous metals and metal products, Spirits, Sugar and molasses, Textile fabrics, Textile fibers, Tobacco, Wines, and Wood):
—annual price indices, 394-395
——percentage change, 131-132, 183-184, 200-201, 221-223, 252-256, 424-425
—commodities included, 13-16
—monthly price indices, 365-387
——cycles in, 263-268, 309-314, 415-423
——fluctuations of, 103, 108-112, 115-117, 119, 121, 122-123, 124-125, 149-151, 178-179, 198-200, 214-218, 236-237, 247-248
Sugar, 153, 168, 337
—Havana brown or muscovado, 67, 72-73, 85-86, 90-92, 292, 294, 296, 327-328, 413
—loaf, viii, 292-296, 327-328
Sugar and molasses (see also Sub-groups):
—annual price index, 394
—commodities included, 13-16
—monthly price index, 374

Tallow, 42, 59
Tar, 42, 60, 67, 68, 72-73, 87, 89-93, 293-297, 308, 327-328, 414
Tariff, 8, 17, 152, 157, 165, 176-177, 235
Tea, 42, 147, 168, 217, 255
—Hyson skin, 61, 67, 68, 72-73, 84, 86, 90-92, 308, 413
—Souchong, 61
Textile fabrics (see also Sub-groups):
—annual price index, 395
—commodities included, 13-16
—monthly price index, 384
—supply of, 147, 152
Textile fibers (see also Sub-groups):
—annual price index, 395
—commodities included, 13-16
—monthly price index, 383
Timothy seed, 337
Tobacco (see also Sub-groups):
—annual price index, 394
—commodities included, 13-16
—monthly price index, 366
Tobacco, 97, 174
—James River, 41, 59, 67, 68, 70-71, 77-78, 79, 89-92, 294-297, 307-308, 327, 411
—Kentucky, 41, 47, 59
Total index, see General index
Trade, foreign (see also Blockades, Demand, Embargo Acts, Non-Intercourse Acts):
—conditions of, vii, 95-96, 104-105, 109-110, 116, 119-121, 123-124, 152-154, 162-163, 170-171, 176, 305
—restrictions on, viii, 5, 95, 121, 125, 142, 143-148, 149, 163-164
Treaty of Ghent, 6, 169
Trotter, Nathan, and Company, 333-336
12-commodity index:
—annual, 396
—commodities included, 300 note
—computation of, 340
—monthly, facing 300, 390-391
—comparison with 20-commodity index, 300-301
20-commodity index:
—annual, 396
—commodities included, 293
—computation of, 339-340
—monthly, facing 300, 388-389
——cycles in, 297-304, 326
Turpentine, 42, 293-297, 327-328

Unemployment, 208
Units of measure, 65, 336-338

Value:
—of gold, 1-2
—of Spanish milled dollar, 1-2
Variability, year-to-year, 45-52, 307, 315, 326
—construction of, 45, 343
Vegetables, 245

War (see also French Revolution):
—Civil, 10, 230, 247
—Crimean, 9, 10, 243, 245, 254
—Mexican, 9, 10, 231
—of *1812*, 6, 17, 22, 52, 150, 151, 152, 167, 168, 168 note, 169, 176, 178, 179, 181, 290, 293, 309, 310
—Revolutionary, readjustment after, 52, 95, 293-294, 297
Warder, John H., 202-203, 205-206
Wars, Napoleonic, viii, 5, 52, 106, 112, 290, 293, 296, 310
Webster, Pelatiah, 96 note, 97 note, 111 note
Weems, James N., 147 note, 152-153, 167 note
Weighting, problem of, 338
Westcott, Thompson, 168 note

Wetherill, Abel P., xi, 332
Wetherill and Brother, xi, 333-336
Wetherill, Samuel, 2, 112 note, 119, 128 note, 144-145, 147-148, 173, 176 note, 177
Wheat, viii, 41, 47, 59, 63, 67, 70-71, 75, 79, 89-92, 97, 104, 109, 113, 124, 153, 174, 294-297, 307-308, 327-328, 411
Whiskey Rebellion, 113 and note, 333
Wilson and Potts, 202 note
Wine:
—claret, 44, 62
—Lisbon, 44, 62, 337
—Madeira, 44, 47, 61, 62, 294-297, 327-328, 337
—Malaga, 44, 61, 337
—port, 44, 337
—sherry, 61, 337
—Teneriffe cargo, 44, 62, 337
Wines (see also Major groups and Sub-groups):
—annual price index, 393
—commodities included, 12-16, 38
—monthly price index, 100-101, 160-161, 196-197, 232-233, 364
Wood (see also Sub-groups):
—annual price index, 395
—commodities included, 13-16
—monthly price index, 381
Wool, 105
Woolen goods, 163

Yellow fever, 5, 17, 113, 116, 120, 305, 333

www.ingramcontent.com/pod-product-compliance
Lightning Source LLC
LaVergne TN
LVHW011822200926
848484LV00005B/1276